REWRITING AMERICAN ARCHITECTURE

REWRITING AMERICAN ARCHITECTURE

CONTESTING THE MYTHS OF NATIONAL CULTURE

Edited by Charles L. Davis II, Kathryn E. Holliday, and Joanna Merwood-Salisbury

University of Texas Press *Austin*

Publication of this book was made possible in part by support from Roger Fullington and a challenge grant from the National Endowment for the Humanities.

Printed in the United States of America
First edition, 2026

Chapter 15 is based in part on Anjelica S. Gallegos, "Designed Assimilation: Southern Utes at the Fort Lewis Boarding School," *Journal of the Society of Architectural Historians* 84, no. 3 (2025): 294–321, published by the University of California Press.

♾ The paper used in this book meets the minimum requirements of ANSI/NISO Z39.48-1992 (R1997) (Permanence of Paper).

Library of Congress Cataloging-in-Publication Data

Names: Davis, Charles L., II, editor. | Holliday, Kathryn E., editor. | Merwood-Salisbury, Joanna, editor.
Title: Rewriting American architecture : contesting the myths of national culture / edited by Charles L. Davis II, Kathryn E. Holliday, Joanna Merwood-Salisbury.
Description: First edition. | Austin : University of Texas Press, 2026. | Includes bibliographical references and index.
Identifiers: LCCN 2025040563 (print) | LCCN 2025040564 (ebook)
ISBN 978-1-4773-3416-4 (hardcover)
ISBN 978-1-4773-3417-1 (paperback)
ISBN 978-1-4773-3418-8 (pdf)
ISBN 978-1-4773-3419-5 (epub)
Subjects: LCSH: Architecture and race—United States. | Architectural criticism—United States. | Architecture—United States—Historiography. | African Americans—United States—Social conditions. | Indigenous peoples—United States—Social conditions. | Architecture and society—United States. | Architecture—Political aspects—United States. | Transnationalism.
Classification: LCC NA2543.R37 R49 2026 (print) | LCC NA2543.R37 (ebook)
LC record available at https://lccn.loc.gov/2025040563
LC ebook record available at https://lccn.loc.gov/2025040564

doi:10.7560/334164

The University of Texas Press gratefully acknowledges the Roger Fullington Endowment in Architecture for its support of this publication.

CONTENTS

Introduction 1
Charles L. Davis II, Kathryn E. Holliday, and Joanna Merwood-Salisbury

Part I: Defining the Profession

1. Spatializing the American Architectural Profession in the Nineteenth Century 25
Kathryn E. Holliday
2. Vernacular Professionalism: Rural Home Economics and the Racial Contract of Expertise 43
Athanasiou Geolas
3. A Cattle Brand and a Cattle Ranch: Land, Race, and Power in Architectural History 61
Kathryn E. O'Rourke

Part II: Reconstruction and Architecture

4. Slavery and Sovereignty in Stone: The Mason Family of Austin, Texas 81
Tara A. Dudley
5. Grand Narratives in Black: The Architectural Histories of John Marrant, Robert Benjamin Lewis, and Martin Delaney 96
Bryan E. Norwood
6. The Black Parti: Reinterpreting African American Placemaking as Design Ideation 111
Andrea Roberts
7. Identifying the Religio-Racial Aesthetics of AME Church Design, 1876–1920 127
Melanee C. Harvey-Fryar
8. Demolishing Historic Architecture: Black Activists' Crusade Against the One-Room Cabin in the Early Jim Crow Era 146
Whitney Nell Stewart

Part III: Transnational Americas

9. Border Crossing: Architecture in Brownsville, Texas, and Heroica Matamoros, Tamaulipas, as a Case Study 163
Stephen Fox

10. Aesthetic Imperialism in the Asia-Pacific: The Coastal Politics of Bernard Maybeck's Architectural Practice 180
Charles L. Davis II

11. Mahogany and the Locations of American Architecture 197
Jonah Rowen

12. Building an Evangelical Utopia: Missionaries and the Racial Destiny of the United States in the "Near East" 214
Yasmina El Chami

Part IV: Building Settler Colonialism

13. The Apple of Discord: Free Labor, Sectionalism, and Anglo-Assimilation in Olmsted's Agricultural Colleges 233
Maura Lucking

14. Confronting Assimilation: The Interplay Between Očéti Ŝakówiŋ and Settler Spatialities in Dakota Territory, 1883–1888 255
Katherine Solomonson

15. Designed Assimilation: The Architecture of Federal Indian Boarding Schools 273
Anjelica S. Gallegos

16. The Native American Ranch House: Dialectics of Architecture, Race, and Land in Southern California, 1850–1935 289
Manuel Shvartzberg Carrió

Part V: Modern Mythologies

17. Jefferson's Ashes and Architecture's Racial Dialectic 311
Peter Minosh

18. Ordering Things: Ethnology, Empire, and Everything Else at the Library of Congress 326
Diana Martinez

19. Chicago Frame: Evolution, Ethnology, and the Idea of the First Skyscraper 342
Joanna Merwood-Salisbury

20. "Americans" and Others: A Prehistory of Frank Lloyd Wright's Usonia 362
Joseph M. Watson

Acknowledgments 375
Index 376

REWRITING AMERICAN ARCHITECTURE

The treatment of the period of Reconstruction reflects small credit upon American historians as scientists. We have too often a deliberate attempt so to change the facts of history that the story will make pleasant reading for Americans. . . .

One reads, for instance, Charles and Mary Beard's *Rise of American Civilization*, with a comfortable feeling that nothing right or wrong is involved. Manufacturing and industry develop in the North; agrarian feudalism develops in the South. They clash, as winds and waters strive, and the stronger forces develop the tremendous industrial machine that governs us so magnificently and selfishly today. . . .

The chief witness in Reconstruction, the emancipated slave himself, has been almost barred from court. His written Reconstruction record has been largely destroyed and nearly always neglected. . . .

All this is reflected in the textbooks of the day and in the encyclopedias, until we have got to the place where we cannot use our experiences during and after the Civil War for the uplift and enlightenment of mankind. We have spoiled and misconceived the position of the historian. . . .

. . . [US history] paints perfect men and noble nations, but it does not tell the truth.

W. E. B. DU BOIS, "THE PROPAGANDA OF HISTORY," *BLACK RECONSTRUCTION IN AMERICA*

INTRODUCTION

Charles L. Davis II, Kathryn E. Holliday, and Joanna Merwood-Salisbury

WRITTEN IN 1935, W. E. B. DU BOIS'S *Black Reconstruction in America* concludes with a searing criticism of contemporary history writing, sharply rebuking both popular and academic authors for their biased portrayal of nineteenth-century US history. Du Bois begins the final chapter, "The Propaganda of History," by reviewing texts he condemns as crafting a comforting narrative of national unity. A child educated using these books, he wrote, "would in all probability complete his education without any idea of the part which the black race has played in America; of the tremendous moral problem of abolition; of the cause and meaning of the Civil War and the relation which Reconstruction had to democratic government and the labor movement today."[1] Du Bois particularly criticizes Charles and Mary Beard's *The Rise of American Civilization* (1927) for its mechanistic interpretation of historical forces, where political events are seen as the result of "cosmic social and economic law."[2] Omitted from this narrative, he claims, are facts in the historical record that do not support the authors' overarching thesis, a thesis that promotes a Progressive Era image of a modern, working democracy in the early twentieth century.

The canonical history of American architecture, which offers a similarly sweeping mechanistic interpretation of the nineteenth century, emerged as part of the same Reconstruction-era propaganda project critiqued by Du Bois. In the United States, the racial theories of national development that shaped European thought also influenced the architectural imagination and practices of this period. From the mid-century, a small group of newly professionalized architects who gathered in New York City rejected what they saw as lifeless imitations of classicism. Instead, they promoted the idea of true "American" architecture as the natural result of evolutionary forces, the product of a unified, or at least unifying, national culture.[3] Influenced by historians such as James Fergusson and Eugène Emmanuel Viollet-le-Duc, postbellum architects working on the "frontier" described American architecture in their professional journals in terms of the westward advance of civilization, seeing the establishment of American towns and cities in new states and territories as the fulfillment of manifest destiny.[4]

In the late nineteenth century, this rhetoric of national evolution and advancement passed from architects to critics and art historians, who constructed a narrative of American architectural genius that rested on the shoulders of a few men, a narrow catalog of examples, and a small geographical area. Writing in the 1880s and 1890s, the critics Montgomery Schuyler and Mariana Griswold Van Rensselaer each established a core aesthetic of progressive American modernism that has influenced historians and architects for generations. They were among the earliest critics of architecture in the United States and shared a focus on what they viewed as the generative originality of architects like H. H. Richardson, Louis Sullivan, and John Wellborn Root. In writing about the architecture of their own time, they, in Schuyler's words, sought to bring American architects' "art more into alliance, more into union, more into identity, with the art of building . . . [to] gain a living, a progressive, a real architecture—the architecture of the future."[5] The "American public" envisioned by Van Rensselaer was "foolish" and "selfish," in need of architects in this "transition stage" in America when the "architectural profession" was "very young."[6] Like Schuyler, Van Rensselaer was deeply embedded in her own contemporary vision of the late nineteenth century and wrote of America as a "new country" with a focus on the future.[7] Schuyler and Van Rensselaer framed the last two decades of the nineteenth century in America as a time of new beginning, based on their wonder at the rise of monuments like the Brooklyn Bridge, skyscrapers, and dense urban commercial districts where none had been before.

Historiographically, Schuyler's and Van Rensselaer's views of their own time have a long shadow. The echoes of their work are found in Talbot Hamlin's *The American Spirit in Architecture* (1926), Fiske Kimball's *American Architecture* (1928), Lewis Mumford's *The Brown Decades* (1931), Henry-Russell Hitchcock's *The Architecture of H. H. Richardson and His Times* (1936), Sigfried Giedion's *Space, Time and Architecture* (1941), Reyner Banham's *Theory and Design in the*

First Machine Age (1960), James O'Gorman's *Three American Architects* (1991), and countless other surveys of American architectural history. What those varied works share is a focus on the 1880s and 1890s as the focal point of the nineteenth century, a focus on highly urbanized places, and an acceptance of the canon established in these critical essays. Though they were writing during Reconstruction and its aftermath, a period when American society confronted and then retreated from the brutal realities of emancipation, both Schuyler and Van Rensselaer approached American architecture as a remarkably apolitical undertaking, disassociated from the devastating violence of the Civil War, the abolition of slavery, postbellum Reconstruction, and the labor disputes of the last two decades of the nineteenth century.

The definitions of America promulgated by Schuyler and Van Rensselaer focus on artistic originality and an aggressive avant-garde rooted in conquering the vast American landscape. In their writing, architecture floats in its own idealistic, artistic sphere, removed from the very real and contentious issues of unionized labor, urban growth, racial and ethnic violence, and territorial acquisition. "American" refers to an identifiable style, visually distinctive and composed of "true forms" that connected Ruskinian notions of purity to an Emersonian rawness and newness unattainable in Europe.[8] Schuyler's and Van Rensselaer's views of American architecture were rooted in the emergence of a new stylistic modernity. In adopting an art historical framework focused on enclaves of avant-garde practitioners, this narrative of the American nineteenth century has exerted a powerful hold that has been difficult to reframe.

Modernist historiography has distorted our ability to assess nineteenth-century architecture on its own terms. The hierarchy of formal and vernacular architectures it reinforced prevents a full accounting of the nineteenth century that centers instead on its competing narratives and identities. Assessing this period in terms of its antecedents to modern architecture, architectural historians like Talbot Hamlin, Fiske Kimball, and Lewis Mumford emphasized a teleological ladder of progress from British colony to American republic, ignoring the Civil War and slavery and the continued social and political upheavals as the United States grew its territory through formal and informal imperialist expansion. Erasing the history of Indigenous architecture, they reconfigured white settler colonists as the true "native" Americans.[9] Operative in intent, their works create a story of conflict moving toward synthesis, diversity moving toward unity, and historicism moving toward pure form. In them, we rarely see the context of the turbulence of nineteenth-century politics and expansionism, where the violent dynamics of race and labor were central to the building of the nation and its constantly shifting borders. This tendency continued well into the late twentieth century, with scholars such as Vincent Scully interpreting Frank Lloyd Wright as a seminal transitional figure toward "a unique American achievement in architecture," largely in comparison with the state of European modernism of the same period.[10] This teleological model of development is implicit in the category of "protomodern" that continues to distort our interpretation of the nineteenth century.

Reinterpreting the Nineteenth Century

"American architecture" is a problematic label in both geographic and symbolic terms. In geographic terms, it masquerades as a neutral category for collecting and identifying all of the material cultures generated within the political boundaries of the United States. Yet the United States is just one of several Americas on the globe. In symbolic terms, this label establishes a canon of built works that most clearly embody the political spirit of the nation's founding—a constitutional republic capable of expanding the franchise of freedom and democracy to the plurality of its citizens. Within the context of historiography, American architecture surveys operate as an allegorical representation of the ethnonational mythologies that are used to police the body politic. The Anglo-American tradition is profiled most heavily in titles of the late nineteenth and early twentieth centuries. And despite the expansions of postwar multicultural surveys, the European pedigree of American art and architecture has continued. Even a cursory survey of style manuals like the perennial bestseller *A Field Guide to American Houses* (Virginia Savage McAlester, 1984) reveals the Eurocentric biases that have fueled developer housing since the mid-eighteenth century. Despite the racial and ethnic diversity found in the nation, US domestic architecture hails from a steady stream of European immigrant material cultures that have seemingly evolved over time to reconstitute the cultural landscape. What are we to make of the paucity of Indigenous, Asian, Arab, Latino, and African American building styles in these canonical texts? And what should we make of the expectation that all people are capable of living in the International Style buildings that later became popular in the interwar and postwar periods? Such texts ask us to believe that the political experiment in American liberalism was an unequivocal success. Such a label inherently provides a systematic means of interpreting the United States as an exceptional space of ethnonational development on the globe.

The historiographic focus on a progressive evolution of formalist movements depends for its definition of modernity on the continued presence of "others"—premodern cultures misunderstood as remaining at a "primitive" stage of evolution—without categorizing their material cultures as anything other than vernacular.[11] This structural codependency is evident in the high/low division of professional culture that persists across architectural discourses and educational institutions, where "modern" and "vernacular" are seen as separate realms of study. Such a division of knowledge has been institutionalized within design studio culture (via the precedents used for contemporary designs) and by the historical surveys of "great men" in professional schools of architecture, which have been taught alongside, but seldom integrated with, studies of "native," "folk," or "regional" architecture. Routinely divided along a binary of "premodern" (origins to 1750) and "modern" (1750 to present) cultural eras, this intellectual framing is reinscribed in studio culture through community workshops that anonymize the suggestions of nonlicensed residents into a singular voice (the community) to legitimize the creative innovations of a canonical voice (the designer). Dating to Ephraim G. Squier and Edwin H. Davis's *Ancient Monuments of the Mississippi Valley* (1848) and Lewis H. Morgan's *Houses and House-Life of the American Aborigines* (1881), histories produced by archaeologists, anthropologists, preservationists, and local historians emphasize typical building types, local materials, and the evolution of construction methods and technologies rather than individually named creators. Valued by architecture critics and historians for their window into premodern craft traditions, these histories are employed to cover, in a patchwork manner, the territories and peoples left out of the canon.

Since the 1970s, activist-scholars of vernacular architecture have sought to correct an overemphasis on artistic avant-gardes by focusing on an "architecture without architects," primarily in an attempt to equalize the scholarly archives available to those documenting contributions to the built environment. Early works such as Dell Upton and John Michael Vlach's *Common Places* (1986) and Upton's *America's Architectural Roots* (1987) showed the varied, rich, folk and indigenous building traditions in rural and nonurban environments, emphasizing the role of immigration and transoceanic cultural exchange in making American architecture. Vernacular studies have subsequently highlighted the importance of intergenerational folk practices that continue to parallel the achievements of licensed architects in the present. Despite serious efforts by learned societies to connect the study of vernacular and avant-garde architectures, which can be seen in thematic issues of the journals *Buildings and Landscapes* and *Journal of the Society of Architectural Historians*, past biases persist through the academic training of doctoral students and specialists. This is manifested in part by the field methodologies of folk historians that insist on accepting and reinforcing the divide between professional architectural practice and the making of the built environment by those without formalized, institutional associations. It is also compounded by architectural masters and doctoral students who are complicit in producing and historicizing, as Mark Jarzombek puts it, a "neo-avant-garde" through a prioritizing of future-oriented technological and formal innovations.[12] Rarely has the inclusion of the unlettered into the architectural survey necessitated a disciplinary recalibration of the core definition of what it means to be an architect.

The failure to redefine architectural expertise has challenged the logical cohesion of even the most heterogeneous surveys of American architecture. Thematic studies of nineteenth-century culture have risen to take their place, but these efforts often remain splintered in the form of individual articles, essays, and encyclopedia posts.[13] New scholarship must fill this gap with a historiographic construction of nineteenth-century American architecture that knits vernacular and elite realms of cultural production back together in studies that are distinctively reflective of the political and cultural realities of the United States during the 1800s. The cities that occupied Schuyler's and Van Rensselaer's attention were being built using capital earned through trade supported by enslaved labor. Ownership and control of both land and people created systemic hierarchies that were codified through land use and architecture. The history of architecture is not only a history of design but also a history of the land and of those who labored to shape it. Unceded Indigenous land was taken and used for agriculture, land-grant universities, and railroad infrastructure. Land colonized and occupied under French, Spanish, and Mexican law was purchased and ceded; the very idea of who architects were and what they could build was constantly reshaped as "America" continually remade itself. Our architectural histories tend to focus on flattering reflections of "Americanness" and the consolidation of territories into the United States rather than on shifting, unstable, and contested identities. We envision "the Americas" as porous and migratory, more characterized by flow than dominated by a singular narrative of nationhood.

Du Bois's *Black Reconstruction in America* carefully cataloged the inadequate, myopic, and self-protective histories written about the Civil War, slavery, and Reconstruction during the early twentieth century that made the voices and experiences of Black people invisible. The "propaganda of history," as he described it, painted a picture of the United States in the nineteenth century at odds with its realities.[14] The Civil War is itself structurally absent in histories of nineteenth-century American architecture. Biographical treatments of Frank Furness, H. H. Richardson, and Frederick Law Olmsted, for example, discuss their personal relationships to the war, but its effects on the profession, its clients, and its systems of labor go unaddressed. Instead, the Civil War provides a periodized demarcation of antebellum and postbellum architectures as "revivalist" and "protomodern" and creates a series of regionalisms associated with Lost Cause narratives that we have passively accepted. The realignment of Black Americans as creators of a hegemonic material culture during Reconstruction is critical to this reassessment. As architectural historians, we are now in a position to question the propaganda of our own historiographies, asking not how architecture reflects the building of a new nation but how architecture reflects the conflicts and contested identities of nation, region, and state.

Answering this challenge, this volume aims to produce a critical history examining the construction of narratives of American architecture during the long nineteenth century, defined from the early republican era to the New Deal. Its purpose is to subvert the synthetic narrative of architectural history based on the ideas of a "nation of immigrants" or the "melting pot" and to recover the complexities of competing debates about nation and nationhood. Rejecting the canonical emphasis on the birth of an American modernism out of industrial and urban growth, we are interested in recapturing the unresolved, contentious character of the nineteenth century and reconnecting its professional and vernacular traditions. Our contributors have accepted this charge by looking at, for example, contested borders, sites of Indigenous agency, and the production of architecture through Black institutions and intellectual traditions. They question accepted histories of architectural progress and recapture untold histories, repositioning the role of institutions. In telling each of these small stories, we are arguing for a new approach to nineteenth-century American architectural history that emphasizes its contested, hybrid character, formed by larger processes of nation-building and territorial acquisition made possible by an interconnected system of production across scales.

New Rubrics

This book is an outgrowth of recent scholarship on American architecture published in the edited volume *Race and Modern Architecture* (2020).[15] A small subset of Americanists who contributed to the volume decided to extend this line of research in a one-day symposium titled "The Whiteness of American Architecture," which was convened at the School of Architecture and Planning at the University at Buffalo in 2019.[16] This event mined the ubiquitous influence of white cultural nationalisms on hegemonic American architecture movements—from the European pedigree of Thomas Jefferson's Virginia State Capitol and the embodiment of frontier ideologies in Frank Lloyd Wright's Prairie-style architectures to the visualization of white women's domestic labor in the Arts and Crafts rhetoric of the Roycroft colony and the coastal politics of West Coast modernisms in California. While we were convinced that a broader critique of whiteness would promote renewed interest in nineteenth-century studies of American architecture, we were less certain that a sole focus on whiteness was sufficient to articulate the extent to which race thinking was foundational to establishing disciplinary debates. The more we looked, the more we were convinced that competing regionalist and countercultural interpretations of national belonging were far more complex, fragmented, and oppositional than protomodernist histories of the discipline would have us believe.

Following up on the efforts of our initial symposium, we expanded the scope of our research by assembling a bibliography that included canonical histories of American architecture, seminal readings in settler colonial theory, and social histories of nonwhite material culture in North America. This literature review enabled us to identify a number of emerging scholars who employed innovative research methodologies to limn the hidden influence of race on architectural production. We invited four of these scholars to become collaborators for a second edited book project, this time completely dedicated to a study of American architecture in the long nineteenth century.[17] In the summer of 2021, these efforts culminated in a virtual publication workshop hosted in collaboration with the Society of Architectural Historians. This workshop, titled "Race and the Historiography of American Architecture," began with a pointed critique of the settler colonial narratives that underwrote progressive histories of modern architectural style—a developmental model that veiled the contingent and conflicted nature of national growth in this period.[18] Our introduction was followed up by four case studies that critiqued the whiteness of the canon and introduced the works of minority builders that presented countercultural definitions of authorship not legitimized by these hegemonic discourses. We closed our session with an open call for papers that yielded the remaining thirteen chapters included in this volume.

It is inevitable that any initial plan for an edited volume will change in response to ongoing scholarly conversations and the editorial processes that are required to finalize a new publication. Pointed questions posed at our publication workshop challenged us to produce "an architectural history that focuses on systems not objects, flows and processes and not individuals," to overcome the bias toward avant-gardist models of development promoted in professional schools of architecture.[19] We struggled with presenting a racial critique of disciplinary histories that did not create an anti-racist alternative that merely reinscribed the principles and rubrics of hegemonic debates. We have responded to this challenge by presenting "architecture" as a collective visual response to the shifting notions of national identity that were implicated in the consolidation of a settler colonial state. This approach enables us to demonstrate the ways that national architectural movements, both built and unbuilt, vernacular and avant-garde, constituted a speculative exercise in what kind of nation a community wished to inhabit. The architectural studies included in this volume collectively embrace what we call a horizontal framework of building expertise that explicitly relates the products of vernacular and avant-garde groups in an interdisciplinary study of national culture. We hope this approach will produce an inclusive conception of American architecture that recovers the complex range of historical actors operating at any one point in time.

Any effort to reexamine the long nineteenth century will require selective editorial decisions on which historic ideas, continuities, and archives to synthesize into a coherent set of themes for a single volume. It requires a principled balance among the desire for rigor, for comprehensiveness, and for an exploration of the most promising analytical frameworks that can guide future research. After careful consideration, we decided to reject creating a new survey of American architecture. It is no longer possible to formulate a comprehensive survey of the nation's architecture culture within a single ideological framework, especially in this age of global histories of architecture. So much work remains to be done before a new synthesis can occur. The previous function of architectural surveys in professional schools of architecture—namely, to identify a fixed canon of monumental works for the present—is antithetical to the inclusive approach we are pursuing in this volume. What we have set out to accomplish instead is a collection of thematic writings that recover the latent themes of nineteenth-century studies of American architecture. These gaps in the literature are collected under the five subheadings of this volume, including the rise of professionalism within the field of architecture, the racial conflicts that defined the postbellum era, the transnational production of American character, the settler colonial ideologies that subtend American nationalism, and the modernist mythologies that have veiled previous research. Our main approach in producing this list was to focus on the historical movements, events, and ideas that reached an apogee at the end of the nineteenth century and then continued to have an effect on architectural production into the first few decades of the twentieth century.

One of the most obvious but consistently overlooked themes in American architecture culture is the influence of race and racial politics on architectural production before and after the Civil War. We have consciously framed one section of this anthology around debates on Reconstruction, which connects the political conflicts over US sectionalism that emerged early in the nineteenth century with subsequent policies and movements during Reconstruction and Redemption in the second half of the long nineteenth century. This theme enables us to foreground the lost contributions of African Americans to the built environment after the Civil War while relating these events to the racial politics associated with the shifting Texas-Mexico border, the white nativist politics of architectural professionalization, and the fears associated with the closing of the American frontier and the rise of Chinese immigration in the second half of the nineteenth century. Our focus on the settler colonial origins of the nation enables us to collect essays that discuss the racial politics subtending the establishment of Indian reservations, Indian reservation schools, and the broader social imaginaries of westward expansion that recast American architecture as an autochthonous movement of "native" (white) peoples. While we have inevitably left out some debates from the early nineteenth century, we hope that our volume opens the way for reexamining such themes with new eyes. As an example, some of the potential themes of future research that are raised but not fully explored in our volume include the racial politics of the Louisiana Purchase, the material cultures associated with the Monroe Doctrine, and the conflicting claims on land ownership, settler identity, and material culture to emerge between settler and Indigenous trade and exploration. All of these areas of study are opened up by our insistence on viewing American culture through the lens of contentious debates and patterns of growth over the century, rather than on the seeds of a germinating modernist style with material roots in rural and early settler material culture.

All of the scholarship featured in this volume strategically builds upon existing scholarship in architectural history, vernacular studies, American studies, and cultural studies. These studies have produced analytical frameworks that reveal the structural inequities connected to the racial, gender, and class biases in the discipline of architecture. Our collection features writings that establish an interdisciplinary framework for architectural history that aims to reform the habitus of two primary disciplinary audiences at once: architectural academies and other professional institutions and scholars within the broader humanities that use architecture as primary evidence for their historical claims (a both/and approach). Disciplinary histories of architecture and social critiques of the built environment are generally written for different audiences and placed in separate publication lists. What is possible if we can get these audiences to speak to one another? Our goal is to build a bridge from the specialized research produced for architects and architectural historians to those studies produced for readers with a broader interest in the built environment. In this spirit, we have purposefully included essays that directly engage with specialized discourses and jargon influential in the discipline of architecture, as well as essays that apply the methodologies of statistical research, fieldwork, and cultural analysis, sometimes within the same subheading. The cross-disciplinary methodologies applied in these sections will resonate with a range of institutional reforms already being undertaken within higher education, from the horizontal framing of high and low building cultures in introductory survey courses to the countercultural seminars that encourage students to think beyond the "great men" of the canon. These pedagogical aims require us not to ignore professional and biographical studies of architects but to recontextualize their study toward the broader contexts of national policies and cultural politics (see chaps. 1, 17, 19, 20). Our hope is that this strategy will encourage the audiences of existing and future survey and elective courses in higher education to expand their gaze toward the wide range of methods that scholars collectively use to analyze the built environment.

Constructing a revisionist historiography of American architecture remains a difficult task, even as calls to bridge the study of high and low building cultures have been circulating for decades.[20] One obstacle is the settler colonial framing of America that veils contentious debates about national belonging in the nineteenth century.[21] Efforts to pluralize the history of American architecture by merely combining the contents of vernacular and avant-garde building surveys fail to destabilize the disciplinary biases and definitions of professional expertise that preserve the institutional categories that successfully segregated national building cultures along racial, gender, and class lines. How can one properly contextualize the story of Indigenous architecture into a survey of American architecture without first challenging the political function of European-inspired canons and stylistic revivals as a settler colonial project? And what countercultural definitions of national building traditions are elided by the maintenance of an assimilative hegemonic model of American character that reinforces the inevitability of racial and gender parity as a final product of American liberalism? Recovering the illiberal trends of nineteenth-century politics frees us to remember the historical stakes associated with experimental building practices and movements.

The historical narratives of Black builders and critics discussed in this volume initiate a contested "potential history," to borrow Ariella Azoulay's term, for the discipline of architecture during the antebellum period, when minority rights for citizenship, voting, and personal freedom were not yet achieved (see chaps. 4–8).[22] And yet these subjects pursued an alternative form of architectural modernity that has yet to be incorporated within existing canons of masterworks. The social imaginaries of Black architectural genius articulated in such writings and buildings provide us with the scaffolding for a new disciplinary culture that is potentially freed of its illiberal biases. Our volume explores the material cultures and political imaginaries of Black subjects living in the United States. This theme substantively reintroduces the historical role of US sectionalism, abolition movements, and manumission and marronage in national building cultures, sometimes without aiming to produce a recognizable new style of building or architectural aesthetic. Examining the spatial innovation of Black cultural landscapes restores the fight for an alternative modernity that is completely elided by the demand for a minority style of building based on abstraction. Documenting this history is an important part of reforming our disciplinary culture.

Another obstacle to reforming the historiography of American architecture is the disciplinary standards that eschew certain kinds of historical phenomena as evidence of architectural genius. The architectural plans and models of licensed architects are rarely offered in this volume as definitive evidence of the public meaning intended by an architect or theorist. The conflicted motivations of a fragmented nineteenth-century public are understood to generate multiple, competing, and coextensive perceptions of the built environment. Emulating the techniques and strategies advanced by the spatial turn in architectural history, several chapters offer a phenomenological accounting of the social and political agencies that result from the situational habitus of nonwhite and Indigenous groups.[23] These settings were capable of exerting tremendous influence on the perceived meaning of settler colonial forms, even as minorities were excluded from shaping these environments directly as marginalized or underresourced public actors. The contributors to this volume have expanded our conception of archival evidence by consulting a broad range of sources, from African Methodist Episcopal newspapers (see chap. 7) and murals about Black master builders (see chap. 4) to literary references to Asian material culture (see chap. 10) and countercultural readings of state archives (see chaps. 14, 16). Broadening the range of actors included within the discipline emulates the revisionist models of expertise put forward by scholars such as Saidiya Hartman, Swati Chattopadhyay, Lewis R. Gordon, Rizvana Bradley, and Ned Blackhawk, to name just a few.[24]

The emergence of fieldwork in folk and vernacular studies of the 1970s and 1980s was a tremendous step toward reforming the potential range of evidence the architectural historian employed for locating actors operating in the built environment. Employing this approach to avant-garde buildings reveals the hidden politics of everyday spaces that bend a building's uses beyond the licensed architect's original intentions—mostly because these possibilities were unaccounted for in their original disciplinary contexts. Women consigned to home economics work are revealed to employ the notational strategies of licensed architects in their management of daily domestics (see chap. 2). The role of place-naming is shown to constitute an understudied yet parallel form of oral parti in regulating the construction of Black freedom towns—a mutuality that only emerges when studied through the collective lenses of architectural theory, urban and environmental planning practice, and statistical analysis (see chap. 6). The Texas ranch is understood to be a physical manifestation of the triad of race, money, and power (see chap. 3). Missionary campuses and congressional libraries are understood to be the materialization of settler colonial aesthetic tropes and motifs and the aestheticization of political projections abroad (see chaps. 12, 18). And the study of mahogany uncovers the common transatlantic routes of slave labor and architectural theory—two phenomena brought together by the economic regimes of racial capitalism in the United States (see chap. 11).[25] This latter framework makes use of recent findings in economics that mine the historical roots of capitalist exploitation in architectural debates.[26]

We hope that embracing a horizontal framework of building expertise not only will assist scholars in constructing a revisionist history of American architecture in the present but also may reveal the inherent transdisciplinary potential of architectural history as an academic field. Histories of the built environment are currently produced in disciplines as distinct as anthropology, sociology, cultural studies, art history, and architectural history. Architectural historians inhabit a unique institutional position within the humanities that is a direct result of their situatedness within professional schools of architecture and design. This institutional habitus has historically been the root of intractable problems in the past, most notably in the inheritance of a racialized model of evolutionary development that promotes the neo-avant-gardist pedagogies of architectural education.[27] Yet such a position places the architectural historian in the enviable position of writing directly to future generations of architects, planners, and preservationists. What models of architecture might the historian offer that depart from the exclusive notions of artistic genius currently canonized within the discipline? How might we write and teach in ways that continue to problematize the discipline's long-standing tradition of self-promotion through history? Perhaps we stand at the precipice of a reformation wherein architectural historians are ethically bound to reject their previous role as keepers of the disciplinary torch. Instead, they might create new hybrid disciplines that provincialize design within a horizontal schema of cultural production. Such an undertaking would represent a new phase of collective public scholarship on architecture.[28]

Structure of the Book

PART I: DEFINING THE PROFESSION

This book's conceptual subdivisions offer new rubrics for interpreting the meaning and importance of American architecture in the nineteenth century. Part I considers how architecture was professionalized in the United States and how that process was shaped by questions of race, gender, and regional identity. Building on our critique of architectural historiography, the chapters in this section examine how the boundaries of the profession were historically constructed through institutions, archives, and ideologies as a means of consolidating authority and cultural legitimacy. In doing so, these chapters uncover alternative sites of expertise, revealing how the architectural profession was always entangled with the political struggles over who counts as an architect and what counts as architecture.

The maturation of American architecture beyond the gentleman architect is linked historiographically to the birth of professionalization in the mid-nineteenth century. Scholars like Mary Woods have tied the creation of the American Institute of Architects (AIA) in 1857 to an explicit distancing of architects from craftsmen, with an emphasis on linking the creation of professional standards of conduct to a removal from working-class labor. In the first chapter, Kathryn E. Holliday looks beyond this dichotomy to reassess the ways that professionalization reflected the tensions of US sectionalism and spatialized the American profession in the urban North through deliberate organizational strategies that located the AIA's activities and membership primarily in New York and, later, in other cities of the urban North such as Philadelphia and Chicago. By asking how this established network of architects imagined and located their practices, she shows that their own conception of "American" reinforced the spatial imaginary that linked American architecture to Eurocentric aesthetics. The resulting self-written and self-published histories promoted the members of AIA and its view of American architectural history, leading to the creation of persistent regional hierarchies and a continued amnesia concerning the full scope of American practice across the South and West.

Beginning in the 1990s, historians such as Dolores Hayden and Annmarie Adams explored alternative histories of architecture that recognized different kinds of expertise in the construction and organization of the built environment, including the female homemaker, the sanitary engineer, and the home economist. Building on the historical momentum of the nineteenth-century women's rights movement, the early decades of the twentieth century saw the establishment of home economics programs at Cornell University and elsewhere as a route to professionalization taken up mainly by middle-class white women. In his chapter, Athanasiou Geolas explores the federal Bureau of Home Economics project to survey women's domestic labor on small family farms during the 1920s. The female home economists who undertook these surveys sought to record women's unrecognized contributions to the national agricultural economy. As Geolas argues, however, these women participated in the same racialized enactment of expertise as the predominantly male architectural profession in the same period. As this example shows, the expansion of professionalization to women in the early twentieth century did not necessarily overcome the assumption of white authority and the privileging of white social patterns and beliefs embedded in the architecture profession.

In her provocative contribution, Kathryn E. O'Rourke asks us to consider the role of archives and archival documents in constructing American architectural history. As she writes, the project to create a racially conscious historiography of nineteenth-century American architecture is hampered by the apparent lack of evidence of nonwhite building culture and by the shifting and highly contested definition of the nation's boundaries in this period, particularly in the Southwest. O'Rourke pairs two very different "objects" to make her case: a cattle brand registered in Texas in 1856 by a "mulata" woman named Margaret Smith Dimery and the enormous King Ranch owned and managed for most of the century by Henrietta King. These two objects, O'Rourke argues, illustrate an expanded conception of nineteenth-century American architecture, one defined by the triad of land, race, and power. In the landscape that made up the shifting territory of Northern Mexico, and then Texas, she writes, architecture may be understood as the accumulation of capital in the form of property and as a statement of power. Attention to the graphic image of the Dimery cattle brand and the numerous buildings that make up the King Ranch as legitimate archival objects allows for an expanded historical account of American architecture that exceeds the limitations of the discipline as it has been traditionally constructed—as one that is dominated by voices and interests from the Northeast.

PART II: RECONSTRUCTION AND ARCHITECTURE

Part II explores the role of Black Americans in the theory, practice, and discourse of building during the Reconstruction era. In her chapter on the Mason family—builders active in Austin, Texas, before and after the Civil War—Tara A. Dudley uses methods from traditional architectural history, historic preservation, and genealogical research to highlight African American contributions to the built environment. This includes the work of enslaved and freed craftsmen in trades such as brickmasonry and stonemasonry, carpentry, plastering, and ironwork. Although some of their work is preserved and respected by local historians and preservationists, professional attribution conventions often leave these craftsmen unnamed. Continuing the theme of seeking evidence beyond traditional archives, the work of uncovering these craftspeople's identities involved exploring genealogical records for information about slaveholding master builders, as well as research into census records and property and probate documents. As Dudley concludes, attention to these alternative research methods allows Black builders and architects to be seen and acknowledged.

Bryan E. Norwood expands the narrative of nineteenth-century American architectural historiography by looking to Black American writers and the counternarratives they created. His close reading of works by three writers—John Marrant, Robert Benjamin Lewis, and Martin Delany—uncovers how they both challenged and drew on the prevailing grand narratives of architectural history. As Norwood shows, Marrant, Lewis, and Delany rewrote the ideology of Freemasonry and its "grand Christian frame" to center Africa and the Black diaspora in their texts. Rereading these texts by Black nonarchitects offers an alternative to the exclusionary narratives embodied in canonical histories of the nineteenth-century American architectural profession.

While Black Americans were excluded from the architectural profession in the nineteenth century, they used alternate means to build thriving communities and towns across the American South. Andrea Roberts uses the idea of the parti to argue that the naming of Black towns should be seen as a practice that expands our understanding of architecture to include Black material culture. In the absence of drawings or other traditional means of interpreting architectural intent, Black placemaking and naming, as preserved in oral traditions and origin stories, provide an alternate means of understanding what she terms "an aspirational Black sense of place."

Using the intellectual framework of Black formalism, which encompasses the communal practices defining Black life in the nineteenth century, Melanee C. Harvey-Fryar examines the role of the African Methodist Episcopal (AME) Church in shaping the aesthetic standards of Black church architecture. Harvey interprets the AME newspaper *The Christian Recorder* as a public expression of a religio-racial identity aimed at achieving cultural mastery. Centering the career of the AME architect John A. Lankford, she explores how his religious and educational buildings promoted modern ideals and supported Black institutional development to combat racism.

In the final chapter of this section, Whitney Nell Stewart examines the complex interplay between historic preservation and racialized ideologies in the United States. As a counterpoint to nineteenth-century white preservationists who equated permanent architecture with civilization and moral superiority, her chapter explores how Black Americans understood the demolition of certain historic structures, such as one-room slave cabins, as essential to their political struggle for rights and racial uplift. By focusing on the Jim Crow–era campaign by Black activists to demolish these cabins, Stewart challenges the traditional preservationist view that values the maintenance of structures as the primary goal, particularly when the historical memory a piece of architecture holds is considered too painful to preserve.

PART III: TRANSNATIONAL AMERICAS

The history of the Americas has been transnational in character since the founding of its earliest societies, from the Asian migrants who first entered North America across the Bering Strait to the European migrants who crossed the Atlantic Ocean to establish satellite colonies for extracting raw materials for modern industry. Even after the historian Frederick Jackson Turner theorized the closing of the American frontier in 1893, the various nations across the Americas maintained active connections with European trading partners and slave traders across the Atlantic, as well as connections across the Pacific toward new protectorates and Asian trade routes. These international developments contributed to active debates on the delineation of political borders and cultural boundaries. Understanding and reframing the border is essential, rather than peripheral, to US architectural history because it asks us to embrace a plural constitution of the Americas rather than a singular American narrative. This point is cogently expressed in Stephen Fox's chapter on border crossings, which mines the contingent identities of white settlers and people of color as the Mexican-American War shifted the boundaries of Matamoros, Mexico, and Brownsville, Texas. Fox shows how racial and ethnic identities were materially inscribed in the built environment, as racial codes of inclusion and exclusion were projected onto physical transformations—manifest in the reconfiguration of building typologies, the redirection of cotton trading routes, and the pluralization of designers and clients along the border's edge.

In the next chapter, Charles L. Davis II places Bernard Maybeck's West Coast modernism—typically examined through the lens of stylistic debates among US coastal elites—within a broader Pacific context. Informed by travels from San Francisco to Honolulu, Maybeck developed an ingenious process for abstracting the formal, spatial, and structural components of Japanese, Hawaiian, German, and English precedents to create a unique, wood-based style of American housing near the University of California, Berkeley. This approach reflected the academic interests of Maybeck's peers in Asian material culture and is perhaps most clearly expressed by public lectures and theatrical performances at the Hillside Club, of which he was a member. Davis suggests that Maybeck's paternalism, a form of progressive cultural appropriation, reveals the racial hierarchies underpinning his experiments with modern American architectural expression.

The last two chapters of this section examine the colonial roots of the material luxuries and religious ideologies imported into and exported from the United States. Jonah Rowen builds upon recent scholarship in American studies by tracing the slave labor and raw materials used to create mahogany finishes in luxury furnishings within the United States. Using three overlapping analytical rubrics—agents, materials, and geographies—Rowen traces the production of luxury spaces for urban elites to the hidden sources of racial and ethnic inequality in slaveholding Caribbean islands.

In the final chapter of part III, Yasmina El Chami highlights the role that extra-continental projects played in the elaboration of a "national" American political and architectural culture. El Chami examines the exporting of white Christian religious ideology through the design and construction of missionary campus architecture abroad. These sites operated as colonial outposts for disseminating Anglo-American religious and political values to the Middle East, primarily as physical embodiments of American exceptionalism, even as they operated as a soft form of social and economic influence.

PART IV: BUILDING SETTLER COLONIALISM

In the earliest canonical histories of American architecture, the notion of American exceptionalism is plainly evident in the intellectual and cultural frameworks used to describe the building cultures of the United States. Montgomery Schuyler's *American Architecture Studies* (1892) and Fiske Kimball's *American Architecture* (1928) are exemplary for their consideration of architecture culture as a continuous line of teleological development from the primitive vernacular structures of English, French, and German settlers into the modernist skyscrapers that made New York and Chicago such economic engines of national development. As a form of settler colonial culture, buildings, landscapes, and town plans naturalized the presence of European precedents in the very spaces that regulated daily life. During the post–Civil War period, this provided a social and political obstacle to the aspirations of recently freed peoples seeking to establish themselves—for example, in the freedmen's towns that emerged in the wake of US sectionalism. As Maura Lucking notes in her chapter, the landscape architect Frederick Law Olmsted desired the social and political function of Southern agriculture to be actively modeled on the landscape principles of New England towns and settlements. Olmsted's failure to properly theorize the position of the Black farmer in this context left his thinking open to the appropriations of New South and free labor apologists in the late nineteenth and twentieth centuries.

Indigenous groups are typically depicted as unilaterally suppressed by the socially assimilative and politically isolative policies of settler colonialism, especially during the long nineteenth century, when the doctrine of Indian removal gave birth to the Bureau of Indian Affairs. Yet Native scholars and historians of Indigenous peoples such as Ned Blackhawk, Roxanne Dunbar-Ortiz, and Kathleen DuVal document the ways that Indigenous subjects continued to find ways of controlling their engagement with foreign trade, conducting themselves as sovereign subjects, and actively resisted settler attempts to unilaterally define their place within the American landscape. In her chapter, Katherine Solomonson analyzes the ways that the Očéti Ŝakówiŋ cleverly employed their use of space in the Dakota Territory to undermine federal attempts to coerce the signing of imbalanced treaties. In carefully articulated close readings, Solomonson reveals the ways that Indigenous spatial practices upend traditional readings of settler space, at times even for the settlers themselves. In light of the biased documentation of Native practices found in the federal archive, this chapter emphasizes the importance of adopting countercultural reading practices to elevate and centralize the Native experience in histories of the national past.

In her chapter, Anjelica S. Gallegos examines the architecture and spatial practices of the federal Indian boarding school system as a deliberate tool of settler colonialism, designed to erase Indigenous spatial practices and enforce assimilation. Contrasting the rigid built environment of Fort Lewis Indian Boarding School in Colorado with the seasonal, reciprocal, and ephemeral spatial traditions of the Southern Ute people, she reveals how Indigenous children were forcibly subjected to identity-altering regimes within spaces that denied their cultural lifeways. Yet Gallegos also highlights acts of resistance and the persistence of Indigenous knowledge. Drawing on newly released federal reports, as well as oral histories and tribal knowledge, the chapter calls for a redefinition of American architectural history to include Indigenous design traditions as distinct spatial and material epistemologies.

Finally, Manuel Shvartzberg Carrió reinterprets the Southern California ranch house as a site of settler colonial domination and Indigenous resistance. Beginning with the romanticization of the Mission style in architectural history, he demonstrates how the ranch house served first as a material tool of Indigenous erasure and later as a bureaucratic instrument of assimilation, particularly through the Dawes Act and New Deal housing reforms. In this way, the chapter reconfigures the ranch house as a contested architectural form entangled in racial capitalism, state power, and Indigenous self-determination.

PART V: MODERN MYTHOLOGIES

The chapters in this section examine a pivotal moment when constructions of American architectural history shifted in response to changing national and imperial ambitions around the turn of the twentieth century. This period saw the emergence of modern mythologies—foundational ideas about architecture's role in expressing national identity, racial hierarchy, and technological progress—that would shape the discourse on American architecture well into the late twentieth century. These myths include the belief in American exceptionalism and manifest destiny and the notion of the United States as a technologically superior and racially distinct civilization.

The figure of Thomas Jefferson holds a privileged position in American architectural history, in which he is often presented as the prototypical American architect. Beginning in the 1970s, historians revealed the presence of slavery in Jefferson's architecture, paying particular attention to how Monticello depended on classical models and at the same time rendered invisible its dependence on enslaved labor. This literature is often presented as a project of historic completion, expanding our knowledge of Jefferson and his work by placing it in its social, economic, and political context. Taking a historiographical approach, Peter Minosh looks beyond Jefferson's biography and built works to explore the constitutive role Jefferson has played in the history of American architecture written during the twentieth century, focusing on texts by Fiske Kimball, Vincent Scully, and Manfredo Tafuri. Minosh writes that this history, although largely silent on the question of slavery, is not merely incomplete. Rather, in its various approaches and methods, it has been shaped by an effort to create an origin story for modern architecture in which the forms and values associated with democracy are privileged as eternal while the legacies of enslavement are rejected as contingent, or historic.

Examining the iconographic program of the Library of Congress, Diana Martinez focuses on its ornamental expression of ideas of American nationhood. Inaugurated in 1897 as the first purpose-built structure for the national library, the Library of Congress was a key expression of the so-called American Renaissance. Designed during a period of post–Civil War reconstruction, this important federal building projected a vision of American civilization as racially ordered and culturally ascendant. Martinez argues that the library's ornamental schema and spatial ordering reflected not only domestic efforts to incorporate formerly enslaved, Indigenous, and immigrant populations into a hierarchical national identity but also international ambitions to extend that racial order abroad. Rather than a neutral container of knowledge, the library building functioned as an architectural projection of the empire, cloaked in the language of scientific progress and civilization.

The final two chapters take on the mythologies of the Chicago School. Joanna Merwood-Salisbury challenges the myth that William Le Baron Jenney's 1885 Home Insurance Building was the first true skyscraper, arguing that its iconic status rests less on structural innovation than on racialized ideas of evolutionary progress expressed through building technology. Through Jenney's own writings, the chapter reveals how nineteenth-century theories of architecture cast the skyscraper as the natural outcome of white American ingenuity—ideas embedded in professional discourse and reinforced by the technological innovations of the Civil War. Though the structural primacy of the Home Insurance Building has been debunked, the evolutionary metaphor remains central to architectural historiography.

In his prehistory of Frank Lloyd Wright's concept of Usonia, Joseph M. Watson traces the racialized and nationalist origins of the term and complicates its association with democratic architectural ideals. Watson shows that Wright did not invent the term, nor was he the first to use it in architectural discourse. Instead, "Usonia" emerged in the late nineteenth century as a racially coded neologism aimed at distinguishing white US citizens from other Americans, particularly in the context of US imperialism and expansion. Watson reveals how Wright adopted and repurposed "Usonia" in the 1920s to promote a vision of architecture rooted in organic, "indigenous" design, while obscuring the term's exclusionary logic. These final chapters challenge the foundational narratives of American modernism, revealing how architecture was central to the construction of national myths that conflated race, empire, and progress. They call for a critical rethinking of the historiographical frameworks that continue to define the field.

Notes

1. W. E. B. Du Bois, "The Propaganda of History," in *Black Reconstruction in America* (Harcourt, Brace, 1935; Routledge, 2017), 637.

2. Du Bois, "Propaganda of History," 638.

3. Horatio Greenough, "American Architecture," *The Crayon* 2 (1855): 224–226; first published 1843.

4. See, for example, Henry Van Brunt, "Architecture in the West," *Inland Architect* 14, no. 7 (1889): 78–80.

5. Montgomery Schuyler, "The Point of View," in *American Architecture Studies* (New York: Harper & Brothers, 1892), 5.

6. Mariana Griswold Van Rensselaer, "Client and Architect," *North American Review* (September 1890); reprinted in *Places*, February 2013, https://placesjournal.org/article/client-and-architect.

7. Van Rensselaer, "Client and Architect."

8. Schuyler, "An American Cathedral," in *American Architecture Studies*, 111.

9. Fiske Kimball, "Beginnings," in *American Architecture* (Bobbs-Merrill, 1928), 19.

10. Vincent J. Scully Jr., *The Shingle Style and the Stick Style: Architectural Theory and Design from Richardson to the Origins of Wright* (Yale University Press, 1955), xxi. See also the multivolume series by William H. Pierson and William H. Jordy, *American Buildings and Their Architects* (Doubleday, 1970–1978), which further canonizes this particular sequence from the early republic through Wright.

11. Marcel Vellinga, "The End of the Vernacular: Anthropology and the Architecture of the Other," *Etnofoor* 23, no. 1 (2011): 171–192; Irene Cheng, Charles L. Davis II, and Mabel O. Wilson, "Racial Evidence," *Journal of the Society of Architectural Historians* 76, no. 4 (2017): 440–442.

12. "A Conversation with Kenneth Frampton: Can There Be a Global Architectural History Today?," lecture at the Canadian Centre for Architecture, Montreal, Quebec, recorded April 19, 2017, posted by CCAchannel, YouTube, https://www.youtube.com/watch?v=QRWp5AqAZjs.

13. A notable exception is Dell Upton's *American Architecture: A Thematic History* (Oxford University Press, 2019), which straddles the format of a general textbook that foregoes a chronological arrangement.

14. Du Bois, "Propaganda of History," 635–651.

15. See Irene Cheng, Charles L. Davis II, and Mabel O. Wilson, eds., *Race and Modern Architecture: A Critical History from the Enlightenment to the Present* (University of Pittsburgh Press, 2020). The opening chapters of the present volume outline the racial epistemologies established by the Enlightenment discourses disseminated in transatlantic debates of the eighteenth century. The European pedigree of these debates legitimized the white cultural nationalisms espoused by modern critics searching for an autochthonous style of American architecture (see chaps. 1–7).

16. The lead organizers of the symposium were Charles L. Davis II, Joanna Merwood-Salisbury, and Kathryn E. Holliday. Mabel O. Wilson and Dianne Harris delivered the opening and closing keynotes, respectively. We would like to thank those who contributed funds and administrative support for this event, including Dean Robert Shibley, Professor Hadas Steiner, Jessie Fisher, and Reinhold Martin with the Temple Hoyne Buell Center for the Study of American Architecture.

17. These scholars—Tara A. Dudley, Bryan Norwood, Katherine O'Rourke, and Joseph Watson—all became contributors to this current volume.

18. We would like to thank the Society of Architectural Historians for accepting our proposal for an SAH Connects online session. Special thanks go to Carla Yanni, Christopher Kirbabas, and Helena Dean for spearheading this effort.

19. This insight was included in a question posed by Louis Nelson. For a transcript of the questions asked during our publication workshop, see SAH Connects Q&A, Society of Architectural Historians, accessed June 30, 2024, https://www.sah.org/docs/default-source/sah-connects—-public/q-a-transcript.pdf.

20. Thomas Carter and Bernard L. Herman, "Introduction: Toward a New Architectural History," *Perspectives in Vernacular Architecture* 4 (1991): 1–6.

21. Patrick Wolfe, "Settler Colonialism and the Elimination of the Native," *Journal of Genocide Research* 8, no. 4 (2006): 388.

22. Ariella Azoulay, *Potential History: Unlearning Imperialism* (Verso, 2019).

23. For an example of a world art history told from a spatial perspective, See David Summers, *Real Spaces: World Art History and the Rise of Western Modernism* (Phaidon Press, 2003). Swati Chattopadhyay tells of a spatial turn in postcolonial critiques of architecture in "New Spatial Histories," *Journal of the Society of Architectural Historians* 73, no. 4 (2014): 461–463. See also Adrienne Brown, *The Black Skyscraper: Architecture and the Perception of Race* (Johns Hopkins University Press, 2019), and Rizvana Bradley, *Anteaesthetics: Black Aesthesis and the Critique of Form* (Stanford University Press, 2023), both of which are racial critiques of traditional phenomenology as it applies to Black spaces in the built environment.

24. Saidiya Hartman, *Wayward Lives, Beautiful Experiments: Intimate Histories of Riotous Black Girls, Troublesome Women, and Queer Radicals* (W. W. Norton, 2020); Swati Chattopadhyay, *Small Spaces: Recasting the Architecture of Empire* (Bloomsbury, 2023); Lewis R. Gordon, *Black Existentialism and Decolonizing Knowledge*, ed. Rozena Maart, Sayan Dey, and Lewis R. Gordon (Bloomsbury Academic, 2023); Ned Blackhawk, *The Rediscovery of America: Native Peoples and the Unmaking of U.S. History* (Yale University Press, 2023).

25. For comparable studies on racial capitalism and architectural materials, see Jennifer L. Anderson, *Mahogany: The Costs of Luxury in Early America* (Harvard University Press, 2012).

26. A good example of this kind of scholarship is Whitney Martinko, *Historic Real Estate: Market Morality and the Politics of Preservation in the Early United States* (University of Pennsylvania Press, 2020).

27. See Mark Jarzombek's critique of this position in "Conversation with Kenneth Frampton."

28. This would be comparable to the bridging function served by the growth of architectural criticism in newspapers and public-facing journals directed toward nonspecialists. See Michael Sorkin's positive assessment in "Critical Mass: Why Architectural Criticism Matters," *Architectural Review*, May 28, 2014; and Mimi Zeiger's social critique of architectural criticism in "'It's Time to Abolish the Architecture Critic,'" *Dezeen*, March 1, 2021, https://www.dezeen.com/2021/03/01/abolish-architecture-critics-newspaper-mimi-zeiger/.

PART I

DEFINING THE PROFESSION

1 SPATIALIZING THE AMERICAN ARCHITECTURAL PROFESSION IN THE NINETEENTH CENTURY

Kathryn E. Holliday

IN 1857, A SMALL GROUP of New York architects met in the office of Richard Upjohn in the Trinity Building on Broadway. Their goal was to establish a professional organization, the American Institute of Architects (AIA), to solidify their status in the rapidly expanding economy of American building and create standards for contracts and ethical practice. They also sought to create standards of aesthetics, taste, and intellectual attainment through the creation of a shared library, a paper series, and discussion of the proper education of potential architects. It was a generative moment for American architecture, one that began to delineate the shared codes by which architects would behave, do business, and design. From this first meeting, generations of architects in the AIA have discussed and debated the same issues, perennially seeking to define the scope of an architect's work relative to the craftspeople, laborers, and engineers who are also necessary to the making of buildings.

The consolidation of this effort to create the AIA in a single place, namely New York City, may seem natural or inevitable, given the city's prominence as a commercial and cultural center today. This essay argues, however, that repositioning the 1857 formation within the context of antebellum US sectionalism allows architectural historians to look anew at our assumptions about definitions of American architecture, the development of regional hierarchies in its historiography, and multiple generations' search for the historical origins of American modernism in the practices of nineteenth-century urban architects. While historians such as Mary Woods and Andrew Saint have examined the formation of the AIA within the context of nineteenth-century professionalization movements, there remain opportunities to link its formation to other theoretical approaches and social contexts.[1] A spatialized framing of architectural practice in the United States, one that reflects the AIA's deliberate retreat from the unstable borders of the South and West, suggests the creation of a defensive bastion of urban architecture culture in New York that could hold itself aloof from the exploitative systems of slavery and labor that translated drawn design into constructed form. While the AIA's creation reflects larger global movements toward professionalization and ownership of knowledge, in Jacksonian America the beginnings of labor organization in the urban North and labor's troubled relationship with abolition and antislavery movements is essential in understanding the structural biases of the organization and profession. As historians, if we do not directly link professionalization to the larger issues surrounding labor and slavery in the United States, we contribute to the depoliticized narrative of architecture that the AIA's founders sought to project.

Understanding American architecture through the profession and its architects, using the structures and definitions reinforced by the creation of the AIA, has historiographically created certain kinds of narratives. The "first architect" is alternately identified as Charles Bulfinch of Boston; Benjamin Henry Latrobe of Baltimore; Peter Harrison of Newport, Rhode Island; or Stephen Hallet of Washington, DC.[2] The first university-based architecture school is at the Massachusetts Institute of Technology (1867), the first trade-based architecture school is in Philadelphia, and the first professional organization is the New York–based AIA (1857). All of these accounts focus on a narrative of the American architectural profession grounded in a stable urban, industrialized center as fundamental to how we understand the making of architecture, a framework that reflects the worldview of the early histories of American architecture, written by figures like Louisa Tuthill and, later, Talbot Hamlin and Henry-Russell Hitchcock, who themselves were largely based in the cities of the Eastern Seaboard of the United States and immersed in Eurocentric systems of design and art history.[3] Those narratives suggest a teleological progress framed by a small, self-defining, elite group of men with a vested interest in aligning American histories of architecture with European histories of architecture in their methodologies and values. Those histories emphasize avant-garde creative innovation, aesthetic expertise, large scales of practice, and links to powerful institutions like cities, governments, museums, banks, corporations, churches, and universities that created permanence in a newly formed country.

More recent scholars have redressed this skewed historiography by building rich traditions of inquiry in vernacular architecture, looking at the long architectural histories created by indigenous builders and documenting regional histories outside the power centers of the urban Eastern Seaboard.[4] These strategies largely turn their back to the question of the American profession and its architects, seeking to decenter the structures of elitism and whiteness that long supported the centrality of their place in the story of American architectural history.[5] But this neglect has not allowed a fuller inquiry into how and why the profession shaped itself the way it did in the United States and what we might learn by asking additional questions about the practitioners of the nineteenth century as well as how and why they constructed the institutions they did. For many historians of architecture, the AIA has been of only peripheral interest, whether because of its perceived lack of influence on canonical design or because of a principled disinterest in the profession as an elitist construct. The AIA is thus central to American architectural history and at the same time peripheral. It is the organization that increasingly regulated architectural production and discourse through its journal, its awards programs, and its networks of members. At the same time, the AIA, in its focus on issues purely architectural, created enormous distance between itself and the context for practice in the United States. Many practitioners chafed at its structure and policies and viewed it as little more than a club for a cliquish group of members.

This essay argues that the formation of the AIA in New York in 1857 and its subsequent regionalized history through the next fifty years encoded mythologized narratives of American architecture that had their roots in antebellum conflicts about race, labor, and slavery. Pre–Civil War divisions between the urbanized North and the rural South shaped the profession's structure and its self-description and informed how practitioners narrated their work—and how historians would later begin to develop histories of the profession. These narratives reflected prevailing cultural norms associated with US sectionalism and presented the AIA and the profession as genuinely separate from the issues that divided the country, led to violent labor demonstrations in city streets, and fomented the coming war. That supposed agnosticism belies what I suggest was a deliberate attempt to distance architecture as a profession from labor not just because of issues of class, as other scholars have well documented, but also, more specifically in the American context, from the issue of slavery and architecture's entanglement with it across the United States. The profession's distance from the abolition movements and from labor reform is critical to its self-positioning as an urban, Northern profession.

These issues are sprawling, and rather than provide a series of definitive answers, this essay seeks to prompt speculations for a future historiography based in a different understanding of the forms of architectural practice, taken in the context of the realities of the nineteenth century in the United States, which was anything but stable. It was a century defined by multiple wars on US soil, dramatically unstable borders at the southern and western edges, genocide of Indigenous peoples, enslavement of millions of African-descended people, massive immigration from Europe and Asia, and violence in US cities over labor and military drafts. The land we call the United States today began the nineteenth century as sixteen states and ended as forty-five. What if American architectural history, instead of focusing on the creation of stability and order, focused on sites of contest, where shifting ideas of what it meant to be American were being formed and tested? What if America, in the nineteenth century, is not well represented by New York but is better represented by New Orleans, as it was traded between Spain, France, and the United States? What if the Texas-Mexico border represents America in the nineteenth century better than Boston does, as it shifted between Spain, Mexico, the Republic of Texas, and eventually the United States?[6] What if, in writing about American architects and architecture in the nineteenth century, we worked from the premise that there was no America, only a constantly contested idea of what it might be in the future? And why have we, as architecture historians, accepted histories that neglect conflict in favor of stability?

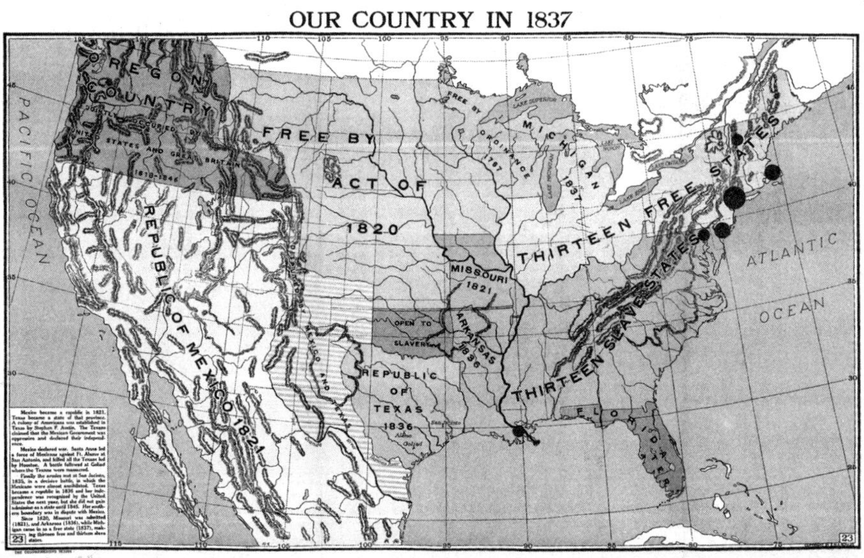

FIGURE 1.1. *The United States in 1837, evenly divided between thirteen free states in the Northeast and thirteen slave states in the Southeast. Territories are shown with light and dark shading, respectively, to indicate free territory (Republic of Texas and the future Midwest) and territory open to slavery (Florida and Oregon Country). Known members of the American Institution of Architects are designated by the dark dots in New Orleans and the Northeast. Map courtesy of the Library of Congress, Geography and Map Division; with additions by the author.*

By comparing the 1857 formation of the American Institute of Architects in New York with a failed attempt to create an American *Institution* of Architects just twenty years earlier, we can see two different self-conceptions of the profession based in differing ways of spatializing professional relationships across the United States. While the AIA formed in 1857 was based in New York and counted its membership entirely from that city (with the exception of a grandfathered membership extended to the Philadelphia architect Thomas U. Walter), the earlier Institution cast a wide net across the entire country, from New Orleans to Vermont (figs. 1.1, 1.2). By recontextualizing the development of the profession within this broader range of political and spatial dimensions, we can reknit the scales and varieties of US architectural knowledge, rather than accepting the divisions and hierarchies of the nineteenth century. We can prompt ourselves, as historians, to think differently about the ways that practice relates to representations of architectural value and to systems of slavery and labor, and the ways that the

FIGURE 1.2. *"Reynolds's Political Map of the United States," based on the 1850 census and published in 1856, showing the extent of slavery after the repeal of the 1820 Missouri Compromise made slavery legal in US territories. The Northern states and California are free, while the Southern states, including Missouri and Texas, are slaveholding. The American Institute of Architects shrank from its earlier incarnation, reducing its footprint to New York City. Map courtesy of the New York Public Library, Map Division; with additions by the author.*

Civil War defined the profession, even in the absence of overt discussion of any of these issues among its members. Only by recovering the intertwining of architecture with the politics of labor, abolition, and slavery can we create an American architectural history that more accurately sees the multiplication of thousands of distinct local histories in the nineteenth century as a more accurate reflection of the highly varied forms of practice and design that created architecture in the United States.[7]

Spatializing American Architecture Through Professionalization

Today's AIA finds its origins in a small group of self-described architects who banded together in New York City in 1857. Called together by Richard Upjohn—an English-born and -trained architect with a large, prosperous practice—at his offices in the Trinity Building in Lower Manhattan, the group of thirteen encompassed figures from across New York's building and design world. They had various kinds of relationships: mentor and mentee, employer and employee, competitors and colleagues, father and son. The thirteen included Richard Upjohn and his son R. M. Upjohn, Edward Gardiner, H. W. Cleaveland, Jacob Wrey Mould, Leopold Eidlitz, Henry Dudley, Frederick A. Petersen, Charles Babcock, Joseph C. Wells, Richard Morris Hunt, John Welch, and J. M. Priest.[8] It was a fractious group, holding meetings intermittently, often not reaching a quorum, and holding debates over papers on topics relating to cast iron, church design, and decoration in architecture that ran well into the night. It added a handful of additional members from New York quickly and invited Philadelphia-based Thomas U. Walter—largely an honorary position acknowledging his former role as secretary of the 1836 American Institution of Architects (Walter attended one early meeting of the AIA in New York on July 7, 1857). The group created a constitution and bylaws and set about trying to establish standards for the profession related to contracts, competitions, ethics, and education. They began holding, or at least scheduling, monthly meetings in Upjohn's office, occasionally rotating to other members' offices. Members began to donate materials for a shared library, which prompted attempts to find a permanent meeting location. Early attempts to secure an official meeting space in the Cooper Institute were unsuccessful, so an itinerant schedule of meetings in Upjohn's and other members' offices continued. Despite its ambitions, the group was largely a debate society, and actions related to the regulation of architecture, construction, and labor largely came from outside its purview.[9]

In studying the minutes of AIA meetings, reading the papers delivered and published by its members, and discovering the alliances and rivalries among them, it also appears that the group considered itself broadly international and worldly in its scope. They represented a transatlantic range of ideas about education and professionalization, comprising English, German, French, and eastern European professional and intellectual cultures. They had personal backgrounds that ranged from the patrician upbringing of Richard Morris Hunt in New York to the more constrained childhood of Leopold Eidlitz in Prague's Jewish quarter. They donated publications on Greece, Japan, and Moorish Spain to the organization's shared library. They did not in any way perceive that limiting their membership to New York skewed their understanding of the American profession. Instead, they operated from an assumption that their debates were in fact willing an American profession into existence through their collective pursuits. Mary Woods has written that the survival of this group in a cultural climate hostile to professionalization was perhaps its greatest achievement.[10] The early AIA might have suggested that it viewed the American profession as interconnected with Europe in much the same way as the newly constructed telegraph network, creating a spatial imaginary that filtered the global history and practice of architecture through their debates in New York (fig. 1.3). Thomas U. Walter's invention of the term "Americo-Roman" to describe New York City Hall (1803–1812) is a reflection of this mindset.[11] Practice in America was an extension of an already established global culture, and the AIA served to connect its members to that long, exalted history.[12]

Absent from any official record of the AIA, and absent from the writing of its membership, was explicit reference to America itself as a place to practice. Richard Upjohn, the group's organizer and president for its first decades, conducted a practice firmly based in New York, with commissions heavily concentrated in

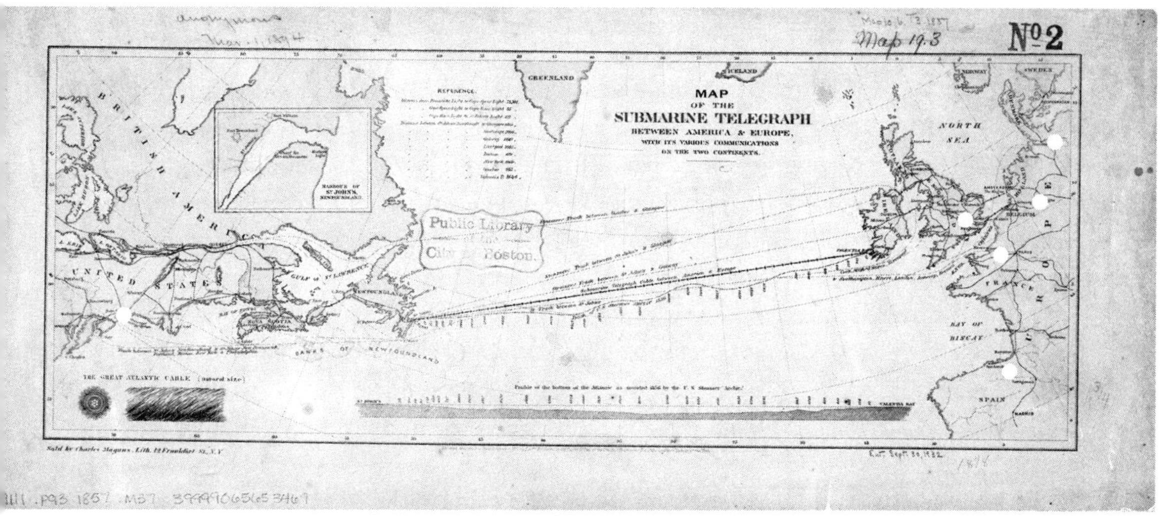

FIGURE 1.3. *Map of the submarine telegraph between America and Europe, published by Korff Brothers, 1857. Members of the American Institute of Architects envisioned themselves as spatially and culturally intertwined with their home countries and the Western history of architecture. Map courtesy of the Norman B. Leventhal Map and Education Center at the Boston Public Library; with additions by the author.*

the Northeast and New England. His book *Upjohn's Rural Architecture* (1852) published plans for small wooden churches, houses, and "rural structures" suitable for building in remote locations. His own practice spatialized the dominance of New York and dissemination of knowledge across the American landscape through drawings. His practice was based not on travel but on correspondence and letters (now preserved at the New York Public Library). Churches in remote, small communities like Fourmile Branch, Tennessee (1852–1853), Aiken, South Carolina (1847–1848), and Cahaba, Alabama (1854), the state's one time capital, rose from plans commissioned from afar and delivered via messenger and post.[13] Upjohn had never seen these rural places, and he envisioned an idealized architecture for them based on his vantage point in New York, filtered through a hegemonic understanding of Christian architecture formed in Augustus Pugin's England (figs. 1.4, 1.5). Though some carpenters have been identified, for the most part it was unknown carpenters, craftspeople, and enslaved people who translated those drawings into architecture, in a process unobserved by Upjohn.[14]

While there are multiple references to the idea of America in the AIA's discussions (perhaps most importantly, in the nationalistic name of their organization), nothing acknowledges the distinctly American systems of labor that made architecture possible—namely, the growth of labor unions and the increasing conflict over slavery. In 1857, the Supreme Court handed down its *Dred Scott* decision, which upheld slavery and denied the possibility of citizenship for Black people. Frederick Douglass published *My Bondage and My Freedom* in the same year. That year also marked the escalation of labor union organization and public protest in New York and across US cities, with demonstrations and marches violently disbanded by police. In this broader context, the AIA's retreat into drawing room debates appears as a deliberate choice. Their meetings and goals did not address how the profession would relate to and negotiate with labor unions. They did not address how architects based in New York could contend with building a national practice across the boundaries of slave and free states established by sectionalism. They did not address differences in building practices in different urban environments with different cultures of labor. They did not take a position on abolition. None of these issues were actually irrelevant to the practice of architecture in the United States. We know that the work of all the New York architects who engaged with the AIA was disrupted by strikes, and that their projects built in slave states were crafted by enslaved men and women.[15] The AIA organized with intentional disregard for these issues and continued to deflect them across the nineteenth century.

The AIA's most direct response to the Civil War came at the conflict's conclusion. In 1867, the New York AIA held a convention that for the first time invited architects from across the country to participate. Upjohn, opening the proceedings, stated,

FIGURE 1.4. *A sample board-and-batten church. Richard Upjohn,* Upjohn's Rural Architecture *(New York: George P. Putnam, 1852). New York Public Library.*

FIGURE 1.5. *St. Luke's Episcopal Church, built to Upjohn's designs in 1854 in Cahaba, Alabama. The church was moved to Martin's Station in 1878, where it served as home to a Black congregation, and then moved again to Marion in 1934. Photo by W. N. Manning, 1933. Historic American Buildings Survey, Library of Congress.*

> From the time of the organization till the year 1867 . . . the only organization of architects in this country was simply local. In that year it was determined to enlarge its powers and under the reorganization it partook of the character of a national convocation. Every architect in the United States [has], therefore, been invited to take part.[16]

It is difficult to believe that this new call for a truly national organization was not directly related to the end of the Civil War and to what the historian Drew Gilpin Faust has described as "a new sense of national destiny, one designed to ensure that lives had been sacrificed for appropriately lofty ends."[17] The AIA and its board of trustees continued to meet in New York during the war, taking few actions but continuing to discuss what the future might hold. That its first action after the war was an attempt at union, calling together architects from across the country in a mirror of postwar reconstruction, is telling.

The actual structure of this union, however, was fragmented and hierarchical and continued to spatialize the profession of architecture through the urban North. The subject of the national organization and the creation of a chapter system consumed the AIA's New York meetings during 1866 and 1867, leading to heated disagreements about specifics of the policy.[18] The national AIA began through a chapter system, in which the national organization remained in New York and a sprawling, distributed system of local chapters could be formed in cities where architects self-organized. The national AIA played no role in encouraging the formation of chapters or advocating for a system inclusive of its geographically dispersed profession. In 1870, those chapters were located in New York, Philadelphia, Cincinnati, Chicago, Boston, and Baltimore, concentrating the AIA in cities closely connected along the Eastern Seaboard and extending through the new railroad to Chicago in the West. Conspicuously absent from this list were St. Louis, the country's fourth-largest city (AIA chapter formed 1884), and New Orleans, its ninth-largest (AIA chapter formed 1909)—both places with extensive networks of architects and builders. The Western Association of Architects formed in 1884, gathering together architects from Chicago, St. Louis, and other inland cities frustrated with the exclusivity of the AIA and its power structure in New York.[19] The Western Association challenged the primacy of the AIA and began to establish Chicago as an alternative power center to New York, but it soon ceded its challenge and was absorbed into the national organization. By 1897, there were nineteen AIA chapters, all in the urban North and Midwest. There were of course hundreds of architects at work in Galveston, New Orleans, Atlanta, Nashville, San Francisco, Seattle, and all points in between, who remained unengaged by the AIA in the nineteenth century.

Why does the formalized, spatialized structure of the AIA matter? The AIA and its chapters very quickly began to write their own histories of American architecture, championing their own members and the works they believed should be valued by the public. AIA conventions in New York, beginning in the years after the Civil War, honored its early members and feted significant careers, penning lengthy encomiums to Upjohn, Hunt, and others. Through a partnership with *The American Architect and Building News* formed in 1876, the AIA promoted these narratives to a broader architectural audience. The Western Association of Architects formed an official partnership with *The Inland Architect and Builder*, "a monthly journal devoted to western interests," beginning in 1884 as part of its agenda to champion its own network of architects and narrate its own accomplishments. Philadelphia's chapter celebrated its own founders, Thomas U. Walter and John Haviland, and created their own narrative of American architecture based in their own city.[20] From the beginning, the AIA consciously kept records, formalizing its history and publishing its proceedings in a variety of partner journals. It was self-conscious about painting a portrait of its permanence and success through the power of the archive and its association with institutions from which it could borrow social capital. For example, Fiske Kimball—architect, architectural historian, architectural educator, and museum director—was also the AIA's first historian. Kimball assembled the AIA's records into an archive in 1926 in partnership with Florence P. Spofford. Kimball's teaching positions in multiple architecture schools across the country, from the University of Illinois Urbana-Champaign to the Institute of Fine Arts at New York University, and his position as director of the Philadelphia Museum of Art linked the history of the AIA to institutions of memory and cultural capital. The records he and Spofford assembled began to document American architecture through the lens of the AIA and its chapters from 1867 forward, heavily skewed toward cities in the urban North, with elite practitioners celebrated by their peers. Rarely do American architects who practiced before 1857 appear in these celebratory histories and catalogs—and never do nonmembers appear.[21]

The organization of the AIA, centered in New York and tilted heavily toward the urban North, was not inevitable. Within its own membership, this organization was continually critiqued as privileging cities over towns and reinforcing existing hierarchies and power structures that favored elite practitioners.[22] As a counterpoint, in 1836, a small group of architects made the first attempt to form a professional organization in the United States, the American Institution of Architects. Invited by New York–based Alexander Jackson Davis and Philadelphia-based Thomas U. Walter and John Haviland, the Institution gathered its membership in a first organizational meeting in New York and a second meeting held soon after at the Pennsylvania Academy of Fine Arts in Philadelphia in 1837. These members hailed from across what was then the United States, from as far west as New Orleans and northward to Vermont. The United States in 1837 was not the United States we know today, but this first Institution found broader geographic representation than the subsequent New York–based Institute (see figs. 1.1, 1.2). Because very few records survive, the exact membership of this early

Institution is difficult to determine, but a handful of letters from invited members remain in the AIA archives, as well as remembrances published by the later AIA's proceedings and chapter newsletters and magazines. Though records indicated a count of twenty-three members, twenty-five honorary members, and two associates, the only additional known members include John Trautwine and William Strickland of Philadelphia; Isiah Rogers, Minard Lafever, Charles F. Reichard, William C. Kramp, F. Schmidt, Thomas Thomas, and his son Thomas Thomas Jr. of New York; Asher Benjamin, Alexander Parris, Richard Bond, and William Sparrell of Boston; Robert C. Long Jr. of Baltimore; James H. Dakin of New Orleans; and Ammi B. Young of Vermont. This was an ambitious undertaking to connect architects across cities and regions, drawing in mentors and mentees who had traveled to and from the borders of the United States in pursuit of work. Very little scholarship exists on these practitioners beyond historic preservation, and their attempt to create a network among themselves provokes intriguing questions about generational shifts in the relationship between architecture and labor.[23] Perhaps most intriguing is how few of the known Institution members from 1836 were also members of the AIA in 1857—or were even remembered by the later AIA in their convention and journal encomiums. In the space of twenty years, the profession seems to have reinvented itself and its heroes entirely, with only a nod to Walter as an elder of the profession.

But the group's quick failure does not mean it is a trivial counterpoint to the later AIA. Historians have accepted Walter's later recollection that the Institution failed because it was too difficult to travel and meet, which suggested that long distances and travel times were a natural barrier to other forms of professional organization: "It was . . . impossible to keep up the meetings with any regularity, and as the consequence, the American Institution of Architects went quietly to sleep."[24] But we know that architects of the early nineteenth century traveled extensively in the United States and that they envisioned their practices as broadly engaged across all the states, both slave and free. This early attempt to organize asks us to look again at the scale of practice in 1837, recognizing the interlocking network of practitioners and labor that already connected slave and free states in industry and agriculture, but also in architecture. Town & Davis, the firm established by Ithiel Town and Alexander Jackson Davis, has been most associated with its work in New York, but through Davis's social connections the firm had extensive business in North Carolina. Town & Davis conducted professional practices enabled by the labor of enslaved men, as we know from documentation assembled by historians examining the construction of their designs for the North Carolina State Capitol (1833–1840) in Raleigh (fig. 1.6).[25] Town, known best to architectural historians as a promoter of the scholarly Greek Revival style in capitol buildings and the US Custom House in New York (1842; today Federal Hall National Memorial), made his fortune not through architecture but as an innovator in bridge construction based on his patent for the Town lattice truss

FIGURE 1.6. *Ithiel Town and Alexander Jackson Davis, North Carolina State Capitol, Raleigh, built with enslaved labor, 1833–1840. Photo by Tim Buchman. North Carolina State University Libraries, Built Heritage of North Carolina: Historic Architecture in the Old North State.*

that allowed the proliferation of railways across the country.[26] Covered wooden railroad bridges throughout the South, constructed by enslaved men, supported the cotton economy and the movement of goods between slave and free states. In about 1820, Town experimented with prototypes for his patent in North Carolina, designing the Clarendon Bridge over the Cape Fear River near Fayetteville, North Carolina—a critical piece of the state's plantation economy burned by retreating Confederate soldiers during the Civil War.[27]

Town & Davis were not alone in their entanglement in the American system of design and construction. Walter, though based in Philadelphia, spent many years focused on Washington, DC, as architect of the US Capitol dome (1855–1866), one of the most visible architectural endeavors of the nineteenth century. The dome and Capitol, as well as many other construction projects in Washington, depended on the expertise and labor of enslaved men—and, indirectly through their support for households, on enslaved women. Both Thomas U. Walter and Robert C. Long Jr. welcomed the new "association of architects from all parts of our country."[28] Ammi B. Young in Vermont and James H. Dakin in New Orleans represented the long reach of the founders.[29] Dakin, who had worked for Town & Davis before moving to Mobile, Alabama, and then on to New Orleans, wrote, "I am much elated to hear that something is doing for Architecture besides drawing and executing, which until now has been the only public demonstration of its existence in our country." Dakin was architect of the Old Louisiana State Capitol (1847–1852) in Baton Rouge and institutional buildings in New Orleans—built, again, with the labor of enslaved men.

Perhaps the greatest failure of the 1836 American Institution of Architects was that it did not tell its own story. The leaders of the 1857 organization had little use for backward-looking histories as they looked to the future, to growth, and to the creation of union in a future America. We can speculate that the AIA failed to tell the story of a profession so deeply rooted in a Jacksonian vision of America and openly tied to its expansionist acceptance of slavery's role in the making of architecture. By ignoring American architecture's history, the AIA could write a new story.

This seemingly trivial event in the history of the US profession provides us with an opportunity to look again at the values and structures embedded in professionalization. We should understand the entire historiography of nineteenth-century American architecture as rooted in US sectionalism: written by architects and architectural historians to justify a particular glossy definition of America that was urban and Northern and that sidelined pressing issues of labor and slavery well known to be integral to practice across the United States. We know that New York was divided over slavery, labor, and the future of a nation wounded by civil war.[30] Beyond this reality, we should also question why subsequent architectural historians and critics adhered to these stories and begin to look more carefully at the nineteenth-century profession, a subject largely neglected in the past several decades of architectural history. Guided by W. E. B. Du Bois's critique of US history, written in his critique of the failed memory of Reconstruction, we have an opportunity to see the architecture profession as historians, not how the profession has asked us to see it: "History," as it is written and taught in the United States, "paints perfect men and noble nations, but it does not tell the truth."[31]

Conclusion

In 1941, the influential public intellectual Lewis Mumford gave a series of addresses on the topic of "the South in architecture" at Alabama College in Montevallo, Alabama. While Reinhold Martin has written about these lectures in the context of modernism, here I suggest we look at the addresses in the context of the American nineteenth century.[32] While Mumford evinced ignorance of the South and claimed a "lack of . . . understanding which only a native Southerner" could have of its architecture, he nonetheless gave a series of four lectures about regionalism and modernism centered in his own understanding of American architecture and its motivations. He identified only two Southern architects, Thomas Jefferson and H. H. Richardson. Although Mumford identified both as "Southern" architects, what made them important was not their association with Southern culture, people, or places but their creation of a "universal" ideal (for Jefferson) and the embrace of a New England–based regionalism that became an "entirely native architecture" for America.[33] Mumford's discourse on nineteenth-century American architecture in the South gingerly skirts the issue of what he calls the "misfortunes" of the Civil War,[34] makes no mention of slavery, and skips one hundred years of the long nineteenth century by jumping from the founding of the republic, as viewed through the lens of Jefferson's 1780s, to the establishment of modernism in Richardson's 1880s.

While these lectures are in some ways minor essays by a prolific critic and writer of great influence on modernist architectural thinking, we should also see them as reflective of the blind spots and prejudices that informed the creation of the historiography of nineteenth-century American architecture. A lack of knowledge and documentation, which Mumford freely acknowledges, compounded with a narrow sense of the meaning of region in the United States, and a profound avoidance of issues of slavery and war, combined to fuel a misreading of "the South in architecture"—and as a result, a misreading of American architecture itself. The proliferation of widely varied architectural practices in the nineteenth century was of no interest to Mumford, whose sense of history, as is well documented, was informed by seeking precursors to modernist ideology.

Mumford's reading of American architecture is spatially and historiographically stunted and reflects both the structures and the spatialization established by the AIA in the nineteenth century. This myopia is reflected in the work of his contemporaries and of subsequent scholars, from Talbot Hamlin to James Marston Fitch, Marcus Whiffen and Frederick Koeper, and William H. Jordy and William H. Pierson Jr., to more recent scholarship that continues to reinforce a narrative of America based in hierarchies of region rather than their interconnectedness. American architectural historians have worked to create a more complex historiography that fills in these blind spots and makes possible a more nuanced understanding of this period. While that literature is too vast to catalog here, it fills out the canon of practitioners, creates new ways of understanding architectural production through vernacular practices, and investigates transnational avenues for the transfer of knowledge and labor. What requires our sustained attention are questions about why Mumford's and the other early historians' conceptions of American architectural practice were so skewed in the first place. Why did Mumford, Kimball, and Hamlin embrace a history of the United States so entirely divorced from its political realities, and what structures allowed them to pursue such blind histories? Contemporary histories of the United States in the nineteenth century did not at all neglect the Civil War, and while we today dispute the conclusions of scholars in the 1940s and 1950s, their attention was certainly engaged by issues of war, slavery, region, and power. Understanding what made architecture different then, and how we can redress those historiographic limitations imposed by authors and institutions, is at the core of a new approach to American nineteenth-century architectural history. This project has already begun, writ large, for the history of modernism; to view the nineteenth century in America as its own subject deeply connected to particularly American conflicts over land, slavery, labor, and race is essential.

Notes

1. Mary N. Woods, *From Craft to Profession: The Practice of Architecture in Nineteenth-Century America* (University of California Press, 1999); Andrew Saint, *Architect and Engineer: A Study in Sibling Rivalry* (Yale University Press, 2007).

2. For example, Harold Kirker writes that "Bulfinch became America's first native-born professional architect." Harold Kirker, *The Architecture of Charles Bulfinch* (Harvard University Press, 1969), 5. Latrobe described himself as "the first who, in our own Country has endeavored and partly succeeded to place the profession of Architect and civil Engineer on that footing of respectability which it occupies in Europe." John C. Van Horne, ed., *The Correspondence and Miscellaneous Papers of Benjamin Henry Latrobe: Vol. 2, 1805–1810* (Yale University Press, 1986), 680. Roger Hale Newton describes the firm of Town & Davis as "our first important 'association to practice architecture professionally.'" Roger Hale Newton, *Town and Davis, Architects: Pioneers in American Revivalist Architecture, 1812–1870* [. . .] (Columbia University Press, 1942), xviii.

3. Early architectural histories of the United States include Louisa C. Tuthill, *History of Architecture: From the Earliest Times; Its Present Condition in Europe and the United States; with a Biography of Eminent Architects* [. . .] (Philadelphia: Lindsay and Blakiston, 1848). For a discussion of early histories of architecture in the United States, see Sarah Allaback, "Louisa Tuthill, Ithiel Town, and the Beginnings of Architectural History Writing in America," in *American Architects and Their Books to 1848*, ed. Kenneth Hafertepe and James F. O'Gorman (University of Massachusetts Press, 2001), 199–215.

4. See, for example, Dell Upton and John Michael Vlach, eds., *Common Places: Readings in Vernacular Architecture* (University of Georgia Press, 1986). Also see the initial publication of the journal *Perspectives in Vernacular Architecture* in 1982 (now titled *Buildings and Landscapes*). Additional work unpacking the racial spatialization of plantations can be found in Rebecca Ginsburg and Clifton Ellis, eds., *Cabin, Quarter, Plantation: Architecture and Landscapes of North American Slavery* (Yale University Press, 2010).

5. Dell Upton, *Architecture in the United States* (Oxford University Press, 1998), esp. 251, and annotated bibliography, 312–315. The historian Jean Baker speculates that the current lack of attention to architects is because "architecture, unlike literature and art, has never been incorporated into social history." Jean H. Baker, *Building America: The Life of Benjamin Henry Latrobe* (Oxford University Press, 2020).

6. Julian Lim, *Porous Borders: Multiracial Migrations and the Law in the U.S.-Mexico Borderlands* (University of North Carolina Press, 2017).

7. I am depending on the rich scholarship from geography and planning that explores the spatialization of capital, labor, gender, and race, looking most specifically at literature connected to place. See George Lipsitz, "The Racialization of Space and the Spatialization of Race: Theorizing the Hidden Architecture of Landscape," *Landscape Journal* 26, no. 1 (2007): 10–23; Katherine McKittrick, *Demonic Grounds: Black Women and the Cartographies of Struggle* (University of Minnesota Press, 2006); Lisa K. Bates, Sharita A. Towne, Christopher Paul Jordan, et al., "Race and Spatial Imaginary: Planning Otherwise [. . .]," *Planning Theory & Practice* 19, no. 2 (2018): 254–288, https://doi.org/10.1080/14649357.2018.1456816. I am also indebted to colleagues who have questioned the dominance of the United States in conceptions of the Americas, and who have pursued retellings of architectural histories of the Americas from an alternative perspective. Those histories include Fernando Luiz Lara, *Spatial Theories for the Americas: Counterweights to Five Centuries of Eurocentrism* (University of Pittsburgh Press, 2024); Fernando Luiz Lara, ed., *Decolonizing the Spatial History of the Americas* (Center for American Architecture and Design, 2021). The essays published in two special issues of the *Journal of the Society of Architectural Historians (JSAH)* also created space for this inquiry. See "Constructing Race and Architecture, 1400–1800: Part 1," *JSAH* 80, no. 3 (2021): 258–279; "Constructing Race and Architecture, 1400–1800: Part 2," *JSAH* 80, no. 4 (2021): 385–415.

8. The meeting minutes are held by the archives of the AIA and show members present at each meeting beginning at the first, on February 23, 1857.

9. In addition to the work of Mary Woods and Andrew Saint, my own research has looked thematically at debates in the AIA about education and other matters. See Kathryn E. Holliday, "The Architect at Mid-Century: The AIA and Architecture Education, 1857 and 1957," in *Histories of Architecture Education in the United States*, ed. Peter L. Laurence (Routledge, 2024); Kathryn E. Holliday, "'Build More and Draw Less': The AIA and Leopold Eidlitz's Grand Central School of Architecture," *JSAH* 65, no. 3 (2006): 378–401.

10. Woods, who has painstakingly outlined the group's founding and influence, writes that the AIA's "limited agenda and selected membership" were keys to its survival in a climate initially hostile to professionalization. Woods, *From Craft to Profession*, 38.

11. Minard Lafever's *The Architectural Instructor, Containing a History of Architecture from the Earliest Ages to the Present Time* (New York: G. P. Putnam, 1856) and Thomas U. Walter's lectures on architecture reflect these attempts to position America as part of the European tradition. Walter's lecture on modern architecture covered Italy, France, Spain, Germany, and England and praised the "Americo-Roman" architecture of New York City Hall. Thomas U. Walter, *The Lectures on Architecture, 1841–1853*, ed. Jhennifer A. Amundson (Athenaeum of Philadelphia, 2006), 188.

12. A recent volume begins to address the origins and development of the idea of global histories: Petra Brouwer, Martin Bressani, and Christopher Drew Armstrong, eds., *Narrating the Globe: The Emergence of World Histories of Architecture* (MIT Press, 2023). Rebecca Roiphe's work on professionalization in the nineteenth-century United States suggested that in a "growingly diverse and intensely divided country," professionalization provided "an arena in which to negotiate these differences and translate them into a common language." The professionalization of architecture suggests that this "common" experience was more limited in scope than Roiphe suggests. Rebecca Roiphe, "A History of Professionalism: Julius Henry Cohen and the Professions as a Route to Citizenship," *Fordham Urban Law Journal* 40, no. 1 (2012): 33–74.

13. On Upjohn, see Everard Upjohn, *Richard Upjohn: Architect and Churchman* (Columbia University Press, 1939); Judith S. Hull, "The 'School of Upjohn': Richard Upjohn's Office," *JSAH* 52, no. 3 (1993): 281–306. Upjohn's work and intellectual position remain ripe for reexamination.

14. Peggy Deamer developed a Marxist critique of the separation of design from work: "Work," in *Architect as Worker: Immaterial Labor, the Creative Class and the Politics of Design*, ed. Peggy Deamer (Bloomsbury, 2015), 61.

15. In architectural history, see especially Joanna Merwood-Salisbury, *Design for the Crowd: Patriotism and Protest in Union Square* (University of Chicago Press, 2019). More generally, in labor history, the following provide many prompts for architectural historians: Joshua Greenberg, *Advocating the Man: Masculinity, Organized Labor, and the Household in New York, 1800–1840* (Columbia University Press, 2008); Sean Wilentz, *Chants Democratic: New York City and the Rise of the American Working Class, 1788–1850* (Oxford University Press, 1984).

16. Richard Upjohn, 1867 remarks, reprinted in "Architects in Council," *New York Times*, November 17, 1869, 2.

17. Drew Gilpin Faust, *This Republic of Suffering: Death and the American Civil War* (Alfred A. Knopf, 2008), 268.

18. According to the AIA meeting minutes held at the AIA archives, the first discussions of how to expand to national membership began at the November 6, 1866, meeting with a suggestion from Emlen T. Littell. See also George Champlin Mason, "Professional Ancestry of the Philadelphia Chapter," *Journal of the American Institute of Architects* 1, no. 9 (1913): 371–386.

19. Woods, *From Craft to Profession*, 38–39; Joanna Merwood-Salisbury, *Chicago 1890: The Skyscraper and the Modern City* (University of Chicago Press, 2009); Joanna Merwood-Salisbury, "Western Architecture: Regionalism and Race in the *Inland Architect*," in *Chicago Architecture: Histories, Revisions, Alternatives*, ed. Charles Waldheim and Katerina Rüedi Ray (University of Chicago Press, 2005), 3–14.

20. See Mason, "Professional Ancestry of the Philadelphia Chapter," 371. For more on Philadelphia architecture culture, see Michael J. Lewis, "The Philadelphia Way of Making Architects: The Birth and Birthplace of American Architecture Education," in Laurence, *Histories of Architecture Education*, 7–25.

21. Roxanne Kuter Williamson's *American Architects and the Mechanics of Fame* (University of Texas Press, 1991) provides some tantalizing investigations of the effects of networks and patrilineal firms on architectural "success." While the conclusions of the study are dubious, the questions asked in it are worth revisiting with new research frameworks. Garry Stevens attempts a long, linear, uncritical narrative of the Western architectural profession in "Review Essay: the Historical Demography of Architects," *JSAH* 55, no. 4 (1996): 435–453.

22. By the 1930s, a full-fledged movement to create a state-based, rather than city-based, AIA system was contemplated to redress these perennial complaints. See the discussion in "Report of the Committee

on State Organization," reprinted in *Weekly Bulletin of the Michigan Society of Architects* 12, no. 29 (1938). Note especially: "The Institute is controlled by the chapters of larger cities and the practitioner from the small town or city has little or no voice in its affairs." And, further: "As long as architects are individuals with little or no interest in the affairs of government outside of the few big cities where they practice, The Institute chapter system has worked. But it has ceased to work by itself, and the state associations have, to a certain extent, and will continue more and more to fill the new needs of the profession" (7).

23. Hafertepe and O'Gorman's *American Architects and Their Books to 1848* is an exception that reenvisions the early nineteenth-century profession through its writing.

24. Thomas U. Walter, "Annual Address," in *Proceedings of the Fourth Annual Convention of the American Institute of Architects, Held in Philadelphia, 1870* (New York: American Institute of Architects, 1871).

25. Davis pursued many commissions in North Carolina, made possible through his friendship with Robert Donaldson, a wealthy North Carolina merchant who built a financial empire in New York and in his home state, supported through plantation economies and enslaved laborers. An article by John Allcott remains the only investigation of the architect's role in building antebellum North Carolina: John V. Allcott, "Architect J. A. Davis in North Carolina," *North Carolina Architect* 20 (November and December 1973). See also Catherine Bishir, *North Carolina Architecture* (University of North Carolina Press, 1990), 289–290. Amelia Peck's exhibition catalog includes none of the work in North Carolina: Amelia Peck, ed., *Alexander Jackson Davis: American Architect, 1803–1892* (Rizzoli, 1992). Roger Hale Newton's *Town & Davis, Architects* remains the sole monograph of the Town & Davis firm's work.

26. John S. Lupold and Thomas L. French Jr.'s *Bridging Deep South Rivers: The Life and Legend of Horace King* (University of Georgia Press, 2004) discusses Ithiel Town's patents for the Town truss bridge and the proliferation of his bridges designed for railroads; see esp. 25–29.

27. On the role of the bridge in the town of Fayetteville, see John A. Oates, *The Story of Fayetteville and the Upper Cape Fear* (John A. Oates, 1972).

28. Robert C. Long Jr. to Thomas U. Walter, November 6, 1836, AIA archives. My thanks to Nancy Hadley, archivist for the AIA, for sharing the scant archival material related to this group's formation.

29. On Young, who practiced in Washington, DC; Boston; and New England, see Daniel Bluestone, "Civic Aesthetic Reserve: Ammi Burnham Young's 1850s Federal Customhouse Designs," *Winterthur Portfolio* 25 (1990): 131–156. On Dakin, see James C. Dakin to Thomas U. Walter, New Orleans, April 20, 1837, AIA archives. Dakin received Walter's letter but not the proposed bylaws and constitution, and therefore did not comment on them. Dakin's extensive work is examined in Arthur Scully Jr., *James Dakin, Architect: His Work in New York and the South* (Louisiana State University Press, 1973).

30. See, for example, Tyler Anbinder, *Nativism and Slavery: The Northern Know Nothings and the Politics of the 1850s* (Oxford University Press, 1992); Eric Foner, *Free Soil, Free Labor, Free Men: The Ideology of the Republican Party Before the Civil War* (Oxford University Press, 1995). Historians have deeply and repeatedly investigated the substantial historiography on these issues; one summary is Michael E. Woods, "What Twenty-First-Century Historians Have Said About the Causes of Disunion: A Civil War Sesquicentennial Review of the Recent Literature," *Journal of American History* 99, no. 2 (2012): 415–439.

31. W. E. B. Du Bois, *Black Reconstruction in America* (Harcourt, Brace, 1935; Routledge, 2012), 645.

32. Reinhold Martin, "Drawing the Color Line: Silence and Civilization from Jefferson to Mumford," in *Race and Modern Architecture: A Critical History from the Enlightenment to the Present*, ed. Irene Cheng, Charles L. Davis II, and Mabel O. Wilson (University of Pittsburgh Press, 2020), 59–78.

33. Lewis Mumford, *The South in Architecture—The Dancy Lectures, Alabama College, 1941* (Harcourt, Brace, 1941), 115.

34. Mumford, *South in Architecture*, 80.

2 VERNACULAR PROFESSIONALISM

RURAL HOME ECONOMICS AND THE RACIAL CONTRACT OF EXPERTISE

Athanasiou Geolas

DRESSED IN FLOWING ROBES AND makeshift wings, a group of female students danced in an open field under the gaze of a fairy queen (fig. 2.1). Organized by the student honors society Frigga Fylgae—meaning Followers of Frigg, the Anglo-Saxon goddess of fertility—these women were celebrating the 1916 graduating class of Cornell University's Department of Home Economics and the beginning of the graduates' professional careers.[1] Anti-modern enactments like these were common among professional organizations in the early twentieth century.[2] Home economics provided an early pathway for rural women (largely of western European ancestry) to develop economic and social independence as professionals. Like the advocates of other Progressive-minded disciplines, home economists championed architecture's leading role in social advancement. Within a rapidly expanding administrative state, they hoped to understand and refashion every-

FIGURE 2.1. *Women's pageant, 1916, held near Beebe Lake on the Cornell University campus as part of an annual fair hosted by the Frigga Fylgae society. Archives Picture Collection, collection no. 13-6-2497, Division of Rare and Manuscript Collections, Cornell University Library.*

day life, linking their expertise in domestic architecture with a new economic theory of consumption. Historians have thoroughly documented the apotheosis of the postwar suburban home and the impact of the racialized, single-family domesticity it exemplified.[3] Although they have also addressed home economics' impact on modern architecture through its use of efficiency studies and rationalization in the home, few have looked beyond urban and suburban contexts to the rural origins of these ideas.[4] Moreover, little scholarship to date has connected the early twentieth-century rise of professionals in architecture and design with home economists' new form of architectural expertise.[5] These women built the groundwork from which they dominated the analysis and design of domestic life from positions within farming communities.

This chapter presents a case study from the summer of 1925 to recontextualize home economics and the place of the professional in the historiography of American architecture. Engaging the rural history of this discipline revises the meaning of the architectural professional, a figure too often limited to the construction industry. This context shifts the focus of existing questions, including what defines the professional as a social category, who is allowed into it, and how it has been narrated. Architectural historians often ground the emergence of the professional in the replacement of eccentric local practices with newly developed standards guaranteed by university education and state regulation.[6] This chapter reconsiders the ongoing distinction between vernacular practices and professional standards in the history of architectural expertise by emphasizing the cultural embodiment of a regionally specific, gendered whiteness. It builds on what Gwendolyn Wright has termed "modern vernaculars" to show that home economists' racialized enactments of expertise embodied tensions that cannot be held apart as opposites. Wright presents the vernacular as both the "domain of the everyday" and a peculiar "language of expertise" that upsets dichotomies while operating "here-and-now, with daily life rather than theoretical abstractions."[7] Likewise, as George Barnett Johnston asserts, "there is no universally applicable model of professionalism."[8] Instead, professional authority must be understood as a multiscalar set of relations operating in specific locations. Asking which everyday relations underwrote rural home economists' practices reveals how these women embodied a form of whiteness that made their professional status suitable to local power dynamics.

Theoretical assumptions in the sociology of professions have heavily influenced the architectural history of North American professionals. These accounts frame professionalism as a jurisdictional dispute requiring the privatization of knowledge and an adherence to a normative model typical across disciplines, continents, and time periods. They call this matrix of components a "mandate," the "monopoly thesis," or, in Judith Blau's more poignant terminology, an "imperialist claim" for the right to privatize, implement, and evaluate a certain kind of specialized knowledge. Magali Sarfatti Larson, a sociologist frequently cited by architectural historians, calls this imperial claim to an invented region of expertise the "professional project." Understood through the metaphor of jurisdiction, the critical determination has been who can be included, who will be excluded, and who gets to make these decisions.[9] This is a compelling explanation foregrounding important realities of ongoing professional formation; it also overlooks any professional discipline that freely distributes knowledge.

Like gender and race, professionalism is a social relation. It is a "cultural style," to use Dell Upton's phrase, continuously adjusting an existing vocabulary to shifting social expectations and institutional systems.[10] I will argue that professionalization may be best understood as a racial contract of expertise. Building on the work of Carole Pateman, the political philosopher Charles W. Mills introduced racial contract theory to address the Western philosophical tradition of the "social contract" and to acknowledge the implicit foundation of whiteness in the theory of social relations and authority it codifies. Mills argues that the whiteness of the contract is revealed in the historical fact that the first contract theorists did not recognize all people as social equals, and that "this apparatus was originally designed for a population with a different history and facing a different set of problems."[11] The whiteness of home economists' professionalism emerges as a form of cultural embodiment designed by a specific group of women with their own imagined and real history who were facing a specific set of perceived problems.

Not all home economists were white. The first home economics program that accepted Black students opened in 1892 in Frankfort, Kentucky. Six such programs existed prior to the development of the term "home economics" itself, which was not coined until an 1899 conference organized in Lake Placid, New York. Of the thirty-four programs established before Cornell's, eight were designated as "colored." By 1914 there were nearly three hundred programs in home economics, including those at historically Black colleges and universities.[12] It was not until

1915 that the US government would hire Black extension agents. As the historian Carmen V. Harris explains, Black women working as home economists were designated with racialized titles. Government reports identified Black women as "negro home demonstration agents," while redacting the racial identity of white home economists, listing them only as "home demonstration agents."[13] The majority of historical research on Black home economists focuses on Southern states.[14] Few Black people migrated to rural New York, and fewer still migrated there to rent or buy single-family farms. According to agricultural census data, from 1910 to 1940, the overall number of "colored" farm operators remained at approximately one-half of one percent of total single-family farm renters or owners in New York state.[15] Although Cornell did train a small number of Black home economists and it did offer winter courses in home economics to nearby Indigenous women, I have found no evidence of Black or Indigenous women working as home economists in rural New York in the early twentieth century.

Racial contract theory offers a paradigm well-suited for narrating home economics expertise because, as Mills explains, it works as a "device of representation." For rural New York home economists, work began by describing the existing material conditions of single-family farm homes. Like racial contract theory, home economics does not map "the ideally just society we want to attain, but the non-ideal, unjust society we already have and want to get rid of."[16] When redeployed for historical analysis, racial contract theory foregrounds otherwise ancillary details of client–professional relationships, including informal and situated means of cultural and racial recognition, while underlining their analytical significance. The question becomes not whether professionalism itself was imbued with racist ideology, or even actively used for this purpose, but how it operated within and according to the values of an already existing racialized social structure. In contrast to deracinated theories of the professional, a racial contract theory of expertise does not presume that those recognized as professionals ought to be counted because of their skill or capacity in a merit-based social system upon which we can all agree. Instead, it only describes those that can be recognized within existing social structures. Rural home economists cultivated their professional standing by navigating social relations extending across US governmental standards, narratives, and funding, as well as local expectations, affiliations, and histories. Although architecture is not at the center of this narrative, the way these women analyzed rural farmhouses was heavily influenced by these relations. In what follows, I will show that professional status is not the product of a standardized, linear path but emerges amid local circumstances.

Although often remembered for rapid urbanization more than bucolic domesticity, the Progressive Era witnessed the rapid expansion of support for home economics. After the Morrill Land Grant Acts of 1862 and 1890, Cornell's program benefited from a series of government appropriations from 1910 to 1936 earmarked for home economics research.[17] The political economist and historian Elizabeth A. Ramey argues that an inexpensive and abundant food supply had become the lynchpin of US economic development.[18] Despite progress in scientific farming, advances in agricultural technology, and an increase in itinerant laborers, food production in the United States remained dependent on small- and medium-sized farms with a permanent rural workforce. The greatest challenge to food production was rural depopulation, as young people moved away from the "drudgery" of farm life. From 1880 to 1920, over one-third of New York's total population had left farms for large cities.[19]

By conceiving of food production through the single-family farm, home economics aligned with other Progressive Era values. While agricultural science was working to maximize productivity, home economics reconceptualized farm life and the single-family home with the phrase "standard of living."[20] Rather than quantifying its output, these professionals focused their attention on the experience and quality of life on the farm. Most single-family farms were composed of more than a single nuclear family—including extended family, siblings and their families, as well as hired men, domestic servants, and itinerant laborers, often all living under one roof. Rural farmhouses expanded and contracted by building or closing off additions to the back and sides of their original stone foundations. Adjusting existing farmhouses to suit the demands of a seasonal labor supply and the need to entice younger generations to remain called for a new form of expertise.[21]

When the United States officially entered World War I in 1917, rationing measures starkly limited domestic access to agricultural commodities. In response to rapidly increasing demand, the secretary of agriculture called on farmers to open new fields and to quickly increase their production. Farmers responded "vigorously." But when the war ended and the export market evaporated, the US Department of Agriculture (USDA) announced that surplus had become "the chief agricultural problem."[22] The conceptual meaning of efficiency shifted, and the secretary of agriculture began to echo the calls of home economists, stressing the relationship between producers, consumers, and economic policy. According to the USDA, ongoing research into efficiency and management practices positioned single-family farms to "help balance supply and demand, guarantee the dependability of production, raise living standards, and aid industry as a whole."[23] In other words, the new discipline of home economics provided a crucial tool to balance production and consumption without the security of a stable market or the flexibility previously provided by product elasticity or labor supply in industrial urban centers.[24]

It was in this context on July 1, 1923, that the USDA announced the formation of the Bureau of Home Economics to orchestrate research in the new science of consumption.[25] Louise Stanley, the first director of the bureau, began with "the economic phases of home economics" as a means of defining a new standard of household consumption—that is, "the average home in a given community uses so many pounds of butter or so many sacks of flour per individual"—and thus estimating "need" across the nation.[26] Correlating household income, expenditure, and consumption, the bureau would first identify demand in local studies, and through this bring together a synthetic portrait of the domestic economy. Previous surveys were insufficient because they had overlooked the unpaid contribution of farm women's reproductive labor in the home. Household management experts saw that an accurate accounting of the "real income" of a single-family farm required them to document the labor value that homemakers' daily chores and other tasks contributed in monetary terms.[27] Reconstructing and then itemizing a farm woman's reproductive labor on a wage basis, in other words, provided a crucial explanatory factor in determining an overall picture of the economic value of the farm, without which a new national portrait would be not just incomplete but erroneous. By setting aside a prescriptive theory of the ideal domestic life, home economists like Stanley sought to articulate a descriptive, nonideal theory of the way the world already existed. As Mills explains, a descriptive approach inverts ideal theories that "imply the moral endorsement of the institutions" they create, and instead "serves to alert us to the structures of systemic institutional oppression, which need to be dismantled."[28] For home economists, descriptive observations were not endorsements of the current structure of the farm enterprise, nor were they an attempt to radically rethink domesticity. Like nineteenth-century domestic scientists, home economists alerted us to the status quo as it was experienced by the homemakers they studied.

From May to June of 1925, a small group of white home economists traveled to the homes of approximately seventy-five white farm women in Chautauqua, Chenango, Madison, Niagara, and Wyoming Counties in central and western New York (fig. 2.2).[29] They were on their way to distribute survey documents for "the study of the use of time, energy, materials, goods, and money" in rural farmhouses.[30] The bureau wrote and then disseminated a series of survey documents to regional experiment stations. Cooperatively developed by Cornell home economists and the bureau, this "Time Study of New York Homemakers" itemizes participants' domestic labor for all twenty-four hours of seven consecutive days in a typical workweek, and it archives the relationship forged between rural women and professional home economists. Once a farm woman volunteered to participate, the process would begin with a visit from a home economist to complete the initial seven-page "Inventory of Working Equipment."[31] The inventories note the details of farm life under seventeen headings. Each presents an aspect of housework, offering three columns to list kitchen equipment, the date it was acquired, and its cost. Most of the headings have several subdivisions further specifying types of appliances, equipment, materials, and finishes. The final three headings document the health, training, and employment history of the housewife, explicitly translating rural homemakers into added value for the farm enterprise.

FIGURE 2.2. *Home economics extension agents arrive by Model T at a rural farm home for a series of home demonstrations, ca. 1920. New York State College of Home Economics Records, 1875–1979, collection no. 23-2-749, Division of Rare and Manuscript Collections, Cornell University Library.*

Shortly after leaving the site, extension workers added qualitative descriptions of the farmhouse and farm woman to the inventory form. Often surprisingly candid, these descriptions indicate how tightly bound objectivity and cultural aesthetics were for these professionals. They referred to "homey" mothers and "hardworking" appearances; to "intelligent grey eyes" alongside poorly planned housing for itinerant laborers. They emphasized "good taste" and acknowledged oppressive husbands. Between farm woman and home economist, there was a sense of shared identity as they sat on a porch discussing "the importance of being business-like about housework," while each evaluated the other in a cooperative effort to establish homemaking as a form of expertise.[32] Surveys like these continued for at least the next thirty years. In a class exercise created to educate would-be home economists, extension specialist Ella Cushman collated similar informal descriptions of participating farm women. Collectively, they "should bring to mind a definite attitude," wrote Cushman. Thus codified into attitudes—or "any relatively habitual overt behavior which indicates what is customarily felt, thought, or done in a given situation"—housewife descriptions reframed informal aesthetic judgments as data for analysis. Whiteness remained implicit in these relationships and judgments. A later collection of surveys includes the word "colored" added to the top of a small percentage of reports, again underlining the

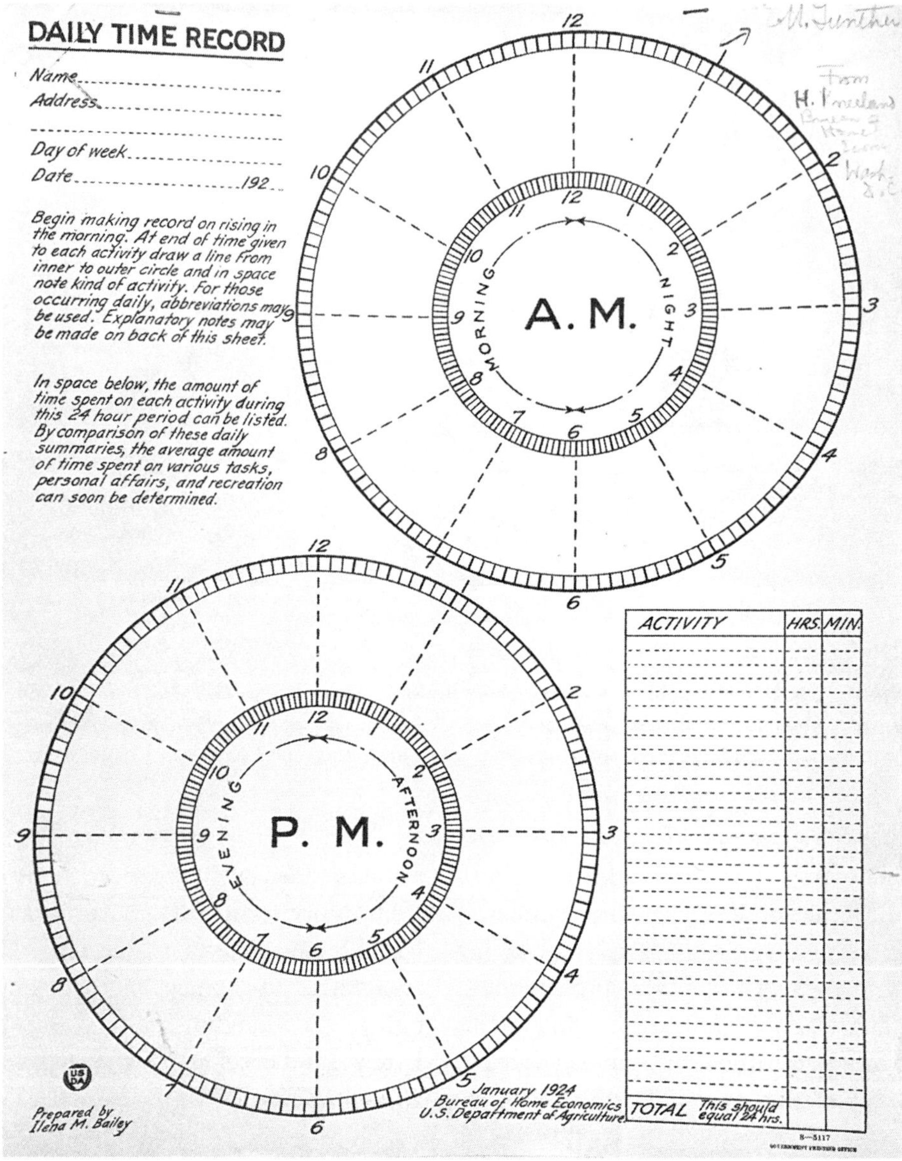

DAILY TIME RECORD

Name.................................
Address..............................
....
Day of week..........................
Date............................192..

Begin making record on rising in the morning. At end of time given to each activity draw a line from inner to outer circle and in space note kind of activity. For those occurring daily, abbreviations may be used. Explanatory notes may be made on back of this sheet.

In space below, the amount of time spent on each activity during this 24 hour period can be listed. By comparison of these daily summaries, the average amount of time spent on various tasks, personal affairs, and recreation can soon be determined.

A. M.
MORNING
NIGHT

P. M.
EVENING
AFTERNOON

ACTIVITY	HRS.	MIN.
TOTAL This should equal 24 hrs.		

Prepared by Ilena M. Bailey

January 1924
Bureau of Home Economics
U.S. Department of Agriculture

FIGURE 2.3. *"Daily Time Record," form created and distributed by the Bureau of Home Economics for time-use surveys in household management research. National Council on Household Employment Records, collection no. 5226, Kheel Center for Labor-Management Documentation and Archives, Martin P. Catherwood Library, Cornell University.*

fact that failing to mention race is tantamount to indicating that the survey participant is white.[33]

Following these initial visits, agents left a set of daily time diaries that looked like two 12-hour clock faces (fig. 2.3).[34] These came with a set of instructions detailing how to record different types of daily activities, illustrated with concrete examples.[35] As with inventory categories, small details within the forms suggest the kind of woman the bureau sought to describe in their national portrait. This woman owned or rented the single-family farmhouse in which she labored. Chores from "cooking and food preparation" to "cleaning," "laundering," or "gardening" were to be carefully distinguished and marked separately from activities "done for pay." Activities including "care of children," "feeding baby," and even "help" referred to the homemaker's own family members. The instructions encouraged her to carefully distinguish between aid "from members of your family and [from] hired help," who were otherwise excluded from these studies. The bureau's understanding of home economics relied on a careful distinction between homemakers and household employees, even as the bureau sought to reveal the hidden reproductive labor of farm women.

This conceptual division remains in the archive today. Cornell University's Division of Rare and Manuscript Collections holds extensive materials on the discourse of home economics, the operations and legacy of household management, and the valorization of unwaged domestic labor. However, for investigation into these same topics concerning those who held jobs or labored within their employers' homes, you have to find your way to the Kheel Center for Labor-Management Documentation and Archives, across Cornell's campus. Documents related to Bureau of Home Economics research in household management, including reports, bulletins, and survey documents, can be found in both archives. The primary difference in the documents at each location is the race and class of the subjects analyzed in the surveys, and the audience the studies intended to address and educate.

Completed inventories and time diaries created a means of interaction between rural farm women, traveling professionals, and bureau specialists. The data gleaned from these documents served as a testing ground to establish generalized design principles. During a speech to rural women, Liberty Hyde Bailey insisted that "we very much need standardized plans for farm dwellings" to ensure that all parts functioned in relation to one another based on "a set of working principles." Although they need not be followed literally, these principles would establish a standard to best fulfill the needs of individual communities, families, and farms, Bailey explained.[36] Helen Binkerd Young, who was trained as an architect in Cornell's Department of Architecture before becoming the director of housing and design in the Department of Home Economics, explained in several rural bulletins the importance of redesigning country life by rearranging the farmhouse interior.[37] Young's publications marked a half step between extension workers in the field and the bureau's national portrait. Like many bulletin authors, Young correlated local research findings with those from other states and bureau reports to refine a new set of design principles that would be applicable to each homemaker's unique circumstances.

Home economists often used plan diagrams to articulate these principles, connecting them to a broader discourse on "convenient kitchens" (fig. 2.4). According to Jan Jennings, the theory of convenience promoted by home

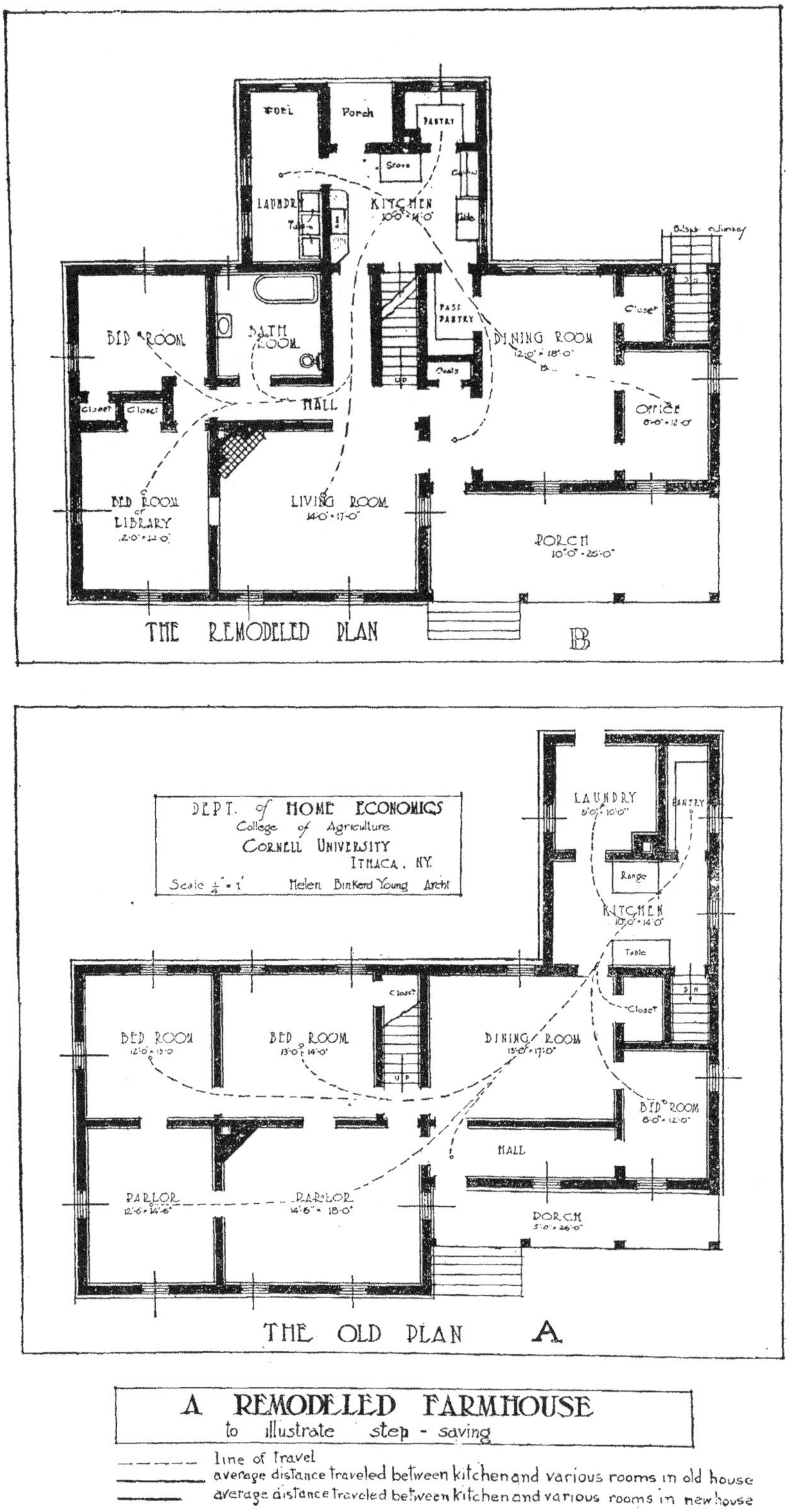

Fig. 61.— *Example of remodeled farmhouse*

FIGURE 2.4. *Diagrams for remodeling a farmhouse, 1913. Helen Binkerd Young, "The Farmhouse,"* Cornell Reading-Courses: Lesson for the Farm Home *2, no. 39 (1913).*

economists "relied on standards of common practices passed down and traditionally used by ordinary people in their homes."[38] Young's understanding of the farmhouse plan was intimately connected with bodies moving through space.[39] The many problems with the New York farmhouses derived from their slow, informal process of construction throughout the nineteenth century. With each additional room, "the kitchen retreated to the rear of the structure, where, by its very distance from the living-rooms, it confined the housewife to her post of duty." "However picturesque a rambling house may be," wrote Young, "it either enslaves the workers or degenerates into a small inhabited area and a large closed-up area that is useless and unhealthful." Young's solution was to relocate the hall to the center of the home, linking it directly to the kitchen and developing the other rooms around this central axis. By rearranging the house interior to better suit existing rural practices, Young calculated that this new arrangement would save the housewife an average distance of fifteen feet per round trip: "Such a saving multiplied by days and years would in the course of a lifetime aggregate a great amount of economy."[40] Jennings explains that this form of architectural expertise "acted as a truth and as a logic endorsed and accepted in the community" and whose "sole validation was the sanction of social approbation and custom."[41]

While design principles can seem disconnected from social and material realities, in this instance, Young plainly stated the desired social impact of new standards for good farmhouse design using a racialized analogy. She reassured her readers that although "health and happiness in the home are not marketable commodities" on their own, "household investments" focused on redesigning the farmhouse to improve the efficiency of daily tasks would accrue "real profit" over time.[42] Young warned rural women that "the mistakes and triumphs of these structures will in turn be passed on for the next generation to cope with or to enjoy." Thus they ought "to build wisely for the future" and not haphazardly. "A well-planned farmstead," she argued, "is more economical, more orderly, more beautiful, and more saleable than one which, like Topsy, 'just growed.'" This critique of makeshift site planning on farms was not just a condemnation of poor foresight, but an adamant declaration of the values implicit in "the order of the day."[43] This order, it seems, found its most apt analogy with a reference to the young Black character named Topsy from Harriet Beecher Stowe's *Uncle Tom's Cabin*. What some may take as a minor detail, upon closer inspection exposes a deeper and more violent set of assumed cultural reference points. In Stowe's novel, when asked about her origin, Topsy replies that "she wasn't born, she just growed." The scene suggests that because Topsy has no mother, she also has no idea that God has made her. For Stowe this dramatizes the crucial link between motherhood and Christianity, while for home economists the young Black character illustrated the opposite of a well-planned farmstead: inefficient, disorderly, dull, and unsalable. At best a callous, offhand remark, Young's racialized analogy reveals a then-popular understanding of the spectrum between informal ignorance and well-informed expertise.[44]

The collaboration between the traveling extension workers and the rural volunteers scrutinizing and documenting their daily lives laid the foundation for these design principles. Traveling by train, horse-drawn carriage, and early-model automobiles, home economists moved freely throughout New York. Increased travel was spurred principally by the building of hard-packed dirt roads and new highways traversing the state's landscape. From 1904 to 1920, a series of legislative initiatives and the USDA provided over $3.6 billion to develop over one million additional miles of rural roads across the country. The expansion of road systems was a fundamental requirement in the rise of professions. These allowed home economists to schedule longer demonstrations and more visits per day by decreasing travel times, which in turn encouraged greater attendance from rural women, who often lived significant distances from one another.[45]

Engaging with rural communities required developing local credibility, something that necessitated more than passing familiarity with local cultural norms. Indeed, extension agents were often from rural backgrounds themselves and consciously integrated themselves into the community before they could begin their work. Extension specialist Helen Vandervort describes the politics of fitting in, explaining how she and other extension agents succeeded because they were from a rural town and knew agricultural work, because they were matter-of-fact and so trustworthy, and because they were action oriented and went there to get things done. At the same time, Vandervort recounts at least one circumstance in which she was viewed with significant skepticism because of her uncle's involvement with the Dairymen's League and their 1917 strike in Lewis County, New York.[46] Even in this instance, however, she could draw on her knowledge of the dairy business and its local pressure points while working under a family name her clients recognized.

Ella Cushman, the future director of the program in household management at Cornell, made this tacit process the foundation of her research methodology.[47] She stridently promoted working directly with the homemaker to propose site-specific, practical solutions to the farm woman's problems. Cushman's strategy hinged on going to stay with someone, learning what problems they faced, and then offering focused propositions.[48] Her method derived in part from living briefly with the industrial engineer and psychologist Lillian Gilbreth and her husband, Frank, to study scientific methods in household analysis in the summer of 1927. According to one oral history, Lillian Gilbreth had recently published a "very stimulating" book, *The Homemaker and Her Job*, and Cushman wanted to learn more about the couple's process—an impulse that reveals at least as much about her own research methods as her interest in the Gilbreths.[49] As one former student explained, Cushman required her students to spend at least half of their time working with the homemaker directly in her home, believing that learning

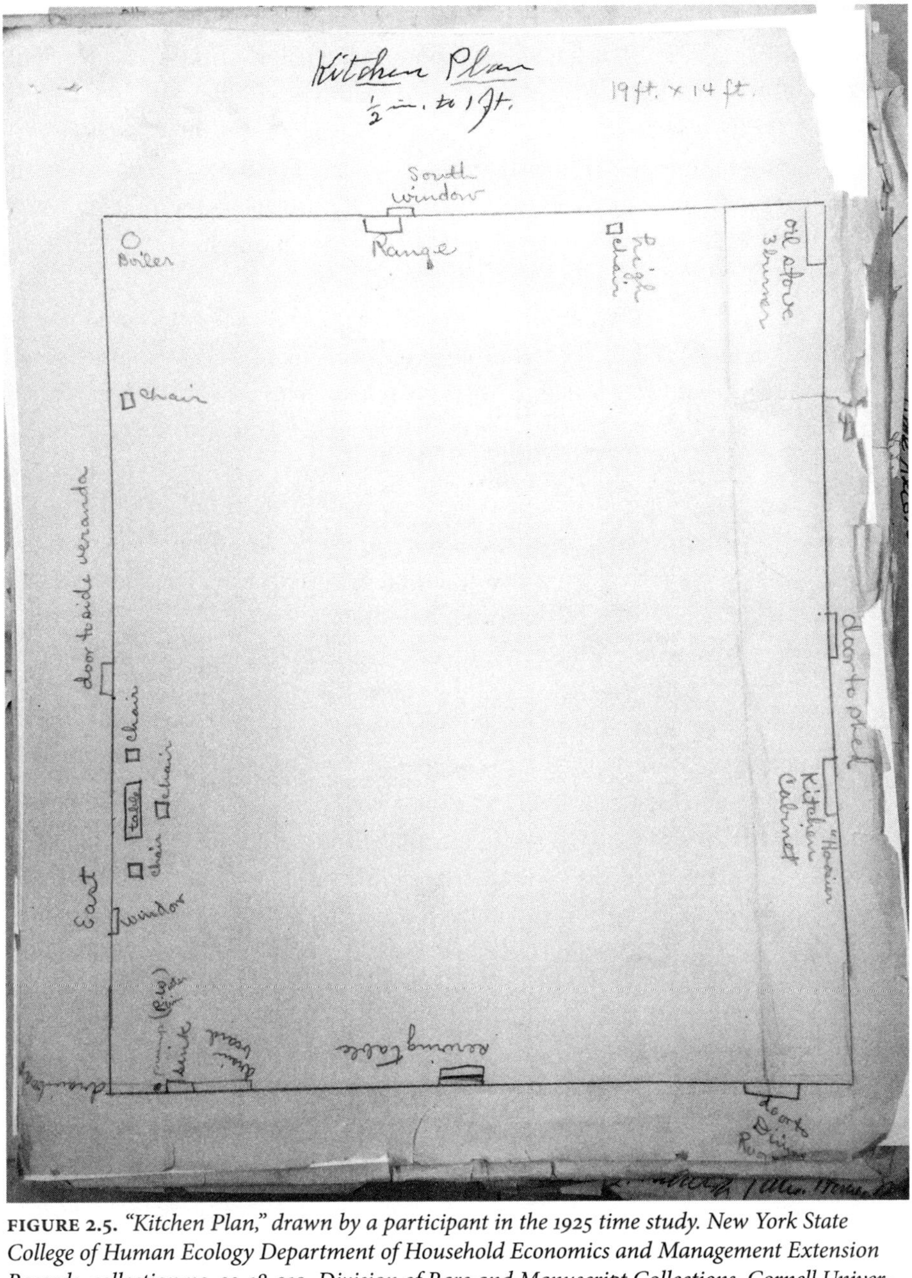

FIGURE 2.5. *"Kitchen Plan," drawn by a participant in the 1925 time study. New York State College of Human Ecology Department of Household Economics and Management Extension Records, collection no. 23-18-919, Division of Rare and Manuscript Collections, Cornell University Library.*

was "not just based on observations, but [on] working with families."[50] Requiring more than the application of abstract scientific principles or a merely "professional" relationship with her clients, Cushman's insights followed directly from the specific rooms in which she collaborated on household management problems. Where class boundaries were cemented in the identification of participants, racial identity remained implicit. For both Vandervort and Cushman, rural New York's relative racial homogeneity eased potential tension in these intimate collaborations. It is easy to wonder whether their methods would have been successful had either the specialists or the families they visited not been white.

One final example brings survey protocols, design principles, and local relationships together in a single artifact. Participants were asked to include rough plan drawings of their kitchens alongside time diary submissions (fig. 2.5). Consisting of freehand sketches made by the housewife (and sometimes her children), they record the distribution of kitchen furniture, appliances, and finishes, as well as architectural features and mechanical equipment. Nearly all use a single line to show the perimeter wall of a rectangular space surrounded by the material accretions of daily labor in the kitchen, drawn as small boxes with textual annotations. Most are casually outlined in pencil, with the title "Kitchen Plan," a general scale, and a north arrow noted in pen afterward by the extension agent. In the top right corner of each drawing appears the name of the housewife written by a third person in red grease pencil, presumably added to correlate the many documents associated with each farmhouse back at the home economist's desk. Anchored by this drawing, housewife and home economist could hold ongoing conversations in person or via correspondence, linking the material specifics of a kitchen, a daily routine, and the scientific design principles of ongoing home economics research across the county, state, and country.

Originally referring to local dialects, the term "vernacular" helps us to interpret these kitchen drawings as well as the relationships and farmhouses they articulate. Scholars have often characterized the use of jargon and abstruse technical visualizations by professionals as a way to maintain control over disciplinary knowledge.[51] In contrast, these kitchen drawings and the conversations they promoted demonstrate a form of vernacular professionalism. Far from top-down systems of abstraction, these drawings produced a common ground and shared language through which the client-housewife and the professional–home economist could document and redesign daily life together. They demonstrate not only spatial, material, and aesthetic dispositions, but also the fact that rural housewives thought with planimetric diagrams of their homes and the many components that made up their kitchens.

In her compelling account of nineteenth-century material feminists, Dolores Hayden criticized the rise of home economics as a normalizing discipline that absorbed the radical practices of cooperative housekeeping. She asserted that "what they lost in socialist ideology, they hoped to pick up in efficiency; what they lost in sisterhood, they hoped to gain in professional status." In a similar vein, David R. Roediger argued that what white, working-class laborers lost in solidarity, they gained in social, economic, and racial status.[52] Taken together, these arguments would suggest that home economists elevated themselves above other rural women by choosing the implicit whiteness of professionalism over community solidarity. This also poses one more teleological narrative in which the only aim can be middle-class social ascension and the only means can be jurisdictional control of knowledge. In some instances, this power dynamic is certainly at work among home economists, but it does not sufficiently explain the emergence of professional women who gained recognition as experts among the same rural women they supposedly rose above. Moreover, it does not seem capable of addressing the simple fact that home economists' primary practice was distributing their disciplinary knowledge free of charge and as widely as possible among equally white clients. And yet their professional status was closely bound up with their gendered whiteness.

By presenting a case study of professional home economists in rural New York State during the opening decades of the twentieth century, this chapter has expanded the scope of professionalization narratives in architectural history. Focusing on professional expertise foregrounds the fluidity of categories too often foreclosed by the concept of professionalization. Looking to the practices of rural home economists defamiliarizes the professional in the historiography of American architecture. It emphasizes the shifting racial contract in the recognition of professional legitimacy and exposes how knowledge problems are social problems. Along with considering rural women's impact on the history of American professionalism, this case study highlights one instance in which directly addressing race and its seeming absence highlights long-held historiographical biases. It demonstrates that the cultural embodiment of whiteness was embedded within the professionalization of home economics. This approach opens the door to a history of the single-family home as a multipurpose tool in the formation of a potent form of architectural expertise.

After the ethereal dancers at the Cornell University pageant stepped to the side, a stream of costumed participants arrived on the field. They were dressed as medieval knights, ancient Greeks, Dutch peasants, Italian Renaissance courtiers, Native Americans, and other ethnic types. Unlike the melting-pot metaphor, the women's pageant does not dramatize the dissolving of these ethnicities into a new type, nor these women's gendered bodies into the technical skills of their discipline. Rather, it reveals how rural professionalism transformed the description of material differences into social and cultural choreography and disciplinary unity. It symbolizes a forgotten understanding of the American professional ideal attuned to Progressive political values. As extension specialist Ruby Green Smith explained in her history of New York home economics, "modern homes cannot be isolated from community life, and modern farms are no longer self-sufficient; both are dependent upon conditions in the community which are reflected, for good or evil, in homes." And, I would add, in the racial contract of professional expertise.

Notes

1. *Cornell Bulletin* 1, no. 24 (May 3, 1916); Helen Vandervort, oral history, no. 47-2-O.H.75, 17–18, Division of Rare and Manuscript Collections, Cornell University Library (hereafter cited as RMC, Cornell). See also Nancy K. Berlage, "Plotting a Better Future for Agriculture, Women, and the Empire State: Historical Pageantry in the 1920s," *New York History* 97, nos. 3–4 (2016): 319–344; John Higham, *Strangers in the Land: Patterns of American Nativism, 1860–1925* (Rutgers University Press, 1955), 131–156.

2. T. J. Jackson Lears, *No Place of Grace: Antimodernism and the Transformation of American Culture, 1880–1920*, 2nd ed. (University of Chicago Press, 2021).

3. See especially Dianne Harris, *Little White Houses: How the Postwar Home Constructed Race in America* (University of Minnesota Press, 2013).

4. Gwendolyn Wright, *Moralism and the Modern Home: Domestic Architecture and Cultural Conflict in Chicago, 1873–1913* (University of Chicago Press, 1980), 254–294; Dolores Hayden, *The Grand Domestic Revolution: A History of Feminist Designs for American Homes, Neighborhoods, and Cities* (MIT Press, 1982), 280–304; Michael Osman, *Modernism's Visible Hand: Architecture and Regulation in America* (University of Minnesota Press, 2018), 1–43; Zeynep Çelik Alexander, "The Larkin's Technologies of Trust," *Journal of the Society of Architectural Historians* 77, no. 3 (2018): 300–318.

5. Anna-Maria Meister, "'Housewives and Architects': Marie-Elisabeth Lüders' Management of the New Architecture from Pot Lid to *Siedlung*," *Architectural Histories* 10, no. 1 (2022): 1–24; Anna Myjak-Pycia, "Forgoing the Architect's Vision: American Home Economists as Pioneers of Participatory Design, 1930–60," *arq: Architectural Research Quarterly* 25, no. 1 (2021): 17–30; Barbara Penner, "The Flexible Heart of the Home," *Places Journal*, May 2018, https://placesjournal.org/article/home-economics-and-flexible-design/; Barbara Penner, "The Cornell Kitchen: Housing and Design Research in Postwar America," *Technology and Culture* 59, no. 1 (2018): 48–94; Sophie Hochhäusl, "From Vienna to Frankfurt Inside Core-House Type 7: A History of Scarcity Through the Modern Kitchen," *Architectural Histories* 1, no. 1 (2013): 1–19.

6. See, for instance, Mary N. Woods, *From Craft to Profession: The Practice of Architecture in Nineteenth-Century America* (University of California Press, 1999).

7. Gwendolyn Wright, "On Modern Vernaculars and J. B. Jackson," *Geographical Review* 88, no. 4 (1999): 480, 477; Gwendolyn Wright, "Modern Vernaculars," *Architecture + Urbanism*, no. 332 (May 1998): 4–9.

8. George Barnett Johnston, "Traveling Professions: How Local Contingencies Complicate Globalizing Tendencies in the Standardization of Architectural Practice," *96th ACSA Annual Meeting Proceedings: Seeking the City* (Association of Collegiate Schools of Architecture, 2008), 15.

9. Judith R. Blau, *Architects and Firms: A Sociological Perspective on Architectural Practices* (MIT Press, 1987), 8; Elliott Freidson, *Professionalism: The Third Logic* (University of Chicago Press, 2001), 22; Magali Sarfatti Larson, *The Rise of Professionalism: A Sociological Analysis* (University of California Press, 1977).

10. Dell Upton, *Architecture in the United States* (Oxford University Press, 1998), 275.

11. Carol Pateman, *The Sexual Contract* (Stanford University Press, 1988); Charles W. Mills, *The Racial Contract* (Cornell University Press, 1997); Charles W. Mills and Carole Pateman, *Contract and Domination* (Polity, 2007).

12. "The History of Home Economics in Colleges," three-page memo in large scrapbook, box 48, collection no. 23-2-749, RMC, Cornell; Benjamin R. Andrews, "Education for the Home," *U.S. Bureau of Education Bulletin*, no. 38 (1914). See also Emma Weigley, "It Might Have Been Euthenics: The Lake Placid Conference and the Home Economics Movement," *American Quarterly* 26, no. 1 (1974): 79–96.

13. Carmen V. Harris, "The South Carolina Home in Black and White: Race, Gender, and Power in Home Demonstration Work," *Agricultural History* 93, no. 3 (2019): 477–501, 493.

14. For the limited existing research, see Oscar Baker Martin, *A Decade of Negro Extension Work, 1914–1924* (US Government Printing Office, 1926); Penny A. Ralston, "Distinctive Themes from Black Home Economists," *Journal of Home Economics* 84, no. 2 (1992): 39–44; Allison Horrocks, "Good Will Ambassador with a Cookbook: Flemmie Kittrell and the International Politics of Home Economics" (PhD diss., University of Connecticut, 2016); Cherisse Jones-Branch, "'An Uneasy Alliance': Farm Women and the United States Department of Agriculture, 1913–1965," *Federal History*, no. 10 (April 2018): 98–114; Harris, "South Carolina Home in Black and White."

15. US Census Bureau, *US Census for Agriculture, 1925: Reports for States, with Statistics for Counties and a Summary for the United States* (US Government Printing Office, 1927).

16. Mills and Pateman, *Contract and Domination*, 7.

17. The most prominent appropriations for rural home economics included the Smith-Lever Act of

1914, which established cooperative extension services, and the Smith-Hughes Act of 1917, Purnell Act of 1925, and George-Deen Act of 1936.

18. Elizabeth A. Ramey, *Class, Gender, and the American Family Farm in the Twentieth Century* (Routledge, 2014), 11.

19. Bruce L. Melvin, *Rural Population of New York, 1885–1925* (Cornell University, 1927).

20. Marina Moskowitz, *Standard of Living: The Measure of the Middle Class in Modern America* (Johns Hopkins University Press, 2004).

21. Sally Ann McMurry, "From Production to Consumption: Progressive Farmhouse Design at the Turn of the Century," in *Families and Farmhouses in Nineteenth-Century America* (Oxford University Press, 1988), 209–221.

22. Office of Information, USDA, "Some Landmarks of Department of Agriculture History (Condensed Version)," abridged as USDA document no. 8, September 1952, 28; Alan L. Olmstead and Paul W. Rhode, "The Transformation of Northern Agriculture, 1910–1990," in *The Cambridge Economic History of the United States: Vol. 3*, ed. Stanley L. Engerman and Robert E. Gallman (Cambridge University Press, 2000), 693–742; Ramey, *Class, Gender, and the American Family Farm*, 88–92.

23. Office of Information, "Some Landmarks of Department," 31–32. See also W. J. Spillman, *Balancing the Farm Output: A Statement of the Present Deplorable Conditions of Farming, Its Causes, and Suggested Remedies* (Orange Judd, 1927); USDA, *Achieving a Balanced Agriculture: How the National Farm Program Meets the Changing Problem* (US Government Printing Office, 1940).

24. Gavin Wright, "American Agriculture and the Labor Market: What Happened to Proletarianization?," *Agricultural History* 62, no. 3 (1988): 182–209; Osman, *Modernism's Visible Hand*, 45–80; Olmstead and Rhode, "Transformation of Northern Agriculture," 726.

25. "News from the Field," *Journal of Home Economics* 15, no. 8 (1923): 458.

26. Louise Stanley, "Plans for the Bureau of Home Economics," *Journal of Home Economics* 15, no. 12 (1923): 679, 680.

27. Stanley, "Plans for the Bureau of Home Economics," 680.

28. Mills and Pateman, *Contract and Domination*, 92.

29. The exact number of women surveyed is unknown. At least forty-eight but fewer than one hundred surveys remain from central and western New York, according to research assistant Faith Williams. Letter from Faith Williams to Martha Van Rensselaer, November 29, 1926, box 9, folder 3, collection no. 23-18-919, RMC, Cornell.

30. Jean Warren, oral history, no. 47-2-O.H.70, RMC, Cornell. See also Ronald Kline, "Ideology and Social Surveys: Reinterpreting the Effects of 'Laborsaving' Technology on American Farm Women," *Technology and Culture* 38, no. 2 (1997): 355–385; Linda L. Stinson, "Measuring How People Spend Their Time: A Time-Use Survey Design," *Monthly Labor Review*, August 1999, 12–19; Peggy S. Berger, "Home Management Research: State of the Art, 1909–1984," *Home Economics Research Journal* 12, no. 3 (1984): 252–264.

31. "Inventory of Working Equipment: Farm Households," document no. 3318, May 13, 1925, New York State College of Home Economics at Cornell University, box 9, collection no. 23-18-919, RMC, Cornell.

32. "Worksheets on Family Attitudes for Miss Cushman's Training School, February 1936," box 3, folder 10, collection no. 23-18-1648, RMC, Cornell. All quotes from the survey forms are found within box 9, collection no. 23-18-919, RMC, Cornell.

33. Survey reports, box 1, folder 28, collection no. 23-18-1648, RMC, Cornell.

34. Letter from Faith Williams to Martha Van Rensselaer, November 29, 1926, box 9, folder 3, collection no. 23-18-919, RMC, Cornell.

35. Letter from Ilena M. Bailey to Mrs. Eva V. B. Hansl, July 31, 1924, box 3, folder 63, collection no. 5226, Kheel Center for Labor-Management Documentation and Archives, Martin P. Catherwood Library, Cornell University.

36. Speech reproduced in Helen Binkerd Young, "The Farmhouse," *Cornell Reading-Courses: Lesson for the Farm Home* 2, no. 39 (1913): 184.

37. Helen Binkerd Young, "Household Decoration," *Cornell Reading-Courses: Lesson for the Farm Home* 1, no. 5 (1911): 43–63; Helen Binkerd Young, "Household Furnishing," *Cornell Reading-Courses: Lesson for the Farm Home* 1, no. 7 (1912): 65–84; Young, "Farmhouse," 153–184. See also Clara Browning Goodman, oral history, no. 47-2-O.H.84, RMC, Cornell.

38. Jan Jennings, *Cheap and Tasteful Dwellings: Design Competitions and the Convenient Interior, 1879–1909* (University of Tennessee Press, 2005), 159.

39. See Annmarie Adams and Don Toromanoff, "Kitchen Kinetics: Women's Movements in Sigrun Bülow-Hübe's Research," *RFR/DRF: Resources for Feminist Research / Documentation sur la recherche féministe* 34, nos. 3–4 (2015–2016): 9–39; Penner, "Flexible Heart of the Home."

40. Young, "Farmhouse," 156. See also Thomas C. Hubka, *Big House, Little House, Back House, Barn: The Connected Farm Buildings of New England* (University Press of New England, 1984).

41. Jennings, *Cheap and Tasteful Dwellings*, 159, 137–166.

42. Young, "Farmhouse," 153. See also David P. Handlin, *The American Home: Architecture and Society, 1815–1915* (Little, Brown, 1979), 333, 332–335; McMurry, *Families and Farmhouses*, 209–222.

43. Young, "Farmhouse," 153, 154.

44. In a letter to Martha Van Rensselaer dated April 8, 1920, Claudia Quigley Murphy, a consultant in home economics, uses the same reference to Topsy, who was "not born" but "just grew," to encourage improved cooperation between teaching staff in home economics and the efforts of commercial industries. Letter, box 37, collection no. 23-2-749, RMC, Cornell. See also Adrienne Brown, *The Black Skyscraper: Architecture and the Perception of Race* (Johns Hopkins University Press, 2017), 3–6, 203n4.

45. Olmstead and Rhode, "Transformation of Northern Agriculture," 693–742; Paul Starr, *The Social Transformation of American Medicine: The Rise of a Sovereign Profession and the Making of a Vast Industry*, 2nd ed. (Basic Books, 2017), 65–71.

46. Helen Vandervort, oral history, 65–76.

47. See Myjak-Pycia, "Forgoing the Architect's Vision."

48. Jean Warren, oral history, 41.

49. Ella M. Cushman, "A Week at Mrs. Gilbreth's, Montclair, New Jersey," unpublished manuscript, nine pages, box 1, folder 1, collection no. 23-18-1725, RMC, Cornell; Jean Warren, oral history, 40–41.

50. Jean Warren, oral history, 66; Ella M. Cushman, *Management in Homes* (Macmillan, 1945).

51. See, for instance, Upton, *Architecture in the United States*, 247–283.

52. Hayden, *Grand Domestic Revolution*, 177–178; David R. Roediger, *The Wages of Whiteness: Race and the Making of the American Working Class* (Verso, 1991).

3 A CATTLE BRAND AND A CATTLE RANCH

LAND, RACE, AND POWER IN ARCHITECTURAL HISTORY

Kathryn E. O'Rourke

CAN LOOKING AT A CATTLE brand registration and a giant Texas ranch together help us write race into the history of nineteenth-century US architecture? What do they say about the limits of architectural history? Can the discipline account for buildings that may not have existed? Should it attempt to try?

These questions emerge in analysis of two objects, paired because they almost, but don't quite, fit together: the cattle brand registration that Margaret Smith Dimery filed in Bexar County, Texas, in 1856, and the King Ranch, roughly one hundred miles north of the present US-Mexico border. Both are associated with Texas, with property, and—implicitly or explicitly—with land. The dynamics of race and power haunt them both. In the different ways they appear in archives and published histories, they function together almost as caricatures of the status of different kinds of objects in the historical record: the ranch, with its superabundance of evidence and interpretation, and the brand, with hardly any supporting information or analysis at all.

The Dimery registration and the King Ranch are pronouncedly asymmetrical. The registration is a single piece of handwritten paper that includes text and the graphic logo of Dimery's brand (fig. 3.1). A tool to identify property, the brand reads as a fused *M* and *D*, the letters presumably chosen because they are Dimery's first and last initials. Margaret Smith Dimery was a free Black woman (she was recorded as a "mulata" in the 1850 US census) born in South Carolina in 1822 or 1823. She was in Nacogdoches, Texas, by early 1838, when Texas was an independent republic, having separated from Mexico (where it was part of the state of Coahuila y Tejas) in 1836. That year she married Allen (Obidah) Dimery, a free Black man who owned two thousand acres of land in Leon County in East Texas, which he sold in the early 1840s. By 1850 he had died, and Margaret had moved to Bexar County.[1] Her registration is one of five such pre-1930 records in Bexar County that the architect and landscape historian Everett Fly has found

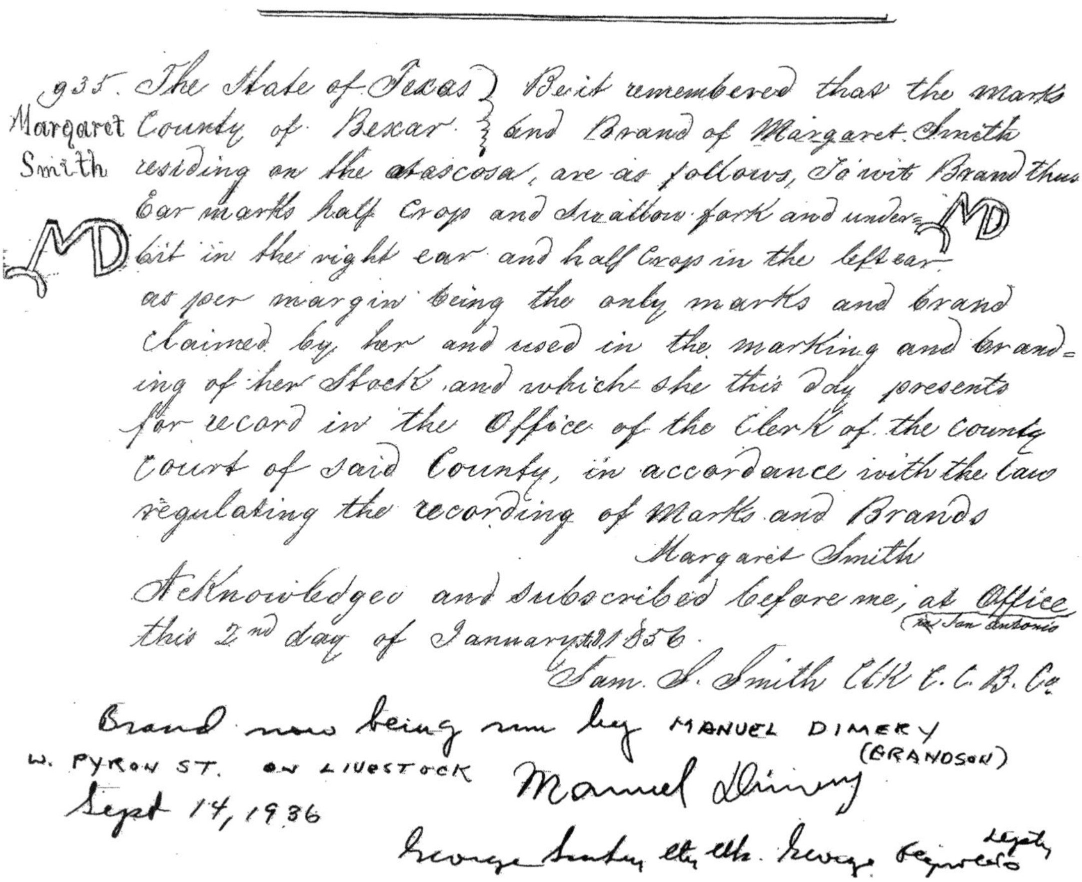
935. The State of Texas } Be it remembered that the marks
Margaret Smith County of Bexar } and Brand of Margaret Smith
residing on the Atascosa, are as follows, To wit Brand thus
Ear marks half Crop and Swallow fork and under
bit in the right ear and half Crop in the left ear.
as per margin being the only marks and brand
claimed by her and used in the marking and branding of her Stock, and which she this day presents
for record in the Office of the Clerk of the County
Court of said County, in accordance with the law
regulating the recording of Marks and Brands
Margaret Smith
Acknowledged and subscribed before me, at Office (in San Antonio)
this 2nd day of January AD 1856.
Sam. S. Smith Clk C. C. B. Co
Brand now being run by MANUEL DIMERY (GRANDSON)
W. PYRON ST. ON LIVESTOCK
Manuel Dimery
Sept 14, 1936
George [illegible] Cty Clk. George [illegible] Deputy

FIGURE 3.1. *Cattle brand registration filed by Margaret Smith Dimery in Bexar County, Texas, 1856. Bexar County Spanish Archives.*

belonging to Black women, and one of seventy registered to Black Texans, many of which were filed before 1870.[2]

When Henrietta King, a white woman and the owner of the King Ranch, died in 1925, her cattle ranch was about the size of Delaware. It encompassed 1,280,000 acres spread across three counties and was anchored by an enormous Spanish Colonial Revival–style house described as the "finest farm home in America."[3] King's was the "world's largest ranch," and she "its woman ruler."[4] Her husband, Richard King, had bought the first parcel of ranchland in 1853 with money he made smuggling cotton over the border to be exported from Mexico for the Confederacy. Working with her son-in-law, Richard Kleberg, and relying on the labor of Mexicans and Mexican Americans, Henrietta King transformed the ranch into the center of a modern industrial network that included a town and railroad. The story of the ranch exemplifies the entwining of race, land, and power in the United States. In this history, architecture is alternately central and peripheral: central insofar as it is understood as property, and peripheral in that only occasionally in King Ranch history did "capital *A*" architecture play a starring role—in the design of the commissary and a stable, and in the main house, by San Antonio architect Carleton Adams.

Reading the ranch and brand together, from within a discipline that has been chiefly concerned with buildings in urban contexts and architectural theory written in cosmopolitan centers, directs our attention to rural contexts during a period when most people in the United States didn't live in cities. The Dimery brand and the King Ranch draw our focus to land and the buildings associated with it, and to its function as a store of wealth. Together, the objects bring architecture into the racially inflected realms of property and money. Such an approach can support scholars as the categories of "high" and "vernacular" forms, creators, and clients merge and intersect in their thinking and method.[5] More fully admitting land as property, and the social and racial structures that attend it, as an analytical frame (as has long occurred in scholarship on twentieth-century urbanism and suburbanization) could help uncover other embedded racial histories in the nineteenth century as well.

Two other problems at the heart of a racially conscious historiography of nineteenth-century US architecture come into view when the Dimery brand and the King Ranch are paired: geography and loss. In the nineteenth century, state and national borders moved repeatedly. The ideological and cultural meanings of place-names evolved in economic, political, and literary texts, as well as in images—in the process, taking on different meanings for different groups. Engaging with the instability of familiar geographic descriptors, including "America" and "Texas," as well as the fact that the rights of most of the people who lived in these places for much or all of the 1800s were denied by state and national governments, can productively animate inquiries into the architecture of that period by helping scholars imagine territory, nation, and identity in new ways. For example, historians of Latin American architecture have long been attuned to the semiotic problems of the term "America." They grapple with the insufficiencies in "Latin America" as geographical descriptor, and with historical periodizations that centralize European colonialism in the hemisphere: for example, "preconquest" and "postconquest."[6] Imperialism is embedded in "America," a word that many people regard as a descriptor of the landmasses of an entire hemisphere, but which continues to be widely used uncritically as the name of the country that attempted to claim dominance over that vast zone. The Monroe Doctrine (1823) was proclaimed just two years after many Spanish colonies declared their independence throughout the Americas. Framed as foreign policy, the doctrine helped lay the conceptual groundwork for the subsummation of difference within a white patriarchy that projected itself continentally and hemispherically.

"Texas," and its status within "America," is equally complicated. Until 1836, Mexico included all of what is today Texas, California, Utah, Arizona, New Mexico, and most of Colorado; by 1853 the present borders of the countries were established. New American histories may be invigorated by new geographies that are flexible, local, and culturally defined.[7] Shifting the ways we understand borders can help us unmask inherited disciplinary colonialisms, rooted in differences between Anglo, Spanish, and French imperialism and racial thinking. An attention to relative geography—the consciousness on the part of architects and clients of living and working in a place that is not some other place—can open modes of inquiry and illuminate differences among specific communities within broad cultural and national constructs. A rigorous interrogation of geography also supports a local approach to history, which can be productively integrated with reflections on broad historical patterns and widely shared theoretical engagements. Many scholars have already pointed the way. To take just one example, Marta Gutman's dynamic model, in which multiple disciplinary histories, geographic and architectural scales, voices, families, and generations are set in motion in relation to one another, makes race a category and context that is always at play in architecture.[8] If not exactly the critical fabulation of Saidiya Hartman, Gutman's model imaginatively takes readers into the streets and spaces of Oakland, even as Gutman keeps them abreast of broad social patterns and relevant developments in law and policy.

Absence manifests in the historical record as nonpresent archival documentation, nonexistent primary accounts, and unwritten histories. It may be experienced by the historian as loss. Insofar as the project of writing race into architectural history is shaped by an ambition to contend with or make up for absence, for now, at least, one subject of a race-conscious history is loss itself. In the case of Dimery, absence and loss are further complicated: Thus far, no building can be associated with her, and yet, with its implication of property (on which cattle would have grazed and upon which some structure surely stood), the brand registration tantalizes us with an evidentiary fragment of a potential architectural history. It invites questions about the methods and bounds of the discipline, and challenges object-oriented historians especially to consider the uses and ethics of an imaginative approach to their work.[9]

Taking the Dimery brand and the image of Dimery as inspiration, and reading them together with the King Ranch, suggests the possibility of coupling a new interpretive triad with the one Vitruvius described, for use in reinscribing race into the history of nineteenth-century US architecture. In the Dimerian Triad, the points of the equilateral triangle are land, race, and power. Imagined in parallel alignment with Vitruvius's familiar metaphorical triangle anchored by *utilitas*, *firmitas*, and *venustas*, the result is a prism through which a more complex, dynamic, and inclusive architectural history may be refracted (fig. 3.2). The Dimerian Triad makes it easier to conceptualize architecture as the racialization of land when it is transformed into real estate under capitalism. When aligned with the Vitruvian Triad, the Dimerian Triad makes it possible to retain in architectural analysis the attention to program, technology, and art that has long undergirded the discipline, and can help bridge the divides between vernacular and high-style buildings, and rural and urban contexts. Because it brings land and landscape further into the domain of architectural history, this additional triad can support scholarship that addresses the ecological implications of architecture. The Dimerian Triad is in part an extension of the Marxist-feminist current that has long coursed through some branches of architectural history and builds on work by scholars including Carl Anthony, Dell Upton, and Louis P. Nelson.[10] But the triad sharpens our focus on the particular conditions in which the architecture and buildings have been constructed, literally and rhetorically, in the United States. The empty interior of the prism symbolically shelters the work of dynamic historical interrogation where six points of architecture are in play. It depicts the spiritual void that nationalism,

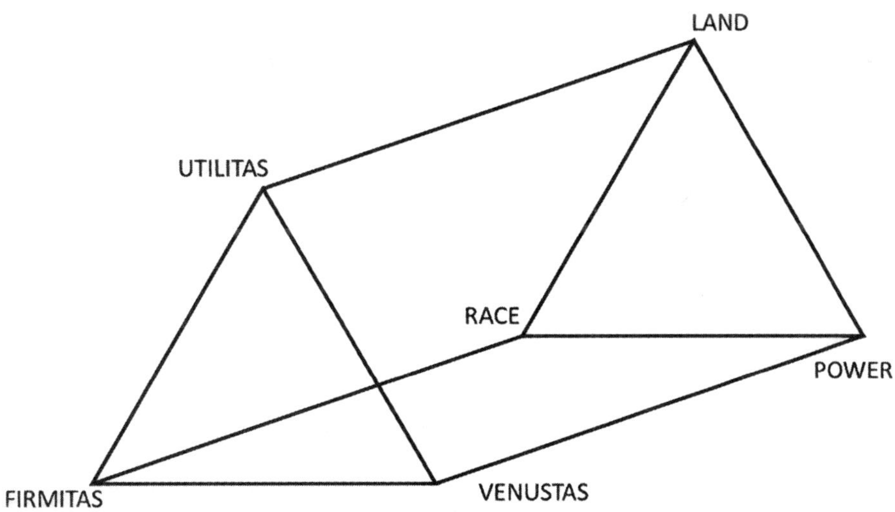

FIGURE 3.2. *The Dimerian Triad aligned with the Vitruvian Triad. Drawing by the author.*

capitalism, and concepts like "America" (when it is used uncritically) are used to fill, and it represents loss, as literal archival and historiographic absence, which is experiential and therefore potentially generative for the scholar.

Land

It is both true and a cliché that one of the most pronounced qualities of Texas south and west of San Antonio—the places where Dimery and King cattle grazed—is the vastness of open sky and land. Roughly 250 miles south of San Antonio, across the Nueces River, continuing to the US-Mexico border at the Rio Grande, the landscape changes as the land flattens and becomes more arid. The dominant experience is of spatial expansiveness, intense sun and heat, and rough, inhospitable terrain. Here, even today, architecture, where it exists at all, seems incongruous—an afterthought to more pressing concerns of survival in and against nature. In few places is it more obvious that concepts such as style, form, building typology, and authorship, which have long dominated academic architectural history in the United States, were invented to explain buildings somewhere else. While the buildings of the great border cities of this part of the state—Brownsville, Roma, and Laredo—bear evidence of their position in a trade-driven, international urban network that included New Orleans and reached deep into the Mexican interior, the expanses that separate these places from nineteenth-century Texas's major cities—San Antonio and Galveston—can appear empty. Coahuiltecan peoples were long established in this region, followed by the later Lipan and Mescalaro Apache, Comanche, and Kiowa.[11] Wild grasses and the ecosystems they supported covered the ground until they were devoured by cattle, first introduced to the Americas by the Spanish in the sixteenth century. Farther south, in central Mexico, along with architecture, chiefly in the form of cities and missions, cows and horses were critical tools of European colonization. While horses facilitated military conquest and missions a spiritual one, the introduction of cattle anticipated the creation of haciendas, the vast agricultural estates owned by wealthy Spaniards, and the antecedents of ranches.

Architectural and spatial hierarchies are built into the concept and practice of the ranch. The term signifies both land and the buildings on it, controlled by a private owner who typically occupies a main house, with workers' houses and buildings such as barns, corrals, and water towers dedicated to ranch operations. Cattle brands were first used in the Americas in 1537, when the Spanish king required cattle owners to brand their cows and register their brands with the viceregal government in Mexico City. In the centuries thereafter, cows roamed north into what would become Texas, where they formed part of the base of modern ranching. Brands functioned like real estate deeds in that they belonged to a widely agreed upon system for identifying ownership of salable property. In the absence of fencing, which began to be used on Texas ranches in the 1880s, brands helped delimit and define property. Cattle owners often designed their own brands, and it was essential that each brand be distinctive and recognizable. Before the rise of typographically driven advertising in Europe in the 1880s, in the US West in the nineteenth century, the practical requirements of branding gave rise to a graphically rich, abstract visual lexicon that communicated wealth, embodied in cattle, and often implied the existence of corresponding, privately owned land on which to keep and graze them.

Legal and ideological constructions of property and land possession—the frameworks through which US architecture has been predominantly understood outside of the academy and profession—themselves support the consolidation of racialized power. Property ownership, land grabs, and settler colonialism had in common with slavery the unwaged labor of women of all colors, the systemic undercompensation of workers (particularly immigrants), and an ambition on the part of an owner to amass capital, often at the expense of others. It is therefore possible to understand architecture as an expression of consolidated wealth, rendered visually and spatially with or without the aid of a professionally trained architect. Land as an interpretive lens brings money into the Dimerian-Vitruvian dynamic. Because access to wealth in the United States has been sharply defined by racialized economic, financial, and social structures, a history that reads architecture in terms of capital can help illuminate the racial dynamics at play in both high-style and vernacular buildings.

Race

> Congress shall pass no laws to prohibit emigrants from the United States of America from bringing their slaves into the Republic with them, and holding them by the same tenure by which such slaves were held in the United States; nor shall Congress have power to emancipate slaves; nor shall any slave-holder be allowed to emancipate his or her slave or slaves, without the consent of Congress, unless he or she shall send his or her slave or slaves without the limits of the Republic. No free person of African descent, either in whole or in part, shall be permitted to reside permanently in the Republic, without the consent of Congress. . . .
>
> All persons, (Africans, the descendants of Africans, and Indians excepted) who were residing in Texas on the day of the Declaration of Independence, shall be considered citizens of the Republic, and entitled to all the privileges of such. All citizens now living in Texas, who have not received their portion of land, in like manner as colonists, shall be entitled to their land in the following proportion and manner.
>
> TEXAS CONSTITUTION OF 1836

Sections 9 and 10 of the General Provisions of the Constitution of the Republic of Texas, written by whites in 1836, explicitly bound race and land, limited citizenship to white men, made it illegal for free Black people to live in Texas without permission of the government, and enshrined the enslavement of Black people as a fundamental right of whites. These sections knitted together the very definition of the republic with white landownership, which the government subsidized. And the new laws pointedly distinguished Texas from the Mexican states of Tamaulipas and Coahuila y Tejas that preceded it, where slavery was illegal. White leaders also understood white landownership as fundamental to the political and economic constitution of the state. Under the state constitution written after the annexation of Texas by the United States in 1845, the legal status of nonwhite people improved little, and enslaved and free people of color were subject to an entirely different code of laws than whites. From 1836 to 1860 in Texas—a span of time in which the first record of Dimery appears in 1856, when she registered the brand—the number of enslaved people increased substantially, from roughly 5 percent to 30 percent.

Understood in this context, Dimery's assertion of personhood and agency as a property owner reads as an act of defiance within the Texas legal system. The importance of her status as a woman of property in the context of Republic-era Texas is underscored by another document seemingly unrelated to architecture: Allen Dimery's 1840 petition to the Republic of Texas to remain in Texas as a free person of color, which, having immigrated to Mexico (where slavery was outlawed) in 1835, he had to file after Texas independence. Indeed, it is likely that Allen was allowed to stay in Texas precisely because he owned land. In the face of enormous obstacles, the Dimery family held on to their property, at least insofar as it was expressed in the brand registration, through the period of the Black Codes (1866), and into the years of segregation that followed their demise during Reconstruction. Margaret Dimery's brand registration was last renewed by her grandson, Manuel Dimery, in 1936, suggesting that the first herd of cattle to be marked with the Dimery brand, during the early years of Texas's statehood, contributed to the creation of intergenerational wealth, much in the same manner that other forms of privately held property, such as buildings, do. The Dimery brand registration and the documents associated with the Dimery family emerge, then, as common dominators between architecture and race in the nineteenth century: land, defined as property and instrumentalized as a tool and symbol of power.[12]

The Dimery brand registration turns on its head one of the archetypal images of the Western United States by inviting us to imagine the cowboy as a Black woman. Scholars have documented the work of Black cowboys, who played particularly important roles in Texas.[13] Nevertheless, against the sheer quantity of landscape paintings, photographs, films, television programs, novels, and advertisements through which (mostly white) men constructed the "West," and the ponderous symbolic weight attached to it, to imagine Margaret Smith Dimery surveying her four-legged, branded property (perhaps from a horse, wearing a wide-brimmed hat) around 1860 feels almost revolutionary. Although we can't quite see her face, or the would-be ranch house and the other ranch buildings she may have inhabited, the prospect of such a scene opens up new conceptual possibilities, even as it is embedded in familiar tropes.

In Mexico, racial inequality was also bound to a system of rural landownership and industry that profited few at the expense of many. In Northern and Central Mexico, haciendas and mining outfits retained colonial structures that relied on the unwaged or minimally waged labor of Indigenous and mixed-race Mexicans to enrich white landowners. The architectural expressions of this system included the hacienda itself—typically with a huge main house, workers' dwellings, and agricultural buildings—and urban palaces, sustained by rural wealth. When Texas separated from Mexico, slavery expanded west, where it met the hacienda system near San Antonio. Mexicans, and later Mexican Americans, taught the techniques used on Spanish haciendas to white and Black ranchers and cowboys in Texas, who adapted them as they developed modern ranching.[14]

Like missions and military forts, haciendas and ranches functioned as outposts of colonial control in areas with few permanent settlements. Indigenous people were typically indentured to the hacienda, headed by the *patrón*, the wealthy male head of the estate. This system of land control and racialized labor relations extended north into Texas into the twentieth century and shaped rural employment patterns in the area between the Nueces River and the Rio Grande, a region claimed by both the United States and Mexico until 1848. The King Ranch was worked by predominantly Indigenous and mixed-race people known as Kineños, who came from the town of Cruillas in the Mexican state of Tamaulipas, and whom Richard King had coaxed or coerced to Texas to work his land in 1854.[15] This arrangement helped entrench the *patrón-péon* system in South Texas and a set of economic, social, and racial structures that bind low-wage laborers who are nearly always Mexican American to a "benevolent," wealthy, usually white landowner. When Henrietta King died, the ranch was staffed by approximately one thousand Mexican American cowboys and ranch hands, many of whom were the descendants of the people from Cruillas, and who lived on the ranch with their families. Unlike the main house, the ranch workers' dwellings were not documented in widely reproduced photographs or splashy society pages. Although they appear to have been few in number, among the employees at the King Ranch were formerly enslaved Black Texans, whose story remains to be told but who presumably lived in conditions similar to those of Mexican Americans.[16]

Some idea of life on the ranch for nineteenth-century Kineños, and the buildings they built and inhabited, can be gleaned from the research that Roberto M. Villarreal conducted in the early 1970s on the experiences of Mexican American ranch workers on the neighboring Kenedy Ranch, founded by Richard King's former partner, Mifflin Kenedy.[17] Villarreal's interviews with elderly former ranch workers and descendants of people who worked on the Kenedy Ranch in the 1800s reveal sharp racialized spatial, architectural, and income divisions between ranch owners and workers. At the Kenedy Ranch, workers' houses had dirt floors, thin walls, and external kitchens, and until 1918, they were heated with cedar coals. While they tended to various tasks on the open land, male workers often slept for long periods of time away from their families. A few lived in small buildings called *ranchitos*. Many more slept in the open air while working on a cow camp, clearing brush, repairing buildings and tools, or constructing fencing. It was only in the 1920s that these workers acquired tents, after advocacy by a Black ranch worker recorded as Evans.[18]

The exploitation of Mexican American laborers in the amassing of white ranch wealth was one component of a larger system of racialized power that crossed classes and borders and had land at its heart. Particularly after 1848, US and Texas law regularly disregarded the rights of Mexican landholders. In 1935, the historian Walter Prescott Webb recorded that "old [Mexican] landholding families found their titles in jeopardy, and if they did not lose to the courts, they lost to their American lawyers." He added that "the Mexicans suffered not only in their persons, but in their property."[19] Legal and physical threats to Mexican Americans were sometimes backed up by extralegal measures, and violence against them was condoned and conducted by the state, via the Texas Rangers.[20] The historian Américo Paredes observed that the Texas Rangers "furnish[ed] the fortune-making adventurers [such as Richard King] with services not rendered by the United States Army or local sheriffs."[21] With reference to Paredes's work, Villarreal wrote in 1972 that "among the Mexicans of South Texas, the official Texas Rangers are known as the 'rinches de la Kinena': or Rangers of the King Ranch, in accordance with the belief that the Rangers were the personal strong-arm men of Richard King and the other 'cattle barons.'"[22]

Power

Under US capitalism, money and power are coterminous. Because it implies property, a cattle brand, like land as real estate and as architecture, can be read as an expression of wealth and therefore of agency within capitalism and the social conditions it produces. As a work of graphic design that its owner may have drafted using her own name as inspiration, the Dimery brand foregrounds the close relationship between authorship and authority. By registering her brand, Dimery formally entered into the land-based system around which racialized power was structured, and in the process claimed far more power than most Black Texans could. This system was of course the same one in which Henrietta King's much greater power was based. What did power look like for Dimery? The act of branding a cow was not only a statement of economic authority. Imagined in Dimery's hand, or that of one of her ranch hands, in the context of 1856 Texas, the brand reads as a gruesome, literal, and symbolic link between the cattle ranch and the treatment of enslaved people, who were assaulted with brands in the name of identifying property. For a Black woman to possess a brand in this context was itself a statement of power. Whether Dimery expressed authority architecturally we do not know. It is likely that any building that may have been associated with Dimery resembled the early and quite modest architecture of the King Ranch. When they first acquired land, Richard and Henrietta King lived in an adobe jacal, a thatched-roof dwelling common in Northern Mexico and South Texas.[23] In 1859 on the King Ranch, work began on a one-and-a-half-story wooden frame house, and it is possible that Dimery and her family lived in a building like this.

Race, land, and power repeatedly came together architecturally in buildings on the King Ranch. Until the building of the new main house, the most architecturally significant structure on the ranch was the stone commissary, built around 1856 (fig. 3.3). Visually, it conveyed colonial control in two registers in a species of multicultural imperial revivalist eclecticism. Its crenellations call to mind Anglo and French castles built during the Crusades, while the arcuated portico evokes the signature element of Spanish American architecture and urbanism. By the standards of Northern Mexican hacienda architecture, the commissary was remarkably up-to-date. After Richard King died in 1885, Henrietta King purchased more land and transformed her ranch into the center of a large, modern, industrial network. Danish-born architect Jules Leffland, who was South Texas's foremost architect in the late nineteenth century, designed new stables on

FIGURE 3.3. *Commissary, King Ranch, Kingsville, Texas, ca. 1856. Flato Family Collection, South Texas Archives and Special Collections, Texas A&M University–Kingsville.*

the ranch in 1909. With an arcade and Mission Revival–style parapet, the stables used a revival style popular among white patrons in the Southwest for its association with colonial Spain. The building thereby implicitly expressed the colonialist character of the ranch and its geographical and cultural dualism.

King commissioned her most architecturally ambitious project, a new main ranch house, known also as the Santa Gertrudis House, to replace one that burned in a 1912 fire (fig. 3.4).[24] More than any other, this eclectic, palatial building symbolically and linguistically affirmed binational colonialism reliant on unwaged and low-wage labor within a system of transactions (or thefts) that cemented economic and political power in the hands of whites. The house combined defensive elements with Spanish colonial forms and decorative references to Anglo control of Texas. Early on, "during the trouble with Mexico" (i.e., the Mexican Revolution), King put guns and a searchlight on the crenellated roof of the central tower.[25] From the tower, in the manner of aristocrats and popes, the family could survey its vast wealth, experienced as an "unforgettable" view: "the land stretching away in a level plain to the horizon, with mesquite and cactus forming the only break. Outhouses cluster like a village about the big house."[26] At ground level, the long arcade of the porch reinforced the association with Spanish colonial precedents in the commissary and stables. Other allusions to Spanish colonial architecture included decorative detailing derived from Islamic architectural patterns, a red tile roof, and a large courtyard with a fountain. With the courtyard, the long interior and exterior galleries, and a stair hall lit by leaded windows designed by Tiffany & Company, the design alternately evoked colonial palace

SANTA GERTRUDIS HOME AND HEADQUARTERS OF THE KING RANCH. KINGSVILLE, TEXAS.

FIGURE 3.4. *King Ranch Main House, designed by Carleton Adams, Henrietta King, and Richard Kleberg, Kingsville, Texas, 1915. Postcard collection of the author.*

types and Southern plantations, giving the building a hybrid spatial character appropriate to the ranch's historical relationships with the systems and economies of Spanish colonialism and slavery.

Even as the new house metaphorically looked south and east, Carleton Adams oriented it associatively toward San Antonio. At the same time, with King and her daughter and son-in-law, the architect developed an architectural and decorative vocabulary that would come to be recognized as distinctively "Texan." Materially, formally, and decoratively, "Texan" meant yoking references to the local landscape, multiple colonial histories, and even Indigenous Mexican history, as if to visually articulate the ranch's historicity and the geographic breadth of its reach, thereby reinforcing its status as a semi-imperial entity. On the outside of the ranch house, a pair of trefoil arches on the vestibule leading to the long porch evokes the entry to Mission Espada, one of the five Spanish missions in San Antonio. Tiny decorative reliefs with images of the missions ornament one wall of the courtyard. Inside, local mesquite wood was used as flooring, along with stone and tile, in the manner of Mexican haciendas. Richard Kleberg commissioned a library rug woven to his design that suggested that the ranch was the historical successor to a series of empires. It centered on an "Aztec motif," around which were emblems referencing Spanish and French colonial control of Texas; beyond these, on the border, was a pattern that recalled the snakelike "running *W*" form of the King cattle brand, a design whose author may have been a Kineño.[27]

Under a ceiling of ornamental plaster ran the long main living room (fig. 3.5). The focus of this space was a large fireplace and an area rug bordered with abstract geometric patterns evocative of Navajo textile designs, with a Texas flag at its center. Above the fireplace hung a huge painting of the Alamo, which was then being romantically reclaimed and reimagined as the foremost symbol of the triumph of Anglo Texans over Mexicans.[28] Framed spatially by the Texas flag and the image of the Alamo in a building that, like executive mansions, accommodated and collapsed distinctions between residential recreation and political and economic planning, Richard King's descendants (and ranch trustees) gathered to discuss ranch management and the further expansion of their empire.[29] In its decoration and furnishings, this room visually and symbolically conflated private power as conferred through vast property ownership, political power as it resided in the state of Texas, and white colonialism, architecturally embodying sections of the 1836 Texas Constitution. The image of the Alamo and the Texas flag in a setting of genteel, white informality—an image reproduced in widely circulated publications—helped cement the myth of the Texas ranch as an integral and even natural part of a state born out of white settler colonialism and ambitions to expand slavery west. With its formal spatial planning, clear distinctions of public and private spaces, and numerous bedrooms, Henrietta King's house reinforced her status as the architect of social and business relationships enacted by her guests and family members within the walls of her house, while its porches, tower, balcony, and

FIGURE 3.5. *King Ranch Main House, designed by Carleton Adams, Henrietta King, and Richard Kleberg, Kingsville, Texas, 1915. King Ranch Collection, South Texas Archives and Special Collections, Texas A&M University–Kingsville.*

views reminded visitors of her status as the ruler of a realm that extended, over land and rail, far beyond its grounds.

Loss and Method

By naming absence, Saidiya Hartman showed poignantly that the presence of archival evidence is proof of power.[30] Having been conceived within and sustained by capitalism, academic architectural history has historically valued the kinds of evidence power and money produce, but the discipline has long been capacious enough to include nonarchitectural objects. At some level, as scraps disengaged from contexts and woven into histories, all of our evidence is fragmentary and partial, even buildings. Dwelling on voids, absences, fragmentation, and a yearning for wholeness as a core constitutive impulse in architectural modernism and in history writing allows us to see relationships between avant-garde theory, with its pose of ahistoricity, and the practice of architectural history: from James Stuart and Nicholas Revett gazing at the ruins of the Philopappos Monument in Athens; to painterly cubism, with its connotation of incompleteness, as foundational for Le Corbusier's history-based theory; to the doctrine of organicism, with its obsession with parts and wholes; to the fragment as fetish in postmodernism. Recognizing the parallels in the history we were taught and the history we practice can bring us closer to understanding disciplinary architectural history as a coproducer of architectural modernity, broadly defined. Does that in turn liberate us to face and unmask the spaces, voids, shards, and fragments inherent in our practices as historians, and to risk engaging with obviously incomplete histories like Dimery's?

Reflecting on the ideas of Michael Ann Holly, Mary K. Coffey observes of loss and scholarship:

> Our writing . . . becomes a compensatory mechanism to make present what is absent, to revivify the object by generating new meaning, not restoring original meaning, even as we recognize that that meaning is arbitrary and contingent upon our own desires. . . .
>
> The relationship to the past we seek to enliven, then, is not empirical, but ethical.[31]

In revivifying—if not resurrecting—via writing, especially in the face of nonpresent evidence, architectural history becomes not fiction but aspiration. This kind of scholarship may require scholars to confront violence, making research and writing not only compensatory but a vocalization of powerlessness, anger, or sadness. History writing then has the potential to be not just an attempt at restitution but an act of revenge. It seems essential to be explicit about the dynamics of scholarly desire and archival absence when thinking about race and architectural history in the United States in the twenty-first century. Thus, to what extent is the study of Dimery's brand an expression of desire for her to have had a ranch and a house, because we might wish Texas had been different in her time, and wish it were different today?

If the years since 2016 have taught us anything, it is that as scholars we must become even more rigorous in our interrogation of sources and relentlessly model evidence-based argumentation in our research, teaching, and public lives. And yet the example of the Dimery brand complicates that dictum. It asks us to move in a different direction: toward a more explicitly imaginative mode of conceiving architectural history. By setting race in dialogue with *venustas*, putting power into play with *firmitas*, or reading land in relation to *utilitas*, and opening up the possibility that all six points operate together, the Dimerian Triad can help us balance our imaginative impulses and our commitment to hard evidence. The Dimerian Triad acknowledges that the reality of land, race, and power as they operated in the United States in the nineteenth century did not produce the kinds of objects that make it possible to read architecture in the ways that make sense when the Vitruvian Triad, or architectural theory, is the privileged disciplinary framework. To more effectively write race into the history of US architecture, we need not give up everything we have been taught. Form still matters, as the King Ranch buildings illustrate, and old art historical tools, such as comparative analysis, remain useful. As a device, the new triad makes it easier to write race into the history of the King Ranch and to bring into the same frame two women who navigated the equivalence of power and property under patriarchy. It does not, however, turn Dimery into an architect or a patron in the usual sense, nor the brand registration into architecture. But by accommodating the absence of a record of Dimery in those roles, it creates historiographic space for naming loss, and perhaps thereby helps make the discipline less indifferent to stories like hers.

The Dimerian Triad, with Vitruvius's, may be the basis of a methodology that is at once flexible and rigorous, eclectic, and capable of coping with instability and absence—in a single reading, essay, monograph, or semester. It holds out the possibility of a historiography that actively grapples with the discipline's imperialisms, and with architectural history's condition as an invention by people of privilege in western Europe and in the Northeastern United States, crafted primarily to describe buildings and conditions in those places. In the ways it stands for loss in the architectural historical record, the empty space of the Dimerian-Vitruvian prism invites us to test disciplinary limits and confront research and writing in the 2020s inflected by the sense of loss—of norms that underpin liberal democracy, of human rights, of lives, of the planet itself—that has come to define the experience of living in the United States for many.

Notes

1. I thank David Carlson of the Spanish Archives in the Bexar County Clerk's Office for his generous assistance in locating documents related to the Dimerys.

2. Kathleen Petty, "Branding History," *San Antonio Magazine*, September 2020, 64. On deeds associated with Black residents of Bexar County, see Edgar Johnson, *African Americans in the Bexar County Texas Deed Records, 1823–1865: A Documentary History* (independently published, 2022).

3. "Mrs. H. M. King Dies in Texas at 93," *New York Times*, April 1, 1925.

4. "Mrs. H. M. King Dies in Texas"; "Greatest Cattle Ranch Loses Its Woman Ruler," *New York Times*, April 19, 1925.

5. Tara A. Dudley provides a model for reading race in the built environment by analyzing property ownership alongside a wide variety of historical sources in *Building Antebellum New Orleans: Free People of Color and Their Influence* (University of Texas Press, 2021).

6. See, for example, Mauricio Tenorio-Trillo, *Latin America: The Allure and Power of an Idea* (University of Chicago Press, 2017).

7. Such an approach might draw from insights in Kevin Lynch, *The Image of the City* (MIT Press, 1960).

8. Marta Gutman, *A City for Children: Women, Architecture, and the Charitable Landscapes of Oakland, 1850–1950* (University of Chicago Press, 2014).

9. The essays in Martin Brückner and Sandy Isenstadt's edited volume *Elusive Archives: Material Culture Studies in Formation* (University of Delaware Press, 2021) offer a variety of methodological approaches to writing history using nonarchival objects and those that do not fit in conventional disciplinary frameworks.

10. "A Way Must Be Found to Broaden Our Perspective: James Ackerman in Conversation with Cammy Brothers," *Art Bulletin* 94, no. 3 (2012): 362–367; Carl Anthony, "The Big House and the Slave Quarters: African Contributions to the New World" (1976), in *Cabin, Quarter, Plantation: Architecture*

and Landscapes of North American Slavery, ed. Clifton Ellis and Rebecca Ginsburg (Yale University Press, 2010), 177–191; Dell Upton, "White and Black Landscapes in Eighteenth-Century Virginia" (1985), in Ellis and Ginsburg, *Cabin, Quarter, Plantation*, 121–139; Louis P. Nelson, *Architecture and Empire in Jamaica* (Yale University Press, 2016).

11. On the Indigenous history of this region, see Daniel J. Gelo, "The Indigenous Borderlands: Cultures Without Boundaries," in *Bridging Cultures: Reflections on the Heritage Identity of the Texas-Mexico Borderlands*, ed. Harriet D. Romo and William A. Dupont (Texas A&M University Press, 2021), 26–49.

12. Antebellum Black Texas ranching families included the Ashworths; see Jason A. Gillmer, "Shades of Gray: The Life and Times of a Free Family of Color on the Texas Frontier," *Minnesota Journal of Law and Inequality* 29, no. 1 (2011): 33–108. I am grateful to Tara A. Dudley for calling my attention to this article.

13. See, for example, Philip Durham and Everett L. Jones, *The Negro Cowboys* (University of Nebraska Press, 1965); Sara R. Massey, ed., *Black Cowboys of Texas* (Texas A&M University Press, 2000).

14. On the Spanish and Mexican roots of Texas ranching, see Jack Jackson, *Los Mesteños: Spanish Ranching in Texas, 1721–1821* (Texas A&M University Press, 1986).

15. On the ranch workers, see Roberto M. Villarreal, "The Mexican-American Vaqueros of the Kenedy Ranch: A Social History" (master's thesis, Texas A&I University, 1972).

16. For example, Walter Rimm, born in San Patricio County, Texas, worked as a cook at the King Ranch for fifteen years. "Federal Writers' Project: Slave Narrative Project, Vol. 16, Texas, Part 3, Lewis-Ryles," 1936, Library of Congress, https://www.loc.gov/resource/mesn.163/.

17. Villarreal, "Mexican-American Vaqueros."

18. Villarreal, "Mexican-American Vaqueros," 42.

19. Walter Prescott Webb, *The Texas Rangers* (Houghton Mifflin, 1935), 14.

20. In the 1910s, possibly as many as five thousand Mexicans and Mexican Americans were murdered in the Rio Grande Valley by white civilians and law enforcement personnel. Monica Muñoz Martinez, *The Injustice Never Leaves You: Anti-Mexican Violence in Texas* (Harvard University Press, 2018); see also "The History," Refusing to Forget, 2024, https://refusingtoforget.org/the-history.

21. Américo Paredes, *With His Pistol in His Hand* (University of Texas Press, 1971), 31.

22. Villarreal, "Mexican-American Vaqueros," 5.

23. Joe S. Graham, "The Jacal in South Texas: The Origins and Forms of a Folk House," in *Hecho en Texas: Texas-Mexican Folk Arts and Crafts*, ed. Joe S. Graham (University of North Texas Press, 1991), 293–299.

24. "Mrs. H. M. King Dies in Texas."

25. "Greatest Cattle Ranch Loses Ruler."

26. "Greatest Cattle Ranch Loses Ruler."

27. "Greatest Cattle Ranch Loses Ruler."

28. L. Robert Ables, "The Second Battle for the Alamo," *Southwestern Historical Quarterly* 70, no. 3 (1967): 372–413; Richard R. Flores, "Private Vision, Public Culture: The Making of the Alamo," *Cultural Anthropology* 10, no. 1 (1995): 99–115.

29. Ranching operations and businesses have continued to expand dramatically since Henrietta King's death in 1925. Tom Lea, *The King Ranch*, vol. 2 (Little, Brown, 1957), 605–706; see also King Ranch website, accessed March 17, 2022, https://www.king-ranch.com.

30. Saidiya Hartman, "Venus in Two Acts," *Small Axe*, no. 26 (vol. 12, no. 2) (2008): 1–14.

31. Mary K. Coffey, *Orozco's American Epic: Myth, History, and the Melancholy of Race* (Duke University Press, 2020), 22–23.

PART II

RECONSTRUCTION AND ARCHITECTURE

4 SLAVERY AND SOVEREIGNTY IN STONE

THE MASON FAMILY OF AUSTIN, TEXAS

Tara A. Dudley

THE STORY OF THE MASON family of Austin, Texas, is one of a forgotten Black community, the men and women who founded it, and a journey that established that family as the builders of some of the most prominent buildings in nineteenth-century Austin. The building blocks of the family's history were seemingly components of disparate narratives. Yet hidden behind the facades of iconic historical buildings (and the Anglo settlers credited with building them), buried beneath an urban landscape altered by industrialization and gentrification, woven in genealogical connections, and written into untapped archives, are Sam and Dicy Mason and their children—founding residents of Austin and architects of the early city's structure and development. Their story can be told through a methodology that more broadly considers the archive: how and where information about African American building practitioners and communities is recorded and stored.[1]

In Search of the "Negro" Master Builder

When the small hamlet of Waterloo was established as Austin in 1839, enslaved Blacks lived throughout the city. After emancipation, newly freed men and women founded over a dozen freedom colonies in and around Austin in the postbellum era.[2] Masontown developed between 1869 and 1871 from property acquisitions by the craftsmen Raiford, Sam Jr., George, and Henry Mason. Once a vibrant settlement, none of the historic fabric of Masontown remains, not even a historical marker to commemorate the bygone community, its inhabitants, and its buildings. The *Handbook of Texas Online* contains one short paragraph on Masontown, but the archivist Michelle M. Mears has expanded this brief chronology with a more detailed narrative of Masontown's history, physical development, and demographics beyond the postbellum era.[3] Nevertheless, a study establishing the deeper context and connection between the Mason family and their community, city, and profession is nonexistent. From their founding of Masontown to their work on the 1887 Texas State Capitol, the contributions of the family of stonemasons seem to be unrelated bookends of a postbellum story. Unbeknownst to me, the family's story proved richer and more far-reaching, extending from North Carolina through Tennessee, before establishing roots and growing in Texas well into the next century. The recovery of this narrative via alternative forms of historiography promotes revisionist criteria to advance interpretation of African American contributions to the built environment.

My early knowledge of the Mason family as builders came from repetitive information in limited secondary sources.[4] The quest to know more began in earnest while I conducted research for several talks on enslaved and free Black builders in nineteenth-century Austin. Austin's continued development—and need for enslaved laborers—was guaranteed when the election of 1850 designated it as the state capital for the next twenty years. Assured of a government presence and steady population, Austin quickly expanded and prospered. State officials approved permanent building construction, including the second Texas State Capitol, built from 1853 to 1855. The contractors for the project were John Brandon, Abner H. Cook, A. W. Moore, Charles L. McGehee, Thomas H. Jones, and John Hendrickson. Except for Brandon and Hendrickson, these men were all enslavers at the time of the 1850 census, holding in bondage men who would have been of age to contribute to the capitol building project.[5]

Abner Cook is the best known of the group of contractors; he became the premier contractor and master builder in Austin by mid-century, supervising construction of Greek Revival–style buildings such as the Texas Governor's Mansion (1854), in addition to the Texas State Capitol.[6] Already familiar with Cook's life and career, I continued to seek specifics on his exploitation of enslaved laborers but focused my analysis on the built works with which his peer Thomas H. Jones was known to have been involved. Upon their arrival in Austin in the mid-1840s,

Jones and his family settled on the Colorado River southeast of Austin. There, in 1852, enslaved masons completed the Joneses' two-story limestone house (fig. 4.1). Those laborers contributed to subsequent projects on which Jones collaborated with other Austin builders. In addition to supervising work on the capitol building, Jones was also the master builder or contractor of record for the first Travis County Courthouse (1855) and the Sampson-Henricks Building (1859) (fig. 4.2). While researching the latter, a review of contemporary photographs yielded an interesting detail: The same masonry pattern on the south facade of the Jones farmstead is present under the cornice on the front facade of the Sampson-Henricks Building. In these locations, the limestone blocks were laid with alternating square and rectangular faces, resembling the Flemish bond pattern of brick masonry construction and suggesting that an individual trained in bricklaying was being required to work with the limestone more readily available in Central

URE 4.1. *Thomas H. Jones House, 1852. Photo by Kenneth ertepe, 2020.*

FIGURE 4.2. *Sampson-Henricks Building, 1859. Photographer and date unknown. Austin-Travis County Collection, Texas Historical Commission; courtesy of the Portal to Texas History, University of North Texas Libraries.*

URE 4.3. *The cornice of the Sampson-Henricks Building ests a brick masonry pattern, indicating the workman- of Sam Mason Sr. Photographer and date unknown. as Historical Commission; courtesy of the Portal to Texas ory, University of North Texas Libraries.*

FIGURE 4.4. *Detail of the west facade of the Thomas H. Jones House. The stonework suggests the same brick masonry pattern present in the Sampson-Henricks Building, indicating the hand of Sam Mason Sr. Photo by Kenneth Hafertepe, 2020.*

Texas (figs. 4.3, 4.4).[7] In 1852, the unidentified author of an editorial describing a journey westward from San Marcos, Texas, through Lockhart to Austin revealed the existence of a master builder whom Jones enslaved and had trained in Nashville, Tennessee (fig. 4.5).[8] In an attempt to discover more about this unnamed master builder, I began to research Jones's biography more deeply by expanding his family tree and searching for archival records that might link him to any enslaved or freedmen builders in Austin.

In the meantime, I turned back to Masontown to develop a more complete chain of title and acquisition history utilizing Travis County deed records, but the Mason family's ownership of properties just north of Masontown offered a significant revelation.[9] In July 1886, Sam Mason Sr. and Jr. sold two adjacent lots to Maria Louisa "Lou" Jones Caldwell, who I knew was a daughter of Thomas H. Jones based on concurrent genealogical research. Navigating the deed transaction and the Jones family tree using county deed records, as well as probate records available in digitized form through Ancestry.com, I found that Lou's sister Olivia "Lilly" Jones had willed those two lots to Sam Mason Sr. and Jr. two years earlier.[10] The 1884 bequest offered a connection between the Mason and Jones families. I wondered if the Masons could have had an antebellum connection to the Joneses

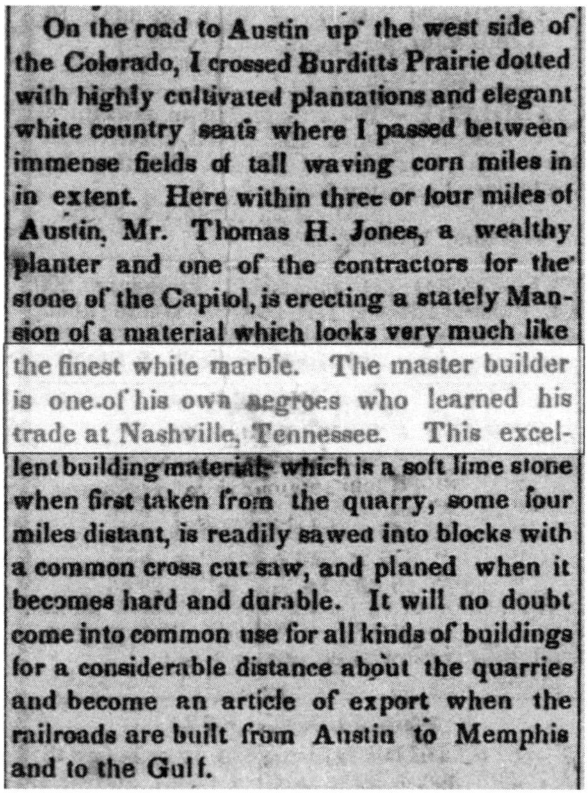

On the road to Austin up the west side of the Colorado, I crossed Burditts Prairie dotted with highly cultivated plantations and elegant white country seats where I passed between immense fields of tall waving corn miles in in extent. Here within three or four miles of Austin, Mr. Thomas H. Jones, a wealthy planter and one of the contractors for the stone of the Capitol, is erecting a stately Mansion of a material which looks very much like the finest white marble. The master builder is one of his own negroes who learned his trade at Nashville, Tennessee. This excellent building material which is a soft lime stone when first taken from the quarry, some four miles distant, is readily sawed into blocks with a common cross cut saw, and planed when it becomes hard and durable. It will no doubt come into common use for all kinds of buildings for a considerable distance about the quarries and become an article of export when the railroads are built from Austin to Memphis and to the Gulf.

FIGURE 4.5. *An unnamed traveler who visited Thomas Jones in the early 1850s and observed his building projects noted that "the master builder is one of his own negroes, who learned his trade at Nashville, Tennessee."* Galveston Weekly Journal, *July 9, 1852.*

and if one of them could have been the "Negro" master builder. One unexpected archival find from digitized probate records—the will of Thomas Jones's father, Edmund Jones—substantiated the Mason-Jones connection. On July 15, 1835, Edmund Jones, a prominent landowner, made out his will in Madison County, Tennessee. He made bequests of human chattel and money to his children and grandchildren. In the eighth provision, he stated, "I give and bequeath to son Thomas H. Jones my negroes, Sam[,] Dicy his wife[,] and child Isham."[11]

North Carolina to Tennessee

Edmund Jones was born in Georgia in 1768. After his marriage, Edmund ultimately relocated to Tennessee in the late 1790s. The Joneses appear to have also resided periodically in North Carolina, the home of Edmund's forebears; Thomas H. Jones was born in Halifax County, North Carolina, in 1812 during one of those stints. Sam and Dicy were also born in North Carolina, around 1820.[12] Sam and Dicy would have been among the fifty-nine enslaved men, women, and children enumerated as Edmund's Tennessee property in the 1830 federal census.[13] The enslaved couple had a young son by the time they were identified in Edmund's 1835 will and transferred to his son Thomas's possession.[14]

Thomas H. Jones lived his childhood and early adult life in Tennessee. He married Maria Louisa Van Zandt, and they would ultimately have nine children. In Tennessee, Sam and Dicy's family also continued to grow, with four sons born from 1837 to 1845: Raiford (b. 1837), Henry (b. 1840), George (b. 1842), and Sam Jr. (b. 1845). The Joneses' maintenance of Sam and Dicy's family unit had long-standing repercussions for all concerned. Sometime between 1835 and 1845, Samuel trained as a brick- or stonemason. It may never be known if Sam had a natural aptitude or if Jones took advantage of his power and connections as an enslaver to have Sam educated in this way. No known historical records prior to Jones's arrival in Texas indicate Jones's experience as a builder. Architectural historian Catherine Bishir has studied the contributions of enslaved craftspeople to the architecture of the Upper South; her body of work may offer context on the relationship between Mason and Jones, as well as insight into the methodologies used to identify and elevate other enslaved builders in North Carolina.[15] Sam, however, may have had limited training in that region, since he would have been around the age of sixteen when the Jones family trafficked him to Tennessee. The Middle Tennessee region, including Nashville, was home to scores, if not hundreds, of skilled enslaved craftsmen, including brickmasons, stonemasons, plasterers, carpenters, builders, and ironworkers.[16] Sam had a direct line to the tradition of masonry construction in both North Carolina and the Nashville and Middle Tennessee region before the Joneses trafficked him and his family to Texas.

Gone to Texas

The establishment of the Republic of Texas following independence from Mexico in 1836 further opened the doors for Anglo settlers from the Southeastern United States to relocate to Texas—bringing with them the individuals they enslaved—and build new cities such as Houston (1836) and Austin. After Texas gained statehood in 1845, Thomas and Maria Louisa Jones made their way to Texas in 1846.[17] The couple established the aforementioned farmstead along the Colorado River below Austin, where Sam erected a house that the family called Riverside: a two-story limestone dwelling with a similar layout on both floors of two rooms flanking a central hall (see fig. 4.1).[18] Unlike most other limestone houses that other enslaved laborers constructed in early Austin, Sam's ability allowed him to build not with rubble or rough-hewn limestone but with smooth ashlar blocks in a pattern that required skill to align the vertical mortar joints for best effect. Undoubtedly, other enslaved laborers worked with Sam on Riverside and Jones's other building projects; Jones enslaved fourteen individuals at the time of the 1850 census, and by 1860 that number had increased to thirty-one.[19]

Enslaved laborers became instrumental to Jones, who transitioned from farmer to builder-contractor, an enterprise made possible with ready access to unpaid labor and a quarry within four miles of his homestead.[20] In the 1850s, Jones contracted for several important stone buildings in Austin. Sam, and others, provided uncredited expertise and labor for the buildings' construction. By 1853, *The Southwestern American* noted of Austin buildings and of the city's main thoroughfare, Congress Avenue, "Our wooden age is passing away, ushering in one of brick and stone."[21] That year, the carpenter John Brandon submitted the winning design for a new state capitol building.[22] Brandon and fellow builder Abner Cook were contracted to complete the woodwork, painting, and glazing; A. W. Moore, the plastering. Charles L. McGehee began the stonework with "handsome white limestone" laid "in the most faithful and workmanlike manner."[23] With McGehee's untimely death in April 1852, new contractors were hired. John Hendrickson completed the exterior stonework. Thomas H. Jones was contracted for the interior stonework and plastering.[24] Sam would have been among Jones's crew.

A few years later, in 1855, Jones was a contractor, with George L. Walton and W. M. Walton, for the first Travis County Courthouse. The newspaper notice announcing that Jones won the contract states that the courthouse was to be brick and that the adjoining jail would have brick exterior walls and a stone interior wall.[25] However, subsequent Sanborn maps depict a stone building with brick interior walls and ground-level floors.[26] Again, Jones's access to a limestone quarry precluded any preference that county officials (or Sam) had for building in brick. Sam's skill was again required four years later, in 1859, when Jones—along with William M. Wilson and Abner Cook—directed the construction of a three-story, Italianate-style general merchandise store for the merchants George W.

Sampson and Abram Henricks on Congress Avenue (see fig. 4.2). Construction commenced in April 1859 on the "fine [edifice] of rock" that newspaper publishers anticipated.[27] When completed in June 1860, the three-story Sampson-Henricks Building featured a primary (east) facade with arched windows set in a wall of ashlar limestone framed with pilasters, detailed with dentiled string courses, and capped with a bracketed cornice.[28] Sam's skill, training, and personal stamp can be seen in the craftmanship of the Flemish bond stonework incorporated beneath the cornice area—the same pattern he laid at the Jones farmstead (see figs. 4.3, 4.4). Such a high-style building required additional laborers; the hands of others—and signs of economy at less public facades—remain visible with the rough-hewn limestone on the north facade and rubble limestone at the rear (west) facade.[29] It is highly likely that among those enslaved laborers were Sam's three oldest sons, Raiford, Henry, and George, who, by 1855, were of age to be trained in stone- and brickmasonry and to work with their father on the Jones-managed projects. On the eve of the Civil War, Congress Avenue's and Austin's prominence and growth were emphasized by the Texas State Capitol and the Sampson-Henricks Building, which were built by Sam and other enslaved craftsmen and laborers, as opposed to the white contractors and developers with whom the buildings are associated (fig. 4.6). As Sam (and his sons) enhanced Austin's built

FIGURE 4.6. *Congress Avenue in the 1860s. Two of the prominent buildings in this view of Austin's main street—the Sampson-Henricks Building at the left middle ground and the second Texas State Capitol at the right background—are projects that Sam Mason Sr. would have worked on under Thomas H. Jones. Photo by the Jordan Company. Chalberg Collection of Prints and Negatives, Austin History Center, Austin Public Library, C00393; courtesy of the Portal to Texas History, University of North Texas Libraries.*

environment with some of the city's finest limestone buildings, Sam and Dicy's family continued to grow, with Harriet (b. 1855), Viny (b. 1856), Charles (b. 1861), Laura (b. 1862), and Louisa (b. 1863).[30]

Building Community

With emancipation, Sam and Dicy welcomed the agency to choose their names. Dicy took the surname of their former enslavers, adapting Jones for her maiden name. Sam embraced his profession and chose Mason for the family name—a badge of honor to signify the trade in which he was skilled and could now practice freely for his own benefit and that of his family. Sam and his sons now had the agency to act on other rights as freedmen. On July 31, 1867, Sam Sr., George, and Raiford purchased three lots in the original townsite at the southwest corner of Water Street (present-day East First Street) and Trinity Street.[31] This was likely the location of the family's first permanent residence after emancipation. Later maps indicate that they constructed a brick house on one of the lots, well within the capabilities of Sam and his sons.[32] Between 1869 and 1871, the Mason sons purchased eight lots in the 1500 block of Cedar and Pine Streets (present-day East Fourth and Fifth Streets) (fig. 4.7).[33] Masontown was the name given to the freedom colony that developed around the family's landholdings. Per their skill and preference, the family erected a brick house on the lot that George acquired.

In the 1870 census, the entire Mason family—into its third generation—resided in Masontown. All of the adult male members of the family except Henry were employed as stone- or rock masons.[34] When the Houston and Texas Central Railway's line came into Austin from the east in 1871, Masontown was bisected and became increasingly industrial.[35] Raiford and Sam Jr., who were listed as stonemasons along with their father in the 1872–1873 city directory, lived on their

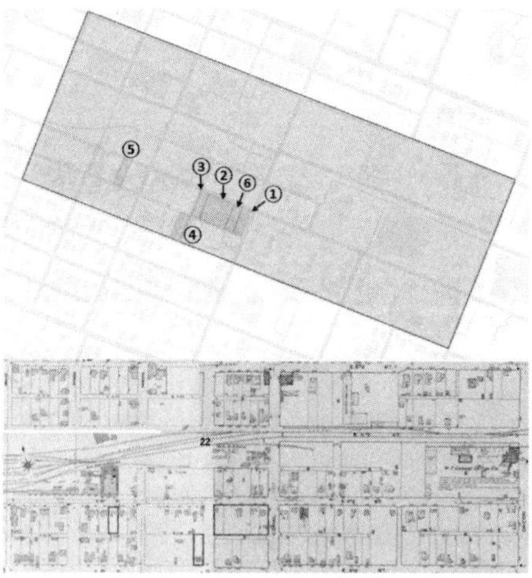

FIGURE 4.7. Top: *The historic boundaries of Masontown, highlighting the locations of Mason family property acquisitions. (1) November 8, 1869 (Sam Jr.); (2) November 8, 1869 (Sam Jr.); (3) January 5, 1870 (Raiford); (4) July 25, 1870 (George); (5) November 19, 1870 (Henry); and (6) September 23, 1871 (Sam Jr.). Google Maps, 2024; with additions by the author.* Bottom: *Mason family properties and the Masontown community on Sanborn Fire Insurance Company maps, 1900 and 1930. Perry-Castañeda Library Map Collection, University of Texas Libraries; with additions by the author.*

properties near the freight depot. In the years after the Civil War, it is possible that the Mason family was employed by Thomas Jones's son Isaac, who briefly followed in his father's footsteps with his involvement in the construction business; he operated a brick manufacturing firm for eight years before turning to the dry goods business and other pursuits.[36] In the postbellum era, the Mason family's entrepreneurial efforts expanded to property ownership, development, and speculation. Raiford and Sam Jr. were both listed as stonemasons in the 1881–1882 city directory. Deed records indicate that they also began to acquire property north of Masontown and outside of the then city limits, farther to the northeast.[37] It was in this period that the Masons received the property from their former enslaver's daughter, a transaction that suggested a connection between the two families and fostered the research that revealed Sam Sr.'s familial and professional origins. When Lilly Jones died in Pennsylvania in July 1884, she willed property in the racially mixed Gregorytown neighborhood to Sam Sr. and Sam Jr.[38] The seventh of eight children and youngest daughter born to Thomas H. Jones and Maria Louisa Van Zandt in 1856, Lilly would have been a young girl when the Masons were freed but would have had plenty of occasions to know them, since presumably they had lived somewhere on her parents' property prior to emancipation. Since her father and mother were already deceased, and she was unmarried with no children, Lilly may have thought of the Masons, who already owned property nearby.[39] City directories indicate the Masons' Gregorytown addresses on Chincapin Street (present-day Rosewood Avenue), even though they retained their primary residences on Trinity Street (Sam Sr.) and Cedar Street (Sam Jr.). The Masons' ownership of these two lots was short-lived; they sold them to Lilly's sister Lou in 1886.[40]

Capitol Craftsmen

In addition to continued real estate endeavors, the second-generation Mason men remained active in the building trades in Austin. Like their father had in 1853, George, Raiford, and Sam Jr. worked as masons during the construction of the current Texas State Capitol, which was completed in 1888. On various occasions, the men appear in payroll records administered by the state of Texas and currently housed at the Texas State Library and Archives.[41] With the absence of the Masons' words about their involvement in the construction of the grand Renaissance Revival building that rivaled contemporary state capitol buildings, one might wonder what they thought about the convict laborers (mostly African American) who quarried the limestone and granite for the building's construction, or about working with the Scottish stoneworkers who were brought in when citizens and craftsmen protested the use of convict labor when law-abiding citizens were ready to do the work. The Masons, and a handful of other African

American craftsmen, were likely hired by the Capitol Building Commission and the project general contractor alongside the Scottish masons because of their skill and reputation as builders, on one hand, and their affordability and availability in light of the controversy over the project, on the other. The Mason brothers may be among the African Americans photographed with the Scottish stoneworkers or with the crowd of dignitaries and craftsmen attending an event before the Goddess of Liberty statue was installed atop the dome of the almost complete capitol building in 1888 (fig. 4.8).

The other major building project in the city at the end of the nineteenth century was the construction of buildings and infrastructure on the campus of the University of Texas at Austin after its founding in 1883. As they did with the state capitol building project, financial records aid the recovery of the Mason family's involvement in early campus construction. The Board of Regents' 1892 biennial report reveals that either Sam Sr. or Sam Jr. worked a total of 11.5 days on the University of Texas campus, earning $14.35; while it is unknown exactly what the man's task entailed, this was equivalent to what other men of any race were compensated for "work on campus."[42] Between March 1893 and January 1894, one of the Sams earned $52.50 for hauling earth, brush, and gravel—tasks related to site excavation—as recorded in the vouchers he received to collect his payment.[43]

Although the Mason family had attained status and a measure of equality by virtue of their skill and connections by the end of the century, the next decades ushered in the end of an era. When family patriarch Samuel Mason Sr. died and was buried on March 23, 1899, the only mention in the local newspaper simply read, "The funeral of Samuel Mason took place yesterday afternoon."[44] While the notice is phrased such that readers likely knew to whom it referred, none of Sam's history, his family's history, or his lifelong accomplishments were mentioned. This may have been due to a loss of stature within a profession increasingly dominated by white craftsmen and professionally educated and trained architects.

FIGURE 4.8. *Dignitaries pose with the Goddess of Liberty prior to the statue's installation atop the Texas State Capitol in February 1888. The photograph includes several African American men (*highlighted*) who were probably craftsmen involved in the capitol's construction—the Mason brothers likely among them. Photographer unknown. Texas State Library and Archives Commission.*

Sam's sons remained part of the tradition of respected African American brickmasons whose ranks were diminishing. In 1902, Prairie View State Normal and Industrial College professor Elijah H. Holmes wrote,

> Brickmasons are fewer than carpenters. This class of workers are in demand, wages are high and discrimination is reduced to a minimum. There are no brick contractors in Houston, and only one or two in the state. Bricklayers in the towns are journeymen and most of them do a good grade of work [and] wages are from $3.00 to $4.00 per day. In the cities wages are a little better.[45]

One would therefore assume that in Austin, the Mason brothers remained prosperous, especially as they still engaged in diversified entrepreneurship in real estate in the early 1900s.[46]

The 1910 census would be the last time that the surviving Mason brothers, Raiford, George, and Sam Jr., were documented; brickmasons Raiford and Sam Jr. still resided in Masontown, while George was a farmer outside of the city limits.[47] According to Oakwood Cemetery burial ledgers, Raiford died a few weeks after the census taker visited in May 1910. George Mason died December 20, 1913. Sam Jr. died February 20, 1917.[48]

Today, the only physical remnants of the Mason family's architectural legacy are the Jones homestead and the Sampson-Henricks Building. Place-names provide clues in the built environment: Masontown at the now-gentrified community they founded, and Mason Avenue at the western boundary of the property they owned in far East Austin. With that absence in mind, the artist Ryan Runcie presents an alternate historiography in the form of a public mural, completed in 2020 as the nation reckoned with racism following the murder of George Floyd (fig. 4.9). Installed on the top-floor exterior of one building within a four-block condominium complex built in 2019, occupying several lots in the neighborhood left vacant by industrialization and gentrification, the twenty-by-twenty-five-foot mural is privately accessible and only partially visible from the ground (figs. 4.10, 4.11). Albeit in a limited way, the depiction of Raiford and Sam Jr. does offer the public a sense of the brothers' "resolve and determination to build a homestead of acceptance and economic stability" for Black Austinites in the late nineteenth century.[49] Like many historiographies of African American builders and craftspeople, the mural is significant for what it presents, as well as what it omits.

Through intentional analysis of diverse primary sources and archival materials, a once-forgotten family legacy can reclaim its place in the canon of Austin's built history. Architectural historians of the nineteenth century must continue to expand our understanding of architectural practice by working against conventional definitions of the profession and by accessing new archives or considering common sources from a new perspective. The tools of historic preservation—

FIGURE 4.9. *Ryan Runcie (Runcie Studios), The Rise of Masontown, 2020. The mural features portraits of Sam and Raiford Mason. Photo by Moyo Oyelola.*

FIGURE 4.10. *The mural's location, marked with a painter's palette icon, at the corner of East Fifth and Attayac Streets within west Masontown (highlighted) and in juxtaposition with the Mason family properties (outlined). Google Earth, 2021; with additions by the author.*

FIGURE 4.11. *Aerial view of the mural on the fourth floor o the Saltillo development. Google Earth, 2021.*

especially the broader consideration of historic context—are fundamental to this methodology, which offers different ways of researching, documenting, and storytelling, and allows Black builders and architects to be seen and acknowledged. In this way, the lives and careers of Sam Mason Sr. and his sons provide not only a counternarrative but a rethinking of authorship and the relationship between canonical architectural histories and histories of the vernacular—a means of diminishing the divide fostered by the professionalization of the US architecture field and the institutionalization of architectural education in the late nineteenth century, which resulted in the creation of and emphasis on canon.

Notes

1. Several recent works by architectural historians frame contemporary discussions on cultural memory, production, and preservation related to Black builders and architects and Black placemaking. See Irene Cheng, Charles L. Davis II, and Mabel O. Wilson, eds., *Race and Modern Architecture: A Critical History from Enlightenment to the Present* (University of Pittsburgh Press, 2020); Mabel O. Wilson, "Race, Reason, and the Architecture of Jefferson's Virginia Statehouse," in *Thomas Jefferson, Architect: Palladian Models, Democratic Principles, and the Conflict of Ideals*, ed. Lloyd De Witt and Corey Piper (Chrysler Museum / Yale University Press, 2019); Clifton Ellis and Rebecca Ginsburg, eds., *Slavery in the City: Architecture and Landscapes of Urban Slavery in North America* (University of Virginia Press, 2017); Andrea Roberts, "The End of Bootstraps and Good Masters: Fostering Social Inclusion Through Counternarrative Creation," in *Preservation and Social Inclusion*, ed. Erica Avrami (Columbia Books on Architecture and the City, 2020).

2. Freedom colonies, or freedmen's communities, "are 'historically significant communities' that were settled by formerly enslaved people during the Reconstruction and Jim Crow eras in Texas following Emancipation." "What Are Freedom Colonies?," Texas Freedom Colonies Project, accessed March 1, 2023, https://www.thetexasfreedomcoloniesproject.com/what-are-freedom-colonies. See also Thad Sitton and James Conrad, *Freedom Colonies: Independent Black Texans in the Time of Jim Crow* (University of Texas Press, 2010). Michelle M. Mears provides one of the first comprehensive histories of freedom colonies located within the current Austin city limits in *And Grace Will Lead Me Home: African American Freedmen Communities of Austin, Texas, 1865–1928* (Texas Tech University Press, 2009).

3. Vivian Elizabeth Smyrl, "Masontown, TX," *Handbook of Texas Online*, April 1, 1995, https://www.tshaonline.org/handbook/entries/masontown-tx; Mears, *And Grace Will Lead Me Home*, 29–35.

4. Additional sources with brief mentions of Masontown are John Mason Brewer, *An Historical Outline of the Negro in Travis County* (John Mason Brewer, 1940); and Delta Sigma Theta Sorority, *A Pictorial History of Austin, Travis County, Texas' Black Community, 1839–1920; The Black Heritage Exhibit* (Austin Alumnae Chapter Delta Sigma Theta Sorority, 1970).

5. Seventh Census of the United States, 1850, series M432, Records of the Bureau of the Census, RG 29, National Archives, Washington, DC, accessed from Ancestry.com, 1850 U.S. Federal Census—Slave Schedules.

6. The historian Kenneth Hafertepe has written *Abner Cook: Master Builder on the Texas Frontier* (Texas State Historical Association, 1992), the definitive biography chronicling Cook's career.

7. This connection between Jones, the unnamed enslaved stonemason, and the unusual limestone pattern was worked out via email correspondence in consultation with Kenneth Hafertepe during the spring of 2021.

8. "Editorial Correspondence: Travis County—Austin City—Railroads, Etc.," *Galveston Weekly Journal*, July 9, 1852, 4.

9. Deed record books are available on microfilm at the Travis County Clerk's recording division, as well as electronically via the Portal to Texas History, a digital repository administered by the University of North Texas that includes archives from across the state.

10. Sam Mason Sr. to Lou Jones, Travis County deed, July 22, 1886, bk. 70, p. 41; Sam Mason Jr. to Lou Jones, Travis County deed, July 22, 1886, bk. 70, p. 42.

11. Tennessee County, District, and Probate Courts, will books, vols. 1–2, 1825–1839, accessed from Ancestry.com, Tennessee, U.S., Wills and Probate Records, 1779–2008.

12. Sam and Dicy's birth dates are estimated from their ages in later census records. It is currently unknown if they were enslaved by Edmund Jones from birth or if they were previously held in bondage by others.

13. Fifth Census of the United States, 1830, Madison, Tennessee, series M19, roll 179, p. 73A, Records of the Bureau of the Census, RG 29, National Archives, Washington, DC, accessed from Ancestry.com, 1830 United States Federal Census.

14. At present, Edmund Jones's will is the only known record that mentions the child Isham, suggesting that he died or was sold and separated from his family before emancipation.

15. See the following works by Catherine W. Bishir: "A Proper Good Nice and Workmanlike Manner: A Century of Traditional Building Practice, 1730–1830," and "A Spirit of Improvement: Changes in Building Practice, 1830–1860," in *Architects and Builders in North Carolina: A History of the Practice of Building*, ed. Catherine W. Bishir, Charlotte V. Brown, Carl R. Lounsbury, and Ernest H. Wood III (University of North Carolina Press, 1990), 48–192; *North Carolina Architecture* (University of North Carolina Press, 1990); "Black Builders in Antebellum North Carolina" and "Severe Servitude to House Building: The Construction of Hays Plantation House, 1814–1817," in *Southern Built: American Architecture, Regional Practice* (University of Virginia Press, 2006), 69–109, 126–156; and *Crafting Lives: African American Artisans in New Bern, North Carolina, 1770–1900* (University of North Carolina Press, 2013).

16. Robbie Jones, email correspondence with the author and Kenneth Hafertepe, May 27, 2021.

17. Thomas H. Jones obituary, *Austin American-Statesman*, March 1, 1883, 4.

18. Other sources claim that the property was inherited via Maria Louisa Van Zandt's family, but that is not the case. Thomas F. McKinney to Thomas H. Jones, deed, February 28, 1848, bk. C, pp. 258–259; "Under Three Flags: Frontier Austin Homes, 1839–1865," brochure, Heritage Society of Austin, Heritage Homes Tour, 1996.

19. Seventh Census of the United States, 1850, Travis County, Texas, series M432, Records of the Bureau of the Census, RG 29, National Archives, Washington, DC, accessed from Ancestry.com, 1850 U.S. Federal Census—Slave Schedules.

20. "Editorial Correspondence," *Galveston Weekly Journal*, July 9, 1852.

21. Joe and Martha Freeman, "Congress Avenue Historic District National Register of Historic Places Nomination," 1978, sec. 8, p. 2, https://www.thc.texas.gov/public/upload/preserve/survey/highway/Congress%20Ave%20Historic%20District%20Austin.pdf.

22. "Editorial Correspondence," 2.

23. "Editorial Correspondence," 2.

24. "Editorial Correspondence," 2.

25. "Editorial Correspondence," 2.

26. Sanborn Fire Insurance Company maps of Austin, 1877 (sheet 1), 1885 (sheet 6), 1889 (sheet 15), 1894 (sheet 14), 1900 (sheet 40), Perry-Castañeda Library Map Collection, University of Texas at Austin, https://maps.lib.utexas.edu/maps/sanborn/texas.html.

27. Texas Historical Commission, Sampson Building historical marker application, 1983, 2, University of North Texas Libraries, Portal to Texas History, https://texashistory.unt.edu/ark:/67531/metapth491804.

28. Sampson Building historical marker application, 3.

29. Sampson Building historical marker application, 2–3.

30. Sam and Dicy's youngest daughter may have been named after Maria Louisa Van Zandt Jones, who died in July 1863.

31. The men purchased lots 7, 8, and 9 in block 182 for $350 from James P. Cope: deed, bk. R, p. 96. They sold half of block 9 on July 20, 1880: deed, bk. 47, p. 404.

32. Sanborn Fire Insurance Company maps of Austin, 1900, sheet 9, Perry-Castañeda Library Map Collection, University of Texas at Austin, https://maps.lib.utexas.edu/maps/sanborn/txu-sanborn-austin-1900-09.jpg.

33. Delta Sigma Theta Sorority, *Pictorial History of Austin*, 7.

34. In fact, George was enumerated twice: once in June, in the same Masontown household as his brother Raiford, and again in August, as brother Sam Jr.'s neighbor.

35. George and Henry Mason were not included in the 1872–1873 Austin city directory.

36. Charlene Carson, "Ike Jones Mill, 1880–1917: All in the Family," *Salado Village Voice*, July 12, 2018, https://saladovillagevoice.com/ike-jones-mill-salado-creek1880-1917.

37. W. J. and Mary A. Tannehill to Raiford Mason, deed, February 1, 1876, bk. 32, p. 26; R. H. Peck to George Mason, deed, October 16, 1882, bk. 53, pp. 374–375; L. W. Simpson to Sam Mason Sr. and Raiford Mason, deed, September 10, 1883, bk. 57, p. 216; C. S. Hardy to George Mason, deed, February 21, 1887, bk. 72, p. 485.

38. Lilly moved with her father (and his second wife) to Bell County, Texas, after her mother died and

was there for the 1870 and 1880 censuses. She lived briefly in Galveston, Texas, nursing her younger sister Emma before the latter died in 1881. When or why Lilly went to Pennsylvania is unknown. Her body was brought back to Austin and interred in Oakwood Cemetery. Gregorytown was a community where many freedmen and their families began to settle in the 1880s. See Mears, *And Grace Will Lead Me Home*, 53–56.

39. Kenneth Hafertepe, email correspondence with the author, November 15, 2021.

40. Sam Mason Jr. to Lou Jones, deed, July 22, 1886, bk. 70, p. 42; Sam Mason Sr. to Lou Jones, deed, July 22, 1886, bk. 70, p. 41.

41. The Texas State Library's records of the Texas Capitol Building Payroll, 1882–1888, have been transcribed to cards organized by individual and are further made accessible via Ancestry.com. The men are recorded as follows: George, Capitol Pay Rolls, 1884, 1887; Raiford, Capitol Pay Rolls, 1884, 1886; Samuel Mason [Jr.], Burnet Granite Quarry Roll, 1884.

42. That amount is equivalent to $495.25 in 2024. *Fifth Biennial Report of the Regents of the University of Texas, December 1892* (Austin: Ben C. Jones, 1893).

43. Vouchers, March 18, 1893, and March 25, 1893, UT Office of Accounting Records, box CDL2/B11, Dolph Briscoe Center for American History, University of Texas at Austin.

44. "Sidewalk Notes," *Austin American-Statesman*, March 24, 1899. According to the records of Oakwood Cemetery, Dicy Jones died in the spring of 1901; she was interred there on April 26, 1901. Austin History Center, Oakwood Cemetery Database, https://www.austinlibrary.com/ahc/oakwood.htm.

45. Elijah H. Holmes, "Local Conditions: Texas," in *The Negro Artisan: A Social Study Made Under the Direction of Atlanta University by the Seventh Atlanta Conference* (Atlanta University Press, 1902), 99.

46. Shortly before his death, Sam Sr. acquired six lots in block 3, outlot 6, division B, located between the Texas State Cemetery and the Tillotson Institute. E. M. E. Garland to Sam Mason Sr., deed, March 4, 1899, bk. 154, p. 425.

47. This was the family property acquired in 1882, located in outlot 23, division B, one mile outside of the city limits on the south side of East Nineteenth Street (present-day Martin Luther King Jr. Boulevard).

48. Delta Sigma Theta Sorority, *Pictorial History of Austin*, 7.

49. The Masontown Mural Project was an urban beautification project coordinated by the nonprofit Raasin in the Sun in conjunction with Six Square (and with sponsorship by Saltillo and Endeavor Real Estate). "The Rise of Masontown, Residences at Saltillo, East Austin, Texas," Runcie Studios, accessed January 3, 2022, https://ryanruncie.com/masontown-east-austin-tx; "Masontown," Raasin in the Sun, accessed January 3, 2022, https://www.raasininthesun.org/masontown.html.

5 GRAND NARRATIVES IN BLACK

THE ARCHITECTURAL HISTORIES OF JOHN MARRANT, ROBERT BENJAMIN LEWIS, AND MARTIN DELANY

Bryan E. Norwood

IN *DARK SPACE* (2016) THE architect Mario Gooden asks if there is a Black American architectural theory, a ground for architectural practice outside of the shadow of the nineteenth-century white gentleman that gave the profession its contemporary body. Gooden, like others, finds important strands of an answer in the communal and fugitive spaces of marronage that permeated the marshy and wooded borders of the plantation system.[1] In the past several decades, architectural history in the Americas has learned much about this aspect of enslaved spatial experience, and it still has much to learn.[2] To this I want to add another layer of nineteenth-century Black spatial practice: the written narration of architectural history itself. Indeed, as Stephen Hall says, while there are good reasons we "often privilege nontextual manifestations of black culture as the dominant modes of early African American historical expression," we should not overlook the numerous instances of antebellum Black American writing.[3] While hush arbors and other architectural appearances of the practices of marronage are foundational to the Black radical tradition, as Cedric Robinson describes, they had textual, historiographical companions in the nineteenth century.[4]

The "bleach bowels of mid-nineteenth-century American intelligentsia" confidently declared, Robinson writes, that "the negro has no history."[5] Framing Africans and their diaspora as historyless was a quintessential tool of white European and Euro-American Enlightenment histories. These racialized grand narratives provided the authors of Enlightenment individualism a smoke screen for slavery and colonialism, ways of formulating an account of human freedom that excluded multitudes from the tropical zone. In these grand narratives, the lack of writing itself was often marshaled through what W. E. B. Du Bois called a "curious assumption" as evidence of a paucity of civilization worth documenting.[6]

European and American architects, in a profession that took shape in the nineteenth century by looking back toward an ancient past for legitimacy, made great use of the structure of these written Enlightenment narratives and their attendant racial regimes. Nineteenth-century Euro-American architectural practitioners, educators, and apologists wrote from the stance that architectural history was a history of progress (albeit marred by backsliding). These grand narratives usually incorporated Africa. In fact, according to a number of these narratives, it was in Egypt that the very project of architecture as we know it was born. Even if it acted as an origin, however, Africa was treated as lost to the past, a historical stepping stone that architectural progress had traveled past millennia ago.

In the early nineteenth century, though, Black American writers were already developing counternarratives to these white plots, counternarratives in which architecture played an important role. Britt Rusert, through the concept of "fugitive science," has suggested that early republican Black theories of history and race were formulated in a way that mirrored the material practices of marronage and flight from capture.[7] Black authors wrote alternate histories and sciences not through a wholesale rejection of white theory but rather by tracing different lines through its pieces and parts. The nineteenth-century Black American writers I look at here—John Marrant, Robert Benjamin Lewis, and Martin Delany—drew on white histories that wove architecture into expansive world narratives, but they twisted these plots. John Ernest describes nineteenth-century Black writers like these three as formulating a "liberation historiography," a history that reappropriated and reimagined the pieces of "white nationalist mythology."[8] Marrant, Lewis, and Delany did not back away from the white grand narratives of architecture but rather cut up and collaged them in new ways, producing a different plot.

In this essay, I use these three authors to think about the challenges of formulating counternarratives in architectural history. Toni Morrison described the pressure to "dredge" up the fact that there is Black history as a kind of misdirection, an energy-wasting demand produced by the ideology of white supremacy.[9]

This demand, as Olúfẹ́mi O. Táíwò describes, is racism doing its work, shaping the thought of racialized people around "answering other people's questions."[10] And Achille Mbembe says this kind of Black apologetic work is a product of a "stark choice." While the "reaffirmation of African humanity" through a historical defense of the "distinct genius" of the "black 'race'" is certainly of consequence, it is also, Mbembe suggests, an approach in which the denials and reaffirmations of African humanity "look like the two sterile sides of the same coin."[11] Are the counternarratives of architectural history that are held out by Marrant, Lewis, and Delany caught in this sterile binary and energy-wasting task? And whether they are or are not, what can we learn from these authors' early nineteenth-century efforts to write outside of the misdirection of white supremacy?

Racial Regimes and Inversion

In a 1789 sermon in Boston, the minister John Marrant wove architecture into a grand historical narrative that was shaped by African American Protestantism, Black Freemasonry, and a nascent Pan-Africanism.[12] In his story, architectural knowledge and practice traveled with religiously devout Freemasons from Eden—which he positioned in Ethiopia—through Babylon, Egypt, Jerusalem, and on to the entire globe, where its continuation and maintenance anticipated the coming reunion of humanity with God in the "great and glorious Lodge in heaven."[13] As Marrant spoke of humanity's expulsion from Eden and the first murder that followed, he not only entered into late eighteenth-century discussions of Freemasonry and Christianity; he also broached the "makeshift patchwork" of racial regimes.[14] Africans were often described as the "Sons of Cain," he said, referencing the eighteenth-century theological idea that Cain's descendants were marked with Blackness for their father's sin of committing murder.[15] And Marrant, in fact, accepted this racialized interpretation: "We admit it if you please." But he reevaluated its implications for the history that followed, for it was from Cain and his sons that the practice of Freemasonry—both speculative and operative—began. "Bad as Cain was," Marrant wrote, "God took not from him his faculty of studying architecture."[16] Cain, while cursed, remained the prime vector of architectural wisdom.

Marrant's use of biblical events to frame his lecture on the world historical narrative of Freemasonry would have made perfect sense to the numerous Black and white Freemasons in his Boston audience.[17] Marrant's foundational truths were Christian, having been converted to the faith by the famed white Anglican revivalist preacher George Whitefield in 1770.[18] Following an itinerant path around the northern Atlantic world as a Black loyalist for the next two decades, Marrant honed his beliefs and his ministerial craft. It was likely not until he arrived in Boston in 1789 that he became intimately acquainted with Freemasonry, so much so that within months he could deliver his famed sermon.[19] Freemasonry in the form that Marrant encountered and taught can be traced back to early eighteenth-century England, when "speculative" masonry took shape by joining, co-opting, and mimicking the actual trade organizations that had been formed by "operative" masons.[20] Shifting the focus from operative trade secrets to grand speculative secrets about morality and world historical order, the white gentlemanly class that shaped speculative masonry's grand narratives used architectural symbolism and building practices to create a medium in which the histories of Christianity and the classical world were intertwined. But Marrant encountered Freemasonry in Boston not through these white gentlemen but rather in Black communities. A couple of decades prior to Marrant's arrival, the formerly enslaved tradesman Prince Hall, along with fourteen other Black men, began meeting with an Irish military lodge in Boston in 1775. After the American Revolution, they would continue to meet without official recognition from any American lodge. Finally, in 1787, Hall and others officially formed the first Black lodge, sponsored from across the Atlantic by the Grand Lodge of England.[21] It was two years after the formation of Boston African Lodge No. 459 that Marrant delivered his sermon at Prince Hall's invitation.

Architecture, as white Freemasons had used it for decades, provided Marrant a way to narrate a grand world history in which Blackness played a central role. In his account, the descendants of Cain, marked by Blackness, brought the secrets of architecture out of Eden and into the modern world. His technique of accepting the racial regime of racists but turning its narrative role upside down would become a common move of early African American writers. That much of the material for these Black counterhistories came from white narration is not surprising. These writers, after all, inhabited a milieu deeply intertwined with their European American counterparts. As Laurie Maffly-Kipp notes, the conversion of African Americans to Protestantism in large numbers in the late eighteenth and early nineteenth centuries took place "at precisely the same historical moment that gave rise to both biologically based theories of race and new conceptions of the 'nation' as a potent form of political identity."[22] Black writers would use the techniques and terminology of white racism and nationalism to write against white hierarchies, producing counternarratives of architectural history.

More than half a century after Marrant's lecture in Boston, the journalist, writer, and physician Martin Delany delivered a lecture over five hundred miles west titled "The Origin and Objects of Ancient Freemasonry," in which he took up and inverted another story of theological racism. Printed in 1853, not long after his oral address to the St. Cyprian Lodge No. 13, Delany's lecture defended the right of Black men to become Freemasons by showing it was from their progenitors that Freemasonry was born. "From whence sprung Masonry but from Ethiopia, Egypt, and Assyria—all settled and peopled by the children of Ham," he said.[23] Accepting a theological idea that dated back to the Middle Ages, Delany embraced the narrative that Noah's three sons—Shem, Ham, and Japheth—were the origins of geographically dispersed ethnic difference. The racialization of Ham's descendants arose from an interpretation of Genesis 9 that took the curse placed on Ham's descendants, because he laughed at his drunk, naked father, to be Blackness. This was a prevalent theological position in the United States in the mid-nineteenth century, particularly among enslavers, who used it to present Black bondage as a "universal truth."[24]

But it was not just enslavers who believed in the Curse of Ham (fig. 5.1). Northerners like Thomas Ustick Walter, architect of the US Capitol from 1851 to 1865 and a key figure in the founding of the American profession, upheld it in their churches.[25] And Northern Black intellectuals like Delany and Marrant accepted it too.[26] But again, Black authors wrote counternarratives using the terms of this racialist theology. For Marrant, it was Ham's grandson Nimrod who first achieved postdiluvian greatness in architecture and city building.[27] While nineteenth-century white racists like the widely read Josiah Priest used the figure of Nimrod to assign the blame for the Tower of Babel to Black people, in Marrant's narrative, this site of blame was the source of architectural wisdom (fig. 5.2). Nimrod was the "grand master of all Masons," Marrant said, and it was through him that knowledge of architecture was historically transmitted. Rewriting racialized genealogies, Black Freemasons turned a narrative of degradation into one of the maintenance of knowledge and skill in an imperfect world.

Book-length publications authored by African Americans began to emerge in the United States in the 1840s, particularly in the Northeast, with the establishment of Black presses and the expansion of free Black associations.[28] One of these antebellum, Black-authored books, Robert Benjamin Lewis's *Light and Truth*, wove architecture into its elaboration of a grand historical narrative in which Black people were the protagonists. While publications like Lewis's were appearing more rapidly by the late antebellum period, Black literacy rates nonetheless remained lower than those of the white population. But the oratory practices of the immensely popular culture of public lectures, which grew in companion with print practices in the early nineteenth century, greatly expanded the reach of Black Freemasons and other intellectuals like Lewis, Marrant, and Delany.[29] Indeed, *Light and Truth* was first published serially in 1836 as Lewis, like thousands of white orators and authors, toured around nineteenth-century New England, lecturing and selling copies of one-hundred-page installments for twenty-five cents each.[30] Like the tours of other Black orators, it is possible that Lewis's lecture circuit would actually have overlapped with white abolitionist circuits in New England. And in 1843, a "committee of colored gentlemen," including the abolitionist Thomas Dalton and the Underground Railroad conductor James Scott, acquired the copyright to *Light and Truth* and published a complete version, describing it in their introduction as a "compilation."[31]

FIGURE 5.1. *Curse of Ham. Josiah Priest,* Slavery, As It Relates to the Negro, or African Race *(Albany, NY: C. Van Benthuysen, 1843). Harvard Library; courtesy of HathiTrust Digital Library.*

FIGURE 5.2. *Tower of Babel. Josiah Priest,* Slavery, As It Relates to the Negro, or African Race *(Albany, NY: C. Van Benthuysen, 1843). Harvard Library; courtesy of HathiTrust Digital Library.*

Light and Truth was not just a compilation of four serialized parts. Each part was itself a kind of textual collage of fragments from numerous other sources. Lewis's description of architectural "order" was copied directly from English masonic manuals, a discourse that masons from England to the United States would study assiduously.[32] In repeating this definition, he accepted the importance of classical Greco-Roman form, like the white American architects of his day.[33] But key for him was that the Greeks learned their architectural principles from the Egyptians. "But for the Egyptians," Lewis said, "Greece might have remained a country of barbarians to this day."[34] If it were not for Black Africans, classicism would not be. Lewis was not alone in making this argument. It was with "the sons of Africa or of Ham" that "learning originated, and was carried then into Greece, where it was improved upon and refined," the Black Freemason David Walker wrote in his 1829 *An Appeal to the Colored Citizens of the World*.[35] Delany put forth similar arguments in both his 1853 lecture and, the year before, his book *The Condition, Elevation, Emigration, and Destiny of the Colored People of the United States*. And Frederick Douglass, in an 1865 lecture, spoke of the "magnificence and stupendous dimensions of Egyptian architecture," which advanced architectural knowledge while Europe floundered in barbarism.[36]

Many eighteenth- and early nineteenth-century white European and Euro-American architectural histories also traced Grecian classicism back to Egypt. Thomas U. Walter, for example, would say in his public lectures on architectural history in the 1840s and 1850s that the "firm foundations" for subsequent architecture were first "laid by the descendants of Ham on the shores of the prolific Nile."[37] But in many of these narratives, North and Northeast Africa remained more closely aligned with Europe than with the sub-Saharan portion of the continent.[38] For some white US writers, such as the "scientific" racist Samuel Morton in *Crania Aegyptiaca* (1844), this even became an avenue for claiming that ancient Egypt's leading citizens were white.[39] But Lewis, Delany, and Marrant all took the genealogy of modern architecture further back in time and further south, to sub-Saharan Africa. Lewis, for example, treated the first great urban construction of Babylon as Ethiopian.[40] And Delany traced the wisdom of the Bible and Freemasonry from Egypt to Ethiopia, where, he said, the very idea of man being created in God's image first developed.[41] Egyptian architecture had a decidedly Black source.

The counterhistoriographical tool these narratives used was to extend a historical genealogy in a way that turned the "one drop" framework of genealogical racism on its head.[42] If the Freemasons, architects, and entire cultures that originated and advanced architecture were Black, then so was architecture's history. White people's "barbarous, soul-sickening treatment of the offspring of their benefactors" under racialized slavery, Lewis said, depended on forgetting the genealogical ubiquity of Blackness.[43] So too did accounts of architectural classicism as if it were white in form.

Exodus and Diaspora

While building in ancient Egypt was a crucial part of architectural history for both white and Black authors, the enslavement of the Jewish people there was even more so for popular historical imagination in the nineteenth-century United States. Exodus analogies were well trodden in colonial North America, comparing Protestants' flight from Europe to the Israelites' from Egypt.[44] And as the Civil War approached in the United States, these analogies proliferated. From David Walker to Harriet Tubman, references to Egypt were repeated and Black abolitionist leaders were often framed as Moses (as were some white figures such as John Brown).[45] Abraham Lincoln, for some Southern slaveholders, was a "modern Pharaoh," the head of a Leviathan intent on enslaving Southern interests to Northern power. For some Northern abolitionists, Lincoln was also a pharaoh because he was more intent on keeping the North and South of his kingdom together than on following moral principle. More common, though, was to see Lincoln as a "modern Moses" and the Emancipation Proclamation as "a pillar of fire" leading to the Promised Land.[46] Used to authorize prayerful quietism as well as violent action and divine retribution, the Exodus analogy religiously structured historical narratives of nation and slavery.[47]

Black narratives of enslavement and exodus also involved architecture, for it was in Egypt that divine chosenness and Blackness were understood to have converged. Marrant, for example, said that although the Israelites lived in tents prior to Egyptian captivity, practicing "very little of the art of architecture," in Egypt they became "expert Masons."[48] In his 1853 lecture, Delany identified Moses, "the fugitive slave," as the specific carrier of the masonic legacy out of Egypt.[49] Indeed, in the masthead of Delany's Pittsburgh newspaper, *The Mystery*, was a verse to which numerous masons and architects, both white and Black, referred: "Moses was learned in all the wisdom of the Egyptians." In fact, for Delany, not only was Egypt itself a colony of Ethiopia, and thus a product of its culture, but the way Moses acquired Ethiopian wisdom was through his "learned wife Zipporah," an Ethiopian princess and priestess who taught him as she "accompanied him by day and by night."[50] Jewish enslavement in Egypt was a historical hinge—the point from which Black origins were inflected via slavery into what would eventually become European form. For Delany, the key figure in the transference of masonic knowledge was a free Black woman.

Marrant, Lewis, and Delany mirrored their account of Egypto-Jewish combination with one of diaspora. Upon the Israelites' flight from Egyptian slavery, Marrant explained, the tabernacle plan was given directly to Moses by God.[51] It was the combination of this divinely given plan of the nomadic holy dwelling with the expertise in masonry that the Israelites acquired under Egyptian slavery that would eventually result in the great work of Solomon's temple. Lewis's detailed description of the temple's materials, ornament, and scale framed it as a key moment in a globalized, multiethnic history of architecture.[52] The architect of the temple, Hiram Abiff, was Ethiopian, he said. And it was from the jobsite he oversaw, Marrant explained, that "high taste of architecture" would spread out to different parts of the world by a multiethnic set of builders who had worked in harmony and brotherly love.[53] This Jewish construction site, under the direction of an Ethiopian architect, was, as Delany put it, a point of architectural diaspora: "Previous to the building of the temple, Masonry was only allegorical, consisting in a scientific system of theories . . . understood only by the priesthood and a chosen few."[54] But after the temple was built, Black knowledge and skill spread across the globe.

Pan-Africanism and the World Citizen

Through selective appropriation and reworking of western European Enlightenment and Romantic thought, Black writers narrated the African diaspora into the center of world history, creating a framework in which they and their ideas were "citizens of the world," as David Walker put it.[55] Bracketing Egypt between a deeper Black origin of architecture in Ethiopia and a multiracial diaspora from Solomon's temple, these narratives rooted the classicism of Europe and its colonial enterprises in African craft.

In one sense, white and Black grand narratives of architecture in the early American republic were the same, as both depended on a grand Christian frame in which the ultimate future was a return to the prelapsarian origin. Marrant described this narrative of return as an act of reconstruction: "One grand end and design of Masonry is to build up the temple that Adam destroyed in Paradise."[56] Lewis took a premillennial stance on this ultimate end, one more akin to the narrative honed by the influential English theologian John Nelson Darby than to the mid-nineteenth century's more popular postmillennialism. The biblical descriptions of the destruction of Jerusalem "allude to the tremendous scenes of judgment, which will introduce the millennium," Lewis said.[57] On this account, it was not improvement but rather collapse that would precede divine return. In both Marrant's and Lewis's case, the end of history was a millenarian return or reconstruction of divine order—a wish image shared with numerous white American narratives.

But what was different between white and Black grand narratives was the penultimate frame. Unlike the common white Protestant narrative in the United States that saw the new nation as the new Israel, Black narratives turned not just on a promised salvation but more specifically on a promise of a diasporic future that sat on the other side of captivity.[58] White Christians certainly believed in a global project, a kind of evangelism that rode on and advanced the waves of imperialism, as Emily Conroy-Krutz describes it.[59] But the Black Christian project was different in the way that it envisioned the past returning in the future. One of the most cited verses in African American religious history comes from Psalms: "Princes shall come out of Egypt; Ethiopia shall soon stretch out her hands unto God." Rather than imagining a progressive globalization of whiteness, Black narratives situated the outstretched hand of Ethiopia as the coming Promised Land. The Black pedagogy that was, still would be.

A key way that this practice of a historical Black fugitive science—of a liberation historiography—worked was through constructing different analogies. Rather than Greece and Rome, it was Ethiopia and Egypt that acted as the ancient pinnacle and the orienting point for architecture in a postlapsarian world. But it would be a mistake to geographically limit an account of a kind of future that figures like Lewis or Delany saw as a return to Egypt or Ethiopia. Narratives like Marrant's, Lewis's, and Delany's emerged in what Maffly-Kipp suggests was a "rediscovery" of Africa by Northern free Black authors and orators who, among Black people in mid-nineteenth-century America, were some of the "most removed from African communities."[60] The idea of Africa that emerged in these narratives, built out of both oral tradition and biblical, masonic, and classical references, was both an abstraction and a vital political agent.

Indeed, this vision of an African diaspora and a return twisted together Black and white interests in multifaceted ways that were both sympathetic and antithetic. The antebellum visions of white organizations like the American Colonization Society and Black authors like Delany appeared to converge at moments, particularly when the differences between the colonization of Liberia and emigration to Africa were elided.[61] But the future that figures like Lewis and Delany saw was not limited to Africa, for the kind of Pan-Africanism they articulated was much wider than the continent itself. Rather, it was a kind of multicontinental Black internationalism, one that involved the undoing of the plantation system but not of globally expansive narratives. Lewis's *Light and Truth* ended with descriptions of Haiti's robust output of commodities and of the political freedom that had been pursued by maroons in Surinam.[62] And Delany, in his 1852 *The Condition, Elevation, Emigration, and Destiny of the Colored People of the United States*, argued extensively for the emigration of Black Americans not just to Africa but also to the Caribbean and Central and South America. A Promised Land to which the enslaved and oppressed were to escape would be constructed around the globe by citizens of the world.[63]

The Challenge of Counterhistories

The lineage of Marrant's, Lewis's, and Delany's historical projects can be followed into the twentieth century through texts like George Washington Williams's *History of the Negro Race in America* (1883), Carter G. Woodson's *The Negro in*

Our History (1922), Du Bois's *The World and Africa* (1947), Martin Bernal's *Black Athena* (1987), and more recently Howard French's *Born in Blackness* (2021).[64] These are projects of reconfiguring a grand narrative, putting Africa at the center rather than in the margins of a Eurocentric historiography. At the beginning of this chapter, I asked if the counternarratives held out by Marrant, Lewis, and Delany were caught in a sterile binary and energy-wasting task. Now we might phrase this question in a more precise way: In narrating an original Blackness from which global architecture came, and in whose image Black internationalism could formulate a global reconstruction, did these writers invert the polarity of the herrenvolk republicanism of white nationalist mythology, or did they undo it?

If the answer is the former, then we can see in Marrant, Lewis, and Delany a "simple dialectical negation" carried out by choosing the other side of the coin.[65] On this interpretation, by taking pieces common to European and Euro-American histories of architecture and realigning them, these writers repeated what they critiqued. Rather than reject historiographical progressivism, Marrant, Lewis, and Delany provincialized Europe only by centering Africa. Because they were caught in a binary, while they shifted content, they nonetheless repeated the framework.

But another possibility is that these histories methodologically worked outside the bounds of herrenvolk nationalism while they talked about it and even appeared to use it. And herein lies a particular task that Cedric Robinson can help us frame. The Black radical tradition, he suggests, performs a "negation of Western Civilization" that is not a "simple dialectical" one. In this type of negation, one has to sidestep rather than flip a coin. Robinson finds in the Black radical tradition—born of resistance, marronage, and even revolution—practices that "cast doubt on the extent to which capitalism penetrated and re-formed social life and on its ability to create entirely new categories of human experience stripped bare of the historical consciousness embedded in culture."[66] No doubt, he says, the intellectual Black radical tradition was born out from under the weight of the white European radical intelligentsia.[67] But, Robinson also argues, it was not buried by either racial capitalism or European radicalism, because rather than trying to counter either directly, it cut new paths through and alongside them. In the task of writing a fugitive science, a liberation historiography, marronage is a foundational way of working. The companion of the hush arbor with which this essay started is a different kind of history. With this interpretation, we might understand Marrant, Lewis, and Delany as sidestepping the framework of white nationalism, even while using some of its rhetoric of racial regimes.

On a more directly architectural level, it's worth noting that Marrant, Lewis, and Delany were not primarily builders by occupation, let alone professional architects. Marrant was an itinerant minister. Lewis was a writer and lecturer, but he worked a host of other jobs—several of which were in building trades—to make ends meet. Through painting, paperhanging, whitewashing, and calcimining, his relationship to the designed environment—which also included cleaning carpets and caning chairs—was one of maintenance and care more than the professional architect's designful production of the new.[68] Delany also had a host of careers, which included attempting to pursue professional medical education at Harvard before student objections forced him and two other Black students to withdraw.

We might see in the work of Marrant, Lewis, and Delany an important intellectual foundation for the experiment in a different form of architectural education at Tuskegee Institute in the Alabama Black Belt that took shape at the end of the nineteenth century—one in which architecture was not treated as a design profession set apart from the world of working-class making and maintenance. Rather, at Tuskegee, architecture was integrated into the laborious processes of extraction, the difficulty of capital accumulation, and the work of construction.[69] This suggests an additional intellectual genealogy, one that might find Black authors influencing those that have made and remade the built environment. This alternate genealogy of architectural education and practice would be shaped not only by different antebellum spatial and oral histories but also by Black historiographical and literary traditions from which architectural history still has much to learn.

For architectural historians, the three authors discussed here suggest one way to think about Robinson's challenge to negate without dialectically opposing. The challenge is to write a different history of architecture while refusing to do so on architecture's professional terms. That is, the challenge is to write a history of architecture from outside its institutional limits, not in order to negate it but rather to see it differently. The challenge is not to write with the task of finding the opposite of the white gentleman who gave the profession its body. Rather, it is to undo the stability of this identity by refusing the immutability of its historical terms. Authors like Marrant, Lewis, and Delany give us one way to approach nineteenth-century architectural historiography in terms other than those produced by the trajectory of professional architectural defense that has a tendency to mire architectural historians' consideration of this period. They are nonarchitects who use one of architecture's primary professional weapons—history—to attack the culture that produced it.[70]

Acknowledgments

I would like to thank Kate Masur for thoughtful comments on an earlier version of this chapter, delivered at the Society for the History of the Early American Republic annual conference in 2019.

Notes

1. Mario Gooden, *Dark Space: Architecture, Representation, Black Identity* (Columbia Books on Architecture and the City, 2016).

2. See, for example, Rebecca Ginsburg, "Escaping Through a Black Landscape," in *Cabin, Quarter, Plantation : Architecture and Landscapes of North American Slavery*, ed. Clifton Ellis and Rebecca Ginsburg (Yale University Press, 2010), 51–66; Stephanie M. H. Camp, *Closer to Freedom: Enslaved Women and Everyday Resistance in the Plantation South* (University of North Carolina Press, 2004).

3. Stephen G. Hall, *A Faithful Account of the Race: African American Historical Writing in Nineteenth-Century America* (University of North Carolina Press, 2009), 3.

4. Cedric J. Robinson, *Black Marxism: The Making of the Black Radical Tradition*, 3rd ed. (University of North Carolina Press, 2020).

5. Robinson, *Black Marxism*, 74–75.

6. W. E. B. Du Bois, *The World and Africa* (Oxford University Press, 2007), 96.

7. Britt Rusert, *Fugitive Science: Empiricism and Freedom in Early African American Culture* (New York University Press, 2017).

8. John Ernest, *Liberation Historiography: African American Writers and the Challenge of History, 1794–1861* (University of North Carolina Press, 2004), 126.

9. Toni Morrison, "A Humanist View," Portland State University, 1975, transcript, https://www.mackenzian.com/wp-content/uploads/2014/07/Transcript_PortlandState_TMorrison.pdf.

10. Olúfẹ́mi O. Táíwò, *Reconsidering Reparations* (Oxford University Press, 2022), 6.

11. Achille Mbembe, *On the Postcolony* (University of California Press, 2001), 12.

12. John Marrant, *A Sermon Preached on the 24th Day of June 1789* [. . .] (Boston: Bible and Heart, 1789). On these three themes, see Laurie F. Maffly-Kipp, *Setting Down the Sacred Past: African-American Race Histories* (Belknap Press, 2010), 3.

13. Marrant, *Sermon Preached on the 24th Day*, 24.

14. Cedric J. Robinson, *Forgeries of Memory and Meaning: Blacks and the Regimes of Race in American Theater and Film Before World War II* (University of North Carolina Press, 2012), xii.

15. Marrant, *Sermon Preached on the 24th Day*, 9.

16. Marrant, *Sermon Preached on the 24th Day*, 10.

17. Peter P. Hinks, "John Marrant and the Meaning of Early Black Freemasonry," *William and Mary Quarterly* 64, no. 1 (2007): 105–116.

18. Hinks, "John Marrant"; Maffly-Kipp, *Setting Down the Sacred Past*, 35–36; Joanna Brooks, "Prince Hall, Freemasonry, and Genealogy," *African American Review* 34, no. 2 (2000): 197–216; Joanna Brooks, *American Lazarus: Religion and the Rise of African American and Native American Literatures* (Oxford University Press, 2003), 87–113.

19. Hinks, "John Marrant," 108–110.

20. Steven C. Bullock, *Revolutionary Brotherhood: Freemasonry and the Transformation of the American Social Order, 1730–1840* (University of North Carolina Press, 1998), 9–49.

21. Chernoh Momodu Sesay Jr., "Freemasons of Color: Prince Hall, Revolutionary Black Boston, and the Origins of Black Freemasonry, 1770–1807" (PhD diss., Northwestern University, 2006).

22. Maffly-Kipp, *Setting Down the Sacred Past*, 12.

23. Martin Robison Delany, *The Origin and Objects of Ancient Freemasonry* [. . .] (Pittsburgh: W. S. Haven, 1853), 30.

24. Thomas Virgil Peterson, *Ham and Japheth: The Mythic World of Whites in the Antebellum South* (Scarecrow Press, 1978), 1.

25. See Thomas U. Walter, "Landing from the Ark," Genesis 8:15–22 and 9:1–16, July 14, 1867, box 21, folder 303, Thomas Ustick Walter Collection, Athenaeum of Philadelphia.

26. There was also resistance to this argument; see Hall, *Faithful Account of the Race*, 64.

27. Marrant, *Sermon Preached on the 24th Day*, 12; Delany, *Origin and Objects of Ancient Freemasonry*, 30. See also Robert Benjamin Lewis, *Light and Truth: Collected from the Bible and Ancient and Modern History* [. . .] (Boston: A Committee of Colored Gentlemen, 1844), 40–41.

28. Maffly-Kipp, *Setting Down the Sacred Past*, 22; John Ernest, *A Nation Within a Nation: Organizing African-American Communities Before the Civil War* (Ivan R. Dee, 2011).

29. Carolyn Eastman, *A Nation of Speechifiers: Making an American Public After the Revolution* (University of Chicago Press, 2010); Donald M. Scott, "The Popular Lecture and the Creation of a Public in Mid-Nineteenth-Century America," *Journal of American History* 66, no. 4 (1980): 791–809.

30. Marnie Hughes-Warrington, "Coloring Universal History: Robert Benjamin Lewis's *Light and Truth* (1843) and William Wells Brown's *The Black Man* (1863)," *Journal of World History* 20, no. 1 (2009): 107. See, for example, the short note in the *Emancipator and Free American*, November 17, 1836, 115; and "Catalogue," *Emancipator and Free American*, April 5, 1838, 192.

31. Lewis, *Light and Truth*, iii. See the notice of copyright transfer in *Emancipator and Free American*, March 14, 1844, 181.

32. Lewis, *Light and Truth*, 289–290. Compare with James Hardie, *The New Free-Mason's Monitor: Or, Masonic Guide* [. . .] (New York: G. Long, 1818), 133–134.

33. Lewis, *Light and Truth*, 289–90; Ernest, *Liberation Historiography*, 101–113.

34. Lewis, *Light and Truth*, 291, 18.

35. David Walker, *Walker's Appeal, in Four Articles* [. . .] (University of North Carolina at Chapel Hill Library, 2011), 24.

36. Quoted in Robert S. Levine, *Martin Delany, Frederick Douglass, and the Politics of Representative Identity* (University of North Carolina Press, 1997), 10–11. See also Margaret Malamud, *African Americans and the Classics: Antiquity, Abolition and Activism* (I. B. Tauris, 2016), 185ff.

37. Thomas U. Walter, *The Lectures on Architecture, 1841–1853*, ed. Jhennifer A. Amundson (Athenaeum of Philadelphia, 2006), 34.

38. Teshale Tibebu, *Hegel and the Third World: The Making of Eurocentrism in World History* (Syracuse University Press, 2011), 171–229; Cedric J. Robinson, *An Anthropology of Marxism*, 2nd ed. (University of North Carolina Press, 2019), 60–87.

39. Samuel George Morton, *Crania Aegyptiaca: Or, Observations on Egyptian Ethnography, Derived from Anatomy, History, and the Monuments* (Philadelphia: John Penington, 1844), 66.

40. Lewis, *Light and Truth*, 42.

41. Delany, *Origin and Objects of Ancient Freemasonry*, 10–11, 30.

42. See Rodney S. Sadler Jr., "Exegesis in Black and White: Dualism in 19th and Early 20th Century African American Biblical Hermeneutics," in *Light Against Darkness: Dualism in Ancient Mediterranean Religion and the Contemporary World*, ed. Bennie H. Reynolds III, Armin Lange, Eric M. Meyers, and Randall Styers (Vandenhoeck & Ruprecht, 2011), 287.

43. Lewis, *Light and Truth*, 291.

44. See, for example, Ezra D. D. Stiles, "The United States Elevated to Glory and Honor (1783)," ed. Reiner Smolinski, University of Nebraska, Electronic Texts in American Studies, http://digitalcommons.unl.edu/etas/41.

45. See John Coffey, *Exodus and Liberation: Deliverance Politics from John Calvin to Martin Luther King Jr.* (Oxford University Press, 2013), 79–180; Eddie S. Glaude Jr., *Exodus! Religion, Race, and Nation in Early Nineteenth-Century Black America* (University of Chicago Press, 2000).

46. Coffey, *Exodus and Liberation*, 140.

47. Albert J. Raboteau, "The Black Experience in American Evangelicalism," in *African American Religion: Interpretive Essays in History and Culture* (Routledge, 1997), 101; Albert J. Raboteau, *A Fire in the Bones: Reflections on African-American Religious History* (Beacon Press, 1995), 17–36.

48. Marrant, *Sermon Preached on the 24th Day*, 13–14.

49. Delany, *Origin and Objects of Ancient Freemasonry*, 28.

50. Delany, *Origin and Objects of Ancient Freemasonry*, 31.

51. Marrant, *Sermon Preached on the 24th Day*, 14.

52. Lewis, *Light and Truth*, 212ff.

53. Marrant, *Sermon Preached on the 24th Day*, 17.

54. Delany, *Origin and Objects of Ancient Freemasonry*, 14.

55. Hall, *Faithful Account of the Race*, 11; Peter P. Hinks, *To Awaken My Afflicted Brethren: David Walker and the Problem of Antebellum Slave Resistance* (Pennsylvania State University Press, 1997).

56. Marrant, *Sermon Preached on the 24th Day*, 16.

57. Lewis, *Light and Truth*, 245.

58. Stephen Kantrowitz, "'Intended for the Better Government of Man': The Political History of African American Freemasonry in the Era of Emancipation," *Journal of American History* 96, no. 4 (2010): 1001–1026; Chernoh M. Sesay, "The Dialectic of Representation: Black Freemasonry, the Black Public, and Black Historiography," *Journal of African American Studies* 17, no. 3 (2013): 380–398.

59. Emily Conroy-Krutz, *Christian Imperialism: Converting the World in the Early American Republic* (Cornell University Press, 2015).

60. Maffly-Kipp, *Setting Down the Sacred Past*, 26–27.

61. See Ousmane K. Power-Greene, *Against Wind and Tide: The African American Struggle Against the Colonization Movement* (New York University Press, 2014).

62. Lewis, *Light and Truth*, 385–400.

63. Ernest, *Liberation Historiography*, 126.

64. Robin D. G. Kelley, "'But a Local Phase of a World Problem': Black History's Global Vision, 1883–1950," *Journal of American History* 86, no. 3 (1999): 1045–1077; Howard W. French, *Born in Blackness: Africa, Africans, and the Making of the Modern World, 1471 to the Second World War* (Liveright, 2021). See also Robinson, *Black Marxism*, 83–85.

65. Robinson, *Black Marxism*, 73.

66. Robinson, *Black Marxism*, 164, 170.

67. Robinson, *Black Marxism*, 175–184.

68. Hughes-Warrington, "Coloring Universal History," 107.

69. See Ellen Weiss, *Robert R. Taylor and Tuskegee: An African American Architect Designs for Booker T. Washington* (NewSouth Books, 2012); Anna Goodman and Maura Lucking, "Images Doing Work," *Journal of Architectural Education* 73, no. 2 (2019): 241–250; Donald E. Armstrong Jr., "Brick-Making and the Production of Place at the Tuskegee Institute," *Arris* 16 (2005): 28–36; Kenrick Ian Grandison, "From Plantation to Campus: Progress, Community and the Lay of the Land in Shaping the Early Tuskegee Campus," *Landscape Journal* 15, no. 1 (1996): 6–22.

70. Cedric J. Robinson, "The First Attack Is an Attack on Culture," in *Cedric J. Robinson: On Racial Capitalism, Black Internationalism, and Cultures of Resistance*, ed. H. L. T. Quan (Pluto Press, 2019), 69–74.

6 THE BLACK PARTI

REINTERPRETING AFRICAN AMERICAN PLACEMAKING AS DESIGN IDEATION

Andrea Roberts

African American Settlement History

The Black town is a "formally organized municipality intentionally created for Black people and by Black people, working either alone or in partnership with people of other races."[1] The Black town movement sought to decenter the white integrationist framework for success, European aesthetics, and state-sponsored naming traditions of their communities. More generally, Black placemaking has been described as "the ways urban Black Americans create sites of endurance, belonging, and resistance through social interaction."[2] These modes of Black placemaking, associated with urban and legally legible places substantiated by plats, surveys, and boundaries, inherently fall outside of professionally recognized standards of town planning and design.

In this essay, I am concerned with what shaped the imagination of those who created freedom colonies in Texas. Rarely were these settlements organized towns or platted developments for which documentation is registered at a courthouse. The Texas State Historical Association defines freedom colonies, freedmen's settlements, Black settlements, or freedmen's towns as historically significant communities across Texas and the South that were established from 1865 to 1930. The freedom colonies' population and status as unincorporated areas (90 percent of the time) often meant land ownership and settlement patterns remained largely invisible and subsumed by white county government leadership. Black Texans founded freedom colonies by obtaining land by adverse possession, typically in flood-prone bottomlands on the edge of plantations and city boundaries. At other times, these rural places were subsumed by indifferent, if not existentially threatening, white-led governments.

In the absence of town charters, sketches, plats, and county meeting minutes attesting to the origin of a community and its name, what might crowdsourced stories about Black place-naming of freedom colonies tell us about the design intentions of early Black placemakers? Oral histories, folk histories, and personal stories passed on through family and informal social networks provide a vehicle for beginning to understand. The following research outlines the ways that freedom colony placemaking conventions are best understood through the mimetic associations of their dominant landscape features and the origin stories of the most enduring institutions anchoring early African American communities, namely their churches and schools.

By analyzing the artifacts and landscape elements featured in public and social histories uploaded to an online hub of Black settlement stories and location data—a database I began in 2012, now called The Texas Freedom Colonies Project Atlas—I reveal the ways place-naming stories foreground important landscape features, such as groves of trees, springs, or brush arbors, and principles of form that persist even when populations decline and structures disappear. Naming is an organizing feature of sentiment and experience that regulates the Black perception of space that continues to live on as a design imprint. I argue that place-naming has a synthetic, regulating effect on Black settlements' architectural form and function, behaving in much the same way that a parti functioned in architectural design and town-planning principles of the same time period. This is important to note, as the literate and professional practices of land-owning whites were made illegal for many Black subjects living in the United States. Thus, an alternative to presiding architectural standards is something one must account for in the historical literature on Black material culture.

The parti is a visual communication tool professional designers employ to share the intention and vision behind the big idea of a project. Its origins are in the French term *parti pris*, or decision made, which originated in the state institution that was established to disseminate the most influential conventions for design in early to mid-nineteenth century France. Before professional schools of architecture opened in the United States, wealthy gentleman architects traveled to France to train under the Beaux-Arts system, and then to train others back home through local apprenticeships. The parti is often a rough drawing, doodle, or diagram used early in the schematic design process to represent a design concept. Inspiration from the physical setting of a site can influence the designer's approach to the parti, such as a natural feature or material present in that space. But what can we understand about the genesis of a place without the physical or scanned archival image of a parti?

The parti is traditionally framed as an indicator of an architect's skill or talent.[3] It is an expression of the projective form of a future space or artifact that regulates the dominant features of the landscape, projecting one's intent into the future through visual inferences of the key relationships that should exist between various elements in a space. Overall, the parti is a totalizing activity that seeks to inspire and create a locus of control. As part of the French Beaux-Arts movement popular in the United States at the end of the nineteenth century, the parti has had one of the most lasting impacts on architectural pedagogy as a methodology for establishing design ideation. The techniques of the École des Beaux-Arts, celebrating neoclassical precedents of historical form, utilized the canonical partis of monumental programs that became proxies for economic and political power in the present. This Beaux-Arts imprint was manifest in design cultures worldwide, even in early twentieth-century Black spaces, originating within the plans and drawings made for industrial schools.[4]

Yet the sketch is only one form the parti can take. Its traditional form privileges the professional separation between a designer who uses drawings to manage a project and the workmen who use artisanal skill sets to translate the master text of the construction drawings. Historical precedents for nonvisual communication of design intent also exist, from the communal construction of a Quaker barn to the settlement pattern of antique African villages. Such examples indicate the possibility that a design idea can be communicated through the act of oral incantation. In the case of historic Black settlements, the stories of a place's origins and naming signal the conceptual function of the architectural parti, but primarily through isolating the features of a place that satisfy the Black subject's perpetual seeking of sanctuary within an anti-Black world. When placemaking is understood as a communal strategy of shoring up protection and safety, then these techniques operate as an oral form of designing in a way that outwardly manifests the active creation of places of safety and refuge. I argue that rather than the spare, Cartesian lines that inspire the building forms of traditional European architecture, the place-naming and origin stories of freedmen's colonies are laden with values about Black advancement through physical design—a strategy that replicates in purpose and function the parti but employs it in a way that is more congruous with the needs of Black modernity in the years following the Civil War.

Black Places, Black Naming

Before considering the results of an analysis of the placemaking entries recorded through a crowdsourcing database, the significance of naming free Black communities in various parts of the United States should be discussed. Naming is among the first intentional acts of self-making among formerly enslaved people. Though at times taking on the names of their former captors, recently emancipated people still exercised agency by sharing these names with those orphaned because of family separation due to the internal slave trade. Naming practices are aspirational because the act suggests an interest in the trappings of American citizenship or in reclaiming citizenship within tribes and fugitive communities before exposure to Western norms or enslavement. M. B. Adams notes naming conventions among Black Seminoles who gave children multiple names, which may have been acquired through Indigenous rite-of-passage ceremonies. In contrast, others retained Gullah terms associated with their Floridian Black ancestors.[5] These naming conventions also reflect what Kevin Mulroy has called "neoteric societies—cultural groups who have survived as a people by weaving together valuable elements of their diverse cultural and symbolic history as they rapidly assimilate to conditions of extreme scarcity or pressure from the outside world."[6] In addition to self-naming, emancipated individuals named the communities they would call home. African American settlements were known as freedmen's towns during the Reconstruction era and have been called all-Black towns in Oklahoma; freedpeople settlements in Louisiana, North Carolina, and Virginia; and freedom colonies in Texas.

Placemaking includes the cultural practice of ascribing toponyms, or names inspired by topographic features. The geographer Derek Alderman explains that "place names represent a form of symbolic capital, a way of giving the landscape a comforting cultural value or image that can be marketed to visitors in order to facilitate the exchange of financial capital for a certain place-based experience."[7] If architecture is thought of as a world-building activity, it stands to reason that a critical component of the infrastructure of Black places would be this symbolic capital manifested in part through the selection of names that would catalyze certain behaviors and actions, such as creating new settlements.[8] But a decline in population and an unincorporated status leads to a deterioration in legibility and recognition and an aesthetic expulsion from mainstream architectural discourses on uses, design, capacity, and intention among Black placemakers, constraining the emancipatory force of naming.

Brian D. Joyner speaks to the Africanisms persisting in African American place-naming practices, using the examples of place-names derived from African words or a mixture of words from several African language groups—for example, Nicodemus, Kansas, a Black town named for an enslaved African prince who purchased his freedom.[9] Naming towns was often honorific yet a significant tribute to Black leadership. For example, Langston City in Oklahoma was named for an African American congressman who favored Black migration to Western states; Allensworth, California, was named for an African American military chaplain. In other cases, towns were named for natural landscape features. Mound Bayou, Mississippi, is named for nearby Indigenous burial mounds and two bayous. In these incorporated towns, their establishment required that they demonstrate the intention of being a municipality, with a plat, clear boundaries, and a name.[10] Thus, as much as a Black town's siting and place form were shaped by a namesake or a landscape feature, the actual place design was dominated by the need for legal recognition, in a way that mimicked traditional siting and design practices. For historic Black settlements known as freedom colonies, their foundational stories reveal a co-naming approach toward churches, landscape features, and places that captures and mobilizes a temporally transgressive architectural moment of settlement as a collective revelation that serves the same purpose as the parti. Naming advances the vision or parti of ancestors and their descendants, detectable through the textual artifact—the oral history transcription or the transfer of memory. The Texas Freedom Colonies Atlas seeks to reveal the nature of place origination and naming; in the absence of traditional siting and platting documentation, it provides a vehicle for exploring the concept of an origin story as parti of Texas freedom colonies.

The Texas Freedom Colonies Project Atlas and Study

This study's Black settlement naming conventions and categorizations emerged from reading the entries in The Texas Freedom Colonies Project Atlas. This online methodology is rooted in ethnographic fieldwork I conducted from 2014 to 2016. The field experience led me to conceptualize an archiving platform for capturing and securing the varied forms of evidence of place origins, existence, landscape features, buildings, and material culture. This later yielded the Atlas 1.0. This ever-changing atlas, comprised of both public and private archival sources, was first developed by reviewing a list of place-names available in the appendices of the book *Freedom Colonies*, along with stories collected through two years of ethnographic research in a two-county area.[11] The resulting list contained 557 place-names organized by county. Of that list, I and a research assistant identified, using publicly available sources, 357 freedom colony locations.[12] These 357 place-names offered evidence of Black settlement in place from 1865 to 1930, were associated with Blackness, and had recorded a predominantly Black population. Next, we invited the public to add their stories and supporting materials through an ArcGIS Survey123 form on the ArcGIS StoryMaps platform to fill in gaps in the public record with oral history and personal archival materials. This platform has since attracted participation from academics, freedom colony residents, founders' descendants, and amateur genealogists. The atlas database reflects local ontologies of place, capturing the variety of terms used to indicate Black settlements, from "Black towns" to "freedom colonies."[13]

Data for this essay comes from the contents of The Texas Freedom Colonies Project Atlas. Rather than a database that answers the question of where all the settlements are and what are their stories, the online platform answers the question of what types of responses you would receive if you sought the names, locations, and origin stories not already in the public record through crowdsourcing a variety of data forms and materials from experts and nonexperts. For this essay, I coded public and social narratives uploaded to the atlas to note the frequency of the structures co-named within settlements.

Method

I borrow from Trevon Logan, Lisa D. Cook, and John Parman's quantitative historical method while also heeding their call for researchers to identify "from the narrative record why these names came to be so common as opposed to others."[14] Their study tracked the frequency of racially distinctive names from the antebellum to postbellum periods. They concluded that name persistence among family members sold and separated during slavery was evidence that racialized naming was a practice of adaptation and fostering collectivity while in bondage and after emancipation.[15] I have applied this same principle of name frequency to reviewing atlas entries about individual settlements.

This theoretical frame, while participatory because it integrates crowdsourced data, is also rooted in critical race theory because it foregrounds experiential storytelling (origin stories) and empirical evidence (frequency of names in the dataset). Creating the parti or big idea behind Black placemaking produces archival proof of what the scholar Cheryl J. Fish calls architextual practice, identified through her studies of the poet June Jordan's architectural sketches of Harlem. Fish uses the term "architextual" "to emphasize architecture as text and text as thickly descriptive, multidimensional (a pre-computer version of hypertext), serving as a scaffold to build a vision of hope and embodied environments."[16] While this study is concerned with settlements during an earlier period, I argue that the efforts to reconstruct the placemaking stories are ones in which oral histories become the architextual evidence of the parti, communicating the overarching big ideas of Black placemaking—intention, aspiration, and inspiration.

Content Analysis of Atlas Origin Stories

A content analysis of entries from The Texas Freedom Colonies Project Atlas, which contains the origin or foundational stories of Black settlements founded in Texas from 1865 to 1930, reveals the parti or organizing idea of Black placemaking. Rather than drawings or sketches, however, the parti is indicated in oral histories and traditions inserted into a publicly available online survey form in the atlas. A content analysis tracks the frequency of terms associated with freedom colony founding. The detected conventions or themes reflect how names establish place character and inform site selection among founders in early African American settlements in Texas. Like the parti, these names and naming stories persist as organizing ideas for settlement programming, cultural reproduction, and meaning making well into the present, even as the traces of once-extant features fade or disappear. When examining the patterns and trends in place design or visioning, I sought to understand whether naming was an adaptive, agentive architectural practice akin to the parti.

At the time of this initial writing, the atlas held 834 unique entries. Of those entries, 5 settlements were marked by contributors as having unknown names, while the remaining 829 were named places. This data is current as of March 19, 2022, but monthly changes occur as new entries are added and verified.[17] Using the atlas's data, I sought to answer the following question: How many settlement features (e.g., churches or cemeteries) also share the settlement's name?

A constant feature across the atlas is the effort made by contributors to establish connections between the names of landscape features (such as churches, cemeteries, schools, and roads) and the names of the settlements (fig. 6.1). Religious themes associated with liberation (e.g., hiding or creating a haven in woodlands, finding complete safety in churches) are pervasive and are particularly pronounced in the crowdsourced place histories selected for this study. A review of a subset of crowdsourced entries reveals that churches are the most common signifiers of place (118), followed by cemeteries (28), schools (22), streams (9), flats (1), and lakes (1). Five settlements are identified by both their church and cemetery. Nineteen settlements' names changed over time. Place-names are most often associated with churches, reflecting how church building and literacy were central to community formation. Such names drew on biblical themes of resilience, divine favor, or the Promised Land as a symbol of the community's new beginning. My analysis further indicates that the ideas of creating a refuge and seeking a guarantee of safety were ways in which placemaking was a precursor to liberation theology among freedom colony founders. But did the church come first or did the settlement? Sometimes they were established simultaneously. At least 26 percent of the settlements (173) were named for their founder or for the individual who provided the initial land to the freedom colony's founders.

FIGURE 6.1. *Pleasant Hill Cemetery, Harrison County, Texas. Photo contributed to The Texas Freedom Colonies Project Atlas by Earnol Brewster.*

The religious concepts referenced in place-names not only indicated the church being the founding institution but also reflected an ethos, intentionality, and design priorities focused on liberation, hope, and environmental pragmatism. Biblical names comprise over 10 percent of the total dataset (70 settlements). Bethlehem, Shiloh, Macedonia, Antioch, Galilee, and Mount Olive predominate. Saints were often part of place-names. St. John occurred most often (5), followed by St. Luke (2) and St. Paul (2), both known as authors of New Testament accounts of the life of Jesus. The most frequent names of settlements across multiple counties are Pleasant Hill, Bethlehem, Pleasant Grove, Shady Grove, and Shiloh. The connotations tell us much about the associations descendants made with founding, placemaking, and building a place. The five most frequently occurring landscape terms represented in the whole dataset are "hill" (40), "chapel" (27), "spring" (22), "colony" (20), and "grove" (20). Other frequently recurring terms include "pleasant" (9), "union" (8), and "hope" (6). Among the recurring evidence of religious themes in place-names is the word "chapel." Other place-names reference natural features that ensure sustenance, such as a spring. The concept of the colony or the grove indicates a place of refuge. The naming reinforces how the settlements' organizing ideas represent an aspirational Black sense of place.

Case Studies: Origin and Naming as Parti

I begin this chapter's case studies of Black place-naming as a design practice with the Shankleville community, which inspired the development of the atlas and its efforts to document place origins and naming stories. Shankleville's foundational story ties its founders' fugitive placemaking to their community's origin story. I then discuss the Pleasant Hill community as an example of co-naming of communities with churches, focusing on the atlas's entries about the community, church, and cemetery.

THE TEST CASE: SHANKLEVILLE

Before establishing the public, online, crowdsourced atlas, I encountered a descendant community in Newton County, Texas, where I first detected a relationship between settlement-creation storytelling and design. Over the course of two years, I became acquainted with the Shankleville community's origin story about its namesakes through engaged ethnographic research with descendants living in the diaspora and in place. The annual commemoration of the settlement namesakes, Jim and Winnie Shankle, consistently attracts descendants back to the community for homecoming celebrations. The origin story tells of an enslaved man who ran away from a plantation in Mississippi in hopes of reuniting with his wife, Winnie, who had been sold to a slaveholder in Texas. Jim reunited with his wife at a spring adjacent to the plantation where she was enslaved. I visited the spring with descendants who gathered to pay tribute to Jim and Winnie's contribution to the place-creation process. The couple engaged in site selection: They sought and found a safe space to hide and gather food on the plantation's edge, surviving enslavement and creating a community nearby in 1867, just two years after emancipation.[18] Jim's intention—during a period in which he wasn't even afforded the human right to have a will or a self-defined purpose in life—was compelling. He undertook an act of romantic marronage, pursuing the woman he loved in a way that overcame the de facto condition of enslavement. This power of intention was also an aspiration. That intergenerational aspiration or seeking is manifest in what remains in the landscape: the spring, a perpetual source of nourishment and the inspiration that reinforces descendants' return to the place.

The settlement naming practice, emerging from this creation story, integrates a family name and two landscape features: tree groves and a spring. The pathway to the spring is densely wooded, and even in the summer, as one approaches the spring, the temperature seems to drop, creating a microclimate that feels more tropical, nurturing, and secure. A video tour led by descendant Elzie Odom describes walking down the "chute" when entering the pathway from the 1920s homestead and two cemeteries down to the path to the spring.[19] Here, Elzie envisions a narrow, steep transition, with the surrounding dense foliage forming the portal to another time and space, where his ancestors sought safety and created the kernel of the settlement. He then notes a clearing and a crepe myrtle, representing both a moment in time and a stunning architextual design moment that reminds the visitor of the passage of time at this place. Elzie arrives at the spring, sharing his genealogical kinship with the Shankles. A series of flows, circulations, and forms define what is still considered the heart of Shankleville, all referenced in his storytelling.

Elzie invokes the parti by verbally sketching out spatial possibilities, functions, freedom of movement, and imagination for what is possible within the settlement. In short, the name operates as an organizing idea. Elzie's storytelling is the evidence of intention, meaning, and landscape that inspired the founding, land use, and spatial provision analogous to the role of the parti or sketch in traditional design processes (fig. 6.2).

Shankleville's origin story is the organizing idea of the settlement as descendants ritualize perpetual return to the water source—the spring—and prioritize the preservation of the nearby cemeteries in ways reminiscent of West African burial practices, which involved placing loved ones near groves of trees. The Shankle ancestors are interred just feet from the thick grove of trees near the cemetery. The scholar Gérard Chouin asserts a spatial correlation between old settlements and groves in Africa, explaining that settlements were often changed into burial grounds and later "recolonized by forest," making their sacredness arise from an association with the ancestors buried in the grove or nearby.[20] Groves also fall into various categories, including those discovered: some are used for ritual purposes, some are associated with a specific event, and others are used as burial grounds and old settlements. Chouin explains that the formation of sacred groves involves a process in which an area is identified as "a point of contact between the invisible and human worlds," followed by the development of a "ritualized alliance with the spiritual entities that dwell there."[21] To arrive at the Shankleville spring, one must be led through thick vegetation, including groves of trees. The descendants who guide visitors to the spring, including Harold Odom, establish an intimate connection with the ancestors—made possible by drinking from the same spring where Winnie is said to have hidden food for Jim (fig. 6.3). At the spring, a consecration occurs as the story is told. The shelter and sustenance the Shankles experienced just beyond the grove is the organizing idea or parti of Shankleville, and it catalyzes the return and reproduction of place meaning through the libation ritual. This communion across time and place is not a solitary, inspired pencil stroke but a sense that one can access placemaking knowledge in the sacred space by conjuring design and preservation intention from one's ancestors at the site of memory.[22] These themes of sustenance, shelter, and refuge are often referenced in the atlas's crowdsourced origin stories, including the church-centered foundings that follow.

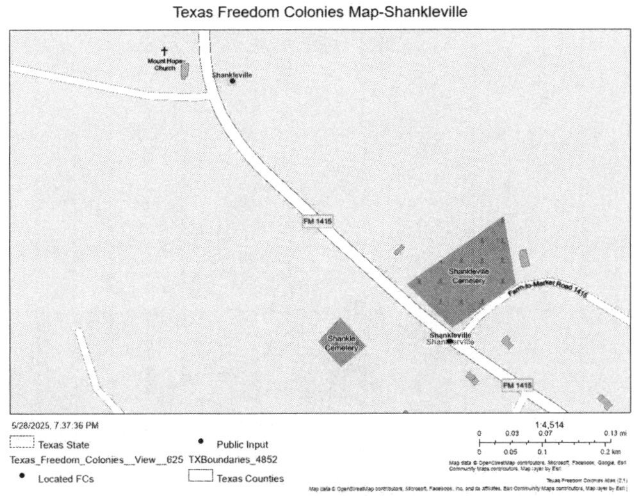

FIGURE 6.2. *Shankleville, Newton County, Texas. Map download from The Texas Freedom Colonies Project Atlas.*

FIGURE 6.3. *Harold Odom at the spring. Photo by the author.*

CHURCH FOUNDING AS PLACEMAKING: PLEASANT HILL COMMUNITY

Visitors to the atlas will see multiple entries for each settlement. In the instance of Pleasant Hill, in Harrison County, there are two entries provided by the descendant and another entry that contains our research team's initial input of publicly available sources, from a state historical marker commemorating individual structures and the place history summarized by the Texas State Historical Association's *Handbook of Texas*. The state historical marker contextualizes the church's founding with information about the community's founding, explaining that

FIGURE 6.4. *Pleasant Hill Baptist Church, Harrison County, Texas. Photo contributed to The Texas Freedom Colonies Project Atlas by Earnol Brewster.*

"within a few months of the 1865 notification of the Emancipation Proclamation, former slave families began to settle in the area later known as the Pleasant Hill community" (fig. 6.4).[23]

Community descendant Earnol Brewster of nearby Hallsville, Texas, writes the following entry about Pleasant Hill Baptist Church in the atlas:

> The year was 1871, the location was under a brush arbor, the occasion was organizing the Pleasant Hill Baptist Church (PHBC), and the first Pastor was Reverend George Pritchett. History reports that soon after emancipation, a few families who loved the Lord had the mind and determination to establish a permanent place to worship God and serve the community. This was accomplished! Over the past 148 years, PHBC has given birth to Pastors, Deacons, and countless other professionals. Not only has PHBC given birth to great people but great opportunities. It was here the community would meet for town hall meetings to address the concerns of our people.[24]

Without other available public gathering places, the church became a focal point for not only church gatherings but also community pursuits such as reading and writing lessons and economic and political meetings (fig. 6.5). The name Pleasant

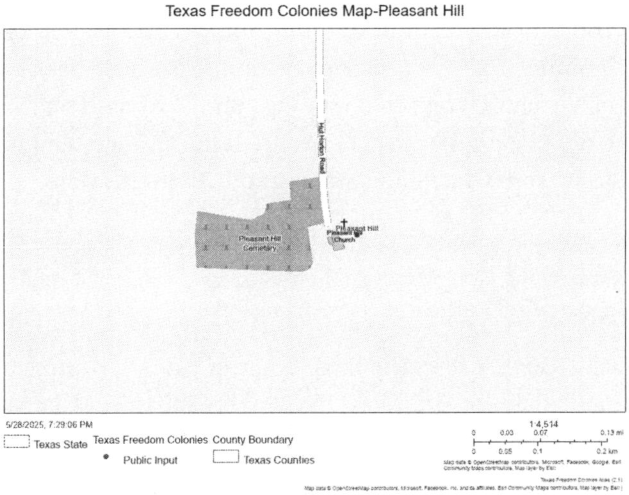

FIGURE 6.5. *Pleasant Hill, Harrison County, Texas. Map download from The Texas Freedom Colonies Project Atlas.*

Hill—one of the most frequently used place-names—is consistent with the slight elevation where the church is located and the sense that the church has been the central defining element of the community for over 150 years. Within the descendant community, the leaders established a permanent institution to anchor decision-making and yield determined people, all required for Black settlements to survive and persist. The adjacent Pleasant Hill Cemetery holds the formerly enslaved people the atlas contributor refers to, including John Clemons, born in 1854, and Patsy Ann Clemons, born in 1862. The Reverend George Pritchett's son, Neal, born in 1875, is also interred at the cemetery.

Interestingly, the founders of the church moved their congregation from private homes to hush or brush arbors. Hush arbors were precursors to the establishment of church buildings. Brush or hush arbor stories appear in several stories of place origins and are present in Federal Writers' Project slave narratives.[25] An exercise in siting, design, and aspiration, brush or hush arbors were primarily located in swamps, ravines, ditches, or thickets. They were called hush arbors because they were safe, quiet places to worship, sustain rituals rooted in African survival, and craft plans to escape before emancipation. The term "hush" connotes the accoutrements of quiet worship, including ring shouts and wet rags clamped over mouths to muffle voices. Wet rags were also hung to form an enclosure.[26] The term "arbor" references the roof formed by a close grove of trees. These spots were chosen because tree branches effectively muffled sound. The enslaved strategically engaged trees and sound to create safety for worshippers and avoid detection by masters.

These meetings leveraged the earth itself to create safe spaces that would later be the sites of churches after emancipation. Pleasant Hill was just west and one hundred feet above nearby Hardin Creek, making it an elevated place of refuge from inland flooding. The creek or stream would also have been a food source. In Pleasant Hill, the church reflects a naming approach based on using landscape features as the organizing idea for the secure, safe, and elevated enclosure in a wooded area away from white populations and rising waterways.

Conclusion

This chapter asks whether the early imaginings of rural African Americans were organized around naming practices. Term frequencies and entries from The Texas Freedom Colonies Project Atlas reveal the naming process as paralleling the critical function of a parti in architectural design, an organizing idea that brings together site placement, order or expansion, progress, land use, and future investment. Placemaking stories in private and public records explain communal motivations for settling in freedom colonies, including the hope invested in religious leaders, the guidance of Christian precepts, and the protection provided by the natural environment, including elevation, tree cover, and ancestral power and presence. These stories, memories, or fragments of origin stories, yielding patterns and trends in naming, offer insight into the organizing principles that shaped the formation of place and the collective will and action of freedom colonies.

In naming places, early Black founders expressed aspirational visions and design imaginaries that drew on opportunities in the landscape, rituals invoking access to ancestral knowledge, and natural features. Black settlement placemaking was accomplished through strategically discrete land accumulation and institution building (churches and schools), and co-naming was part of the placemaking process. Naming reinforced the existence of founders' partis or organizing ideas by perpetually invoking the reason for founding—be it landscape feature, founding family, or church establishment. Sample origin stories explaining settlement naming processes from The Texas Freedom Colonies Project Atlas, an online countermapping and counternarrative dataset, capture the twin naming of settlements and sacred spaces that yield homesteads and collective church founding in natural surroundings. Church and place foundings were often simultaneous or prefaced by earth-based partis like the brush or hush arbor and the sacred grove.

This project of recording community stories, inviting descendants' participation, and investigating crowdsourced material encourages visitors to the atlas and readers of this chapter to shift their attention to non-elite place-naming practices. These originally extralegal naming practices offer a way to reintroduce historical Black placemaking and design into humanistic discussions of the meaning, regulation, historical significance, and legitimacy of endangered Black settlements.

Such engagements with naming are part of an overall effort to accelerate place preservation and protection for emancipatory landscapes by framing their origination as intentional and as reflecting innovations worthy of recognition and land use protections. The findings and entries in the atlas introduce to architecture the possibility that architectural education might foreground, in its earliest stages, these partis as a core design practice discernible through the elevation of ethnographic inquiry. Freedom colonies' communitarian naming practices subvert the notion of the singular stroke of genius, indicating that design agency rests not only with the trained designer but also with those whom architects, builders, and clients once held captive.

Notes

1. Melissa N. Stuckey, "Black Towns," in *International Encyclopedia of the Social Sciences*, vol. 1, 2nd ed., ed. William A. Darity Jr. (Macmillan, 2007); Melissa N. Stuckey, "Boley, Indian Territory: Exercising Freedom in the All-Black Town," *Journal of African American History* 102, no. 4 (2017): 510.

2. Marcus Anthony Hunter, Mary Pattillo, Zandria F. Robinson, and Keeanga-Yamahtta Taylor, "Black Placemaking: Celebration, Play, and Poetry," *Theory, Culture & Society* 33, nos. 7–8 (2016), https://doi.org/10.1177/0263276416635259; El-Ra Adair Radney, "A Place in the Sun: Black Placemaking in Pan African Detroit," *Journal of Black Studies* 50, no. 3 (2019): 316.

3. Hyungmin Pai and Hyŏng-min Pae, *The Portfolio and the Diagram: Architecture, Discourse, and Modernity in America* (MIT Press, 2002), 45. Pai and Pae offer an account of how Stanford White ignored precedents and formulas, instead speedily composing a sketch and handing it off to others in the office to implement. With this speed and sense of accomplishment, White elevated himself in the hierarchy of the architectural office.

4. Angel David Nieves, *An Architecture of Education: African American Women Design the New South* (University of Rochester Press, 2018), 10.

5. Mischa B. Adams, "Naming Practices Among the Black Seminole of the Texas-Mexico Border Region," in *Big Bend's Ancient and Modern Past*, ed. Bruce A. Glasrud and Robert J. Mallouf (Texas A&M University Press, 2013), 228.

6. Kevin Mulroy, *Freedom on the Border: The Seminole Maroons in Florida, the Indian Territory, Coahuila, and Texas* (Texas Tech University Press, 1993).

7. Derek H. Alderman, Stefanie K. Benjamin, and Paige P. Schneider, "Transforming Mount Airy into Mayberry: Film-Induced Tourism as Place-Making," *Southeastern Geographer* 52, no. 2 (2012): 222.

8. Lisa K. Bates, Sharita A. Towne, Christopher Paul Jordan, et al., "Race and Spatial Imaginary: Planning Otherwise [. . .]," *Planning Theory & Practice* 19, no. 2 (2018): 254–288, https://doi.org/10.1080/14649357.2018.1456816.

9. Brian D. Joyner, *African Reflections on the American Landscape: Identifying and Interpreting Africanisms* (US Department of the Interior, 2003).

10. "Black Towns," Encyclopedia.com, accessed April 3, 2022, https://www.encyclopedia.com/history/encyclopedias-almanacs-transcripts-and-maps/black-towns.

11. Thad Sitton and James H. Conrad, *Freedom Colonies: Independent Black Texans in the Time of Jim Crow* (University of Texas Press, 2005).

12. Andrea Roberts and Mohammad Javad Biazar, "Black Placemaking in Texas: Sonic and Social Histories of Newton and Jasper County Freedom Colonies," *Current Research in Digital History* 2 (2019), https://doi.org/10.31835/crdh.2019.06.

13. Andrea R. Roberts, "Count the Outside Children! Kinkeeping as Preservation Practice Among Descendants of Texas' Freedom Colonies," *Forum Journal* 32, no. 4 (2018): 64–74. For instance, in Brenham, Washington County, the historical record refers to freedom colonies as "additions." In East Texas, sites on the edges of incorporated areas were known as "Black pockets" (a term that emerged from my discussions with local kinkeepers).

14. Lisa D. Cook, John Parman, and Trevon Logan, "The Antebellum Roots of Distinctively Black Names," *Historical Methods: A Journal of Quantitative and Interdisciplinary History* 55, no. 1 (2022): 9.

15. Cook, Logan, and Parman, "Antebellum Roots of Distinctively Black Names."

16. Cheryl J. Fish, "Place, Emotion, and Environmental Justice in Harlem: June Jordan and Buckminster Fuller's 1965 'Architextual' Collaboration," *Discourse* 29, no. 2/3 (2007): 331. Among others who have explored these architextual and inspirational design terrains, bell hooks has written about aesthetic inheritances associated with her grandmothers' quilting. Isabel Elson writes about Italo Calvino's concept of "the constructive capacity of utopic thinking" at play in the creation of Soul City in North Carolina. Isabel Elson, "Fifty Years of Soul City: Lessons of a Black Utopia," in *"Invisible Cities" and the Urban Imagination*, ed. Benjamin Linder (Springer International, 2022), 135.

17. Texas Freedom Colonies Project Atlas, v. 2.1, https://www.thetexasfreedomcoloniesproject.com/atlas. The atlas's data continually changes through constant additions from the public.

18. Odom Family Trust, "Shankleville, Odom House SBR National Register of Historic Places Registration Application," Texas Historical Commission National Register Program, January 2012.

19. Andrea R. Roberts, "Performance as Place Preservation: The Role of Storytelling in the Formation of Shankleville Community's Black Counterpublics," *Journal of Community Archaeology & Heritage* 5, no. 3 (2018): 1–20.

20. Gérard Chouin, "Archaeological Perspectives on Sacred Groves in Ghana," in *African Sacred Groves: Ecological Dynamics and Social Change*, ed. Michael J. Sheridan and Celia Nyamweru (Ohio University Press, 2008), 179.

21. Chouin, "Archaeological Perspectives on Sacred Groves," 179.

22. Pierre Nora, "Between Memory and History: *Les Lieux de Mémoire*," *Representations*, no. 26 (1989): 7–24.

23. "Details for Pleasant Hill Baptist Church: Historical Marker—Atlas Number 5203010206," Texas Historic Sites Atlas, Texas Historical Commission, accessed November 2, 2025, https://atlas.thc.texas.gov/Details?atlasnumber=5203010206.

24. Pleasant Hill, Harrison County, crowdsourced entry from Earnol Brewster, Texas Freedom Colonies Project Atlas.

25. Maya Cunningham, "The Hush Arbour as Sanctuary," *Sonic Histories of Occupation: Experiencing Sound and Empire in a Global Context*, ed. Russell P. Skelchy and Jeremy E. Taylor (Bloomsbury, 2022), 59–60. Cunningham shares the oral account of a formerly enslaved man, William Ford III, a Texas-based minister who describes the prayer space within the hush arbor as a site of rebellion amid slavery and an effort to create a sacred space.

26. Cunningham, "Hush Arbour," 63.

7 IDENTIFYING THE RELIGIO-RACIAL AESTHETICS OF AME CHURCH DESIGN, 1876–1920

Melanee C. Harvey-Fryar

DURING THE LAST QUARTER OF the nineteenth century, the African Methodist Episcopal (AME) Church, one of the oldest African American institutions and religious organizations in the United States, published articles on architecture in their newspaper, *The Christian Recorder*. With an expansive subscription base and readership consisting of friends of the denomination and church members totaling 561,550 by 1900, the architectural discourses circulated in this weekly news outlet demonstrate a substantive engagement with broader discussions on the national character of Black church architecture. This body of writing initiated a denominational building boom from 1876 to 1924, with heightened awareness of the need to integrate modern architectural standards. From 1880 to 1890, up to 170,506 new churches were built.[1] Additionally, the denomination reported that 126,804 churches were constructed in 1900 and 1901 alone.[2] This chapter interprets the historiography of AME architectural discourse as an intellectual framework for regulating the material form, symbolic meaning, and visual circulation of AME structures that spatially marked the modernization of denominational building production.

In this chapter, I argue that the AME denomination actively shaped a "religio-racial" aesthetic practice in their published literature and mobilized AME membership around building projects of cultural significance from the Reconstruction era to the turn of the century.[3] AME communities marshaled textual and image-based accounts of construction efforts to record institutional growth as well as document the geographic and social mobility of Black racial advancement. This initiative also served the practical work of educating African Americans on modern architectural history and trends to illustrate the capacity for architecture to improve the quality of life within Black spaces. The AME architectural tradition from this period represents one segment of a longer aesthetic history of AME members promoting a shared legacy of Black formalism in art and architecture.

Black formalism framed the cultural life of the AME Church, evident in the social histories that unfolded throughout its national circuit of churches and educational sites.[4] Imani Perry defines Black formalism as the communal practices that came to define Black life in the nineteenth century. Black formalist practices originated from the diverse cultures geographically connected by the transatlantic slave trade, but were syncretized to meet the cultural demands of modern Black life. Perry asserts that the "social graces and rules of engagement" that comprised the rituals of Black formalism

> were not the property of the elite. . . . Formalism was deeply rooted in the communities that black folks imagined and carefully crafted from the late nineteenth century through most of the twentieth century and that continue in more modest form today. In particular, I'm interested in black formalism as part of the culture attached to institutions like schools, churches and civic organizations. Appropriately, given the creole forms of black life in the Americas, black formalism included elements of European cultural forms, though in its constitution it became something distinctly black American. . . . Black formalism, then, was not based upon hierarchical ideas of culture that marked some cultures as more worthy than others. Rather, the distinctions were made about time and appropriateness. . . . Although black formalism was engaged in across the lines of socio-economic class and education, the increased access to formal education, literacy, and property that emerged in the postbellum period unquestionably aided the development of black formalism.[5]

AME architecture, as well as the images and cultural rituals that established meaning in these spaces, employed the "rich mix of performance and mastery" at the core of Black formalism.[6] Black formalism provides an analytical structure for understanding how the architectural discourse informed the architectural character of this nationwide African American community.

In the context of AME architecture, Black formalism is the appropriation and transformation of popular aesthetic conventions to create specific places and spaces that facilitate AME religious practice and historical revision. Close attention to the architectural discourse in AME-affiliated publications, as well as attention to the career and designs of the African American architect John A. Lankford (1874–1946), reveals a cultural record of the functions and mechanisms of Black formalism. In the case of this study, which replaces Perry's discussion of performance with an examination of visual representation, Perry's emphasis on public projections of identity facilitated by comprehensive cultural knowledge provides a useful interpretive frame for AME art and architecture. Akin to AME music and liturgical traditions, the selection and use of popular architectural styles and visual idioms moved beyond mimesis to engage in the active cultural work of contesting racist misrepresentations popular in American culture. This use of Black formalism as a lens to understand the role of architecture in AME communities is informed by Perry's acknowledgment of churches and educational spaces as central to the cultivation of autonomous cultural expression. My application of Black formalism to interpret aesthetic histories diverges from standing literature on nineteenth-century African American art and self-fashioning. Scholars like Aston Gonzalez and Jasmine Nichole Cobb have examined African American representation as an expression of the politics of respectability, which Evelyn Brooks Higginbotham defines as a modification of one's behavior and public presentation to negotiate socioeconomic and cultural norms.[7] Whereas the politics of respectability often demonstrated a preoccupation with middle-class cultural practices, Black formalism offers an alternative means to acknowledge the necessity of cultural adaptation and horizontal diffusion across class.

The Black religious community constructed a network of urban cathedrals and educational campuses to serve as sanctuaries where philosophical and cultural ideas were exchanged. These sites provided a space of autonomy where everyday life could be structured and value systems promoted. Recognizing the life of AME schools and churches is integral to a more expansive, inclusive understanding of the American built environment. These architectural histories advance new narratives of African American patronage, thus expanding the cast of actors who shaped the nation's architectural landscape. This study begins by introducing the development of architectural discourses in *The Christian Recorder*, from essays republished from periodicals like *The Atlantic Monthly* and *The Presbyterian Banner* in the 1860s to entries authored by AME ministers and members from the 1870s to the 1890s. Literature addressing architecture in *The Christian Recorder* established a knowledge base for AME members and their readership. Access to this body of architectural knowledge informed and encouraged the first generation of licensed African American architects and the AME congregations who would act as their patrons.

The chapter then evaluates the career and publication history of John A. Lankford as evidence of the representational strategies and architectural mastery at the core of Black formalism. As the only supervising architect appointed by the denomination, Lankford crafted a modern AME architectural identity that marshaled stylistic diversity and design efficiency to improve the quality of AME spaces in denominational commissions, including educational structures such as Arnett Hall (1910) at Wilberforce University and the Chappelle Administration Building (1922) at Allen University, and the 1923 reconstruction of Atlanta's Big Bethel AME Church. This analysis culminates by addressing the visual mechanisms of Black formalism proposed in the architectural pattern book authored by the denominational architect, *Lankford's Artistic Churches and Other Designs* (1916). Lankford's book textually and visually promoted modern ideals and expectations for AME Church building practices during the early decades of the twentieth century, emphasizing healthy and functional spaces. AME clergy and members visually documented their structures and circulated images, illustrating institutional development in an effort to combat racism.

Shaping the AME Architectural Landscape Through Black Formalist Discourse

The architectural discussions that took place in *The Christian Recorder* advanced the Black formalist objective of pursing aesthetic mastery by enhancing general architectural knowledge among AME clergy and congregations. This study contributes to a larger body of scholarship that interprets the cultural significance of African American religious spaces as repositories of material and visual history. In his examination of AME print culture, Eric Gardner asserts that

> these physical congregations, church buildings and ministers were also often sites/agents for "imagined" rituals that were crucial to not only the spiritual lives of individual congregants but also to the material circumstances of those congregants. . . . Church members were sometimes incredibly mobile, and they expected their ministers, church structures and church hierarchy to follow suit.[8]

Akin to Gardner's argument that AME churches created a sense of unity and facilitated mobility, this chapter investigates how AME architecture and visual culture were employed as cultural strategies for sustaining AME communities as autonomous sites forged out of a protest tradition and collective self-definition.

AME building activity during the late nineteenth and early twentieth centuries attests to a material response to denominational architectural discourse that developed within the pages of *The Christian Recorder* from 1861 to 1902.[9] Religious studies scholar Julius H. Bailey interprets *The Christian Recorder* as a platform for communal discussions of ideologies and cultural styles. He interprets *The Christian Recorder* as a "discursive space" where notions about African American identities were developed across a vast readership.[10] Bailey contends that

> from the early struggles of the AME periodicals, the *Christian Recorder* emerged as a discursive space in which contributors debated and discussed how to best uplift the race. . . . The *Christian Recorder* would provide a distinctive type of historical writing in which narratives were created, interrupted and reframed at varied points with an eye toward shaping the future trajectory of the race and denomination.[11]

Aesthetics and architecture figured prominently in the discursive space of *The Christian Recorder*. The periodical published over one hundred articles on architecture that varied in length and analytical depth. These entries can be categorized under the following thematic headings: informational entries on historical global architecture; promotional coverage of appropriate architectural styles; charges for improved building practices to reflect the development of African Methodism and promote a modern design; documentation of AME architectural activity, as well as building efforts from other African American institutions; and accounts of the realities of construction, including project delays and financial difficulties.

From the 1860s through the 1880s, *The Christian Recorder* published a series of articles that educated its readership on architecture around the world and prominent models of sacred architecture. In the midst of the Civil War, the newspaper published architectural accounts that would inform how the denomination influenced the architectural landscape during the Reconstruction and post-Reconstruction eras. In November 1863, a series titled "Church Antiquities" provided readers with three installments on the ancient history of Christianity that referenced architecture from a contributor affiliated with *The Lutheran and Missionary*. Beginning with the influence of early Christian apostles proselytizing in public spaces and conducting liturgical rituals in private domestic spaces, this initial entry culminated by discussing the diversity of Christian architecture stretching from the Byzantine basilica to the Russo-Greek church and concluding with the development of Romanesque structures.[12] By the 1870s, the denominational newspaper reported on "the mania for pilgrimages" as Catholic devotees traveled across France and Germany to visit European cathedrals.[13]

In order to provide a broad range of architectural insight, the editor of *The Christian Recorder* maintained the practice of offering a variety of Protestant perspectives. For instance, Michigan-based Episcopalian layman Crumell Lambert penned an article titled "The Pyramids," which introduced the architectural features of the Giza funerary complex. Lambert framed the entry with a narrative structure that mimicked travel literature, including detailed information on the approach to the Giza Plateau and the monumentality of the pyramids.[14] Considering that Lambert's account was published two years after Egyptian explorations by William Matthew Flinders Petrie, a pioneering British archaeologist, this coverage informed readers about ancient architectural legacies.[15] These essays collectively functioned as a form of artistic education, establishing an aesthetic foundation for AME members and leaders to build upon in future construction initiatives.

During the 1860s and the first half of the 1870s, *The Christian Recorder* republished commentaries on European architecture from other Protestant religious publications, such as *The Presbyterian Quarterly Review*. Protestant Episcopal minister C. C. Tiffany authored a reflection on Christian church architecture, concluding, "The Gothic style is churchly in all its forms."[16] He offered suggestions concerning the specifications of a Protestant church informed by medieval architecture, exemplified in the following passage: "There should be a diminution in the size of churches, and the removal of columns, or the placing of them in the form of pilasters against the walls. We should retain a well-defined chancel. The pulpit, the symbol of prophecy, should stand forth conspicuous."[17] The endorsement of revival styles such as Gothic Revival architecture demonstrates an interest in solidarity with broader Methodist trends while reserving space for AME interventions in cultural meaning.[18] Jeanne H. Kilde explains how mainstream Protestant denominations employed Gothic Revival styles to articulate socioeconomic or political status, noting that

> Gothic Revival buildings . . . were intended to attract congregants by appealing to these new aesthetic and formalistic interests of this growing middle class. . . . In this way, aesthetic and social motivations intertwined as churches competed for congregants in the religious marketplace. For Protestants, then, historicism provided a means of addressing concerns about Christian unity and the desire to attract and retain members.[19]

Revival styles allowed Black Protestant denominations to simultaneously join in broader Protestant agendas and express cultural distinction through the use of space and iconographic style.

In almost thirty-five articles discussing Gothic or Gothic Revival architecture from the 1860s to the 1880s, the AME church aimed to influence the architectural contours of a religious body that was rapidly expanding. The newspaper frequently reported descriptions of new church construction, detailing the buildings' dimensions, layout, and architectural style. These reports note how AME churches employed similar design strategies as their white Methodist counterparts, extending design around the Methodist sanctuary core of the chancel with pulpit and nave or audience chamber.[20] For example, in 1872, G. M. Alexander reported on the success of Mr. Bertha, whom the author classified as an "architect . . . [and] a colored man," in designing St. Paul's Chapel in St. Louis, Missouri.[21] An unidentified contributor to *The Christian Recorder* reported on the church's completion, framing the announcement in terms of architectural advancement:

> It is our material growth, which marks more substantially the improvement we are making. In this connection, the erection of St. Paul's Chapel is a fair indication of the strength, resources and self-reliance of the colored people of St. Louis. It is an edifice commanding and beautiful, and reflects admirably the substantial growth and enterprise of the colored people. . . . The chapel is ninety feet in length, and fifty-eight feet wide, and is built of St. Louis stock brick. The basement is fifty-five by eighty feet, twelve feet in the clear, and is two feet above the ground; it is well ventilated, and will be used for lectures, Sunday schools and prayer meetings. The main audience chamber is eighty by fifty-five feet with a gallery in front. . . . In the chancel and behind the pulpit an innovation is made upon the established custom of the Methodist church in the shape of a baptistery, of ten feet ten inches by five feet two inches, eight inches deep and lined with lead. The roof is gothic and slated, and has two ventilators. The chapel will seat comfortably fifteen hundred persons, and is a model of grace and tasteful decoration. It is well arranged for acoustics, and reflects unmeasured credit on the board of trustees, and the noble women, and congregation generally, who carried the great undertaking forward to successful completion.[22]

This description exemplifies numerous instances of *The Christian Recorder* providing specific documentation of the evolving architectural character of the denomination, citing the Gothic Revival, auditorium-style church as "a model of grace and tasteful decoration."[23] Moreover, this passage reflects the development of auditorium-style churches to accommodate the social functions of religious communities but also the shifts in hierarchical structures of the AME denomination and local congregations. These types of descriptive announcements provided congregations with empirical examples of impressive church designs that could inform building initiatives. These descriptive inventories of dedicated areas and liturgical objects illustrate the material aspects of Black formalism that signal communal traditions such as baptism and communion. Additionally, reports on ritualistic aspects of church construction such as cornerstone ceremonies and dedication services indicate the impact of new AME structures in mobilizing African American communities around public celebrations of architectural advancements.[24]

The Christian Recorder frequently published articles that encouraged AME congregations to construct churches that reflected the style and functional attributes of modern architecture. Early entries from the 1860s discuss the aspiration of AME congregations to construct churches in "a modern style of architecture."[25] In 1863, the newspaper published "Warming and Ventilating Churches," encouraging congregations to place as much consideration into heating and ventilation as into exterior design. The author opens with these words:

> Thousands [of dollars] are expended in constructing and adorning churches: lavished upon tower and spire; organ and bells; upon pulpit and altar; upon stained glass; gas fixtures; upholstering and painting; nor are the acoustic properties of the audience chamber neglected. No expense is spared to make our churches externally attractive or internally beautiful. All these are matters of importance and should be pressed to the utmost ability of the congregation to pay for them. Unfortunately, the matter of warming and ventilation generally receives but a small share of attention, from either architect or building committee.[26]

The remainder of the text provides readers with instructions for how to consider heat and air circulation by way of three structural examples. *The Christian Recorder* supplied AME congregations with usable building practices and promoted enhancements in design quality to produce more efficient and serviceable spaces.

AME church pastors published reports boasting of architectural projects that reflected modern convenience as a sign of racial equality. In 1890, the Reverend James M. Henderson announced the completion of a new edifice for Bethel AME Church in Detroit, remarking,

> Bethel AME Church, Detroit, is one of the most commodious churches in the beautiful City of Straits. It is a brick structure with stone trimmings. It contains a spacious auditorium with circular pews, lecture room, parlors, class rooms, pastor's study, reading room, kitchen, pantry, and [is] heated by steam. The architecture is purely modern and provision is made for every convenience commonly found in a church. There is no better mark of true advancement among a people than increased attention to their moral culture and this elegant house of worship shows Bethel Society to be thoroughly progressive.[27]

Here, the author submitted the architectural arc of this religious community, from an antebellum inherited property to the contemporary modern structure, as evidence of racial advancement and communal moral rectitude. In the newspaper layout, the description of interior spaces that served sacred and secular needs of the Black community in Detroit was augmented by the inclusion of an elevation illustration of the Romanesque Revival structure (fig. 7.1). These descriptions and images provided subscribers and members with a visual index of ideal architectural models and standards. The comprehensive textual and visual presentation of Detroit's Bethel AME Church exhibits Black formalism's concern with representation and working knowledge of contemporary cultural forms.

The top tier of AME leadership, the episcopacy, also actively promoted architectural discourse in *The Christian Recorder* across a range of forms, including "Episcopal Reports." In March 1897, the AME Council of Bishops published an address that provided a comprehensive state of affairs for the institution, including standards for architectural projects. This edict advises:

6 THE CHRISTIAN RECORDER | February 20 1890

Missionary { READ! EASTER DAY. April 6, 1890. } Appeal

TO THE BISHOPS, PRESIDING ELDERS, PASTORS AND CONGREGATIONS OF THE AFRICAN METHODIST EPISCOPAL CHURCH—GREETINGS!

Beloved Fathers, Brethren and Saints; Grace, Mercy and Peace through our Lord Jesus Christ.

The Missionary Department respectfully but earnestly solicits your sympathy, co-operation and help in the good work in which the department is engaged. The preaching and teaching the Scriptures and the consolation here and hereafter in a pure and religious life among a poor but worthy class of persons in this and foreign lands. This work in behalf of Christ's kingdom is one that appeals to ...

Church News.

BETHEL, DETROIT.

REV. JAMES M. HENDERSON, PASTOR.

Bethel A. M. E. church, Detroit, is one of the most commodious churches in the beautiful City of Straits. It is a brick structure with stone trimmings. It contains a spacious auditorium with circular pews, lecture room, parlors, class rooms, pastor's study, reading room, kitchen, pantry, &c., heated by steam. The architecture is purely modern and provision is made for every convenience commonly found in a church.

There is no better mark of true advancement among a people than increased attention to their moral culture, and this elegant house of worship shows the Bethel Society to be thoroughly progressive.

Organized in the dark ante-bellum days it has exerted a wide influence in the intellectual and moral culture of Afro-Americans throughout the State of Michigan. Detroit has among its citizens some of the most cultured and substantial members of the race and many of these are communicants in Bethel church. The organization of this society dates as far back as 1839, when they worshipped in an old building given them by the city authorities, which had been used for the City Hall. They found many warm friends among the citizens who aided them in securing a permanent place of worship.

In 1845 they purchased the site of their old church an Champlain street for $300. Four years later they were regularly incorporated and continued to worship here until December, '88, when they sold to Thomas Lorimer for $7,000. In January '89, they purchased the site of their new church building from John Darraugh for $3,500 cash. They used the building they found on this property for church services until they were ready to clear the ground for their new church.

The new edifice cost $18,000. Of this amount $12,000 is already provided for. $7,062 was raised at the laying of the corner-stone and the society expects to be able to raise the remainder at the dedication, for which arrangements are now being made.

The following has been the succession of pastors: Jeremiah Thomas, 1844–'46; Edward Davis, '46–'47; Peter Gardner, '47–'48; Edward Hart, '48–'50; J. Bowman, '50–'51; M. F. Newsome, '51–'52; Isaiah Williams, '52–54; John A. Warren, '54–'55; Nelson H. Turpin, '55–'57; A. R. Green, '57–'59; J. A. Warren, '59–'61; R. A. Johnson, '61–'73; H. J. Young, '63–'64; Enoch McIntosh, '64–'66; W. S. Lankford, '66–'68; G. C. Booth, '68–'71; A. T. Hall, '71–'72; Theodore Crosby, '72–'73; W. C. Trevan, '73–'75; W. Revels, '75–'77; Johnson Mitchem, '77–'79; D. P. Roberts, '79–'82; A. A. Burleigh, '82–'84; Jesse Bass, '84–'86. James M. Henderson, the present pastor, assumed charge in August, 1886.

Much credit is due Bishop John M. Brown for the large success which has attended the Bethel Society in Detroit. He began his ministry here in 1844 and was an assistant pastor for three years. During this time their first property was purchased largely under his direction. He has also manifested a vigilant interest in the new edifice.

LITERARY NOTES.

"The City of St. Paul will be the subject of a four-page supplement, by William Willard Howard, in the number of *Harper's Weekly* to be published February 19th. The article will be profusely illustrated.

Poultney Bigelow will contribute to the number of *Harper's Weekly* to be published February 19th an article on "The German Reichstag," with a picture of a scene during a session of the Reichstag, and with portraits of Barth, Bamberger, Richter, Virchow, Windthorst, and Stoecker.

Benjamin Constant's picture, "A Funeral in Morocco," has been reproduced in a double-page engraving for the number of *Harper's Bazaar* to be published February 21st. Mary Gay Humphreys will contribute to to the same number an article on "Plaster Casts, and How to Use Them."

Mrs. Arthur Brooks will contribute an article on "The Berkeley Ladies' Athletic Club" to the number of *Harper's Young People* to be published February 18th. "Empty Bottles"—a story of a great magician and an ambitious student—written and illustrated by Howard Pyle, will appear in the same number.

Professor William Knight, of St. Andrew's University, Scotland, editor of the great standard edition of Wordsworth, writes to Dr. William J. Rolfe, in regard to the latter's recent work, *The Select Poems of William Wordsworth:* "Your selection is *excellent*, and must do great good. No better service can be done than to popularize Wordsworth in America."

"*Our Suffering Sisters*," is the title of a little pamphlet issued by the Medical Missionary Society, 118 East 45 St., New York. It is written by Mrs. Geo. D. Dowkontt. It unfolds some of the hororrs of the life of women in heathen countries. It can probably be gotten by writing for it without money; though it would be cheap at 10 cts. Women, read it.

EDUCATIONAL NOTES.

The number of *State* students appointed by the Ohio legislature to the State Normal school at Wilberforce University this year more than doubles that of any former year.

Some of the former contributors to Wilberforce University have this year doubled their annuity.

Wilberforce received a small financial donation from a lady in Europe recently.

The city of Norfolk is well represented at Wilberforce University. Thanks to Brother Cook.

Money.

Recommendation.

Tutt's Liver Pills

I CURE FITS!

STRAWBRIDGE & CLOTHIER

Printed Cotton Goods

FOR

THE SPRING OF 1890

Long rows of shelves and counters are piled high with the latest and choicest creations in Printed Cotton Fabrics, France, England, Scotland and America, have contributed their finest products to make up a stock which, it is believed, has no counterpart this side of Paris.

A few of the many beautiful fabrics are mentioned, although this list can convey but a faint idea of the extent and beauty of the display.

Cashmere Ombres—

one of the very newest cotton fabrics, manufactured exclusively for our own sales in this market. The cloth closely resembles woolen fabric in weight and finish, though more beautiful in effect than any fabric made of wool can be. They are in softly shaded Figures, Stripes, Plaids, &c., in all the new Spring and Summer shadings.

Melanels Fabric

This is a beautiful material with a soft henrietta finish, in fast black with white figures. The designs, which are all new, are copied directly from nature.

Cotton Brocade.

An entirely new and very choice mourning Fabric, in black ground only, with small brocade figures, sprays, dots, &c.

French Printed Satines.

We are showing a choice line of all the *Latest French Novelties* in styles and combinations ever before produced in these goods.

A full line of *Plain colors* included.

Scotch Novelties.

These goods, which excel any materials of the kind heretofore shown, are exhibited in

Brocaded Weaves, Stripes, Plaids and Figures,

embracing all the choicest colorings, and the most beautiful and almost bewildering assortments of shadings produced by the leading English and Scotch manufacturers.

We call attention to many other styles, quieter in effect, but very choice, which have been selected with great care, and represent the newest and choicest styles in Stripes and Plaids. Included are medium and fancy effects in all the newest combinations and colorings produced by the best Scotch and English makers.

We also display a choice line of

Deep Black and Second Mourning Goods

in all shades ranging from black to the lightest shades of lavender and gray.

Also a full line of

Anderson's Latest Novelties in Stripes and Plaids.

STRAWBRIDGE AND CLOTHIER.

EIGHTH AND MARKET STREETS, PHILADELPHIA, PA.

FIGURE 7.1. *Layout from* The Christian Recorder, *February 20, 1890. Digitized by History Commons, African American Newspapers Collection.*

> Architecture is the art of building according to principles which are determined, not merely by the ends the edifice is intended to serve, but by consideration of beauty and harmony, so declared an eminent architect of France. The proper construction of our houses of worship should claim our attention more than it does. Often times money and materials are wasted simply because no care is taken as to manner and style of erecting houses of worship. In building our church edifices, though not costly nor commodious, comfort and taste should not be overlooked. On account of the credence which so widely prevails among us in the ill constructed as well as ill ventilated church buildings, we are drifting into irreverence and carelessness of worship. It is a long standing custom of Methodism to kneel while at prayer, but owing to the disregarding of these principles it is a matter of impossibility, much to the regret of a large class of humble and devout worshippers, to approach the throne of heavenly grace in the attitude which is in harmony with their Christian belief. In the future more attention ought to be paid in the building of churches to the proper seating and ventilating.[28]

The AME bishops established expectations for church construction, emphasizing the equal importance of style and function. They suggest a direct correlation between the efficiency and comfort of the structure and the success of liturgical exercises.

The architectural information and debates printed during the last four decades of the nineteenth century constituted an alternative historical narrative that acknowledges the masterful architectural legacy established by enslaved African Americans and those beyond the professional boundaries of the gentleman architect and nascent architectural profession. These accounts provide a resource-rich repository that would influence subsequent generations of African American builders and architects who would draft designs and oversee construction of AME edifices. In fact, *The Christian Recorder* documents a small network of African American builders and architects who were lauded for representing the achievements and future potential for the race in this professional sector. Only months after the conclusion of the Civil War, AME minister and army chaplain Henry McNeal Turner recognized the contribution of often-unidentified Black builders in the South, remarking, "In short, the ablest historian, the greatest orator, and the most skillful architect and mechanic I have ever seen, were all slaves in the South. Having travelled through all the slave States except Texas, prior to the war, my observations have been extensive."[29] Turner's report carried substantial weight, as he was emerging as a race leader in the years following the Civil War. Ascending into the leadership ranks of the denomination in the 1870s and 1880s, Turner carried this counterhistory of African American contributions to the built environment with him as he became a leading voice in advocating for the creation of the denominational supervising architect position in the early twentieth century.

AME voices outside of the leadership also advanced revisionism in architectural discourse in the pages of *The Christian Recorder*. Two months after Turner's report, a correspondent from Charleston, South Carolina, reported on the city's newly constructed Emanuel AME Church, identifying the architect as Robert Vesey, the son of Denmark Vesey, an AME member, carpenter, and organizer of the 1822 Charleston slave rebellion.[30] During the 1880s, two African American builder-architects were acknowledged in *The Christian Recorder*: Robert Sims, who designed an AME church in West Point, Mississippi, and George Lucas, who was heralded as a "first class architect" practicing in Salem, Oregon.[31] The denominational newspaper also recorded a tradition of AME ministers who served as builder-architects for AME projects, including the Reverend G. D. Jimmerson, a "master builder" who oversaw construction of the AME church in Eastville, Virginia.[32] Throughout the 1890s, the AME minister F. P. Main was identified as a "well known mechanic, builder and architect" who designed the AME church in Bridgeton, New Jersey.[33] Main also penned two statements for the newspaper, reflecting on this commission and his collaborative engagement with the church pastor.[34] The architectural discourse in *The Christian Recorder* provides a counternarrative that corrects the absences and voids in American architectural historiography around African American architectural contributions. Pioneering Black institutions like the AME Church were committed to revising and reconstructing historical narratives through Black formalist strategies of visualizing and materializing racial equality through spirituality and aesthetics.

Informed by the Black architectural history and legacy outlined through editions of *The Christian Recorder*, African American carpenters and master builders paved the way for subsequent generations of licensed architects who would shape the architecture of the denomination in the twentieth century. By 1902, *The Christian Recorder* mentions the growing reputation of the African American architect John A. Lankford. In the early decades of the twentieth century, Lankford would gain the distinction of being the first professionally licensed African American architect in Virginia and the District of Columbia. He marks a new chapter in the AME denomination's approach to architecture as the first and only supervising architect for the AME Church.

John A. Lankford, Denominational Architect

John A. Lankford was a leading figure of the first generation of professionally trained African American architects.[35] He studied at several institutions between 1896 and 1902, earning bachelor of science degrees from Shaw University (Raleigh, NC), Morris Brown College (Atlanta, GA), and Wilberforce University (Wilberforce, OH), and a master of science degree from Alabama A&M University (Huntsville, AL). Shortly after completing his architectural training, Lankford married Charlotte Josephine Upshaw, the granddaughter of army chaplain and AME bishop Henry McNeal Turner.[36] Capitalizing on the authority of the episcopacy, Lankford was appointed supervising architect for the institution around 1906.[37] During the 1910s and 1920s, Lankford was a leading proponent of AME Black formalist aesthetic practice through his architectural practice, publication record, and visual representational strategies.

Although Lankford received commissions from AME congregations as early as 1907, his work on an institutional level began with his designs for structures on the campus of Wilberforce University in 1910. He designed and oversaw the construction of the women's dormitory and the campus's heating tunnel system.[38] Wilberforce University published reports that identified Lankford as the architect and supervisor for Arnett Hall, a three-story, multiuse structure with women's boarding accommodations as well as parlor spaces, classrooms, kitchens, and dining facilities (fig. 7.2).[39] The exterior facade, constructed of stone and brick, was designed in a Romanesque Revival style, consistent with the stylistic direction established by the African American architect Robert R. Taylor at Tuskegee Institute (later Tuskegee University) at the turn of the twentieth century.[40] Arnett Hall was anchored by a central tower with rounded arches, and a portico supported by Ionic columns marked the main entrance. The 1911 institutional report advertised this building as reflecting "modern convenience," as the structure provided hot water and was sufficiently heated for frigid Ohio winters.[41]

ARNETT HALL AT WILBERFORCE UNIVERSITY

FIGURE 7.2. *John A. Lankford, Arnett Hall, 1910, Wilberforce University, Wilberforce, Ohio.* Annual Catalogue of Wilberforce University, Wilberforce, Ohio, 1911–1912 *(Wilberforce University, 1912). The Rembert E. Stokes Library and Information Commons, Wilberforce University.*

Both Lankford and Wilberforce University publicized the construction of Arnett Hall as experiential learning, since carpentry work was executed by students under the tutelage of the architect.[42] By 1916, Lankford depicted his teaching record and architectural practice at Wilberforce by juxtaposing a photograph of students in his architectural and mechanical drawing course with a model elevation for an imposing exposition building. This layout presents Lankford as a race man shaping the minds of future generations to innovate spaces that serve African American needs and foster their imaginations. Wilberforce and other historically Black educational institutions followed the lead of Tuskegee Institute in circulating photographs of industrial education as visual proof of post-Reconstruction development.[43] Lankford continued to develop AME university campuses in the 1920s, as evidenced by his design for the Chappelle Administration Building at Allen University in Columbia, South Carolina (fig. 7.3). This four-story edifice was constructed from 1922 to 1925.[44] It was one of several university structures that faced public thoroughfares.[45] The structure included classrooms, an assembly hall, administrative offices, and a printshop, as well as a kitchen and dining hall.[46] Lankford enlarged his mark on the Allen University campus by also designing a chapel.[47]

In 1916, John Lankford extended AME Black formalism through architectural literature with his *Lankford's Artistic Churches and Other Designs*, one of

FIGURE 7.3. *John A. Lankford, Chappelle Administration Building, 1922, Allen University, Columbia, South Carolina. Historic American Buildings Survey, Library of Congress, SC-397.*

the earliest-known architectural pattern books produced by an African American architect. The 1916 edition was followed by a second edition in 1924. The book was structured as a branding opportunity for Lankford and an educational resource for AME congregations and other African American institutions, as he included a biographical sketch, an essay, patron references, architectural plans, and photographs of completed projects. Although this book does not focus exclusively on AME building practices, over one-third of the photographs and plans represent AME structures.[48] *Lankford's Artistic Churches and Other Designs* features a lengthy essay titled "The Church Edifice," in which Lankford provides recommendations for building commodious churches based on function under the following subject headings: "Practical Points"; the "Sunday School"; the "Social Side"; "Should We Have a Gallery?"; and "Heating, Lighting and Fixtures." Demonstrating his historical knowledge as an AME member, he contextualizes the architectural efforts of the AME Church in relation to the denominational origin narrative, asserting,

> [Bishop Richard] Allen and his followers wanted religious freedom, without discrimination on account of race and color, and ever since Allen . . . called his meeting in that little blacksmith shop in Philadelphia, using his anvil as a pulpit stand, the old wagons and buggies as the pews for his congregations . . . from that day we have been building better churches, and today scarcely any minister or trustee board would be so stupid as to attempt to plan or build a church edifice or a school without a competent architect's advice.[49]

Lankford offers a rich description of foundational AME material and spatial traditions that can be traced to the autobiography of AME founder Richard Allen.[50] The architect emphasizes the historical arc for the denomination's architectural evolution, suggesting a shared understanding about the necessity and value of the architectural profession in improving the quality of AME structures. This spatial and material evolution narrative situated the AME Church among world religious traditions that develop from modest, mundane, private spaces to monumental religious structures.[51]

Extending the architectural discourse established in *The Christian Recorder*, Lankford encourages congregations to insist on designs that ensure comfort. Framing this imperative in terms of racial advancement, he closes the essay by stating,

> A church edifice which is poorly lighted and ventilated, is a germ and disease carrier and distributor. The mortality in the Negro race is said to be higher today than that of the Caucasian, and we have logical reasons to believe that our poorly lighted and ventilated churches and school

buildings are some of the principal reasons for it. . . . As one of the most progressive Negro organization[s] along about every line . . . [every AME member] should lend a helping hand by advocating better churches, parsonages and school buildings . . . so we can better beautify, cultivate and refine the taste and ideas for these the coming generations of God and man.[52]

Emphasizing the importance of architecture and public health to racial advancement, Lankford informed readers about designs like those in the illustrated pages of his pattern book that accommodated the social function of Black religious communities as well as modern architectural standards. This directly contested popular racist misconceptions that the inferiority of African Americans was visible in physical appearance and habitation conditions.[53] Lankford educated readers and equipped them with scientific logic and new standards for healthy spaces.[54]

Photographs of Lankford in the pattern book achieve the representational and performative aims of Black formalism. Lankford was an active participant in shaping the landscape of the New Negro movement in Washington, DC, during the 1900s and 1910s. The architect visited Washington's preeminent African American photographer, Addison Scurlock, to sit for a quarter-length portrait that would appear in *Lankford's Artistic Churches and Other Designs*. The pattern book also includes two additional photographs of Lankford in the following settings: in the drafting room of his Washington, DC, architecture office and in front of his temporary architectural and administrative headquarters at the 1912 AME General Conference in Kansas City, Missouri. In the latter image, Lankford and his staff, dressed in their crisp professional attire, are poised to usher prospective patrons onto a pathway toward African American material advancement (fig. 7.4). Representing commercial space defined by African American profession-

FIGURE 7.4. *"Our Headquarters at the General Conference at Kansas City, Mo." John Lankford,* Lankford's Artistic Churches and Other Designs, *second edition (Hamilton Print, 1924), 19. Stuart A. Rose Manuscript, Archives, and Rare Book Library, Emory University.*

OUR HEADQUARTERS AT THE GENERAL CONFERENCE AT KANSAS CITY, MO., 1912

als put forth an additional type of African American structure and space that demonstrates Black formalist principles of public presentation of mastery.

In 1923, Lankford drafted reconstruction plans for the 1891 structure that housed Big Bethel AME Church in Atlanta's historic African American neighborhood Sweet Auburn. This project extended Lankford's contribution to shaping the AME architectural landscape in the Southern United States, during an era of anti-Black terror in which African American–owned properties such as churches were often targets of arson.[55] AME members understood this reality as an enduring historic threat to AME edifices, with nineteenth-century examples such as the 1865 arson of the Wilberforce University Main Building.[56] On February 16, 1923, only one day after the insurance policy for the structure expired and only a month after the completion of Lankford's renovations, Big Bethel AME Church was destroyed by fire.[57] Lankford designed a Romanesque Revival church with an asymmetrical facade and an auditorium-style sanctuary for Atlanta's new AME cathedral. The semicircular orientation of church pews around the chancel and pulpit facilitated religious liturgy, which culminated in preaching as well as social events such as concerts and community meetings. The addition of a cross and textual signage on the spire marked a shift in AME architecture and demonstrated Lankford's awareness of contemporary trends in architectural detailing prominent among Pentecostal churches.[58] The construction was particularly symbolic of racial advancement for the denomination, as both the architect and the building contractor, Alexander Hamilton (ca. 1840–1944), were African American. The 1924 edition of *Lankford's Artistic Churches and Other Designs* visualized

1.…Big Bethel Church before the fire, Feb. 16, 1923
2. After the fire looking west.
3.…Rev. R. H. Singleton, D.D., Pastor
4.…Ruins after fire.
5. After fire, looking north

The above pictures show Big Bethel A. M. E. Church of Atlanta, Ga., and the Pastor after the great destruction Feb. 16, 1923. The church had just been completed by the Pastor and Prof. John A. Lankford as Architect. Prof. Lankford was immediately called back to Atlanta by Dr. Singleton and the church was redesigned. The new plans which were made for the church edifice, beautified and enlarged the structure, with a seating capacity for several hundred more, and was rushed to completion in order to accommodate the Bishops' Council which met there February 1924.

FIGURE 7.5. *Layout featuring Big Bethel AME Church, Atlanta, Georgia, 1924. John Lankford, Lankford's* Artistic Churches and Other Designs, *second edition (Hamilton Print, 1924), 2. Stuart A. Rose Manuscript, Archives, and Rare Book Library, Emory University.*

this cycle of destruction and reconstruction through a series of photographs (fig. 7.5). This layout design echoes the historical framing of racial progress consistent in AME architectural discourse and denominational historical narratives.

Conclusion

Through *The Christian Recorder* and AME-affiliated publications, the AME denomination promoted architecture as a means to publicly articulate and affirm racial histories of self-definition. AME religious communities used architectural education in their press outlets to uplift and cultivate a more informed religious body that would commission more modern, healthier spaces for Black life. Furthermore, AME architectural discourse and the circuit of AME structures served as a beacon for revisionist counterhistories that illuminate African American contributions to the American built environment. AME-affiliated publications such as *Lankford's Artistic Churches and Other Designs* provided readers with scientific logic and recent advancements in designing healthy spaces that privileged light and ventilation. Photography served a pivotal role in visualizing and advancing Black formalist aesthetics by recording structures, promoting architectural style, and circulating visual evidence of improved quality of life in enhanced, modern spaces. Black religious institutions like the AME Church employed similar religio-aesthetic strategies to create formal space for the Black formalist rituals that ushered in new modern cultural paradigms like the New Negro movement.

The architectural history of the AME denomination is chronicled in denominational publications and African American archival collections. This requires historians of American architecture to expand the sources that comprise American architectural history and to consider the range of ways African American builders and architects were in dialogue with national discourses on church architecture. Moreover, it is important to recognize how African American institutions like the AME Church influenced perspectives and ideals for American architecture. As indicated by the example of *Lankford's Artistic Churches and Other Designs*, by the 1920s, African Americans had crafted narratives that used architecture as evidence of racial advancement. Recovering and engaging Black architectural discourse in various publications is necessary to broaden our understanding of architecture's meaning in the everyday life of African Americans and to embrace a more expansive definition of American architecture.

Notes

1. W. E. B. Du Bois, ed., *The Negro Church: Report of a Social Study Made Under the Direction of Atlanta University* [. . .], (Atlanta University, 1903), 126.

2. Du Bois, *Negro Church*.

3. Although Judith Weisenfeld uses the term "religio-racial" to describe religious communities outside of mainstream Protestant denominations (e.g., Father Divine's Peace Mission Movement), she

acknowledges the usefulness of "religio-racial identity" to describe religious practice more broadly in the United States, stating, "In some sense, all religious groups in the United States could be characterized as religio-racial ones, given the deeply powerful, if sometimes veiled, ways the American system of racial hierarchy has structured religious beliefs, practices and institutions for all people in its frame." Judith Weisenfeld, *New World A-Coming: Black Religion and Racial Identity During the Great Migration* (New York University Press, 2016), 5–6.

4. Imani Perry, *May We Forever Stand: A History of the Black National Anthem* (University of North Carolina Press, 2021) 8.

5. Perry, *May We Forever Stand*, 11–12.

6. Perry, *May We Forever Stand*, 9.

7. Aston Gonzalez, *Visualizing Equality: African American Rights and Visual Culture in the Nineteenth Century* (University of North Carolina Press, 2020); Jasmine Nichole Cobb, *Picture Freedom: Remaking Black Visuality in the Early Nineteenth Century* (New York University Press, 2015); Evelyn Brooks Higginbotham, "African-American Women's History and the Metalanguage of Race," *Signs: Journal of Women in Culture and Society* 17, no. 2 (1992): 251–274; Evelyn Brooks Higginbotham, *Righteous Discontent: The Women's Movement in the Black Baptist Church, 1880–1920* (Harvard University Press, 1993).

8. Eric Gardner, *Black Print Unbound: "The Christian Recorder," African American Literature, and Periodical Culture* (Oxford University Press, 2015), 15–16.

9. Julius H. Bailey, *Race Patriotism: Protest and Print Culture in the AME Church* (University of Tennessee Press, 2012), xvi, 23. Bishop Benjamin Tucker Tanner maintains a prominent position in the historical narrative of African American aesthetics as the father of the first internationally renowned African American painter, Henry Ossawa Tanner. Bishop Tanner's tenure as editor of *The Christian Recorder* coincides with his son's matriculation as one of the first African American students to attend the Pennsylvania Academy of Fine Arts. Informed by his son's interest and commitment to a career in the arts, Bishop Tanner gave great consideration to cultivating an awareness about aesthetics among AME members and the readers of *The Christian Recorder*.

10. Bailey, *Race Patriotism*.

11. Bailey, *Race Patriotism*, 17.

12. Bailey, *Race Patriotism*.

13. "Pilgrimages," *Christian Recorder*, February 6, 1873, 4; Ryan K. Smith, *Gothic Arches, Latin Crosses: Anti-Catholicism and American Church Designs in the Nineteenth Century* (University of North Carolina Press, 2011).

14. Crummell Lambert, "The Pyramids," *Christian Recorder*, October 12, 1882, 1.

15. Petrie was famous for employing the modern technologies of photography and X-ray to gather accurate measurements and descriptions of the Giza necropolis.

16. Rev. C. C. Tiffany, "Church Architecture," *Christian Recorder*, March 25, 1875.

17. Tiffany, "Church Architecture."

18. Smith, *Gothic Arches, Latin Crosses*, 8.

19. Jeanne H. Kilde, *Sacred Power, Sacred Space: An Introduction to Christian Architecture and Worship* (Oxford University Press, 2008), 166.

20. Jeanne H. Kilde, *When Church Became Theatre: The Transformation of Evangelical Architecture and Worship in Nineteenth-Century America* (Oxford University Press, 2002), 146.

21. G. M. Alexander, "St. Louis Communication," *Christian Recorder*, July 27, 1872, 2.

22. "St. Paul's Chapel," *Christian Recorder*, August 10, 1872, 1; Kilde, *When Church Became Theatre*, 146.

23. "St. Paul's Chapel," 1.

24. Examples of such announcements include the following: Rev. Walter Thompson, "Dedication of a Church," *Christian Recorder*, February 15, 1877, 6; "The New Emanuel Laying of the Corner-Stone on Monday by Shekinah Lodge No. 6," *Christian Recorder*, September 10, 1891, 6; Amos Wilson, "Corner Stone Laying," *Christian Recorder*, July 20, 1876, 2.

25. Rev. F. Meyers, "AME Notes," *Christian Recorder*, December 21, 1867, 2; Prof. J. W. Morris, "Dedication at Georgetown," *Christian Recorder*, June 28, 1883, 1.

26. "Warming and Ventilating Churches," *Christian Recorder*, January 4, 1868, 1.

27. Rev. James Henderson, "Bethel, Detroit," *Christian Recorder*, February 20, 1890, 6.

28. Bishop Henry McNeal Turner, Bishop Wesley Gaines, Bishop Benjamin Arnett, et al., "Episcopal Address," *Christian Recorder*, March 11, 1897, 1. I was unable to locate any specific references to prominent French architects like Eugène Viollet-le-Duc in *The Christian Recorder*. AME bishops, editors, and contributors may have had access to English translations of the writings of French architects, but the newspaper does not explicitly list these sources. *The Christian Recorder* did advertise Frederick C. Withers's 1873 text *Church Architecture*.

29. Chaplain Henry McNeal Turner, "Army Correspondence," *Christian Recorder*, August 5, 1865, 1.

30. "Charleston Correspondence," *Christian Recorder*, October 4, 1865, 1.

31. Byron W. Force, "West Point (Miss.) Letter," *Christian Recorder*, April 9, 1885, 1; "Personal," *Christian Recorder*, September 8, 1887, 1.

32. "Second Episcopal District News," *Christian Recorder*, July 31, 1902, 1.

33. "Notes and Comments," *Christian Recorder*, November 30, 1893, 2.

34. Rev. F. P. Main, "The Bridgeton AME Church, New Jersey," *Christian Recorder*, December 20, 1894, 6; Rev. F. P. Main, "The Bridgeton AME Church, NJ," *Christian Recorder*, January 3, 1895, 4.

35. John Anderson Lankford, *Lankford's Artistic Churches and Other Designs*, 2nd ed. (Hamilton Print, 1924), 3.

36. Paul Kelsey Williams, "John Anderson Lankford (1874–1946)," *African American Architects: A Biographical Dictionary, 1865–1945*, ed. Dreck Spurlock Wilson (Routledge, 2004), 254.

37. Williams, "John Anderson Lankford." Paul Kelsey Williams attributes Lankford's familiar connections to Bishop Henry McNeal Turner as a plausible explanation for his appointment as supervising architect. Lankford garnered notice in 1908 for being selected to serve as supervising architect alongside Robert R. Taylor for the National Negro Fair in Mobile, Alabama, although the fair was canceled due to lack of financing.

38. Williams, "John Anderson Lankford," 257.

39. *Annual Catalogue of Wilberforce University, Wilberforce, Ohio, 1910–1911* (Wilberforce University, 1911), 79.

40. Charles L. Davis II, email correspondence with the author, October 4, 2023; Ellen Weiss, *Robert R. Taylor and Tuskegee: An African American Architect Designs for Booker T. Washington* (New South Books, 2012), 60–61; "Tuskegee Normal School," *Christian Recorder*, May 15, 1890, 3. *The Christian Recorder* published several reports on the development of Tuskegee's campus in the 1890s.

41. *Annual Catalogue of Wilberforce University*, 79.

42. *Annual Catalogue of Wilberforce University*.

43. "Original Buildings at Tuskegee Inst. in 1882," Photographs of Tuskegee Institute, American Antiquarian Society Illustrated Inventory, https://www.americanantiquarian.org/tuskegeecollection/items/show/59. The 1882 photograph of Tuskegee Institute predates early photographs of historically Black college and university campuses that become prevalent in the 1890s.

44. Nenie Dixon, "National Register of Historic Places Inventory Nomination Form: Allen University," April 1, 1975, 5–6.

45. Dixon, "Nomination Form."

46. Dixon, "Nomination Form."

47. Williams, "John Anderson Lankford," 255. Archival sources do not list a date of construction for this building.

48. Lankford, *Artistic Churches*. This pattern book included seventy-one images or plans for a range of structures, including churches, banks, schools, professional office buildings, and residences. In terms of religious structures, it contained twenty-eight AME buildings, five Baptist churches, three AME Zion structures, two Methodist Episcopal churches, and one Presbyterian church.

49. John Anderson Lankford, "The Church Edifice," in Lankford, *Artistic Churches*, 4. Lankford was a member and church officer at the Metropolitan AME Church in Washington, DC.

50. Richard Allen, *The Life, Experience, and Gospel Labours of the Rt. Rev. Richard Allen* [. . .] (Philadelphia: Martin and Boden Printers, 1833), 17.

51. Charles L. Davis II, email correspondence with the author, October 4, 2023.

52. Lankford, "Church Edifice," 5.

53. Barbara Burlison Mooney, "The Comfortable Tasty Framed Cottage: An African American Architectural Iconography," *Journal of the Society of Architectural Historians* 61, no. 1 (2002): 1.

54. Charles L. Davis II, email correspondence with the author, October 4, 2023.

55. Christopher B. Strain, *Burning Faith: Church Arson in the American South* (University Press of Florida, 2008).

56. "Wilberforce University," *Christian Recorder*, April 29, 1865, 2; "The Ohio Annual Conference," *Christian Recorder*, April 29, 1865, 1. The denominational news outlet reported, "Scarcely had the first shock subsided, ere the intelligence reached us that Wilberforce University had been fired by some wicked and heartless scoundrel, and reduced to ashes."

57. Lankford, *Artistic Churches*, 2.

58. Lauren Elizabeth Beaupre, "Saints and the 'Long Civil Rights Movement': Claiming Space in Memphis," *Journal of Urban History* 38, no. 6 (2012): 971–1002.

8 DEMOLISHING HISTORIC ARCHITECTURE

BLACK ACTIVISTS' CRUSADE AGAINST THE ONE-ROOM CABIN IN THE EARLY JIM CROW ERA

Whitney Nell Stewart

AMERICANS HAVE BEEN PARTICIPATING IN and advocating for historic preservation for over two centuries, and over those many years, their goals have always been as much about the present and the future as the past. The maintenance of old structures, as Whitney Martinko and others have argued, is part of "a process of making historical memory: the creation of a usable past for a contemporary purpose," one that shapes generations to come.[1] It is about maintaining something that exhibits not only who you were but also who you are today and who you hope to be tomorrow.

But what happens when the needs of a community's present and future dictate not preservation but *destruction* of historic architecture? The answer to that question has long been obscured by the racialized overtones of preservationists, who embedded white supremacist ideologies into the built environment. For nearly its entire history, the historic preservation movement has been overwhelmingly white, focused on saving structures associated with white Americans, and consequently, as architectural historian and preservationist Brent Leggs notes, it has "neglected and undervalued Black sites."[2] And as Martinko shows, there is a long history to this, for nineteenth-century white preservationists crafted a racialized dichotomy wherein "savages and barbarians exhibited self-interest with temporary structures and architectural destruction . . . [while] civilized people advanced the commonweal with permanent architecture."[3] And in the nineteenth century, "savages and barbarians" was code for Indigenous and Black Americans, whose domestic architecture was epitomized in what white Americans regarded as flimsy, hastily constructed, and impermanent tipis and slave cabins. Permanent architecture—and, importantly, the maintenance of it—was seen as the morally superior option, one that reified the claims of racial superiority that undergirded the denial of citizenship and human rights to those deemed unworthy.

In ways that both challenged and upheld these conceptions of architecture and preservation, Black Americans in the late nineteenth and early twentieth centuries vociferously argued that obtaining rights required destroying historic structures. Acting as architectural historians and preservationists, they crafted a usable past that could demonstrate progress and improve the lives of Black Americans. Importantly, though, that usable past did not need material form in the present, for the lingering historical connection between slavery and architecture impaired the political project of racial uplift. By eliminating one form of historic and historical architecture from the landscape, they sought to construct a better present and future for their people.[4]

This essay focuses on an unrecognized moment in American preservation and architectural history: Black activists' Jim Crow–era crusade to demolish one-room cabins across the US South. While demolition is antithetical to preservation in its most rudimentary sense, destruction is an integral part of the practice of and scholarship on historic preservation. Indeed, as Max Page and Marla Miller suggest in their forward-looking anthology *Bending the Future: Fifty Ideas for the Next Fifty Years of Historic Preservation in the United States*, one of the most problematic and difficult matters for preservationists is "When do we let buildings die?"[5] Still, scholars have often ignored or minimized this question for those in the past, assuming (just as so many white nineteenth-century Americans did) that not preserving was somehow a less worthy choice.[6] But preservation is always a choice, never a given, and exploring moments when Americans decided in the negative provides us with new avenues to contemplate the meaning and function of architecture, history, and memory. It also encourages us to consider the underlying racialized assumptions of these fields that associate people's preservation choices with morality, intelligence, and civilization, or a lack thereof.

It was a bright, cloudless day in March 1896 when nearly one thousand Black men and women convened in the chapel of Tuskegee Normal and Industrial Institute's Porter Hall. They had come to Alabama from across the country for the fifth Tuskegee Negro Conference.[7] This annual meeting was an increasingly important and influential event, one that would help chart the path forward on a range of pressing issues for rural Black Southerners, from education and economy to public roads and the poll tax.[8] But when the Committee of Declarations announced the discussion topics for this year's convening, it was housing and a particular architectural form that topped the list: the one-room cabin.[9] For decades after emancipation, the majority of Black Southerners continued to live in one-room cabins similar to, or in many cases the exact same houses they had lived in under slavery. And this was seen as a major culprit holding back the race. "We are more and more convinced," the committee argued, "that we shall secure our rightful place as citizens in proportion as we possess Christian character, education, and property." Key to that, they declared, was "doing away with the one-room cabin," for this architectural form "is preeminently one source of the moral degradation of the negro."[10] The conference attendees proclaimed that much progress had been made on this front across the South, yet the issue's position atop the list of declarations made clear the work still to be done. Black Americans' progress, their present and their future, depended on it.

But it was in part the one-room cabin's connection to the past that made it such a target for Black activists. As Clark University professor William Henry Crogman maintained, "The first thing that should interest us is the fact that thousands of colored families in the South are still living in one-room cabins. Though the South is filled with our professors, ministers and smart politicians, yet few have attempted to teach these people the difference between a slave cabin and a Christian home."[11] The slave cabin was still pervasive across the rural South by 1901, when W. E. B. Du Bois further connected one-room cabins to Black Americans' past and present, arguing that it was "the home . . . which slavery bequeathed to freedom."[12] This architecture was so deeply and clearly connected to bondage that its continued existence and use was a hindrance to realizing the possibilities of emancipation. The one-room cabin materially represented the enslaved past that had morphed into the pernicious Jim Crow present: disfranchisement, segregation, lynching.

As they documented this present issue, what writers and activists like Crogman and Du Bois articulated was an architectural history. Of course, this was a housing form not exclusively constructed or lived in by Black people, but the connection between the one-room cabin, slavery, and Blackness was ensconced in American culture by the mid-nineteenth century. Jim Crow–era activists were well versed in the cultural products of this earlier age, when artists, writers, and cultural producers presented slave dwellings as dilapidated log cabins with a single disheveled, dirty, and uncomfortable room, often inhabited not by family but by random individuals forced to make these terrible living conditions livable.[13] For instance, Northern transplant Joseph Sadd had found that in the 1830s, enslaved Missourians "live generally in miserable huts, which are without floors, and have a single apartment only, where both sexes are herded promiscuously together."[14] In this way, abolitionists focused on one-room slave dwellings as a useful visual for clarifying the horrors, deprivations, and inhumanity of slavery.[15] Popular illustrated books like *Uncle Tom's Cabin* likewise circulated this idea and image around the nation and beyond, as did the material culture produced around the book and later play, including engravings, needlepoint, wallpaper, and transferware plates, which often featured small log cabins as the singular type of housing for slaves (fig. 8.1).[16] Although American culture at the time associated other individuals

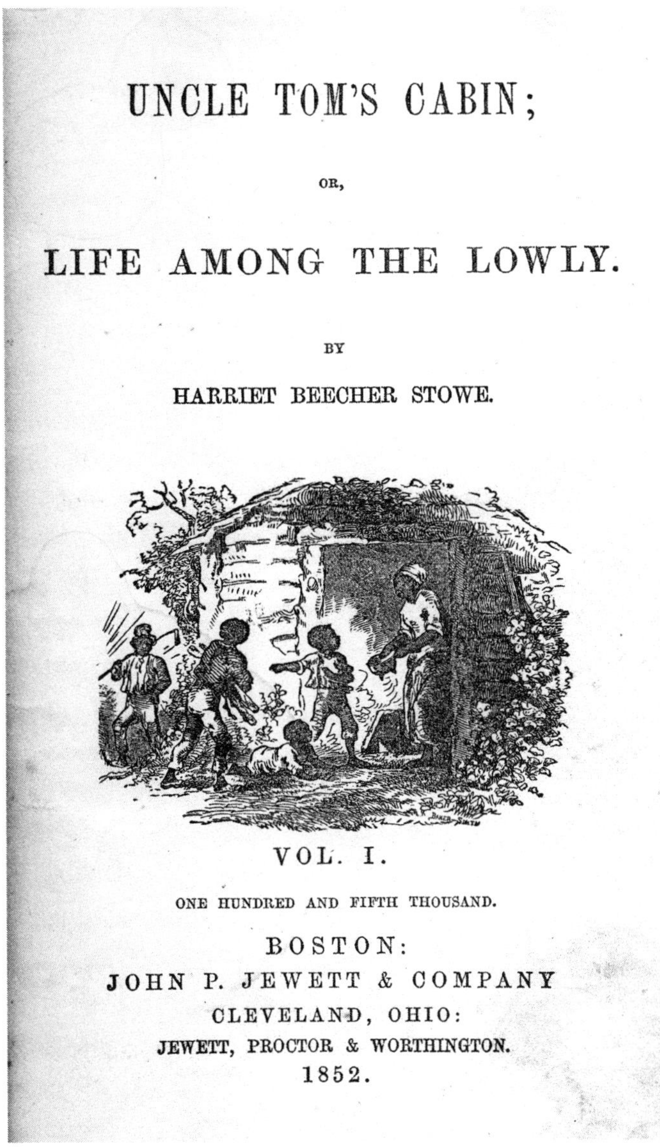

UNCLE TOM'S CABIN;

OR,

LIFE AMONG THE LOWLY.

BY

HARRIET BEECHER STOWE.

VOL. I.

ONE HUNDRED AND FIFTH THOUSAND.

BOSTON:

JOHN P. JEWETT & COMPANY

CLEVELAND, OHIO:

JEWETT, PROCTOR & WORTHINGTON.

1852.

FIGURE 8.1. *Title page featuring a very small log cabin. Harriet Beecher Stowe,* Uncle Tom's Cabin; or, Life Among the Lowly *(Cleveland, OH: John P. Jewett, 1852).*

and groups with the log cabin—for example, William Henry Harrison and Abraham Lincoln—it maintained a firm association with the peculiar institution in the nineteenth century, including after abolition.[17] Postbellum cultural products such as novels, travel accounts, sketches, paintings, photographs, postcards, and plays (including the wildly popular theatrical version of *Uncle Tom's Cabin*) continued to picture a small log cabin as the quintessential slave dwelling.[18] Indeed, the plethora of memoirs produced by Black writers in the decades after the Civil War contained discussions and drawings of the small houses they were born in, thereby utilizing the architectural form as a representation of their lives in slavery.[19] In so doing, Black Americans expressed and reaffirmed the historical connection between the one-room cabin and bondage, wielding this architectural history for their own purposes.

But this history was not confined to the past. Slavery and its attendant evils seemed to linger in the present one-room cabins prevalent in the Jim Crow South, and Black activists and writers demonstrated that continuation by wielding language strikingly similar to that of antebellum writers. Postbellum Black periodicals, conference proceedings, missionary and school reports, and memoirs described and pictured contemporary one-room cabins as cramped, unclean, and poorly ventilated or as overexposed living quarters with inadequate furnishings and a lack of privacy. Like Joseph Sadd four decades earlier, Frances Ellen Harper reported that the houses she encountered while traveling throughout the South in the 1870s were often "without a single window pane, where a whole family are living, parlor, chamber, and kitchen, all combined in one, and if you want light, you open the door, and the light and air both enter together through the cabins."[20] Du Bois, in *The Southern Workman*, included photographs of decrepit one-room dwellings along with descriptions of the "single rooms of logs or unceiled boards, with sometimes a small additional room, without glass windows, without stoves and with little furniture, [that] form the homes of the majority of the Negroes" (fig. 8.2).[21] Mary Church Terrell connected the materiality of the dwelling to the morality of its inhabitants, asserting in *The Southern Workman* that "when families of eight or ten men, women and children are all huddled promiscuously together in a single apartment, a condition common among our poor all over the land, there is little hope of inculcating morality and modesty."[22] The same exact language about materiality and morality—including the cabin's herding or huddling of people "promiscuously together"—had been used to describe slave dwellings throughout the antebellum South. Clearly, to these and other Black activists, "the old slave cabin [was] still the prototype of the present homes" of Black Southerners.[23]

The historical and contemporary connection between the one-room cabin and unfreedom informed the preservation pursuits of Black Americans during the Jim Crow era, and in this case the choice was to *not* preserve the material remains of their past. This did not signify that they wanted to erase or forget their

536 Southern Workman

The machinery of the state judiciary was, in many cases, after the withdrawal of the Freedmen's Bureau, used to place Negroes under the control of the state. "Vagrancy," theft, loitering, "impudence" and assault were the easily proven charges which forced large numbers of Negroes into penal servitude. The next step was to hire the labor of these persons to private contractors; thus was born the Convict Lease System. Many large planters conducted their plantations with such labor, and erected for them "barracks" and "stockades"—i. e., large enclosed quarters, guarded by high fences and crowded with inmates. These quarters were wretched, unsanitary and small, and the death rate of convicts was enormous. The Convict Lease System was however found to be better suited to certain large operations such as brickmaking, road building and mining, than to ordinary farming, and its use on the regular plantations was therefore limited, although not entirely discarded even to-day.

The share and rent systems of farming gradually came to replace the slave system in most cases. The best class of masters entered into contracts with their freed slaves and the latter worked on as hired laborers. There were, however, difficulties in the carrying out of this plan. The Negroes naturally felt like seeing something of the world after freedom came. To stay on the old plantation and pursue the same dull round of toil had little attraction for a people fired with new thoughts and new ambitions. It was therefore very difficult to stop the roving instinct of the new laborers. To some extent this was accomplished by offering better wages and better houses. Frame cabins and board floors came gradually to replace the worst of the slave

FIGURE 8.2. *W. E. B. Du Bois, "The Problem of Housing the Negro: III; The Home of the Country Freedman,"* Southern Workman *30, no. 10 (1901), 536.*

history writ large; in fact, this preservation choice was part of Black Americans' quest to find or create a usable past after slavery had prevented or destroyed so many individual, family, and community histories.[24] This quest took form through the burgeoning academic Black history movement led by scholars like Du Bois and Carter G. Woodson, but also through a rise in appreciation and publication of more vernacular and folk history methodologies.[25] Historical awareness and production did not necessarily equate to a desire to retain the material remains of it, however. The Black women and men who articulated an antipreservationist vision believed that demonstrating the race's progress from slavery was pivotal to securing rights, which meant getting rid of the lingering architectural stain of slavery in the Southern landscape. Thus the "abolishment of the one-roomed cabin and its attendant evils," as the Tuskegee Negro Conference proclaimed in 1896, became a central objective of reform-minded Black men and women.[26] That same year, the National Association of Colored Women proclaimed a "vigorous crusade" against the one-room cabin.[27] Six years later, in a speech at the

1902 Negro Young People's Education Congress, the urgency of this crusade was reasserted:

> The home is a citadel of strength[,] the castle of virtue and patriotism. Without it both society and the state must crumble; with it the high ideals of life must thrive. While home must not be judged by the height of the walls or the decorations thereof, still I am here to maintain that no families can be prepared for the battles of life with from six or seven living in one room. There is progressive work to be done along this line. More rooms: better homes.[28]

This kind of uplift would produce results beyond improvements in architecture. As Anna Julia Cooper noted in 1892, "We must point to homes, average homes, homes of the rank and file of horny handed toiling men and women of the South (where the masses are) lighted and cheered by the good, the beautiful, and the true,—then and not till then will the whole plateau be lifted into the sunlight."[29] In building better homes in the rural South, they could uplift all Black Americans during an era that sought to drag them back into the darkness. The present-day politics of Jim Crow, of having to demonstrate aptitude for rights and citizenship even after decades of freedom, therefore shaped Black Americans' relationship to their history and historic architecture.

In the Jim Crow present, not preserving one-room cabins was more important, more necessary, than preserving them. There was no talk of keeping the material remains of these historic buildings, even though many of them had in fact been witnesses to Black Americans' trauma in and triumph over slavery.[30] Instead, the one-room cabin's continued existence seemed to keep working-class Black Southerners in a subjugated state, unable to fully flourish and prove that they were deserving of the equality and rights they were currently denied. So, more and more, Black Southerners worked to rid the landscape of this architectural residue of slavery. By 1898, Black Virginians in Farmville had "established a building and loan association made up of men of their own race and are as rapidly as possible abandoning the old one-room cabin for frame houses with two or more distinct rooms."[31] The Tuskegee conference of that year noted "constant growth" in "replacing the one room cabin."[32] A 1901 article titled "One-Room Cabins Passing Away" described changes in rural Alabama, where one could "clearly see that the [Booker T.] Washington idea of doing away with the one-room cabin is largely put into practice."[33] A year later, another *Southern Workman* article proclaimed that "no greater evidence of progress, thrift and prosperity can be found" throughout the South than by the fact that "the one-room cabins that once constituted the homes of the colored people have given way to neat, clean, well-painted cottages—comfortable, and in many instances attractive homes."[34] The architecture of Black Americans' past was being replaced by an architecture of the future

FIGURE 8.3. *"Evolution of Farmers' Homes." Taken near Tuskegee Institute, this photograph shows the evolution of rural Black houses, from the one-room cabin of the past in the background to the multiroom houses of the present and future in the foreground. Courtesy of the American Antiquarian Society.*

(fig. 8.3).[35] This era required new dwellings, ones with multiple rooms that would "put into permanent form a record of [Black Americans'] remarkable progress under freedom."[36] As Morgan London Latta declared in his 1905 memoir, "It is time for us as a race to improve our condition, and forget the past and look forward to the future."[37]

Yet improving today and looking forward to a better tomorrow, one with houses of many rooms, did not mean completely erasing the past. It meant narrating a history that was useful for the present. And with the political project of racial uplift, Black activists knew they needed a *usable* history, for a progress narrative needed both before and after pictures. So even as they argued for the replacement of the one-room cabin in the contemporary landscape, they preserved and drew on primary sources that documented the architecture in its historic form. This included drawings of slave dwellings, which men such as Morgan London Latta, Thomas William Burton, Scott Bond, Peter Bruner, and even Booker T. Washington used in their memoirs to represent life in slavery (fig. 8.4). Several pages later appeared photographs of their current dwellings: painted, multiroom houses with windows, shutters, decorative features, and much more square footage, all meant to demonstrate that Black Americans had the capacity

THE OLD LOG CABIN IN WHICH THOMAS WAS BORN.
The little fellow by the door is Thomas.

FIGURE 8.4. *"The Old Log Cabin in Which Thomas Was Born." Thomas Burton,* What Experience Has Taught Me: An Autobiography of Thomas William Burton *(Cincinnati, OH: Jennings and Graham, 1910), 16.*

for improvement that freedom allowed and even necessitated (fig. 8.5).[38] Beyond the page, Booker T. Washington's grand, two-story, Queen Anne–style, red-brick home, built in 1899 and known as the Oaks, functioned as one of Tuskegee's social centers and as an example to all who passed through the institute that progress from slavery was not only possible but very real.[39] Plus, Tuskegee students learned architecture and carpentry, and visitors who attended the annual conferences likewise left with printed copies of building plans, all of which helped inculcate the architectural skills necessary to replace the old one-room cabins still dotting the rural South with the preferred multiroom houses that Washington and other activists argued for.[40]

For Jim Crow–era Black writers and activists, a usable architectural history of slavery was one relegated to books and photographs, no longer part of the Southern landscape. They saw their work as today and tomorrow oriented, just as many modern-day historians and preservationists do. The architect Paul Bentel, for instance, asserts that "historic preservation . . . [is] rooted in the issues of heritage politics in the present," while the National Park Service goes further to declare, "Historic preservation is a conversation with our past about our future."[41] In other words, we preserve what we want of the past in order to make the present better and build the kind of future we want. But with the one-room cabin connected to the evils of slavery that stubbornly persisted so long after emancipation, these Black Americans determined preservation was not the right choice for their people.

DR. THOMAS W. BURTON'S RESIDENCE,
Springfield, Ohio.

FIGURE 8.5. *"Dr. Thomas W. Burton's Residence." Thomas Burton,* What Experience Has Taught Me: An Autobiography of Thomas William Burton *(Cincinnati, OH: Jennings and Graham, 1910), image after p. 114.*

Their present- and future-oriented approach to the past has remained persistent, even as preservation debates and decisions about one-room cabins have changed over time. Remarkably soon after enacting a crusade to eradicate one form of historic architecture, the same activists launched the Black preservation movement with the quest to save Cedar Hill, the impressive and imposing mansion of Frederick Douglass.[42] But it would be decades before nonheroic sites of Black life, including one-room slave cabins, were regarded with the same preservationist fervor.[43] It would take the power and success of the civil rights movement to encourage the simultaneous growth of Black studies, social history, and vernacular architecture alongside community-led initiatives, a surge in monuments and memorials, and increasing attention from federal programs, all of which together produced a desire not only to study but to conserve the material remains of those long left out of the traditional historical narrative.[44]

It was not until the 2010s, though, that a true slave cabin preservation movement was underway, as public historians, preservationists, and descendants such as Joseph McGill Jr. and Jobie Hill called for these historic artifacts be preserved to tell a fuller history and create a better world. McGill, a public historian in South Carolina, gained national attention with the Slave Dwelling Project, whose mission is to promote the preservation of slave cabins to help tell "a more truthful and inclusive narrative of the history of the nation that honors the contributions of all our people." McGill believes that changing the historical narrative can help to change our nation, for in preserving slave dwellings, he means to "engage people in honest conversations about slavery, race, racism and racial equity in search of improved racial relations."[45] At the same time, Hill, an architectural historian and preservationist, was creating the Saving Slave Houses project, which seeks to document every extant slave dwelling in the country and in the process work to save them. As with McGill, Hill sees her work as simultaneously past, present, and future oriented: "It is vital for our national self-worth to give a voice to enslaved individuals and to recognize and present authentic and truthful accounts of slavery. Stories of enslaved people, told in part by the houses they inhabited, have the capacity to facilitate our nation's efforts to collectively move forward from the legacy of slavery."[46]

Over the past decade, more historic sites and museums have likewise sought to preserve slave dwellings and to interpret the history they represent—not the heroic narratives of those like Douglass or Washington, but rather the ordinary Americans who lived, loved, labored, and lost within these buildings they called home.[47] Perhaps most visibly, the highly anticipated National Museum of African American History and Culture ran an extensive publicity campaign about their 2013 acquisition of a one-room slave cabin from South Carolina (fig. 8.6). No one famous had lived there and nothing groundbreaking had happened there, but the Smithsonian had wanted it badly. In fact, it would be a central feature—or, as *Smithsonian* magazine called it, the "crown jewel"—of the new museum.[48] The museum saw this slave cabin is a crucial part of the history of African Americans and a particularly useful way of narrating that past, but it also looks toward tomorrow.[49] Lonnie G. Bunch III, the museum's founding director, felt that even

FIGURE 8.6. *Cabin from Point of Pines Plantation in Charleston County, South Carolina, 1853, restored and displayed at the National Museum of African American History and Culture. Collection of the Smithsonian National Museum of African American History and Culture, Gift of the Edisto Island Historic Preservation Society.*

though the cabin represents a difficult history, "it's ripe with optimism. It's ripe with hope."[50] And nothing is more future oriented than hope.

It has been more than a century since Black writers and activists launched a crusade against the one-room cabin, and times have changed. Twenty-first-century preservationists, historians, and others now argue that our own time necessitates a different usable past, one that preserves slavery's material remains. And yet the underlying mission remains the same: to craft a history that combats the persistent white supremacist logics that continue to undergird American society, and hopefully to construct a better world in the process.

Through their campaign against the one-room cabin, Black activists in the Jim Crow era developed unique arguments about preservation and architecture that scholars need to grapple with. These Black women and men are rarely, if ever, found in our scholarly canons. And that's because Black architectural history and preservation didn't always look or sound or function like those of white folks. Examining Black Americans' crusade against the one-room cabin reveals a more complicated history of architecture and historic preservation in the United States, one in which the racial politics of the Jim Crow present demanded the demolition of the historic built environment rather than its preservation. That history encourages us to expand the scope of what and who constitutes architectural history and preservation, to center the power and role of the political, and to expose the ways that historic preservation is never *only* about preservation. Sometimes, what we decide to tear down is just as important as what we keep.

Notes

1. Whitney Martinko, *Historic Real Estate: Market Morality and the Politics of Preservation in the Early United States* (University of Pennsylvania Press, 2020), 5.

2. Brent Leggs, "Growth of Historic Sites: Teaching Public Historians to Advance Preservation Practice," *Public Historian* 40, no. 3 (2018): 94. See also Elizabeth A. Lyon and Frederick W. Williamson, "The Preservation Movement Rediscovers America," in *African American Historic Places*, ed. Beth L. Savage (Preservation Press, 1994), 67.

3. Martinko, *Historic Real Estate*, 5.

4. I use the term "historic and historical architecture" here to signify how both those in the past and those in the present have understood Black Southerners' nineteenth-century one-room cabins. Black activists in the Jim Crow era saw them as historical: They were often older buildings directly associated with the past (the era of slavery, in this case). Today, preservationists, historians, descendants, and activists argue that these same buildings are in fact historic: They are places of deep significance to the history of families, communities, and the nation.

5. Max Page and Marla R. Miller, introduction to *Bending the Future: Fifty Ideas for the Next Fifty Years of Historic Preservation in the United States*, eds. Max Page and Marla R. Miller (University of Massachusetts Press, 2016), 17.

6. The National Park Service, for instance, argues that there are only four types of intervention with historic structures: "preserving, rehabilitating, restoring, and reconstructing." Anne E. Grimmer, *The Secretary of the Interior's Standards for the Treatment of Historic Properties*, rev. ed., parts 1 and 2 (US Department of the Interior, 2017). See also Norman Tyler, Ilene R. Tyler, and Ted J. Ligibel, *Historic Preservation: An Introduction to Its History, Principles, and Practice* (Norton, 2018).

7. John Quincy Johnson, *Report of the Fifth Tuskegee Negro Conference, 1896* (Baltimore: The Trustees, 1897), 7–10.

8. Over time, the conference focused more on political and social issues, rather than solely on moral,

educational, and material ones. See Emmett J. Scott, *The Tuskegee Negro Conferences* (Tuskegee Institute Press, 1904). See also Allen Jones, "Improving Rural Life for Blacks: The Tuskegee Negro Farmers' Conference, 1892–1915," *Agricultural History* 65, no. 2 (1991): 105–114.

9. Johnson, *Fifth Tuskegee Negro Conference*, 12–15.

10. Johnson, *Fifth Tuskegee Negro Conference*, 13.

11. William H. Crogman, *Progress of a Race or, The Remarkable Advancement of the Afro-American Negro* (Atlanta, GA: J. L. Nichols, 1898), 204.

12. W. E. B. Du Bois, "The Problem of Housing the Negro: II; The Home of the Slave," *Southern Workman* 30, no. 9 (1901): 493.

13. Some of the many nineteenth-century slave narratives that describe enslaved people's dwellings in this way include Charles Ball, *Fifty Years in Chains* (New York: H. Dayton, 1859); John Brown, *Slave Life in Georgia* (London: W. M. Watts, 1855); Martha Griffith Browne, *Autobiography of a Female Slave* (New York: Redfield, 1856); Lewis Garrard Clarke, *Narrative of the Sufferings of Lewis Clarke* (Boston: David H. Ela, 1845); Francis Fedric, *Slave Life in Virginia and Kentucky* (London: Wertheim, Macintosh, and Hunt, 1863); Josiah Henson, *Uncle Tom's Story of His Life* (London: "Christian Age" Office, 1876). Twentieth-century interviews with formerly enslaved people (including Works Progress Administration narratives) also typically depicted slave dwellings in this way. Eileen Southern and Josephine Wright have noted that artists illustrating the domestic lives of the enslaved typically did so by showing individuals or families gathered inside the small, often single apartments of living quarters or in front of a cabin. Eileen Southern and Josephine Wright, *Images: Iconography of Music in African-American Culture, 1770s–1920s* (Garland, 2000), 30–31.

14. Theodore Dwight Weld, *Slavery as It Is: Testimony of a Thousand Witnesses* (New York: American Anti-Slavery Society, 1839), 43.

15. The abolitionist Theodore Dwight Weld provided fourteen different witness testimonies about the reality of slave living conditions across the South, and more than half explicitly described the dwellings as containing a single room or apartment. Weld, *Slavery as It Is*, 43–44.

16. See John W. Frick, *"Uncle Tom's Cabin" on the American Stage and Screen* (Palgrave Macmillan, 2012), 21.

17. For more on the log cabin as both icon and shelter, particularly in nineteenth-century America, see Alison K. Hoagland, *The Log Cabin: An American Icon* (University of Virginia Press, 2018).

18. Of course, the reality of housing for enslaved people was not so homogenous, as the variety of dwellings and sleeping spaces for enslaved people throughout the American South and beyond was vast. For more, see John Michael Vlach, *Back of the Big House: The Architecture of Plantation Slavery* (University of North Carolina Press, 1993).

19. Dozens of examples can be found through the Documenting the American South database (https://docsouth.unc.edu/neh), including the use of cabin imagery in titles such as Peter Randolph, *From Slave Cabin to the Pulpit* (Boston: James H. Earle, 1893), and William H. Robinson, *From Log Cabin to the Pulpit* (James H. Tifft, 1913). In addition to books, newspapers also ran uplift stories that set their protagonists' beginnings in a cabin. For example, the *Afro-American* description of the "Remarkable Rise of a Man Who Came Up from a Log Cabin in Missouri to High Place of Honor in the Service of the National Government." R. Thompson, "Career and Work of W. T. Vernon," *Afro-American*, February 19, 1910.

20. Frances Ellen Watkins Harper, "Communications," *Christian Recorder*, December 24, 1870.

21. W. E. B. Du Bois, "The Problem of Housing the Negro: I; The Elements of the Problem," *Southern Workman* 30, no. 7 (1901): 393.

22. Mary Church Terrell, "Club Work of Colored Women," *Southern Workman* 30, no. 8 (1901): 436.

23. Du Bois, "Problem of Housing the Negro: I," 393. Du Bois is often juxtaposed with Booker T. Washington and the racial uplift movement at the core of the one-room cabin crusade, but his work relating to housing did have some tinges of uplift. In fact, the historian Shawn Michelle Smith complicates the image of Du Bois as a complete radical who refused racial uplift, particularly through analyzing his use of images, including photographs of dwellings. Shawn Michelle Smith, *Photography on the Color Line: W. E. B. Du Bois, Race, and Visual Culture* (Duke University Press, 2004).

24. For more on enslaved people's estrangement from personal or shared histories, see Orlando Patterson, *Slavery and Social Death: A Comparative Study* (Harvard University Press, 1982).

25. Jeffrey Aaron Snyder, *Making Black History: The Color Line, Culture, and Race in the Age of Jim Crow* (University of Georgia Press, 2018). For more on Black Americans' early twentieth-century quest for a usable past, particularly through folk and vernacular culture, see Catherine A. Stewart, *Long Past Slavery: Representing Race in the Federal Writers' Project* (University of North Carolina Press, 2016).

26. B. M. H., "The Tuskegee Negro Conference: From a Special Correspondent Declarations," *Outlook* 53, no. 12 (1896): 526; "The Colored Workers," *New York Times*, March 8, 1901.

27. Terrell, "Club Work of Colored Women," 436.

28. *Afro-American*, August 23, 1902.

29. Anna Julia Cooper, *A Voice from the South* (Xenia, OH: The Aldine Printing House, 1892), 31.

30. The phrase "witness to history" often refers to histories, interviews, and artifacts associated with the Holocaust, though architectural historians and theorists have applied it more broadly to what buildings can do. See Pierre von Meiss, *Elements of Architecture: From Form to Place + Tectonics*, 2nd ed., trans. Theo Hakola (EPFL Press, 2013), 196.

31. "A Study of Negro Life," *New York Times*, January 30, 1898.

32. "Farmer's Conference," *Christian Recorder*, March 24, 1898.

33. L. S. Peterson, "One Room Cabin Passing Away," *Star of Zion*, August 15, 1901.

34. J. C. Napier, "Real Estate," *Southern Workman* 31, no. 1 (1902): 11.

35. The final or end point of this evolution was not yet determined, as progress was still ongoing. Du Bois argued, for instance, that the final form and contribution of Black culture would not be a "servile imitation of Anglo-Saxon culture, but a stalwart originality." W. E. B. Du Bois, *The Conservation of Races* (Washington, DC: The Academy, 1897). This parallels but does not fully map onto progress or evolution narratives of architecture penned by white Americans in the early twentieth century, including Fiske Kimball, who was also highly influential in the era's developing historic preservation and historic house movements in the United States. See Lauren Weiss Bricker, "The Writings of Fiske Kimball: A Synthesis of Architectural History and Practice," *Studies in the History of Art* 35 (1990): 215–235.

36. This quote, from the preface to Crogman's book, refers specifically to the role of history and books in demonstrating progress, but the dozens of photographs of houses that Crogman included suggest that he and others also saw the power of architecture in making their arguments. Crogman, *Progress of a Race*, iii. Du Bois certainly did, including dozens of photographs of Black homes in his highly acclaimed Exhibit of American Negroes at the 1900 Paris Exposition. W. E. B. Du Bois, "The American Negro at Paris," *American Monthly Review of Reviews* 22, no. 5 (1900): 576–577.

37. Morgan London Latta, *The History of My Life and Work* (Rev. M. L. Latta, 1903), 107.

38. Latta, *History of My Life and Work*; Thomas William Burton, *What Experience Has Taught Me* (Jennings and Graham, 1910); Dan A. Rudd and Theophilus Bond, *From Slavery to Wealth: The Life of Scott Bond* (The Journal Printing Company, 1917); Peter Bruner, *A Slave's Adventures Toward Freedom* (N.p., 1918); Booker T. Washington, *The Story of My Life and Work* (W. H. Ferguson, 1900).

39. Ellen Weiss, *Robert R. Taylor and Tuskegee: An African American Architect Designs for Booker T. Washington* (New South Books, 2012), 177–178.

40. Ellen Weiss, "Tuskegee: Landscape in Black and White," *Winterthur Portfolio* 36, no. 1 (2001): 20.

41. Paul Bentel, "Where Do We Draw the Line? Historic Preservation's Expanding Boundaries," *Future Anterior: Journal of Historic Preservation History, Theory, and Criticism* 1, no. 2 (2004): 44–45; "What Is Historic Preservation?," National Park Service, https://www.nps.gov/subjects/historicpreservation/what-is-historic-preservation.htm.

42. In 1917, the National Association of Colored Women, the very same organization that had called for the "vigorous crusade" against the one-room cabin two decades earlier, spearheaded the effort to preserve Cedar Hill. Leggs, "Growth of Historic Sites," 91.

43. Robert Weyeneth encourages us to move beyond the preservation of what he calls "heroic architecture," or material examples of success, progress, and other "heroic" narratives. Robert R. Weyeneth, "The Architecture of Racial Segregation: The Challenges of Preserving the Problematical Past," *Public Historian* 27, no. 4 (2005): 40.

44. James O. Horton, "Social History and the African American Experience," in Savage, *African American Historic Places*, 17–23; Lyon and Williamson, "Preservation Movement Rediscovers America," 68–75; Dell Upton and John Michael Vlach, eds., *Common Places: Readings in American Vernacular Architecture* (University of Georgia Press, 1986); Dell Upton, *What Can and Can't Be Said: Race, Uplift, and Monument Building in the Contemporary South* (Yale University Press, 2015).

45. "About Us," Slave Dwelling Project, https://slavedwellingproject.org/about-us.

46. Home page, Saving Slave Houses, https://www.savingslavehouses.org.

47. Kristin Gallas and James DeWolf Perry, eds., *Interpreting Slavery at Museums and Historic Sites* (Rowman and Littlefield, 2014); Jennifer L. Eichstedt and Stephen Small, *Representations of Slavery: Race and Ideology in Southern Plantation Museums* (Smithsonian Institution Press, 2002); National Summit on Teaching Slavery, "Engaging Descendant Communities in the Interpretation of Slavery at Museums and

Historic Sites," *History News* 74, no. 1 (2019): 14–21; Julia Rose, *Interpreting Difficult History* (Rowman and Littlefield, 2016).

48. Haleema Shah, "This South Carolina Cabin Is Now a Crown Jewel in the Smithsonian Collections," *Smithsonian*, November 2, 2018, https://www.smithsonianmag.com/smithsonian-institution/south-carolina-cabin-has-become-crown-jewel-smithsonian-collections-180970681.

49. "Slave Cabin Donated to National Museum of African American History and Culture," National Museum of African American History and Culture, May 13, 2013, https://nmaahc.si.edu/about/news/slave-cabin-donated-national-museum-african-american-history-and-culture.

50. Shah, "This South Carolina Cabin."

PART III

TRANSNATIONAL AMERICAS

9 BORDER CROSSING

ARCHITECTURE IN BROWNSVILLE, TEXAS, AND HEROICA MATAMOROS, TAMAULIPAS, AS A CASE STUDY

Stephen Fox

WHERE DO WORKS OF ARCHITECTURE that do not figure in US architectural history fit in the historiography of US architecture? Nineteenth-century buildings in the adjoining border cities of Brownsville, Texas, and Heroica Matamoros, Tamaulipas, lie outside the historiographic canons of both nations. Yet these buildings materialize processes of horizontal cultural exchange precipitated by historical flows of commerce and migration, war and conquest, race and ethnicity, and individual subjectivity and agency that would eventually seep into the canon.[1] Matamoros and Brownsville, situated twenty-five miles upstream from the mouth of the Rio Grande / el río Bravo del Norte, constitute a provocative case study in challenging the epistemological borders of US architectural history: a geographical territory that, one hundred years after its initial European settlement in the middle of the eighteenth century, was forcibly divided between competing nation-states following the US victory in the US-Mexico War of 1846–1848. The architecture of the two cities and their hinterland demonstrates that the plural Americas, rather than a singular America, is a relevant historiographical frame in which to reconsider US architectural history in transnational terms.[2]

El Seno Mexicano / Nuevo Santander / Tamaulipas / Texas

Between 1821 and 1848, territory lying on the northeast (left) bank of the Rio Grande in what is today Texas transited from Spanish to Mexican to US control. As cultural geographer Daniel Arreola indicates, the Nueces River, 120 miles north of the Rio Grande, was fixed by Spanish colonial authorities in 1805 as the boundary between the Spanish viceregal provinces of Texas, to the north, and Nuevo Santander (known until 1749 simply as el Seno Mexicano, or the Mexican Gulf), to the south.[3] El Seno Mexicano / Nuevo Santander lay largely in the littoral between the Gulf of Mexico and the Sierra Madre Oriental mountain chain. The Sierra Madre isolated the Seno Mexicano from Nuevo León to the west, where the Spanish had established settlements by the end of the sixteenth century. On becoming a state of the Estados Unidos Mexicanos in 1824, Nuevo Santander was given a new Indigenous name: Tamaulipas.[4]

When US immigrants to Mexican Texas rebelled against Mexico between 1835 and 1836, they claimed the Rio Grande as the border between Texas and the rest of Mexico. Yet even after establishment of the Republic of Texas in 1836, Mexican settlements on both sides of the Rio Grande remained under Mexican jurisdiction.[5] In preparation for the US annexation of Texas in December 1845, the US Army landed at the mouth of the Nueces River, then marched south to the Rio Grande to claim the intervening territory for the United States, precipitating the US-Mexico War. The Treaty of Guadalupe Hidalgo, signed in February 1848, ended the war. Under the treaty's terms, the United States annexed over half of what had been Mexico's territory prior to the Texan rebellion. All of Tamaulipas northeast of the Rio Grande was incorporated into the new US state of Texas, including Matamoros's gulf port at Brazos de Santiago on the Laguna Madre.[6] Mexico in the nineteenth century was the world's foremost producer of silver.[7] Despite chronic political instability following independence from Spain in 1821, Mexico possessed enormous potential both as a source of minerals critical to the global economy and as a market for foreign goods. Annexing Matamoros's harbor at the Barra de Santiago gave the United States control of the maritime gateway to Northeastern Mexico.

Precolonial: El Seno Mexicano

Martín Salinas, in his book *Indians of the Rio Grande Delta*, cataloged thirty-one Indigenous communities living along the Lower Rio Grande by the middle of the eighteenth century.[8] Spanish colonial officials in 1747 and 1757 noted one community based on the right bank of the river, between the future site of Matamoros and the gulf, whose members were described as *negros* (Blacks) because of their dark skin. The Spanish presumed they were descendants of Africans who survived the wreck of a slave ship near the mouth of the river and were assimilated into Indigenous society.[9] Salinas observed that the *negros* affected regional material culture by introducing a new hunting instrument.[10] The Atlantic slave trade was one form of horizontal cultural exchange. As a result of this trade, African-descended people resident on the Lower Rio Grande preceded European-descended communities.

Settler Colonialism in the Eighteenth Century: Nuevo Santander

European occupation of the Seno Mexicano involved a deliberate program of settler colonialism organized from 1746 to 1748 by the Spanish Crown through its Kingdom of New Spain to populate the Seno Mexicano with European-descended families.[11] The settlement program was led by a Spanish-born military officer, José de Escandón y Helguera. Between 1749 and 1755, Escandón authorized the formation of twenty-two communities in the Seno Mexicano, to which he gave a new name: Nuevo Santander. Five of Escandón's communities, the northernmost outposts in Nuevo Santander and collectively known as the *villas del norte* (cities of the north), lay along or near the Rio Grande. Escandón did not locate any settlements in the broad delta of the Rio Grande because this coastal plain landscape was subject to the river's flood cycle.[12]

In 1767 Mexico's viceregal government authorized the distribution of private property to Escandón's settlers.[13] Privatization entailed surveying townsites for all settlements in Nuevo Santander, introducing versions of the plaza-centered, gridded townsites associated with Spanish colonial settlement, as architectural historian Jesús Franco Carrasco has shown.[14] In addition, Crown surveyors laid out *porciones*—long-lot tracts with frontage on streams—bracketing the townsites. The *porciones* provided pasturage for the town dwellers' livestock, since livestock raising was Nuevo Santander's primary economic activity.[15]

The surveying of plazas, streets, blocks, lots, and *porciones* functioned as a tool of colonialism by inscribing European concepts of spatial order and property ownership onto the land.[16] Once built up with one-story houses, town lots and the streets they faced lent themselves to the spatial shaping of urban community. Today the *villas del norte*—Laredo in Texas and Camargo, Mier, and the remnants of Guerrero Viejo in Tamaulipas—are defined as historic Mexican towns by their straight, narrow streets lined with one-story houses constructed of locally quarried sandstone.[17] Here, architecture materializes the "legal structure and social customs of land ownership."[18] Architecture also served to "construct, structure, and enforce ideas of racial difference," spatially distinguishing Nuevo Santander's "invasive settler society" from Indigenous *rancherías* (campsites) along the Lower Rio Grande.[19] The building type described in eighteenth-century documents as *cal y canto con azotea* (lime mortar and stone with a roof-deck) was supplemented by the jacal, a more common house type constructed of vertical wood stakes infilled with wood cordage, plastered outside and inside, and covered by a pitched roof thatched with grasses or palm fronds.[20] As is apparent today in the inner-city neighborhoods of Laredo, the homogeneous spatial continuity of masonry houses lining streets signified elite space. Lower-income neighborhoods were marked by freestanding structures, resulting in heterogeneous spatial gaps between buildings and along street fronts.

Privatization drew ambitious cattle ranchers from Camargo and Reynosa into the delta to claim territory lying beyond the network of *porciones*. In 1774, thirteen stock owners from Camargo and Reynosa secured 490,000 acres on the southwest bank of the Rio Grande, extending forty miles upstream from the river's mouth, which they subdivided into eight ranches. By 1784, the townsite of San Juan de los Esteros Hermosos was surveyed on the river's southwest bank on one of the ranches. In 1793, San Juan was renamed Congregación del Refugio. When it was chartered as a *villa* (city) in 1826, el Refugio was renamed again: Matamoros, to commemorate the Mexican independence patriot, Mariano Matamoros.[21] Along the Lower Rio Grande, town formation in the eighteenth century functioned as a technology of settler colonialism, spatially marking the imposition of new regimes of political, economic, and cultural authority.

Mercantile Colonialism: Trade and Architecture

Matamoros received authorization as a port that could engage in international trade in 1823.[22] New Orleans merchants drove this mercantile colonial process as they sought access to Mexican markets that Spain had kept closed to foreigners. Ramón Lafon, a French immigrant to New Orleans, is credited with discovering that the Laguna Madre, just inside the Barra de Santiago and north of the mouth of the river, provided the best natural harbor for gulf navigation.[23] In 1839, the Mexican novelist, economist, and public official Manuel Payno additionally credited Lafon with introducing brickmaking to Matamoros, compensating for the lack of stone in the alluvial soil of the delta.[24] At Matamoros, mercantile colonialism was overlaid on the earlier project of settler colonialism. In a speech delivered in April 1844, US Senator Thomas Hart Benton identified Matamoros's special role in North Atlantic trade. Benton described Matamoros as critical to the triangular trade involving slave-grown cotton from the Mississippi River Valley, exported through the port of New Orleans to textile mills in Europe, then shipped back through the port of New Orleans as finished fabric to be exported to Matamoros and other Mexican gulf ports in exchange for silver.[25] Benton asserted that nearly 80 percent of US silver imports, essential for the minting of American coinage and the stabilization and expansion of the domestic economy, entered the United States from Mexico through the port of New Orleans.[26]

In an article published in a Mexico City newspaper almost concurrently with Benton's speech, Manuel Payno described Matamoros's rapid transition from a village composed of jacales to a city in which "bricks were made and lumber was imported to build as if by magic, houses, some as magnificent and beautiful and almost equal to those of the United States."[27] The most substantial Matamoros houses reproduced the two-story New Orleanian Creole merchant's house type. Matamoros's Casa Lojero of 1836 bore a striking resemblance to the Perrilliat House of 1825 in the French Quarter of New Orleans.[28] Matamoros also had its versions of the one-story Creole cottage framed by gabled brick end walls rising in raking parapets above pitched, wood-shingled roofs.[29] Unlike the flat-roofed, plaster-faced stone houses of the *villas del norte*, the exterior surfaces of Matamoros's brick houses were articulated with creolized classical detail. Pilasters with molded brick caps rose from bases. The pilasters framed entablatures constructed with courses of molded brick.[30] In 1821, the parochial vicar of Matamoros's parish, Nuestra Señora del Refugio, contracted with a French-born New Orleanian master builder, Mateo Passement, to build a new brick church facing the Plaza de Armas (now the Plaza Hidalgo). The church (now Catedral de Nuestra Señora del Refugio) was completed in 1833.[31]

The emergence of Matamoros as a mercantile colonial outpost of New Orleans resonates with a point that Benton emphasized in his speech: The Matamoros trade was driven by transnational market flows rather than US government policy.[32] It was the potential for profit that Matamoros possessed as the trade gateway to Northern Mexico, and as a conduit for Mexican silver, that generated the flow of US and European merchants and goods into Matamoros. The aggressive economic imperialism advanced by transnational agents can be inferred from the density of brick Creole merchant houses and side-gabled, one-story, brick cottages that still stand in the center of Matamoros—architectural evidence of the impact of horizontal exchange emanating from New Orleans.[33]

Interconnected History of Place and Race

Matamoros's transnational architectural legacy incorporates a racial stratum that inverted the legally constituted racial hierarchy of the United States. As state, parish, and local governments began to suppress the liberties of free people of color in Louisiana following the Louisiana Purchase, there was a diaspora of Afro-Creoles from New Orleans to Matamoros and to Tamaulipas's other port city, Tampico.[34] The Matamoros architect and engineer Alfredo Bartolomé Passement (1800–1868) was part of this diaspora of free people of color. According to a death notice published in Brownsville's *Daily Ranchero* newspaper on August 2, 1868, and reprinted in New Orleans's *Daily Picayune*, Bartolo Passement was "one of a number of Creoles of Louisiana who came to Matamoros about the year 1832. Many settled and remained here, while others went into the interior."[35] The report ascribed to Passement the design of Nuestra Señora del Refugio (he seems to have reconstructed the church's facade and towers, which were toppled in the hurricane of August 1844). An indication of Passement's standing in Matamoros was his participation as one of three prominent citizens called on to persuade the Texan rancher Juan Nepomuceno Cortina to curtail an armed attack Cortina mounted on Brownsville on September 28, 1859.[36] Although only fragmentary information about Passement's career has yet been discovered, it is clear that the impact he made on contemporaries was sufficient to rupture the code of silence that would otherwise have prevailed in the US press when it came to acknowledging the life of a distinguished immigrant to Mexico of African descent.

Mercantile Colonialism: The Nineteenth-Century Accommodationist Strategy

Cortina's attack on Brownsville was an outgrowth of the US victory in the US-Mexico War. The war changed social, political, and architectural dynamics along the Lower Rio Grande as new towns were founded opposite Matamoros and the *villas del norte* along what had become an international border.[37] Brownsville was initially the most important of these new trade centers. The historian David Montejano has described the consensus that emerged on the Texan side of the Lower Rio Grande as a "peace structure": "an accommodation between the victorious Anglos and the defeated Mexican elite" that entailed "the subordination of Mexicans to Anglos in matters of politics and authority, and . . . the accommodation between new and old elites." Montejano identifies one mechanism for achieving such accommodation: "American merchants and lawyers . . . intermarried and became an extension of the old elite."[38] Assimilation facilitated mercantile colonialist priorities and deflected the impact of Anglo-American settler colonial attitudes and practices along the new border, where people of Mexican descent remained the overwhelming majority of the numerically small population; where Spanish, not English, was the primary language; and where Mexican and US currencies were interchangeable because both were minted in silver.[39] Accommodation did not prevent episodes of violent resistance, such as Cortina's raid, which in turn provoked equally violent, and often indiscriminate, reprisals.

Brownsville's architectural development contrasted spatially with that of Matamoros. Brownsville's gridded town plan was surveyed in August 1848 for Charles Stillman, a US merchant from Wethersfield, Connecticut, who had immigrated to Matamoros in 1828. The Brownsville townsite adjoined Fort Brown, the new US Army post opposite Matamoros's steamboat landing, and had frontage on the Rio Grande a mile upriver from Matamoros. Two of the new city's streets—Levee and St. Charles—bore the names of streets in New Orleans.[40] In a show of US nationalism, most of the streets parallel to Levee and St. Charles were named for US presidents. Only one street, Frontón, bore a Spanish name.[41] Unlike Matamoros, with its hierarchical array of parish church and *palacio municipal* (city hall) facing each other across the Plaza de Armas, Brownsville's town plan was all business. When Brownsville was incorporated as a city in 1850, the new city government carved Market Square out of the center of one of Stillman's town blocks.[42]

The Brownsville streets nearest Front Levee, facing the Rio Grande, were lined with one- and two-story brick business houses occupied by US and European merchants. Brick-built merchants' houses served primarily as business buildings, although Stillman lived in his no-longer-extant, patio-centered brick compound on Front Levee, as did the Spanish immigrant merchant José San Román Palacio, who occupied a brick New Orleanian-type merchant's house (1850) with raking side parapets and a pitched roof on Elizabeth Street, a block from Front Levee. The Mexican-born merchant Francisco Yturria built his two-story brick business house (1854) in the same block of Elizabeth Street as San Román's. Brownsville's dominant dwelling house type, however, was the Anglo-American wood cottage with side-gabled roof and front veranda, even though the milled lumber from which such houses were constructed had to be shipped from New Orleans, Mobile, or Florida.[43]

Brownsville's City Market House (1850–1852), constructed in Market Square, exemplified the hybridization of type, materials, construction technique, and building professionals that first appeared in Matamoros and was then translated to Brownsville. The City Market House was erected by John P. McDonough, an English immigrant carpenter, and Adolphe Seuzeneau (1807–1879), a New Orleanian brickmason who transited between New Orleans and Matamoros before moving to Brownsville after the US-Mexico War. In its original configuration, the City Market House was an arcaded, two-story, Anglo-American public building type. But it was built according to Matamoros construction practices.[44] Fusing Mexican, US, New Orleanian Creole, and European techniques and typologies into a transnational architectural vernacular, the border-brick style was a cultural hybrid that straddled national categories, making the plural Americas more relevant than the singular America in framing this development.

In contrast to this accommodationist approach, the most impressive work of architecture built in Brownsville in the 1850s conceded little to local practice. The Immaculate Conception Church (now Cathedral), built between 1854 and 1859, is an example of the modern revival of Gothic architecture. Richard Cleary has examined the career of the French immigrant priest and architect Pierre-Yves Kéralum (1817–1872), who designed and built Immaculate Conception Church. The adjoining rectory, the Oblate Community House (1861, altered), exemplifies border-brick-style practices, introducing an architectural dichotomy between the modernity of the church (and Father Kéralum's awareness of contemporary European and US architectural discourses) and the "hyperlocal" vernacular practices materialized in the rectory, which, like the City Market House, is an architectural hybrid.[45]

In comparing mid-nineteenth-century Brownsville to Matamoros, it is apparent that Brownsville inverted Mexican urbanization practices by displaying greater architectural/typological and urban/suburban spatial heterogeneity than did Matamoros, despite the strong imprint of Matamoros building practices on Brownsville. Spatial heterogeneity in Brownsville did not signal reduced social status. Instead, it distinguished between commercial and residential precincts, a typological difference that did not pertain in Matamoros. In Brownsville, brick construction was not socially superior to wood construction. Rather, each was associated with different building types, mirroring the work/home duality of middle-class Anglo-American culture.

Reverse Flow: The Matamoros Cotton Trade

Brownsville and Matamoros were transformed by the US Civil War because Matamoros was the port closest to the Confederacy not subject to the US Navy's blockade of Southern shipping. Matamoros became the gateway through which Confederate cotton flowed to Europe and the United States. This ignited an economic boom lasting from 1862 until the defeat of the Confederacy in spring 1865.[46] Wealth generated by the flow of Confederate cotton through Matamoros attracted a new generation of building professionals from New Orleans.[47] The Massachusetts-born Henry A. Peeler (1833–1907), an engineer from New Orleans, designed the major cultural institution erected in nineteenth-century Matamoros, the Teatro de la Reforma (1865, demolished), and, across the street from it, the expansive Matamoros business house (1866) of the Brownsville merchant Francisco Yturria.[48] Two other building professionals—the Pennsylvania-born, Ohio-raised Samuel W. Brooks (1829–1903) and the Norwegian-born Martin Hanson (1825–1902)—migrated during the war from New Orleans to Matamoros, where they were joined by a Scottish immigrant to Texas, George More (1826–1872). Brooks, Hanson, and More spent the rest of their careers in Brownsville and Matamoros.

Peeler, Brooks, Hanson, and More renewed the architectural accommodation strategy visible in Brownsville in the 1850s, assimilating to prevailing typologies, especially the Matamoros merchant's house type—updating ornamental details, as architectural historian Eduardo Alarcón Cantú observes, but adhering to received construction techniques.[49] This was evident in More's two major institutional buildings in Brownsville, St. Joseph College (1868, demolished) and the Convent of the Incarnate Word and Blessed Sacrament (1869, demolished), both examples of the Matamoros border-brick base-pilaster-and-entablature system.[50] Within a few years of beginning his forty-year career on the Rio Grande, S. W. Brooks won the contract to build the Post Hospital at Fort Brown (1869), an architectural hybrid. As architectural historian Willard B. Robinson has determined, the design of the hospital was based on diagrams published by the US Surgeon General's Office in 1867.[51] But Brooks built the one- and two-story building with Matamoros-type brick pilasters framing an arched ground-floor gallery.

Brooks was aware of broader trends, as architectural historian Margaret Culbertson discovered when she identified a published source for one of Brooks's major surviving houses, the two-story Casa Cross in Matamoros (1885).[52] Casa Cross stands out in the fabric of Matamoros's Zona Centro because it is a freestanding villa, set in a fenced garden, in contrast to the typology of continuous street fronts and interior patios that dominates the center of the city. The house architecturally marked the family of Melitón H. Cross and his wife, Marie Eduwiges Lamarque, a New Orleanian Creole, as US immigrants to Mexico. The Crosses became Mexican because M. H. Cross's father, John S. Cross, a South Carolinian who came to Texas in 1848 via Lowndes County, Mississippi, was the father of four children by his enslaved companion Lydia. In the US census of 1850, Lydia and three of their children, including Middleton (M. H. Cross's birth name), were enumerated in the slave schedule.[53] From a US perspective, Casa Cross was radical in subverting the use of architecture as a tool of segregation. The house symbolically refutes the proposition that racial difference constituted an impediment to social equality and respectability. It spatially challenged the unequal distribution of resources naturalized by the (white) sociopolitical construction of the US racial hierarchy.

Until the end of his career, Brooks perpetuated assimilationist architectural practices. His typologically "American" buildings include surviving brick houses in Brownsville's West End for Emilia Campbell and Louis Kowalski (1893) and for María Josefina Glaevecke de Browne (1894). Among his typologically "Mexican" designs is El Alamo, a one-story brick merchant's house (1893), built for Manuela Alcalá de Bouis, the Matamoros-born widow of a Mexican immigrant grocer.[54]

Martin Hanson's body of work is not as well documented as that of Brooks. If a later architectural attribution is accurate, Hanson may have been responsible for a series of substantial, two-story brick corner store complexes erected in the residential neighborhoods of Brownsville in the early 1890s—most built for Spanish immigrants and all perpetuating the Matamoros merchant's house type.[55] Brooks's and Hanson's masonry buildings were consistently detailed with the creolized classical attributes of the Matamoros border-brick style. After the US Civil

War, Matamoros-type brick buildings based on Mexican typologies and exhibiting border-brick details spread upriver to Hidalgo, Rio Grande City, Roma, and Laredo, Texas, as well as to Camargo and Nuevo Laredo, Tamaulipas.[56] Although the lack of Spanish surnames among Brownsville building professionals identified in nineteenth-century Anglophone newspaper reports stands out, *The Brownsville Herald* did note in May 1894 that Brooks had received a photo of a new house in San Antonio, sent by the Brownsville-born Baltasar Torres (1860–1926). The photo's inscription read, "This being my first work is respectfully dedicated to my teacher S. W. Brooks. Baltasar Torres, Arch. and Bldr., San Antonio."[57]

Reports in *The Brownsville Herald* in the 1890s referring to Brooks and to Martin Hanson Jr. (1857–1916), who succeeded to his father's practice after the elder Hanson retired to New Orleans in 1892, used different professional identifiers—architect, engineer, contractor, surveyor—related to the type of work each news report described. In addition to functioning in different disciplinary capacities, More, Brooks, and the younger Hanson also held public office. More served as a city alderman, and Brooks and Hanson held various appointed positions. During the 1890s Brooks was also regional agent for the Springfield Architectural Iron Works of Springfield, Ohio.[58] Such professional nonspecialization suggests the range of moneymaking skills that building professionals drew on to remain gainfully employed. Drafting designs for buildings and administering their construction were too tenuous economically to be practiced in isolation.[59]

The economic imperative of being multifaceted and flexible was out of step with the trajectory of professional specialization in the decades after the Civil War, not only in the largest cities in the United States but also in those of Texas. The continued use of such old-fashioned practices on the Lower Rio Grande reflected the sharp decline of Brownsville and Matamoros as economic gateways after railroad connections between the United States and Mexico—first at Laredo in 1881, two hundred miles upriver from Brownsville, then through El Paso and Eagle Pass, Texas, even farther upriver—diverted trade routes. Located on the wrong side of the Sierra Madre Oriental, Brownsville and Matamoros were geographically marginalized. For the last two decades of the nineteenth century, Brownsville and Matamoros subsisted in what might be termed the long 1870s, a condition reflected in the perpetuation of pre–Civil War architectural practices and typologies in both cities. Because Brownsville and Matamoros would not gain access to the rail systems of their respective nations until 1904, economic flow in the South Texas borderlands moved from the city to the countryside during the 1880s.

Urban to Rural: Capitalist Ranching

The wealth generated by the Matamoros cotton trade contributed to the capitalist transformation of cattle ranching in the 1870s in the *llanos mesteños* (wild horse plains), the sand plains between the Rio Grande Delta and the Nueces River. The Brownsville steamboat captains Mifflin Kenedy and Richard King invested their wartime profits in aggressively expanding their livestock operations in the *llanos mesteños*.[60] King multiplied his holdings, which amounted to 614,000 acres at the time of his death in 1885.[61] Kenedy and his Mexican-born wife, Petra Vela, assembled the 440,000-acre Rancho La Parra in 1882.[62] Both King and Kenedy were modernizers, improving livestock herds through scientific management, fencing their pastures with barbed wire, installing windmills to pump groundwater, and investing in railroad construction. Railroads made it possible to ship livestock to meat-processing centers rather than herding them on long-distance cattle drives or simply harvesting their hides, horns, hooves, bones, and tallow.[63] Barbed-wire fencing, a potent new technology for enforcing the prerogatives of property, ended the open-range pasturing of livestock practiced since the eighteenth century, squeezing out smaller (usually Mexican-descended) ranchers.[64] The arid climate of the *llanos mesteños* additionally exposed cattle owners to crises of sustainability, evident when a prolonged drought that began in 1888 intersected with the Panic of 1893, a global economic contraction, and led to the collapse of markets for agricultural commodities and agricultural land values. The historian Armando C. Alonzo has correlated this convergence of cycles with the steepest decline of Texas Mexican land ownership in South Texas counties as ranchers defaulted on loans during the 1890s or sold their land to pay off debts.[65]

The capitalist ethos with which Mifflin Kenedy pursued ranching operations, and his involvement in constructing railroads across the South Texas borderlands prior to his death in 1895, displayed his capacity for entrepreneurial innovation. Kenedy's son and successor, John G. Kenedy, and his New Orleanian wife, Marie Stella Turcotte, marked their economic standing by commissioning the San Antonio architect Henry T. Phelps (1871–1944) to design a grandiose California Mission–style house at Rancho La Parra in 1917, clearly influenced by the even grander Mission-style house that Richard King's widow, Henrietta Chamberlain King, and her son-in-law, Robert J. Kleberg, built at the adjoining Santa Gertrudis Ranch in 1912.[66] In the *llanos mesteños*, the modern California Mission style architecturally advertised the ranch owners to an Anglo-American audience as patriarchal inheritors of a century-and-a-half-long tradition of Mexican livestock ranching, even though their fortunes derived from the intersection of wartime commodity and transportation flows. The long-term economic dividends of the Matamoros cotton trade spilled over the historic borderline of the Nueces River to be materialized in architecture recognized in the canon. In 1899, Charles Stillman's Brownsville-born son and heir, James Stillman, bought the former Merchants Exchange Building at 55 Wall Street in New York City, commissioning McKim, Mead & White to double its size in 1904 to become headquarters of the National City Bank, of which Stillman and subsequently his grandson and namesake, James Stillman Rockefeller, were presidents.[67]

Horizontalizing the Historical Frame

What does the historiography of architecture in the United States gain by taking Brownsville and Matamoros into account? Inverting historiographic narratives and horizontalizing frames of reference demonstrate that the diversity of historical subjects and the contingencies of history are as relevant to interpreting the past as to understanding the present. Town founding and the descriptive, legal, and architectural tactics employed to naturalize claims to property and privatization stand out as space-shaping practices applied in different formats by successive generations of newcomers, empowered by regimes of legal authority to confirm or overturn prior arrangements. When railroads arrived in Brownsville and Matamoros in 1904, they set off a new cycle of settler colonialism in South Texas that eclipsed previous episodes because of the newcomers' systematic efforts to subordinate and segregate the region's Mexican-descended and Mexican immigrant population. The nineteenth-century buildings of Matamoros and Brownsville materialize the cyclical flows of capital and populations and distinguish between the totalizing practices of eighteenth-century (and twentieth-century) settler colonialism and the assimilationist strategy of nineteenth-century mercantile colonialism. Successive iterations of what constitutes the modern track expanding scales of operation.

The history of architecture along the Lower Rio Grande highlights the inadequately studied role of New Orleans as a center of American capital and cultural flows during the long nineteenth century.[68] On the Rio Grande, the formation and replication of a transnational architectural vernacular, the Matamoros border-brick style, materialized the New Orleanian Creole connection, as do the careers of the building professionals who extended these practices into the first decades of the twentieth century.[69] In bringing classical and vernacular streams together in a contrapuntal narrative, the border-brick style materialized places, transnational communities, and building professionals not represented in canonical surveys.[70]

Matamoros inverted the oppressive racial hierarchy that still prevails in the United States by subverting white US stereotypes of racial and ethnic inferiority. In nineteenth-century Matamoros, such African-descended people as the architect Bartolo Passement and the merchant, architectural client, and former slave Melitón H. Cross were agents of cosmopolitan cultural modernization, as had been the eighteenth-century *negros*.[71]

The creolized classicism of nineteenth-century borderlands architecture calls attention to a broad spectrum of US architecture derived from *novohispano* (colonial Spanish) practices—from St. Augustine and Pensacola, Florida, to New Orleans, the Mississippi River Valley, Texas, New Mexico, Arizona, and California. This US cultural landscape was marked architecturally by encounters with Indigenous, Cuban, Haitian, Franco-Canadian, Mexican, and Anglo-American cultural streams. What is apparent, even in a simple listing, is the hybrid, contingent, noncanonical orientation of this body of material culture, in contrast to the exclusionary tendencies associated with what the Brownsville-born literary critic José David Saldívar humorously describes as every canon's need of a disciplinary "border patrol."[72] Canonical border crossing is one method of horizontalizing historiographic frames of research and interpretation. Resisting exclusion is another. Hyperlocalized histories may narrow the range of works of architecture to be examined. But they also have the capacity to expand the critical perspectives from which such works can be surveyed.

Acknowledgments

The author is grateful to the organizers of the Society of Architectural Historians' Race and the Historiography of American Architecture project—Charles L. Davis II, Joanna Merwood-Salisbury, and Kathryn E. Holliday—and to Kathryn O'Rourke and other participants in the sessions of July 28, 2021, and August 25–26, 2022. Their concepts, critiques, and in many cases exact words shaped this essay. The author also thanks Daniel D. Arreola, Juan Ignacio Barragán Villarreal, Patricia Brady, Frank Briscoe Jr., Edward R. Burian, Thomas B. Carroll, Augustine Celaya III, Richard Cleary, Margaret Culbertson, Tara A. Dudley, Eugene Fernández, Gregory Free, Adrián Garza Dragustinovis, Virginia Haynie Gause, George R. Gause Jr., Mary Gehman, Mary Carolyn Hollers and W. Eugene George, Nydia Tapia-Gonzales, Miguel Angel González Quiroga, Manuel Humberto González Ramos, Manuel Hinojosa, Patrick Kelly, Anthony Knopp, Lawrence V. Lof, Rafael Longoria, Mark Lund, Katherine Moore and James A. McAllen Jr., Mary Margaret McAllen, Roman McAllen, Reba Cárdenas McNair, Clemente Rendón de la Garza, Carlos Rugerio Cázares, Martín Salinas Rivera, Mario L. Sánchez, Anatole Senkevitch Jr., Alexander Stillman, Eduardo Valent, Juan Vélez, Ambrosio Villarreal, Frank D. Yturria, and Antonio Zavaleta.

Notes

1. Prospectus, "Race and the Historiography of American Architecture Publication Workshop," Society of Architectural Historians, July 28, 2021 (hereafter cited as "Race and Historiography Workshop").

2. Kathryn E. Holliday, "Race and Historiography Workshop"; Charles L. Davis II, "Race and Historiography Workshop."

3. Daniel D. Arreola, *Tejano South Texas: A Mexican American Cultural Province* (University of Texas Press, 2002), 28–30.

4. Octavio Herrera Pérez, *Tamaulipas: Historia breve* (Fondo de Cultura Económica, Fideicomiso Historia de las Américas y Colegio de México, 2010), 67.

5. A. Ray Stephens, *Texas: A Historical Atlas* (University of Oklahoma Press, 2010), 70–121.

6. Jerry D. Thompson, "Historical Survey," in *A Shared Experience: The History, Architecture, and Historic Designations of the Lower Rio Grande Heritage Corridor*, ed. Mario L. Sánchez (Texas Historical Commission, 1994), 40–46.

7. Mario Cerutti, "Comercio, guerras y capitales en torno al río Bravo," in *El norte de México y Texas (1848–1880)*, by Mario Cerutti and Miguel A. González Quiroga (Instituto Mora, 1999), 25. Cerutti singles out LeRoy P. Graf, "The Economic History of the Lower Rio Grande Valley, 1820–1875" (PhD diss., Harvard University, 1942), as identifying the key economic factors driving the development of Matamoros's port city economy. See also Octavio Herrera Pérez, *Matamoros: Historia de una ciudad heroica, leal e invicta en la frontera y noreste de México* (Quintanilla Ediciones, 2018), 46–47; David Montejano, *Anglos and Mexicans in the Making of Texas, 1836–1986* (University of Texas Press, 1987), 16, 18; Miguel Angel González Quiroga, *War and Peace on the Rio Grande Frontier, 1830–1880* (University of Oklahoma Press, 2020), 56–57, 93–94.

8. Martín Salinas, *Indians of the Rio Grande Delta: Their Role in the History of Southern Texas and Northeastern Mexico* (University of Texas Press, 1990). Salinas underscores the extent to which the river, the only perennial stream for 120 miles to the north and 75 miles to the south, sustained communal life in the delta, the flat coastal plain, and the arid uplands of the Rio Grande plain. Pre-European Indigenous architectural types survive in Tamaulipas in the form of the *ramada*, a brush arbor shelter. Jesús Franco

Carrasco also identifies the Indigenous groups associated in historical records with the communities of Nuevo Santander in *El Nuevo Santander y su arquitectura* (UNAM, Instituto de Investigaciones Estéticas, 1991), vol. 1, 58–66. In addition, see Dylan Baddour, "Forgotten Keepers of the Rio Grande Delta," *Texas Observer* 116 (May/June 2024): 20–29.

9. Salinas, *Indians of the Rio Grande Delta*, 30, 54–55, 126, 132, 136.

10. Charles L. Davis II, "Race and Historiography Workshop." According to Salinas, Spanish colonial sources noted that the *negros*, unlike other Indigenous communities along the river corridor, used spears, presumed to be a weapon of West African origin, in addition to bows and arrows. Salinas, *Indians of the Rio Grande Delta*, 55, 126.

11. John W. Reps, *Cities of the American West: A History of Frontier Urban Planning* (Princeton University Press, 1979), 71–75.

12. The river's delta comprises the Texas counties of Hidalgo and Cameron (the Lower Rio Grande Valley of Texas) and the Tamaulipecan *municipios* of Reynosa, Río Bravo, Valle Hermoso, and Matamoros. Herbert Eugene Bolton, *Texas in the Middle of the Eighteenth Century: Studies in Spanish Colonial History and Administration* (Russell & Russell, 1962), 291–303; Lawrence Francis Hill, *José de Escandón and the Founding of Nuevo Santander: A Study in Spanish Colonization* (Ohio State University Press, 1926); Florence Johnson Scott, *Historical Heritage of the Lower Rio Grande Valley* (Texian Press, 1966).

13. Escandón encountered resistance from his *novosantanderino* settlers because of his reluctance to grant titles to private property. The historian Octavio Herrera Pérez argues that Escandón feared that property ownership would lead to competition and conflict within settlements. Herrera Pérez, *Tamaulipas*, 49.

14. Franco Carrasco, *El Nuevo Santander*, vol. 1, 196–201, and vol. 2, 345–352, 395–400, 407–411.

15. Armando C. Alonzo, *Tejano Legacy: Ranchers and Settlers in South Texas, 1734–1900* (University of New Mexico Press, 1998), 75; Jack Jackson, *Los Mesteños: Spanish Ranching in Texas, 1721–1821* (Texas A&M University Press, 1986).

16. Kathryn E. Holliday, "Race and Historiography Workshop." Because the *porciones* were not fenced, livestock owners used branding irons to identify their animals, which grazed in common herds rather than on individual owners' property. Material culture in the form of branding irons and the ownership insignia they impressed extended the regime of European concepts of property.

17. A sixth settlement among the *villas del norte* was a ranch, the *hacienda* of Dolores, which never attained the status of *villa*. Reynosa, which today is the largest city in Tamaulipas, retains little of its nineteenth-century fabric. Because of persistent flooding of the townsite surveyed in 1767, Reynosa was relocated to its present site in 1802.

18. Kathryn O'Rourke, "Race and Historiography Workshop."

19. Joanna Merwood-Salisbury, "Race and Historiography Workshop"; Charles L. Davis II, "Race and Historiography Workshop."

20. Joe S. Graham, *El Rancho in South Texas: Continuity and Change from 1750* (University of North Texas Press, 1994), 21, 85–86; Antonio Tamez Tejeda, *De piedra, adobe y barreta: Arquitectura noresteña* (Instituto de Investigaciones Históricas, Universidad Autónoma de Tamaulipas, 2003).

21. Herrera Pérez, *Matamoros*, 26–40, 45–65; Omar S. Valerio-Jiménez, *River of Hope: Forging Identity and Nation in the Rio Grande Borderlands* (Duke University Press, 2013), 55, 57; Manuel Humberto González Ramos, *Cartografía histórica Matamoros, 1772–2004* (Consejo Ciudadano para el Desarollo Cultural de Matamoros, 2004), 3–8.

22. Herrera Pérez, *Matamoros*, 46; Valerio-Jiménez, *River of Hope*, 64–65, 111.

23. Victor M. Rose, *A Republication of the Book Most Often Known as Victor Rose's History of Victoria*, ed. J. W. Petty Jr. (Book Mart, 1961), 152; Valerio-Jiménez, *River of Hope*, 113.

24. Herrera Pérez, *Matamoros*, 72; Eduardo Alarcón Cantú, *Arquitectura histórica en un espacio de encuentro: Ciudades fronterizas del bajo río Bravo* (El Colegio de la Frontera Norte, 2004), 19.

25. "Texas and the United States, Letter from Senator Benton," *Alexandria Gazette and Virginia Advertiser*, May 1, 1844, 4.

26. The territorial gains made by the United States in the US-Mexico War transferred Mexican mineral wealth to US control, as was immediately evident from the California Gold Rush (1848), followed by the Pike's Peak Gold Rush in Colorado (1858) and the Comstock Lode silver discovery in Nevada (1859). For a thorough analysis of Mexico's importance to the US economy during the 1820s and 1830s, see Linda K. Salvucci and Richard J. Salvucci, "The Lizardi Brothers: A Mexican Family Business and the Expansion of New Orleans, 1825–1846," *Journal of Southern History* 82, no. 4 (2016): 759–788.

27. Manuel Payno, *El Puerto de Matamoros en 1844* (Instituto Tamaulipeco para la Cultura y las Artes, 2013). Payno worked as an accountant in the Matamoros customhouse from 1839 to 1842.

28. Eliseo Paredes Manzano, "Across the Rio: A History of Matamoros by Eliseo Paredes," in *A Blast from the Past: Windows to Yesteryear from the Archives of the Brownsville Historical Association*, vol. 1

(Brownsville Historical Association, 1996), 52; Molly Reid, "Room to Grow: The Collection Celebrates Its Newest Addition, the Perrilliat House," *Historic New Orleans Collection Quarterly* 19, no. 3 (2012): 2–5.

29. The cultural geographer Terry Jordan posited a different genealogy for the side-gabled cottage. See Terry G. Jordan, "A Gabled Folk House Type of the Mexico-Texas Borderland," *Yearbook Conference of Latin Americanist Geographers* 14 (1988): 2–6.

30. Matamoros's merchant houses represent a thick, artisanal version of the attenuated neoclassical details visible on early nineteenth-century merchants' houses in the French Quarter of New Orleans. Valerio-Jiménez, *River of Hope*, 67–68.

31. "Matamoros, Diócesis de," in *Enciclopedia de México*, vol. 9 (Sabeca International Investment Corporation, 1998), 5072–5073.

32. "Letter from Senator Benton," 4.

33. Senator Benton's assertion verifies Kathryn Holliday's observation that change in the nineteenth century was propelled as much by economic flows as by narratives of nationhood. Kathryn E. Holliday, "Race and Historiography Workshop"; Valerio-Jiménez, *River of Hope*, 113.

34. Joseph Logsdon and Caryn Cossé Bell, "The Americanization of Black New Orleans, 1850–1900," in *Creole New Orleans: Race and Americanization*, ed. Arnold R. Hirsch and Joseph Logsdon (Louisiana State University Press, 1992), 207–208; Mary Gehman, "Visible Means of Support: Businesses, Professions, and Trades of Free People of Color," in *Creole: The History and Legacy of Louisiana's Free People of Color*, ed. Sybil Kein (Louisiana State University Press, 2000), 209, 212.

The US abolitionist Benjamin Lundy lived in Matamoros for five months in 1834 and 1835 and left a record of its African American community in an autobiography, *The Life, Travels and Opinions of Benjamin Lundy, Including His Journeys to Texas and Mexico* [. . .], ed. Thomas Earle (Philadelphia: W. D. Parrish, 1847), 143. The presence in Mexico of Afro-Creole migrants from the United States represents a wave of emigration that does not figure in US historiography—Americans who departed their homeland in search of the liberty and opportunity they were denied because of racial oppression and exclusion. The existence of a community of color in nineteenth-century Matamoros was not registered in histories of the city until Herrera Pérez, *Matamoros*, 73. See also Alice L. Baumgartner, *South to Freedom: Runaway Slaves to Mexico and the Road to Civil War* (Basic Books, 2020).

35. "Don Bartolo Passement," *Daily Ranchero*, August 2, 1868. This brief article was reprinted in the August 14, 1868, issue of *The Daily Picayune*. Passement is listed in the US census of 1830 for Orleans Parish, Louisiana, as A. B. Passement, the head of a household of eleven people, nine categorized as free people of color and two as enslaved women. He is listed in the New Orleans city directory of 1830 as A. Passement, bricklayer, living at what was then 350 Bourbon Street. In property records from 1826 and 1828, he is listed as the grandson of Madame Rosette Gallaud, a free woman of color born in New Orleans about 1761, and one of eight children of Madame Gallaud's deceased daughter, Euphrosine Gallaud, a free woman of color. Passement was party to a lawsuit, *Rabassa v. Passement*, decided on appeal by the Louisiana Supreme Court in 1830. In Matamoros, Passement married María Trinidad Sixtas Farías-Sánchez of Laredo in 1835, the great-granddaughter of the founder of Laredo, don Tomás Sánchez de la Barrera y Garza, and the aunt of Manuela Farías Benavides, the second wife of the Coahuila rancher don Evaristo Madero, whose grandson by his first marriage, Francisco I. Madero, was president of Mexico from 1911 to 1913. María Trinidad Farías and Bartolo Passement were the parents of at least five children. One son, the merchant Alfredo M. Passement Farías, served as mayor of Matamoros in 1891. One of Passement's daughters, Irene Passement Farías, married General Pedro Argüelles de la Garza, governor of Tamaulipas from 1902 to 1908. The nature of the relationship between Mateo Passement and Bartolo Passement is not presently clear. Thanks to Gregory Free for sharing his research on the Passements and to the historian Mary Gehman for sharing her knowledge of Afro-Creole emigration from Louisiana to Mexico.

36. "Guerilla Attack upon Brownsville," *American Flag*, October 1, 1859, Extra Edition; Joseph E. Chance, *José María de Jesús Carbajal: The Life and Times of a Mexican Revolutionary* (Trinity University Press, 2006), 101–127; Jerry Thompson, *Cortina: Defending the Mexican Name in Texas* (Texas A&M University Press, 2007), 34–66. Bartolo Passement's involvement in this negotiation lends circumstantial weight to the architectural historian Gregory Free's attribution to Passement of the design of the no-longer-extant ranch house of Cortina's mother, doña Estefana Goseascochea de Cortinas, upriver from Brownsville at El Carmen, Texas. Although externally a classic example of the Matamoros border-brick style, the Carmen ranch house, as Free has recognized, was in plan a two-room Creole cottage with back-to-back center fireplaces and a pair of rear cabinet rooms flanking an inset arched *petite galerie*. The Carmen ranch house was documented in the Historic American Buildings Survey in 1934.

37. The new, postwar towns founded in Texas were Brownsville (1848), opposite Matamoros; Hidalgo (1852), originally called Edinburgh, opposite Reynosa; Rio Grande City (1848), near Camargo; Roma (1848), near Mier; and Zapata (1858), originally called Bellville, near Guerrero. War also brought changes

on the Mexican side of the border. Nuevo Laredo, Tamaulipas, was incorporated as a city in 1848 in what had been the cross-river suburb of what became, after 1848, Laredo, Texas. And the surveyor and military adventurer José María de Jesús Carbajal founded the *villa nueva* (new town) of Camargo, upstream on the río San Juan and on the opposite bank from the historic plaza of Camargo.

38. Montejano, *Anglos and Mexicans in the Making of Texas*, 34.

39. Alonzo, *Tejano Legacy*, 110.

40. Dell Upton notes that the waterfront street in New Orleans now called Decatur was known in the nineteenth century as Levee Street. Dell Upton, "'The Master Street of the World,' the Levee," in *Streets: Critical Perspectives on Public Space*, ed. Zeynep Çelik, Diane Favro, and Richard Ingersoll (University of California Press, 1994), 280.

41. Nomenclature and geometry concealed an instability tied to disputes over land ownership. When Matamoros was elevated to the status of a city in 1826, its municipal government exercised its legal authority to annex a commons surrounding the city. Because the properties affected were all in private ownership, the city government became involved in lengthy litigation over compensation to affected owners. One dispute that had not been resolved by 1848 affected the portion of the Potrero del Espíritu Santo grant occupied by the Brownsville Town Company's townsite. The litigation migrated to US courts and was not resolved until after Stillman's death in 1875. Sara C. Bronin, "Land Grab: The Untold Story of Fort Brown," *Latino Book Review*, 2022, https://www.latinobookreview.com/8203land-grab-the-untold-story-of-fort-brown-by-sara-c-bronin—latino-book-review.html.

42. Betty Bay, *Historic Brownsville: Original Townsite Guide* (Brownsville Historical Association, 1980), 100–101, 105–106. Charles Stillman platted a four-block reserve, Washington Square, at the geographical center of the Brownsville townsite, but it remained at the edge of continuous settlement until the end of the nineteenth century.

43. Caleb Coker, ed., *The News from Brownsville: Helen Chapman's Letters from the Texas Military Frontier, 1848–1852* (Texas State Historical Association, 1992), 107, 174; Kyle B. Carpenter, *Globalizing the Lower Rio Grande: European Entrepreneurs in the Borderlands, 1749–1881* (University of North Texas Press, 2024), 106.

44. Eugene Fernández, National Register of Historic Places nomination form for Brownsville City Hall and Market House, 2018, https://atlas.thc.texas.gov/NR/pdfs/100004474/100004474.pdf.

45. Richard Cleary, "Texas Gothic, French Accent: The Architecture of the Roman Catholic Church in Antebellum Texas," *Journal of the Society of Architectural Historians* 66, no. 1 (2007): 60–83; Kathryn E. Holliday, "Race and Historiography Workshop."

46. The US Navy could not intercept shipping by neutral parties in the Gulf of Mexico or on the Rio Grande. From 1864 to 1866, Matamoros was occupied by the French as part of France's effort to install Archduke Maximilian of Austria as emperor of Mexico. The last land battle of the Civil War was fought at Palmito Ranch on the Rio Grande downriver from Brownsville on May 13, 1865. See David Montejano, "How Do Markets Trump Warfare? On the Wartime Business of Confederate Supplier Charles Stillman," *Southwestern Historical Quarterly* 127, no. 1 (2023): 32–54; John Mason Hart, *Revolutionary Mexico: The Coming and Processes of the Mexican Revolution* (University of California Press, 1987), 111–112.

47. New Orleans was captured by US Army forces in May 1862 and was occupied by the Union until the end of the war.

48. "The New Theater," *Daily Ranchero*, August 22, 1865, 2; Eddie Valent, "Teatro de la Reforma Was Place to Be Proud Of," *Brownsville Herald*, January 28, 1975, 3E.

49. Alarcón Cantú, *Arquitectura histórica en un espacio de encuentro*, 35–39.

50. "Catholic College," *Daily Ranchero*, May 25, 1867, 2; "Bishop Dubuis," *Daily Ranchero*, February 26, 1868, 4; "The New Convent," *Daily Ranchero*, March 5, 1868, 2.

51. Willard B. Robinson, *Texas Public Buildings of the Nineteenth Century* (University of Texas Press, 1974), 18.

52. "American Bracketed Villa," in *Hobbs's Architecture: Containing Designs and Ground Plans for Villas, Cottages, and Other Edifices* [. . .], by Isaac H. Hobbs and Son (Philadelphia: J. B. Lippincott, 1876), 164–165. M. H. Cross and his father were business partners in the major US-owned commission house in Matamoros, which also maintained a branch in Brownsville.

53. Edith Smith and Vivian Lehman documented the Cross family history on a website, No Land, Only Slaves, that is no longer available. In the slave schedule of the 1850 US census of the Rio Grande Valley in Cameron, Starr, and Webb Counties, J. S. Cross is listed as "John J. Ross." Published biographical profiles of the Crosses make no reference to the family's mixed race. See W. H. Chatfield, *The Twin Cities of the Border—Brownsville, Texas, and Matamoros, Mexico—and the Country of the Lower Rio Grande* (New Orleans: E. P. Brandao, 1893), 21–22; John Henry Brown, *Indian Wars and Pioneers of Texas* (Austin: L. E. Daniell, ca. 1895), 481–482.

54. As was not unusual among second-generation members of elite Brownsville families, Mrs. Kowalski and Mrs. Browne were the daughters of Mexican-born mothers.

55. "Historic House: Cueto Building Built for Store, Home," *Brownsville Herald*, November 25, 1945, 1.

56. The best-documented building professional working in the border-brick style after the Civil War was the German immigrant Enrique Portscheller (1840–1915), who was active in Roma, Rio Grande City, Mier, and Laredo. See W. Eugene George, *Master Builder of the Lower Rio Grande: Heinrich Portscheller* (Texas A&M University Press, 2016). See also Mario L. Sánchez, "Settlers, Artisans, and Immigrants: Evolution and Cultural Continuity in the Building of South Texas," in *Itinerant and Immigrant Artists and Artisans in 19th-Century Texas* (Museum of Fine Arts, Houston, 2014), 32–59.

57. "A Former Resident of Brownsville," *Brownsville Herald*, May 2, 1894, 3. Spanish-surnamed building professionals operating in Brownsville during the late nineteenth and early twentieth centuries include Atilano Rendón (1863–1933), Modesto S. Adame (1869–1953), Tomás Montes (1873–1947), Domingo V. Farías (1876–1917), José Colunga (1882–1946), and Severiano Escobar (1885–1938). Of these, only Escobar seems to have identified himself professionally as an architect.

58. "About Town," *Brownsville Daily Herald*, October 16, 1893, 3.

59. On the senior Martin Hanson, see "Drowned in the River," *Brownsville Herald*, November 22, 1902, 3. On S. W. Brooks, see "Death of S. W. Brooks," *Brownsville Herald*, February 16, 1903, 3.

60. Evan Anders, *Boss Rule in South Texas: The Progressive Era* (University of Texas Press, 1982), xiii–xiv; Tom Lea, *The King Ranch* (Little, Brown, 1957), 322; John Salmon Ford, *Rip Ford's Texas*, ed. Stephen B. Oates (University of Texas Press, 1963), 468.

61. Lea, *King Ranch*, 104, 108; Bruce S. Cheeseman, "King, Richard," *Handbook of Texas Online*, updated May 17, 2017, http://www.tshaonline.org/handbook/online/articles/fki19.

62. H. Minot Pitman, *Charles Stillman, 1810–1875* (N.p., 1956), 30; Jane Clements Monday and Frances Brannen Vick, *Petra's Legacy: The South Texas Ranching Empire of Petra Vela and Mifflin Kenedy* (Texas A&M University Press, 2007), 278–282.

63. Hart, *Revolutionary Mexico*, 120–121.

64. Fencing fixed territory and stabilized the internal borders of private property, halting the trail drives characteristic of the 1870s that had herded livestock across Texas and Indian Territory to the railhead in Kansas. Livestock owners could no longer sustain herds that exceeded the grazing capacity of their individually owned properties. Armando Alonzo comments on the contrasting attitudes of Mexican American and Anglo-American ranchers with regard to private property ownership. Alonzo, *Tejano Legacy*, 66–67.

65. Alonzo, *Tejano Legacy*, 234, 256–258.

66. "Building News," *Industrial Record* 22 (May 1917): 15; "Santa Gertrudis Ranch—The Home of Mrs. H. M. King," *Architectural Record* 49 (July 1916): 767–783; Clive Aslet, *The American Country House* (Yale University Press, 1990), 234–235.

67. Leland Roth, *A Monograph of the Works of McKim, Mead & White, 1879–1915* (Benjamin Blom, 1973), plates 295–300; Leland M. Roth, *The Architecture of McKim, Mead & White, 1870–1920: A Building List* (Garland, 1978), 101.

68. Tara A. Dudley makes a case for New Orleans's importance in *Building Antebellum New Orleans: Free People of Color and Their Influence* (University of Texas Press, 2021).

69. The triumvirate of nineteenth-century American architectural mythology all had connections to New Orleans: Thomas Jefferson bought it, H. H. Richardson grew up there, and Louis H. Sullivan designed the New Orleans passenger station of the Illinois Central Railroad, which linked the competing mid-continental metropolises of New Orleans and Chicago.

70. Prospectus, "Race and Historiography Workshop."

71. Even on the Texan side of the Rio Grande, a series of mixed-race ranching communities established in Hidalgo County in the 1850s sought to evade state laws that made interracial marriage illegal and made it extremely onerous for free people of color to live in Texas. See Thomas Daniel Knight, "Immigration to South Texas, 1850–1900," in *Still More Studies in Rio Grande Valley History*, ed. Milo Kearney, Anthony Knopp, and Antonio Zavaleta (Texas Center for Border and Transnational Studies, 2014), 49–96.

72. José David Saldívar, *Border Matters: Remapping American Cultural Studies* (University of California Press, 1997), 20. The historian Sarah Deutsch explores the socioeconomic efficacy of a border consciousness in *Making a Modern U.S. West: The Contested Terrain of a Region and Its Borders, 1898–1940* (University of Nebraska Press, 2022), 9, 18, 62, 93. Deutsch's third chapter, "Being American in Boley, Oklahoma," 95–116, captures the sense of fluid plurality characteristic of the South Texas border in describing the dilemma outsiders to Boley experienced in trying to define racial and ethnic identities.

10 AESTHETIC IMPERIALISM IN THE ASIA-PACIFIC

THE COASTAL POLITICS OF BERNARD MAYBECK'S ARCHITECTURAL PRACTICE

Charles L. Davis II

THE GERMAN AMERICAN ARCHITECT BERNARD MAYBECK is lionized for pioneering a regional style of modern architecture on the West Coast of the United States.[1] Given the modest output of his architectural practice, at least in comparison to some of his peers who also traveled west to look for work, this is decidedly high praise. Perhaps his best-known project is the Palace of Fine Arts (1915), a building so magnificent that it survived its function as a temporary pavilion for the Panama-Pacific International Exposition in San Francisco to become a permanent feature of the Northern California skyline. Designed to fall into ruin as it aged in place, the plaster detailing of the palace was meant to be something of a stage set. So it is not entirely surprising that it was eventually converted into a permanent theater in 1970, when the building underwent a major renovation to shore up its permanence. For an architect who built very few theaters, this is no mean feat. What is perhaps less well known, however, is that the Palace of Fine Arts also served many municipal functions over a century of use.

After World War II, the largely open function of the palace enabled it to meet the conflicting demands of a temporary pavilion, a military storage depot, and a permanent theater. In this sense, the flexibility of the space prompts the question of what political associations undergirded this beautiful design. The bright lights that animated its surfaces during the exposition suggested to many that Maybeck possessed an inherent sensibility for dramatically staging color and light in a major civic architectural space. Archival documents reveal that Maybeck was in fact fascinated with theatrical design throughout his career, a theme evident in his designs for stage sets, his correspondence on the architectural standards of theater buildings, and his penchant for performing in historical dress for private audiences at home and in local clubhouses. Given the historical relationships that implicitly connect regionalism, theater design, and military action in Maybeck's most memorable project, it is not entirely unreasonable to explore the deeper basis upon which these relationships proliferated in the broader context of Northern California and its national position as a threshold to the Asia-Pacific.

In 1922, less than a decade after the deposed Hawaiian Queen Liliuokalani's death, the architect Bernard Maybeck set sail for Honolulu on the SS *Wilhelmina*, a passenger ship that had been commissioned for wartime naval use and was now resuming commercial travel (fig. 10.1). Maybeck was part of an esteemed party of modern architects charged with adjudicating the design competition for the War Memorial Natatorium in Waikiki, a structure that still stands today. The building was commissioned to honor the valiant sacrifices of local Hawaiians in the military defense of the nation in the Asia-Pacific during World War I. The award-winning Beaux-Arts structure, designed by the Midwestern architect Lewis Hobart and completed in 1927, adorns an ocean-water swimming pool with a European revivalist structure that was described by the jury as creating a noble frame that surrounds and "reflects the highly individual color and flavor of Hawaii and Honolulu."[2] In his travels to Hawaii, Maybeck traversed the military theater that had silently animated his architectural practice in California—an influence that is still understudied today, perhaps because it only remains explicitly evident in his Asian-inspired projects.[3]

The following research mines the latent influence of coastal politics on Bernard Maybeck's architectural practice. I argue that Maybeck's regional style of modern architecture was in part reliant upon an aesthetic imperialism that resulted from his artistic borrowings of Asian motifs within a racially stratified cultural landscape. Using the daily itinerary of the architect's transpacific voyage aboard the SS *Wilhelmina* as a maritime framework for analysis, this chapter demonstrates the persistent influence of coastal politics on Maybeck's architectural practice by

FIGURE 10.1. *The* Wilhelmina *at the Charlestown Navy Yard, Boston, Massachusetts, 1919. US Naval History and Heritage Command, NH 103411; courtesy of the Naval Historical Foundation.*

interspersing the racialized events of the *Wilhelmina* cruise with historical asides that document the architect's professional entanglement with Sinophilia from the 1890s to the 1930s.

Between the historically inspired houses of the mid-1890s and his work on theater sets and designs in the early 1900s, Maybeck developed an innovative approach to architectural precedents that used the visual patterns of color and shade to synthesize the features of Western and non-Western building elements into a unique style of modern architecture. While this approach was socially progressive in comparison to standard Beaux-Arts interpretations of historical precedents, in part for its potential to be culturally inclusive along new aesthetic principles, Maybeck's architectural regionalism was often racialized by its segregated context. Many of his wealthy white clients internalized racial biases against Chinese laborers that were becoming common in Northern California. The spatial dynamics of Maybeck's architectural projects were thus inherently tipped toward preserving the power dynamics of white elites while expropriating the material culture of nonwhite peoples. Within the broader political context of the Asia-Pacific, this would have tremendous effects on the social and political agency of Asian migrants in advancing the history of West Coast modernism.

As Sara Ahmed notes in her essay "The Phenomenology of Whiteness," the ways that architectural spaces and forms are used to stabilize white supremacy can be measured by the ways these practices privilege the comfort of white subjects over others. This is especially true in social contexts that hold the potential for nonwhite spatial occupations that could operate to destabilize the spatial dynamics of white supremacy.[4] The yellowface performances that took place on board the *Wilhelmina* during the vessel-wide costume parties echo broader patterns of extractive labor practices in California and Hawaii. Telescoping in and out of Maybeck's maritime voyage across the Pacific enables us to see the subtending influence of coastal politics on his principled aesthetic vision for West Coast modernism.

June 7–13, 1922—SS *Wilhelmina* from San Francisco to Honolulu

Like most international trips, Maybeck's began with a parting of family members at the pier. On June 7, 1922, he was joined by Ellis Fuller Lawrence, an MIT graduate and dean of the School of Architecture at the University of Oregon, and Walter Ross Baumes Willcox, architect and partner of Willcox & Sayward, to travel from San Francisco to Honolulu to adjudicate an architectural competition. Willcox made himself responsible for keeping daily notes on their travels, later sending copies to Maybeck and Lawrence for posterity. The three architects met three women on their trip, together forming the core of what Willcox called the "Sextette of Table #18."[5]

Over the course of their journey on the *Wilhelmina*, the group engaged in various party games, poetry readings, political debates, musical performances, and other forms of distraction. Lawrence was very fond of reading short stories and poetry, including passages from Hugh Walpole's latest book, *The Thirteen Travellers* (1920), and Frederick Henry Pilch's much older *Homespun Verses* (1882). Both Maybeck and Lewis produced sketches of sites and figures along the way, including sketches by both men of a Hawaiian woman sitting at table 18. (Unfortunately, no such material survives in the Maybeck archive at the University of California, Berkeley.) Of all the recorded events, however, one particular incident stands out for special scrutiny for the ways in which it indexes the conflicted notions of American character operating within the Asia-Pacific—a conflict enacted through an artistic performance aboard the ship.

On the evening of Saturday, June 10, the ship's crew hosted a masquerade dance that challenged attendees to dress up in costumes for a juried competition. Of the guests sitting at table 18, only four were noted as active participants: Bernard Maybeck and the three women who had joined his table, one of whom was a Hawaiian-born woman traveling to the island from California to visit her family. Mrs. Langford—or "Fifi," as she was affectionately called by Willcox in his diary—participated in Maybeck's costume drama as one of three ancient Roman women snatched from antiquity:

> While thought of by those immediately concerned in their costuming as a family of a Roman senator, some of the onlookers at least grasped the significance of the disguise, and greeted M [Maybeck] as Socrates. He thereupon introduced the ladies as Helen of Troy, Clytemnestra, and another of the celebrated women of ancient Greece, whose name the Scribe was not fortunate enough to hear. Others, less discerning, were heard to refer to M as Bacchus, Nero, and by one he was mistaken for the representation of Jesus Christ, which naturally called forth expressions of horrified surprise mixed with considerable amusement on the part of those within hearing.[6]

While this performance enabled Maybeck to continue to connect with his Western roots, such an occasion likely provided Fifi with the challenge of presenting herself as a cross-racial figure in disguise.

Even more salacious was the "motley array" of historical tropes the other guests and members of the crew performed for this event: "negroes and negresses, Spanish troubadours, with their ladies, cowboys, Mexican cattle men, Japanese dames, Chinese women, a Mephistopheles or two—one of them the Ship's Doctor, who looked the devil some said he was—and the company of Romans who brought up the rear and made a fitting finale to the procession."[7] What is interesting about the broad array of characters on display here is the regional specificity of its selection. Every figure represented on the boat was rooted in political conflicts or regional cultures emerging along the West Coast, from the US annexation of Mexican territory representing former Spanish colonies to the in-migration of Japanese and Chinese laborers. To identify alternative possibilities, Willcox notes that there was jazz music played on the trip to and from Honolulu. And yet he makes no note of women dressed as flappers or men dressed in suspenders and baggy suits. The social imaginary represented here is partial to the figures representing the Far West. In addition, the representation of nonwhite figures on board the *Wilhelmina* was completed by a manifest of crew members and guests that largely consisted of white people. This suggests that many of the participants likely engaged in acts of Blackface, brownface, and yellowface to compete in this costume party. Maybeck and his team later won the competition but passed on the prize when they learned that it could not be shared among multiple guests. In their place, the prize was given to an individual who provided a "lovely portrayal of a Japanese geisha girl"—yet another fetishized depiction of Asian identity.[8]

The theatrical character of the costume party aboard the *Wilhelmina* rehearses some of the cross-cultural themes that emerge during Maybeck's architectural career, some of which explicitly relate to the broader milieu of the Asia-Pacific. As mentioned at the outset of this essay, Maybeck's use of color in the Palace of Fine Arts suggested to some of his clients that he was qualified to undertake a

FIGURE 10.2. *Bernard Maybeck, design for an amusement park in Guangzhou, China, 1914. Courtesy of the Bernard Maybeck Collection, Environmental Design Archives, University of California, Berkeley.*

theater project. In an undated letter to Maybeck, Christine Wetherill Stevenson cited the architect's Palace of Fine Arts in her decision to solicit a meeting with him to commission "an Oriental looking theater facing a beautiful canyon" in Daisy Dell in the Cahuenga Pass, purportedly to stage the play *The Light of Asia*—an adaptation of an epic poem written in 1879—to depict the life and religious philosophy of the Buddha for an English-speaking audience.[9] Stevenson had previously directed this material at the Krotona Institute in 1918 and wanted to continue this work in her current position as the head of the Theatre Arts Alliance. The alliance board had located sixty acres of land and performers to undertake this performance in perpetuity. When conflicts between Stevenson and members of the board made her initial bid for an Oriental theater impossible, she commissioned Maybeck to complete a design for an outdoor theater on twenty-nine acres nearby to stage *The Pilgrimage Play*, this time on the life and times of Jesus Christ.

Unfortunately, there is no evidence of what Maybeck's "Oriental looking theater" would have looked like. But the architect did complete beautifully vibrant color studies of Asian-inspired architectural scenes for international fairs. This included a commission for an amusement park in Guangdong, China, in 1914; color studies of San Francisco's Chinatown in 1933; and site planning as a consulting architect for the Golden Gate International Exposition, held in San Francisco from 1939 to 1940 (figs. 10.2, 10.3). Each example demonstrates Maybeck's mastery of color, volume, and contrast in studying Asian sources. The expo scene exemplifies the eclectic character that planners wished to use to represent San Francisco as a crossroads of cultural mixing, from Spanish colonial and Asian migrants to the integration of various global planning models.

FIGURE 10.3. *Bernard Maybeck, color study of Chinatown, San Francisco, October 5, 1933. Courtesy of the Bernard Maybeck Collection, Environmental Design Archives, University of California, Berkeley.*

On June 11, 1918, Maybeck wrote a letter to Henry Bishop, who served as the director of the Bishop Playhouse, an enclosed theater on Franklin Street in Oakland, California. Bishop initially became famous for building the first permanent rotating stage in the United States, an innovation he claimed to have seen in "revolving Kabuki stages during a trip to Japan."[10] Maybeck's letter discussed aesthetic principles for regulating the use of stage lighting to amplify the political meaning of important scenes in *The Mikado*, a Gilbert and Sullivan piece then playing at the Bishop Playhouse. Having served as an advisor for theater spaces in the past, Maybeck notes the importance of changing lighting conditions during especially dramatic moments in the play:

> For example, at the opening scene of the "Mikado" the stage was in a subdued light. Everyone seemed delighted. After a little while the bright lights were turned on to show all of the different makeshifts and faults of the scene. Suppose the same mind that conceived of the first setting continued the same method of analysis and made change after change of lighting in harmony with the moods of the play. When discouragement comes, a cloud passes over the stage; when the hero appears, the light is centered not upon him but near him at his feet or an object nearby. The stage must be kept in a low tone until the grand climax and then all is brilliant.[11]

We know from newspaper stories that Maybeck was eventually employed to create "special scenery" for *The Mikado*, although no surviving drawings or photographs exist in his archive. His continuing interest in theater design is also evidenced in other private letters, including one to Willis Polk containing a "request for data on theaters" and one from H. H. Robinson informing Maybeck of a talk on stage lighting by the technical director of the San Francisco Players Guild.[12] Most of this work took place within a decade of Maybeck's trip to Honolulu, all of which culminated in the design of the outdoor Pilgrimage Theater in the 1930s.

June 14–22, 1922—Deliberating the Natatorium Competition

Outside of the official work of adjudicating the War Memorial Natatorium competition, Maybeck and his peers engaged in a series of exploratory trips on the island of Oahu. Some of these trips were organized by the Honolulu mayor's office, which organized the competition. On one such trip, Willcox observed several things about the local culture found in Hawaii. He explicitly discusses race in the context of visiting a normal school on the island. He was surprised that this building brought together "Hawaiians, Tahitians, Samoans, Japanese, Chinese, Portuguese, and descendants from American and English forebears," and yet Willcox saw no sign of racial tensions between these groups.[13] This suggests that he was well aware of the racial tension that separated white and Asian groups living in California. Willcox later records a comment made by one of the teachers that the racial mixture of "Hawaiians and the Chinese" was thought to be the most advantageous because its progeny were "well developed physically and seemed possessed of the finer qualities of mind and temperament."[14] It was at this point that the group learned that the press announcement for the finalist of the war memorial project would take place in the former palace of the deposed Queen Liliuokalani, an ironic development, given the political significance of the project.

Willcox proved to be a keen observer of Hawaiian vernacular culture, as evidenced by his comments on local flora, fauna, building culture, and the vernacular roots of the public function of the natatorium. This included documentation of and speculation on local lanai culture on the island. There was also no shortage of Japanese tea gardens, workshops, and novelty stores dedicated to Asian folk culture. The potential value of the Hawaiian lanai for a regional style of building around the University of California, Berkeley, was recognized as early as 1904 with the publication of Charles Keeler's *The Simple Home*. This publication formalized more local efforts to standardize Maybeck's approach to house design through pamphlets, news articles, and exhibits at the Hillside Club.

Some scholars have taken Keeler's text as a self-initiated popularization of Maybeck's approach to housing design, but there is some evidence that Maybeck was collaborating with Keeler. Keeler and Maybeck had been personal acquaintances for years, which the former claims began with a shared ferry ride that eventually led to a private commission for the Charles Keeler House in 1895. Keeler was a well-known naturalist who spent time with figures such as John Muir, William Keith, John Burroughs, and Francis Fisher Browne. The Keeler home synthesized the structural features of medieval European structures with the tectonic profiles of Hawaiian houses and the landscape features of Hawaiian lanai porch culture. In many ways, Keeler's career as a naturalist, ethnographer, and reporter prepared him to explore a synthetic combination of Western and non-Western building motifs. From 1900 to 1901, "he made a voyage with his family to the South Seas, visiting Tahiti, New Zealand, Australia, Samoa, and Hawaii. While on this voyage, he worked as a reporter for the *San Francisco Chronicle*, sending back articles about the natives of those lands, the most notable of which were his experiences among the Maoris of New Zealand."[15] Keeler initially endorsed a climatic reading of the California landscape that suggested it was a natural environment for promoting a pluralistic approach to horticulture and gardening: "The coast of California has a climate of such temperatures that an extraordinary variety of exotics will thrive, Bamboo, palms, dracaenas, magnolias, oranges, bananas, and innumerable other fragrant or show plants of New Zealand and Australia, of Africa, South America and the Indies."[16] But this reading was only directed toward the literal flora and fauna that could grow on the mainland.

In a complement to his observations on the climate in California, Keeler claimed that its future architecture would be based principally on the "spirit" of various architectural precedents that could be harmonized on a slightly different logic: "The whole pointed effect of Gothic architecture is, in a measure at least, a means of expressing the ideal of aspiration. . . . If the Gothic spirit is to be introduced and perpetuated in California, it will have a temperamental rather than a climatic rationale."[17] The archive of Maybeck's early housing designs contains many notes that document his desire to achieve a particular ethnic character or spirit for a project, even when the structural details or ornamental motifs for such historical precedents were omitted from a final design.[18] For Keeler, this spiritual rationale was expressed by the strikingly similar visual character of particular architectural elements constructed by peoples living across the world in different climatic regions. Keeler specifically wondered at the "natural genesis of roof lines" found in "savage architectures" of the Tlingit Indigenous people of Alaska, the Maori of southern New Zealand, Hawaiians, and Indigenous groups of Norway.[19] Whether these houses were built of grass, clapboard, or masonry, they displayed a similar "steep slope" that gave them a common architectural character.

Keeler's formalist catalog of structural typologies is paralleled by Maybeck's personal use of color and shade to analyze the architectural elements of historical precedents. In comparison to the functionalist basis by which many Beaux-Arts-trained architects selected historical precedents, which was based on an association between historical elements and contemporary use of a building or space, Maybeck developed a visual methodology by which to compare the similar color variations, hues, and shadows generated by architectural elements across time. This approach suggested a primarily visual basis for synthesizing global architectural elements. A few of Maybeck's color and shadow studies of the library stairwell at Principia College and the front elevation for the Palace of Fine Arts exemplify the analytical value of this approach in breaking down the formal and structural elements that define architectural character in particular settings (figs. 10.4, 10.5).

Using this pattern-based analytic, it is possible to interpret the potential sources of the strong profiles created by the steep pitch of historic gable roofs that influenced the designs of the Charles Keeler and Williston Davis Houses, which consciously recall medieval Gothic precedents as well as the exposed wooden structures of Asian vernacular buildings—something both Keeler and Maybeck suggested in textual form on different occasions and would have been seen in various contexts on the West Coast (fig. 10.6).[20] These cross-cultural references provide an aesthetically embodied interpretation of architectural typologies that credits a building's visual effects not to its structural system per se but to the creativity embedded in the social and cultural contexts of its making. Maybeck's analytical technique juxtaposes many of the conflicting cultural identities circulating within his Asia-Pacific context without fully resolving them into a rationally synthetic style. Instead, they are effectively collaged or montaged into a combination of elements that achieves the same "feeling" or "spirit" as its predecessor, sometimes by arriving upon a new modern form. One can imagine Maybeck using this embodied approach to architectural elements to develop unprecedented structural solutions that could produce the visual effects he desired in a speculative parti. The cantilevered framing of ceiling joists alongside the windows of the George H. Boke House is just one example of his skill with manipulating architectural elements.

Despite the formal ingenuity of his visual interpretation of historical precedents, Maybeck labored against a social and political context that contained heavy biases toward people of Asian descent. The imperial West seemed to offer a

FIGURE 10.4. *Bernard Maybeck, undated pencil drawing of stairwell at Principia College Library. Courtesy of the Bernard Maybeck Collection, Environmental Design Archives, University of California, Berkeley.*

FIGURE 10.5. *Bernard Maybeck, undated charcoal lighting study of stairwell at Principia College Library. Courtesy of the Bernard Maybeck Collection, Environmental Design Archives, University of California, Berkeley.*

FIGURE 10.6. *A Hawaiian house on display at the Bishop Museum, Honolulu, showing the beginning of the thatching on the front side. William T. Brigham,* The Ancient Hawaiian House *(Bishop Museum Press, 1908), plate 27. Courtesy of the University of Texas Libraries.*

convenient home to many Asia enthusiasts, from Henry Pike Bowie, US diplomat to Japan, to Christine Wetherill Stevenson. Maybeck was a founding member of both the Hillside Club and the Bohemian Club, two volunteer organizations that did much to educate the public on Asian art and material culture. Over time, members arranged public symposia, talks, and exhibits on Asia. In keeping with the modernist appreciation of Asian art, Bowie organized "an exhibit of Japanese color prints" at the Bohemian Club.[21] Maybeck himself was a member of the Arts Committee for the Hillside Club, which regularly hosted exhibits that included the display of lent Asian curios.

This progressive love of Asian art was offset by a regressive opposition to the racial integration of Asian immigrant laborers in the wealthy enclave of North Berkeley. Local immigrants who could afford to enter this neighborhood were viewed with suspicion and at times became the subject of targeted discriminatory laws and local mandates. In 1908, leading members of the Hillside Club rallied to sponsor a bill limiting the public display of signage and billboards associated with businesses such as Chinese laundries in North Berkeley. What began as an issue of public urban beauty quickly expanded to a broader effort to limit the presence of working-class Chinese businesses as a whole: "A fight has also been begun by the members of the Hillside Club against the establishment of laundries and other commercial enterprises in the pretty villa section of the city."[22] Apparently, only the most refined aspects of Chinese culture were welcome in this exclusive section of the city.[23]

On Wednesday, June 21, 1922, Maybeck left his group of travelers in Hawaii to "see the work in a pineapple canning factory," perhaps to document the modernization of food production in the United States.[24] There were many newspaper articles on the technological advancements that enabled food to be preserved for long periods of time, a holdover of wartime reporting on local efforts to support the nation during World War I. Looking through the architect's personal correspondence, however, reveals a more personal connection to the daily reality of canning in the Hawaiian Islands, one that exposes the racial character of plantation labor. Maybeck received a letter dated November 1920 from Lloyd, a family friend who worked on a pineapple plantation in the region.[25] In this letter, Lloyd mentions hiring a Japanese maid and cook: "From now on we will have a Japanese girl to help, as they only cost $25.00 a month and board themselves." Lloyd also discusses his life on pineapple plantations on Oahu, where "8 white men" were hired to oversee the work of "2,500 Japs [*sic*], Chinese, Philipinos, Koreans, Portuguese and natives." The use of an epithet to describe Japanese migrants is very telling of white racial attitudes toward this ethnic minority. Lloyd describes the attitudes of the Japanese on the island as more "servile" and deferential to white men than those of other Asian groups found in California. Such language mirrors that used to describe African slavery in the American South and is just one reminder of the strife-ridden racial context of Maybeck's practice.

June 22–28, 1922—Return Trip to San Francisco

Of the myriad events to take place on the *Wilhelmina*'s return trip to San Francisco, just two are worthy of note here: an additional masquerade ball (though covered in less detail than the first in Willcox's account) and a play wherein Maybeck and Lawrence played a pair of Arab seers. On this occasion, Maybeck himself is documented as performing the cross-cultural identity of a nonwhite figure on board the *Wilhelmina*. In typical fashion, this performance does include orientalized depictions of Arab natives:

> M's [Maybeck's] idea was to have a scarecrow galvanized into life by the black, or other, magic of a couple of Arab seers,—parts assigned to M and L. [Lawrence],—gradually quickening it to action and then to speech. To this framework the idea of the Red Cross nurse as an aid to them was added, in order to give the lady of the quartet a proper place in the fun.[26]

Willcox's notes offer no indication of what the Arab costumes included. What is more interesting in comparison to the documented activities occurring during the first leg of the trip is the departure from ready-made tropes of the American Far West. Arab players were a bit more "exotic" than those rehearsed in either masquerade ball. Upon returning to the shore, Maybeck, Lawrence, and Willcox were met by "their trusty friend, Schnaittacher, who had been in charge of the Competition business."[27] At the end of their voyage, "they presented him with a little blue [cloisonné] jewel box," a characteristic ending to a trip across the Pacific.

During the nineteenth century, the term "theater" accrued a double meaning for representing national events in the history of American empire. This duality was present in both the immediate social implications of this building typology and its use as a metaphor for military conflict. At the level of the building, a theater is a structure or outdoor space in which plays and other dramatic performances are held. Outdoor theaters were a regular feature of settler culture in Northern California.[28] The balmy weather of the region permitted designers to experiment with a wide range of architectural forms and programmatic solutions, from historical revivalist assemblages to extremely minimal landscape solutions that integrated the stage and seating within its natural surroundings. By the late nineteenth century, the term "theater" became associated with military actions in the Asia-Pacific to describe the geographical areas demarcating the space for war, particularly naval battles, and other forms of international conflict. In both senses, the theater constituted a relational space wherein an actor performed a set of actions that were interpreted by an audience on what was considered an international stage of cultural production. In California, the geographical limits of the Far West established the continental boundaries of a transpacific theater of naval power that extended from the shores of the United States to the shores of eastern Asia. Within this maritime context, the Asia-Pacific contained both literal theaters for expanding the repertoire of American arts and letters and a metaphorical stage upon which American naval power was to be exercised to ensure US dominance in the Pacific Ocean.

Given the social implications of theater culture in the visualization of American identity, particularly in the sort of plays that were performed in this regional context, it is important to consider the ways these spaces enabled people to calibrate their understanding of national identity over the course of the long nineteenth century. Colonial settlements in the Far West were constituted by a demographic mix of peoples coming from various parts of the world. These people and their cultures often collided with one another in social and cultural terms. Such is true of the "Concord people" migrating from the East of the United States to modernize California and the "coolie" and itinerant laborers migrating east from China, Japan, Korea, and islands in the Pacific Ocean to fill the gap left by previously enslaved African laborers across the Americas.[29] These Asian travelers often found themselves exiled within the United States as perpetual onlookers upon the predestined Christian drama of manifest destiny. Prevented from becoming legal citizens by recurring exclusion laws, yet conscribed as essential laborers for the California Gold Rush, the intercontinental railroad, and regional fruit plantations on various Pacific islands, Asians were forced to live permanent lives as temporary aliens. This life of precarity was paralleled by the cultural fetishization of antique Asian material culture, especially within socially progressive, white, elite circles. There is historical evidence of avant-garde displays of "Oriental curios" in regional clubhouses, in university museums, and even in private homes, curated by diplomats to Asia and enthusiasts of Asian culture to reflect the revered philosophies of Eastern culture. Within this context, it is not surprising that Edwin Arnold's epic poem *The Light of Asia* became a popular subject of East Hollywood's outdoor theater culture.[30]

The trend of Sinophilia in Northern California was manifest in a string of Asian-themed plays, set designs, and architectural motifs, sometimes through the borrowing of historical typologies that enabled white settlers to appropriate the visual and material culture of Asia.[31] The popularity of outdoor theater culture prompted the question of what visual aesthetic was perceived to be the most appropriate for generating regional forms of Far Western culture. How did American architects respond to the shifting contexts of Western civilization as their migrations approached the geographical boundaries of the Asia-Pacific? Would modern architecture be represented by a single, hegemonic movement or style, or by a panoply of visual experiments synthesizing different currents? And what role did Asian material culture, if not Asian subjects themselves, have in this historical process?

If the lectures, exhibits, and plays hosted by California's local art and culture clubs are any indication, there was a bifurcated public reception of Asian culture by modern architecture critics: The expressive and material cultures of ancient China, Japan, and Korea were taken as evidence of high cultural output, while contemporary waves of Asian migrants were viewed with suspicion and fear, largely for their potential to contaminate the purity of Anglo-American culture, either on race-, class-, or health-based terms. This fractured model of cultural reception constitutes what I call the aesthetic imperialism of modernist theory—the explicit visual borrowing of antique Asian culture alongside the social exiling of new waves of Asian migrants—which enabled white settlers to police the boundaries of American character as it collided with the social, political, and economic milieus of the Asia-Pacific. In this sense, the Hawaiian Islands constituted both an exotic locale for Western visitors outside of the North American continent, an economic opportunity for rising industrialists, and political evidence of the increasing global influence of American power in the region.

Within the militarized context of the Pacific Ocean, the West Coast of North America constituted the bounding edge of an impending conflict zone between established powers in Asia and the United States. The term "Pacific Theater of Operations" would become official terminology for US naval operations shortly after the nation entered World War II in the 1940s. But the assumption of international conflict was already evident in the frenetic construction of US military bases in the Pacific and the annexation of island protectorates nearly half a century before the war. After the official closing of the American frontier in 1890, national leaders faced a difficult choice on how to expand their influence around the world. Would the United States need to engage in traditional colonialism to ensure its safety in the Asia-Pacific, or would strategic military alliances be enough to create a buffer between itself and naval power in China and Japan? The ports and slips of California's West Coast pragmatically operated as the new geographical frontier of American imperialism, and this power was extended into the Pacific Ocean through the formation of new protectorates.[32]

As Amy Kaplan notes, the political category of protectorate skirts the line of extracontinental military expansion without constituting the formation of an outright colony in the Pacific Ocean.[33] Instead of extending the rights of citizenship to those born on the island, its residents were cast into an ambiguous middle ground where they lacked the autonomy for sovereignty but were reliant on the benevolence of the federal government. This logic added Hawaii as a buffer within the Pacific against foreign threats, even as it was itself seized through overt military action to secure its raw materials and economic potential. In her biography of Hawaii, the deposed Queen Liliuokalani notes the military coup that effectively made her a political prisoner in 1898.[34] Despite her protests and appeals to international bodies for relief, she was forced to witness the foreign modernization of her homeland from her palace home until her death in 1917.

Having arrived at the end of Maybeck's voyage on the SS *Wilhelmina*, we are now better positioned to identify the latent influence of coastal politics on his architectural oeuvre. In each of the projects mentioned here, from the set designs and lighting direction he created for Asian-themed plays and theaters, to his Asian-inspired exposition designs and color studies, Maybeck invested his coastal architecture with a sense of theatricality and drama that synthesized the cultural details of the Western and non-Western material cultures that intersected in Northern California. His principled approach to analyzing the figural patterns of architectural precedents enabled him to develop uniquely modern details that expressed the historical "feeling" or "spirit" most related to his clients' needs. Yet the social contexts of these projects nearly guaranteed that the Asian-inspired features of his designs could only be experienced by the "Concord people" who commissioned these works. This segregated reception of Maybeck's socially progressive designs provides an indication of the negative inertia that often binds innovative architecture to the hegemonic discourses of its day. In the case of Maybeck's architectural practice, a bona fide American architecture may still emerge when these projects become equitably bound to the ethnic communities he borrowed from in the early twentieth century. Who knows what material and spatial innovations these actors have yet to bring to the long history of West Coast modernism? I hope there will be a scribe capable of writing down the details of this journey. Perhaps then we can compare Willcox's journal with what they have yet to say to us.

Notes

1. See Kenneth H. Cardwell, *Bernard Maybeck: Artisan, Architect, Artist* (Hennessey + Ingalls, 1977); Richard Longstreth, *On the Edge of the World: Four Architects in San Francisco at the Turn of the Century* (MIT Press, 1983); Sally Byrne Woodbridge, *Bernard Maybeck: A Guide to Modern Ideas, Movements, and Buzzwords, 1848–1944* (Abbeville Press, 1992); Mark Anthony Wilson, *Bernard Maybeck: Architect of Elegance* (Gibbs Smith, 2011).

2. Walter Ross Baumes Willcox, account of trip to Hawaii with Bernard Maybeck (hereafter cited as Willcox account), 1922, paginated copy, box 1, folder 12, Bernard Maybeck Collection, Environmental Design Archives, University of California, Berkeley (hereafter cited as Maybeck Collection, Berkeley).

3. Maybeck designed an amusement park commissioned by the Chinese city of Guangzhou (then known in English as Canton) in 1914. This work paralleled his participation in the Panama-Pacific International Exposition in the same year. Drawings of both projects are held in the Environmental Design Archives at the University of California, Berkeley.

4. Sara Ahmed, "The Phenomenology of Whiteness," *Feminist Theory* 8, no. 2 (2007): 149–168.

5. Willcox account.

6. Willcox account, 17–18.

7. Willcox account, 17.

8. Willcox account, 18. Asian women were not initially allowed to immigrate to the United States for fear that they would either start families with male "coolie" laborers or marry white men and seek citizenship. See Gary Y. Okiro, *American History Unbound: Asians and Pacific Islanders* (University of California Press, 2015), 1–20.

9. Although Stevenson's letter contains no date, she must have written to Maybeck before he began his design of the Pilgrimage Theater for her in 1917. Christine Wetherill Stevenson to Bernard Maybeck, box 4, folder 3, Maybeck Collection, Berkeley.

10. Chad Randl, *Revolving Architecture: A History of Buildings That Rotate, Swivel, and Pivot* (Princeton Architectural Press, 2008), 56.

11. Bernard Maybeck to Bishop Playhouse, June 11, 1918, Maybeck Collection, Berkeley.

12. Bernard Maybeck to Willis Polk, 1912, box 4, folder 3, Maybeck Collection, Berkeley; H. H. Robinson to Bernard Maybeck, 1928, box 2, folder 3, Maybeck Collection, Berkeley.

13. Willcox account, 32.

14. Willcox account, 32.

15. Dimitri Shipounoff, introduction to *The Simple Home*, by Charles Keeler (Paul Elder, 1904), xxxii–xxxiii.

16. Keeler, *Simple Home*, 12–13.

17. Keeler, *Simple Home*, 25–26.

18. In a handwritten note about the S. H. Erlanger House, Maybeck discusses the architectural elements that contributed to the character of the home. Although this dwelling would never have been present in England, he describes it as having an "English feeling." The lower wing is a chapel-form living room of a type greatly used in an early period of English history, and the ceiling of the room is very similar to one in Samlesbury Hall, Lancashire. The second-story windows are of iron, like those of their English prototype. The building and its setting among the trees loudly proclaim the good taste of the Erlangers, from whom the suggestion came. Bernard Maybeck, handwritten note, 1916, box 13, folder 4, Maybeck Collection, Berkeley.

19. Keeler, *Simple Home*, 25–26.

20. William T. Brigham, *The Ancient Hawaiian House* (Bishop Museum Press, 1908).

21. Joan Levy, "The Bowie Scandal Shocked 1920 Society," *Daily Journal* (San Mateo, CA), June 14, 2004.

22. "Residents Oppose Ugly Billboards: Hillside Club Members Plan a Campaign Against Unsightly Signs in Northern Berkeley," *San Francisco Call*, September 12, 1908.

23. Two years earlier, the rigid perception of beauty held by prominent members of the Hillside Club was manifest in the notorious opposition to constructing Arts and Crafts–style affordable housing (called "portable housing" by its architect, Paul Needham) in North Berkeley, primarily because the dwellings departed from Maybeck's and Keeler's formal aesthetic for the district. See "Invasion of Portable Houses Seeks to Disrupt Hillside Club: Strife Besets Fashionable Berkeley," *San Francisco Call*, October 9, 1906.

24. Willcox account, 45.

25. Lloyd [full name unknown] to Bernard Maybeck, November 1920, box 1, folder 3, Maybeck Collection, Berkeley.

26. Willcox account, 70.

27. Willcox account, 74.

28. See, for example, Emerson Knight, "Outdoor Theaters and Stadiums in the West," *Architect and Engineer* 78, no. 2 (1924): 53–92.

29. The phrase "Concord people" was used to describe the white settler groups who migrated from the East Coast to build a life in California. See Hal Johnson, "Berkeley's Forgotten Man," *Berkeley Daily Gazette*, May 9, 1949. "Coolie" was a term initially used to describe indentured or enslaved Indian laborers working in the British colonies. It was later extended to enslaved Asian laborers in Latin America and the United States when this labor force was tapped to replace the labor of previously enslaved Africans. See Katharine Coman, *The History of Contract Labor in the Hawaiian Islands* (Macmillan, 1908).

30. Edwin Arnold, *The Light of Asia* (London: Trübner, 1879). Evidence of plays hosted in East Hollywood can be found in the newspaper article "The Light of Asia," *Los Angeles Times*, July 1, 1918.

31. See, for example, Horatio F. Stoll, "Transplanted Japan," *San Francisco Sunday Call*, March 30, 1913. This article describes the construction of Japanese gardens for the Panama-Pacific International Exposition, as well as local gardens emulating this pattern.

32. For a historical summary of the imperial associations of California's seaports, see Grey Brechin, *Imperial San Francisco: Urban Power, Earthly Ruin* (University of California Press, 2006), 71–120.

33. Amy Kaplan, *The Anarchy of Empire in the Making of U.S. Culture* (Harvard University Press, 2005), 1–22.

34. Liliuokalani, *Hawaii's Story: Written by Hawaii's Queen* (Boston: Lothrop, Lee & Shepard, 1898).

11 MAHOGANY AND THE LOCATIONS OF AMERICAN ARCHITECTURE

Jonah Rowen

Solid mahogany! . . . For all its magic there lingers about it a sense of crudity, of aggression and strife which attaches it to the foundations rather than to the superstructure of civilization.

MEYRIC R. ROGERS, PREFACE TO *MAHOGANY ANTIQUE AND MODERN: A STUDY OF ITS HISTORY AND USE IN THE DECORATIVE ARTS*

The Black Africans are not compared to trees that are alive in a forest and radiant in their branches, but to *wood*, to the *matter* that is extracted from the living being and will be used to supply the Plantation's workshops and houses.

MALCOLM FERDINAND, *DECOLONIAL ECOLOGY: THINKING FROM THE CARIBBEAN WORLD*

LONDON'S WEST INDIA DOCKS OPENED in 1802 to funnel raw materials harvested by enslaved Black people in the Americas into British warehouses, and on to purchasers, manufacturers, and consumers. At the incitement of enslaver-importers with goods stuck in the crowded Thames, London's urban administrators authorized construction of more efficient ship-to-shore transfer facilities. The initiative took on greater urgency in light of the risk posed to merchants from unloaded cargoes' susceptibility to looting, to destruction by fire or damp, or to devaluation by other means.[1] Fifteen years after the warehouses' initial opening, the complex was complemented by the Mahogany Shed, a fully integrated mechanized structure (fig. 11.1).[2] Designed by the engineer John Rennie, the technologically advanced building included gantry cranes for hoisting and moving the heavy mahogany logs, mounted on tracks that were also the bottom cords of the roof trusses.[3] The fire-resistant materials that constituted the shed, brick and cast iron, testify to the preciousness of the structure's contents. Rennie's son declared that "the saving of labour alone very soon paid the cost" of the mechanical-architectural contraptions, emphasizing the obviation of human exertion, delegated instead to the overhead devices.[4] The subtext of that celebration of mechanical advantage, however, was the labor that the cranes did *not* save: that of the coerced lumberjacks of African and Indigenous American descent in the Caribbean.[5] Yet such quantitative balances, and economic historians' admirable efforts to compute the share of Caribbean produce during this period, overlook the incommensurability of the extraction-enslavement economy, let alone its environmental tolls.[6] American foresters' exertions were impregnated into the wood that was cut down and dressed for white merchants' and craftspeople's profits, and in commodities for white metropolitan consumers. The trolleys mounted in the Mahogany Shed absorbed the strain of lifting and moving logs at the London wharf. The mechanisms at the Mahogany Shed, which eased the burden of handling that lumber, only further obscured the places where the wood came from and the people whose labor made it available.

The West India Docks Mahogany Shed was a nexus between the realms of production and consumption. From there, importers transported logs to sawyers' mills for drying and rough-cutting, and on to craftspeople's workshops for carving, joining, polishing, finishing, fastening, fitting, and upholstering, depending on the ultimate use of the material in the luxurious, or at least petit bourgeois, interior that would be its final destination. Arriving at warehouses, the lumber remained a raw material. Coerced lumberjacks had imbued the wood with value by procuring it from forests at speculating enslavers' behest. The process of felling trees, extracting them from heavy brush, loading logs onto ships, and unloading them onto metropolitan urban shores transmuted the wood into a commodity. In spite of its unique features of color, figure, and texture, upon entering the space of transatlantic trade, the material became fungible. And while distinguishing the subspecies of mahogany is difficult even through microscopic analysis, per-

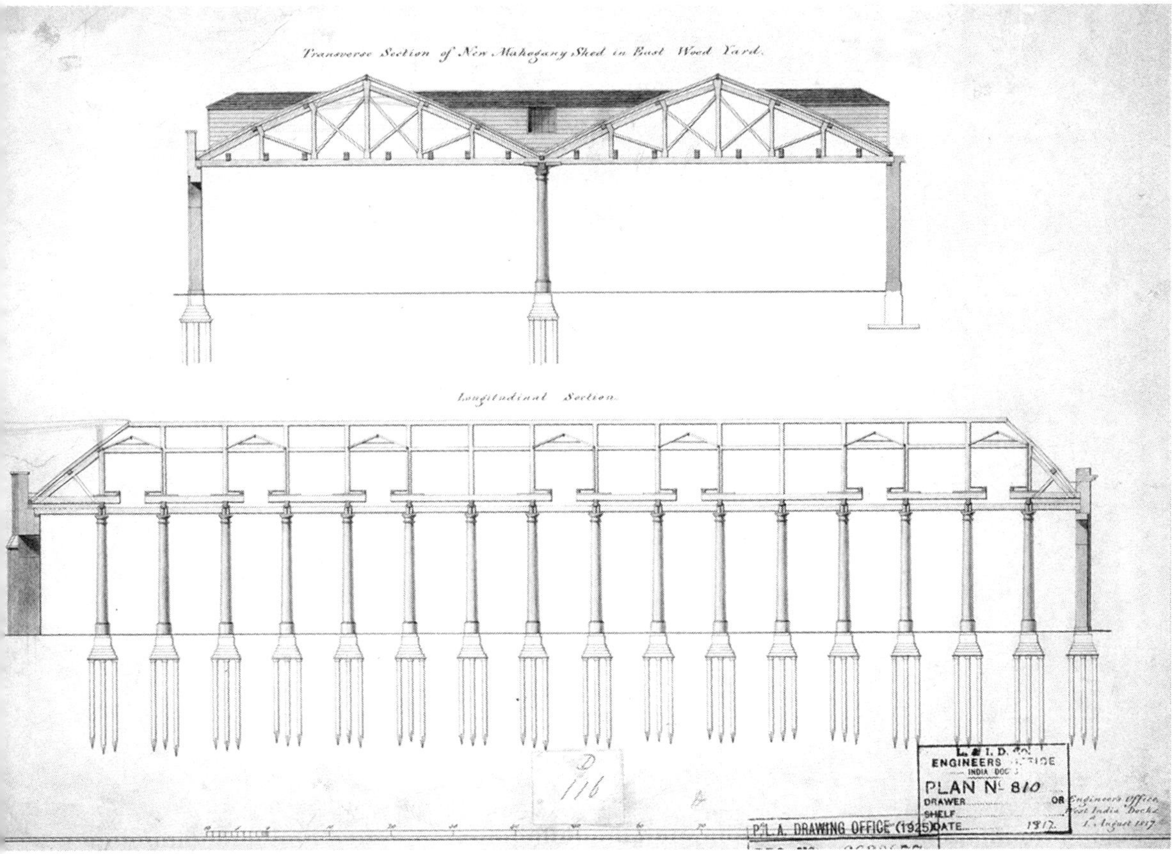

FIGURE 11.1. *John Rennie, West India Docks Mahogany Shed, London, 1817. Port of London Authority Collection, London Museum Docklands.*

ceptions of quality and scarcity have lent the wood a mystique that enhanced its fungibility at every turn.[7]

Along the mahogany supply chain, the identifiability of the various tradespeople who handled the wood corresponded to consumer proximity. Whereas joiners' and designers' inscriptions on salable goods, and signatures on drawings, justified the objects' value, the enslaved or free American workers had no opportunity to mark the material they had obtained. An 1853 woodworking manual read, "No wood extensively used in cabinet-making is better suited thus to exercise the judgment of the workman than mahogany."[8] A craftsperson, that is, could convey their unique skill and distinction in an object's very shape, or even in the selection of wood from which they fashioned one piece or another. The foresters who sought out the solitary trees from dense growth likewise exercised discerning judgment, but those skills were subsumed into the lumber's exchange value as it was shipped to metropolitan destinations for further sale.

While successive transfers between types of workers paralleled the gradual "refinement" of colonial produce into forms fit for urbane settings, such material exchanges were nevertheless multidirectional. As one scholar of US domestic patterns has observed, "Mahogany, an exotic wood closely associated with wealth, linked the furniture to the cosmopolitan tastes and merchant culture of the Atlantic world."[9] The early twentieth-century architectural historian Talbot Hamlin suggested that the wood occupied an integral place in the formation of a national paradigm.[10] Yet by placing it in the context of "American empire" aesthetics, Hamlin likewise intimated its transcontinental connections. At the same time, the wood's transformations detached resources from the labor of Black and Indigenous people and domesticated them for white consumers. Two paradoxes of material history thus emerge. First, the wood was valuable in itself but required human agency to render its inherent qualities perceivable, and thus monetizable. And second, mahogany commodities were both of the trees' sites of growth and removed from them; distance lent cachet, but retaining its recognizability as Caribbean-sourced hardwood remained essential to that cachet. Irene Cheng makes much the same point in her analysis of Greene & Greene houses through the lens of teak production—equally applicable to mahogany.[11] As mahogany left the realm of generalized, nondescript lumber to be processed into specific architectural accoutrements, its value increased. In other words, the further removed from its sources in the Americas it was, the more it was worth—and yet its value derived, inescapably, from the trees' native soil. Carving and finishing deracinated mahogany from the Caribbean Basin into architectural interiors, but its roots remained apparent in the wood's grain.

A single column in an 1847 issue of *Scientific American* illustrates these simultaneous dynamics of obfuscation and rootedness. In a chance encounter owing to pagination, the article "Origin of Negro Slavery" directly precedes the column on "Mahogany," separated only by an unrelated heading. The latter credits one Dr. Gibbons as "the first that brought from the West Indies some mahogany logs to London for ballast."[12] Finding the wood unworkable for architectural applications to build Gibbons's house, the carpenters discarded it, but Gibbons's wife persuaded him to use it for a candle box and furniture. "No other wood excels it yet," the brief essay concludes. In an alternative origin story, mahogany "was first used to repair some of Sir Walter Raleigh's ships at Trinidad."[13] The subtext of colonial exploitation is conveyed in both the geographic setting and the assertion of its "first" use—naturally, by British "explorers." The *Scientific American* article on mahogany says nothing about enslavement, nor does the article on slavery discuss mahogany. But their juxtaposition encapsulates the disparities between the labor of extraction and that of construction. Those who cut down the trees are elided, while Dr. Gibbons and his wife metonymically receive credit for importation. Recognition of the wood's value only occurs upon encounter with the trained eye of an unnamed master craftsman, "a cabinet maker," who made the candle box and then a bureau. The material thus embodied racial divisions of labor and class hierarchies.

This essay builds upon recent histories of mahogany by Jennifer L. Anderson, O. Nigel Bolland, and Daniel Finamore by concentrating on architecture.[14]

These authors have each admirably traced mahogany craft artifacts to Caribbean ecosystems, detailing processes of finding and felling trees, extracting them from forests, shipping logs to warehouses, and carving the wood into salable commodities. Considering those processes through overlapping lenses of race and architecture, however, this study devotes attention to the *spaces* where labor, transactions, and leisure occurred. The environments where workers rendered the wood a commodity were mahogany's physical context as much as its sites of installation. Rather than connecting geographic dots between growth, transfer, carving, and possession, therefore, this focus on architecture emphasizes frictions that precluded seamless transactions. Such barriers in the conversion of mahogany from a "raw" material to the domesticated elements of metropolitan buildings were also instruments of exclusion, allowing bourgeois white consumers to racialize logging teams in the Caribbean. Stopping points in between, such as port towns, ships, mahogany sheds, and merchants' warehouses, reflected the same geographic-racial distribution. At successive stages of mahogany's production, the dynamics of refinement gradually excluded the various people involved. It is appropriate, then, that mahogany so commonly became doors—architectural devices for discretionary exclusion.

Mahogany's geographic dispersion has historiographic implications for American architecture in three mutually intersecting categories: agents, materials, and geographies. First, the agents to whom we attribute architecture must include the workers who performed the labor to produce buildings' constitutive materials. Howard W. French observes, "Without African peoples trafficked from its shores, the Americas would have counted for little in the ascendance of the West."[15] The human exertion required to exploit the hemisphere's material wealth substantiates this assertion. Thus Black and Indigenous enslaved, formerly enslaved, and free people were indispensable to the era's architectural aesthetics. Second, our architectural histories must account for the ideologies of extraction that allowed for delineation between sites of production and sites of consumption, along lines of racial division of labor. Third, while "American" architecture includes buildings sited in the Americas, the incorporation of materials extracted from forests in the Americas makes British rural estates comparably "American" to their counterparts in New York. Attending to architectural materials, we may understand buildings not just as historical objects that reflect broader systems of racialization, but, further, as artifacts for extrapolating the presence of people whose humanity they have historically obscured.

Fittings and Furniture

By the early nineteenth century, when the West India Docks Mahogany Shed was completed, capitalists had exhausted the most desirable mahogany resources in Jamaica. Nevertheless, London's industrial-scale port infrastructure attests to the alternative Honduran varietal's relative abundance across Central America through the mid-nineteenth century. In the decades prior, mahogany had become a marker of elegance and distinction for the wealthy in the Caribbean, Europe, and North America. The wood's sumptuous reputation led to greater demand, persistent despite depletion of the most prized species. Bolstered by increased lower-quality stock, however, importers could rely on an expanded consumer market. One 1832 article noted, "If we had been speaking about . . . mahogany, thirty or forty years ago, we should have expected only to have interested the rich. . . . Now, what tradesman, or mechanic, or even cottager, does not possess some article of mahogany[?]"[16] Yet even as perceptions veered toward stuffy formality, mahogany retained airs of luxury. The 1853 woodworking manual ascribed Vitruvian superlatives: "the chief of furniture woods, whether considered in regard to beauty, utility, or durability."[17] Despite veneer's increasing popularity, mahogany's attainability in large-enough masses for carving entire components distinguished it from other precious woods.[18]

Mahogany's value exceeded financial quantification or projection of social status. Jeremy Bentham regarded mahogany as "an agreeable folly" that justified colonization.[19] Elsewhere, Bentham urged imperial powers to relinquish colonies and replace compulsory labor with wage payment. Despite exhortations against colonialism's inefficiencies, he conceded that "the mahogany which ornaments our apartments" was a source "of enjoyment, and the pleasure which results from these objects of luxury is in part the profit of colonization." Because climates conducive to mahogany trees are so different from Britain's, colonial agriculture complemented domestic production and therefore extenuated other disadvantages of retaining control over remote territories. An 1832 article deemed it an acceptable extravagance for the "labouring man" who, having saved up, "may afford his wife a mahogany tea-table."[20] Bentham agreed: "Novelty and variety are sources of pleasure," and mahogany fulfilled those desires.[21]

Through the eighteenth century, mahogany accumulated prestige from association with well-known designers and aristocratic consumers. In 1751, George William Coventry, sixth Earl of Coventry, inherited Croome Court in the West Midlands, and in 1760 he hired Robert Adam to appoint it. The Coventry family capitalized on colonial exploitation in India and later married into Caribbean wealth, and in 1835 descendants received compensation for Black people whom they claimed as possessions in Jamaica.[22] Adam's renovation included sundry mahogany items, the largest a wraparound bookcase manufactured by royal cabinetmakers William Vile and John Cobb.[23] Replete with Ionic pilasters, a frieze, pediments, and finials, its neoclassical detailing, combined with its spanning around the room's corners, created an immersive architectural environment (fig. 11.2). If the entire interior was not to be covered in solid mahogany, the bookcase approached the effect of encasement inside a figured mahogany block. Adam's

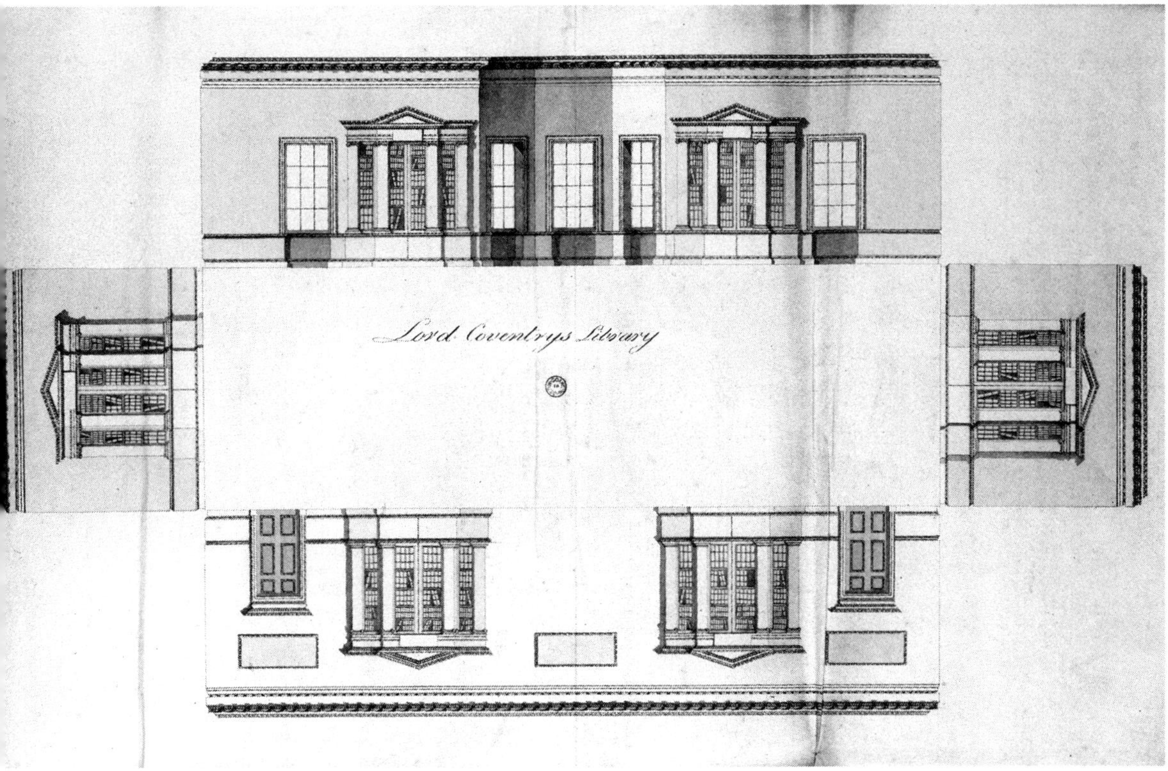

FIGURE 11.2. *Robert Adam, Lord Coventry's Library, Croome Court, Worcestershire, England, 1761. © Sir John Soane's Museum, London.*

drawing combining the room's plan and its interior elevations corroborates this interpretation. Robin Evans describes such "developed surface interior" drawings as "a way of turning architecture inside-out."[24] In late eighteenth-century English aristocratic society, these drawings created insular interiors: "Each room is its own little empire of activity, allusion, and colour; each a totally encompassing enterprise."[25] Although Evans's subject is not British imperialism, his invocation of "empire" suggests that these rooms at once bracketed the outside world and created imperial dominion in miniature. "Introverted and boxed in," Evans argues, the illusion of self-containment detaches the interior from its context, separated and deracinated.[26] In that sheltered space, mahogany fittings retain their exotic enchantment while also constituting the mansion's owner's "own little empire."

By the nineteenth century, mechanization played a role in mahogany production, following trends signaled by the West India Docks' industrial import facility. Mahogany was a major constituent material in the 1851 Crystal Palace. Iron balustrades were capped by Honduran mahogany handrails and newel posts. On-site workers operated a machine specially designed to plane, bevel, and round off the wood. Contemporary descriptions underscore the rhetorical consumption of the wood: Pressure rollers had "teeth," and cutters "form[ed] . . . the jaws of the hollow cylinder . . . , constantly swallowing lengths of rough mahogany."[27] Moreover, stair treads were made of a Caribbean-derived wood, sabicu, casually identified as mahogany. Visitors to the Crystal Palace literally grasped mahogany and treaded on it underfoot, thus manifesting the wood's ambivalent value and abundance.

At the Great Exhibition of the Works of Industry of All Nations in London, what counted as "industry" varied, depending on the place represented. The Crystal Palace exhibited a number of mahogany manufactured items, attributed to where they were carved and joined. Whereas mahogany doors and furniture appeared as European contributions, the Caribbean was represented by sugarcane, pitch, and other raw materials—including unfinished Trinidadian and Dominican mahogany samples—and mahogany appeared in the nondenominated "Vegetable and Animal Substances Used in Manufactures" section.[28] The American "industry" that felled trees for export was celebrated only for furnishing opportunities to increase exchange value by transforming the material into consumer commodities. The Great Exhibition catalog cited the artisans who crafted the objects on display, but the Americans who obtained the wood remained nameless.

Just before the Great Exhibition, William Makepeace Thackeray's 1847 poem "The Mahogany Tree" wistfully memorialized a party enjoyed around a mahogany table. Slightly bucking more prevalent indifference to the material's sourcing, the Christmas "Weather without" contrasts against an acknowledgment that "Once on the boughs / Birds of rare plume / Sang, in its bloom."[29] If not precisely about resource extraction, the lyrics' juxtaposition of the tropical wood as backdrop with a wintry England scene demonstrates the material's capacity to refer to the remote Americas.[30] The wooden table acts as a receptacle of memories of both the joy of present festivities and mahogany's path from the Caribbean to England. The comfort of the familiar piece of furniture is counterbalanced by mahogany's foreignness: not simply wood, but a tree, and an entire ecosystem.

Forced Labor and Forests

Prospectors gradually consumed nearly all Jamaican mahogany through the eighteenth century to clear land for yet more lucrative sugarcane fields.[31] Some landowners capitalized on that scarcity by using mahogany to hedge against bad crops of their primary products.[32] Merchants' attempts to pass off inferior-quality wood as Jamaican backfired, diminishing the onetime highest-value category's status.[33] The shift of mahogany extraction to British Honduras (present-day Belize) and elsewhere, and British emancipation from 1834 to 1838, brought changes to the logging business. Yet even after full emancipation, the majority of mahogany harvesters were formerly enslaved people and their children.

The 1827 *Honduras Almanack*, published in an edition of seventy-two, of which only three survive, narrated mahogany lumber acquisition. The tree was so significant to British Honduras, the *Almanack* explains, that it crowned the colony's escutcheon, flanked by Indigenous male lumberjacks and emblazoned with cutting tools, a Union Jack, and a ship: in all, a heraldic visualization of extraction. (Today's Belizean flag retains all of those symbols except the British standard.) Mahogany's size and characteristics were otherworldly, apparently "designed by Nature for the use of a race, of more colossal proportion than the present."[34] Oak, erstwhile "King of the Forest," compares poorly—a notable remark, given English national identification with that species since the future Charles II evaded the Roundheads by hiding in a so-called Royal Oak. The burgeoning English Navy, whose ships were largely oak, bolstered that mythology. Yet if oak "dwindle[d] to insignificance in . . . comparison" to mahogany, felling the trees was testament to humanity's triumph over the natural world, and human ingenuity transformed the wood from obscure, exotic vegetation into an essential economic motor.[35] After brief remarks on botany and history, the *Almanack* details "a most extensive branch of British commerce . . . the Cutting and preparing of the Mahogany."[36] What follows draws from that account.

Finding mahogany trees required its own architecture (fig. 11.3). Cutters set up camps with huts thatched with grass or leaves, hammocks, and cooking areas. The *Almanack* admired the "much rural taste" of the uniform yet variegated architecture, "invariably form[ing] a conspicuous figure." From this "small village," as *The Family Magazine* called the camps in 1836, workers used cutting tools and fire to clear roads to the mahogany trees.[37] They often destroyed other valuable lumber in favor of the larger prize, except when smaller trees were useful for building bridges over streams. A captain, sometimes free, sometimes enslaved,

MAHOGANY ESTABLISHMENT ON THE RIVER ULUA, HONDURAS. [From our own Correspondent.]

FIGURE 11.3. *"Mahogany Establishment on the River Ulua, Honduras."* Ballou's Pictorial Drawing-Room Companion, *May 21, 1859, 328.*

directed the work, delegating a "hunter," the "most intelligent of his fellows," who excelled in navigation, to scout out trees. Teams of foresters ventured out on expeditions during the dry season—August until early spring—when logs were likely to remain intact when they fell. By December, the majority of the felling work would be finished, and cutters turned to trimming and squaring the logs, strapping them to ox-drawn carts, and floating them to ports.

The Family Magazine acknowledged workers, if only for their cost: "A great portion of the price of this timber must be made up of the cost of the labour required for transporting it from its native forests to the place of embarkation."[38] Yet the laborers' value to eventual profiteers lay in their specialized knowledge of locating mahogany trees among dense thickets and transporting logs for export. Financiers nevertheless typically compensated workers with goods rather than cash, to decrease labor costs.[39] Construction ability and spatial acuity over vast landscapes contrast with joiners' much smaller-scale expertise carving blocks into fittings for even more spatially confined "little empires."

An 1855 account underscored the division of labor: "Of all occupations known to man, that of the mahogany-cutter is perhaps the wildest in its nature, and yet among the most systematic in its arrangements."[40] Tasks were divided by gender as well as by capabilities.[41] Hunters searched forests for eligible trees by climbing trees, scouting out targets, and guiding teams to them. The job entailed considerable autonomy, and enterprising hunters pitted capitalists against one another when they located mahogany trees. Axmen performed the strenuous work of chopping into the trees' girth, some ten feet off the ground, balanced on precarious stilts (fig. 11.4). Below that point, trunks were irregular and tougher, whereas above, they were more cylindrical.[42] Others then trimmed limbs and branches, roughly squaring lumber into logs. This process likewise involved skill, to balance loads borne by draft animals. During the carting stage, haulage occurred overnight to take advantage of cooler temperatures. By day, workers gathered animal feed. Another specialized task was tending and driving the livestock to waterside holding grounds. These were the bases for the second phase of the extraction process, from March until May: sending logs downriver for longer-distance portage.[43] Women and children participated, clearing brush to reach trees and then making paths for hauling felled ones out. At camps, women and young people also cultivated edible crops and prepared food.[44] Enslaved Black people developed other skilled occupations related to mahogany cutting, including blacksmithing to maintain tools and carpentry.

The contemporary scholar Malcolm Ferdinand, discussing the animalization of Black people, refers to "hunting" as a lens through which white people have racialized others.[45] Indeed, the "hunter," and all of the workers and working animals who contributed to the domestication of mahogany trees into quantifiable, commodified lumber, attests to these people's subjugation. That is, these laborers

FIGURE 11.4. *J. McGahey, "Felling Mahogany, Honduras," 1850. Courtesy of the American Antiquarian Society.*

were coerced into performing a "hunt" that parallels the apprehension and capture of dehumanized objects of value (animals, people, or otherwise).

Although large portions of the mahogany harvested from forests around the Caribbean Basin were exported to metropolitan markets for greater capitalization, some remained local. In the midst of emancipation, a white tourist in 1835 remarked on Black people's inhospitality to white visitors but described "huts . . . by no means incommodious, uncleanly, or ill furnished. In some I have seen mahogany four-post bedsteads, mahogany chests of drawers, . . . [etc.] which are not to be found . . . even in the cottage of an English peasant."[46] An 1810 description of Belizean merchant-class mansions portrayed houses raised on sturdy mahogany piles, about ten feet off the ground.[47] The literal perch of such buildings on mahogany foundations recalls the axmen's precarious platforms. An enslaver's 1816 diary entry mentioned a church in Spanish Town, Jamaica (likely St. Jago de la Vega or St. Catherine's), with "walls lined with fine mahogany."[48] The 1829 edition of *The Honduras Almanack* described the metropolitan church St. John's (built 1812–1815; consecrated 1826; as of 1891, the Anglican cathedral) as "the first building of note in Belize," featuring mahogany railings, pews, doors, and a "moveable Mahogany circular Font of beautiful workmanship."[49] The church's bricks arrived in Belize from England as nearly worthless ballast. Using "expenses defrayed by the inhabitants" of Belize, enslaved people unloaded those bricks and used them to construct the building.[50]

The West India Docks Mahogany Shed, Croome Court, and the Crystal Palace would not have existed as such without American timber harvested by people of African and Indigenous American descent. Conversely, the Jamaican and Belizean churches were built by African Americans from combinations of English and local materials on American sites. Architecture inevitably consolidates substances and people from near and far into roughly bounded spaces. The qualities of mahogany, however, inhere in the material, prompting historical observers to recall the factors of its production and where it came from.

Factors and Figure

Mahogany occupied a particular place in the economy, delineated from both the general field of wood suppliers and the craftspeople who specialized in hewing it into interior fittings. One observer noted that US mahogany yards were specialized businesses, as opposed to those in England, where builders also acted as importers and timber merchants.[51] Dockside in metropolitan ports, merchants auctioned off the choicest hunks of mahogany.

Artisans' premises, often fire resistant, bore few distinguishing architectural characteristics, simply well-fenestrated "room[s] of greater or lesser length."[52] In 1844, *The Penny Magazine* described a large, perhaps atypical site in Newcastle that had, among other buildings, its own mahogany shed, as well as a "manager's room, so placed as to give a sort of 'panopticon,' as Bentham would have called it."[53] A view shows workers at benches with scattered tools and furniture parts, broadly visible across a bright, open floor.[54] Machines like lathes incorporated mahogany, as the wood's density absorbed vibrations. The complex included workers' housing, planned for ventilation, and evoked "a general air of comfort."[55] Such corporate-paternalist governance evokes Samuel Bentham's initial reasoning behind the Panopticon, to prevent dockyard workers from pocketing scraps for off-hours sale. It also invites comparison to the foresters' camps, which, notably, escaped the authoritative gaze of a "manager."

In North America, the neoclassical fronts depicted in an unattributed watercolor of the prominent importer-woodworker Duncan Phyfe's Manhattan stores communicated the "refinement" that Phyfe's clients could expect (fig. 11.5). Ample windows suggest a showroom exhibiting wares to passersby. The rightmost building's skylight would have enabled fine benchwork, and basement fenestration allowed for five stories of working floors. Three white, fashionably dressed figures examine klismos chairs, while next door, white workers peek out of the warehouse door. The range of social classes on display belies the idealization of Phyfe's workforce. His most prolific periods coincided with the legal, if moribund, insti-

FIGURE 11.5. *"Shop and Warehouse of Duncan Phyfe, 168–172 Fulton Street, New York City," ca. 1817–1820. Watercolor, black ink, and gouache on white laid paper, 15⅝ × 19⅝ inches (39.7 × 49.8 cm). Rogers Fund, 1922 (22.28.1). © The Metropolitan Museum of Art. Image source: Art Resource, NY.*

tution of slavery in New York, and enslaved and free Black artisans commonly worked for such enterprises.[56] Phyfe made interior fittings for enslavers' labor camp–plantation houses in the Southern United States.[57]

The free Black North Carolina furniture maker Thomas Day, who also worked in mahogany in the first half of the nineteenth century, presents a companion example to Phyfe's.[58] Both an enslaver himself and an employer of enslaved workers, Day purchased raw materials from merchants rather than importing his own. Yet Day and Phyfe each profited from mahogany by shaping it into geometric forms, detaching it from its sources while leveraging its inherent qualities to produce value.

No mere building material, mahogany encapsulated an entire system of economy and culture. To signal the degree of "civilization" that the English colonial Sierra Leonean settlers had attained by the 1850s, one writer remarked on the "considerable sprinkling of mahogany furniture of European workmanship . . . to be found in" comparatively wealthy American Africans' houses.[59] Its Caribbean origins notwithstanding, mahogany had to undergo all of these successive phases—and receive the imprimatur of whiteness—to become a facilitator of civilization.

Finish

Lewis Mumford begins *The Brown Decades* by observing that by the later nineteenth century, mahogany's bright hues had become outmoded, replaced by dark, somber walnut.[60] Indeed, walnut signified opulence at the Freedmen's Savings Bank building in Washington, DC (1871; demolished 1899), which Frederick Douglass appraised as "one of the most costly and splendid buildings of the time . . . finished on the inside with black walnut . . . with all the modern improvements."[61] The allure of mahogany declined as other "exotic" woods became increasingly available globally. Jennifer L. Anderson explains contraction in demand for mahogany through the combined dynamics of conflating mahogany with people—echoed by Malcolm Ferdinand—and, over the nineteenth century, growing antislavery sentiment.[62] Mahogany still elicited admiration, particularly the nearly extinct Jamaican variety, but it belonged to a bygone epoch.

At the same time that mahogany's currency was declining, its identifications with geographic sources were increasingly hollow.[63] Distinguishing types from one another proved difficult even among experts, resulting in convincing substitutions. The detriment to mahogany merchants nevertheless affirmed the arbitrariness of the subspecies' relative value. Climatological and botanical factors, of course, transcend designations like Jamaican, San Domingo, or Florida mahogany, as such territorial classifications bear little empirical validity. But mahogany's defiance of national borders demonstrates the capaciousness of the designation of American mahogany in three ways. First, the wood has grown across the islands and continental mainland of the Caribbean Basin, generally considered parts of the Americas, and is thus American. Second, its American-ness is definitively not restricted to the United States. Although an American wood, it never grew predominantly in the United States, even after land grabs of Florida in 1819 and Puerto Rico in 1898. Third, buildings and spaces situated in England, for instance, and thus not American, like several cases discussed here, were built from American components. People in the Americas, many forcibly transported there, whose American identity was imposed on them by Europeans, made those materials available. Another truism: Indigenous lumberjacks likely did not think of themselves as American. Questioning the historicity of "American architecture" unsettles the colonial categories ideologically instilled in architectural history.

Mahogany's lasting allure stems from the material's indelibility—its "memory," if not its "brain"—which persistently links it back to its sites of growth.[64] The towering trees that entrepreneurs coveted through the eighteenth and nineteenth centuries were marvels of the Caribbean landscape, and the difficulty of extracting felled timber only compounded that inextricability, even when the material was physically removed. The wood's use in architecture, an ineluctably sited form of material production, is therefore particularly thorny. Whether the wood constituted the space, as at Croome Court, or it was the object of more mobile mechanical functions, like at the West India Docks, connoisseurs perpetually referred to its wildness, exoticizing it and relishing its elusive resistance to relocation.

These themes of situatedness and sitelessness, material memory and forced labor, and the narratives inherent in objects were central to the artist Cameron Rowland's 2020 exhibition *3 & 4 Will IV c. 73*. One piece, *Encumbrance*, featured a set of Georgian mahogany doors leased from the British Crown Estate and installed at the London Institute of Contemporary Arts. Rowland's accompanying essay calls mahogany "one of the few commodities of the triangular trade that continues to generate value for those who currently own it."[65] Arranging for a mortgage on the mahogany items, Rowland deliberately impeded the dynamics of capital accumulation, separating their value as artifacts from their value-earning potential as objects of investment or stores of capital. This transposition may or may not add value to the doors in the long term. But wresting them out of their historical context while leaving them in roughly their physical historical environment at once acknowledges the material's enduring commodification while imbuing it with historical consciousness. Doors, architecture's most rudimentary moving parts, signify passage; and mahogany doors, doubly so. Their recognizable materiality is a constant reminder of their sourcing. The architectural spaces fashioned from mahogany thus encase the wood as valuable while deflecting back outward to the sites, the processes, and the people who imbued that value.

Acknowledgments

Special thanks to Aleksandr Bierig, David Brody, Erica Morawski, and Peter Minosh, as well as the editors and contributors to this volume for indispensable feedback. I developed this project as a UCLA Getty-Ahmanson Fellow with Stella Nair, Paul Niell, and Bronwen Wilson, and my colleague David Sadighian. Alyce Englund gave generous access to the Metropolitan Museum of Art's holdings.

Notes

1. See Nathaniel Hibbert, *Report of the Select Committee on Foreign Trade* (London: J. M. Richardson, 1823), esp. 53.

2. Tom F. Peters, *Building the Nineteenth Century* (MIT Press, 1996), 352.

3. "The West India Docks: The Buildings, Sheds," in *Survey of London: Volumes 43 and 44; Poplar, Blackwall and Isle of Dogs*, ed. Hermione Hobhouse (London County Council, 1994), 300–310.

4. John Rennie, *The Theory, Formation, and Construction of British and Foreign Harbours* (London: J. Weale, 1851), 250.

5. See Robert Naylor, "The Mahogany Trade as a Factor in the British Return to the Mosquito Shore in the Second Quarter of the 19th Century," *Jamaican Historical Review* 7, no. 1 (1967): 45n7.

6. See, for example, Klas Rönnbäck, "On the Economic Importance of the Slave Plantation Complex to the British Economy During the Eighteenth Century: A Value-Added Approach," *Journal of Global History* 13, no. 3 (2018): 309–327; Joseph E. Inikori, *Africans and the Industrial Revolution in England: A Study in International Trade and Economic Development* (Cambridge University Press, 2005).

7. See Adam Bowett, *Woods in British Furniture-Making, 1400–1900: An Illustrated Historical Dictionary* (Royal Botanic Gardens, Kew, 2012), under "Mahogany."

8. P. Thomson, *The Cabinet-Maker's Assistant* (Glasgow: Blackie and Son, 1853), 35.

9. Bernard L. Herman, *Town House: Architecture and Material Life in the Early American City, 1780–1830* (University of North Carolina Press, 2005), 223.

10. Talbot Hamlin, *Greek Revival Architecture in America* (Dover, 1964), esp. 34, 128.

11. Irene Cheng, "Architectures," in *A Concise Companion to Visual Culture*, ed. A. Joan Saab, Aubrey Anable, and Catherine Zuromskis (John Wiley & Sons, 2021), 177–199, esp. 193.

12. "Mahogany," *Scientific American* 2, no. 34 (1847): 269.

13. See *The Honduras Almanack, for the Year of Our Lord 1827* (Belize: N.p., 1827), 4–5. Quote from *The Builder's Practical Director; or, Buildings for All Classes* [. . .] (Leipzig: A. H. Payne, 1855), 147.

14. Jennifer L. Anderson, *Mahogany: The Costs of Luxury in Early America* (Harvard University Press, 2012); O. Nigel Bolland, "Timber Extraction and the Shaping of Enslaved People's Culture in Belize," in *Slavery Without Sugar: Diversity in the Caribbean Economy and Society Since the 17th Century*, ed. Verene A. Shepherd (University Press of Florida, 2002), 36–62; O. Nigel Bolland, "Slavery in Belize," in *Colonialism and Resistance in Belize: Essays in Historical Sociology* (University of the West Indies Press, 2003), 50–77; Daniel Finamore, "Furnishing the Craftsman: Slaves and Sailors in the Mahogany Trade," *American Furniture*, 2008, https://chipstone.org/article.php/582/American-Furniture-2008/Furnishing-the-Craftsman:-Slaves-and-Sailors-in-the-Mahogany-Trade; Daniel Finamore, "'Pirate Water': Sailing to Belize in the Mahogany Trade," in *Maritime Empires: British Imperial Maritime Trade in the Nineteenth Century*, ed. David Killingray, Margarette Lincoln, and Nigel Rigby (Boydell Press, 2004), 30–47.

15. Howard W. French, introduction to *Born in Blackness: Africa, Africans, and the Making of the Modern World, 1471 to the Second World War* (Liveright, 2021).

16. "The Mahogany Table," *Penny Magazine*, June 16, 1832, 107–109. See also Anderson, *Mahogany*, 2, 58–63.

17. Thomson, *Cabinet-Maker's Assistant*, 27.

18. See Jennifer Y. Chuong, "The Nature of American Veneer Furniture, Circa 1790–1810," *Journal 18*, no. 9 (Spring 2020), https://www.journal18.org/4733.

19. Jeremy Bentham, *The Manual of Political Economy*, in *The Works of Jeremy Bentham*, vol. 3, ed. John Bowring (Russell & Russell, 1962), 52.

20. "On the Choice of a Labouring Man's Dwelling," *Penny Magazine*, April 7, 1832, 16.

21. Bentham, *Manual of Political Economy*, 52.

22. "Hon. Anna Maria Coventry (Née Eves)," Legacies of British Slavery Database, https://www.ucl.ac.uk/lbs/person/view/18374.

23. Geoffrey Beard, "Decorators and Furniture Makers at Croome Court," *Furniture History* 29 (1993): 88–113.

24. Robin Evans, "The Developed Surface: An Enquiry into the Brief Life of an Eighteenth-Century Drawing Technique," in *Translations from Drawing to Building* (Architectural Association, 1997), 202–203.

25. Evans, "Developed Surface," 207.

26. Evans, "Developed Surface," 208.

27. Peter Berlyn and Charles Fowler Jr., *The Crystal Palace: Its Architectural History and Constructive Marvels* (London: James Gilbert, 1851), 79.

28. *Official Catalogue of the Great Exhibition of the Works of Industry of All Nations, 1851* (London: Spicer Brothers, 1851), 175.

29. William Makepeace Thackeray, "The Mahogany Tree," *Punch* 12 (January 1847): 13.

30. Thackeray would witness US Southern slavery in ensuing speaking tours in the 1850s, although his impressions were not wholly negative. James Grant Wilson, *Thackeray in the United States, 1852–3, 1855–6* (Dodd, Mead, 1904), 145, 298–301.

31. See Edward Long, *The History of Jamaica*, vol. 3 (London: T. Lowndes, 1774), 842; William Beckford, *A Descriptive Account of the Island of Jamaica*, vol. 2 (London: T. and J. Egerton, 1790), 260.

32. See Anderson, *Mahogany*, 78.

33. See Edward Long, *The History of Jamaica*, vol. 1 (London: T. Lowndes, 1774), 498.

34. *Honduras Almanack for 1827*, 3.

35. *Honduras Almanack for 1827*, 3–4.

36. *Honduras Almanack for 1827*, 3–4.

37. *Honduras Almanack for 1827*, 10–11; "Mahogany," *Family Magazine* 3 (1836): 470.

38. "Mahogany," *Family Magazine* 3 (1836): 469.

39. See Naylor, "Mahogany Trade," 45.

40. E. G. Squier, *Notes on Central America* (New York: Harper & Brothers, 1855), 173.

41. See Anderson, *Mahogany*, 64, 80, 160–161, 166; Bolland, "Timber Extraction"; Bolland, "Slavery in Belize," esp. 56–57; Edward Chaloner, *The Mahogany Tree: Its Botanical Characters, Qualities and Uses* [. . .] (Liverpool: Rockliff and Son, 1850), 40–41.

42. *Honduras Almanack for 1827*, 8. See also "The Mahogany Forests with the Carib Lumbermen of Honduras," *New York Times*, January 27, 1889, 6.

43. *Honduras Almanack for 1827*, 12–13.

44. See Bolland, "Timber Extraction," 44.

45. Malcolm Ferdinand, *Decolonial Ecology: Thinking from the Caribbean World*, trans. Anthony Paul Smith (Polity, 2022), 217–218.

46. R. R. Madden, *A Twelvemonth's Residence in the West Indies* (London: James Cochrane, 1835), 185–186.

47. George Henderson, *An Account of the British Settlement of Honduras* (London: R. Baldwin, 1811), 16–17.

48. Matthew Gregory Lewis, *Journal of a West-India Proprietor* (London: John Murray, 1834), 161.

49. *The Honduras Almanack, for the Year of Our Lord 1829* (Belize: N.p., 1829), 18–20, 26.

50. "View of St. John's Church in Belise, Honduras," frontispiece, *The Honduras Society for Promoting Christian Knowledge*, 1825.

51. Henry Bradshaw Fearon, *Sketches of America: A Narrative of a Journey of Five Thousand Miles* [. . .] (London: Longman, Hurst, Rees, Orme, and Brown, 1819), 23.

52. "Sopwiths' Cabinet-Factory," *Penny Magazine Monthly Supplement*, August 1844, 342–344.

53. "Sopwiths' Cabinet-Factory," 342.

54. See Rosamond Allwood, "Thomas Sopwith of Newcastle 1803–1879," *Furniture History* 26 (1990): 1–9.

55. "Sopwiths' Cabinet-Factory."

56. See Shane White, *Somewhat More Independent: The End of Slavery in New York City, 1770–1810* (University of Georgia Press, 2012), 160.

57. Frances F. Bretter, "Patrons of the Cabinet Warehouse," in *Duncan Phyfe: Master Cabinetmaker in New York* ed. Peter M. Kenny, Michael K. Brown, Frances F. Bretter, and Matthew A. Thurlow (Metropolitan Museum of Art, 2011), esp. 144–152.

58. Patricia Phillips Marshall and Jo Ramsay Leimenstoll, *Thomas Day: Master Craftsman and Free Man of Color* (University of North Carolina Press, 2010), 26–31, 68, 228n29.

59. J. Leighton Wilson, *Western Africa: Its History, Condition, and Prospects* (London: Sampson Low, 1856), 424–425, 427.

60. Lewis Mumford, *The Brown Decades: A Study of the Arts in America, 1865–1895* (Harcourt, Brace, 1931), 8.

61. Frederick Douglass, *Life and Times of Frederick Douglass* (Hartford, CT: Park, 1882), 488.

62. Anderson, *Mahogany*, 293–299; Ferdinand, *Decolonial Ecology*, 58–61.

63. See Anderson, *Mahogany*, 308–315.

64. Karl Marx, *Capital: A Critique of Political Economy*, vol. 1 (Moscow: Progress, 1887), ch. 1, sec. 1.

65. Cameron Rowland, "3 & 4 Will. IV c. 73," Institute of Contemporary Arts, London, 2020, https://www.ica.art/media/03104.pdf.

12 BUILDING AN EVANGELICAL UTOPIA

MISSIONARIES AND THE RACIAL DESTINY OF THE UNITED STATES IN THE "NEAR EAST"

Yasmina El Chami

RECENT SCHOLARSHIP ON US SETTLER colonial history has encouraged a reexamination of the nation's historiography and that of its built environment, yet the simultaneous movement of outward expansion and soft imperialism that the American nation began in the early nineteenth century, and the role of extra-national, non-European projects in the formation of an "American" architectural and national culture, remain little explored. Focusing on questions of style and representation, architectural historians have highlighted the role of architecture in articulating the question of who was to be included and represented in the nation's political body, and the racialized perspectives underpinning the work of white Euro-American architects in this period.[1] The elaboration of an "aesthetic of whiteness" in nineteenth-century American architecture, in parallel with the efforts to locate an American style within a presumed timeline of civilizational progress, has been understood as the result of evolving ideas of scientific racism, influenced by European (secular) intellectual thought as well as by the American nation's particular reliance on settler colonialism and slavery.[2] Missing in these architectural histories is the fundamental role of religion within these perspectives, and the important role that missionary societies had in refining national ideas in nineteenth-century America, through their work both at home and overseas.[3]

Indeed, the notion of a divine mission had been central to the establishment of the Puritan colonies as well as the political trajectory of the American republic. From the early missions among the "Indians" to the eighteenth- and nineteenth-century millennial revivals, education, evangelical conversion, and territorial conquest had been necessarily intertwined.[4] Within the North American continent, the expansion of the United States had importantly relied on the growth of industrial power, capital, and technology in parallel with the spread of evangelicalism toward the "frontier."[5] But while early eschatological thought viewed the United States itself as the land of divine providence—the site for a "new Zion"—by the late eighteenth century, the American Revolution, continuous colonial expansion, and the steady growth of industrial wealth of the nation had transformed the evangelical understanding of divine destiny from "a nation that itself was elect to a nation of elect individuals."[6] In parallel, the notion of a biblical Promised Land, which had held wide currency in the early establishment of the nation, also transformed, from a metaphor to be re-created within North America to an ancient territory to be itself reclaimed.[7] In 1810, the first overseas missionary society, the American Board of Commissioners for Foreign Missions (ABCFM), was formed at Andover Theological Seminary by elite college men who saw themselves as divinely appointed to lead America's renovation of the whole world. In that sense, the American overseas missionary movement begun in the early nineteenth century was from its inception simultaneously a racial, religious, and colonial project. Its foundations were a unique synthesis of national and Protestant belief in the white Anglo-American race as representative of a superior civilization divinely appointed to renovate the whole world.[8]

Complicating the understanding of Moorish or Near Eastern motifs in early modern American architecture as indicative of a vague association with a Jewish past, this chapter aims to show that the evangelical association of Anglo-Americans with the "Near East" was much more than a distant or superficial echo.[9] Rather, taking the ideas of evangelical millennial thought seriously shows that nineteenth-century Anglo-American elites aspired in very tangible and real ways to understand, experience, and eventually transform the "Holy Land." This materialized as an extensive spatial, material, and architectural project that established the United States as a dual Anglo-American and evangelical empire from the beginnings of the nineteenth century. The chapter examines the beginnings of this American transnational, proto-imperial architectural history through the prism of American evangelical missionaries' activities in Ottoman Syria, focusing on the architectural and patronage networks undergirding their building activities in Beirut. I explore, in particular, the activities of a small group of missionaries and philanthropists of the so-called Progressive Era that were central to the elaboration and construction of the Syrian Protestant College, founded by missionaries of the ABCFM in 1866. The chapter uncovers the complex web of ideas regarding race, religion, science, and architecture that shaped seemingly unrelated educational and architectural projects in the United States and Beirut. I argue that the elaboration of exceptionalism in the United States and the intersection of Gilded Age and Progressive Era narratives were intimately related not only to a settler colonial expansionist ambition at a territorial level within the North American continent, but also theologically and materially to the Near East and the Holy Land, through the networks of evangelical-industrial-philanthropic patronage underpinning this dual national-universal project. This dual project relied on a specific relationship between its moral and spatial-material dimensions: Scientific knowledge was both the ideological basis for narratives of civilizational superiority and the spatial technology materializing civilizational spread overseas. In this sense, Progressive Era ideas of civilizational uplift and the industrial wealth undergirding the architecture of the Gilded Age were two sides of the same coin. The Syrian Protestant College, an early manifestation of the evangelical interest in the Near East, by virtue of its proximity to Palestine, as well as its liberal transformation, is an ideal entry point to examine how evangelical notions of divine destiny transformed into a dual racial-material project by the turn of the twentieth century. Focusing especially on the design of the Science Hall at the college in Beirut in conjunction with a memorial chapel for Columbia University in New York, this chapter illustrates how science, education, industrialism, and architecture were crucial in this project of othering and reformation, of "civilization" and colonialism.

The Syrian Protestant College: A Model and an Experiment

American missionaries of the ABCFM arrived in Beirut in 1823, after attempting and failing to settle in Jerusalem, but their efforts at conversion for the first forty years were not fruitful.[10] In 1866, following various political events in the Ottoman Empire, a decision was made to establish a college independently from the mission, which would work on evangelization through education.[11] The new college was incorporated in 1864, and a board of trustees was constituted with the help of William E. Dodge, a partner at Phelps, Dodge & Company, whose son had befriended the missionaries in Beirut during a trip to Palestine. The men involved in the Syrian Protestant College Board of Trustees were all part of the same circle of New York and US Northeastern evangelical elite: They had been educated at the colleges of Princeton, Harvard, and Yale; were part of the US House of Representatives or held extensive industrial and business assets; sat on boards of temperance and philanthropic societies, as well as the American Colonization Society; and championed so-called Progressive ideas, especially after the US Civil War.[12] William Dodge's son, David Stuart Dodge, served as the first treasurer of the college, leading its day-to-day operations from his office in New York, in close collaboration with the new college president, Daniel Bliss.

The college in Beirut was envisioned by David S. Dodge as both a model and an experiment in the renewed millennial project of reforming the whole world. What Dodge called the "advance of the race" would be achieved through the progress of missions; this was to be simultaneously a moral-educational and a material-spatial project.[13] From the center, in the United States, appropriate men were to be recruited, preferably from Princeton's and Yale's seminaries. This need contributed to the establishment of the Teachers College in New York in 1887, begun by Dodge's niece, Grace Hoadley Dodge. Incorporated in 1892 by a board made up of many of the same philanthropic families who sat on the boards of the Syrian Protestant College, the American Colonization Society, and the ABCFM, it was established as an experimental institute for the teaching of "lesser" races. Similar to the college in Beirut, it was not meant to create men who would be considered equals in the American missionaries' eyes. Rather, the pedagogical project was part of a broader Christian civilizationism doctrine that appointed white Anglo-America as morally responsible for "civilizing" the "lower" races, while remaining culturally superior.[14] But while within the United States missionary work highlighted the racial limits of Christian universalism, overseas, especially in the "biblical lands," it was through religious civilizational hierarchies that "heathen," "Mohammedan," and "nominal Christian" people would need to be othered and reformed.[15] It was precisely through education, increasingly liberal and scientific, that such a project could be achieved. Architecture was the prime site in which this displacement could both take place and be represented, and unsurprisingly, architects figured prominently in the tight network of familial evangelical philanthropy that sustained such educational projects. Two projects designed by Isaac Newton Phelps Stokes and John Mead Howells for the Syrian Protestant College and Columbia University illustrate how architecture was crucial in building up an imagined evangelical American civilization at home and overseas.

Archaeology, Science, and the Architectural "Advance of the Race"

The project for a science museum at the Syrian Protestant College in 1896 showcased the growing importance of scientific knowledge for liberal evangelicalism and American civilizational claims. The new Science Hall was conceived to house the extensive and growing geological, botanical, archaeological, and zoological collections of George E. Post, one of the founding professors of the college; to accommodate teaching in existing scientific disciplines; and to contribute to a newly proposed Department of Biblical Ethnology. Forming an "object of special interest to Orientals," with "as full a display as can be made of objects illustrating the Ethnology of Asia and Africa," the hall would contain public exhibition rooms on the ground floor and lecture rooms on the second story.[16] Similar to previous campus buildings, its design was entrusted to New York architects who were both part of Dodge's social and family entourage and active in the design of other educational and charitable buildings in the United States (fig. 12.1). I. N. P. Stokes was Dodge's cousin Anson's son, and his firm, Howells & Stokes, was "planning a noble building for the Teachers' College in the *Oxford* style."[17] Like the Science Hall, the building had received donations from Stokes's aunts, Olivia and Caroline Phelps Stokes, who would later fund St. Paul's Chapel at Columbia, also designed by Howells & Stokes.[18] The Science Hall's design was a reflection of the architects' orientalist evangelical imaginings rendered through architecture, much as its collections represented its curator's "biblical orientalism" and scientific racism through ethnology.[19]

As John Davis and others have shown, the Americans' particular relation-

FIGURE 12.1. *Syrian Protestant College, Beirut, campus panorama from the sea.* Left to right: *Medical Building (1873), Science Hall (1902), Chapel (1890), and Main Building (1873).*

ship to the lands of the Bible and increasing interest in pilgrimage to Palestine had found special fulfillment in the focus on landscape, which allowed them to sidestep the reality that the lands of the Bible were presently occupied by older European Christian orders, "nominal Christians," Jews, and Muslims.[20] The missionaries of the ABCFM had been among the first to develop a botanical literature focusing on the flora of Syria, Mesopotamia, and Palestine.[21] While George E. Post was particularly proud of his own growing collections of specimens and had expressed an early interest in the botany of the region since the founding of the Syrian Protestant College, by the end of the century this had become a more scientific project, a necessary result of the intense interimperial contestation over the exploration of the Holy Land.[22] The need to claim a distinctly "American" project in this respect was reflected both in the establishment and framing of the museum's collections as well as in its architecture.

This relationship between science, civilization, and evangelical imperialism was especially clear in the covert motivations of the architects in accepting the commission. Stokes was a keen member of the American Geographical Society and was seemingly as deeply interested in designing the Science Hall as in joining Post on an American "scientific exploration" being organized for central Syria, headed by the American archaeologist Howard Crosby Butler.[23] According to Dodge, Stokes was "one of the prime movers in it, but they deem[ed] it wise to give the expedition no publicity here or elsewhere."[24] Though he would not end up joining the trip, Stokes acted as one of its four patrons and was perhaps later inspired by its findings. Unlike the early travelers and explorers of the Holy Land, for whom the survey of landmarks and the landscape was a means to verify the truths of the Bible, the novelty of Stokes's, Post's, and Dodge's claims and ambitions illustrated the transformation of biblical attraction into a scientific colonization project by the end of the century. Each member of the party seemed driven by his own interest and ambition in projecting his scientific and disciplinary control over the Holy Land and its "civilization."

The general goal of the archaeological expedition was to "follow up the researches" of the Marquis de Vogüé, who had written an important history of ancient architecture based on his travels in Syria in 1861 and 1862.[25] The party aimed to verify, "corroborate," and "extend" this work, perhaps by way of answering the question that had been posed at a recent meeting of the American Geographical Association, regarding what "part [Americans] will play in the . . . full study and development of our earth."[26] Post accompanied the exploration party in order to acquire further botanical and geological specimens for his collections, half of which were then sent to the Museum of Natural History in New York.[27] Meanwhile, Stokes was not simply content to act as a patron for the exploration trip, but clearly imagined his and his associate's architectural design as part of a renewed American claim on the region. As relayed by Dodge to Bliss, "the novelty of having a building erected under their plans, becoming a feature in this group on Oriental soil, quite captivate[d] them."[28] Yet Stokes's claims on the Holy Land had to materialize by proxy, through the design and construction of the science museum in Beirut. Science, in the Science Hall, was no longer simply about the methods of collecting, classifying, and organizing the past, but was also the driving force in shaping and representing a superior civilizational future.

Howells & Stokes were assigned the task of transforming the proposed brief and initial sketch of the hall into a detailed set of plans, with complete structural and manufacturing details. Though the exterior walls were to be built of local stone, similar to the older buildings on campus, the architects proposed an elaborate structural system that consisted of large timber trusses for the roof, twin iron girders for the long spans of the lecture halls, and thin steel columns in the ground-floor exhibition rooms, all in combination with exterior load-bearing walls. For Dodge and the architects in New York, the Science Hall had to conform to perceived American standards of construction and spatial experience, and it was equally important that the structural components be completed according to the detailed specifications of the architects and under their full oversight. The architects were "concerned at any thought of having [their] iron work prepared abroad. They fe[lt] the necessity of overseeing this important feature and they doubt[ed] the possibility of foreign Firms taking American plans and figures and succeeding in giving accurate and satisfactory results." Even if it entailed "a slight increase of cost," it would be wiser to order the iron girders and components in the United States, where they "would be made under exact supervision."[29] The movers of the project in the United States thus seemed to view the structure of the building and its production as the defining feature of its "American" character.

While the architects viewed the project from a distance as a didactic and symbolic marker of their own cultural imprint on a vague "Oriental soil," the concerns of the curator, Post, were focused elsewhere. He was eager to exhibit his detailed knowledge of the natural, ethnological, and archaeological history of this biblical land that he now partly considered his own. For Post, the scientific and civilizational role of the Science Hall clearly rested as much in the lecture rooms as in the material displays themselves, and he was reluctant to have columns punctuating his displays. After much debate, the architects agreed to reconsider the structure of the ground floor. The new design included "great girders" that necessitated a further thickening of the walls and a redesign of the openings and windows.[30]

Although the parties supplying iron for the Teachers College building in New York "were anxious to have [their] contract," the Science Hall's iron beams and girders were ultimately commissioned to Andrew Carnegie, who "tried hard to strike as low as he could."[31] Jeffrey Cody has shown how the last decades of the nineteenth century, especially after the World's Columbian Exposition in Chicago, saw an increase in the global exportation of American construction technologies, contributing to the growth of an American "informal empire."[32] As evidenced by the design process of the Science Hall, these activities held an additional civilizational dimension, as they were often conducted by the very same men leading the dual evangelization and cultural reformation of the world. Echoing Henry Van Brunt's notions regarding the specific character of American architecture being linked to "commercial experimentation," the Science Hall's design centered the superiority of American structural and industrial production as one of its defining features.[33] The hall simultaneously projected its architects' self-perceived architectural superiority while ensuring the expansion of American industry, in a continuous, mutually reinforcing loop.

The final plans proposed a three-part rectangular volume punctuated by towers at the corners and a continuous line of crenellations across the roofs (fig. 12.2). The building's dark stone and imposing scale contrasted with the lighter and plainer buildings of the college. Though the Science Hall exhibited a distinct Tudor Gothic (or perhaps "Oxfordian") style, its form and proportions recalled the Crusader forts that dotted the cities and landscapes that the exploration party had just been surveying. Dodge perceived it as having "somewhat the air of one of the Khedive palaces," reinforcing the notion that the building was to be perceived

FIGURE 12.2. *Howells & Stokes, Science Hall, 1902. Syrian Protestant College, Beirut, view from the northeast.*

as a “palace of science.”[34] He also saw the hall contributing to the representation of American civilizational advance more didactically: “Our row of buildings will furnish enough different styles of architecture to make a valuable study. . . . Each has some good qualities and the whole tell a most interesting story.”[35]

Inside, the missionaries hoped the “lofty ceilings,” the “long vistas through archways and corridors,” and the “ample space” given to the various collections would make the building as “attractive to the public” as it would be “scientifically valuable to the professors.”[36] Post’s collections were displayed in several long series of dark American timber cases across the ground-floor exhibition rooms, with the classrooms and laboratory spaces fitted in American timber furniture, in a sharp contrast that emphasized the difference and relationship between the ancient civilization on display and the superiority of the one undertaking its study (fig. 12.3). That the deforestation of the region had coincided with the Persian invasion, according to Howard Crosby Butler, resulting in the “barrenness” of the land and its subsequent reliance on stone in the “Mohammedan era,” perhaps made the lavish use of timber as a frame for the museum’s artifacts, as well as Post’s insistence on their uninterrupted arrangement, all the more significant.[37] Thus, the interior presented the curator’s reinterpretation of “Oriental” civilization and its history, only made legible as an object of scientific knowledge once it had been processed, classified, and framed by the American missionaries. Linda

FIGURE 12.3. *Interior of the Science Hall and archaeological museum, 1902, showing roof structure and timber display cases.*

Nochlin has argued that the depictions of the Orient as a picturesque locale by European artists implied a particularly deceitful violence, as the bodies, relics, and scenes portrayed could only become picturesque—or consumed as such—once their representative cultures had been destroyed and displaced, precisely by the policies and colonial practices of these European artists' nations.[38] Here, the Science Hall's interior and its ethnological displays operated in a similar way, displaying to the college's students and (select) visitors their land's natural and historical artifacts as remains of an "ancient civilization" no longer present, as it was being displaced and replaced by the American science, knowledge, and moral values that the hall's exterior and construction represented. Dodge reveled in "the entire suit[e] of photographs" commissioned to mark the hall's completion, which presented a "marvelous view" of the transformation of the "original barren bluff and straggling native houses."[39] In the necessary battle of "civilization . . . over barbarism, . . . the plans [were] already well started towards Syria," he concluded.[40]

Mastering the East: An American Holier Land

While the science museum disclosed its varied commissioners' fantasies about renovating the Orient, the design of a memorial chapel for Columbia University built between 1903 and 1907, also by Howells & Stokes, revealed how these experiments and ideas shaped civilizational ambitions back in the United States. Funded once again by Stokes's aunts, Olivia and Caroline, in memory of their parents, St. Paul's Chapel adopted a "Byzantine" style and plan, distinct from the neoclassical buildings of Columbia's new campus in Morningside Heights (fig. 12.4).[41] According to a *New York Times* article announcing its completion, "The new chapel mark[ed] a departure in church architecture in this country."[42] Interestingly, the choice of a Byzantine style seemed related both to the archaeological expedition financed by Stokes and to his wider efforts at situating the United States within an architectural civilizational hierarchy. According to Butler's archaeological report, "The various influences that cooperated to produce the developed style of the sixth century in Northern Syria cannot all be traced to their original sources." But "one source, that which was made the basis of the development, is easily traced; that is the Greco-Roman source, which is evident in what we shall call . . . the classic elements."[43]

Even more tellingly, in a commentary on the chapel published in *The Architectural Record* in 1907, Russell Sturgis dedicated a full piece to a discussion about the chapel's construction methods and superior structural concept in relation to a (racial) genealogical understanding of the Byzantine style, stating "that nothing better has ever been done in New York than this building and finishing of the St. Paul's Chapel."[44] Sturgis began with a long overview of the Byzantine style and its imperfect use in Syria and the East, before detailing at length how the style, in the expert hands of Howells & Stokes, and the novel construction techniques of

FIGURE 12.4. *Howells & Stokes, St. Paul's Chapel, 1907. Columbia University, New York, exterior view from the southeast.*

wooden centering used for the chapel's domes, had allowed it to become at once structural and ornamental (fig. 12.5):

> When we build in the unmodified way of the early time, in the fifth and immediately following centuries, we cannot make our decorations seem constructional. We are always hoping for that very thing, constructional ornament; but indeed, the men of the East who used this simple and obvious construction which we praise so highly and long to see revived, could only adorn their interiors by applications made after completion of the work. . . .
>
> But the architects of the St. Paul's Chapel have set themselves to a system of decoration wholly constructional, built up with the walls and identified with weight-carrying arches and the very shell of the structure. And this desirable and admirable scheme could only be carried out by the use of wooden [centering] and in the freest and most scientific modern way.[45]

'ig. 9.—The Summit of the Centering for the Dome.

Fig. 10.—The Inner Shell of the Dome Near its Spring.

FIGURE 12.5. *Images from the construction of St. Paul's Chapel, 1907. Russell Sturgis, "St. Paul's Chapel: Columbia University,"* Architectural Record *21, no. 8 (1907).*

The choice of the Byzantine style can thus be seen as an attempt to capture the "original" Christian style of the Holy Land, to be reedified in the United States in a more scientific and modern way. Sturgis's commentary combines the narratives of Eastern decline, pseudoscientific construction histories, and civilizational fantasies that had similarly shaped the report of Butler's expedition in Syria, illustrating the way architecture was used to construct civilizational hierarchies in this period.

But the chapel also fit perfectly into Stokes's broader ambitions and practices. This attempt to order cultures and create a civilizational narrative was echoed in his subsequent projects, especially those he completed after St. Paul's Chapel. According to his obituary, not only had Stokes become a leading figure within New York's tenement housing and slum clearance developments after separating from Howells, but through his work as president of the Phelps-Stokes Fund, he had devoted his life to the "education of the Negroes of Liberia, the Indians of the West, and Southerners of all colors." He was, more importantly, an "inveterate collector," collecting "stamps, armor, oriental art, and even an entire Tudor manor house which he brought to America."[46] In many ways, these collecting urges could all be understood as part of Stokes's attempts to understand and construct an image of art and architecture as direct illustrations of civilizational hierarchies. Stokes was not content to only understand ancient civilizations and their architectures, his own designs, as seen in St. Paul's Chapel, seemed to be an attempt to master and surpass them.

The chapel, in other words, was the material and spatial representation of how the knowledge and mastery of the "imperfect" civilizations of the East had become the basis for the perfection of American civilization, to be held up and shaped by modern, scientific, architectural, and structural knowledge. That this testament to American civilizational advance would materialize in an evangelical chapel, on the grounds of an American university, funded by the Phelps-Stokes network and their associates, was indeed a perfect embodiment of how racial, evangelical, and industrialist-scientific ambitions combined to serve as the imperial foundations of American philanthropy in this period. Conceived and designed by the same representatives of the evangelical-industrialist tycoons of the Progressive Era United States, the Science Hall at the Syrian Protestant College and St. Paul's Chapel at Columbia University ultimately illustrated the intrinsic relationship between civilizational advance at home and abroad. While both were rooted in simultaneously evangelical and scientific notions of civilization, they relied on divergent stagings of architecture as civilization to construct an image of a universal civilizational hierarchy. Whereas the science museum illustrated the implantation of American power in the Holy Land, simultaneously displacing and reforming its present "heathens," the chapel reinforced the notion of the United States as the theological and civilizational inheritor of the Holy Land, leading the way toward a superior moral and scientific future.

While liberal education and scientific knowledge were the ideological tools subtending the moral-cultural reformation of the world, an industrially superior architecture was the material and spatial technology allowing evangelical Americans both to construct this universal Anglo-American utopia and to maintain the notion of American civilization as superior. Thus, Progressive Era notions of civilizational uplift and the industrial superiority undergirding the wealth of the Gilded Age were two sides of the same coin. The Syrian Protestant College, one of the earliest testing grounds for the articulation of US interests in the Near East, became a primary site for the elaboration of this relationship. Throughout the evolution of the project, religion and race were fundamentally intertwined, as the dual bases of an Anglo-American civilization divinely appointed to lead the renovation of the whole world. The Progressive dimension of this nineteenth-century iteration of the project, illustrated in this chapter, was the transformation of Anglo-American evangelical ideas into pseudosecular civilizational and scientific values and their establishment as a new universal good. Yet, as this chapter has shown, the moral-civilizational and industrial-scientific dimensions of the project went hand in hand. If today we fail to recognize the United States as both a historical and an ongoing empire, it is only because the unitary religious roots of its contemporary military-industrial complex and moral-civilizational project—which continue to shape so much of the Middle East—have been for so long forgotten and obscured. By revealing this crucial nineteenth-century relationship between industrialism, science, civilization, and architecture, the case study of the Syrian Protestant College can help us understand the foundational role that the Holy Land—real and imagined—has played in building up American civilization not only in the Middle East but in the United States as well.

Notes

1. See, for instance, Irene Cheng, Charles L. Davis II, and Mabel O. Wilson, eds., *Race and Modern Architecture: A Critical History from the Enlightenment to the Present* (University of Pittsburgh Press, 2020).

2. See especially chapters by Irene Cheng, Charles L. Davis II, Joanna Merwood-Salisbury, Peter Minosh, and Mabel O. Wilson in Cheng, Davis, and Wilson, *Race and Modern Architecture*. See also Martin A. Berger, *Sight Unseen: Whiteness and American Visual Culture* (University of California Press, 2005); Charles L. Davis II, *Building Character: The Racial Politics of Modern Architectural Style* (University of Pittsburgh Press, 2019).

3. There is a huge literature on this dual role of American missionary societies. See, for instance, Derek Chang, *Citizens of a Christian Nation* (University of Pennsylvania Press, 2011); Emily Conroy-Krutz, *Christian Imperialism: Converting the World in the Early American Republic* (Cornell University Press, 2015); Matthew Frye Jacobson, *Barbarian Virtues: The United States Encounters Foreign Peoples at Home and Abroad, 1876–1917* (Hill & Wang, 2000).

4. The literature on the parallel theological and political trajectory of the United States is too broad to fully cite here. See, for instance, Thomas S. Kidd, *The Great Awakening: The Roots of Evangelical Christianity in Colonial America* (Yale University Press, 2008); Paul Frymer, *Building an American Empire: The Era of Territorial and Political Expansion* (Princeton University Press, 2017). For an illuminating history of the theological roots of Harvard and the colonial college, see George H. Williams, *Wilderness and Paradise in Christian Thought* (Harper, 1962). For the role of the American college in the colonial expansion of the United States, see Frederick Rudolph, *The American College and University: A History* (Knopf, 1962). For a comprehensive history of American missions, see William R. Hutchison, *Errand to the World: American Protestant Thought and Foreign Missions* (University of Chicago Press, 1987).

5. Frederick J. Turner, *The Frontier in American History* (Holt, 1920). See also Michael Adas, *Dominance by Design: Technological Imperatives and America's Civilizing Mission* (Belknap Press, 2006); Jacobson, *Barbarian Virtues*; Amy Kaplan, "'Left Alone with America': The Absence of Empire in the Study of American Culture," in *Cultures of United States Imperialism*, ed. Amy Kaplan and Donald E. Pease (Duke University Press, 1993), 3–21.

6. David W. Kling, "The New Divinity and the Origins of the American Board of Commissioners for Foreign Missions," *Church History* 72, no. 4 (2003): 801–802. See also Hutchison, *Errand to the World*, 57–59.

7. On the impact of these ideas on the early geography of colonial America, as well as their appropriation by very different groups, see John Davis, *The Landscape of Belief: Encountering the Holy Land in Nineteenth-Century American Art and Culture* (Princeton University Press, 1996), chap. 1.

8. Hutchison, *Errand to the World*, 45.

9. Berger, *Sight Unseen*.

10. For a comprehensive history of the American mission in Syria, see Abdul-Latif Tibawi, *American Interests in Syria, 1800–1901: A Study of Educational, Literary and Religious Work* (Clarendon Press, 1966). For the history of the Syrian Protestant College campus's construction, see Yasmina El Chami, "A Mutual Project: Architecture and the Imperial Foundations of American Missionaries in Nineteenth-Century Beirut," *Journal of the Society of Architectural Historians* 83, no. 4 (2024): 481–504.

11. The role of education was a point of contention between the missionaries and the secretary of the board, who did not understand the importance of the missionaries' educational activities in Syria.

See Tibawi, *American Interests in Syria*; Hutchison, *Errand to the World*. For more on the evolution of missionary conversion into liberal theology and scientific education, see William R. Hutchison, *The Modernist Impulse in American Protestantism* (Oxford University Press, 1976).

12. See the list of American Colonization Society board members in *Forty-Fourth Annual Report of the American Colonization Society* (Washington, DC: C. Alexander, 1861).

13. David S. Dodge to Daniel Bliss, April 26, 1898, box 7, folder 4, Daniel Bliss Collection, AA: 2.3.1, Archives and Special Collections, American University of Beirut (hereafter cited as Bliss Collection).

14. Keita Takayama, "Beyond Comforting Histories: The Colonial/Imperial Entanglements of the International Institute, Paul Monroe, and Isaac L. Kandel at Teachers College, Columbia University," *Comparative Education Review* 62, no. 4 (2018): 459–481.

15. For more on the racial dimensions of American missionary history, see Chang, *Citizens of a Christian Nation*; Jacobson, *Barbarian Virtues*; Terrence Keel, *Divine Variations: How Christian Thought Became Racial Science* (Stanford University Press, 2018).

16. Annual Report of the Board of Managers of the Syrian Protestant College, 1901, Archives and Special Collections, American University of Beirut.

17. Dodge to Bliss, March 13, 1900, box 8, folder 1, Bliss Collection.

18. Dodge to Bliss, June 8, 1900, box 8, folder 2, Bliss Collection.

19. See David Grafton, *An American Biblical Orientalism: The Construction of Jews, Christians, and Muslims in Nineteenth-Century American Evangelical Piety* (Lexington Books, 2019).

20. Davis, *Landscape of Belief*, chap. 2; Berger, *Sight Unseen*, 98. On this view of the land, see Ussama Makdisi, "Reclaiming the Land of the Bible: Missionaries, Secularism, and Evangelical Modernity," *American Historical Review* 102, no. 3 (1997): 680–713. For more on American attitudes toward the materiality of the biblical landscape, see James S. Bielo, "Flower, Soil, Water, Stone: Biblical Landscape Items and Protestant Materiality," *Journal of Material Culture* 23, no. 3 (2018): 368–387; Annabel J. Wharton, "Relics, Protestants, Things," *Material Religion* 10, no. 4 (2014): 412–430.

21. Grafton, *American Biblical Orientalism*; Heleen Murre-van den Berg, "William McClure Thomson's *The Land and the Book*," in *New Faiths in Ancient Lands: Western Missions in the Middle East in the Nineteenth and Early Twentieth Centuries*, ed. Heleen Murre-van den Berg (Brill, 2006), 43–63.

22. The British and Americans had divided the exploration between themselves, but other powers were at work as well. See Davis, *Landscape of Belief*, chap. 8; Bruce Kuklick, *Puritans in Babylon: The Ancient Near East and American Intellectual Life, 1880–1930* (Princeton University Press, 1996).

23. Dodge to Bliss, March 23, 1900, box 8, folder 1, Bliss Collection.

24. Dodge to Bliss, March 30, 1900, box 8, folder 1, Bliss Collection.

25. Howard Crosby Butler, "Report of an American Archaeological Expedition in Syria, 1899–1900," *American Journal of Archaeology* 4, no. 4 (1900): 415–440; Howard Crosby Butler, *Part II of the Publications of an American Archaeological Expedition to Syria, 1899–1900* [. . .] (Century, 1903).

26. "Transactions of the American Geographical Society, 1900," *Journal of the American Geographical Society of New York* 32, no. 1 (1900): 88–100. On the broader anxieties of American archaeologists around developing a separate tradition from the Germans, see Kuklick, *Puritans in Babylon*, 176–190.

27. Annual Report of the Board of Managers of the Syrian Protestant College, 1901, Archives and Special Collections, American University of Beirut. Martin Berger's discussion of the Metropolitan Museum of Art and its construction of whiteness misunderstands the link to the Israelite metaphor, as well as the reality that many of the artifacts hosted by America's museums were sourced in the Near East itself; see Berger, *Sight Unseen*, chap. 3. For more details on America's archaeological expeditions in the Near East, see Zeynep Çelik, *About Antiquities: Politics of Archaeology in the Ottoman Empire* (University of Texas Press, 2016); Kuklick, *Puritans in Babylon*, chap. 7.

28. Dodge to Bliss, March 27, 1900, box 8, folder 1, Bliss Collection.

29. Dodge to Bliss, June 8, 1900, box 8, folder 2, Bliss Collection.

30. Dodge to Bliss, June 22, 1900; June 26, 1900; August 28, 1900, box 8, folder 2, Bliss Collection.

31. Dodge to Bliss, April 24, 1900, box 8, folder 1, Bliss Collection.

32. Jeffrey W. Cody, *Exporting American Architecture, 1870–2000* (Taylor & Francis, 2003), chap. 1. On the notion of informal empire, see Yasmina El Chami and Sara Honarmand Ebrahimi, "Architectures of Informal Empire," *Architectural Theory Review* 28, no. 3 (2024): 335–345.

33. Charles L. Davis II, "Henry Van Brunt and White Settler Colonialism in the Midwest," in Cheng, Davis, and Wilson, *Race and Modern Architecture*, 109. Mary Woods also discusses the importance of industrialists and merchants in the establishment of an American professional culture in the nineteenth century. See Mary N. Woods, *From Craft to Profession: The Practice of Architecture in Nineteenth-Century America* (University of California Press, 1999). See also Jacobson, *Barbarian Virtues*, chap. 1.

34. Dodge to Bliss, March 13, 1900, box 8, folder 1, Bliss Collection. The Khedive refers here to the viceroy of Egypt in this period.

35. Dodge to Bliss, November 7, 1900, box 8, folder 2, Bliss Collection.

36. Annual Report of the Board of Managers of the Syrian Protestant College, 1901, Archives and Special Collections, American University of Beirut.

37. Butler, *Part II of the Publications*, 9–10. For timber's special significance at the college in Beirut, see Yasmina El Chami, "An American 'Garden' in an Oriental 'Desert': The Modernity of Timber at the Syrian Protestant College of Beirut," *Architectural Theory Review* 25, nos. 1–2 (2021): 199–215. For timber's broader significance in Euro-American nineteenth-century architectural theory, see Davis, *Building Character*, 31–68.

38. Linda Nochlin, *The Politics of Vision: Essays on Nineteenth-Century Art and Society* (Harper & Row, 1989), 49–51.

39. Dodge to Bliss, October 24, 1900, box 8, folder 2, Bliss Collection.

40. Dodge to Bliss, July 20, 1900, box 8, folder 2, Bliss Collection.

41. On the architecture of Columbia's campus, see Francesco Passanti, "The Design of Columbia in the 1890s, McKim and His Client," *Journal of the Society of Architectural Historians* 36, no. 2 (1977): 69–84.

42. "New Columbia Chapel a Stokes Memorial," *New York Times*, February 4, 1907, 6.

43. Butler, *Part II of the Publications*, 18.

44. Russell Sturgis, "St. Paul's Chapel, Columbia University," *Architectural Record* 21, no. 8 (1907): 83–95.

45. Sturgis, "St. Paul's Chapel," 95.

46. C.K.S., "Obituaries: Isaac Newton Phelps Stokes," *Proceedings of the American Antiquarian Society* 55, part 1 (April 1945): 47–50.

PART IV

BUILDING SETTLER COLONIALISM

13 THE APPLE OF DISCORD

FREE LABOR, SECTIONALISM, AND ANGLO-ASSIMILATION IN OLMSTED'S AGRICULTURAL COLLEGES

Maura Lucking

BY THE TIME FREDERICK LAW OLMSTED was called in by the trustees of the Massachusetts Agricultural College in the spring of 1866, the school was already in trouble. Chartered by the commonwealth three years prior, the college was the product of debate over how to best implement the 1862 Morrill Act, otherwise known as the Land-Grant Agricultural and Mechanical College Act. There had been an interest in developing practical higher education for the indigent and working classes in Massachusetts since the 1820s, but the impetus of modest funding from the sale of federal lands provided the opportunity to force the issue. Following the end of the Civil War on its major fronts, there was finally the political will—and the return of 150,000 veterans and potential students—for reform-minded civic projects once again.[1] The project had stalled when trustees couldn't agree on a campus layout; but what appear to be organizational and aesthetic minutiae are revealed, through Olmsted's intervention, as more fundamental disagreements about who constituted skilled workers and how they might be appropriately trained, lodged, and acculturated into the social and economic norms of the state that figured itself as the "cradle of liberty."

Fulfilling the terms of the act to provide agricultural and industrial coursework had already divided state legislators, many of whom felt that the money was best spent on expanding the state's extant urban universities.[2] The matter was split even among farmers, with an editorial in *The New England Farmer* opining that such a school would sow class division and become "an apple of discord amongst learned professors and influential politicians, and an object of merriment to the practical farmer."[3] The state's Board of Agriculture won the day, securing more than two-thirds of the total land scrip of 360,000 acres to establish the rural college that would became the flagship institution of the University of Massachusetts. They chose a location in the center of the state, rather than in Boston, where expenses would be lower and land for a model farm could be acquired. Yet their site outside of Amherst remained undeveloped, without an adopted campus plan or adequate funding in place for construction.[4] Without quick action, the agriculturalists would be forced to resign their Morrill Act funds, which required a physical plant for all schools within five years of appropriations.[5]

Retaining Olmsted, the celebrated gentleman farmer and landscape architect—and a close friend of the act's sponsor, fellow New Englander Justin Morrill—to create a campus plan made sense both practically and politically. The organizers' personal entreaties to Olmsted sought validation for various design possibilities: a monumental stone building sited on the highest point like a country estate; a new, curvilinear approach road that might obliquely frame the south-facing building; and a plan to integrate the property's large, mature chestnut trees into a unified landscape scheme.[6] These were reasonable requests for the man known for introducing English landscape gardening to the United States and for integrating such rural naturalism (including a fondness for Stone Creek granite) into the winning Greensward Plan for Central Park.

Olmsted, however, came to the agricultural college shortly after resuming his landscape practice for the first time since 1860. He had most recently superintended a California mining operation and spent most of the war as secretary of the US Sanitary Commission, a volunteer organization providing medical aid and improving troop conditions. During the intervening years, he had also become known as a leading public voice on the material conditions of enslavement following the abridged publication at the onset of the war of his collected journalism on travels through the slave states, *Journeys and Explorations in the Cotton Kingdom* (1861). While eager to resuscitate his faltering prospects as a landscape designer, he was also perhaps not yet satisfactorily able to sublimate his experiences of the war into purely aesthetic terms.

Instead of design drawings, Olmsted provided a written rejection of the trustee's existing scheme as too urban and "incongruous" with its site in scale and material (like a "jail or reformatory") and as impractical on its architectural merits, being too far from campus access points and other functional spaces in ways both inconvenient and expensive to construct. He made an impassioned argument instead for arranging the college as a New England village, making the most of existing site conditions to cluster modest, framed buildings downhill along the existing public roadway toward the town of Amherst and making the hillside to the west a naturalistic rather than architectural focal point—an outstretched westward horizon (fig. 13.1).[7] And while the plan did provide a treatment for the model farm, he insisted that the college's mission must amount to "more than oral instruction and practical demonstration in the science of agriculture."[8]

Olmsted's primary concern was the social and moral imperative of educat-

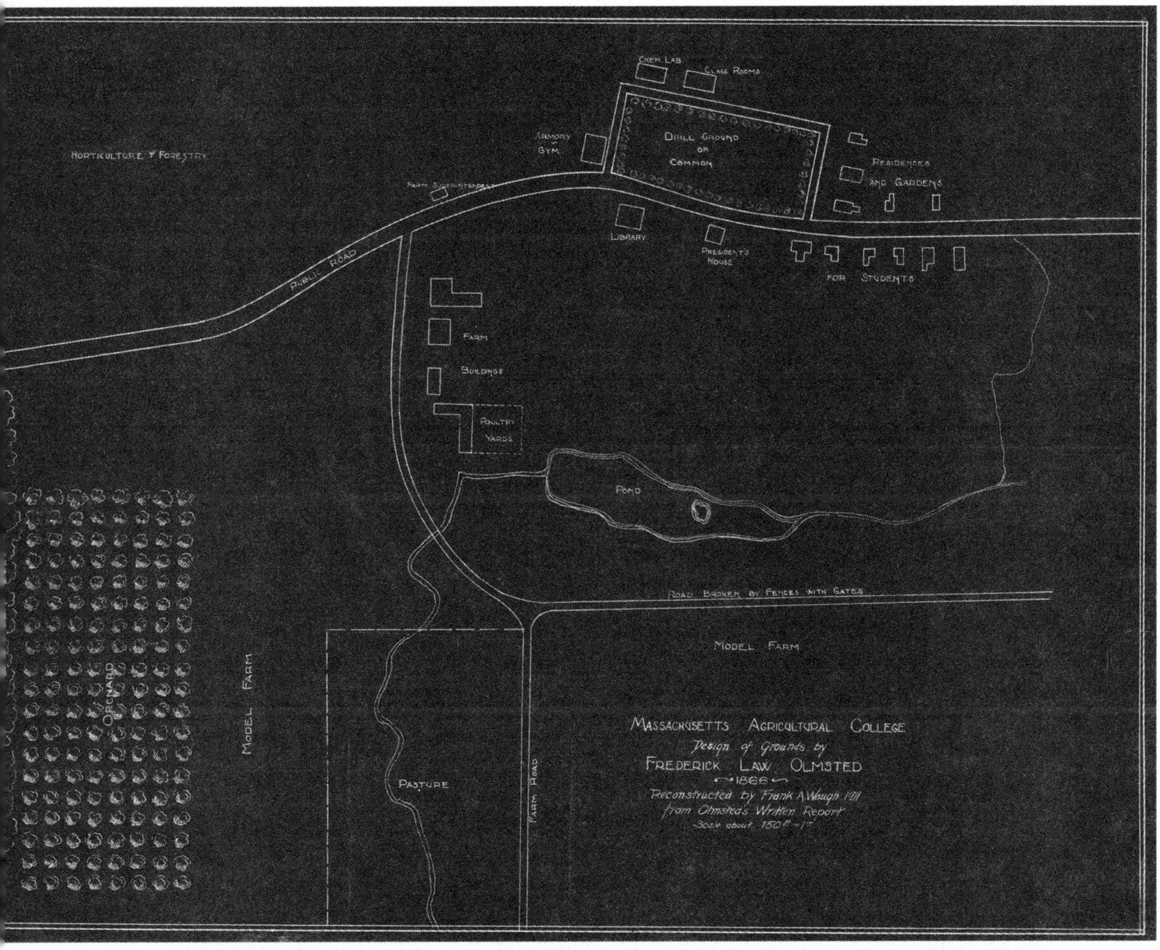

FIGURE 13.1. *Frank Waugh and Warren Manning, re-creation of Frederick Law Olmsted's lost 1866 site plan for the Massachusetts Agricultural College, 1910. Olmsted Archives, National Park Service.*

ing a new class (and, I argue, race) of farmer—the emblematic Northern "free" worker—a central prewar rhetoric of economic self-determination and freedom through the pursuit of capital made material through the postwar collegiate promise. The transubstantiation of free labor from an ideology promising emancipation through business ownership and smallholding to a subject position that might be flexible enough to assimilate new economic citizens—including those actually emancipated—was a central issue of Reconstruction. Instead of the farm field or classroom, Olmsted contended this work began with the design of student living spaces. His residential campus village—and its proximity, through the common road, to "meeting houses, public grounds . . . monuments, libraries, and lyceums"—would shape "tastes, inclinations, and designing abilities," emphasizing that ownership and management of private property and collective commitment to the civic institutions of rural life were of equal or greater importance to these newly enrolled students than to the professional class at existing urban universities.[9]

The trustees ultimately disregarded Olmsted's plan, despite ostensibly sharing his politics. Governor and president of the board John A. Andrew had been a founder of the Free Soil Party, a leader in legal challenges against the Fugitive Slave Law, and the organizer of the much-mythologized Fifty-Fourth Regiment of Black soldiers during the war; and yet he was disinterested in what he saw as Olmsted's overwrought site plan, more concerned with the dual "practicalities" of building out a complex of barns and at least one major stone building to legitimize their legislative success and the new social status of agriculture in Massachusetts as an equal to industry. Following the rejection of another design by Olmsted's sometime partner Calvert Vaux and the Boston architect Joseph R. Richards, the campus would move forward without a presiding architect.

Olmsted's little-remembered proposal for the Massachusetts Agricultural College provides an opportunity to reintegrate the breadth of his Republican politics into the most prolific period of his landscape career, after more than a century of historiographical separation from his prior renown as a journalist, entrepreneur, and public servant. Moreover, the debate over this and Olmsted's other agricultural college designs of the 1860s reveals the fraught anxieties over racial integration, nativism, and labor that shaped the land grant movement in the wake of the Civil War. It also foreshadows in some important ways how these schools would become sites of erasure of the racial violence of the preceding decades, building a sectional mythology of Northern agriculture that presupposed Northern industrial wealth as locally sustained, rather than deeply dependent upon Southern enslaved plantation agriculture.

This rejection of Olmsted's commissioned proposal elicited the resignation of his local advocate, university president (and partner in the "art of drainage" at his own model farm, Tosomock) Henry Flagg French.[10] Olmsted, for his part, was furious. He expanded his proposal to the building committee into a self-published pamphlet, *A Few Things to Be Thought of Before Proceeding to Plan Buildings for the National Agricultural Colleges* (1866), followed by early fall with several anonymous editorials in *The Nation*, the legacy abolitionist newsweekly at which Olmsted served as an editor—including the delightfully confrontational "How *Not* to Establish an Agricultural College," sandwiched between gossip pages from Paris and a debate on universal suffrage for veterans.[11]

In these texts, Olmsted laid out his deeply sectionalist, Northern vision of the public college campus as the space of "free labor"—a machine for acculturating the farmer, as a premodern, agrarian artifact, wholesale into the systems of industrialization, modeling social mobility without the loss of control or need for wage work.[12] He moved fluidly between descriptions of his proposed physical plan (including his reasoned rejection of the trustees) and its associations: for example, that an isolated building sited in relation to its agricultural context rather than its larger community was objectionable because it replicated the values and sociability of the Southern plantation (fig. 13.2).

Olmsted, as a moneyed Protestant, moved in Republican circles, for whom free labor was integral to the rejection of the South—not only the institution of slavery but the moral decadence of the slaveholder as a false American aristocracy. This aversion to clannish social hierarchies and subjugated labor (which extended to wage workers) also led many Republications to reject the Irish Cath-

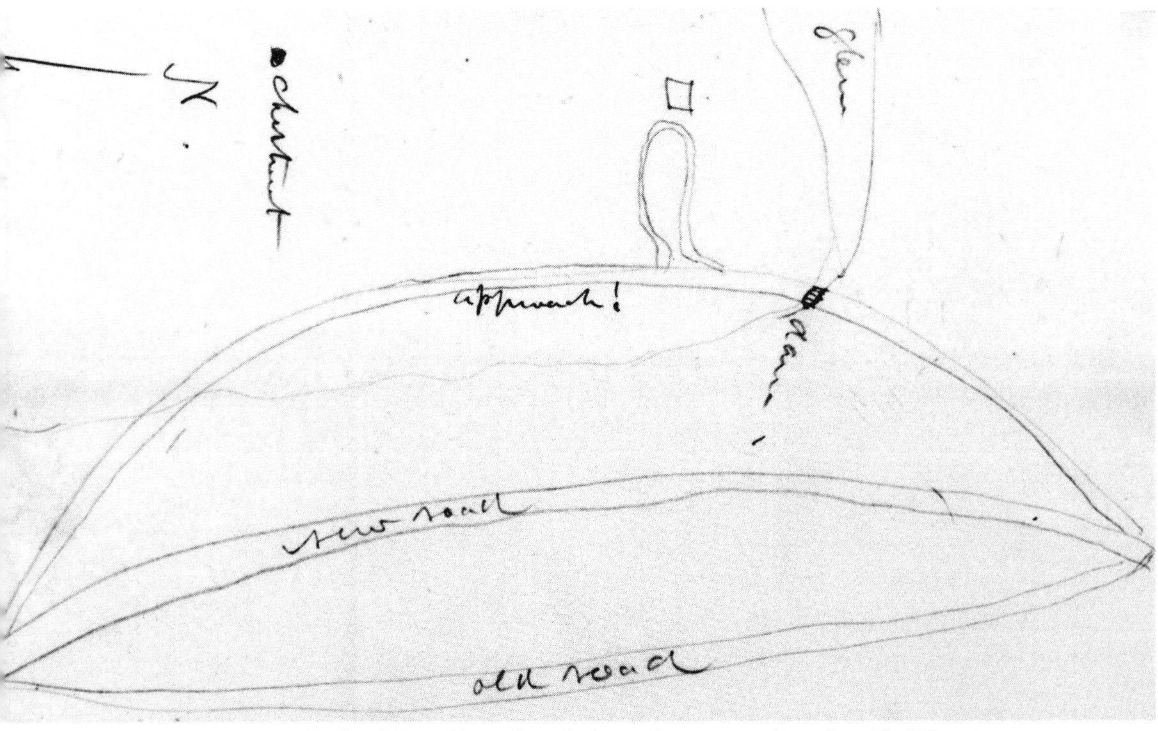

FIGURE 13.2. *Frederick Law Olmsted, study for various approach road and building sites, as proposed by the Massachusetts Agricultural College Board of Trustees, 1865. Library of Congress.*

olic urban base of their rival Democratic Party. Olmsted's organizational rejection of the plantation on feudal, classed terms, rather than because of its associations with racial terror, is telling of the underdevelopment of the subjectivity or social status of the Black worker, despite an abiding interest in the superintendence of the formerly enslaved.[13] It also reveals the extent to which "free labor," as reimagined after the war by Olmsted and his contemporaries, was a theorization instead of an expansive, assimilative whiteness in the wake of its destabilization—part of what Nikhil Phal Singh calls the "haunting of the capitalist imagination" by the constant renegotiation of "free" and "unfree" labor as a stand-in for racialized hierarchies of domination.[14]

The Republican North was imagined as a dynamic, expanding capitalist society led by a constellation of business owners, artisans, and farmers across their own small towns and cities—an effort to be buoyed by colleges educating these upwardly mobile classes. While Jefferson's "academical village" at the University of Virginia had also considered the business acumen and moral formation of citizens, the definition of citizenship (through the extension of voting rights to the propertyless, the foreign-born, and, on the horizon, the formerly enslaved) had so drastically changed over the intervening half century as to necessitate not only a new curriculum but also a more self-effacing architectural language.[15] Rather than educate the new nation's leadership in the European tradition, the land grant colleges were to instill a national culture in even the lowliest farmer by inventing an American tradition that might be reproduced in proximity to their own small town.

Olmsted's own farm was just a few miles from his family home; he worked to drain and grade the seventeenth-century property in the hopes of cultivating rare fruit tree specimens for a nursery business. It proved a commercial failure, but the experiments would ultimately inform his design practice. The Hartford-born son of a prosperous dry goods merchant might respectably enter farming (and consequently, if nearly by accident, landscape architecture) precisely because of its association with the free labor ideal, as one among many possible ventures. In his campus treatise, Olmsted reflected on the elevated social status of the Northern farmer, and the necessity of making the calling appealing to a generation of urban and suburban young people increasingly disinterested in rural pursuits: "It is desirable," he wrote, "that the farmer and his household should be debarred as little as possible from those enjoyments of intellect and taste which are common to men engaged in any professional calling. . . . The question is not whether this [proposed campus design] is at once wholly practicable; it is, what can be done in the ground-plan of your college to bring farmers nearer to it?"[16]

A national bill funding public agricultural colleges provided an opportunity to propagate what Heather Cox Richardson refers to as the "bucolic model of political economy" during Reconstruction.[17] For Olmsted, creating a design precedent with one of the earliest new-build campuses organized with Morrill Act funds could have broad ramifications. The act sought to provide "liberal and practical education to the industrial classes," which in the free labor tradition would not have referred to the freeholding yeomanry but to wage earners.[18] US class politics in the nineteenth century often obliquely subtended racial politics; the North's social promise, in Olmsted's view, was the rapidly assimilative capacity of labor upon its lowest class, foreign-born European peasants. He regularly compared the productivity of "Irish and German laborers" of the North favorably against that of enslaved Africans and African Americans in his reporting on Southern cotton, a reminder that immigrants may have held greater proximity to whiteness but were racialized nonetheless—their emigration a continuation rather than a rupture with earlier configurations of racial capitalism.[19] In *A Journey in the Back-country* (1860), Olmsted expounded:

> Out of twenty Irish proletaires, of whose history for five years after their arrival and *removal to the country* [emphasis added] I have been intimately cognizant, only two, both of whome were over fifty years of age, have lived out that period without beginning to acquire wealth and becoming superior in their ambition and habits to the lowest order, which I believe to include a majority of the whites in the plantation districts of the south.[20]

This passage demonstrates two things: the presence of a racial hierarchy between the Irish and the Southern white workers, both considered major barriers in Republican thinking to the antislavery cause, and Olmsted's fervent belief in environmental determinism. The key to Anglo conformity was in immersion within the physical and cultural environment of the countryside and the small-scale farming to be found there.

Olmsted's pamphlet suggests he was primarily concerned with the agricultural college as a reformative space for Irish Catholics and other European immigrants. Although he faults the traditional urban prison's psychologically stultifying effects ("straight-sided, evenly-balanced, many-sided structure[s] of stone"), he also names several recent reformatory designs as precedents.[21] Such designs used cottages and farmhouse buildings, he argued, as part of "radical improvement[s] . . . to [deal] with those classes of our population whom it is most difficult to influence favorably."[22] Three out of four of these modern institutions were focused on disciplining (and converting) the Irish under the guise of reform: petty criminals and religious dissidents at Mountjoy Prison outside Dublin, Irish Republican political prisoners sent to the Norfolk Island penal colony in New South Wales, and abandoned, orphaned, and delinquent immigrant children relocated to the countryside by the Children's Aid Society of New York.[23] Each design was set in rural environs, with an open-air plan and a regime of manual agricultural labor. While Olmsted admitted that his own design served "young men of comparatively healthy intellects," his embrace of the village model adopted these racial as well as economic motives.[24] As a nineteenth-century planning typology, the campus kept one foot in the world of total institutions even while appealing to utopian reorganizations of work and social life.[25]

Olmsted had long held an interest in the relationship between labor and race. While his 1850s writings are cited as demonstration of his antislavery position, it was his work as a social scientist rather than a moralist that drove those investigations, both on plantations and on labor forces under his own supervision. During his time at the Sanitary Commission from 1860 to 1863, Olmsted devised a questionnaire for inspectors to gather information on the ethnicity and physical traits of enlisting soldiers, requiring invasive measurements and a spirometer reading, in order to produce statistics about their performance in the field.[26] He considered the resulting dataset his private property, the continuation of previous research on the four thousand largely immigrant workers under his supervision at Central Park.[27] Olmsted wrote that his role as commissioner and architect-in-chief of the park provided an "excellent opportunity" for "obtaining statistics of the poorest class of American working-men," something he planned to expand after the war into "a sort of treatise on the established tendencies of the European races in the United States."[28] This suggests, too, that Olmsted was beginning to understand free labor as an embodied trait in alignment with race science rather than as merely a political ideology—one that positioned the organizer of public works and their attendant labor forces in a unique position of conversion.

Yet Olmsted the designer and Olmsted the politicker were historicized separately from the beginning. His first biographies were published around the centennial of his birth in two nascent areas of scholarship: landscape history and history of the Civil War. Frederick Law Olmsted Jr., his son and business inheritor, and Theodora Kimball Hubbard, a Harvard librarian and sister of the architect Fiske Kimball, formally categorized his parks among European precedents and reorganized unwieldy municipal practices as the product of a singular mind.[29] Their edited volume *Frederick Law Olmsted: Landscape Architect, 1822–1903* (1922) culminated with a selection of the designer's papers on the design and construction of Central Park, historicized as the apotheosis of a "municipal park movement" traced across public walks and open spaces in England and Germany from the sixteenth century.[30] Thus, Olmsted was severed from his American influences and collaborators even as he was celebrated as the father of a national school. When excerpts from his earlier experiences in farming or journalism were referenced, it was to demonstrate a nascent interest in "landscape improvement."[31] After 1857, the year Olmsted was appointed superintendent of Central Park, the volume's subject matter turned exclusively to his landscape commissions, ignoring his wartime service and continued political activity.

The historian Broadus Mitchell, conversely, characterized Olmsted as primarily a critic of the Southern cotton industry, in his biography *Frederick Law Olmsted, a Critic of the Old South* (1924).[32] This, too, had little need for social context, as it constructed New South narratives of the war as economically motivated rather than concerning the maintenance of racial supremacy. Mitchell used Olmsted as a proxy for his argument for the negative effects of forced labor on, paradoxically, slaveholders themselves. This position allowed Southern historians to hold on to Lost Cause romanticism without its dubious politics: for example, Mitchell's claim that Olmsted believed "Southern slavery was an ingrained social institution for which no set of men was to blame."[33] Olmsted's farming was simply fallow time, spent reading labor histories and exchanging ideas with neighbor William Lloyd Garrison.[34] Mitchell stressed Olmsted's leadership and taste for discipline, developed in the Sanitary Commission while organizing military hospitals and camps, facilitating transport of the wounded, and providing supplies.

Much recent scholarship on Olmsted has centered his antebellum writing on slavery and the American South during his two trips across Georgia, Virginia, North Carolina, and the Texas borderlands; however, placing equal emphasis on his formative wartime service—a period that overlapped with or directly preceded his professional landscape practice—helps unpack the vexatious relationship between social reform and social engineering that runs underneath much of his work.[35] As secretary of the Sanitary Commission, Olmsted organized one of the largest bureaucracies in the United States—one understood to rival the governance and scale of the railroads—dedicated to studying and caring for the conditions of a widely dispersed army. He hired and managed his own veritable army of physician-inspectors in the field and female volunteers in the hospitals, aided by architects and civil engineers he recruited from his time at Central Park.

After the Union army's disorganized and bloody loss at Bull Run in July of 1861, Olmsted undertook his first large-scale survey of the participating units. The resulting *Report on the Demoralization of the Volunteers* focused on the interrelationship between the physical environment and the mental condition of troops, finding that poor living conditions—in addition to insufficient training and a lack of supplies—were to blame:

> The groups [of men] were formed around fires made in the streets, and burning boards wrenched from citizen's fences. . . . There was the effect of an entire change of air and habits, of food and drink, irregular sleep, and exposure to excessive heat, alternating with exposure to cool, damp, and malarious night-air, or the mephitic atmosphere of crowded and unventilated tents.[36]

While Olmsted and his contemporaries used the report to secure support for the army's medical department, it also piqued his longtime interest in the biopolitics of social science. His physician-inspectors reported that climatic dissimilitude from soldiers' native environments influenced the likelihood of illness; an outsized number of patients from Maine "especially suffered" in the summer heat and humidity of northeastern Virginia, experiencing "depression and nostalgia."[37]

The Morrill Act, passed the following year, was in many ways a response to the poorly prepared and untrained Army of the Potomac. Military training was required as a provision of funding, both in strategy and practical drills. The earliest land grant schools were thus directly intended to aid and abet the Union's military cause in any future conflict. In Olmsted's postwar plan for Massachusetts, as well as a design for Maine the following year, drill and parade grounds directly abutted the public road. But it is his treatment of the residential spaces of the college, and indeed the administration and discipline of its students, that most conveys these wartime influences. His plans suggest that the organization of people—as much as, or more than, space—was of the utmost importance.

In Orono, Maine, he acknowledged the military camp as his most immediate precedent:

> A careful study of the subject, which I made as an official duty during the war, led me to the conclusion that the element of their theoretical responsibility in which regimental and company officers at its commencement most failed; in which they most needed instruction; in which they acquired instruction by experience with the most difficulty; and in which their ignorance caused the most misery, the greatest waste of the national resources and the most melancholy loss of life, *was just this of boarding and lodging.*[38]

This military observation didn't necessarily require a military solution, however; mass barracks were to be avoided at all costs, though he suggested the pitched-roof officer's cottages used in military cantonments as a model, with their right-angled clusters of mess halls, commissaries, and study rooms. Olmsted remained adamant that in order for residents to develop a personal sense of responsibility for their surroundings, lodging should be limited to no more than ten students per building, recommending that the university build three new one-and-a-half-story cottages of fifty-six by twenty-six square feet for every forty-person increase in enrollment.[39] Picturesque groupings—simply meaning asymmetrical—he wrote, were useful insofar as they better accommodated piecemeal expansion than quadrangles, advocating the same pragmatism that had convinced Jefferson to adopt the village form. Dormitories also provided a potent didactic environment. Buildings of a domestic character—landscaped with "arbors, trellises, summer-houses, dove-cotes, martin-boxes, bowling or croquet greens, terraces, hedges, ice-houses . . . pots of window plants, a Wardian case or two, cages of singing birds, and some not expensive musical instruments in each house; a bed of hardy ferns and delicate evergreens on the north side, and a few tender shrubs on the lawn"—would favorably affect the esprit de corps. Visible integration with the more formal spaces of the academic commons would develop a sense of pride in "public edifices and public works" he felt was currently lacking from farm communities.[40] In addition to form and character, Olmsted prescribed the care and maintenance of campus spaces—mowing lawns, trimming hedges, and raking gravel paths—as a crucial part "of the duty and of the education of the students."[41] The recommendation combined Olmsted's shrewd labor practices with a modified design pedagogy emphasizing the responsibilities of property ownership while simultaneously improving campus grounds.

Olmsted couched these choices in the rhetoric of the New England village. The village was, in his eyes, the model environment of the yeoman, the family farmer glorified two decades earlier by Alexis de Tocqueville. To build his case for a tightly nucleated village along the public road at the property's easternmost edge, Olmsted provided extensive topographical analysis for farming, identifying appropriate hill lands to the northwest for horticulture and forestry, central tillage grounds for demonstrating economic agriculture's principles of crop rotation, a westernmost windbreak and orchard, lowland marshy pasture, and a central ornamental pond for aquatic animals, drinking water, and irrigation. The organizational focus of the grounds, he argued, could then be on academic and residential buildings arranged together along the existing public road; the required drill ground might play the part of the classic village green, with a building housing the armory, gymnasium, and assembly hall at its head as a stand-in for the traditional meeting hall. Three other buildings would ring the green as stand-ins for the center village, housing necessary programs: lecture halls and professors' offices, a library and reading rooms, and laboratories with an adjoining specimen museum. From this low vantage point, students might observe the gardens, orchards, vineyards, nurseries, and woods surrounding them, a point he doubly emphasized in Maine with a gentle artificial grade. This siting would reinforce the sense of bucolic isolation by interrupting the sight line to the actual village and the competing Amherst College—representative of the classical educational model rejected by Morrill Act schools—less than a mile to the south. While this scenographic naturalism resonated in some ways with the English landscape tradition, the country estate was not to be emulated, because of its remote location and hierarchical social structure—too like the plantation.[42] The treatment of the president's own house down winding gravel paths or at a remove from other campus buildings or student housing should therefore be avoided and the residence instead integrated among the student housing and academic buildings around the green.

Despite rhetorical associations with the rural township as the transformative site of wilderness, the seventeenth-century village form as conceived by Olmsted was in fact a nineteenth-century fiction.[43] Colonial records used the term "village" as an administrative unit: any settlement of a specified size within a country district, politically subordinate to a larger town. These villages showed a great diversity of spatial organization, from dispersed to linear, only later coming to reference the presence of a local parish or meetinghouse. Indeed, the proximate village of Amherst, incorporated in 1759, was arranged axially along two intersecting public roads.[44] It was not until the Romantic pastoral revival that well-known villages like Concord and Litchfield were rebuilt as dense town centers around a central green, creating a uniform aesthetic ideal to match their political and ideological import (fig. 13.3). The literary qualities of the picturesque landscape were also present in the village ideal; the novelist Nathaniel Hawthorne wrote in 1831 of the visible circles of industry, nature, and society emanating from the central spire of the village church, revealing "cultivated fields, villages, white country seats, the waving line of rivulets, little placid lakes, and here and there rising ground."[45] Never mind that such vistas would have been obscured by old-growth forest until the industrial-scale agriculture of Olmsted's own time, or that improved acres of farmland were rapidly exhausted in the Northeast by the middle of the nineteenth century.

While Olmsted saw the educated farmer as an integral part of both the modern economy and the modern social order, his adoption of the village ideal reveals the operational nostalgia latent within his vision of the land grant college. Olmsted was a fierce supporter of the rural agricultural model for land grant funding, but his site selection often had speculative commercial purposes. He recommended that Maine build near an important junction of the future European and North American Railway, for example, where graduates might be interconnected with the former St. Lawrence Riverway in order to compete for Eastern markets. While

FIGURE 13.3. *The reconstructed village green of Concord, Massachusetts, 1840. John Warner Barber,* Historical Collections, Being a General Collection of Interesting Facts, Traditions, Biographical Sketches, Anecdotes, &c. *(Worcester, MA: Dorr, Howland, 1840).*

initially rural, the campus was imagined as proto-industrial, a landscape itself in flux. If Olmsted's anti-urban vision for many of his parks would have been the return of what Sara Burns calls "Anglo-Saxon, middle-class norms [of] nature, decorum, and democracy [to] the youth of the slums," the rural land grant campus might become the origin point for a new, alternative urban or quasi-urban modernity.[46] Wartime farming in New England had taken on a new, industrial identity through the introduction of mechanization to replace labor-intensive farming in an effort to reduce reliance on Southern agriculture. Training in these specialized tools—planters, reapers, threshers, grain drills, hay loaders, cord binders, and listers—was indeed a major motivation for agricultural higher education in congressional debates. While only 40 percent of the population still worked in farming, by 1860 these family farms outproduced the rest of the nation in corn, wheat, and oats that served—and transformed—the central city into a growing peri-urban periphery.[47]

There remains another unnamed influence on Olmsted's early campus designs, one curiously at odds with his racially assimilative agenda: freedmen's villages. They provide an important footnote to this story by resisting the simple characterization of the campus as a disciplinary space, suggesting that Olmsted's plan was intended for some measure of self-determination. Among his greatest wartime preoccupations had been the superintendence of the enslaved; specifically, the men and women held as "contraband" by the Union army on the sites of abandoned rice and cotton plantations in the theater of war. The largest of these camps was in an area known as Port Royal in the South Carolina Sea Islands, and it operated as a refugee camp, a working farm, and eventually a school.[48] Olmsted drew on his expertise as a farmer, a designer, a student of plantation economies, and a wartime administrator, advocating on behalf of the refugees before Congress as the coauthor of an 1862 bill on wartime relief to African Americans.

In Olmsted's eyes, Port Royal was an opportunity to guide these men and women in their transition to freedom, demonstrating the superiority of free labor to the watchful eyes of the nation. It was in effect a kind of model farm. The bill, sponsored by Senator Lafayette S. Foster of Connecticut, outlined a framework for the management of the estate and its "contrabands," outfitting the refugees with supplies for planting cotton and a system of commissioners who would rent or manage plantation lands and guarantee employment for refugees as farmworkers. Commissioners would also be responsible for the sick and aged and coordinate with aid groups and missionaries to provide education and moral training. In a letter to Lincoln in support of his bill, Olmsted wrote of the Union's responsibility "to train or educate [refugees] in a few simple, essential, and fundamental social duties of free men in civilized life."[49]

The subdivided plantations remained largely unchanged under the management of the secretary of war, continuing monoculture cultivation against Olmsted's recommendation for "more objects of industry, more varied enterprises."[50]

The refugee camps, called "freedmen's villages," that sprung up alongside them were more transformational to Southern land use.[51] Built with scavenged materials, military-issue tents, and government-supplied lumber, these camps became models for what emancipation might look like (fig. 13.4). Mitchelville, just two miles from Port Royal, had planned streets and quarter-acre lots along a central public road, filled with groupings of residences lined by their own small flower beds and kitchen gardens.[52] The Port Royal experiment and freedmen's villages nationwide became integral to changing the hearts and minds of Northerners about Black racial identity and labor. At the outset of the war, popular sentiment found slavery abhorrent, yet racist attitudes about the perceived inferiority of Black workers persisted. By its end, the industriousness of the formerly enslaved in building, education, and community development had significantly shifted public opinion.[53]

Olmsted never referenced Port Royal in his writings on the agricultural colleges. Indeed, he likely thought them unrelated. His private correspondence with Henry Flagg French remained tightly circumscribed by the situation at hand: strategizing and compromising his plan to accommodate the desires of the Massachusetts Board of Agriculture.[54] Yet the two projects both make tenuous connections between spatial organization, agricultural labor, and administrative planning across multiple spheres of practice. The relationship between Port Royal and Mitchelville, between industry as a straightforward expression of modern agricultural production relatively unchanged from the plantation, and *industriousness* as not only the formation but the expression of a new Republican conception of citizenship, permeates Olmsted's focus on the residential buildings of the

FIGURE 13.4. *Alfred R. Waud, "Freedman's Village Seen from the Road," Arlington, Virginia, 1864. Library of Congress.*

agricultural college and informs his hope, however simplistic, that these would be self-made spaces.

The reintegration of Olmsted's designerly and political selves brings this project to the fore in a new way; it is worth noting that neither of Olmsted's early biographers mention his significant campus work—not the failed plan for the Massachusetts Agricultural College, nor the other ten campus designs he would produce in the following decade, the staggering 355 produced by his various firms, or the innumerable others visibly influenced by his approach.[55] Reading the Massachusetts Agricultural College against the freedmen's village underscores the centrality of the formerly enslaved to Olmsted's theorization of Northern free labor, despite his lack of direct engagement with them in his writings as anything other than a productive foil to the white working poor. This absence of explicit theorization, particularly after the war, from an otherwise prolific figure is, in many ways, what allowed for these heavily bracketed historicizations of Olmsted's separate practices to take hold.

Olmsted's suggestions for the land grant campus were not reducible to the formal landscape typologies that Hubbard and Olmsted Jr. hung their narrative on: Olmsted makes no direct references to English or German estates or hunting grounds and rejects the transverse roads and oblique approaches that the coeditors characterized as most innovative in his parks. For Mitchell, Olmsted's attitudes toward slavery were purely economically motivated, which centered Mitchell's history squarely on sites of production and entirely in the South. The book ends with Olmsted's time in Texas in 1853 and 1854, considering the German settlement of Neu Braunfels, a community of revolutionary émigrés Olmsted singled out as a viable white labor alternative to enslaved cotton cultivation. While Mitchell emphasized Olmsted's statistics that German-grown cotton fetched a higher market price, his closing lines also inadvertently demonstrated Olmsted's searingly racialized social interests. Olmsted advocated for empowering German immigrant communities ("there is no philanthropic enterprise that promises half so thankful a return") and for assimilating rather than further displacing the untapped Indigenous labor force that remained in the Texas Hill Country. "Having been forced back from the hunting-grounds and the fertile soil," Olmsted wrote of formidable Comanche raiders, "it is no wonder they are driven to violence. . . . The power of even a little education on these chaotic, malicious idiots and lunatics can hardly be over-estimated."[56]

These competing, and often contradictory, impulses between Olmsted's landscape projects and his ideologies of race and labor were both present in the philosophy of education he espoused for the agricultural college. He concluded that the land grant project was no less than the training of men for freedom versus slavery, of both labor and the mind:

> There have been in this country two distinct and opposing tendencies of social progress. In both, the advantage of fitting men by a special class training to serve the commonwealth, the advantage, that is to say, of a systematic division of labor, is recognized. In one, however, there is an effort to secure not only the special training of each class . . . but distinctions of general conditions and habits. . . . In the other, such artificial distinctions . . . are considered undesirable to be perpetuated.[57]

Olmsted cited two American educators and their institutions to demonstrate this divergence—Southern versus Northern. William Harper was a proslavery jurist and former chancellor of the University of South Carolina whom Olmsted bitterly admonished for condemning common schooling as "not only . . . wasted, but . . . positively detrimental to the interests of society at large."[58] Olmsted contrasted Harper with the industrialist Abbott Lawrence, characterized as the beneficent founder of the Lawrence Scientific School at Harvard University, established in 1847 as the nation's first degree-granting program for practical arts in the applied sciences and engineering. Lawrence had advocated for the expansion of higher education to include technical trades that would have once been associated with freeholding mechanics, small business owners, and farmers, yet scholars have shown that was hardly the intention of his generous $50,000 gift to Harvard. The businessmen responsible for funding the expansion of public education were primarily interested in training qualified men to staff their growing industrial empires.[59] Lawrence was a textile manufacturer and mercantilist with deep economic ties to Southern cotton who maintained warehouses in New Orleans to supply his Lowell, Massachusetts, mills.[60] If the Lawrence Scientific School exemplified the prewar mechanical development of the mill system, the agricultural schools funded by the Morrill Act managed the economic and labor transition of Reconstruction, diversifying farming in the North and Midwest until reliable cotton imports from Egypt and India could be established, and creating robust new industries for patent-protected seeds, fertilizers, and pesticides in their agricultural experiment stations.[61] The renewed emphasis on education in scientific and mechanized agriculture was not only a patriotic contribution to the supply chain but also a public (and publicly funded) act of forgetting on behalf of industrialists like Lawrence, who were able to remake themselves as Republican supporters of free labor and to distance themselves from their capital's origins on Southern plantations.[62]

The campus of the Massachusetts Agricultural College as built retained some resonances with Olmsted's proposal. The large, four-story academic building took pride of place along the new, oblique frontage road with its back toward the westward vista—now an undecorated brick facade with stone quoins on the school's meager budget (fig. 13.5). South College, as it was called, combined nearly all of Olmsted's program areas into a single building, complemented by a wood-frame agricultural chemistry laboratory and a four-story dormitory with a dramatically pitched roofline, officious in a neat quadrangle irrespective of the gently sloping road. Further east, however—Olmsted's preferred site—a motley group of small and midsize boardinghouses, barns, and greenhouses took shape over the summer and early fall of 1867 to meet the pressing Morrill Act deadline, rehabbing existing structures and adding new ones as needed. With the later construction of the campus pond and the transformation of the surrounding tillage into meadows for hay and grazing, the central campus ultimately took on the nucleated village form and common green Olmsted had intended.[63]

The tension between the east and west sides of the campus—one urban, one rural; one academic, one bucolic—reflects the competing visions behind the land grant movement (fig. 13.6). Olmsted's Republican campus machine ultimately aestheticized and spatialized his ideological dissonance with the emerging curricular goals of the college. Although his design plan was rejected, his curricular suggestions for student-led work on buildings, tillage, and grounds were implemented by the college trustees. Members of the first class were divided into working "squads" of six or seven (clearly modeled on enslaved jobbing gangs) that rotated throughout the day to "dig up old apple trees, husk and sort corn, pick apples, dig ditches for draining, fork over manure heaps, etc."[64] Each student was required to labor, without pay, for two hours every other day. Yet this fantasy of student life as educative preparation for free labor was directly at odds with young men who were beginning to understand their position as farmers in solidarity with other forms of labor; the grange movement for agricultural advocacy was particularly active in Massachusetts, and the self-styled "pioneer class" were

FIGURE 13.5. *South College, Massachusetts Agricultural College. Photo by John Lyman Lovell, ca. 1868. Special Collections and University Archives, University of Massachusetts, Amherst.*

FIGURE 13.6. *Early view of Massachusetts Agricultural College campus. Photo by John Lyman Lovell, ca. 1868. Jones Library, Amherst, Massachusetts.*

known locally for their political progressivism relative to the Amherst College students down the road.[65]

In the spring of 1870, the entire class went on strike, withholding their labor (and their tuition payments) for two months until the college's administration removed all compulsory farmwork and building maintenance from the curriculum unless explicitly required along "educational lines."[66] Far from Olmsted's fantasy of urban transformation, 40 percent of that first class came from a twenty-mile radius around Amherst, and more than 75 percent reported previous farming experience.[67] Yet they perceived higher education as an escape from that work, rather than its refinement. Of the graduating class of thirty-five, only three would become full-time farmers, the rest working in manufacturing, mechanical and civil engineering, insurance, sales, academia, and civil service and as the founder and president of a fertilizer company.[68]

For a state known for its ardent support of abolition and for its not-insignificant free Black population, the Massachusetts Agricultural College would remain a white-only space throughout Reconstruction, emboldened by a charter that gave the board full power over "provision for . . . the manual labor of the students . . . as they deem just and reasonable."[69] This distinctly unfree-sounding stipulation deterred many Black farmers from attending—including a young W. E. B. Du Bois, who would choose Jim Crow Tennessee over Amherst for his education, despite his family's homestead in nearby Great Barrington and his visible presence on the campus today as the namesake of the research library and the Department of Afro-American Studies.

The campus's contradictions crystallize the descent of the free labor ideal into an exclusively white racialization and its role in the turn toward more virulent strains of racism and nativism by middle-class Northerners over the following decade. Workers conditioned to expect that their individual efforts would produce value, whether as business owners or as respected employees, instead found themselves increasingly at odds with managers in a highly articulated chain of command. The land grant student (perhaps Irish or German American) rose within that system, moving closer to white identity through a complex class and race hierarchy that increasingly looked like the industrialized workplace. Those that did not (newer immigrants and African Americans) were seen as rejecting free labor. Olmsted's denunciation of Southern land use in favor of the invented New England village played into a uniquely Northern fiction that racialized configurations of free and unfree labor could be removed from the making of capital—one that convinced the technocratic managers of a newly remade Republican industry that they were still just civilized yeomen.

Notes

1. The secondary literature on the land grant program is immense, and I won't attempt to rehearse it conclusively here. The hegemonic narrative of democratization through access to education at the land grant schools has its origins in Earle Dudley Ross, *Democracy's College: The Land Grant Movement in the Formative State* (Amo Press, 1969). I draw on a recent shift in that historiography that has moved to study the land grant schools through the emergence of a working-class consciousness in US labor history, exemplified by the work of Nathan Sorber, as well as extending Craig Stevens Wilder's argument for the American university as one of the core spatial and institutional tools of empire. Nathan Sorber, "Early Land-Grant Colleges and Students in the Northeastern United States: A History of Regional Access and Mobility Patterns in Maine, Massachusetts, and New York, 1862–1878," *Agricultural History* 92, no. 1 (2018): 101–123; Nathan Sorber, *Land-Grant Colleges and Popular Revolt: The Origins of the Morrill Act and the Reform of Higher Education* (Cornell University Press, 2018); Craig Stevens Wilder, *Ebony and Ivy: Race, Slavery, and the Troubled History of America's Universities* (Bloomsbury, 2013). The role of the land grant college as a spatial and organizational logic for resource extraction and industrial development has also recently been taken up in architectural history by Reinhold Martin in "Sources: A Political Ecology of Cultivation," in *Knowledge Worlds: Media, Materiality, and the Making of the Modern University* (Columbia University Press, 2021).

2. Massachusetts land grant funds were ultimately split, with two-thirds of scrip proceeds going to the Massachusetts Agricultural College and the remaining one-third to the Massachusetts Institute of Technology, chartered just before the war in 1861; early debates between legislators favored providing all funds to Harvard University.

3. *New England Farmer* 15 (1863): 167.

4. On the early history of the University of Massachusetts Amherst, formerly the Massachusetts Agricultural College, see Harold Whiting Cary, *The University of Massachusetts: A History of One Hundred Years* (University of Massachusetts, 1962).

5. Morrill Act of 1862, 7 U.S.C. § 301.

6. F. H. Fowler, "The Massachusetts Agricultural College," *College Signal* 18 (1907): 6; Henry Flagg French to Frederick Law Olmsted, July 2, 1866, General Correspondence, July–August 1866, Frederick Law Olmsted Papers, Library of Congress.

7. Frederick Law Olmsted, *A Few Things to Be Thought of Before Proceeding to Plan Buildings for the National Agricultural Colleges* (New York: American News Company, 1866), 6–7.

8. Olmsted, *A Few Things*, 13, 11.

9. Olmsted, *A Few Things*, 14. The last property qualifications for voting were in fact only removed just before the Civil War and would shortly return in Black Codes after Reconstruction. Richard K. Scher, *The Politics of Disenfranchisement* (Taylor & Francis, 2015).

10. French was widely credited with inventing the French drain, implemented at Olmsted's own farm on Long Island. Henry Flagg French, *Farm Drainage: The Principles, Processes, and Effects of Draining Land with Stones, Wood, Plows, and Open Ditches* [. . .] (New York: Orange Judd, 1859).

11. David Schuyler reports that the pamphlet "circulated widely," and it is often cited as the reason for the Olmsted firm's 355 later campus commissions. David Schuyler, "Frederick Law Olmsted and the Origins of Modern Campus Design," *Planning for Higher Education* 25, no. 2 (1996–1997): 1–10; "How *Not* to Establish an Agricultural College," *Nation*, October 25, 1866, 335.

12. Eric Foner, *Free Soil, Free Labor, Free Men: The Ideology of the Republican Party Before the Civil War* (Oxford University Press, 1971). On American architectural style and free labor ideology, see Joanna Merwood-Salisbury, "The 'New Birth of Freedom': The Gothic Revival and the Aesthetics of Abolitionism," in *Race and Modern Architecture: A Critical History from the Enlightenment to the Present*, ed. Irene Cheng, Charles L. Davis II, and Mabel O. Wilson (University of Pittsburgh Press, 2021), 116–133.

13. Indeed, the only sustained engagement with free Black labor in Olmsted's writings was with a white farmer in Virginia who, despite pledging to employ only free workers, ranked the skill level of free Black workers below the Irish, the German, and the enslaved, superior only to native white workers. Frederick Law Olmsted, "Free Labor Farm in Virginia," *A Journey into the Seaboard States* (New York: Mason Brothers, 1856), 94–103.

14. Nikhil Pal Singh, "On Race, Violence, and So-Called Primitive Accumulation," *Social Text* 24, no. 3 (2016): 27–50. Elements of this argument are also implicit in Sylvia Wynter, "Unsettling the Coloniality of Being/Power/Truth/Freedom: Towards the Human, After Man, Its Overrepresentation—An Argument," *CR: The New Centennial Review* 3, no. 3 (2003): 257–337.

15. The physiocratic origins of free labor are, however, present in Jefferson's Rockfish Gap Report, where he lists the objects of the university as providing training in business, improving the morals of students, and communicating duties to both neighbors and country. Thomas Jefferson, "Report of the Board of Commissioners for the University of Virginia to the Virginia General Assembly," August 4, 1818, Papers of Thomas Jefferson, National Archives.

16. Olmsted, *A Few Things*, 11–12.

17. Heather Cox Richardson, *The Death of Reconstruction: Race, Labor, and Politics in the Post–Civil War North, 1865–1901* (Harvard University Press, 2001).

18. Morrill Act of 1862, 7 U.S.C. § 301.

19. "A railroad contractor in one of the best cotton districts of the United States told me, that having begun his work with negroes, he was substituting Irish and German laborers for them as rapidly as possible, with great advantage." Frederick Law Olmsted, *A Journey in the Back Country* (New York: Mason Brothers, 1854), 349.

20. Olmsted, *Journey in the Back Country*, 349 (emphasis added).

21. Olmsted writes that such a design will impose "quite unnecessary inconvenience and fatigue upon those who are to occupy it." Olmsted, *A Few Things*, 6.

22. Olmsted, *A Few Things*, 7.

23. Olmsted does not make direct reference to the inhabitants of these institutions, but all were well known for serving Irish inmates. Of all prisoners over the history of Norfolk Island's second phase, from 1825 to 1855, one-third were Irish political prisoners. Anne-Maree Whitaker, "Swords to Ploughshares: The 1798 Irish Rebels in New South Wales," *Labour History*, no. 75 (November 1998): 9–21. Likewise, the Archdiocese of New York accused the Children's Aid Society in 1863 of targeting the Irish Catholic children of draft protestors. Marilyn Irvin Holt, *The Orphan Trains: Placing Out in America* (University of Nebraska Press, 1994).

24. Olmsted would go on to design another campus, intended as a direct engagement with orphans, children in foster care, and indigent children: the Industrial Home School in Washington, DC, built in 1881.

25. The organization of unruly, hostile labor forces characterizes both utopian socialist projects like Robert Owen's New Harmony, Indiana (1825), and industrial workers' towns like Pullman, Illinois (1880); the tension between these perceived top-down and bottom-up projects, both rural and peri-urban, are characteristic of the emergence of planning in this historical moment.

26. A blank version of Form E is reproduced in Jane Turner Censer, ed., *The Papers of Frederick Law Olmsted: Volume 4; Defending the Union* (Johns Hopkins University Press, 1986), 292–293. Filled-out versions of Form E are captured in the records of the US Sanitary Commission: Statistical Bureau Archives, 1861–1869, Physical Examinations, January 1863–May 1866, US Sanitary Commission Records, New York Public Library Archives and Manuscripts.

27. Leslie A. Schwalm, "A Body of 'Truly Scientific Work,'" *Journal of the Civil War Era* 8, no. 4 (2018): 647–676.

28. Quotes drawn from correspondence with the essayist and antislavery activist John Jay Chapman, as excerpted in Jane Turner Censer's introduction to Censer, *Papers of Olmsted: Vol. 4*, 51.

29. The relationship of Theodora Kimball Hubbard to Fiske Kimball is not incidental, as the latter had written the first monograph on Thomas Jefferson just five years earlier, to great acclaim; both were engaged in the production of an "American" architectural and landscape history. Theodora Kimball Hubbard and Frederick Law Olmsted Jr., eds., *Frederick Law Olmsted, Landscape Architect, 1822–1903: Early Years and Experiences* (G. P. Putnam's Sons, 1922). The impetus of the authors to scientifically professionalize landscape architecture with the publication has been discussed in Edward Eigen, "Frederick Law Olmsted and the Origins of Landscape Architecture," in *On Accident: Episodes in Architecture and Landscape* (MIT Press, 2018), 10–49; and in Heidi Hohmann, "Theodora Kimball Hubbard and the 'Intellectualization' of Landscape Architecture, 1911–1935," *Landscape Journal* 25, no. 2 (2006): 169–186. Hohmann notes that the project was essentially promotional and self-financed, commenting that the younger Olmsted could not find a press that thought the book had a viable audience.

30. Hohmann, "Theodora Kimball Hubbard," 180.

31. For example, the natural beauty of wild sweetbriar and Cherokee roses in Central Texas or the planting of ornamental trees and the scenic relocation of buildings at Tosomock. "Farming," 84–87, and "Southern Trips," 111–117, in Hubbard and Olmsted, *Frederick Law Olmsted.*

32. Broadus Mitchell, *Frederick Law Olmsted, a Critic of the Old South* (Johns Hopkins University Press, 1924). Mitchell was affiliated with Columbia University's so-called Dunning School, which would historicize Reconstruction rather than the antebellum era as the pivotal moment of social discord. See Laura F. Edwards, "Southern History as U.S. History," *Journal of Southern History* 75, no. 3 (2009): 533–564.

33. Daniel Joseph Singal, "Broadus Mitchell and the Persistence of New South Thought," *Journal of Southern History* 45, no. 3 (1979): 353–380; Mitchell, *Frederick Law Olmsted*, 71.

34. "A chief interest in the Staten Island farm lies in the fact that here Olmsted's attention was first drawn in an engrossing way to Southern slavery." Mitchell, *Frederick Law Olmsted*, 44.

35. See Sara Zewde, *Cotton Kingdom, Now* (forthcoming); John Dean Davis, "Olmsted in the South, Olmsted at War," in *Military Landscapes* (Harvard University Press, 2021), 173–199. On Olmsted and social engineering, see Dorceta E. Taylor, "Central Park as a Model for Social Control: Urban Parks, Social Class and Leisure Behavior in Nineteenth-Century America," *Journal of Leisure Research* 31, no. 4 (1999): 420–477.

36. "Report on the Demoralization of the Volunteers," September 1861, quoted in Censer, *Papers of Olmsted: Vol. 4*, 165.

37. Censer, *Papers of Olmsted: Vol. 4*, 173.

38. "Architect's Report," in *Annual Report of the State College of Agriculture and the Mechanic Arts*, 46th Maine State Legislature, 1867, 24 (emphasis added).

39. "Architect's Report," 24.

40. Olmsted, *A Few Things*, 13.

41. Olmsted, *A Few Things*, 21–22.

42. This marked a departure from the other great advocate of English landscape design in the nineteenth-century United States, Andrew Jackson Downing, who emphasized the position of both buildings and plantings to frame or produce the sense of long vistas in his rural residential designs. Andrew Jackson Downing, "Further Hints on the Gardens and Grounds of Cottage Residences," in *Cottage Residences: A Series of Designs for Rural Cottages and Cottage Villas* [. . .] (New York: John Wiley, 1852), 189–210.

43. Joseph S. Wood, "'Build, Therefore, Your Own World': The New England Village as Settlement Ideal," *Annals of the Association of American Geographers* 81, no. 1 (1991): 32–50.

44. Henry Francis Walling, *Map of the County of Hampshire, Massachusetts* (New York: H. & C. T. Smith, 1860).

45. Nathaniel Hawthorne, "Sights from a Steeple" (1831), quoted in Wood, "'Build, Therefore,'" 38.

46. Sarah Burns, *Pastoral Inventions: Rural Life in Nineteenth-Century American Art and Culture* (Temple University Press, 1989), 313.

47. These were both breadbasket crops and feed that supported wool production and dairying, the most profitable and productive outputs of Northern farms at midcentury. R. Douglas Hurt, *American Agriculture: A History* (Purdue University Press, 2002).

48. Willie Lee Rose, *Rehearsal for Reconstruction: The Port Royal Experiment* (University of Georgia Press, 1999); Laura Wood Roper, "Frederick Law Olmsted and the Port Royal Experiment," *Journal of Southern History* 31, no. 3 (1965): 272–284.

49. Frederick Law Olmsted to Abraham Lincoln, March 8, 1862, quoted in Charles Beveridge, ed., *Frederick Law Olmsted: Writings on Landscape, Culture, and Society* (Library of America, 2015), 186. Olmsted would weigh in on the issue of African American education after the war; see "Education in the Rebel States," *Nation*, March 22, 1866.

50. Frederick Law Olmsted, *Journeys and Explorations in the Cotton Kingdom* [. . .], vol. 2 (New York: Mason Brothers, 1861), 270.

51. Quoted in Rose, *Rehearsal for Reconstruction*, 226. Amy Murrell Taylor, *Embattled Freedom: Journeys Through the Civil War's Slave Refugee Camps* (University of North Carolina Press, 2018); Chandra Manning, *Troubled Refuge: Struggling for Freedom in the Civil War* (Vintage Books, 2017).

52. Michael Trinkley and Debi Hacker, *The Archaeological Manifestations of the 'Port Royal Experiment' at Mitchelville, Hilton Head Island, South Carolina* (Chicora Foundation, 1987).

53. Richardson, *Death of Reconstruction*, ix.

54. For example, "Can't you adapt your village to our new road, by moving your public square?" Henry Flagg French to Frederick Law Olmsted, July 16, 1866, General Correspondence, July–August 1866, Frederick Law Olmsted Papers, Library of Congress.

55. "Master List of Campus Projects," in *The Master List of Design Projects of the Olmsted Firm, 1857–1950*, ed. Charles Beveridge and Carolyn Hoffman (National Association for Olmsted Parks, 1987). On the influence of Olmsted's campus designs, see Richard Longstreth, "From Farm to Campus: Planning, Politics, and the Agricultural College Idea in Kansas," *Winterthur Portfolio* 20, no. 2/3 (1985): 149–179.

56. Frederick Law Olmsted, *A Journey Through Texas; or, A Saddle-Trip on the Southwestern Frontier* (1857), quoted in Mitchell, *Frederick Law Olmsted*, 155–156.

57. Olmsted, *A Few Things*, 10.

58. Olmsted, *A Few Things*, 10.

59. "Epilogue: Cotton Comes to Harvard," in Wilder, *Ebony and Ivy*, 275–288.

60. The Lawrence Company's holdings in the South are detailed in the Lawrence Manufacturing Company Records, Baker Library Special Collections and Archives, Harvard University.

61. Lous A. Ferleger, "Higher Education for an Innovative Economy: Land Grant Colleges and the Managerial Revolution in America," *Planting the Seeds of Research: How America's Ultimate Investment Transformed Agriculture* (Anthem, 2020).

62. This impetus—to free capitalism from its debt to slavery—is the major historiographical correction of a body of scholarship beginning with Eric Williams in 1940 and connected most recently to the "new history of capitalism." Eric Williams, *Capitalism and Slavery* (University of North Carolina Press, 1940); for an example of the latter, see Sven Beckert and Seth Rockman, *Slavery's Capitalism: A New History of American Economic Development* (University of Pennsylvania Press, 2016).

63. The meadows were landscaped with native wetland plants and tree species by Olmsted employees Warren Manning and Frank Waugh, creating a unifying campus landscape plan they referred to as "Central Park." Frank Waugh, *Grounds of MAC (Studies for the Improvement of) from 1864–1911*, 1911, box 7, Frank A. Waugh Papers, Robert S. Cox Special Collections and University Archives Research Center, University of Massachusetts Amherst.

64. Lily B. Caswell, *Brief History of the Massachusetts Agricultural College on Its Semicentennial* (F. A. Bassette, 1917), 11.

65. "They tended to be more radical than their average fellow-Americans; they read the writings of free-thinking Charles Bradlaugh and those of the violent agnostic Robert Ingersoll, as well as the novels of that 'woman of sin,' George Eliot. They would walk miles to hear the magnificent orations of the reformers Wendell Phillips and Henry Ward Beecher. They smoked pipes, chewed tobacco, imbibed, and grew mustaches, beards, and 'burnsides.'" Cary, *University of Massachusetts*, 51.

66. Cary, *University of Massachusetts*, 46.

67. Cary, *University of Massachusetts*, 38.

68. Cary, *University of Massachusetts*, 38.

69. The state's free Black population was 8,256, according to the 1860 census. For treatment of that community in the state economy, see Jacqueline Jones, *No Right to an Honest Living: The Struggles of Boston's Black Workers in the Civil War Era* (Basic Books, 2023); *Commonwealth of Massachusetts, Acts and Resolves Passed by the General Court* (Boston: Wright & Potter, 1863), 517–520. It wasn't until the period immediately after the college's incorporation as a university in 1947 and the *Brown v. Board of Education* decision of 1954 that Black enrollment increased, as the university accepted scholarships from Southern states that intended to keep Black residents out of their own state schools. Indeed, the Massachusetts Agricultural College student newspaper *Aggie Life* argued on behalf of the Black Codes and for federal disenfranchisement, claiming that Southern Black people were "improvident, depraved, and strenuously resist any attempts at education," and calling them a "body of people unprepared for freedom." The article alleged that "the giving of the unqualified ballot to a people totally unfitted and unprepared for it was a direct blow against intelligent Republican government." *Aggie Life*, December 14, 1892, 79–81.

14 CONFRONTING ASSIMILATION

THE INTERPLAY BETWEEN OČÉTI ŜAKÓWIŊ AND SETTLER SPATIALITIES IN DAKOTA TERRITORY, 1883–1888

Katherine Solomonson

ON SEPTEMBER 4, 1883, THREE HUNDRED Lakȟóta and Dakȟóta people from the Standing Rock Agency of the Great Sioux Reservation rode into Mandan, Dakota Territory, a boomtown adjacent to the Northern Pacific Railroad just west of the Missouri River (fig. 14.1). With them were the US Indian agent James McLaughlin, who left an account of this event; and the Huŋkpapȟa Lakȟóta Chief Sitting Bull (Tȟatȟáŋka Íyotake), who seven years earlier had been one of the prime movers behind the battle that defeated the US Seventh Cavalry at Pezi Sla (Greasy Grass, a.k.a. Little Bighorn). Leaving their horses behind, the travelers commenced the long wait for their train.[1] As they waited, Pullman cars filled with European and American "ladies and gentlemen," fresh from Yellow-

FIGURE 14.1. *Beck & Pauli,* Bird's-Eye View of Mandan, Dakota Territory, *1883. The railroad depot is visible on Main Street at center left. Lithograph published by J. J. Stoner, 1883. Geography and Map Division, Library of Congress.*

stone National Park, pulled up to the Northern Pacific's new depot, a shingle-clad structure designed in New York by McKim, Mead & White (fig. 14.2).[2]

An architectural history of this event might begin with the puzzle of how a building like this came to be in Mandan. Focusing on the architects, their client, and a singular building—a firmly established method in the production of architectural history—would reveal how Northern Pacific President Henry Villard hired McKim, Mead & White to design Mandan's depot and other buildings for the railroad in the early 1880s, and how they served the railroad's symbolic and functional purposes, especially during the excursion Villard organized to impress his backers and celebrate the rail line's completion.[3]

Such an account would focus on white capitalists and politicians in the East who supported the Western railroads and possessed the means, from afar, to influence the Trans-Mississippi West's future. Looking at this through the lens of scholarship on settler colonialism uncovers how, directly and indirectly, the buildings they commissioned contributed to advancing American imperial expansion, white migrants' settlement of Indigenous lands, and by extension the genocidal violence of Indigenous displacement and environmental despoliation. Many white Americans justified these processes—endemic to settler colonialism—by asserting their own racial superiority and their divinely sanctioned right and responsibility to "civilize" the continent.[4]

Scholarship in settler colonial studies has been generative for numerous fields since the 1990s,[5] and more recently for American architectural history as well.[6] At the same time, scholars in Indigenous studies have pointed out that too many accounts like the one above reproduce settler colonialism's "elimination of the Native" (to quote Patrick Wolfe) by focusing on settlers' actions and Indigenous

FIGURE 14.2. *McKim, Mead & White, Northern Pacific Railway Depot, Mandan, North Dakota, 1882, demolished. Photo by F. Jay Haynes, 1894. Photographic Archives, Montana Historical Society.*

victimization, with little or no recognition of Indigenous agency, resistance, and resilience.[7] Tracey Banivanua Mar and Penelope Edmonds, among others, have demonstrated that one way of countering this is to uncover the specific local, material, and spatial ways that Indigenous people have contended with the broader processes of settler colonialism while sustaining their own cultures.[8]

Another way of approaching this essay, then, is to focus on the interplay between Indigenous and settler spatialities during the 1880s, when the stream of white settlers became a torrent and Indigenous people throughout the West faced increasing pressure to give up millions of acres of common land, "live like white men," and assimilate to dominant American values and practices. At that time, Standing Rock was part of the Great Sioux Reservation, the territory of the Lakȟóta and Dakȟóta people who formed the western Očéti Ŝakówiŋ Oyate—the people of the Seven Council Fires. Because both Lakȟóta and Dakȟóta people lived at Standing Rock, I refer to them collectively as Očéti Ŝakówiŋ, more specifically as Lakȟóta or Dakȟóta, and individually by identifying their people (e.g., Sisitoŋwaŋ Dakȟóta).[9] The activist and historian Nick Estes (Kul Wicasa / Lower Brule Sioux Tribe) has traced the people of Standing Rock's long history of resilience and resistance to settler colonialism, capitalism, and federal authority.[10] I build on his work from the vantage point of a settler and outsider to the Očéti Ŝakówiŋ Oyate, and as a historian of architecture, landscape, and material culture.

Four well-documented events offer the opportunity to examine the production of Očéti Ŝakówiŋ and settler spatialities relationally and dynamically. One event unfolded in the town of Mandan, where Indigenous people from many places wove in their own geographies, followed by another event across the river in Bismarck, where settlers endeavored to incorporate the Očéti Ŝakówiŋ into their own triumphalist narrative. Two others unfolded sixty-five miles south at the Standing Rock Agency, where the Očéti Ŝakówiŋ enlisted long-standing spatial practices to transform federally funded agency spaces and undermine congressional agendas. All of these events offer views of Očéti Ŝakówiŋ and settler spatialities as they coexisted, clashed, and intertwined through dynamic processes that altered Indigenous-settler power relations. Natchee Blu Barnd has demonstrated how "Indigenous geographies have quietly overlapped and coexisted in tension with the geographies of the settler colonial state."[11] In Dakota Territory's contested spaces, these processes could be subtle or far from quiet.

Mandan, Dakota Territory, September 5, 1883

Returning to the travelers from Standing Rock: As they waited for their train, they spent four hours in Mandan, a new colonial town laid out on a grid superimposed on still-visible remnants of Mandan and Hidatsa villages, which were expunged in the idealized bird's-eye view of 1883 (see fig. 14.1). The town was designed by and for white settlers and travelers, who used the depot as a gateway to claims on Indigenous lands. Even as they encountered hostility, Očéti Ŝakówiŋ people produced their own spatialities in and around Mandan through adaptation, appropriation, and performance. Standing Rock's travelers could have visited tipi camps that reconfigured "unimproved" land at the edge of town; entered the urban grid to trade with travelers; greeted a chief who was shaking hands outside Mandan's best hotel; conversed in Plains Indian Sign Language with people from other reservations; and checked in with Lakhˇóta teamsters, whose trajectories intersected with settler systems of trade at the freight depot, redefining the open space around it through paths and arrangements of their own making.[12]

Meanwhile, a few Huŋkpapȟa Lakȟóta travelers were waiting at the passenger depot (see fig. 14.2). With its fish-scale shingles, broad hipped roof, dormers, and a shaded platform that resembled a long wraparound porch, the depot echoed aspects of the "modernized colonial" buildings McKim, Mead & White were designing for fashionable Eastern seaside resorts. Some settlers associated this style with a narrative that featured racially superior Anglo-Saxon pilgrims who landed at Plymouth Rock and laid the foundation for the American values and institutions their descendants would carry westward. Not many passengers would have connected this racialized narrative specifically with the depot, but people in luxurious Pullman cars may have recognized that the building evoked what the Northeastern elite and their Western counterparts defined as genteel taste.[13]

McLaughlin decided to introduce Sitting Bull to the gentility of Mandan's depot and, later, the best hotel in Bismarck. His strategy for assimilation involved co-optation as well as overt control, for he believed that exposure to the achievements of the "white man" would "overawe" Native people and make "them amenable to the government's demands."[14] Along with four tribal policemen and two soldiers from Fort Yates, McLaughlin escorted Sitting Bull and his family into the depot's main waiting room, a large space with arched windows overlooking the tracks and Mandan's City Park Square. There, Sitting Bull, who had become a celebrity in the American press, was both sequestered and on display. Spotting him in the waiting room, the passengers from the Pullman cars disembarked and surrounded him.[15] Though he was the object of tourists' curious gazes, he set the terms for the interactions. It is easy to imagine, for reasons I will discuss below, that for a few hours the waiting room became his. As people approached him, he remained quietly seated. When they asked for his signature, he charged a firm $1.50 for each. That day and the next, he made a total of about $150.00, the equivalent of nearly $5,000 dollars in 2025.[16] Some might have assumed that Sitting Bull was developing the habits of individual acquisitiveness that white reformers and agency staff were trying to inculcate in Indigenous people. Exchanging his signature for American cash was one of the many ways he engaged with changing conditions, for his own reasons. As Christopher Pexa (Bdewákaŋtuŋwaŋ Dakȟóta, Spirit Lake Nation) has observed, Dakȟóta responses to an assimilationist regime could be "decolonial translations that were less acts of resistance than they were nuanced and covert acts of endurance, relinkings to the past, and resurgent movings toward the future." Such acts could be meaningful to Indigenous people who understood how to read them, while remaining illegible to settlers.[17] Sitting Bull was known to make money when he could and then give it away, sustaining Očéti Ŝakówiŋ values and communal practices while performing one of his most important roles as a chief: caring for his people.[18]

Bismarck, Dakota Territory, September 6, 1883

When the Očéti Ŝakówiŋ from Standing Rock boarded their train at 6:00 p.m., it was the first railroad trip for most of them. In addition to sensing the vibrations, noise, smells, and speed of train travel, those who looked out the window would have seen their familiar Mníšoše (Missouri River) seventy feet beneath them as they crossed the iron bridge to Bismarck. There they set up camp while trains from the East arrived bearing hundreds of dignitaries who were part of Villard's celebratory excursion that would continue on to the site where former President Ulysses S. Grant would pound in the Northern Pacific's ceremonial last spike.[19]

The convergence of all of these people in Bismarck was timed to coincide with the cornerstone-laying ceremony for a new territorial capitol building, which would soon become the statehouse for the new state of North Dakota. The Očéti Ŝakówiŋ were there at the invitation of the mayor and the territorial governor. The next morning some of them found themselves incorporated into festivities infused with a triumphalist narrative that juxtaposed US modernity and imperial expansion with their "primitivism" and defeat. Sitting Bull's contingent—"once war-like savages in their aboriginal dress," according to *The Bismarck Tribune*—took their places near the front of the long procession to the capitol building's site (fig. 14.3).[20] There the town had erected a platform that raised that day's most eminent dignitaries high above the crowd. According to the caption for a *Harper's Weekly* illustration of the event, "All around were grouped cow-boys, citizens, frontiersmen, visitors from afar, and natives of the soil," who demonstrated the "closeness with

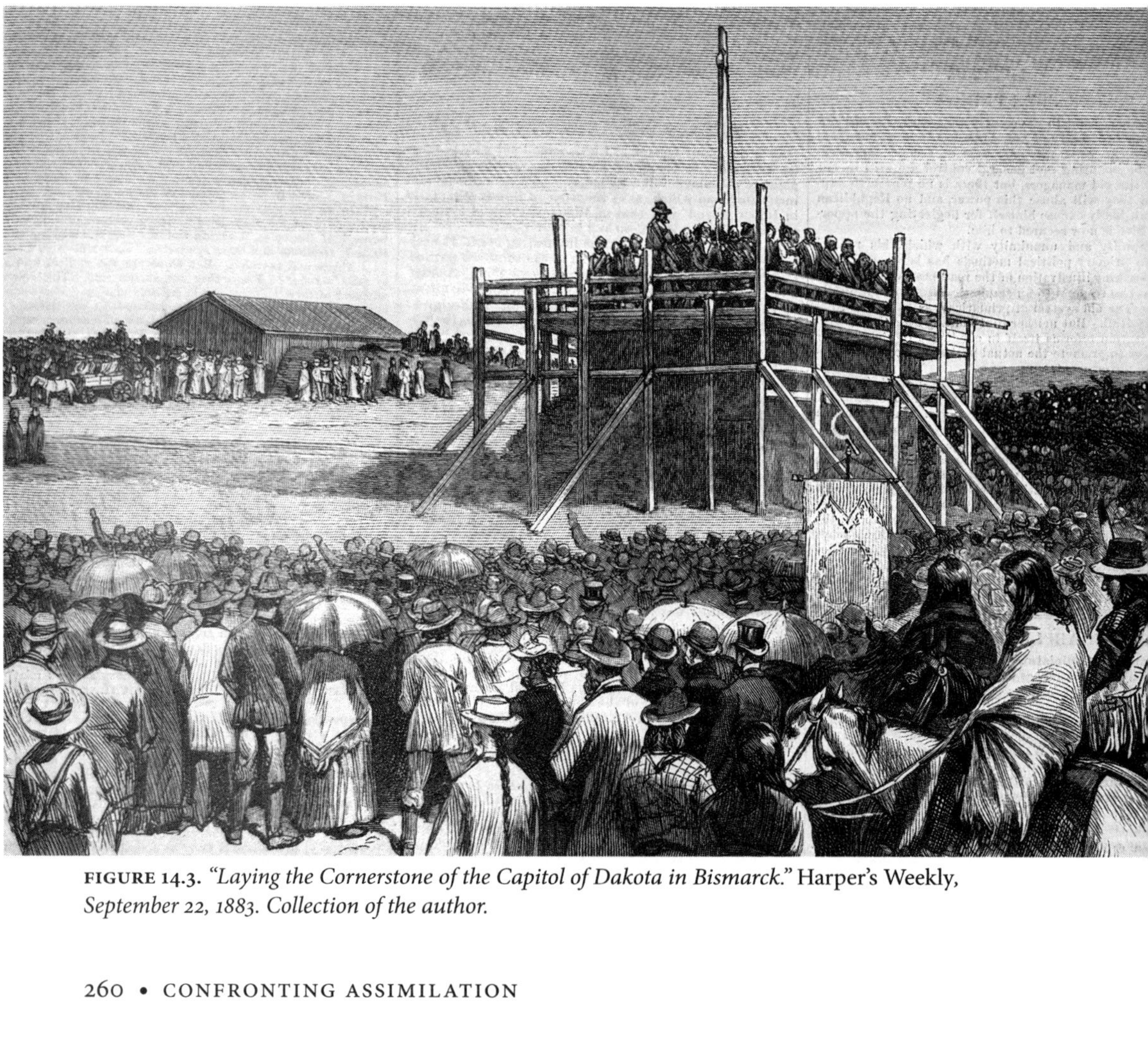

FIGURE 14.3. *"Laying the Cornerstone of the Capitol of Dakota in Bismarck."* Harper's Weekly, *September 22, 1883. Collection of the author.*

which modern civilization jostles barbarism on the frontiers of the republic."[21] The Očéti Ŝakówiŋ people from Standing Rock, like the Indigenous men featured prominently in the illustration, were positioned to enhance the contrast.

Sitting Bull was invited to join Henry Villard, Grant, and other champions of American expansionism up on the platform. To reach them, he mounted a long stairway, a kinesthetic and visual experience that may have seemed alien to someone who, like other chiefs, customarily conducted his interactions on a level playing field.[22] From on high, various speakers extolled the Northern Pacific's achievements.[23] When the crowd clamored for Sitting Bull to speak, his words—as they came out in McLaughlin's translation—assured his listeners that he would always be a friend of the "white man."[24] Afterward, the *Harper's Weekly* reporter sounded a death knell for the Očéti Ŝakówiŋ way of life: "It is not long since these chieftains claimed for their people the vast valley of the Missouri." But now "the shrill call of the railroad whistle, the clatter of trains, and the whir of manufacturing industry will dispel forever the primeval silence of the land of the Dakotas."[25]

Both this event and its reenactment in the press inserted the Očéti Ŝakówiŋ into a celebration of their own pacification, the relegation of their culture to the past, and implicitly, their future incorporation into the expanding settler state. This was underscored by the display of Sitting Bull as a subdued warrior on the platform from which the new capitol building's cornerstone was lowered.

Standing Rock Agency, August 1883

The Bismarck event and its telling were quite different from what had been happening on the Great Sioux Reservation. There the Očéti Ŝakówiŋ were actively resisting federal policy and settlers' thirst for their land.

Three weeks earlier, a US Senate select committee disembarked at Mandan's depot and traveled sixty-five miles south to the Standing Rock Agency, the northernmost part of the Great Sioux Reservation. The committee's chair was Senator Henry L. Dawes from Massachusetts, and its charge was to check on reservation conditions, to determine whether the Očéti Ŝakówiŋ had been forced to sign an agreement the year before (they had), and in the process to show that it was in their best interest to move onto individual allotments of land and give up millions of acres of "surplus" common land to settlers. Dawes and others were preparing a bill that would advance this. In addition to providing legalized means for a massive land grab, this legislation was also meant as a mechanism for assimilating Indigenous people into mainstream Christian civilization. These goals were informed by a concept of race recently promulgated by Lewis Henry Morgan. Morgan rejected the notion that races (defined by physiognomy and skin color) had inherent and intractable character traits and that northern European "stock" was superior to that of all other races. Instead, he contended that all people were capable of attaining a civilized state once they went through three distinct stages: savagery, barbarism, and finally civilization, which he identified with a number of factors, including architecture.[26] Picking up on this, assimilation proponents argued that education and allotments would further this process by fracturing communal bonds, promoting individual property ownership, obliterating Indigenous cultures, and absorbing the assimilated into the cadastral space of the settler state—cultural genocide writ large.[27]

Traveling through the reservation on the way to the Standing Rock Agency, the Senate committee would have seen tipi camps, a few log houses and farms, and broad expanses of open, commonly held land—a landscape that was largely defined by long-standing Očéti Ŝakówiŋ practices, with adaptations to new conditions (fig. 14.4). The landscape changed as they approached the agency's headquarters. The agency and nearby Fort Yates—bounded rectilinear spaces with brick and wood-frame buildings and fences—were extensions of settler geometry and federal authority into Očéti Ŝakówiŋ territory (figs. 14.5, 14.6).[28] From there Standing Rock's Indian agent McLaughlin exercised power reinforced by his management (and withholding) of rations, the visible presence of military force, and the disciplinary control that the Catholic Church, schools, and the rectilinear buildings themselves endeavored to exert over Indigenous minds and bodies.

When the committee arrived, they summoned Očéti Ŝakówiŋ men to the Standing Rock agency's headquarters, where they met in a building that served as a council house. Transcripts of what people said and did during their meetings were published in the *Congressional Record*.[29] These texts were mediated by translators, transcribers, and the publisher and absorbed into the state's colonial apparatus. But read with this in mind, they offer glimpses from several perspectives of how Očéti Ŝakówiŋ leaders and white federal officials contended with differing assumptions about sovereignty, space, and race.

On the first day, sovereignty came to the fore when Sitting Bull rose to speak. He expected the committee to recognize him as a chief and to treat him with the appropriate respect. The committee refused; to do so would have been to recognize the chiefs' authority—Sitting Bull's in particular—and Očéti Ŝakówiŋ sovereignty, which they denied. In response, Sitting Bull gave them a demonstration of his continuing power. With a mere wave of his hand, most people left the room and the meeting came to a close. In effect, he took over a space that representatives of the federal government had defined and controlled.[30]

Resuming the meeting the next day, Dawes asked loaded questions to get his own points across while evading fundamental questions for which the Očéti Ŝakówiŋ needed answers. His first exchange with Chief John Grass (Mathȟó Wathȟákpe, Sihásapa Lakȟóta) is telling:

> DAWES: Do the Indians expect to keep all of their land and not do anything toward taking care of themselves?

FIGURE 14.4. *Sitting Bull's camp at the Standing Rock Agency, Great Sioux Reservation, 1880s. Photo by David F. Barry. Western History Collection, Denver Public Library, call no. B-773.*

FIGURE 14.5. *Standing Rock Agency and Fort Yates, 1880s. Photo by David F. Barry. Western History Collection, Denver Public Library, call no. B-842.*

FIGURE 14.6. *Fort Yates parade ground, 1880s. Photo by David F. Barry. Western History Collection, Denver Public Library, call no. B-848.*

Grass: We have been arguing about the boundary lines of our reservation, and we have come to ask you to make them plain for us.

Dawes [deflecting the question]: Would you and your people like to live as white men live?[31]

Dawes posed the last question to his interviewees over and over. By this he meant abandoning a communal way of life in favor of houses on separate land holdings—a drastically different way of configuring space and life, which Dawes explicitly racialized as white.

Responses varied. Most people said yes to farming. They had little choice now that commercial hunters' decimation of the bison had so radically changed their lives. Many pointed out that after years of unfulfilled promises for equipment, farm animals, houses, and training, it was impossible to achieve this. Several people reminded the committee that they were well aware of how prosperous white people lived. They knew what equipment was needed for white farmers to succeed; they had seen houses on their visits to Washington, DC; they commented on the quality of the commissioners' own clothing; and they compared all of this to their own poverty. None of this meant that they wanted to jettison their communal way of life. When asked whether they were willing to part with reservation land, many were firm in their unwillingness to do so, or to negotiate at all, until promises made through past treaties were fulfilled.[32]

At the Cheyenne River Agency, Chief Charger (Waanatan II, Yangtonai and Sisitoŋwaŋ Dakȟóta), like the others, answered Dawes's question in the affirmative and then shifted tack to make a larger point: "I want to ask you something," he said. "Do you take us for men or beasts?" Dawes evaded the question. Charger pushed harder: "I want to know what the white people think of us." The response: "The white people in Washington want to have the Indians learn how to work, and to live as they do." In so many words, Dawes was saying that you become a fully human adult only when you cease to be and live like an Indian. Toward the end of the interview, Charger used Dawes's racialized terms against him to underscore the commission's racism and hypocrisy: "I think we are treated like dogs. God made us all, both whites and Indians; and if he should look into this matter he might get angry at the way we have been treated."[33]

Standing Rock, July and August 1888

By 1887, Dawes and his allies had managed to push the General Allotment Act (also known as the Dawes Act) through Congress. In addition to providing for allotments and the sale of millions of acres of tribal land to settlers, it also carved the Great Sioux Reservation into six separate reservations. According to the 1868 Fort Laramie Treaty, which had created the Great Sioux Reservation, for this to go forward three-quarters of the reservation's men needed to agree to the Dawes Act's terms. Aiming to secure their assent, a newly formed congressional commission planned to arrive at Standing Rock in July 1888. This time the chair was Richard Henry Pratt, founder of the United States Indian Industrial School in Carlisle, Pennsylvania, the model for the extensive US system of off-reservation boarding schools. Očéti Ŝakówiŋ chiefs were already familiar with Pratt and his project. Pratt had come to the Great Sioux Reservation previously, and its children had been among the first to arrive at Carlisle in 1879.[34]

The most voluminous documentation of the commission's meetings at Standing Rock is the report Pratt prepared afterward. Like the 1883 records mentioned above, this included extensive transcripts that record people's words and actions, as mediated by the translator and those involved in the publication. Newspaper reports, firsthand accounts, and contemporary photographs provide other perspectives.[35]

Before they arrived, the commission sent documents and maps that explained the General Allotment Act's terms. They wanted the reservation's men to be informed and ready to cast individual votes for or against the implementation of the Dawes Act. This modeling of a (male) citizen's participation in an American political process might have been intended as an educational step toward assimilation and citizenship. But it also shows how profoundly the commission underestimated the ongoing strength of the Očéti Ŝakówiŋ chiefs and system of governance, which was based on communal consensus building, not individual votes. Accordingly, before the commission arrived, chiefs throughout the Great Sioux Reservation convened a council to discuss the Dawes Act and its implications for land they planned to preserve for future generations. The goal was to reach a consensus, which the chiefs would convey to the committee on behalf of their people.[36]

Council circles were fundamental to Očéti Ŝakówiŋ governance (figs. 14.7, 14.8). The circle, signifying the essential interrelatedness of all things, was the primary geometric form that organized Očéti Ŝakówiŋ space.[37] According to Luther Standing Bear (Mathȟó Nážiŋ, Sičháŋǧu and Oglála Lakȟóta), who lived on the Great Sioux Reservation around that time, a council began by passing the ceremonial pipe to reinforce communal and spiritual connections. The most important leaders would take honorary places within the council tipi, if there was one, but they did not dominate the proceedings. As they conferred, all were on the same plane and most were visible to one another. Speakers rose and stepped into the circle, surrounded by those they were addressing. Though disagreements could become heated, the expectation was for respectful behavior, attentive listening, and consensus: a decision "done by the people," a binding agreement with which all would comply.[38]

Even though responses to changing colonial conditions varied and Standing Rock's agent was fomenting factionalism, the council reached a consensus: They

FIGURE 14.7. *Očéti Šakówiŋ council tipi and circle, probably at the Standing Rock Agency, 1880s. Photo by David F. Barry. Western History Collection, Denver Public Library, call no. B-734.*

FIGURE 14.8. *Očéti Šakówiŋ council circle, Standing Rock Agency, 1880s. Photo by David F. Barry. Western History Collection, Denver Public Library, call no. B-188.*

would not accept the Dawes Act's terms. Four chiefs would speak to the commission on behalf of the Očéti Šakówiŋ at Standing Rock: John Grass, Gall (Phizí, Húŋkpapȟa Lakȟóta), Big Head (Nasúnatȟáŋka / Yanktonai Dakȟóta), and Mad Bear (Matȟó Gnaskíŋyaŋ, Yanktonais Dakȟóta). Sitting Bull played an important

FIGURE 14.9. *Council meeting between the Očéti Ŝakówiŋ Oyate and a congressional commission in front of a gabled building that is probably the council house, Standing Rock Agency, 1888. Photo by David F. Barry. Western History Collection, Denver Public Library, call no. B-747.*

role as well. All had been at the Battle of Greasy Grass, a feat of military strategy and diplomacy that had united thousands of people against a common threat. This is what they aimed to do now at Standing Rock.

On the first day of the council with the commission, some seven hundred men crowded into the agency's council hall. On the second day, Chief Running Antelope (Thatȟóka Íŋyaŋke, Húŋkpapȟa Lakȟóta) informed the commission that the Očéti Ŝakówiŋ preferred to meet in the open air. They wanted space for more people to attend the meetings, including women—who had a voice in Očéti Ŝakówiŋ affairs—and children.[39] Not surprisingly, Pratt wanted to stay within the confines of a more familiar and controllable rectilinear space. But the next day they met under an open sky in a space that afforded the Očéti Ŝakówiŋ greater spatial agency. David F. Barry, a white photographer who had a studio at nearby Fort Yates, documented the meeting. One photograph shows a crowd that appears to be informally arrayed before a large building, probably the council hall (fig. 14.9). Playing up axial symmetry, the photograph centers on the prominent gable, which creates a frame for a map of the reservation tacked on the building's facade, and below it, a platform elevating the commission and a table that forms a barrier between these visitors and everyone else. From there, the commission holds a dominant position in relation to an audience. This monodirectional, hierarchical arrangement was not unlike the familiar setups for politicians' stump speeches and evangelists' camp-meeting preaching—both of which, like the commissions' orations, were all about persuasion and conversion.

A different perspective reveals that what appears to be a crowd is actually a council circle that merges with the platform and includes—and hems in—the commissioners (fig. 14.10). The circle opens up sight lines that enable Očéti Ŝakówiŋ people to see one another and the commissioners, and vice versa. But it also spatializes two incompatible forms of decision-making and governance. This was not a council in the Očéti Ŝakówiŋ sense. The commissioners announced that there would be no negotiation of the act's terms, and no working toward a consensus, regardless of the fact that the Očéti Ŝakówiŋ Oyate had no input.[40] Elevated

FIGURE 14.10. *Oblique view of the council, with council circle, Standing Rock Agency, 1888. Photo by David F. Barry. Western History Collection, Denver Public Library, call no. B-193.*

on their platform, the commissioners went through the Dawes Act in exhaustive detail. When the chiefs rose to speak to the commission, the position and height of the platform would have compelled them to turn their backs on the circle, to stand in an inferior position, and to tilt their heads back to look up as they spoke of the value of their land and the inequities of the Dawes Act vis-à-vis what they were still owed from earlier treaties. Increasingly frustrated, Pratt raised his voice and shook his fists in the face of perceived intransigence.[41] This display violated Očéti Ŝakówiŋ council decorum. According to Standing Bear, at councils people "were quiet and dignified in manner," and "loud talking and exaggerated or boisterous actions were considered very unseemly."[42] Reporters picked up on this. The *New-York Tribune* was not alone in commending the chiefs for their dignity and eloquence while ridiculing the commissioners for their insulting and threatening behavior.[43]

Pratt may have believed that he was in control, but greater power was generated through councils the Očéti Ŝakówiŋ held separately at night. An undated photograph suggests how one of these might have looked (see fig. 14.8). Bodies form a thick, round wall, producing an ephemeral counterhegemonic space in the midst of agency headquarters. Newspapers reported that some council circles, held amid Očéti Ŝakówiŋ camps one to two miles out, were far larger than this. Celebrated orators spoke to assemblies of thousands in voices that produced a soundscape that reached far beyond the circle.[44] Not everyone was in agreement, but the council circle, where all could see one another, facilitated mutual accountability and solidarity. During a council that lasted all night, "every Indian was asked his opinion [and] the spokesmen were well prepared to give the Commissioners a definite answer."[45]

The answer was a unanimous no; there was thus no reason to vote. When the chiefs reported this to Pratt the next morning, he refused to accept it for two reasons. One was that it was not the answer he wanted. The other was that to him the chiefs' word was not valid. He believed that they exerted undue influence over their people, and he partly blamed the council circle for this. Because the chiefs were so visible there, Pratt thought that seeing them was enough to discourage people from voting their own mind, or voting at all. The only way forward was to break the chiefs' power. So the haranguing from the platform continued. Finally, Pratt decided to break up the circle and set up separate voting stations near the two corrals where everyone received their beef rations. What Pratt would not or could not understand was the way the Očéti Ŝakówiŋ council process worked across scales to produce a binding agreement that reached from the reservation's Očéti Ŝakówiŋ Oyate and grand council to the individual, and vice versa. Although council circles were ephemeral, even after they disbanded their binding power persisted. In the end, only 22 out of 1,133 eligible men cast a vote.[46]

Epilogue

For some of the Lakȟóta and Dakȟóta people who opened this essay, the train ride to Bismarck was their first but not their last. The railroad, an agent of settler colonialism, became an instrument of Indigenous resistance. Railroad travel and mail delivery strengthened and extended alliances and contributed to organized resistance to the General Allotment Act at a national scale.[47] Eventually, however, federal officials—issuing threats, unfulfilled promises, and diminished rations—obtained the votes needed from Standing Rock's men.

The systematic assignment of allotments did not begin there until 1906. Ella Cara Deloria (Aŋpétu Wašté Wiŋ / Beautiful Day Woman, Yangton Dakȟóta), an anthropologist who spent her early years at Standing Rock, observed that in 1900 the reservation remained "a predominantly Dakota picture, in spite of a scattering of log houses, schools, and churches."[48] By the time surveyors superimposed their cadastral grid over the reservation, the Očéti Ŝakówiŋ had made homes and spaces informed by their own values and practices for decades and generations. As implementation proceeded, people at Standing Rock continued to contest the terms of the Dawes Act, and they succeeded in altering it by securing land for married women.[49] In the long run, however, the result was a fragmented landscape.

Even so, as Nick Estes has shown, unified resistance persisted. In 2016, plans for the Dakota Access Pipeline, which would carry oil beneath the Missouri River near Standing Rock, threatened sacred places and the health of the land and water. To block the pipeline, water protectors and their allies formed decolonial spaces of resistance and resurgence.[50] Although the pipeline eventually went forward, they had galvanized a global movement for Indigenous environmental justice reaching far beyond Standing Rock.

Acknowledgments

Many thanks to Charles L. Davis II (insightful editor for this essay), John Archer, Greg Donofrio, Gail Dubrow, Jessica García Fritz (Cheyenne River Sioux Tribe / Itazipco), Tom Erickson, Jason Tippeconnic Fox (Comanche and Cherokee), Anne Marshall, David Monteyne, and Abigail Van Slyck for comments, conversation, and work that has expanded my thinking. Any errors of fact or interpretation are my own.

Notes

1. James McLaughlin described the events in Mandan and Bismarck in a letter dated July 12, 1917, reproduced in Clement Augustus Lounsberry, *Early History of North Dakota: Essential Outlines of American History* (Liberty Press, 1919), 418–420. The number of Očéti Ŝakówiŋ travelers ranged from twenty in newspaper accounts to three hundred in McLaughlin's letter. See, for example, "Sitting Bull at Bismarck," *Morris Tribune*, September 8, 1883; *Press and Daily Dakotaian*, September 8, 1883.

2. "Guests of Uncle Rufus," *New York Times*, August 10, 1883, 8.

3. Katherine Solomonson, "The American Renaissance in the West: Capital, Class and Culture Along the Northern Pacific Railroad," *Architectural History* 64 (2021): 137–162.

4. Reginald Horsman, *Race and Manifest Destiny: The Origins of American Racial Anglo-Saxonism* (Harvard University Press, 1981), 1–6, 85, 92, 301.

5. Patrick Wolfe, "Settler Colonialism and the Elimination of the Native," *Journal of Genocide Research* 8, no. 4 (2006): 387–409; Lorenzo Veracini, *Settler Colonialism: A Theoretical Overview* (Palgrave Macmillan, 2010); Lorenzo Veracini, "'Settler Colonialism': Career of a Concept," *Journal of Imperial and Commonwealth History* 41, no. 2 (2013): 313–333.

6. For example, Charles L. Davis II, "Henry Van Brunt and White Settler Colonialism in the Midwest," *Race and Modern Architecture: A Critical History from the Enlightenment to the Present*, ed. Irene Cheng, Charles L. Davis II, and Mabel O. Wilson (University of Pittsburgh Press, 2020), 99–115; Solomonson, "American Renaissance in the West"; Manuel Shvartzberg Carrió, "Theorizing Decolonial Modernity: Towards an Architectural History of Jurisdictional Technics," *Dialectic* 9 (Spring 2021): 36–44; Manuel Shvartzberg Carrió, chap. 16 in this volume.

7. For example, Corey Snelgrove, Rita Dhamoon, and Jeff Corntassel, "Unsettling Settler Colonialism: The Discourse and Politics of Settlers, and Solidarity with Indigenous Nations," *Decolonization: Indigeneity, Education & Society* 3, no. 2 (2014): 26–27; Mishuana R. Goeman, "Disrupting a Settler-Colonial Grammar of Place: The Visual Memoir of Hulleah Tsinhnahjinnie," in *Theorizing Native Studies*, ed. Audra Simpson and Andrea Smiths (Duke University Press, 2014), esp. 238; Jean M. O'Brien, "Tracing Settler Colonialism's Eliminatory Logic," *American Quarterly* 69, no. 2 (2017): 249–255; George Vizenor, *Survivance: Narratives of Native Presence* (University of Nebraska Press, 2008).

8. Tracey Banivanua Mar and Penelope Edmonds, "Introduction: Making Space in Settler Colonies," in *Making Settler Colonial Space: Perspectives on Race, Place and Identity*, ed. Tracey Banivanua Mar and Penelope Edmonds (Palgrave Macmillan, 2010), 1–18. An excellent example of this is Elizabeth Kryder-Reid, *California Mission Landscapes: Race, Memory, and the Politics of Heritage* (University of Minnesota Press, 2016).

9. Names, affiliations, and spellings can vary over time and from source to source. For this essay I have been guided particularly by the extensive research and writings of a Húŋkpapȟa Lakȟóta historian, who knew many of the people she mentions. See Josephine Waggoner, *Witness: A Húŋkpapȟa Historian's Strong-Heart Song of the Lakotas*, ed. Emily Levine (University of Nebraska Press, 2013).

10. Nick Estes, *Our History Is the Future: Standing Rock Versus the Dakota Access Pipeline, and the Long Tradition of Indigenous Resistance* (Verso, 2019).

11. Natchee Blu Barnd, *Native Space: Geographic Strategies to Unsettle Settler Colonialism* (Oregon State University Press, 2017), 1.

12. The examples in this paragraph are drawn from articles published in the *Mandan Daily Pioneer* in 1883. Each deserves further analysis.

13. Solomonson, "American Renaissance in the West," 137–162.

14. McLaughlin's letter, in Lounsberry, *Early History of North Dakota*, 418–419.

15. William Hardman, *A Trip to America* (London: T. Vickers Wood, 1884), 179–181.

16. "CPI Inflation Calculator," Official Data Foundation, accessed May 19, 2025, https://www.officialdata.org/us/inflation/1883.

17. Christopher J. Pexa, *Translated Nation: Rewriting the Dakhóta Oyáte* (University of Minnesota Press, 2019), 58.

18. On acquisitiveness, see Karen V. Hansen, *Encounter on the Great Plains: Scandinavian Settlers and the Dispossession of Dakota Indians, 1890–1930* (Oxford University Press, 2013), 11. On giving money away, see Stanley Vestal, *Sitting Bull: Champion of the Sioux* (Houghton Mifflin, 1932), 250–251; Robert M. Utley, *Sitting Bull: The Life and Times of an American Patriot* (Macmillan, 2008), 362–363, 368, 370.

19. McLaughlin's letter, in Lounsberry, *Early History of North Dakota*, 418–419.

20. "Bismarck's Day," *Bismarck Tribune*, September 7, 1883; *Harper's Weekly*, September 22, 1883, 603.

21. "The Capitol of Dakota," *Harper's Weekly*, September 22, 1883, 603.

22. F. Jay Haynes, "Laying Cornerstone of Territorial Capitol, Bismarck, Dakota Territory," photograph showing back of platform, September 8, 1883, State Historical Society of North Dakota, no. C0865.

23. "Bismarck's Day."

24. McLaughlin's letter, in Lounsberry, *Early History of North Dakota*, 419.

25. *Harper's Weekly*, September 22, 1883, 603.

26. Lewis H. Morgan, *Houses and House-Life of the American Aborigines* (Washington, DC: Government Printing Office, 1881), esp. vii, 258; C. Joseph Genetin-Pilawa, "'Friends' and Fistfights: Federal Indian Policy Debates and Late Nineteenth-Century State Development," *Journal of the Gilded Age and Progressive Era* 14, no. 4 (2015): 512–520; Eric Oland, "From Savage Space to Governable Space: The Extension of United States Judicial Sovereignty over Indian Country in the Nineteenth Century," *Cultural Geographies* 9, no. 2 (2002): 133, 136, 138–141.

27. D. S. Otis, *The Dawes Act and the Allotment of Indian Lands* (University of Oklahoma Press, 1973); Alan L. Neville and Alyssa Kay Anderson, "The Diminishment of the Great Sioux Reservation: Treaties,

Tricks, and Time," *Great Plains Quarterly* 33, no. 4 (2013): 237–251; Daniel Heath Justice and Jean M. O'Brien, *Allotment Stories: Indigenous Land Relations Under Settler Siege* (University of Minnesota Press, 2022).

28. William H. Truettner, "Plains Geometry: Surveying the Path from Savagery to Civilization," *Winterthur Portfolio* 38, no. 4 (2003): 199–220.

29. "Testimony Taken by a Select Committee of the Senate Concerning the Condition of the Indian Tribes in the Territories of Montana and Dakota Under Resolution of the Senate of March 2, 1883," report no. 48–283, in *Reports of the Committees of the Senate of the United States for the First Session of the Forty-Eighth Congress, 1883–1884* (Washington, DC: Government Printing Office, 1884).

30. "Testimony Taken by a Select Committee," 71–72.

31. "Testimony Taken by a Select Committee," 67.

32. "Testimony Taken by a Select Committee."

33. "Testimony Taken by a Select Committee," 102.

34. In 1892, Pratt delivered his now most infamous pronouncement: "Kill the Indian in him, and save the man." R. H. Pratt, "The Advantages of Mingling Indians with Whites," in *Proceedings of the National Conference of Charities and Correction* (Boston: George H. Ellis, 1892), 46.

35. R. H. Pratt, "Report of the Commissioners, November 24, 1888," in *The Executive Documents of the Senate of the United States for the Second Session of the Fiftieth Congress and the Special Session of the Senate Convened March 4, 1889* (Washington, DC: Government Printing Office, 1889), esp. 56ff. An important counternarrative to Pratt's appears in T. A. Bland, *A History of the Sioux Agreement: Some Facts Which Should Not Be Forgotten* (Washington, DC: T. A. Bland, 1888).

36. Pratt, "Report of the Commissioners," 3.

37. On the significance of the circle and of council circles, see James R. Walker, *Lakota Belief and Ritual* (University of Nebraska Press, 1991), 22–23, 59, 204; Ella Cara Deloria, *Speaking of Indians* (Friendship Press, 1944), 38–39; Jessica Dawn Palmer, *The Dakota Peoples: A History of the Dakota, Lakota and Nakota Through 1863* (McFarland, 2008), esp. 63–64. On the camp circle in relation to the *thiyóšpaye* (extended family) and cultural cohesion, see David C. Posthumus, "The Ritual Thiyóšpaye and the Social Organization of Contemporary Lakota Ceremonial Life," *Journal for the Anthropology of North America* 22, no. 1 (2019): 4–21.

38. Luther Standing Bear, *Land of the Spotted Eagle* (University of Nebraska Press, 1933), 23, 127–129; Catherine Price, "Lakotas and Euroamericans: Contrasted Concepts of 'Chieftainship' and Decision-Making Authority," *Ethnohistory* 41, no. 3 (1994): 449–452.

39. Pratt, "Report of the Commissioners," 56ff. There is much more to say about gender than is possible here.

40. Pratt, "Report of the Commissioners," 2–4.

41. Pratt, "Report of the Commissioners," 110.

42. Standing Bear, *Land of the Spotted Eagle*, 23.

43. "No Treaty for the Sioux," *New-York Tribune*, July 29, 1888, 1.

44. "The Sioux Object," *Bismarck Tribune*, July 27, 1888, 1; "The Sioux Remain Resolute," *Wahpeton Times*, August 2, 1888, 5; "The Great Spirit," *Bismarck Tribune*, August 3, 1888, 1; "Indians Refuse to Sign the Sioux Treaty," *Bottineau Pioneer*, August 9, 1888, 2. It is possible that most of Standing Rock's 4,545 Očéti Šakówiŋ residents attended, some with visitors.

45. "No Treaty for the Sioux," 1.

46. Pratt, "Report of the Commissioners," 8. The report did not say whether the twenty-two votes were pro or con.

47. Justin Gage, *We Do Not Want the Gates Closed Between Us: Native Networks and the Spread of the Ghost Dance* (University of Oklahoma Press, 2020).

48. Deloria, *Speaking of Indians*, 85.

49. Stephen L. Egbert and Joshua J. Meisel, "'The Indians Complain, and with Good Cause': Allotting Standing Rock—U.S. Policy Meets a Tribe's Assertion of Rights," *Geographies* 4, no. 3 (2024): 411–440.

50. Estes, *Our History Is the Future*; Pexa, *Translated Nation*, introduction.

15 DESIGNED ASSIMILATION

THE ARCHITECTURE OF FEDERAL INDIAN BOARDING SCHOOLS

Anjelica S. Gallegos

BETWEEN 1819 AND 1969, THE United States operated or supported 417 federal Indian boarding schools as part of a twin policy of Indian territorial dispossession and Indian assimilation. Under the auspices of the federal Indian boarding school system, often through force or coercion, the United States removed Indian children from their communities and confined them in the boarding schools. During a nearly fifty-year period, known as the Allotment and Assimilation Era (1887–1934), the government, religious organizations, and other institutions instrumentalized the architecture of the federal Indian boarding schools as a tool to change and control the lives and practices of American Indian, Alaska Native, and Native Hawaiian children; their relatives; and Indian tribes, Alaska Native villages, and the Native Hawaiian community. At the same time, the government signed Indian treaties and agreements that led to the dispossession of one billion acres of land from Indian tribes.[1] The twin aims of forced assimilation and territorial expansion are legible in the history of the Fort Lewis Indian Boarding School, a former US Army post in Hesperus, Colorado, which the federal government repurposed as a boarding school campus. The architecture and spatial practices of the Fort Lewis Indian Boarding School were rooted in a militarized disciplinarianism, standing in opposition to the seasonal, reciprocal, and ephemeral spatial practices of the Southern Ute people who were confined there. By comparing these two systems, this study reveals how architecture was a central tool in the US government's assimilationist agenda and how Indigenous culture and spatial knowledge resisted and survived this imposition.

This analysis prioritizes and centers American Indian voices and authorship over conventional academic histories. It also relies on newly available government reports, an archive of records, and a decades-old surveying project, examined in parallel with traditional knowledge sources. In 2022 and 2024, the US government released investigative reports of the federal Indian boarding school system. In these reports, for the first time, the US government acknowledged the historic intentions of the system, which laid the groundwork for a formal apology issued by President Biden in November 2024 on behalf of the United States to Indian tribes. My research also draws on the work undertaken under the auspices of the Colorado Wickiup Project, whose members have comprehensively documented Indigenous wooden feature sites in Colorado since 2003. While Colorado is the homeland of the Southern Ute Indian Tribe, the Ute Indian Tribe of the Uintah and Ouray Reservation (Northern Ute), the Ute Mountain Ute Tribe, and other tribes, the contemporary Colorado-based Ute tribes are the focus of this essay because of both the availability of published resources and their proximity to the Fort Lewis Indian Boarding School. As sovereign nations with a constitutional, legal, and political relationship with the United States, publicly shared tribal community sources and the expressions of tribal representatives are given the same weight as federal sources. Intergenerational traditional knowledge, including oral histories, has long documented the abuses and violence of the boarding school system; these new federal records allow us to better understand enrollments, curricula, and their relationship to the militarized space of the school landscape.

The Federal Indian Boarding School System

The boarding schools evolved from the success and failure of the earlier federal Indian day school system.[2] Federal records envisioned the federal Indian day school system in architectural terms: "To the day school the Indian child comes fresh from the tepee and finds himself at once amid new and strange surroundings."[3] Federal Indian day schools resembled schools built in US cities and towns, providing an intentional contrast to the "tepee." They stood on Indian reservations and introduced assimilation practices close to Indian children's parents and communities and explicitly did not have the housing or boarding facility component. But federal officials found that the day school system was not a success. In its place, they developed a policy of removing children from their families, spaces, homelands, and familiar sites in an effort to manipulate the behavior of Indian children to conform to the norms of the boarding school system. The federal boarding school system practiced identity-altering methods, including the following: (1) discouraging or preventing Native language use, religious expression, and cultural practices; (2) removing tribal- and parent-given names and renaming Indian children with English-language and often religious names; (3) cutting the hair of Indian children; and (4) organizing Indian and Native Hawaiian children into units to perform military drills.[4]

The boarding schools were constructed using a variety of materials and methods. While some new buildings were constructed, sometimes using recycled or repurposed materials, others were moved onto school sites from other places. These included Russian Empire facilities, other federal Indian boarding schools, US military installations and facilities, and the grounds of religious institutions. Architecture displayed an array of programmatic lineage relating to foreign, US military, and religious operations.[5] The ad hoc practice of using buildings for purposes other than those for which they were intended was not conducive to educating and housing Indian children up to the age of twenty-one.[6] Rampant physical, sexual, and emotional abuse; disease; malnourishment; overcrowding; and lack of healthcare in Indian boarding schools are well documented.[7] Abuse included the directive from authorities for older students to surveil and physically abuse younger students, a practice that originated on a military base, as described below.

Since the introduction of President Thomas Jefferson's policy of assimilation, the Public Land Survey System used the formal military tactic of the grid to subdue, divide, and sell land.[8] With no regard for the meanings of land and landscapes, the grid removed all traces of Indigenous occupation and use so as to create a "blank landscape," "devoid of any content or logics that might resist any new intent applied to them," and thus available for government use.[9] The government used this ancient planning system, with roots in Roman military encampment design, to assimilate and create identity-less constituents, thereby producing order and enforcing obedience. In this way, the grid is a methodical and spatial process of cultural erasure. A symbol of order, it spatially supported obedience and was used on tribes eventually confined to reservations and on Indian children of the boarding schools.

Of the 417 federal Indian boarding schools, 105 were located in the Four Corners region of New Mexico, Arizona, Utah, and Colorado (fig. 15.1).[10] This extraordinary density of boarding schools meant that existing buildings were often reused and repurposed to serve as infrastructure. As the government built schools, it also constructed military posts. Over half of the schools in the Four

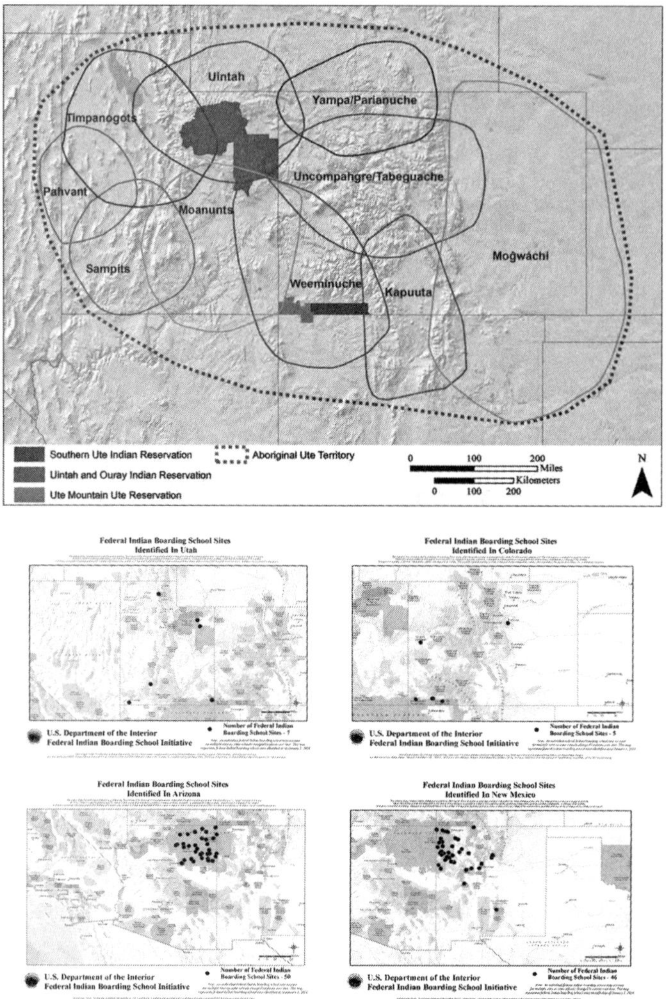

FIGURE 15.1. *Ute territory and the federal Indian boarding schools of the Four Corners.* Top: *Ute territory during the early nineteenth century as mapped by Alden Naranjo, Jr. Cultural Preservation Department, © 2025 Southern Ute Indian Tribe.* Bottom: *Locations of boarding schools in Utah, Colorado, Arizona, and New Mexico. Bryan Newland,* Federal Indian Boarding School Initiative Investigative Report: Volume 2 *(US Department of the Interior, 2024), appendix D, 6, 9, 34, 47.*

Corners were reused buildings, with the majority of those being prior day schools (table 15.1). Former military spaces were the next most often reused building type. The relationship between military posts, Indian removal, and cultural eradication can be traced to the creation of the Bureau of Indian Affairs. When it was founded in 1824, the bureau was housed in the War Department. It was transferred to the Department of the Interior at the department's establishment in 1849. By that point, the hostile relationship between the US government and tribes was reflected in the reuse of military spaces, the very spaces that supported the intention to gain territory and control or eradicate tribes.[11]

Federal Indian Boarding Schools of the Four Corners						
State	Number of schools	Building type: previous day school	Building type: new construction	Building type: reused nonmilitary space	Building type: previous military space	Schools open today
New Mexico	45	20	20	4	1	24
Arizona	48	26	16	4	2	28
Utah	7	1	5	1	0	1
Colorado	5	0	2	1	2	0
Total	105	47	43	10	5	53

Source: Bryan Newland, Federal Indian Boarding School Initiative Report: Volume 1, *US Department of the Interior, 2022, apps. A, B, C.*

Note: "Building type" refers to the type of building in place when the school opened. Unless the school's building type was otherwise specified, it is assumed to be new construction. Military spaces are properties previously held by the US Department of War.

In 1879, Captain Richard Henry Pratt led the conversion of the US Army's Carlisle Barracks in Pennsylvania into the notorious Carlisle Indian Industrial School. The former military base, superintended by the military from 1757 to today, became the prototype of the boarding school system from 1879 onward, regardless of whether a boarding school's infrastructure was newly built or repurposed from existing environments.[12] As the father of the boarding school programming, Pratt first implemented his assimilative tactics of military standards and reform over a group of Apache, Cheyenne, Kiowa, Comanche, Arapahoe, and Caddo prisoners of war at Fort Marion in St. Augustine, Florida, in 1875.[13] Standards of reform included "military haircuts and uniforms, drills, English language education, and a guard system where Native men monitored each other" (fig. 15.2).[14] While some of the prisoners of war were held captive for alleged crimes, without trials, a large number were confined on the principle that "prevention is better than cure."[15]

The principle of "prevention," paired with Pratt's "kill the Indian, save the man" approach, shaped the experience of Indian children confined at boarding schools. Indian children, especially those belonging to families of tribal leadership, were targeted as political actors by the federal government in an attempt to control Indian tribes. In order to coerce children's attendance at boarding schools, government officials offered gifts and payment to families or, alternatively, withheld rations and annuities, denied resources like horses and shelter, removed tribal leaders from their positions, sent tribal leaders to prison, and took children from their homes at gunpoint.[16] Children were treated as political prisoners and housed in military spaces that were either modeled after or had been historically utilized for violent control and surveillance of prisoners of war.

FIGURE 15.2. *Indian prisoners and students at Fort Marion and Carlisle.* Left: *Prisoner-students at Fort Marion, St. Augustine, Florida, ca. late 1800s. "Indian Prisoner Students at Fort Marion,"* Regional Review *5, no. 6 (1940).* Right: *Male students in front of their quarters at Carlisle Indian Industrial School, Carlisle, Pennsylvania, 1880. Photo by John N. Choate. Archives and Special Collections, Waidner-Spahr Library, Dickinson College.*

The Architecture of the Southern Ute People

For Ute children, each season indicated the occupation of different natural and built environments, alongside different spatial and programmatic practices. Staying stationary for more than one season and spending a significant amount of time indoors was unfamiliar. Informational learning stemmed from the occupation of and participation in the natural environment. The Ute primarily traveled in the warmer seasons of spring and summer, while late in the fall, family units would begin to move out of the mountains into sheltered areas for the cold winter. During the winter, more band members would camp together, allowing for more efficent allocation of fuel resources and a better line of defense. Settlements were often built in piñon pine and juniper forests, located at elevations ranging from approximately 5,000 to 6,500 feet. During the time spent indoors, people repaired tools and weapons and made new garments. Winter was a time for rejuvenation and strengthening of tribal customs. Family members shared experiences of travel and social and religious events. Tribal leaders announced plans for major community events, such as the Bear Dance, which marks the beginning of a new cycle or year, when Mother Earth starts to blossom and animals emerge from hibernation after a long winter. In early spring, Ute bands would move closer to suitable riparian areas. Men would hunt large game such as bison, elk, deer, and antelope, while Ute women would gather plants and hunt smaller game. The summer meant travel; bands would disperse and move to higher elevations to follow game herds and access maturing floral resources.

Ute architecture and spaces included wickiups, domed shelters, tipis, menstrual huts, domed sweat lodges, lean-tos, windbreaks, ramadas, hide-processing poles, meat-drying racks, cooking tripods, animal-control features, naturally sheltered sites, and culturally modified trees. Among the Ute's primary dwellings were the *ivikani*, or stick lodges, also known as "wickiups," after the Proto-

FIGURE 15.3. *Southern Ute people and their structures.* Left: *Southern Ute Indian Tribe Women and Children, "Southern Ute Indian Tribe History," Cultural Preservation Department, © 2025 Southern Ute Indian Tribe, https://www.southernute-nsn.gov/history.* Right: *A traditional Ute* noa-ivikan *(*ivikani*), or stick lodge. Photo by Hillers, Powell Expedition, 1873. National Anthropological Archives, Smithsonian Institution, cat. no. 1547.*

Algonquian word for "house" (fig. 15.3).[17] As the formal built environment for learning, the Ute lodge complemented the efficient, travel-bound lifestyle of the Ute, including their hunting practices. The Ute people often alternated their hunting and food-gathering sites, allowing for the animal population to stay healthy and the earth's soil to replenish. Overharvesting and wastefulness were contrary to Ute practices and their regard for the natural environment and other beings. Thus, every part of a hunted animal was used as food, clothing, tools, or building materials, as seen in the building skin of some lodges.

As a mechanism of grounded normativity, ephemerality was intentional during the construction and deconstruction of structures. Grounded normativity is defined as "the modalities of Indigenous land-connected practices and longstanding experiential knowledge that inform and structure ethical engagements with the world and our relationship with human and nonhuman others over time."[18] Consistent with the sustainable principles of material use, respect for the natural environment, and belief that the earth provides, a building was not designed to be permanent or to stand apart from the site. This has proved to be challenging in terms of the preservation of these structures, the identification of sites where structures occur, and the recognition of these lodges as architecture—an architecture that holistically includes the landscape. In the tribes' own words, "the Utes believed that they didn't own the land, but that the land owned them."[19]

Site selection was often on secure, higher ground and close to natural resources such as fresh water. Signifiers of sites and signage for routes were subtle and virtually indistinguishable for those who did not already know the route or particular campsite. Overturned metates served as site signifiers, as they likely originated from the site and were too heavy to be transported elsewhere. A metate is made of stone, typically resembling a shallow bowl, and used with a mano, a rounded stone, to grind grain or corn by hand.[20] Synonymity between the signifiers of the land and the very land they marked was intentional.

The lodges' building material was partially determined by what surrounding natural resources were available.[21] Regina Lopez Whiteskunk of the Ute Mountain Ute Tribe notes that "one wickiup will not look like the next because there's different trees."[22] Living trees, especially pine trees, were not cut down to construct the Ute lodge but were incorporated into the structure as support when available. Resources for the construction of lodges were already provided and simply needed to be erected. There was minimal preparation or transformation of building materials. The detailed exterior identity of the often asymmetric wickiups was uniquely nonuniform, like a site's particular configuration of natural elements: stones, grasses, shrubs, and trees. The branched membrane featured foliage and branches that were naturally varied, resulting in a heterogeneous screen that softly separated the interior and exterior environments.

The majority of poles were constructed from juniper, with a select few made from piñon at lower elevations and aspen at higher elevations. Freestanding wickiups sometimes had pole ends pushed slightly into the ground, while stones lined the outside periphery of the structure to support the poles, acting as weights for the building skin coverings. In section, the dwelling materials were also a collage of materials gathered at the site. Owing to materials, the distinction between indoor and outdoor space was a gradient rather than sharply defined. The perfectly fibrous vertical striations of the red-toned *wa'ap(ü)*, or juniper, and the horizontal cadence of the deep-brown knots and white-powdered skin of the *süav(ü)*, or aspen, created a collage of natural patterns seen from the interior and exterior of the lodge alongside the trees on-site.[23]

Wickiups were conical—distinctly nonrectilinear shapes with space experienced at an angled perspective. Although there is a wickiup construction method, the construction's flexibility allowed the architect to account for seasons, household size, and habitation period. Several wickiup communities have been found that comprise groupings of up to six wickiups.[24] The interior structure of the wickiup usually consisted of three to twenty-two poles formed in a conical shape.[25] Wickiups varied in length from around three feet up to twenty feet, while the height could be as much as fifteen feet tall.[26] Door placement, smoke holes, floors, and framework were details that varied. Acute-angled walls culminating at the apex created the iconic shape of the wickiup. The concave space was experienced at an acute angle, where the top of the structure was smaller than the base, resulting in a space that opened up toward the earth.

Ute architectural design stemmed from the central value of reciprocity with nature and stands in contrast to the standard European and colonialist practices of site alteration and attempts at environmental control. Reciprocity is distinct from the English term "camouflage," developed to describe the military practice of concealing troops and equipment during the First World War. Camouflage is "the disguising, especially of military equipment or installations with paint, nets, or foliage," as well as an "artifice designed to deceive or hide."[27] "Camouflage" stems from a French word for "disguise" used in the nineteenth century, meaning to "conceal the personal identity of, by changes of guise or usual appearance, with intent to deceive."[28] The concept of using disguise to blend in with surroundings has a long history, with roots in natural animal behavior, hunting, and human military tactics.[29] The etymology of "camouflage" and "disguise" suggests that the human intent to blend with nature is tied to both defensive and offensive concealment strategies, reflecting a synonymity with nature, from clothing to structures. The way Ute lodges are described in English is limited; the Ute language restores foundational information to understand the Ute perspective and worldview. The design of Ute lodges was refined over generations and intentionally stemmed from reverence for nature, operating within natural limits, as opposed to concealing oneself within nature for the purposes of armed conflict.

The Architecture of Fort Lewis Indian Boarding School

Fort Lewis opened in 1878 as a base from which federal troops attempted to control the Southern Ute Indians. After the alleged "final removal" of the remaining Utes from their ancestral lands of Colorado to Utah in 1881, the US Army decommissioned the military post and transferred it to the Department of the Interior to become part of the federal Indian boarding school system.[30] Fort Lewis Indian Boarding School opened in 1892 and operated until 1909. In 1911 it was replaced by Fort Lewis High School, which would evolve into today's Fort Lewis College. It is the only military post that developed into an Indian boarding school to remain an educational institution in Colorado. Several iterations of the fort and school occurred, and the school's history is among the most well documented.

The school planned to enroll children of the Southern Utes, the geographically closest tribe.[31] The boarding school was equipped with items from a day school on the Southern Ute Indian Reservation that had closed the previous year. With twenty-two extant buildings, the school could accommodate three hundred resident children.[32] At the opening, approximately one-quarter of the students were Southern Ute, more than half were Mescalero Apache, and the remainder were White River Ute and Navajo.[33] Although the inaugural student body represented tribes originating from the Four Corners region, the community eventually included children from twenty different tribes.[34] Federal records confirm that communities of Indian children were artificially divided into groups so as to encourage them to speak English as a common language; to discourage relationships with other tribal members, so as to reduce the chance they would eventually have "full-blood" quantum offspring; and to discourage the continuation of specific tribal practices and quash the exchange of tribal knowledge.[35] May Lee

Mountain of the Northern Ute Tribe recalls, "Our people were forced to never use their language because it was not supposed to be used at all, it was forbidden. We were supposed to learn the English language. My first language I could not use. I lost my identity. . . . The power of the language for any nationality—it's the most powerful thing one can carry."[36]

The contrast between the home architecture and culture of Southern Ute children and that of the boarding school is stark. Boarding schools, and other environments where children would live and learn separate from the family, were unknown to the Ute people. As part of a traveling society, Ute children lived with and were educated by their family unit and close relatives, often in small bands.[37] The Utes lived across the states of Colorado, New Mexico, Arizona, Utah, and Wyoming, and the Great Basin in Nevada, as well as beyond the Four Corners. According to tribal history, "There is no migration story, we were placed here in the mountains, we have always been here, we will always be here."[38] Through direct, lived experience in their territorial homelands, Ute children learned societal principles, social and religious lessons, traditional ecological knowledge, and ways of collecting food, constructing architecture, hunting game, and conducting intertribal relations.[39] The Utes' harmonious seasonal living within three distinct biomes reflected a sophisticated society with a vast base of cultural and ecological knowledge grounded in language and geography.[40]

The spatial organization of Fort Lewis Indian Boarding School was at odds with the Ute children's experience of the landscape and architecture. All school activities occurred in the military buildings that were constructed between 1880 and 1890 (fig. 15.4).[41] The original square of the fort was rotated off-center from the cardinal directions, pointing forty-five degrees east, with the Rio de la Plata flowing from the south of the site to the east at a diagonal. The uniform central square was complemented by adjacent, offset roads, juxtaposed with roads that were diagonally offset from the river. Washing facilities, barracks, and quarters were along the periphery of the parade grounds—one of the largest in the United States at 500 by 150 yards.[42] Food-processing buildings were to the north, the hospital to the south, and merchants and shops to the east, alongside the river.[43]

Six large buildings were reused for the boarding school, including the officers' quarters, the hospital, three sheds and barns, the old jail building, and a commissary building.[44] Military records indicate that several of the original six buildings were constructed by soldiers with conditioned lumber sourced from the sawmill on base. Barns were made of stone, brick, and wood from the sawmill, and the commissary building was constructed with granary stone.[45] The hospital served as the girls' dormitory, with a foundation of concrete and sandstone.[46] Records do not indicate which building served as the boys' dormitory at the school's opening, but the officers' quarters appear to be the likely place. The stockade, commissary, and barn had long, rectangular floor plans and side gable roofs. The rectangular military hospital foundation was approximately thirteen feet north–south by ten

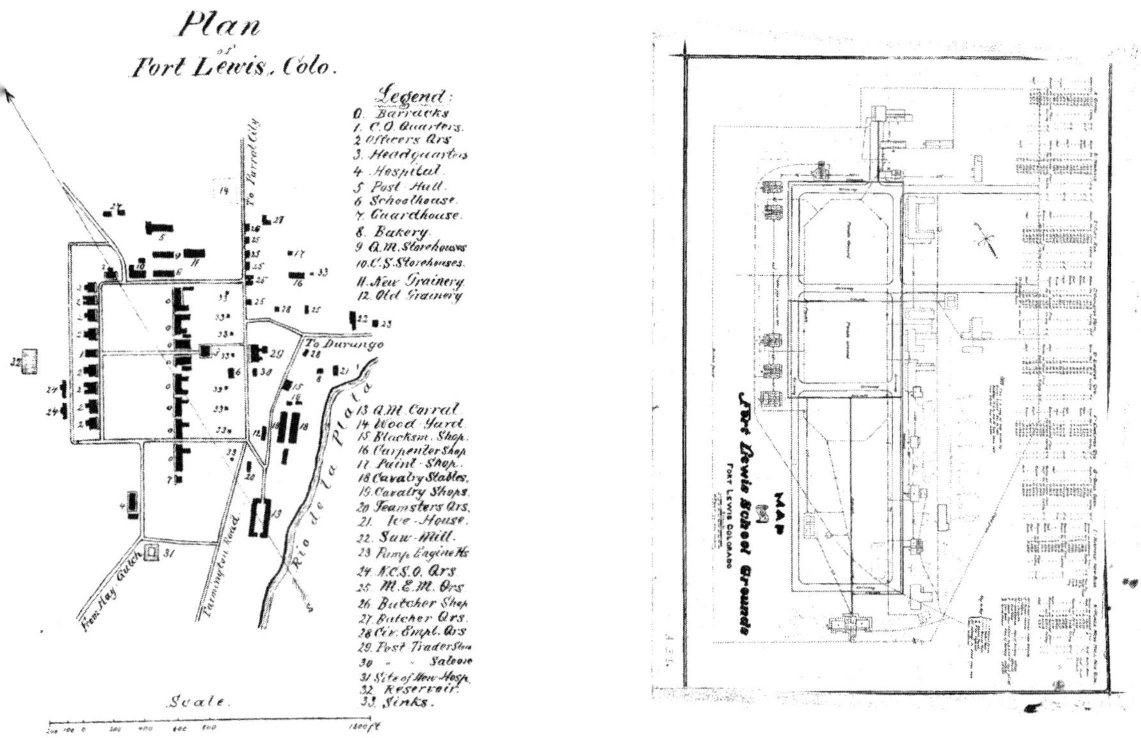

FIGURE 15.4. *Fort Lewis as a military fort and a boarding school.* Left: *Layout of Fort Lewis, before 1887. Jill Seyfarth,* A Historic Buildings Survey of Old Fort Lewis, Hesperus, Colorado *(Office of Community Services, Fort Lewis College, 2007), 11.* Right: *Layout of Fort Lewis Indian Boarding School. Seyfarth,* Historic Buildings Survey, *17.*

feet east–west.[47] New buildings constructed at Fort Lewis exclusive to the Indian boarding school were not designed for Indian student use but for use by administration and staff.

The building's rectilinear floor plans and right-angled, flat, planar walls resulted in a use of space wholly different from the wickiup: rectangular, exposed, and larger in scale, with hard boundaries between inside and outside. The fort's buildings had a massive volume compared to wickiups, amplifying the altered perception and experience of space. Unlike the undulating wall thickness of the lodge, the perpendicular gypsum-board walls of the hospital visually provided a homogenous and stark slate of uniformity without visual access to the exterior. Although Ute children experienced other orthogonal spaces, such as the traditional lodge, the use of the grid as a strict organization of architecture and spatial experience was likely never experienced to this extreme (fig. 15.5). Access to direct air and visual access to the exterior were strictly controlled by windows and doors. While the granary stone, wood, and brick are considered regional materials from immediate and surrounding sites, the materials went through processes of transformation to be considered usable for permanent building

FIGURE 15.5. Left: *Fort Lewis Indian Boarding School children and grounds, 1895. Courtesy of Center of Southwest Studies, Fort Lewis College.* Right: *A view of the Fort Lewis Indian Boarding School in an undated photo. Courtesy of History Colorado.*

purposes. The perpendicular and repetitive patterns of stone, brick, and wood slats communicated rigid order for Indian children. Masonry visually reinforced the regularity they experienced as students in the disciplined programming of the school.

The Fort Lewis regimen for kindergartners through sixth graders included a half day of academic study and a half day of vocational topics.[48] The boys were taught agricultural skills, including how to operate horse-drawn machinery and tend livestock, in addition to carpentry, shoemaking, and blacksmithing. The girls learned domestic skills, including laundry, kitchen work, baking, and sewing. The boarding school was responsible for raising and producing the majority of its own food, as well as tending commercial crops for the vocational education program.[49]

Domestic activities and agricultural skills were taught to equip children for the "outing" system, where they would graduate from the school and be placed with non-Native families to become contributing members of society.[50] Recalling this experience, Russell Box Sr. of the Southern Ute Indian Tribe states, "A lot of us went through mental, emotional, and spiritual experiences. They were trying to take the Indian out of the person and put them into the main society."[51] Domestication discouraged a seasonal traveling lifestyle and promoted the settlement of land and a sedentary lifeway. Monoculture and planting crops systematically in a bound grid for efficient production and expedited consumption perpetuated a one-way transactional relationship with ecology. It is likely that the boarding school residents cultivated grains, corn, hay, and vegetables. Growing plants or food at a surplus for the sake of production to sell was not a traditional practice. Traditionally, plants used for food and medicinal purposes—chokecherry, wild raspberry, buffaloberry, yampah, yellow pond lily, amaranth, wild onion, and *Orogenia linearifolia*—were harvested on-site, where they naturally grew, and were only harvested when needed.[52]

The Fort Lewis Indian Boarding School practiced total immersion away from the primary Ute learning space, the wickiup, through a variety of programmatic and construction methods. Built environments physically distanced from a Southern Ute child's community supported alienation from the family unit and culture. Separate built environments promoted isolation as an individual and set a nontraditional standard for separation based on gender and age. The practice of traditional ecological knowledge relating to seasonal change and lifeways ceased to exist as students were confined to a single built environment and forced to participate in nonseasonal, regimented, repetitive activities. The amount of time spent in the built environment increased, as if the winter season were occurring all year round. The children's interaction with the natural environment and with different biomes diminished. The traditional Southern Ute understanding of being part of an impartial collective and its supportive knowledge was forbidden, while new knowledge systems of individualism and production were enforced. Experiencing the life and death of Southern Ute architecture, connecting sustenance, shelter, and relationship to site, was erased. The Fort Lewis school's built structures provided a foreign spatial experience and identity, advocating identity-altering practices and perpetuating a curriculum rinsed of Southern Ute knowledge and architecture.

Conclusion: Resistance and Method

The Southern Ute people's fortitude and resistance eventually helped close Fort Lewis Indian Boarding School. Almost immediately after the school opened, tuberculosis and trachoma took the lives of two Ute children, while three succumbed to blindness and one became both deaf and blind.[53] This spurred the withdrawal of Ute students from the school by tribal leadership. Ute Chief Mariano was "adamantly opposed to both schooling and agriculture, and was often reported traveling into the mountains where he and his people were out of reach of the federal government."[54] There, Mariano and the Southern Utes likely returned to their original architecture.

The architecture and spatial practices of the Fort Lewis Indian Boarding School, rooted in militarized spatial control, were designed to dismantle Indigenous cultural practices and stood in opposition to the seasonal, reciprocal, and ephemeral spatial practices of the Southern Ute people. At a time when Indian tribes were going through a forced foundational shift in their way of life, Indigenous architectures were similarly exiled and becoming dormant. Instead of experiencing architecture as a perpetuation of identity and a mediator to the natural world, a foreign architecture was deployed to break the bond between Indian children, their Indian tribes, and the natural environment—a design of assimilation.

This chapter's architectural analysis of Ute lodges and Fort Lewis was made possible by the foresight of historians who valued these structures, as well as the release of records from the federal government and the state of Colorado. Without publicly available oral histories, the perspective of the Indian children and tribes who experienced the boarding schools during this era would be limited or nonexistent. The Southern Ute Indian Tribe has shared its knowledge with the public, making it possible to describe their belief system and way of life from their own perspective. Within the historical context of colonization, the exploitation of Indigenous knowledge, and the lack of authoritative consideration of tribal sources in public foundational education, tribes do not owe the public their knowledge. If tribes do choose to share selective information with the public, it will only heighten the American consciousness of its own history. Knowledge can return a rich specificity to land, ecology, and sustainable spatial and living practices. As sovereign nations that represent themselves, their own history, and their own spatial practices, sources from Indian tribes—including publicly shared community resources, oral histories, and expressions of official tribal representatives—carry the same weight as federal sources.

Regardless of Indigenous structures' Western categorization as "architecture" or their inclusion in the canon of "American" architecture, tribes have their own design processes and architecture that predate engagement with foreign entities, including Russia, Spain, the United States, and other countries. American Indian architecture has a standing as its own spatial and material epistemology. As a people inextricably tied to the land base, with intergenerational knowledge refined for over a millennium, the inclusion of American Indian architecture in the history of nineteenth-century American architecture will instill a new depth of ecological knowledge in the built environment and help restore the identity of the American landscape. The support and expansion of national, state, and tribal archives, libraries, and information collections, as well as the documentation and digitization of these records, are vital for the reflection, limited understanding, and continuation of Indigenous structures more broadly. The canon of nineteenth-century American architecture must be revised to include Indigenous design traditions as a distinct spatial and material epistemology.

Architecture is not a neutral field or mechanism. It contributed toward Indian territorial dispossession, starting in the sixteenth century, and attempted Indian assimilation in the nineteenth century, including through militarized confinement of Indian children as political prisoners. Experiencing the deployed design of the federal Indian boarding schools subsequently disrupted the Indian child's experience of the world and the generational relationship with Western education. Within grounded normativity and having a limited understanding of the original language of Indigenous structures, historians and policymakers have a responsibility to preserve the remaining structures and documents of the federal Indian boarding school era. While the knowledge of these structures may not be passed on to the next generation the same way as prior generations, it can contribute toward a restorative healing, renaissance, and continuation of Native spatial identities that are accurate reflections of the people who have no migration story and of an America beginning to examine and know itself.

Notes

This chapter is based in part on Anjelica S. Gallegos, "Designed Assimilation: Southern Utes at the Fort Lewis Boarding School," *Journal of the Society of Architectural Historians* 84, no. 3 (2025): 294–321, published by the University of California Press.

1. US Senate Committee on Labor and Public Welfare, *Indian Education: A National Tragedy—A National Challenge*, S. Rep. No. 91-501 (1969), 143.
2. Bryan Newland, *Federal Indian Boarding School Initiative Investigative Report*, US Department of Interior, 2022, 14.
3. *Annual Report of the Commissioner of Indian Affairs*, US Department of the Interior, 1904, 392.
4. Newland, *Investigative Report*, 7.
5. Newland, *Investigative Report*, 19.
6. Newland, *Investigative Report*, 36.
7. US Senate Committee, *Indian Education*, 10–13; Lewis Meriam, *The Problem of Indian Administration*, US Department of the Interior, 1928, 189–195; Ursula Running Bear, Janette Beals, Carol E. Kaufman, Spero M. Manson, and AI-SUPERPFP Team, "Boarding School Attendance and Physical Health Status of Northern Plains Tribes," *Applied Research in Quality of Life* 13, no. 3 (2018): 633.
8. Newland, *Investigative Report*, 21.
9. Nicole Sylvia, "The Grid," *Site Magazine*, December 2019, https://www.thesitemagazine.com/read/the-grid.
10. Newland, *Investigative Report*, apps. A, B.
11. "Agencies—Indian Affairs Bureau," *Federal Register*, www.federalregister.gov/agencies/indian-affairs-bureau.
12. "Carlisle Barracks History: U.S. Army Carlisle Barracks," US Army, 2023, https://home.army.mil/carlisle/about/history.
13. F. Hilton Crowe, "Indian Prisoner-Students at Fort Marion," *Regional Review* 5, no. 6 (1940), https://www.nps.gov/parkhistory/online_books/regional_review/vol5-6c.htm.
14. "Richard Henry Pratt Papers," Beinecke Rare Book and Manuscript Library, accessed July 20, 2025, https://beinecke.library.yale.edu/collections/highlights/richard-henry-pratt-papers.
15. Crowe, "Indian Prisoner-Students."
16. Kristin Jones, "How Ute Tribes in Colorado Resisted U.S. Boarding Schools," *Collective Colorado*, February 12, 2024, https://collective.coloradotrust.org/stories/how-ute-tribes-in-colorado-resisted-u-s-boarding-schools.
17. Sean O'Meara, Maren P. Hopkins, Michael C. Spears, and T. J. Ferguson, *Ute Ethnographic and Ethnobotanical Research in the Bonita Peak Mining District*, Southern Ute Indian Tribe, 2021, 24.
18. J. Jeffery Clark and Elise Boxer, introduction to *From the Skin: Defending Indigenous Nations Using Theory and Praxis*, ed. J. Jeffery Clark and Elise Boxer (University of Arizona Press, 2023), 5.
19. Southern Ute Indian Tribe, "History," accessed November 3, 2025, https://www.southernute-nsn.gov/history.
20. *Merriam-Webster Dictionary*, "metate," accessed November 3, 2025, https://www.merriam-webster.com/dictionary/metate.
21. "Colorado Experience: The Wickiup Investigation," posted February 1, 2019, by Rocky Mountain PBS, YouTube, https://www.youtube.com/watch?v=hrOojfEo_MA&ab_channel=RockyMountainPBS.
22. "Colorado Experience: Wickiup Investigation."
23. *Ute Mountain Ute Dictionary*, "juniper" and "aspen," accessed November 3, 2025, https://dictionary.utelanguage.org/; O'Meara et al., *Ute Ethnographic and Ethnobotanical Research*, 61.
24. Curtis Martin, Richard Ott, and Nicole Darnell, *The Colorado Wickiup Project: Volume I; Context, Data Assessment and Strategic Planning*, Colorado Historical Society and US Bureau of Land Management, 2004, 12.
25. Martin, Ott, and Darnell, *Wickiup Project*, 12.

26. Martin, Ott, and Darnell, *Wickiup Project*, 14.

27. *Merriam-Webster Dictionary*, "camouflage," accessed November 3, 2025, https://www.merriam-webster.com/dictionary/camouflage.

28. *Etymonline*, "disguise," accessed November 3, 2025, https://www.etymonline.com /word/disguise.

29. Martin Stevens and Sami Merilaita, "Animal Camouflage: Current Issues and New Perspectives," *Philosophical Transactions of the Royal Society B: Biological Sciences* 364, no. 1516 (2009): 423–427.

30. Southern Ute Indian Tribe, "History."

31. Holly Kathryn Norton, *Federal Indian Boarding Schools in Colorado: 1880–1920*, History Colorado, 2023, 65.

32. Norton, *Federal Indian Boarding Schools*, 77.

33. Jill Seyfarth, *A Historic Buildings Survey of Old Fort Lewis, Hesperus, Colorado*, Office of Community Services, Fort Lewis College, 2007, 14.

34. Norton, *Federal Indian Boarding Schools*, 78.

35. Newland, *Investigative Report*, 39.

36. "Colorado Experience: The Original Coloradans," posted June 14, 2013, by Rocky Mountain PBS, YouTube, https://www.youtube.com/watch?v=lWLdijamdcQ.

37. Southern Ute Indian Tribe, "History."

38. Southern Ute Indian Tribe, "History."

39. Southern Ute Indian Tribe, "History."

40. Clark and Boxer, introduction to *From the Skin*, 5.

41. Mona C. Charles, James Gustine, Danielle Sheptow, and Alexis Schank, *A Cultural Resource Inventory of 247 Acres of the Old Fort Lewis, La Plata County, Colorado*, State Historical Fund, 2008, 22.

42. "Military Fort," Fort Lewis College, accessed November 3, 2025, https://www.fortlewis.edu/the-old-fort/about/history-of-the-old-fort/military-fort.

43. Newland, *Investigative Report*, 11.

44. Seyfarth, *Historic Buildings Survey*, 24.

45. Seyfarth, *Historic Buildings Survey*, 24.

46. Charles et al., *Cultural Resource Inventory*, 22.

47. Charles et al., *Cultural Resource Inventory*, 22.

48. Seyfarth, *Historic Buildings Survey*, 14.

49. Seyfarth, *Historic Buildings Survey*, 14.

50. Newland, *Investigative Report*, 39.

51. "Colorado Experience: The Original Coloradans."

52. Southern Ute Indian Tribe, "History."

53. Norton, *Federal Indian Boarding Schools*, 116.

54. Norton, *Federal Indian Boarding Schools*, 113.

16 THE NATIVE AMERICAN RANCH HOUSE

DIALECTICS OF ARCHITECTURE, RACE, AND LAND IN SOUTHERN CALIFORNIA, 1850–1935

Manuel Shvartzberg Carrió

HISTORICALLY, THE UNITED STATES WAS configured through settler colonial policies against Indigenous peoples, their cultures, and their political-economic systems. In the nineteenth century, US policy toward Native American nations shifted from one of foreign diplomacy, as attested by both genocidal wars and treaties, to one of internalization within the state, including establishing Indian boarding schools and policies of allotment of tribal land as private property. The ranch house played a key role in this history, one of the material vehicles by which settlers imagined assimilation in the mold of the Jeffersonian self-sufficient yeoman farmer. While the Homestead Act of 1862 and the transcontinental Pacific Railway Act of 1862 enabled white ranch settlements on the frontier, the Dawes Act of 1887 implicitly mobilized the ranch house through allotments, making it a tool for racializing Native Americans as *potentially* white, if they would only cast aside Indigenous architectures and modes of holding property. The Indigenous "rural" home underwent a settler colonial transformation that was premised on a racialized understanding of both architecture and land. In turn, this reconfigured status of the Indigenous home also modulated the place of Native Americans within the US body politic.

The architectural history of the ranch house in Southern California shows how race was mobilized in this period: first, as a tool of displacement and elimination, by erasing Indigenous lives and architecture; and second, by internalizing Indigenous peoples within the state as a "racial minority group [requiring] the protection of an adequately organized system of government amelioration," as Commissioner John Collier of the Bureau of Indian Affairs would later put it.[1] These two approaches were not sequential but fed off each other as two sides of the same coin, coexisting as tools for the uneasy management of the "Indian problem" in the United States. Together, they illustrate the function of racialization under modern liberalism—attempting to incorporate difference without equality.[2] The history of Indigenous anti-colonial opposition in Southern California shows that abolitionist approaches to the white supremacist state mounted an implicit challenge to the dominant architectural historiographies of the ranch house, a dialectic of architecture and land mediated by racial capitalism.

The Mission Ranch in Architectural History: Racial Elimination

The racialized dimensions of this historiography not only lay in omissions and dissimulations but were positively designed into the architecture of the ranch, orchestrating Native American displacement both territorially and culturally. Territorially, prefabricated construction turned the ranch into a literal technology of settlement.[3] Culturally, the ranch became the opposite architectural symbol of the lifeways of Native American peoples, who were represented as lacking yeomen farmers' virtues of self-improvement and self-reliance.

By 1953, 88 percent of all new American houses were built in the ranch style: sprawling, single-story homes on individual lots.[4] The same year, the landscape historian J. B. Jackson famously articulated the ranch house's centrality to settler history and cosmology as a perennially "westward-moving house."[5] Though Jackson conspicuously elided any discussion of race, this aspect had been very explicit in the most influential American architectural histories on the ranch house until just a few years earlier. Looking at the architectural historiography of what we might call the "eastward-moving house"—the ranch houses developed under the influence of California's Spanish Catholic mission system and also by its Indigenous peoples—we can more accurately understand the dialectical nature of the ranch type in this period.

One of the most influential authors to have addressed this historiography was

David Gebhard, among the first to try to create a genealogy connecting Native American architecture to the European avant-gardes and related modernist movements in the United States.[6] According to Gebhard and other historians in his wake, the interest of early California modernists such as Frank Lloyd Wright, Richard Neutra, and Rudolph Schindler in vernacular and "primitive" architectures was part of the broader wave of American, English, and Austrian Arts and Crafts movements in the late nineteenth century.[7] These connections were key to the emergence of the Spanish and Native Americanist revivals at the turn of the century: the "Spanish Colonial," "Mission," or "Pueblo" styles.[8] Thus, for Gebhard, a key thread between all these different strands of early twentieth-century architecture in Southern California—connecting a universalist Arts and Crafts ethos with specific regional-historical variations—was the magazine *The Craftsman*. Founded and edited by the furniture maker Gustav Stickley, *The Craftsman* achieved phenomenal influence and served as a key forum of debate among architects, designers, and writers during its period of publication from 1901 to 1916.[9] Indeed, the term "Mission style" was first coined by George Wharton James in a 1903 article in *The Craftsman*.[10]

After the magazine's demise in 1916, the most influential author for establishing the Mission style was the architectural historian Rexford Newcomb. Trained as an architect, Newcomb moved to Southern California in 1911, where he soon turned to academia. In 1918 he moved to Chicago as a professor at the University of Illinois, becoming dean of the College of Fine and Applied Arts in 1931, a position he held until his retirement in 1954.[11] Newcomb, whom some have called the "father of regional architectural history," dedicated his career to narrating the history and describing the architecture of the Spanish missions and the Mexican houses, ranchos, and haciendas of California.[12] His many books on the subject employed architectural drawing, photography, and writing to renew the mythologies surrounding life in Southern California, including the relation between the colonizers and the colonized.[13]

While many of Newcomb's works can be read as practical how-to manuals of style and construction,[14] his more scholarly works are guided by a remarkably clear objective: to assess the pedigree of new architecture built in territories previously under Spanish and Mexican rule. Newcomb's most elaborate and comprehensive survey, *The Old Mission Churches and Historic Houses of California* (1925), contains four hundred pages of mostly narrative exposition explaining how the missions emerged, how they changed under Mexican rule, and finally, how they—as he put it elsewhere—"witnessed the advent of conquerors of entirely different blood, history and ideals."[15] Indeed, from the very beginning of his treatise, Newcomb rehearsed a nineteenth-century discourse correlating racial hierarchy and environmental conditions, describing the Native peoples whom the Spanish encountered in California as "inferior" to those of New Mexico and Arizona. Among other highly racialized descriptions, he singled out the former for their "below . . . average height" and "poorly developed limbs," and further asserted that among the peoples of California, "the northern Indians were superior to the southern; the mountaineers, to the plainsmen or coast-dwellers."[16] This racial discourse systematically portrayed Native Americans not just as physically inferior but also as existing in a state of perpetual infantilism or nonhumanity. Indeed, Newcomb completely ignored Indigenous architecture as well as the multiple histories of resistance to the missions' "reductions" (as the forced mass abductions were called), falsely claiming that Native Americans "were easily brought under the influence of the missionaries. There is little record of physical resistance, their subjugation being accomplished more by persuasion than by force."[17]

In Newcomb's racial teleology, the end of Spanish California would give rise to the most "charming, romantic period of Californian history, the period of great days at San Diego and Monterey, the period of the fandango and cascarone balls, the guitar and the serenade, the time to which every mind turns when the old days of California are recalled."[18] It was this Mexican period from 1822 to 1848 that sowed the seeds for the kind of architecture that would be reminisced about in the early twentieth century. The charm of the style, however, was not merely aesthetic: It resided in a particular political and economic relation between land ownership and land use. While there had been few private land developments in the Spanish period (as land was monopolized by the Spanish Crown for military rather than commercial use), the Mexican period saw the proliferation of large "ranch houses" and "haciendas," which together with the missions were used as informal hotels by the incoming migrants and new settlers. It was this privately managed hospitality—turning religious, agrarian, and farming structures into mythologized sites of freedom for the new settlers—yet infused with Old World idiosyncrasies, that formed the imaginary fulcrum of the "Mission style" over fifty years later.

Accordingly, Newcomb's review of the post–Mexican period is centered not on the abandoned missions but on the "historic houses" of the new landed Californio aristocracy—places where white virility could safely coexist with noble Natives and Mexican women.[19] Newcomb described this typology with characteristic attention to its simplicity and craft:

> In the early days of California each *ranchero* (farmer) or *poblador* (town-dweller) was his own architect and builder, and, like the mission fathers, he favored the time-honored and easily acquired sun-dried brick as a structural material. Little wood was used except for window and door frames, doors, and roofing timbers. The timber-framed roof was usually covered with burned tiles, but roofs of tule thatch were used upon occasion. . . . In general the dwellings were far simpler than the mission structures and unadorned. The houses were plastered inside and out, and whitewashed.[20]

Despite the apparent empiricism, this account glorified colonial state authority and craft while systematically neglecting the role of Indigenous peoples' construction techniques, land practices, and political arrangements in the development of these structures.[21] Thus Newcomb's selective historiography concisely performed the task of legitimizing the ranch type's architectural lineage in racial terms: the result of a "peculiar background of geography and climate, with its specific materials at hand, its definite racial and, therefore, historical, religious, social, and political influences."[22] This particular regional and racial mix—predicated on the physical and cultural elimination of Indigenous peoples—had allowed California to capitalize on "her architectural heritage," harnessing "the real spirit of this delightfully simple, virile, and honest folk expression," which was the Mission style as the true archetype for the ranch house. The result, Newcomb claimed, was that "California cities are blossoming forth in a 'Renaissance' of Spanish-Colonial."[23]

The Mission Ranch in State Administration: Racial Assimilation

Newcomb's inflated rhetoric and contrived genealogy over the Mission and ranch styles had a sober contemporary institutional correlative with the development of philanthropic organizations to manage the growing problem of Native housing, as allotment policies resulted in the loss of two-thirds of Native Americans' entire land holdings in just a few decades. By the late 1920s and 1930s, precisely when Newcomb was writing racial histories that systematically excluded Indigenous architecture, state-related organizations were beginning to reconfigure the issue of Native housing as something internal to their purviews. Most notably, the Brookings Institution's Meriam Report (1928) detailed the staggering underinvestment and mismanagement in the state's approach to Native housing nationwide, pointing to necessary changes in policy and administration at the federal level.[24] With the appointment of the progressive reformer John Collier as the new commissioner of Indian Affairs in 1933, the state became formally invested in planning Native housing at a federal level for the first time. Yet despite repealing the policy of allotment, Collier's "Indian New Deal" inaugurated a more insidious mode of technocratic racial assimilation. Although Collier's plans did not reproduce Newcomb's explicit racism, by focusing on the single-family ranch house type as the socioeconomic unit of Native integration into the United States, Native housing became bureaucratically anchored to colonial epistemologies of architecture, property, land, and racial-class formation.[25]

If Newcomb's racialization of Native Americans had resulted in their systematic exclusion from architectural textbooks, Progressive Era racialization worked through a selective incorporation of Native realities into formal state records, and thus policy. This mode of racialization involved other media, especially photography, ethnographic writing, and social surveys, with architecture being deployed as key evidence for illustrating Native living conditions and the policy responses required to address them.

One important avenue for this evidentiary use of architecture was the effort of the Bureau of Indian Affairs to record Native housing conditions in reservations, beginning in the 1920s and becoming more developed in the 1930s. Hundreds of photographs of homes, contrasting deficient accommodations with new ones procured by the state, were taken by the bureau's technocrats in those decades (figs. 16.1, 16.2). The photos dramatized the work of federal agents and Native Americans as they tackled the most pressing issue facing California's Native peoples at the time: precarious housing conditions.[26] Taken by bureau field agents for the purpose of representing local progress to federal officials in Washington, DC, the photographs were key media for securing funding for local Bureau of Indian Affairs agencies. Yet, in so doing, the photographs also constructed a visual archive of an idealized Native American domesticity modeled on representations of Western ranch life: an ideal of the self-sufficient farmer that was implicitly racialized as white and heteronormative. Native people were portrayed standing in front of their new homes as nuclear family units, as opposed to the broader networks of kin they actually belonged to, and as enmeshed in networks of state-sponsored debt, assimilated to the national economy as responsible consumers. This classed and racialized coding served to decouple the geopolitical relation between home and land, and thus the larger problem at stake: Indigenous nations' struggles for land-based sovereignty. The photographs thus structurally reformulated Native Americans as aspiring middle-class racial minorities instead of sovereign nations.

This shift in the racialization of Native American housing, from extreme otherness to one premised on subordinated integration, was mediated by racialized representations of Southern California Native workers and their putative architectures. These elements were threaded together in the development of New Deal Indian housing, but were the result of a much longer process of dispossession with roots in early US colonialism in California. After the Mexican-American War and California's statehood in 1850, the new state passed its first piece of legislation, the Act for the Government and Protection of Indians, which legalized the kidnapping, indenture, and enslavement of Native Americans.[27] Then in 1852, the United States secretly left unratified eighteen treaties signed with California's tribes that included large land bases and duties to provide Native housing.[28] In 1875, the Mission Indian Agency was set up to manage Bureau of Indian Affairs policies in Southern California (fig. 16.3). As with the unsigned treaties, however, its agents disregarded tribal concerns with shrinking land bases, and they addressed housing issues in an ad hoc and residual manner, as an individual problem to be solved through self-sufficient farming or waged employment. Thus, instead of fulfilling its treaty promises, the bureau addressed housing as

FIGURE 16.1. *Photograph taken by supervisors from the Mission Indian Agency documenting new housing construction, procured by the Bureau of Indian Affairs under "Indian New Deal" legislation, at the Pala Indian Reservation (Luiseño and Cupeño), 1935. Original caption reads, "Steven Lugo's 5 room adobe house under construction. (Picture taken 9/6/35) Gov't loan $400 to construct house." National Archives at Riverside.*

FIGURE 16.2. *New housing construction at the Pala Reservation, 1935. Original caption reads, "Steven Lugo IR&R [Indian Relief and Rehabilitation] program repair job." National Archives at Riverside.*

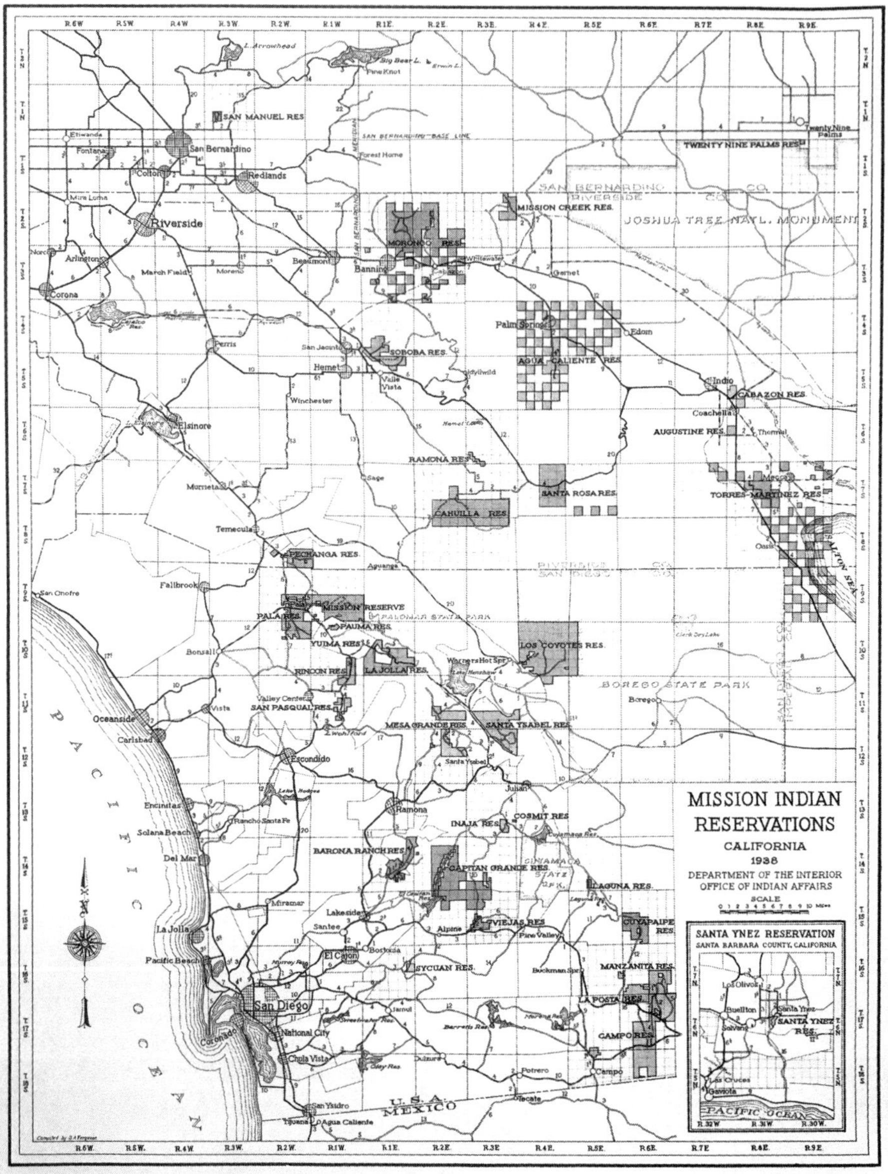

FIGURE 16.3. *Map of the Mission Indian Agency jurisdiction in Southern California, 1938. National Archives at Riverside.*

part of the moral aims of assimilation—subsuming it in educational initiatives rather than in construction programs or a dedicated Native housing agency.[29]

With their legal rights to land systematically undercut, Native Americans became the dual targets of a racial "war of extermination" and the efforts to exploit them as a cheap, indentured labor force for the state's new market economy.[30] As the register of the General Land Office in Los Angeles put it, "The location of an Indian family or families on land upon which a white man desires to settle is, in law, no more a bar to such settlement than would be the presence of a stray sheep or cow."[31] This dehumanization was only tempered by the widespread perception that Southern California's Native peoples had been "patiently taught" in multiple trades and skills by the Spanish missionaries, making them an excellent source of agricultural, construction, and domestic labor for white settlers.[32] Native Americans had been redeemed from "savagery" by the missions, and Indigenous homes demonstrated their skills for rural life and enterprise, even if they appeared poor. Thus, for example, in 1873 Charles Nordhoff, an American travel writer, described the homes of Luiseño people in Southern California as

> mostly constructed of reeds and barley-straw, laced with long poles. You will see, if you enter, a single dark room, without windows or chimney; the fire planted at one end, and smoke escaping by the door; the stone on which grain is ground for tortillas, near the door; the beds on the floor occupying half the space within; the women and children, and on Sunday the men, sitting around the fire.[33]

Nordhoff was particularly concerned to convey how Native homes, despite their poverty, were in fact full of signs of incipient "civilization," not only in their systematic modes of construction and maintenance but in how they displayed a capacity for independent ranch life that would be useful to hypothetical white employers. As Newcomb would do through his textbooks fifty years later, Nordhoff also developed a typological framework for California's ranch homes based on race: "As you ride through the country," he advised his reader, "you can tell at a distance the character of the inhabitants of a house you are approaching." Materials correlated with ethnicity: "If the house is of reeds and straw, the owner is an Indian; if it is of adobe, it is a Spaniard who lives there; if it is of frame, be sure it is an 'American.'" This understanding was not a simple reflection of racial hierarchy, however, as it confounded expectations; despite appearances, "often the wooden house is a mere box, smaller and less comfortable than the Indian's straw hut."[34] Here architecture constituted evidence of racialized progress, as Nordhoff attributed Native Americans' architectural sophistication to having "learned cleanliness from the old Spanish Californians," being well-organized and generous hosts, a characteristic they shared with the higher-class Californio ranching families, despite their relative poverty.[35]

Like many other anthropologists and journalists in his wake, Nordhoff fixated on the discrete materiality and layout of single California Native homes, claiming that the typical Native "house is planted seemingly by chance, anywhere, without relations to any thing except usually another house just like it."[36] This interpretation, however, was misguided; settlement patterns in Native Southern California villages constituted more complex arrangements between housing and land than Nordhoff presumed for a ranching market economy, with each home occupying its own large lot for overseeing cattle. This was a rural conception at odds with the reality of Luiseño urbanism, where homes were set close together, often with clearly marked streets and surrounded by carefully planted "trees, vegetables, and flowers in their yards."[37] While it was true that Native Californians were known for their good ranching skills, this did not mean that their architecture and urbanism corresponded with the Spanish, Mexican, or Anglo-American ranch housing typologies. Instead of building discrete ranch houses far away from each other, Native urbanism organized relations between housing and land by spatially configuring dense kinship networks.

The ethnographer David P. Barrows wrote about a layout similar to Luiseño architecture and urbanism in his seminal studies of Cahuilla life in the Colorado Desert. Barrows described densely articulated multifamily dwellings on a single level. Brush homes were built around open-air courtyards for accommodating extended families, with "two or three" buildings that "usually face each other about a little patio or court." This patio, Barrows continued,

> is, except in cold or stormy weather, the meeting place of all the family. It is surrounded by a low brush fence or wall, which wards off the wind and also serves as a clothes line, utensil rack, etc. In summer time the patio is roofed over and partially inclosed by an airy booth, known everywhere throughout southern California by the Spanish word *ramada*, from *ramas*, "boughs" or "branches." The Coahuillas [*sic*] call it *táish-kish-la*. It is the most comfortable of summer houses. The breeze draws through it, keeping it cool and pleasant, when outside of this leafy retreat the sun may be beating with scorching heat upon the valley. It is made square with flat top. The frame work is of light poles, tied with yucca spines, and the roof and walls are of willow boughs.[38]

A structure with a semiopen courtyard was photographed by Charles C. Pierce in 1895 in the Luiseño village of Pechanga (fig. 16.4). It shows a multigenerational group posing for the camera in front of a brush house, half of it with a pitched, thatched roof, and half of it—the semiopen patio—covered with a flat ramada roof.

While this photo depicts a single structure, Pierce also photographed densely clustered homes and a school at the same village that same year (fig. 16.5)—an image that confounds Nordhoff's typology not just in terms of the homes' settlement pattern but also in their materiality; they were made of adobe brick with thatched roofs and large adobe chimneys on their sides. Other elements of the photograph also challenge the caricature of Native housing offered by Nordhoff. For example, a Native American cowboy is featured atop a black horse in the foreground, while an American flag flies over the school building in the background. On the edges of the image, two ramada structures are also visible: one on the right, attached to an adobe home, and the other seemingly freestanding. In the

FIGURE 16.4. *Charles C. Pierce, "Pachango [Pechanga] House," 1895. C. C. Pierce Collection of Photographs, Huntington Library.*

FIGURE 16.5. *Charles C. Pierce, "Part of the Village of Palatingiva [Pechanga] with a School House with an American Flag," 1895. C. C. Pierce Collection of Photographs, Huntington Library.*

center of the image, a low-level fence made of wooden stakes delineates a garden space or compound framing the side of one or two of the homes.

These architectural and photographic articulations of materiality, form, settlement pattern, and social signifiers speak of a much more complex ethnic, racial, cultural, and economic reality than those identified by either Nordhoff or Barrows. In each case, whether through travel writing, ethnography, or photography, the representations exceeded the available architectural epistemologies offered for understanding them: either as specimens of the Mission-style ranch house or as "authentic" Indigenous homes, according to architectural historians and anthropologists. This epistemic disjuncture, which was key to the racialization of the tribes as potentially white ranch property owners, conformed with a discourse of "salvage ethnography" in the media of photography, popular and academic writing, and architectural history, which continued to disconnect the ranch house from the deep land struggles in which Native Californians were enmeshed.[39]

The anthropologist Alfred L. Kroeber, for example, reproduced the objectification of Cahuilla architecture as disconnected from Cahuilla urbanism in his own photographs of "modern houses in the desert" from 1908 (fig. 16.6).[40] Kroeber photographed four Cahuilla homes and depicted them separated from

MODERN HOUSES IN THE DESERT.

FIGURE 16.6. *"Modern Houses in the Desert." A. L. Kroeber,* Ethnography of the Cahuilla Indians *(University of California Press, 1908), plate 14.*

their surrounding environment. This time, no people were portrayed around the structures, with Kroeber reporting briefly in the text that the "houses of the desert Cahuilla remain very much as described by Dr. Barrows [in 1900]."[41] The images thus tend to reduce the Cahuilla's historicity, aiming to establish a pseudo-objective representation of them as a "vanishing race" that continued to build homes in their traditional ways, even in "modern" times.

This was the architectural equivalent to the influential ethnographic portraits of the photographer Edward S. Curtis's *The North American Indian*, whose twenty volumes presented Native Americans as entirely traditional, and thus racialized, figures. In such portraits, Indigenous subjects were presented in elaborate traditional dress, decontextualized from the complex mix of tradition and modernity they actually experienced—as if they had been frozen in time before colonization.[42] Sometimes their homes and "habitats," as Barrows put it, were also depicted as an integral part of these performances of tradition. By observing and depicting Cahuilla architecture in the same way, Cahuilla architectural and urban practices, inherently tied to Indigenous land governance systems, were also disregarded and excluded from view—as were the fraught struggles over allotments that divided entire tribal communities and created complex hybrid conditions between new farming economies and traditional lifeways (fig. 16.7).

FIGURE 16.7. *Charles C. Pierce, "Colorado Desert Indians [Cahuilla] Cultivating the Land [Allotted] Them by the Government near Indio, California," undated. C. C. Pierce Collection of Photographs, Huntington Library.*

In this sense, the Mission Indian Agency agents' photographs of new reservation housing construction during the 1920s and 1930s continued the tradition of salvage ethnographic photography by rehearsing some of its storied conventions, repeating a semiotic structure—figures, domestic implements, homes, and habitats—that had come to signify a pseudo-objective mode of representation for white society. But they also critically shifted it in a new direction, as it ingrained photography and architecture in the project of building the settler colonial state by giving tribes a stake in this construction, though as racial minorities rather than sovereign nations.

This was a multimedia effort where photography and other tools such as social surveys would recontextualize Native housing uniquely in terms of ranching. Thus, from the epistemic disjunctures of Newcomb and Nordhoff, premised on *mis*representation, Collier's Indian New Deal shifted to technocratic *over*representation—aiming to fully represent tribes in ways that could define them as modern housing clients of the state. In 1933 and 1934, Bureau of Indian Affairs superintendents carried out a large "economic and social survey" of their jurisdictions to "collect information [on] the Indians' . . . [living] conditions."[43] In order to help gather and consolidate this information, the bureau designed a standardized form with predetermined questions to be filled out by field agents. Unlike the extensive narrative reports previously used by the bureau in the vein of traditional ethnographies, the standardized form was a self-contained single sheet of paper printed on both sides. Notations on housing comprised about half of the information in the survey and included items such as the size of house; building materials; numbers of windows, doors, and rooms; water supplies; sanitation facilities; and implements and furniture (fig. 16.8).[44]

Through this social-scientific survey, the form appeared to do away with the focus on narrative reporting, and with it, the paternalistic prose on civilizational progress. On the surface, then, the initiative seemed entirely contrary to the racist handbooks of California ranch housing produced by Newcomb. Yet the survey forms translated the project of Indigenous assimilation into a set of specific metrics that assumed ranch-style dwellings and livelihoods, surreptitiously entrenching the inherent racism of the ranch type as a historical instrument of colonial settlement and disregarding Indigenous modes of urbanization, politics, and economics. While both Newcomb's and the bureau's narrative reports were pitched as moralizing *descriptive* documents that mostly ignored actual Native housing arrangements, the survey forms offered a *prescriptive* outline for what Native life ought to be—implicitly structuring options over Indigenous life by imposing discrete categorizations. Nowhere was this clearer than in how the forms prefigured a pastoral lifestyle for Indigenous peoples—an assumption that was patently simplistic for Southern California's Indigenous tribes. Focused on housing conditions associated with cattle ranching and farming, the forms assumed a subsistence mode of production that did not reflect the highly diversified economies

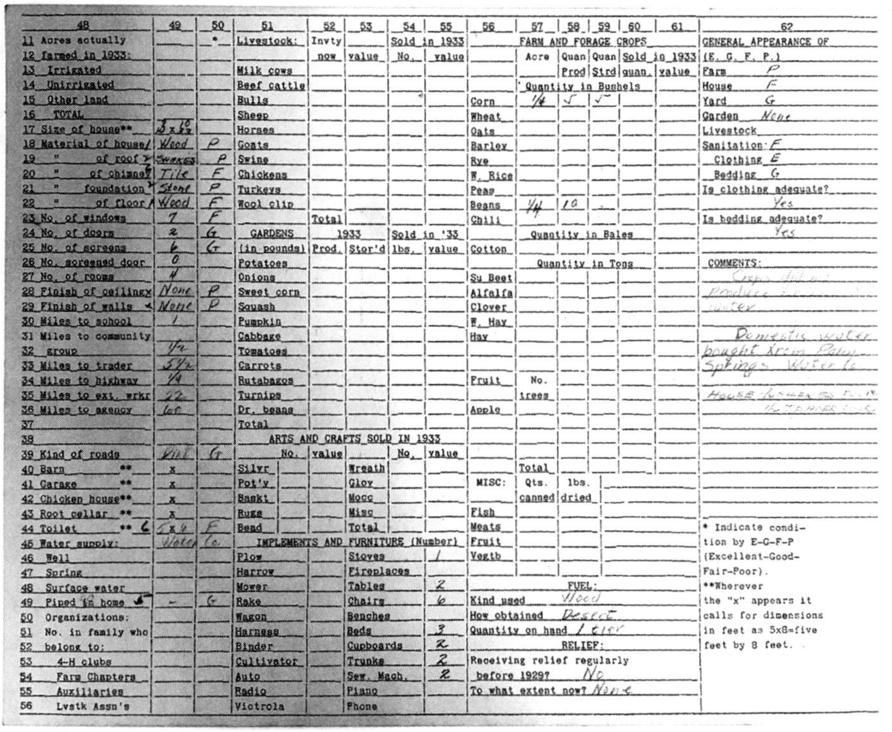

48	49	50	51	52	53	54	55	56	57	58	59	60	61	62
11 Acres actually		*	Livestock:	Invty		Sold in 1933			FARM AND FORAGE CROPS					GENERAL APPEARANCE OF
12 farmed in 1933:				now	value	No.	value		Acre	Quan	Quan	Sold in 1933		(E. G. F. P.)
13 Irrigated			Milk cows							Prod	Strd	quan.	value	Farm P
14 Unirrigated			Beef cattle						Quantity in Bushels					House F
15 Other land			Bulls					Corn	1/4	√	√			Yard G
16 TOTAL			Sheep					Wheat						Garden None
17 Size of house**	3 x 16		Horses					Oats						Livestock
18 Material of house/	Wood	P	Goats					Barley						Sanitation F
19 " of roof	Shakes	P	Swine					Rye						Clothing E
20 " of chimney	Tile	F	Chickens					W. Rice						Bedding G
21 " foundation	Stone	P	Turkeys					Peas						Is clothing adequate? Yes
22 " of floor	Wood	F	Wool clip					Beans	1/4	10				
23 No. of windows	7	F		Total				Chili						Is bedding adequate? Yes
24 No. of doors	2	G	GARDENS	1933		Sold in '33			Quantity in Bales					
25 No. of screens	6	G	(in pounds)	Prod.	Stor'd	lbs.	value	Cotton						
26 No. screened door	0		Potatoes						Quantity in Tons					COMMENTS:
27 No. of rooms	4		Onions					Su Beet						
28 Finish of ceilings	None	P	Sweet corn					Alfalfa						
29 Finish of walls	None	P	Squash					Clover						
30 Miles to school	1		Pumpkin					W. Hay						
31 Miles to community			Cabbage					Hay						Domestic water
32 group	1/2		Tomatoes											bought from Palm
33 Miles to trader	5 1/2		Carrots											Springs Water Co
34 Miles to highway	1/4		Rutabagas					Fruit	No.					
35 Miles to ext. wrkr	22		Turnips						trees					
36 Miles to agency	1/4		Dr. beans					Apple						
37			Total											
38			ARTS AND CRAFTS SOLD IN 1933											
39 Kind of roads	Dirt	G		No.	value		No. value							
40 Barn **	x		Silvr			Wreath			Total					
41 Garage **	x		Pot'y			Glov		MISC:	Qts. canned	lbs. dried				
42 Chicken house**	x		Baskt			Moce								
43 Root cellar **	x		Rugs			Misc		Fish						
44 Toilet **	6 x 6	F	Bead			Total		Meats						* Indicate condition by E-G-F-P (Excellent-Good-Fair-Poor). **Wherever the "x" appears it calls for dimensions in feet as 5x8=five feet by 8 feet.
45 Water supply:	Water Co.		IMPLEMENTS AND FURNITURE (Number)					Fruit						
46 Well			Plow			Stoves	1	Vegtb						
47 Spring			Harrow			Fireplaces								
48 Surface water			Mower			Tables	2	FUEL:						
49 Piped in home	✓	G	Rake			Chairs	6	Kind used Wood						
50 Organizations:			Wagon			Benches		How obtained Desert						
51 No. in family who			Harness			Beds	3	Quantity on hand 1 cord						
52 belong to:			Binder			Cupboards	2	RELIEF:						
53 4-H clubs			Cultivator			Trunks	2	Receiving relief regularly						
54 Farm Chapters			Auto			Sew. Mach.	2	before 1929? No						
55 Auxiliaries			Radio			Piano		To what extent now? None						
56 Lvstk Assn's			Victrola			Phone								

FIGURE 16.8. *Survey of Albert Patencio and family, Agua Caliente Indian Reservation, 1934. Page 2 of survey, box 221, Records Relating to the 1934 Economic and Social Survey, 1933–1934, National Archives at Riverside.*

of tribal members, many of whom had been working as wage laborers or small business owners for decades.[45]

The Mission Indian Federation: Abolition

Out of this colonial contradiction emerged the Mission Indian Federation, a pan-Indigenous political organization founded in 1919 by thirty different Native nations from across Southern California to abolish the Indian Bureau and to protest the US neglect of treaties and the imposition of allotments.[46] With a focus on material conditions and political sovereignty, the federation displaced conceptualizations of ranch housing as a tool of both exclusionary and assimilationist racialization. Instead, they denaturalized the very proposition of the ranch house as the natural architectural type offered by the state, suggesting a much more situated and complex vision of Indigenous sovereignty that openly wrestled with the Progressive Era's contradictions.

The group was organized as a federated system of Native self-government with its own political and administrative leadership. It was not a new type of organization but rather a new iteration of regularly occurring defensive geopolitical arrangements among Southern California's Native nations against colonialism.[47] Though they lacked formal recognition from the United States, they enacted diplomatic, governmental, cultural, and physical modes of organization and resistance, agitating for "Home Rule and Human Rights"[48]—their official motto. The state vigorously persecuted them; in the 1920s, officials brought formal charges of sedition against federation members.[49]

This prosecution stemmed from an inability by US agents and institutions to see or accept the Mission Indian Federation as a legitimate sovereign political entity, a misperception that had been cultivated through a racialized and capitalist understanding of housing and land. The main impetus for joining the federation was opposition to allotments, which were integrally tied to land dispossession and the thwarting of Native urbanisms. While California's economy grew exponentially, by "1920, the Mission Indians received the least attention from Indian agents and the smallest per capita federal aid of any group of recognized Native nations in the United States."[50] The necessity of migrating for jobs and "decades of neglect by the federal government allowed squatters to gain title to lands surrounding and between villages, thus eliminating the possibility of a large reservation that joined multiple villages together."[51] Thus, rather than be pacified with allotments, the federation explicitly agitated for restitution of the land bases agreed to in the treaties of 1852. But instead of upholding the treaties, the state forced a conflict on the tribes in the form of a choice between land *or* housing: Governmental housing was offered as the very prize for accepting the Faustian bargain of allotments, thus enshrining the history of colonial land dispossession and preventing land reconsolidation. As a prominent federationist put it, "The [government's] favorites and sycophants on each reservation are permitted to select their allotments [and] in many instances they are given the old home of another."[52] Thus, the Indian New Deal's surveys and promises of ranch housing, far from being a mere projection of exoticized pastoralism, became a highly charged weapon of class warfare wielded against and within the federation itself.

The federation's trenchant abolitionism, however, did not mean that it lacked its own projects for how to allocate land and housing. Rather than allowing it to be subsumed within the ranch house as a naturalized type, housing was part and parcel of a different architectural epistemology that could not be separated from place-based modes of governance. The organization, as one historian put it, was designed as "an Indigenized form of federalism. . . . [It expanded] village-oriented forms of government, [and] formalized traditional governance into a more cohesive, unified system."[53] Their methods for designing arrangements over land and housing did not reflect a "transitional period" between an undeveloped tribalism and a fully developed "world democracy," as Collier imagined, but rather they denaturalized unmediated equations between the single-family home, individual property ownership, and US sovereignty.[54] Not only were the government's suggested home and farm layouts strange to them, but their purposeful siting as remote homesteads was contrary to the more centralized planning that federation tribes tended to employ, setting homes around social and environmental commons, as in the Luiseño village of Pechanga.[55] These compact settlements followed traditional Native Southern California urban arrangements.

Contrary to many tropes from nineteenth-century ethnographers, homes were usually placed around open-air spaces for accommodating urban life, rather than scattered in the landscape. The federation's political and social organization thus reflected this village urbanism structure. The villages included their own autonomous tribal political organizations, although both Native villages and provinces cooperated on economic, diplomatic, and social matters through specific strategic meetings that occurred at least twice yearly. Such meetings were—and continue to be—crucial not just for political and cultural exchange but also for the administration of life in the desert, attending to the contingencies of droughts, floods, and earthquakes, as well as wars, economic arrangements within the nation, and negotiations with other neighboring nations. Regimes of common property and land ownership were designed to protect ecological biodiversity through economic specialization and cooperation; for example, neighboring villages were responsible for distinct trades, specific food-gathering sites, agricultural fields, and hunting grounds. Through well-maintained trails, they established long-term trade and cultural relations among themselves and with other nations. Foods and products would then be shared or exchanged between villages and provinces at regular meetings so that reciprocity among people, animals, and land was both symbolized and enacted. This kind of social relation with and through the land constituted a very different kind of urbanism than the one imported by settlers, which imposed a rigid separation between the private (social-domestic) sphere and the public sphere of formal political institutions in far-flung places of settler power such as Los Angeles, San Francisco, and Washington, DC.

Thus the idea of "home" for members of the Mission Indian Federation conjured a different set of political and economic formations than those racialized projections of architectural historians like Newcomb and technocrats like Collier. The federation rejected the Faustian dialectic of land *or* housing, which entrenched a racially subordinated status in the US body politic while upholding the property-owning individual as its core normative subject. Instead, their activism pointed to a different understanding of urban-rural density and sociotechnical assemblages of land and governance that did not fit the dominant epistemologies of architecture—whether in built form or through the reifications of architectural historians.

Notes

1. John Collier, Circular No. 3537, "Planning," November 15, 1943, 1, box 163, Overall Post War Work Program Records, 1942–1946, Mission Indian Agency Papers, RG 75, National Archives at Riverside.

2. Jodi Melamed, *Represent and Destroy: Rationalizing Violence in the New Racial Capitalism* (University of Minnesota Press, 2011).

3. See, for example, Dolores Hayden, "Mail-Order and Self-Built Suburbs," in *Building Suburbia: Green Fields and Urban Growth, 1820–2000* (Pantheon, 2003), 97–127; Gilbert Herbert, *Pioneers of Prefabrication: The British Contribution in the Nineteenth Century* (Johns Hopkins University Press, 1978).

4. Dianne Harris, *Little White Houses: How the Postwar Home Constructed Race in America* (University of Minnesota Press, 2013), 48. On the American ranch house as an architectural type, see Barbara L. Allen, "The Ranch-Style House in America: A Cultural and Environmental Discourse," *Journal of Architectural Education* 49, no. 3 (1996): 156–165.

5. John Brinckerhoff Jackson, "The Westward-Moving House," in *Landscape in Sight: Looking at America*, ed. Helen Lefkowitz Horowitz (Yale University Press, 1997), 81–105.

6. David Gebhard, "The Spanish Colonial Revival in Southern California (1895–1930)," *Journal of the Society of Architectural Historians* 26, no. 2 (1967): 131–147. Many architectural historians in the early postwar period wove their own narratives connecting the Indigenous and the modern. See, for example, Sibyl Moholy-Nagy, *Native Genius in Anonymous Architecture* (Horizon Press, 1957); Sigfried Giedion, *The Eternal Present, Volume II: The Beginnings of Architecture* (Pantheon, 1964).

7. Thomas S. Hines, *Architecture of the Sun: Los Angeles Modernism, 1900–1970* (Rizzoli, 2010), 138.

8. Gebhard, "Spanish Colonial Revival," 140, 131; Chris Wilson, *The Myth of Santa Fe: Creating a Modern Regional Tradition* (University of New Mexico Press, 1997), 274–275.

9. T. J. Jackson Lears, *No Place of Grace: Antimodernism and the Transformation of American Culture, 1880–1920* (Pantheon, 1981), 59–96.

10. George Wharton James, "The Influence of the 'Mission Style' upon the Civic and Domestic Architecture of Modern California," *Craftsman* 5 (1903): 458–469.

11. Marc Appleton, introduction to *Mediterranean Domestic Architecture in the United States*, by Rexford Newcomb (1928; Acanthus Press, 1999), xiii.

12. Vincent B. Canizaro, introduction to "Regionalism in American Architecture," by Rexford Newcomb, in *Architectural Regionalism: Collected Writings on Place, Identity, Modernity, and Tradition*, ed. Vincent B. Canizaro (Princeton Architectural Press, 2013), 80. Newcomb's "Regionalism in American Architecture" was originally published in *Regionalism in America*, ed. Merrill Jensen (University of Wisconsin Press, 1951), 273–295.

13. Rexford Newcomb, *The Franciscan Mission Architecture of Alta California* (1916; Dover, 1988); Newcomb, *The Old Mission Churches and Historic Houses of California: Their Story, Architecture, and Lore* (J. B. Lippincott, 1925); Newcomb, *Mediterranean Domestic Architecture*; Newcomb, *Spanish-Colonial Architecture in the United States* (J. J. Agustin, 1937).

14. Appleton, introduction to *Mediterranean Domestic Architecture*, xiv.

15. Newcomb, *Spanish-Colonial Architecture*, 36.

16. Newcomb, *Old Mission Churches*, 10.

17. Newcomb, *Old Mission Churches*, 10. The missions were not charitable to Native Americans, and there were many riots and rebellions. Andrés Reséndez, *The Other Slavery: The Uncovered Story of Indian Enslavement in America* (Mariner Books, 2016).

18. Newcomb, *Old Mission Churches*, 68.

19. Jason E. Pierce, *Making the White Man's West: Whiteness and the Creation of the American West* (University Press of Colorado, 2016). On the mission landscapes as romanticized ruins, see Elizabeth Kryder-Reid, *California Mission Landscapes: Race, Memory, and the Politics of Heritage* (University of Minnesota Press, 2016).

20. Newcomb, *Old Mission Churches*, 309.

21. See, for example, Charles Sepulveda, "Our Sacred Waters: Theorizing *Kuuyam* as a Decolonial Possibility," *Decolonization: Indigeneity, Education & Society* 7, no. 1 (2018): 40–58, 43; Yve Chavez, *Indigenizing California Mission Art and Architecture* (University of Washington Press, 2025); George Harwood Phillips, *Vineyards and Vaqueros: Indian Labor and the Economic Expansion of Southern California, 1771–1877* (University of Oklahoma Press, 2010); Catherine R. Ettinger, "Hybrid Spaces: Indigenous Contributions to Mission Architecture," in *Architecture, Physical Environment, and Society in Alta California: Proceedings of the 22nd Annual Conference of the California Mission Studies Association*, ed. Rose Marie Beebe and Robert M. Senkewicz (California Mission Studies Association, 2005), 77–89.

22. Newcomb, *Old Mission Churches*, 355.

23. Newcomb, *Old Mission Churches*, 358.

24. Lewis Meriam, *The Problem of Indian Administration: Summary of Findings and Recommendations* (Institute of Government Research, 1928).

25. Mark Rifkin, *The Politics of Kinship: Race, Family, Governance* (Duke University Press, 2024).

26. John W. Dady, *Narrative Section Annual Report, Fiscal Year Ending June 30, 1935* (Mission Indian Agency, 1935), 3.

27. Madley, *An American Genocide*, 157–163.

28. Sean Milanovich, "The Treaty of Temecula: A Story of Invasion, Deceit, Stolen Land, and the Persistence of Power, 1846–1905" (PhD diss., University of California, Riverside, 2021); Damon B. Akins and William J. Bauer, *We Are the Land: A History of Native California* (University of California Press, 2021); Joel R. Hyer, *"We Are Not Savages": Native Americans in Southern California and the Pala Reservation, 1840–1920* (Michigan State University Press, 2001).

29. Virginia Davis, "A Discovery of Sorts: Reexamining the Origins of the Federal Indian Housing Obligation," *Harvard Blackletter Law Journal* 18, no. 211 (2002): 211–237.

30. Madley, *An American Genocide*, 173.

31. Valerie Sherer Mathes and Phil Brigandi, *Reservations, Removal, and Reform: The Mission Indian Agents of Southern California, 1878–1903* (University of Oklahoma Press, 2018), 4.

32. Charles Nordhoff, *California: For Health, Pleasure, and Residence; A Book for Travellers and Settlers* (New York: Harper and Brothers, 1873), 158.

33. Nordhoff, *California*, 156.

34. Nordhoff, *California*, 157.

35. Nordhoff, *California*, 157.

36. Nordhoff, *California*, 156.

37. Hyer, *"We Are Not Savages,"* 288.

38. David P. Barrows, "The Ethno-Botany of the Coahuilla Indians of Southern California" (PhD diss., University of Chicago, 1900), 37.

39. Samuel J. Redman, *Prophets and Ghosts: The Story of Salvage Anthropology* (Harvard University Press, 2021).

40. A. L. Kroeber, *Ethnography of the Cahuilla Indians* (University of California Press, 1908).

41. Kroeber, *Ethnography of the Cahuilla Indians*, 64.

42. Edward S. Curtis, *The North American Indian*, 20 vols. (Edward S. Curtis, 1907–1930). Curtis covered Southern California in volume 15 of the series (1926).

43. Davis, "Discovery of Sorts," 228.

44. Survey documents, box 221, Records Relating to the 1934 Economic and Social Survey, 1933–1934, Mission Indian Agency Papers, RG 75, National Archives at Riverside.

45. Nordhoff, *California*, 156; James R. Young, Dennis Moristo, and G. David Tenenbaum, eds., *An Inventory of the Mission Indian Agency Records* (UCLA American Indian Studies Center, 1976), 15; Nicolas G. Rosenthal, *Reimagining Indian Country: Native American Migration and Identity in Twentieth-Century Los Angeles* (University of North Carolina Press, 2012).

46. Tanis C. Thorne and Heather Ponchetti Daly, *El Capitan: Adaptation and Agency on a Southern California Indian Reservation, 1850–1937* (Malki-Bellena Press, 2012).

47. Terence Robert Przeklasa, "Reservation Empire: The Mission Indian Federation and Native American Conservatism" (PhD diss., University of California, Riverside, 2015); Florence Connolly Shipek, *Pushed into the Rocks: Southern California Indian Land Tenure, 1769–1986* (University of Nebraska Press, 1988); George Harwood Phillips, *Chiefs and Challengers: Indian Resistance and Cooperation in Southern California, 1769–1906* (University of Oklahoma Press, 2014).

48. Heather Ponchetti Daly, "Fractured Relations at Home: The 1953 Termination Act's Effect on Tribal Relations Throughout Southern California Indian Country," *American Indian Quarterly* 33, no. 4 (2009): 427–439.

49. Tanis C. Thorne, "On the Fault Line: Political Violence at Campo Fiesta and National Reform in Indian Policy," *Journal of California and Great Basin Anthropology* 21, no. 2 (1999): 182–212.

50. Przeklasa, "Reservation Empire," 102.

51. Przeklasa, "Reservation Empire," 102–103.

52. Richard A. Hanks, "This War Is for a Whole Life: The Culture of Resistance Among Southern California Indians, 1850–1966" (PhD diss., University of California, Riverside, 2006), 193.

53. Przeklasa, "Reservation Empire," 5–6, 88.

54. Collier, Circular No. 3537, "Planning."

55. Thorne and Daly, *El Capitan*, 34, 72.

PART V

MODERN MYTHOLOGIES

17 JEFFERSON'S ASHES AND ARCHITECTURE'S RACIAL DIALECTIC

Peter Minosh

AN 1856 PRINT BY EDWARD SACHSE, *View of the University of Virginia, Charlottesville, and Monticello Taken from Lewis Mountain*The Miriam and Ira D. Wallach Division of Art, Prints and Photographs: Print Collection, The New York Public Library. (fig. 17.1). The campus extends across the length of the sheet. Its ten Pavilions are faithfully reproduced with their accompanying hotels and the iconic curving walls separating the gardens in between. The university is a didactic tool for aspiring architects lacking access to the antiquities of Europe. The Pavilions reconstruct a history of classical architecture in a consistent palette of brick and painted-white wooden details to promote comparative study. The campus's central building, the Rotunda, is the focus of this image; its scale is exaggerated to distinguish it from the Pavilions lining the great lawn and to lend a monumental presence. We can read into this print Jefferson's attempt to formalize his own ad hoc architectural training that synthesized the builder's guides and architectural treatises assembled in his architectural library, his tireless explorations of contemporary buildings in Paris, and his interest in antiquities. The Pavilions are

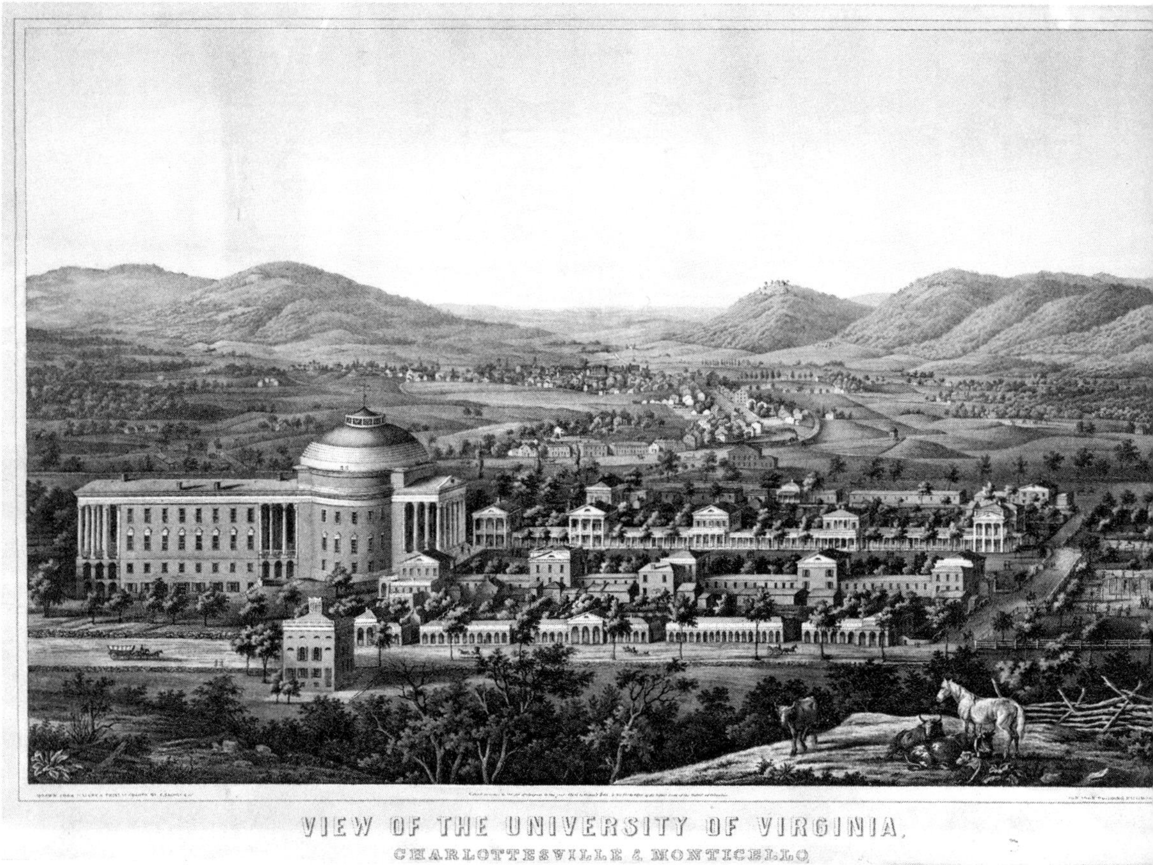

FIGURE 17.1. *Edward Sachse,* View of the University of Virginia, Charlottesville, and Monticello Taken from Lewis Mountain, *1856. The Miriam and Ira D. Wallach Division of Art, Prints and Photographs: Print Collection, The New York Public Library.*

shown as minor works where the Rotunda is their culmination, rooted in precedent but original in composition.

We can also read this print recessionally, from the foreground to the horizon. An elevated ridge atop Lewis Mountain serves as the vantage point of the print. Grazing livestock and a post-and-rail fence indicate small-scale agriculture. The university makes up the middle ground of the composition, with the village of Charlottesville directly behind. Jefferson's Monticello is perched atop a hill at the terminus of this view. This offers a dialectical vision of Jefferson's vision for an American Enlightenment in which the yeoman, or small-scale family farmer, would serve as the source of republican values. The gaze of the independent farmer passes across the university to arrive at Monticello. The autonomous individual, given access to the Enlightenment, attains the condition of the ennobled yeoman, exemplified by Jefferson himself. We can read in this another aspect of Jefferson's architectural production. In his Land Ordinance of 1785, a uniform, abstract grid of thirty-six square-mile units would overlay undeveloped Western lands. One-square-mile lots would be put up for purchase for further division into acreage for farming. The lot numbered 16 would be reserved for a public school. The infrastructure for education would precede the nation's westward expansion, guaranteeing that farmers retained the teachings of the Enlightenment necessary to carry with them the condition of the yeoman.

Gentleman architect and yeoman individual—these narratives are well rehearsed in Jefferson scholarship. Yet the details of this print offer another narrative. The cultivated land at the base of Monticello indicates Tufton Farm, the western extent of Jefferson's lands. Rather than the family farm of an autonomous yeoman, the print depicts an enslaving plantation—remnants of Jefferson's own, and likely labored on by the descendants of people whom Jefferson enslaved. Ad hoc construction sits among the curving walls of the university's Pavilion Gardens. There, enslaved workers tended to the upkeep of the university and to the needs of the professors who resided and taught in the numbered Pavilions.[1] From these details lurking among the heroic narratives of the Jeffersonian ideal, we build another narrative. Jefferson's American Enlightenment, and its notion of the yeoman individual as the basis of American republicanism, is built upon the regime of chattel slavery.

Jefferson holds a privileged place in the history of American architecture. Fiske Kimball declared him "the father of our national architecture" for his admixture of American ingenuity and a republican ethos. Jefferson here becomes the precursor of an American modern architecture that encompasses Daniel Burnham, Frank Lloyd Wright, and Buckminster Fuller. This chapter explores the historiography of Jefferson spanning the twentieth century—from his framing as an antecedent to modernist rationalism at its beginning to his place as postmodernist allegory at its end.

Several scholars have unpacked the role of slavery in Jefferson's architecture. In his groundbreaking 1976 article on American plantation architecture, Carl Anthony employed George Washington's Mount Vernon and Jefferson's Monticello to situate domestic slavery at the seat of American political power.[2] He highlighted the ways that Monticello projected the idea of an American gentleman farmer by employing architectural devices to render invisible the enslaved labor required to maintain it. Dell Upton cast Monticello in the tradition of the tidewater plantation house that differentiated social positions in space; the house demarcated the "indoor family" of relations from the "outdoor family" of the enslaved domestic workers.[3] More recent scholarship informed by critical race theory and whiteness studies has continued this line of research. Irene Cheng and Mabel Wilson, respectively, have interrogated Jefferson's notion of an American Enlightenment. Cheng shows the racial and class precepts of his architectural geometry.[4] Wilson uses the example of the Virginia State Capitol to unpack constructions of racial whiteness in Enlightenment aesthetics.[5] Maurie McInnis and

Louis Nelson show the centrality of enslaved labor in the construction and operations of the University of Virginia.[6]

This chapter examines the diverse roles Jefferson has played in histories of modern architecture, how his place in the enslaving regime has been omitted, and how the history of modern architecture has been shaped and formed through these omissions. What follows here is an exploration of strategies that historians employed to partition Jefferson's role as an enslaver from their analysis of his architecture. If we can read the historiography of Jefferson's architecture through its silences on slavery, we can begin to outline how these lacunae were constitutive in shaping its approaches and methodologies. American architectural history becomes the project of maintaining modernist narratives by navigating around questions of race and histories of enslavement. These narratives themselves become conscripted into the project of white supremacy.

Geographies of Classicism

William Lambeth and Warren Manning, the first historians, in 1913, to treat Jefferson seriously as an architect were also the first to note the aesthetics of invisibility in Jefferson's work. Architectural devices throughout Monticello maintained the invisibility of slavery. Enslaved workers moved from the underground service corridors to the main house through narrow staircases tucked within coves. The sitting room was equipped with a revolving door and a dumbwaiter for enslaved servants to deliver food to Jefferson and his guests without being seen.

> Jefferson's conception was a step forward in the art of home-building. The colonists had crowded about themselves offices and shops for the conduct of a planter's business: weaving, dyeing, distilling, shoemaking, tailoring, blacksmithing, and wagonmaking. Jefferson began by concealing all these handicrafts, removing the symbols which suggested service, veiling the materials of our lower activities, perfecting and minimizing the labor in them, while he prevented their overflow into, and their hard intrusion upon, the spirit of a home. Not only did Monticello do this but it went farther by obscuring those that performed the labor. Dishwashers and cooks, butlers and maids came quietly through concealed passages; with wood, water, food, and ashes they ascended and descended stairs which had been cunningly tucked away in unobtrusive fashion. The old-time Virginian required for his own living, as well as for the entertainment of his guests, that troops of slaves be moving in all directions with wood for fires, cans for ashes, cold water for drinking, warm water for bathing, and hot water for shaving.[7]

This "step forward in the art of home-building" is the use of architecture as a device to build overlapping yet separate spheres for enslaved workers and their enslaver. Lambeth and Manning celebrate Jefferson's use of architecture as an apparatus to build the distinction between Black labor and white leisure. This is ultimately accomplished by treating enslaved workers as components of the house itself. They are mere utility, domestic technologies like the dumbwaiters and the revolving service doors that Jefferson built into his design.

Within this approach that celebrates Jefferson's innovations, a current of scholarship remains little changed since Fiske Kimball's 1916 *Thomas Jefferson, Architect.*[8] Kimball offers a concise chronological history of Jefferson's architectural influences and works, along with a thorough catalog of his architectural library and architectural drawings and renderings. He describes the Virginia estates that Jefferson knew as a child, the buildings he saw in England and France during his appointment as American ambassador to the court of Louis XVI, and the influence of Palladio's *I quattro libri* on his design methodology. His analyses of Jefferson's principal architectural works note the history of their design and construction and their spatial and formal organizations. Kimball offers a heroic narrative. The Virginia State Capitol, for instance, serves as a frontispiece to all of Virginia, having the dignity, expressiveness, and majesty adequate to the sovereign republican state and representing the classical culture of its builders.[9] The current iteration of these approaches dominates the 2019 publication edited by Lloyd DeWitt and Corey Piper, titled, in a nod to Kimball, *Thomas Jefferson, Architect.*[10]

Howard Burns opens the DeWitt and Piper volume with a broad intellectual biography of Jefferson detailing the range of influences on his architectural thought. These include the colonial American buildings he encountered in his youth and the French neoclassical and Roman architecture he saw as ambassador to France. Burns pays particular attention to Jefferson's active engagement with Palladio's *I quattro libri* as both a catalog of precedents and a tool for experimentation. Guido Beltramini describes the scope of Palladianism in the eighteenth century. Palladio could be a model, a precedent, or a catalog of available forms and elements. For Jefferson, according to Beltramini, Palladianism was a system. It offered a set of rules and guidelines, such as the sizes and proportions of architectural elements and the standardization of room sizes, to assist the builder in composing architectural forms and spaces and to determine the relationship between social rank and representation. Richard Guy Wilson follows Jefferson's journeys through England. He discusses the Palladian architecture and picturesque gardens that Jefferson visited and traces their influence in his work. Lloyd DeWitt extends this travelogue through the continent, looking to the works in the Netherlands, Paris, and Southern France that Jefferson admired—giving particular attention to the Maison Carrée in Nîmes as Jefferson's influence for the Virginia State Capitol. The volume concludes with chapters by Mabel Wilson and

Louis Nelson describing the place of slavery in Jefferson's works. It reads as an afterthought; by that point the book's theme has been set.

This scholarship hinges around a debate over whether to situate Jefferson's thought within the English Whig or French Enlightenment tradition. Palladianism was practiced largely in the private realm of Whig country estates. Tying Jefferson to the Palladian tradition associates his architecture with an English liberty that enjoyed political power, celebrated freedom of trade, and deferred abstractions of universal rights. Placing Jefferson in the French tradition puts him in the public space of civic monumentality, where universal rights were practiced with revolutionary vigor. These approaches elide a discussion of the enslaving plantation world in which Jefferson spent most of his life and realized all his architectural works.

The Dialectics of Liberty

Comparing Jefferson's Monticello to Frank Lloyd Wright's 1901 Ward W. Willits House in Highland Park, Illinois, Vincent Scully argued in 1970 that "an archaeologist of some later age, with only these ghosts to go on, might be led to believe that they revealed a century which was wholly single-minded in its speculation about a single theme."[11] This theme was freedom. More specifically, it was the political freedom of republicanism as articulated in the open composition of volumes. With the shift away from Jefferson's agrarian ideal over the ensuing century, this formal liberty—"always recessive but always there"—became the vehicle that carried forward a freedom no longer accessible to politics. Scully follows this framing of Jefferson's architecture as a precursor to an American modernity predicated on reason and ingenuity through the nineteenth century. To do this, he carefully limits his profuse examples of permutations of an American style to the Yankee North while suppressing the place of slavery in Jefferson's architecture.

Scully's methodology combines rigorous historical research with narrative leaps; the studious gaze of the connoisseur with an eye toward the fanciful; erudition with eclecticism. His tools are Heideggerian phenomenology, Freudian psychoanalysis, Jungian archetype analysis, and Kublerian prime objects and replications.[12] For Scully, broad historical movements and forces serve as the ultimate agency underlying a dialectical process of formal development. One can then read larger social and political movements in architecture's formal organization and tectonic expression. Scully employed domestic architecture to describe a dialectic through the nineteenth century between a uniquely American vernacular and an imported European classicism. Jefferson's Monticello initiates this dialectic; Wright's Willits House resolves it.

According to Scully, the American vernacular found its impetus in the wide expanse and boundless possibility of the American landscape. It reached after the endless horizon of the American West. Its formal markers included the interpenetration of volumes, spatial flow, horizontal continuity, interweaving of moldings, and elements that tie diverse volumes together. Its ideological stakes were explicitly the pioneer ideology and implicitly the manifest destiny of continental hegemony over North America. Opposed to this is an architecture imported from Europe. Its cubic volumes, strict order, geometrical uniformity, and heavy verticality intone the authoritarianism and limitations of old-world order. These forms were monarchical, privileging inherited power and received ideas over liberty and invention.

Thus the vernacular impetus for freedom is always trying to escape the bounds of classical authority, versus the classical order seeking to curtail wanton formal liberties. The American vernacular is spatial; its inventiveness comes in its expansion across the landscape. European architecture is temporal; it seeks stable forms legible across generations. Monticello plays a key role in these oppositions. Scully observes that "the completed Monticello shows a contradiction" in the fusion of the sprawling horizontal vernacular instinct native to the American landscape with a monumental and vertically aligned classicism that insists on looking back to Europe. In containing both sides of these divergent forces, it initiates the historical dialectic between them. This "contradiction" of liberty and authority that motivates the duality of American architecture through the nineteenth century seems a cipher for Jefferson's foundational contradiction that espoused universal liberty within an enslavement regime. For Scully, the *architectural* contradiction would be happily resolved through the long arc of the nineteenth century.

The vernacular remains hidden but ever present through periods of the consolidation of power by capital and the state. The democratic impetus—alienated from the political sphere—is sublimated in the tectonics of architecture. It quietly experiments with new forms until conditions are ripe for its reemergence. This occurs in the 1901 design for the Willits House, which appears as a synthesis of vernacular elements: cross-axial plan, interpenetrating spaces, interwoven details, and unifying roofs. After the doldrums of late nineteenth-century classicism, it points a way forward for American cultural rebirth through a formalizing of the vernacular into a progressive modernist impulse. It is also a replication of Monticello: a cross-axial plan expressing horizontal extent behind a protruding central bay. As Jefferson did in Monticello, Wright has the second-story windows read as clerestories to emphasize the ground floor. But Wright omits classicizing elements and reduces architecture to the human scale. "Jefferson's columns and domes are gone. . . . Jefferson's contradictory objectives have also disappeared."[13]

Jefferson's "contradictory objectives," as we have seen, are treated as purely formal, and Scully's dialectic between liberty and authority partitions the question of race. Scully can describe Monticello as a monument to "a man owning the earth" without mentioning the enslaved people subjected to that ownership. He can discuss architecture's horizontal reach to the extent of the landscape without having to bother about the Native American people displaced in its appropriation. Since all these crises and obstacles exist only at the formal level, their resolution can also be formal.

Jefferson's world was the plantation world. The houses he knew best were those of the plantation enslavers that were of his station, and Monticello maintained all the hierarchies and divisions developed in those houses.[14] To include domestic architecture of the South would mean to highlight those plantation houses. There, the admixture of classical and vernacular elements—in the tradition of Monticello—would play out against the backdrop of slavery. Those houses would be both domestic architecture for enslavers and sites of labor for the enslaved. The desire to reach across the landscape would necessarily read as the western expansion of the slave regime. The Dionysian drive for freedom that motivated nineteenth-century architecture would be couched within the organization of enslaved plantation labor and the violent control of enslaved people.

In his later lectures, Scully fully acknowledges the centrality of the Southern slave economy in Jefferson's thinking about architecture. His session on Jefferson in his celebrated Modern Architecture course at Yale followed the outline of his 1970 essay. In a lecture filmed shortly before his 2009 retirement, Scully modifies his argument to pointedly situate Jefferson and his works within an enslavement regime. He describes Monticello as an idealized enslaving plantation—Jefferson's own Vaux-le-Vicomte "modified by slave labor." He casts the University of Virginia in the image of a Southern village, and hence a slave village. The burden of the enslavement economy also takes on material expression in Scully's formalist methodology. He contrasts the heaviness of the low-resting domes at Monticello and the University of Virginia—signifying the entrenchment of an oppressive slave regime—with the light and airy dome at Charles Bullfinch's Massachusetts State House that stood at the center of the Northern abolitionist movement and New England transcendentalism.[15]

With this inclusion, we can imagine a different history. The formal liberty connecting Jefferson to Wright becomes white liberty predicated upon an enslaving plantation system and concluding in the white domination of the American West. The originating crisis of Jefferson might find its place in a narrative of the manifest destiny of white liberty. Enslavement might become a prominent factor in architecture's dialectical transformations through the nineteenth century. Wright's architecture might give tectonic expression to the legacies of enslavement in settler colonialist ideology.

Scully, however, needs a direct path from Jefferson to Wright in order for the westward development of the United States to be a progressive project. This narrative moves from Virginia to Illinois through the Yankee North. Partitioning slavery allows him to tell that story as the gradual realization of a uniquely American form fueled by the relationship to the frontier. Shaking off classical expression, finding a uniquely American form, and realizing a democratic architecture could not have occurred alongside a history of dispossession. Methodologically, the consideration of architecture solely upon the formal and aesthetic plane is what allows Scully to partition the politics within which these buildings were imbricated.

Jefferson's Ashes

Treating Jefferson in primarily formal terms was practiced on all sides of the architectural debates of the 1970s. In Manfredo Tafuri's 1973 *Architecture and Utopia*, Jefferson represents a term within a larger schematic that marks modern architecture's dialectical transformation toward the instrumental logic of capital.[16] Tafuri follows Max Horkheimer and Theodor Adorno's *Dialectic of Enlightenment*, where the Enlightenment contains within itself its own negation. For Tafuri, the central dialectic is the opposing forces of capitalist necessity and the bourgeois values that spring simultaneously from the project of Enlightenment. Modern architecture plays the ideological role expressing anguish at its participation in the bourgeois order while sublimating its internal conflict to the aesthetic plane. In his chapter "Reason's Adventure: Naturalism in the City in the Century of Enlightenment," the stakes of this dialectical movement were the sublimation of the instrumental logic of the capitalist city to the image of naturalism.

Piranesi and Jefferson occupy two opposing positions in this dialectic: Piranesi warns us of the crisis of the Enlightenment, while Jefferson seeks to resolve it. Piranesi anticipates the crisis of the Enlightenment at the moment of its origin. His *Il Campo Marzio* transforms the rational architectural systems that Durand would later codify into a science of type as "sublime uselessness." His *Carceri d'invenzione* are more "Prisons of Invention" than the common "Imaginary Prisons"; Enlightenment reason becomes oppressive and inescapable. Lastly, his *Capricci* signal the endgame of the Enlightenment's dialectic in the reduction of architecture's capacity to mean "a universe of empty signs." For Tafuri, Jefferson's classicism is always at the service of social values. At Jefferson's "monument to agrarian utopia," the "villa-farmhouse" of Monticello, the incorporation of modern technical innovations into neoclassical form hints at the social uses of classicism. With the Maison Carrée realized as political representation in the Virginia State Capitol, public reason became a diffusible social value. The varying Pavilions at the University of Virginia all realized in the same material style represent the permanence of classical values within the flexibility of its models.

We could go point by point through these examples. Briefly, the "monument to agrarian utopia" was anything but; the Virginia State Capitol governed a plantation world, with its classicism articulating a racialized culture of taste; the University of Virginia, where the sons of Southern planters could get a classical education without receiving abolitionist ideas, was run and maintained entirely by an enslaved workforce.[17] All of this was well known in 1976—particularly to a theorist so astute at uncovering architecture's role in alienation. Tafuri's Jefferson enters this argument as an abstraction, a resolution of opposing instincts by maintaining bourgeois values while contesting the capitalist necessity they are based upon. Jefferson's neoclassical buildings realized at the domestic scale offer a rearguard utopia that "acknowledges the foundations of the democratic system while opposing its concrete manifestations."[18] All of the examples that Tafuri cites to draw this conclusion were built around the organization and logistics of slavery. The legacies of enslavement must be partitioned from their neoclassical expression.

Piranesi's anticipation of the crisis of the Enlightenment and Jefferson's effort to resolve it comprise the main arc of Tafuri's 1980 *The Sphere and the Labyrinth*.[19] Its first chapter expands upon Tafuri's earlier writing on Piranesi; Jefferson remains in the background of its concluding chapter (written between 1976 and 1978, just after the publication of *Architecture and Utopia*) to describe a path not taken by modern architecture. Instead, Piranesi's *Capricci* come to life in the empty speech of the New York Five "sinking into the bottomless well of the autonomy of form."[20]

> All of this demonstrates that the "domestic" propositions of Thomas Jefferson, aimed at placating the *Dialektik der Aufklärung* [Dialectic of Enlightenment] no longer have any place in an America that nevertheless seeks consolation from them, among the repechages of the Bicentennial. The solitary games of the intellectuals fascinated by the cobra on the verge of striking them down no longer know what to make of the "ashes of Jefferson."[21]

The ashes of Jefferson are the failure of modern architecture to take that alternate path, to follow the example of Jefferson in reconciling the mobility of values with the stability of principles, and to avoid the fate so clearly outlined by Piranesi.

Tafuri ultimately needs Jefferson to stand at the origin of a historical avant-garde. Jefferson's resolution of bourgeois values with capitalist necessity represents a model for modern architecture to maintain a progressive social function. Alienation and enslavement must be partitioned to maintain the claims of this project. Reinhold Martin describes Tafuri's racial blindness as ideological: "For Tafuri, Thomas Jefferson was not first and foremost a slave owner, nor was he first and foremost white; rather, he was an abstraction, an allegory of the proto-bourgeois artist-intellectual and a precursor to the Euro-American avant-gardes."[22] For this abstraction to play its role as a marker in Tafuri's negative dialectic, it must be stripped of all opposing qualities. If Jefferson's "radical America" was in ashes, his *racial* America remained fully intact.

Thought and Sensation

Contemporary histories have continued to assign Enlightenment autonomy and disinterestedness to Jefferson's thought by partitioning discourses on race. In an analysis culled from excerpts of letters, diary entries, political writings, and practical treatises, Kenneth Hafertepe proposes that Jefferson's aesthetics derive largely from those of the 1762 *Elements of Criticism* by the Scottish Enlightenment thinker Henry Home, Lord Kames.[23] Jefferson, according to Hafertepe, differentiated between two types of beauty: formal and functional. Formal beauty included harmonious form, good proportion, and elegant ornament. The sense of formal beauty was universal and innate in all people. Functional beauty included the accuracy of a painting or the utility of a building. Functional beauty is found in the faculty of reason. These terms mirror Kames's terms of intrinsic beauty, dependent upon an innate and universal human sensibility, and relative beauty, dependent upon reason.[24]

The category of intrinsic beauty allowed Jefferson to disassociate elegant architectural forms from the political regimes in which they were produced. Hafertepe offers the example of the Maison Carrée as an appropriate model for a state capitol representing the people of Virginia. Its intrinsic beauty is independent of any Roman imperial associations. Functional beauty, found in reason, would allow the architect to fashion it as a site for democratic governance. According to Hafertepe, "It was didactic not because it appealed to the moral sense but because it appealed to the sense of beauty; by providing the citizenry with a concrete example of universally approved beauty." Neoclassical forms could be universally appreciated across political systems.[25] We might add that this works both ways; the formal beauty of enslaving estates could be considered separately from their utilitarian functions. Monticello, for Hafertepe, illustrates a formal beauty based upon Kames's criteria of uniformity and variety. The symmetry of the facade and the use of classical orders lends the building uniformity, while the formal buildup to the central pavilion and the use of different orders on the wings offers variety.[26] The innovations that resolved the classicism of Monticello with the requirements of an enslaving estate would constitute functional beauty.

Kames formulated his notions of intrinsic and relative beauty within an Enlightenment tradition that sought to identify a universal beauty, considering the variation among forms across and within cultures. Claude Perrault, for instance, had formulated his similar positive and arbitrary beauty to describe a common sense of beauty in classical orders despite wide variation in their proportions.[27] For Kames, different cultures realized universal intrinsic beauty by applying their reason to resolve its specificity. Jefferson found in Kames the tools to formulate a uniquely American architecture that would serve a didactic role in projecting universal beauty. Following Kames, he partitioned intrinsic beauty from morality, and hence from any political nature. For Kames, however, relative beauty requires "an act of understanding and reflection" and depends upon the capacity to reason.[28] Looking to Jefferson's writings on race, we can also see the ways in which this formulation allowed Jefferson to racialize his ideas on beauty by partitioning its aspects based upon reason from those that are universal.

Jefferson considered Black Africans and their descendants to be unfit for democratic participation and was at pains to distinguish them from Europeans and Native Americans, who he believed could hold a place in his agricultural democracy. In drawing these distinctions, Jefferson described Native Americans as "neither more defective in ardor, nor more impotent with his female, than the white reduced to the same diet and exercise."[29] He considered it likely that they were of the same species as his quasi-scientific category of "Homo sapiens europeaeus," the only distinction from Europeans being cultural. He thus thought that by promoting agriculture and trade with Native Americans, he could induce them to take up sedentary farming and integrate them into the US agricultural economy. In contrast to his optimism for Native American contributions to the United States, he saw no similar possibility for a free Black American population. Making the case that formerly enslaved people should never be integrated into American civil society, Jefferson noted the political obstacle of long-standing animosities that could only end "in the extermination of one or the other race." To this he added a far lengthier set of reasons that were "more physical and moral" than political:

> In general, their existence appears to participate more of sensation than reflection. To this must be ascribed their disposition to sleep when abstracted from their diversions, and unemployed in labour. An animal whose body is at rest, and who does not reflect, must be disposed to sleep of course. Comparing them by their faculties of memory, reason, and imagination, it appears to me, that in memory they are equal to the whites; in reason much inferior, as I think one could scarcely be found capable of tracing and comprehending the investigations of Euclid; and that in imagination they are dull, tasteless, and anomalous.[30]

Throughout this passage he distinguishes the capacity to reason possessed by Europeans and Native Americans from the base sensation experienced by Black people. Both Native Americans and Black people displayed bravery, but where in the case of the former it was a product of advanced strategy, for the latter it was the product of recklessness derived from a lack of foresight. For Jefferson, Black Americans could only experience things sensually—either in the immediate experience of the world or in carnal instincts and base passions. In his view, the love experienced by Black individuals kindled only the senses and not the imagination.

In his discussion of Jefferson, Hafertepe neglects to mention the instances of these categories being employed to dismiss the works of Black artists—and there are many.[31] Where a Black artist or author displayed undeniable talents, Jefferson presented them as emotive rather than intellectual. The works of the formerly enslaved abolitionist and author Ignatius Sancho, for instance, "do more to honor the heart than the head."[32] Reason, the marker of the Enlightenment, was reserved for others. In an enlightened republic, the capacity of reason that serves the basis of democratic self-governance is racialized.

Jefferson never wrote a formal treatise on aesthetics, nor even formulated a cohesive set of theories on the subject. But he may have set forth a theory of sentiments that employed artistic production as evidence of innate human difference. Hafertepe constructs this "Jeffersonian aesthetics" after the fact, through an analysis culled from the holdings of Jefferson's library and fragments of his letters that touch upon aesthetics as well as proximate inquiries into ethics and morals. He identifies a broad sensibility across Jefferson's written work and identifies it with thinking more clearly articulated by Kames. In this selective process, a Jeffersonian aesthetics follows Enlightenment precepts of autonomy and disinterestedness. Kames's aesthetics offered Jefferson racialized criteria in which the capacity for reason was circumscribed within the category of whiteness. In doing so, Hafertepe normalizes what is for Jefferson a racial distinction between sensation and thought by presenting them as autonomous aesthetic categories.

Conclusion

The historiography of Jefferson does not simply constitute an effort to partition him from the realities of enslavement; it is a broader effort to maintain claims upon architecture's modernity by carefully cultivating its origins. Jefferson stands at the origin of diverse historical projects, each posing arguments about modern architecture's foundations and potentials. These arguments have depended upon the omission of slavery. Through this, we can begin to consider how our understanding of modern architecture has been discreetly imbricated within the legacies of enslavement.

Historians have silently shaped the dialectics of modern architecture around the unacknowledged institution of slavery. For Lambeth and Manning, Monticello's "step forward in the art of home-building" was in the integration of the logistics of the enslaving plantation into the private sphere of the home. Enslaved people carrying "wood for fires, cans for ashes, cold water for drinking, warm water for bathing, and hot water for shaving" pose an alternate history of building systems where ducts, conduits, and plumbing are hidden from view. For Scully, the Apollonian and Dionysian interplay that drove a historical dialectic toward an autochthonous American form was motivated by the enslaver's control over the land. Scully never takes up the evolution of the plantation house—in which Monticello would play a key role. Instead of the plantation world, Monticello must take place against the backdrop of Yankee liberty. Hafertepe constructs a Jeffersonian aesthetics to transform observations on race into objective aesthetic criteria. Through aesthetic criteria, Jefferson could claim to distinguish the capacities for self-governance between the sensual African versus the European intellectual. Tafuri describes a negative dialectic that left only ashes in its wake and defeated Jefferson's "radical America" without affecting or acknowledging his racial America. Tafuri's methodology was singularly concerned with describing the historical arc of alienation. To consider race would have undermined the motivating dialectic that he set up in *Architecture and Utopia*. He preferred instead to adjudicate internecine debates between the neo-avant-garde "Whites" and "Greys"—ironically, accusing both sides of shirking political engagement in favor of autodidactic formal exercises. In each of these cases, historical method is maintained by partitioning the question of slavery. Modernist and postmodern histories, in general, were formed through this omission, making the legacy of enslavement central to those historical projects by the very effort of its omission. Slavery becomes structural to our inherited thinking about the possibilities and potentials of modern architecture, formulated within the racialized act of removing all traces of enslavement. The enslavement regime is a silent force that organized and configured the architectural forms of the nineteenth century and the historical thought of the twentieth. Despite the efforts to render enslavement invisible, we can still read its outlines through the absences and lacunae it has left behind in modern architecture's historiography.

Notes

1. Louis P. Nelson, "The Architecture of Democracy in a Landscape of Slavery: Design and Construction at Jefferson's University," in *Thomas Jefferson, Architect: Palladian Models, Democratic Principles, and the Conflict of Ideals*, ed. Lloyd DeWitt and Corey Piper (Chrysler Museum of Art; Yale University Press, 2019).

2. Carl Anthony, "The Big House and the Slave Quarters: Part I, Prelude to New World Architecture," *Landscape* 20, no. 3 (1976).

3. Dell Upton, *Architecture in the United States* (Oxford University Press, 1998).

4. Irene Cheng, "Race and Architectural Geometry: Thomas Jefferson's Octagons," *J19: The Journal of Nineteenth-Century Americanists* 3, no. 1 (2015): 121–130.

5. Mabel O. Wilson, "Notes on the Virginia Capitol: Nation, Race, and Slavery in Jefferson's America," in *Race and Modern Architecture: A Critical History from the Enlightenment to the Present*, ed. Irene Cheng, Charles L. Davis II, and Mabel O. Wilson (University of Pittsburgh Press, 2020).

6. Maurie McInnis and Louis P. Nelson, eds., *Educated in Tyranny: Slavery at Thomas Jefferson's University* (University of Virginia Press, 2019).

7. William A. Lambeth and Warren H. Manning, *Thomas Jefferson as an Architect and a Designer of Landscapes* (Houghton Mifflin, 1913), 17–18; quoted in Anthony, "Big House and the Slave Quarters," 14.

8. Fiske Kimball, *Thomas Jefferson, Architect* (1916; Da Capo, 1968).

9. Kimball, *Thomas Jefferson*, 41–43.

10. DeWitt and Piper, *Thomas Jefferson*. My discussion of this volume follows my review in *The Burlington Magazine*. Peter Minosh, review of DeWitt and Piper, *Thomas Jefferson*, *Burlington Magazine* 162, no. 1407 (2020): 549–550.

11. Vincent Scully, "American Houses: Thomas Jefferson to Frank Lloyd Wright," in *The Rise of an American Architecture*, ed. Edgar Kaufmann (Praeger, 1970), 163–209.

12. Eeva-Liisa Pelkonen, "Vincent Scully Detonates the Past," *Joellho*, no. 13 (2022): 43–58. Pelkonen situates Scully within art history's psychoanalytic turn.

13. Scully, "American Houses," 188–190.

14. Dell Upton, "White and Black Landscapes in Eighteenth-Century Virginia," *Places* 2, no. 2 (1985): 59.

15. "Vincent Scully | Thomas Jefferson (Modern Architecture Course)," lecture at Yale University ca. 2000–2009, posted May 12, 2018, by Vincent Scully Lectures, YouTube, https://youtu.be/Go8U42hPIDo.

16. Manfredo Tafuri, *Architecture and Utopia: Design and Capitalist Development*, trans. Barbara Luigi La Penta (MIT Press, 1976); Manfredo Tafuri, *Progetto e utopia: Architettura e sviluppo capitalistico* (Laterza & Figli, 1973).

17. Anthony, "Big House and the Slave Quarters"; Wilson, "Notes on the Virginia Capitol"; Nelson and McInnis, *Educated in Tyranny*.

18. Tafuri, *Architecture and Utopia*, 26.

19. Manfredo Tafuri, *The Sphere and the Labyrinth: Avant-Gardes and Architecture from Piranesi to the 1970s*, trans. Pellegrino d'Acierno and Robert Connolly (MIT Press, 1987); Manfredo Tafuri, *La sfera e il labirinto: Avanguardie e architettura da Piranesi agli anni '70* (G. Einaudi, 1980).

20. Tafuri, *Sphere and the Labyrinth*, 295.

21. Tafuri, *Sphere and the Labyrinth*, 300.

22. Reinhold Martin, "Drawing the Color Line: Silence and Civilization from Jefferson to Mumford," in Cheng, Davis, and Wilson, *Race and Modern Architecture*, 59–60.

23. Kenneth Hafertepe, "An Inquiry into Thomas Jefferson's Ideas of Beauty," *Journal of the Society of Architectural Historians* 59, no. 2 (2000): 216–231.

24. Hafertepe, "Jefferson's Ideas of Beauty," 217–218.

25. Hafertepe, "Jefferson's Ideas of Beauty," 224.

26. Hafertepe, "Jefferson's Ideas of Beauty," 220.

27. Claude Perrault, *Ordonnance for the Five Kinds of Columns After the Method of the Ancients*, trans. Indra Kagis McEwen (Getty Center for the History of Art and the Humanities, 1993); Claude Perrault, *Ordonnance des cinq especes de colonnes selon la methode des anciens* (Paris: Chez Jean Baptiste Coignard, 1683). See also Joseph Rykwert, *The First Moderns: The Architects of the Eighteenth Century* (MIT Press, 1980), 23–53; Alberto Pérez-Gómez, introduction to Perrault, *Ordonnance for the Five Kinds of Columns*, 1–44.

28. Hafertepe, "Jefferson's Ideas of Beauty," 218.

29. Thomas Jefferson, *Notes on the State of Virginia* (London: John Stockdale, 1787), 97.

30. Jefferson, *Notes on the State of Virginia*, 231–232.

31. Simon Gikandi discusses the ways that Jefferson's dismissals of Black artists and intellectuals worked to configure a white "culture of taste." Simon Gikandi, *Slavery and the Culture of Taste* (Princeton University Press, 2011).

32. Jefferson, *Notes on the State of Virginia*, 234.

18 ORDERING THINGS

ETHNOLOGY, EMPIRE, AND EVERYTHING ELSE AT THE LIBRARY OF CONGRESS

Diana Martinez

THOUGH IT MOST OFTEN PASSES without notice, the home of the nation's most important repository of knowledge is also a remarkably explicit monument to the white supremacist foundations of US empire. Inaugurated on November 1, 1897, the Library of Congress Building bore a particularly heavy representational burden,[1] not only because it was the nation's first purpose-built structure for the congressional and soon-to-be national library, but also because it was the first major project to be built in the US capital following the completion, in 1866, of Thomas Ustick Walter's expansion of the US Capitol building. Announced in 1873, a competition to design the library building forced architects to consider, for the first time since the conclusion of the Civil War, what a monumental image of the nation (that was not a Civil War monument) should look like. Themes of national unification that preoccupied architects for a scant generation were replaced by a desire to present an American civilization ascendant. In the short interim between the end of the Civil War and the preparation of the library's foundations, race was reconfigured as a scientized master narrative that combined an evolutionary logic with a desire to link an American cultural development to Western classical origins. This new civilizational order both organized the library's spaces and facades at the same time that it revealed the emerging ideological basis for the nation's still-nascent imperial ambitions.

At least initially, the call for a freestanding building for the Library of Congress was a response to a crisis of matter. In a report presented to the US Congress, Ainsworth Rand Spofford, the librarian of Congress, complained that his job had been reduced to "presiding over the greatest chaos in America"—one generated by the passage of an 1870 law that required that all books filing for American copyright send two copies to the Library of Congress.[2] In 1873 the library, still housed in an apartment inside the Capitol building, received 19,826 new items—a number that with the full industrialization of the printing trade increased dramatically each year.[3] Quite suddenly, the erudition of the librarian, once the calling card of the profession, was outmoded as data management became the object of the rapidly developing discipline of library science. What was once a collection organized according to Enlightenment-era systems of classification—ones that aligned with the presumed mental faculties of the learned readers who used the library—was transformed by copyright law into a potentially infinite repository of information. The shift of the library's contents from meaningfully ordered knowledge to alphanumerically (i.e., arbitrarily) ordered information constitutes what Zeynep Çelik Alexander has argued was a reconstruction of the world according to new regimes of data management.

Though Alexander's insights are essential to understanding an epistemic condition specific to the industrialization of print and an accompanying compulsion to keep everything printed, it is an assessment that treats the building itself as an insufficient shell—one unable to contain the nearly infinite and entropic growth of its contents. The building itself, and in particular its program of decoration, is important to understand, however, precisely because it was an attempt to impart meaning to this reconstruction, one that collided (not coincidentally) with the historical conclusion of the Reconstruction era. The building's richly decorated interior and exterior walls became a prominent canvas on which to represent a new ordering logic conceived to organize not books but rather a unifying conception of an increasingly diverse American society. The importance of the building as a monument was not trivial. The building was celebrated not on account of its revolutionary solutions to problems of storage and access, but for the cultural significance of its well-ordered facade, for the quality of its handcrafted ornament, and for the grandness of its reading rooms, meeting rooms, and monumental circulation spaces, all of which were presented as evidence of a great "civilizational achievement." In the end, the library's densely packed iron stacks—the building's ostensible reason for being—took up a scant quarter of the final building's total volume. The rest of the building was given over to a purely communicative function: as a showcase for "statues of illustrious authors . . . graphic paintings . . . sculptured emblems . . . [and] inscriptions drawn from the writings of the great scholars of the world"—a trove of symbols that broadcasted and forever enshrined American greatness on Capitol Hill, the nation's most prominent pedestal.[4]

A Modern Library or a "National Monument of Art"?

That the building would be both a monument and a storage facility was never a foregone conclusion. William F. Poole, librarian of the Chicago Public Library and leader of the modern library movement, vigorously advocated for a simple, energy-efficient, tightly packed brick warehouse, absent the lofty (and expensive to heat) reading rooms that defined the still relatively new national libraries of France and England. Frugal congressmen—wary of creating a pretentious "national library in imitation of European monarchies"—agreed. On the opposing side were congressmen like Newton W. Nutting of New York, who wanted to offer a grand gift to the public, arguing that the library "ought to be our largest and best building" to "emphasize the value that we set upon the education of our people." On this point Spofford was obstinate. The librarian wanted not only an efficient container but also a monument that would allow the United States to lay claim to a "foremost rank in civilization."[5] The competition brief included Spofford's suggestion to combine Poole's densely packed stacks with a reading room inspired by the British Museum Library's massive, circular, domed space. In 1873, when Spofford announced the competition to design the library, the debate was still unresolved.

Almost immediately upon winning the competition, the newly formed firm of Smithmeyer & Pelz encountered seemingly endless and irresolvable debates over potential sites, styles, material choices, and projected cost, frustrations that led Spofford to announce a second competition in 1886, which yielded the same result as the first, with Congress ultimately approving an only slightly modified version of the first prize-winning design.[6] The following years continued to be mired in delays, controversies, and debates, ultimately motivating Congress to fire Smithmeyer & Pelz. Congress placed the project in the hands of the "administration," enlisting the US Army Corps of Engineers, under the leadership of Brigadier General Thomas Lincoln Casey Sr. and civil engineer Bernard Green. As a team, Green and Casey had earned a reputation for efficient management and execution after completing the long-delayed construction of the Washington Monument, and though Casey did not work closely with Green on the Library of Congress Building, his thirty-one-year-old son, Edward Pearce Casey, would—a nepotism that was deeply resented by the embattled Smithmeyer & Pelz.

Ordering the Exterior

Despite the turmoil, the completed library is a remarkably unified monument. This was in part due to the clarity of Smithmeyer & Pelz's original design: Its parti pris, or organizational strategy, arranged the building's main and auxiliary programs into a logical progression of spaces that conformed to the conventions of Beaux-Arts design (fig. 18.1). The building's decorative program, however, was little more than a sketch by the time Green and Casey took over the project. Edward Casey, who had just returned from Paris where he trained at the Ècole des Beaux Arts, was deeply influenced by the dramatic last gasps of a nineteenth-century academic Romantic movement that grappled with the transfer of civilizational meaning from the walls of the cathedral to the pages of the book, a crisis that, as Victor Hugo famously argued, was instigated by the invention of the printing press.[7] At the Bibliothèque Sainte-Geneviève, Henri Labrouste aimed to reclaim the cultural significance of architecture through the introduction of modern innovations, including gas lighting and structural iron, and most pointedly, by directly addressing the significance of the printing press. Toward this end, Labrouste's most notable, or at least noticeable, contribution was the building's remarkably flat facades—plain surfaces on which he engraved the library's catalog—a move that absorbed the significance of the book into the walls of the building itself. Though the idea for the US national library was tackled only twenty years after

FIGURE 18.1. *Smithmeyer & Pelz, design for the Library of Congress Building, approved in 1886. Prints and Photographs Division, Library of Congress, LC-DIG-ppmsca-31513.*

the completion of the Sainte-Geneviève library, the US architects of the Library of Congress aimed to address a different set of historical conditions. In a nation with few architectural monuments to begin with, architecture would serve as proof of cultural achievement. At a moment when the United States was impatient to push past its difficult history, a new freestanding building for the Library of Congress presented the ideal vehicle with which to express the positive direction of a civilization ascendant.

Under these conditions, it would seem that the choice of style would be particularly fraught. Smithmeyer & Pelz, however, argued that their selection of an "Italian Renaissance" style was purely arbitrary. Indeed, they had prepared renderings on the same plan with twelve different architectural styles, including modern Renaissance, German Renaissance, Romanesque, German Gothic, and Victorian Gothic.[8] Despite this apparently random selection, the style's conventions afforded Green and Casey a clear structure with which to order a yet-to-be-determined content. The structural hierarchy of the palazzo's typical tripartite elevation, for example, was arranged to represent an evolutionary timeline. The visitor's first encounter with this timeline is preceded by an introduction to the library's metaphorical foundation: A fountain dedicated to Neptune animates the nation's claim to classical origins. Staircases on either side of the fountain pause at the level of the building's first floor, where the visitor finds little decoration, save for the rock-faced finish of the masonry itself. This rustication conveys not only the building's *firmitas* but also, by virtue of its supermateriality, the materiality of stone as such—a nod to deep, geological time (fig. 18.2). The entrance stairs vault over this first level and over a porte cochere to arrive at an entrance plaza, which allows the visitor a spectacular vantage point from which to view the entrance pavilion at the same time that it allows patrons to enter at the building's second level—typically, the piano nobile. The meaning of the basement's geological theme is clarified by the temporal progression revealed by the piano nobile, which is dedicated to various representations of primordial life. This is revealed in part by vermiculated quoins. The worm track–like mason's marks suggest an animate modification of nature, though one closely tied to an unconscious manipulation of matter. Though this form of rustication is commonly used, especially in Beaux-Arts architecture, it is given special significance in relation to the piano nobile's most striking ornamental elements: a series of thirty-three "ethnological heads" (fig. 18.3). Like many of the details of the exterior's decorative program, the idea for the ethnological heads was the impromptu suggestion of Bernard Green. Recalling the genesis of the idea in an interview with the journalist George Alfred Townsend, Green explained:

> It became necessary . . . to put something upon the keystones of windows as large as those, and it has been the habit in the past to carve fantastic heads such as people in the middle-ages were thinking about with their

FIGURE 18.2 (LEFT). *Southeast corner of the Thomas Jefferson Building of the Library of Congress, showing the tripartite division of the facade and its three different kinds of rustication. Photo by the author.*

FIGURE 18.3 (BELOW). *"Ethnological heads" produced for the exterior of the Library of Congress Building. Prints and Photographs Division, Library of Congress, LC-USZ62-101889.*

mixture of piety and diabolism (and) it occurred to me that over [at] the National Museum were models taken from the life of nearly all the races—at least all the American races, and I suggested to the custodian in ethnology there, that we use these heads upon the public library. He warmly entered into the idea, for he is strong in that hobby.

So, we have had the granite carved in the front of the building with

> types of white races, the European you may say; in the rear we have put the black races, at the pavilions we have put the intermediate races.[9]

Deeply satisfied that he was able to represent the work of a neighboring institution, "these faces," Green effused, "work right in with the National Museum which is not very long-established." For Green, the ethnological heads exemplified how "the library *unconsciously* develops ideas as we go along," as part of a process that responded to unfolding "actualities." This "unconscious" process excited Townsend, who took it as "happy evidence . . . that we are getting a national university without knowing it." Elaborating, Townsend wrote that his own interest in the national library was that it was part of "the general substitute of facts for names" that organically "come(s) together like the wise men of the East, traveling by the star till they came upon the child who was to be the new era." In other words, Townsend viewed the library, along with the racial order that it "unconsciously" promulgated, as proof of an ineluctable and providential mandate for the nation. That Green placed little emphasis on his own authorial role was a means of legitimizing a process presented as a sort of channeling of the nation's spirit. Underscoring the idea that this project was sanctioned by the divine winds of a "new era," Townsend pointed to the seemingly cosmic coincidence that "there are just 33 windows requiring these carved keystones," which matched "oddly enough with the fact that there are about 33 races of men."[10]

Installed as mascarons above arched windows that wrap around the building, the ethnological heads were, according to the official *Handbook of the New Library of Congress*, "unique" as "a first instance of a comprehensive attempt to make ethnological science contribute to the architectural decoration of an important public building."[11] Carved by the sculptors William Boyd and Henry J. Ellicott, the heads, the *Handbook* explained, were not portraits but rather the result of "data accumulated by the curator of the National Museum's ethnology department." For six months the curator, Otis Tufton Mason, worked closely with Ellicott and Boyd, poring over books, photographs, "carefully verified measurements . . . [and] life sized models, chiefly of savage and barbarous peoples." Detailing the rigorous process of producing the heads, the *Handbook* continued:

> Any attempt at dramatic or picturesque effect, except what was natural to the type portrayed, was felt to be out of place. Each head was subjected to the strict test of measurement—such as the ratio of breadth to length and height, and the distance between the eyes and between the cheek bones—this being the most valuable criterion of racial differences. All portraiture was avoided, both as being somewhat invidious and unscientifically personal, and, more especially, because no one man can ever exemplify all the average physical characteristics of his race.[12]

In other words, these heads were not intended to be representations of people who were members of a race, so much as they were intended to be representations of a racial construct, or an *idea about race*. Though the idea of a racial construct is today a familiar commonplace, in this instance it was explicitly the case, as these faces were supposedly synthesized averages of racial data. Though the heads were intended to be viewed as statistically generated, they were also to be understood as *natural* categories. These categories were verifiable, according to Daniel Brinton's *Races and Peoples* (the ethnological textbook to which the *Handbook* refers), on account of the "common observation that . . . to our eyes all Chinamen look alike . . . [and] one cannot distinguish an Indian 'buck' from a 'squaw.' But you can recognize very well the one as a Chinaman, the other as an Indian."[13] That the "traits of a race overslaugh the variable characters of the family, the sex, or the individual" was, Brinton argued, the "corner-stone" of the science of ethnography.[14] Brinton's confidence about the concreteness of racial characteristics was apparently not shared by the artists themselves. A close examination of Mason's collection exposed that most of the heads were in fact not generated from compiled measurements but modeled after actual people.[15] What biographical notes remain of them reveal that the "Esquimaux" was likely modeled after a man named Yoo-Ka-Lucke from South Labrador, who was a practicing Christian educated at a missionary post in his Native village. The name of the "Hindu" closely resembled D. Joseph, an East Indian who, along with his wife, had been placed on display at the Columbian Exposition's Ceylon Building exhibit and tearoom on the Midway Plaisance. The "Modern Egyptian," was a near identical match to the photograph of Mahomet el-Bashe, who had also been put on display on the Midway, as a camel driver in the "Cairo Bridal Procession."[16]

Methodically arranged according to strict racial divisions, the four races considered white were installed on the elaborately decorated entrance pavilion—the building's tallest and most prominent volume. Twenty-four "intermediate" races were installed on the slightly shorter corner pavilions, and the five races considered Black were placed on the rear facade (fig. 18.4). The groups were not only separated but also ranked within their respective groups: Relative proximity to the front and center was a mark of superiority. Thus, the "Blonde European" and "Brunette European," who represented the end of racial evolution, directly face library patrons as they enter the building. Meanwhile, the "Russian Slav" and "Circassian" heads, representative of white races of a slightly lower order, occupy the sides of the entrance pavilion.

Just as the significance of the rock-faced rustication was revealed by the piano nobile's narrative of evolution, the significance of the ethnological heads (and their ordering) is laid bare by the ornament of the entrance pavilion's topmost register. There, the busts of nine great white worthies embody the apotheosis of American civilization. Each bust is set within an oculus that breaks the apex of its own

FIGURE 18.4. *Detail of the rear elevation of the Thomas Jefferson Building of the Library of Congress, showing the five representative heads of the "primitive races." Photo by the author.*

miniature temple front. Putti, foliate volutes, and festoons overburdened by heavy fruit conjure the fertility of their minds. Hand-selected by Spofford, these representative men are arranged in symmetrical pairs. On either side of the portico were Demosthenes and Dante—classical bookends. Ralph Waldo Emerson and the Scottish writer Sir Walter Scott (adjacent to his American disciple Washington Irving) are inset into the portico's pavilions.[17] At the very center is Benjamin Franklin, presented as the embodiment of a distinctly American practical genius (fig. 18.5). He is flanked on the left by Thomas Babington Macaulay, the famed statesman and Anglo chauvinist, and on the right by the great Saxon Goethe. To the further left and right are Irving and his fellow American Nathaniel Hawthorne.

Carved in a manner similar to Roman senatorial portraits, each veristic bust emphasized the experience and vibrant internal life of the man depicted. That Spofford, who was appointed to his post by Abraham Lincoln, was an abolitionist of some renown is worth noting here.[18] As was the case with Emerson, Spofford's valorization of Anglo-Saxon scholarship was to the exclusion of everything and everyone else. Spofford's opprobrium for chattel slavery—a position shared among all of the American worthies he selected—was not an indication of a commitment to racial egalitarianism. As Nell Irvin Painter argues, for abolitionists like Emerson and Spofford, slavery was a relic of barbarism and was thus incongruous with the values of an advanced Anglo-Saxon civilization.[19] Whatever the case, in failing to identify worthies from the Black or "intermediate" races, Spofford and Green precluded the possibility that representatives of these races were capable of high levels of cultural achievement. Spofford's curation of the names was particularly important when viewed against the increasingly chaotic collec-

FIGURE 18.5. *Bust of Benjamin Franklin, placed at the center of the nine great worthies selected by Ainsworth Rand Spofford to adorn the facade of the Library of Congress Building. Prints and Photographs Division, Library of Congress, LC-DIG-highsm-01922.*

tion housed within the library. In canonizing white achievement, the entrance pavilion completed a cosmogram of a racially ordered American civilization.

The racial hierarchy of the exterior is not easy for the everyday visitor to grasp, mostly on account of the prominence of the entrance pavilion. The ethnological heads of the "intermediate" races, for example, are both set back from the projecting entrance and separated from it by a seven-bay intermezzo. Thus they are barely visible to visitors entering the building. Likewise, it is difficult to observe the precise meaning of placing the Black races on the back of the building, a significance revealed only if one observes the building in the round. The decoration of the entrance pavilion is likely the only part of the building that the everyday visitor gets to see up close. When viewed in isolation, the entrance leaves the visitor with the impression that the building simply excludes other races, rather than assimilating other races into a precisely ordered, hierarchical logic (fig. 18.6).

A Coordinated Interior

If the racial ordering of the exterior is rendered indecipherable by the sheer scale of the building, then the message is multiply reinforced within the building's inte-

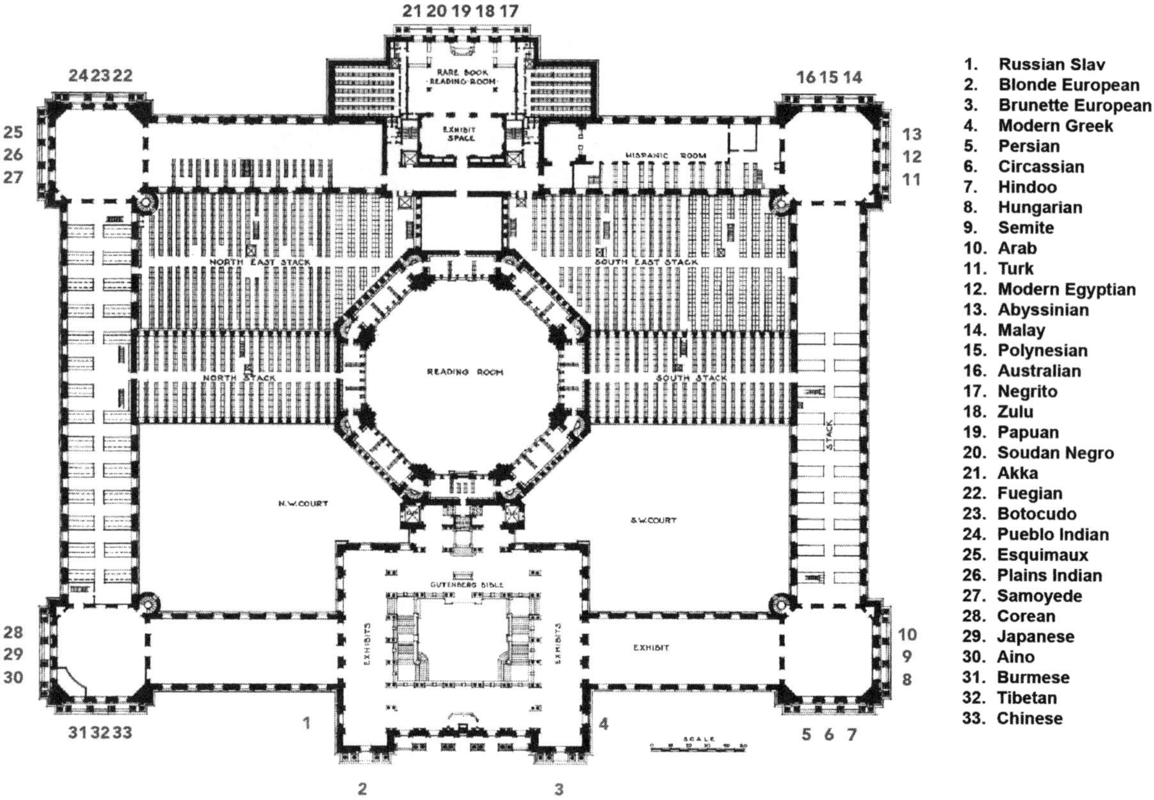

FIGURE 18.6. *Plan showing the locations of the "ethnological heads" on the facade of the Library of Congress Building. The "white" races are numbered 1–4, the "intermediate" races are numbered 5–16 and 22–33, and the "primitive" races are numbered 17–21. Plan from the Prints and Photographs Division, Library of Congress, LC-USZ62-109562; with additions by the author.*

rior.[20] By 1893, when exterior work was about half complete, Green and Casey had saved enough money to fund a lavish program of ornament. Fortunately for them, it was not difficult to find artists. All of those who worked on the interior decoration of the library had just completed work on the World's Columbian Exposition. Three of the most prominent among them, John Quincy Adams Ward, Olin Levi Warner, and Augustus Saint-Gaudens, were charged with overseeing hundreds of individual commissions.

One of the first and largest of these was a set of three massive bronze doors that serve as the library's main entrance. Here the visitor first encounters a compact and thus more legible composition of an American racial order, which was here combined with an evolutionary history of media. Warner designed the tympana on the left and right side, representing the oral tradition and writing, respectively, while Frederick William MacMonnies carved the center tympanum, representing printing—the most modern media. For the oral tradition, Warner places six figures in a tightly grouped sacra conversazione, or sacred conversation, a Venetian Renaissance convention wherein saints from different historical epochs sit in the relaxed company of an enthroned Virgin and Child.[21] In Warner's version, a woman in classical garb sits with a putto resting against her knee. On her left side sits a Native American figure holding arrows next to a "prehistoric man" with a stone axe lying by his side. On her right side sit representatives considered to be of relatively more advanced cultures: a Norseman wearing a winged steel cap and a shepherd with his crook who represents the "nomadic, pastoral races."[22] All sit in rapt attention, ready to receive the lesson of civilization. Remarkably, though the Norseman, prehistoric man, and shepherd are all generic figures, the *Handbook* takes care to note that the face of the Native American is understood to be a portrait of Chief Joseph of the Nez Perce, from a sketch made from life by Warner in 1889 (just seven years before the completion of the library). This was, in other words, a historical allegory depicting contemporary conditions.

The doors prepare the attentive visitor for their first encounter with the building's spectacular interior—the Great Hall—a soaring, two-story arcade of white and pale-gray marble sandwiched between two saturated zones of color: a floor of polished, inlaid stone and a coved ceiling covered in frescoes. On the first level, the arches are supported by Ionic pilasters and engaged columns superimposed upon robust piers. The solidity of the lower floor is relieved by the airiness of the upper level, where arches spring from slender pairs of Corinthian columns. The room is dominated by images of youth; a parade of putti ascend along the room's two grand staircases. Conceived by Philip Martiny (whose plaster models were copied by government stone carvers), the first and largest group consists of sixteen putti carved in high relief into the stair railing. Depicting various "occupations, habits, and pursuits of modern life," the putti, who gaily go about their work, are broadly representative of the nation's growing force of free labor.[23] They are met at the top by six figures representing the fine arts, and thus the apotheosis of culture. Comedy, poetry, and tragedy occupy the balustrade of the north landing, while painting, sculpture, and architecture occupy the south. The most striking of the putti groups—the only marble sculptures in the round—are two pairs of racialized putti personifying America, Africa, Asia, and Europe (figs. 18.7, 18.8). Carved at roughly twice the scale of the putti in the railings, each couple sits atop a buttress that marks each staircase's intermediate landing. The *Handbook* describes the group thusly:

> *America* is an Indian, with a tall headdress of feathers, a bow and arrow, and a wampum necklace. With one hand he shades his eyes while he gazes intently into the distance, awaiting, one may fancy, the coming of his conqueror, the white man. *Africa* is a little negro, with a war-club and his savage necklace of wild beasts' claws. *Asia* is a Mongolian, dressed in flowing silk robes, the texture of which, as the visitor will notice, is very perfectly indicated by arranging the folds of the marble so that they receive the proper play of light and shade. In the background is a sort of dragon-shaped jar of porcelain. *Europe* is clad in the conventional classic costume, and has a lyre and a book; and a Doric column [*sic*] is intro-

duced beside him—the three objects symbolizing, specifically, Music, Literature, and Architecture, and, more broadly, the pre-eminence of the Caucasian races in the arts of civilization generally, just as the dragon-jar on the other side of the globe stands for the admirable ceramic art of China and Japan; and, also, as the wampum and bow of the Indian indicate his advance in culture over the stage of evolution typified by the rude war-club and savage necklace of the negro.[24]

Here Martiny was able to elaborate the master narrative through a more robust use of classical conventions than was available to the sculptors of the ethnological heads. The lyre, Ionic colonnette, book, dragon jar, wampum bag, "war club," and "savage necklace" are meant to assist the viewer in assigning each personification a spot on a racial hierarchy. Europe, with its putto's attributes of architecture, literature, and music, has attained the highest level of civilization. Asia's dragon jar, meanwhile, provides evidence of an ability to produce fine crafts, though Martiny provides no attribute suggesting intellectual achievement. This is of course even less so the case with America and Africa. All of the figures except for one look down onto the floor of the foyer. The exception is America, who shields his eyes as he looks off into the distance. Though the *Handbook* proposes that he is "awaiting . . . the coming of his conqueror," *America* is also looking directly at the entrance, toward the guests who enter the library, but also toward the Capitol building beyond, which lies due west of the library. While this direct address of the library patron has been interpreted as a simple greeting,[25] it also suggests that those who enter the building, by encountering an image of Native America, are also entering into the narrative of manifest destiny.

Ordered Races and the Ineluctable Empire

The racial ordering of the Library of Congress Building was not only a reflection of an evolving narrative of racial progress but also a projection of an order onto the world. The abolition of slavery and the ostensible end of the Indian Wars did not mark the beginning of an era of racial egalitarianism. To the contrary, those "closing" events gave way to a hierarchical integration not only of the nation's Black, Native, and immigrant subjects but also of people and places increasingly subject to American "intervention." On this matter, Spofford believed that the library played a necessary role. One of Spofford's specific laments about the library's lack of comprehensiveness was that there was not enough material for congressmen to fully grasp international political conditions in which the Congress had an increasing interest. He used the example of the outbreak, in 1895, of the British-Venezuelan border crisis, when it was found that "two-thirds of the books relating to Venezuela and its border-countries in South America, needed for ref-

FIGURE 18.7. *Racialized cherubs representing Asia and Europe in the interior decoration of the Library of Congress Building. Prints and Photographs Division, Library of Congress, LC-DIG-highsm-01979.*

FIGURE 18.8. *Racialized cherubs representing the Americas and Africa in the interior decoration of the Library of Congress Building. Prints and Photographs Division, Library of Congress, LC-DIG-highsm-01759.*

erence by the Venezuelan Commission, were not in the Library of Congress." It is unclear whether those books would have affected the outcome of the Venezuelan crisis, which the United States "resolved" by invoking the Monroe Doctrine to force the British to accept the US terms of arbitration. What was made clear at this moment was the nation's full embrace of its new role as a world power.[26]

Fully assuming this new role, only six months after the library building's inauguration, the United States declared war on Spain. The US challenge to a deteriorating Spanish Empire was a war of imperial aggression, declared, it seems, without locating details of legal precedent, economic data, or historical knowledge now made easily accessible in the Library of Congress's "comprehensive" collection. In this respect, all of the information contained within the library's scientifically ordered stacks has less to reveal about the course of US empire than did the meanings and messages expressed in the library's heavily articulated decorative program, a projection of a new era of reconstruction—one that signaled the unequal integration of the world's diverse populations into the US empire's new racial order.

Notes

1. In June of 1980, the library building was renamed the Thomas Jefferson Building.

2. Ainsworth Rand Spofford, quoted in Zeynep Çelik Alexander, "Stacks, Shelves, and Restructuring the Library of Congress," *Grey Room* 82 (Winter 2021), https://www.greyroom.org/issues/82/144/stacks-shelves-and-the-law-restructuring-the-library-of-congress/.

3. Today the Library of Congress adds ten thousand new items to its collection each day. See "About the Library," Library of Congress, https://www.loc.gov/about.

4. Today, the Library of Congress's collection of 171 million cataloged items far exceeds what in 1873 was thought to be the original building's generous accommodation of 2 million books. See "General Information," Library of Congress, https://www.loc.gov/about/general-information.

5. Ainsworth Rand Spofford, "The Function of a National Library," in *Handbook of the New Library of Congress*, by Herbert Small (Boston: Curtis & Cameron, 1897), 124.

6. See John Y. Cole, "Smithmeyer & Pelz: Embattled Architects of the Library of Congress," *Library Quarterly: Information, Community, Policy* 80, no. 4 (2010): 301–310.

7. Hugo's argument that the printing press would kill architecture ("Ceci tuera cela," or "This will kill that") was famously staged in his 1831 novel *Notre-Dame de Paris*.

8. Though Smithmeyer & Pelz had selected an "Italian Renaissance" style and had determined positions for the placement of architectural sculpture, neither Smithmeyer nor Pelz felt that the ornament was integral to the design. The twelve different stylistic variations presented by Smithmeyer & Pelz were, as they testified, an exhausting attempt to satisfy the different desires of fickle and frugal congressmen. Thirteen years after Smithmeyer & Pelz won the initial competition, Congress approved a design that was an only slightly modified version of their initial entry. Cole, "Smithmeyer & Pelz," 301–310.

9. George Alfred Townsend, "Townsend's Letter: Congressional Library Half Completed," *Boston Daily Globe*, October 4, 1891, 26.

10. Townsend, "Congressional Library," 26.

11. Small, *Handbook of the Library of Congress*. Not only were the ethnological heads novel, but so was the use of architectural sculpture. As Michele Bogart points out, in the first half of the twentieth century, American architects produced relatively unadorned, neoclassical structures. The style did not preclude sculptural ornamentation, but the decoration seldom featured statuary. In the mid-twentieth century, major architects like Andrew Jackson Downing and Alexander Jackson Davis worked in the Gothic and Italianate styles and enhanced their structures with ornamental brackets, moldings, and multicolored patterns of brick and roof tiling, but not with figural sculpture. See Michele Bogart, "In Search of a United Front: American Architectural Sculpture at the Turn of the Century," *Winterthur Portfolio* 19, no. 2/3 (1984): 151–176.

12. Small, *Handbook of the Library of Congress*, 14.

13. Brinton, *Races and Peoples* (New York: N. D. C. Hodges, 1890), 18. The terms "buck" and "squaw" were derogatory words for Native American men and women, respectively.

14. Brinton, *Races and Peoples*, 18.

15. John J. Wayne, "The Jefferson Building's Keystone Heads at 100: A Detective Report," *Library of Congress Information Bulletin* 50 (1991): 458–464. This inspection was conducted in 1991, as part of a commemoration of the centenary of the installation of the heads.

16. John J. Wayne, "The Jefferson Building's Keystone Heads at 100: A Detective Report," *Library of Congress Information Bulletin* 50 (1991): 458–464.

17. Scott's *Ivanhoe* not only influenced Irving but also led legions of Southerners to romanticize their Anglo heritage. In his book *Life on the Mississippi*, Mark Twain blamed Scott for nothing less than actually causing the Civil War, arguing that by valorizing white roots that had little to do with the reality of Southern culture, Scott caused "measureless harm; more real and lasting harm, perhaps, than any other individual that ever wrote." Mark Twain, *Life on the Mississippi* (New York: Grosset & Dunlap, 1874), 375.

18. Spofford was the author of *The Higher Law: Tried by Reason and Authority* (1851), an at first anonymously published pamphlet written in response to the Fugitive Slave Act of 1850.

19. Indeed, ridding the world of slavery in "less advanced" nations was used as a moral justification for the US colonization of the Philippines. See Michael Salman, *The Embarrassment of Slavery: Controversies over Bondage and Nationalism in the American Colonial Philippines* (University of California Press, 2001).

20. The natural comparison here is to the front elevation of the Palais Garnier (1861–1875), where all of the ornament is systematically integrated into a facade that is very much about music and about preparing the visitor for the experience inside the building. On account of the Palais Garnier's compactness, it is a far more legible composition.

21. Thomas P. Somma, "American Sculpture and the Library of Congress," *Library Quarterly* 80, no. 4 (2010): 311–335.

22. Small, *Handbook of the Library of Congress*, 19.

23. Small, *Handbook of the Library of Congress*, 26.

24. Small, *Handbook of the Library of Congress*, 25. Note that the column behind the Europe figure is an Ionic column, as distinguished by the capital's volutes (exaggerated in scale) and by the column's fluting and slender proportions.

25. Somma, "American Sculpture," 335.

26. See Spofford, "Function of a National Library," 124.

19 CHICAGO FRAME

EVOLUTION, ETHNOLOGY, AND THE IDEA OF THE FIRST SKYSCRAPER

Joanna Merwood-Salisbury

THE IDEA THAT WILLIAM LE BARON JENNEY'S Home Insurance Building, completed in Chicago in 1885, was the first skyscraper ever built is one of the most entrenched myths in the history of American architecture. The myth, which rests on the erroneous belief that it was the first wholly skeleton-framed building, took hold soon after the Home Insurance Building was demolished in 1931 and the building's owners commissioned a committee of experts to examine the building's structural system (fig. 19.1).[1] Written by Chicago architect and architectural historian Thomas Tallmadge, the committee's report became a central plank in the rhetoric of technological advancement and originality that supports the concept of a "Chicago School" of architecture. The claim was popularized by an exhibition of Chicago architecture mounted by the Museum of Modern Art in New York in 1933, in the wake of the better-known International Style show displayed the previous year.[2] Cocurated by Henry-Russell Hitchcock, the exhibition was centered on the desire to find an American basis for modern architecture in Chicago's innovative commercial structures of the 1880s and 1890s. Key to its message was the idea of material and tectonic progress from masonry to skeleton-framed structures, as shown in the famous photograph of the architect and curator Philip Johnson standing in front of models made for the MoMA show (fig. 19.2). Though this exhibition is little remembered today, its influence is significant. Its ideological agenda was to posit an explicitly American structural technology as the key formal signifier of an apparently depoliticized modern style. As Colin Rowe wrote, by the 1950s the "Chicago frame" had become the universal expression of modern architecture, and the attributes of American architecture came to be seen as transnational ones.[3]

FIGURE 19.1. *The American architect Andrew Nicholas Rebori, with others, examines a column of the Home Insurance Building at the southwest corner of the building's fifth floor in 1931. Getty Images.*

FIGURE 19.2. *The architect and curator Philip Johnson with models demonstrating the structural "evolution" of the skyscraper. The models were commissioned for the exhibition* Early Modern Architecture: Chicago, 1870–1910, *at the Museum of Modern Art in New York, January 18 to February 23, 1933. Getty Images.*

The myth of the Home Insurance Building as the first skeleton-framed skyscraper has been endlessly repeated across all media imaginable. Although challenged in academic publications, beginning with the work of Gerald R. Larson in the 1980s, it continues to have a powerful hold on the popular imagination.[4] As Dell Upton has written, in the historiography of the discipline, American architecture is defined by its originality: the idea that at some undefined point in the late nineteenth or early twentieth century, it assumed a unique and distinctive form. The persistence of this definition is perplexing, Upton notes, since in most areas of intellectual life, apart from right-wing politics, the idea of American exceptionalism is rejected. But "in the study of American architecture it has not yet been dismissed, in part because the nationalist discourse in architecture has played out historically in ways that have made it difficult for architectural thinkers to abandon it."[5] In this discourse, the suburban house and the skyscraper play important roles as built signifiers of exceptionalism—the only types that the nation could plausibly claim as its own. The suburban house embodied America's distinct political identity and values, encapsulated by the term "democracy," and the skyscraper embodied the development of a functional and pragmatic architecture characterized by American technological ingenuity. Since the 1930s, Jenney's Home Insurance Building has served as an exemplar of those characteristics.

At the heart of the mythology surrounding Jenney's iconic building is the biological analogy central to the design theory of the modern movement: the belief that architectural forms and technologies, like living organisms, adapt or evolve according to their environment.[6] Imported from European design theorists, the desire to escape from history by discovering universal "first principles" of design derived from biological science dominated the rhetoric of American architecture in the second half of the nineteenth century. As Gregory Dreicer and Irene Cheng have pointed out, respectively, two nested ideas dominate these discussions: the belief that architecture, as a primary and palpable form of technological production, may be understood as a marker of evolutionary advancement; and the belief that technological ingenuity, or progress away from a so-called primitive state, differs according to innate racial and cultural capabilities.[7] Transposed from biology into diverse forms of social organization and cultural production, the concept of technological evolution became the primary framework through which to assess national progress.

Although Jenney holds secondary status in histories of American architecture because his built work is seen as aesthetically inferior to that of the Chicago architects he mentored, his writing contains a clear explanation of the way in which ideas of architectural evolution were employed in professional circles. In texts published from 1885 to 1891, Jenney set out to explain the practical origins of the skeleton-framed skyscraper, as well as its evolutionary significance. These texts demonstrate the intellectual influence of his European education, the mutual influence of the close-knit circle of professional architects in Chicago, and the broader sociopolitical context of the rise of technological expertise and professionalism in the years following the Civil War. Performed on a grand stage, the conjoined ideas of architectural and ethnographic progress rehearsed in Jenney's essays were enacted in the exhibitions and lectures presented at the World's Columbian Exposition of 1893. Here, anthropological and architectural concepts of evolution were first used to explain the rise of Chicago as an industrial metropolis, prefiguring the idea of the Midwestern metropolis as the place where the modern style first emerged.[8] Transmitted via the mythology of the Chicago School, the analogy of evolution is a constant in histories of American architecture.[9] Even today, this concept is routinely used in discussions of the Chicago frame and other structural systems, with little recognition that it was once defined in explicitly racial terms.

From Engineering to Ethnology: Jenney and the Evolutionary Narrative

To understand the endurance of the Home Insurance Building myth, we must examine how ideas of evolutionary progress were embedded in Jenney's own writings and professional context. The analogy of evolution was not imposed upon the iconic building after the fact but was embedded within it. In 1884, Jenney was commissioned by the Central Deposit Vault Company (a real estate financing company) to prepare plans for a ten-story, fireproof office building for the Chicago headquarters of the New York–based Home Fire Insurance Company, to be erected on a site at Adams and LaSalle Streets in Chicago.[10] The building would house two large banks on the principal story, with well-lit offices above. This commission coincided with a series of lectures Jenney offered at the University of Chicago, where he was on the faculty during the 1883–1884 academic year.[11] A graduate of the École Centrale des Arts et Manufactures, Jenney was deeply influenced by Eugène Emmanuel Viollet-le-Duc's and James Fergusson's ethnographic versions of architectural history, quoting these authorities in support of an argument about the vital link between architectural style, the scientific theory of evolution, and distinct racial characteristics.[12] In summarizing the architecture of the classical period, Jenney wrote, "Each style has been evolved from what has gone before, under the influence of race traditions, the religion, the available building materials, and the requirements of the civilization; in short, what the zoologists call 'the environment.'"[13] The vital link between architectural history and ethnography was an idea he would return to again and again throughout the course of the twelve lectures, a rapid and eclectic survey of the architecture of the "savage tribes," Egypt, Assyria, Greece, Rome, and the Middle Ages.

Assembled from respected European sources, it is not surprising that Jenney's history was an operative one: He was, after all, not primarily an academic but a practitioner. Though he would later be criticized for his lack of artistry and cast as primarily an engineer, despite his formal training in Paris and his long professional experience, in 1884 Jenney was a significant figure among Chicago's professional architects. His belief that racial progress could be measured through technological development reflected the dominant worldview of his peers, many of whom gave speeches and published widely on the future of "American architecture" in contemporary journals. The lectures he delivered at the University of Chicago were republished in the first volume of *The Inland Architect and Builder*, the official journal of the Western Association of Architects. Intended to inspire both students and colleagues, these lectures advocated for the development of a new "native" architectural style, one shaped by the local climate, material conditions, and social aspirations of the American Midwest.

Jenney's explicit employment of racial terms included a description of contemporary Americans as hybrid descendants of the three "great building races of the ancient world": the Turanians (including the Egyptians), the Celts, and the Aryans. Mixing with the methodical nature of the Turanians and the lively artistry of the Celts, the intellectual and practical Aryans had produced, in ancient Greece, the most brilliant civilization the world had ever seen. Appearing most recently in northern and western Europe, the descendants of this hybrid race were on the move, "migrating westward and spreading themselves over the United States from the Gulf of Mexico to Canada and the Pacific to produce a new center of civilization; and if we could but cast its horoscope, we should see a future whose dazzling brilliance would eclipse all that had gone before."[14] Although Jenney's lectures are based on the relationship between ethnology and architectural development, he makes no mention of the Indigenous occupants of this massive land area. In his history of architecture, they simply have no place, even among the so-called savage tribes. As for races not descended from the favored Turanian-Celtic-Aryan intermarriage, Jenney made a claim that erased them from narratives of American architectural history constructed in biological terms: "To the zoologist the differences of the Aryans, the Semites and the Negro are sufficiently marked and persistent to establish distinct species in the genus homo."[15] In other words, for Jenney, the descendants of eastern European Jews and the peoples of the African continent were, and would always remain, distinct biological races, with distinct and unalterable hereditary characteristics, including differences in temperament and intelligence.

These ideas were far from unusual among academics and professionals during this period. For example, the Harvard geologist Nathaniel S. Shaler, an advocate of race science and an expert on stone used for building, published widely on the supposed links between climate, geography, and racial advancement. Unlike Jenney, Shaler did incorporate the Indigenous inhabitants of North America into his narrative. The success of colonization, he claimed in 1888, was due to the fact that the colonizers were better able to deal with the difficult environment than the Indigenous people, who had hardly advanced beyond a primitive level of civilization. Talking of the passing of "craft" architecture and the rise of the specialist building professionals in 1888, he spoke of the "inventiveness which is the most striking intellectual mark of the American [and] is a measure of his independence of the past; the best use he can make of the ancestral traditions is to get his foot upon them that he may mount to a higher plane of action."[16] Shaler was also an apologist for slavery, arguing that the practice had enabled white colonizers to make the most of unforgiving agricultural land across much of the country.[17] But this is where the geologist and the architect parted ways: For Jenney, the way to ensure the brilliant future of the American nation was industrial development, overcoming reliance on indentured slavery as the basis of the national economy.

In a paper delivered at the 1885 annual convention of the American Institute of Architects in Nashville and reprinted in *The Inland Architect and Builder*, Jenney applied the principle of environmental adaptation to his own practice and that of his Chicago colleagues. Moving from the long history of architecture to the context of the contemporary profession, he jumped from describing building as the result of embedded racial characteristics and abilities to the superior way in which the contemporary "American" (with his innate engineer's mindset and artistry) was able to adapt traditional construction methods to the difficult local environment. The analogy of evolution was pervasive in nineteenth-century writing on architecture and design, and in this paper, Jenney explained its operation in the context of his own city. Titled "The Construction of a Heavy, Fireproof Building on Compressible Soil," it used the Home Insurance Building as an illustration of these ideas.

It is important to note that in this paper, Jenney does not describe the Home Insurance Building as the "first" of a new type but as "the successful application of methods in use, with some variation in detail" (fig. 19.3).[18] Because the building relied heavily on brick walls to take wind and some gravity load, as well as to provide resistance to combustion, it is best described as a hybrid building rather than wholly skeleton framed. Jenney begins by noting the use of a system of "independent piers" for the foundations, along with an iron "skeleton" throughout the entire building, except for the party walls, with every piece of iron covered in masonry as fire protection. Fireproofing was obviously an important concern: The commission for the Home Insurance Building came relatively soon after the Great Chicago Fire of 1871, which forced the company to pay out $2.5 million in claims.[19] Besides providing protection for the building itself, it was vital that the company's headquarters model good fire-safety practices, and it is possible to argue that the desire to fireproof buildings drove the adoption of skeleton framing in this period.[20]

In 1891, Jenney returned to the Home Insurance Building for a lecture given to the twenty-fifth annual convention of the American Institute of Architects, held in Boston.[21] While the content was essentially the same as the paper delivered

FIGURE 19.3. *Exterior view of the Home Insurance Building, Chicago, before the additions of 1891. Photo by J. W. Taylor, ca. 1890. Chicago History Museum, ICHi-000989.*

six years earlier, the title was now "The Chicago Construction, or Tall Buildings on a Compressible Soil." In 1885 he had emphasized innovations in foundation design, but now he focused on the construction system that Chicago architects had developed to deal with complex environmental conditions—principally, poor soil. Borrowing from railway bridge technology, he wrote, the so-called Chicago construction "consists of a fireproofed steel skeleton so arranged that all the load, including the walls and partitions, is carried story by story on the columns. The foundations as far as practicable are on isolated piers."[22] Referencing a pamphlet published by the architect Frederick Baumann in 1873, Jenney explicitly acknowledged that the foundation system of isolated-pier foundations had been trialed a decade earlier.[23] And, as he acknowledged, steel by itself was practically useless as a structural material without a sheathing of plaster and brick or terracotta-clay tiles, as seen in the paper's accompanying diagram (fig. 19.4).[24] In other words, the "ingenuity" of the Western architect and engineer utilized several materials acting in concert. Together, steel and masonry gave the structure adequate lateral strength and made it fireproof.

Though Chicago architects debated the point in the 1880s, by the 1890s many

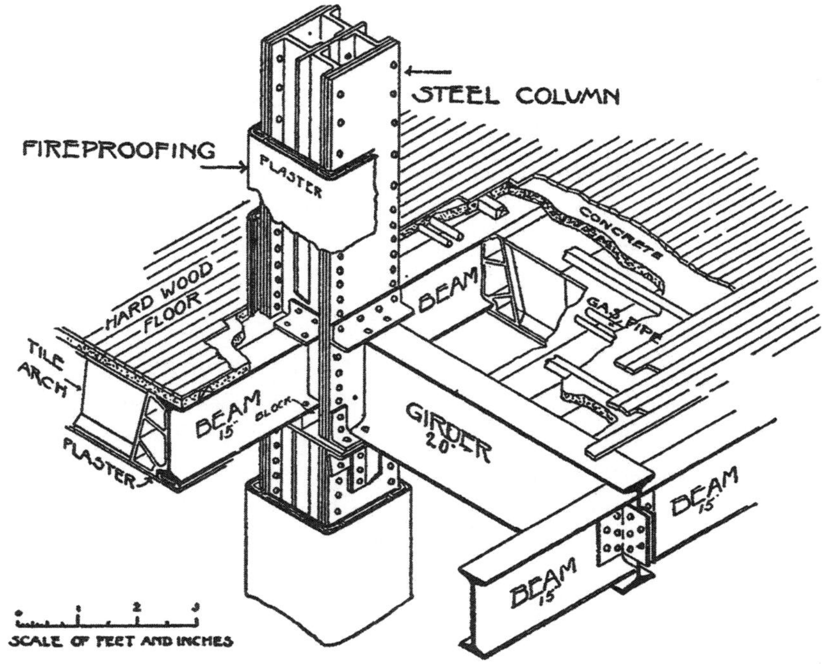

FIGURE 19.4. *The interior structural configuration of the Home Insurance Building. William Le Baron Jenney, "The Chicago Construction, or Tall Buildings on a Compressible Soil," in* Proceedings of the Twenty-Fifth Annual Convention of the American Institute of Architects *(New York: American Institute of Architects, 1891), 33.*

agreed a new style would develop out of this form of construction, one based in the expression of structural lightness.[25] This lightness would enable taller buildings and satisfy the demand for well-lit buildings on the part of their clients. Noting the change in Chicago buildings constructed before and after 1880, including the introduction of the elevator and the "new system of Chicago construction," *Industrial Chicago* called the result a "revolution in the building arts."[26] Even though the steel frame was augmented by the reinforced-concrete frame around the turn of the twentieth century, a single material, steel, would come to signify the modern building type. Although steel was always used in conjunction with other materials, such as concrete, its symbolic value was entrenched as a material indicator of progress and modernity.

In Jenney's description of the incremental development of Chicago construction, we can see the nineteenth-century understanding of the "evolutionary" process in architecture that remains operative today. The general problem of the tall office building called for "a different method of construction from those in general use," Jenney wrote: "This method of construction has been improved upon; each architect using it has added something, particularly to the details. The manufacturers of steel, terracotta and fireproofing have improved their material and adapted it more especially to this style of construction."[27] In other words, the Chicago construction was not the invention of an individual or of the architecture or engineering professions alone, but of a close cohort of specialists working in response to a particular environment. This environment is defined in terms of not only ground conditions but also the availability of materials, as well as real estate practices and building regulations. This understanding of structural evolution as a networked activity responsive to local conditions persists in contemporary scholarship. As the structural engineer Robert Mark puts it, practical experience with past structures influences how new ones are built, and earlier buildings serve as models for new designs, modified according to circumstance.[28] This modification is understood as a form of "adaptation" or "survival of the fittest," where the "fittest" is defined as the most effective, or structurally stable, solution.

In the context of postbellum American society, the analogy of evolution in architecture and engineering applied not only to structural forms but also to the racial, cultural, and nationalist characteristics of those who conceived them. While the Civil War era is referred to in modernist architectural histories as the nadir of good taste, the height of historical eclecticism, it was also valued as an era of technological experimentation. Less often scrutinized, however, is the context of this experimentation in processes of settler colonization, including land appropriation and warfare. Yet Jenney's evolutionary thinking was not merely theoretical: It was rooted in his lived experience and shaped by the practical demands of war, which provided a powerful framework for architectural innovation.

The Civil War and the Formation of Technical Expertise

Jenney's military service during the Civil War played a foundational role in shaping his approach to architectural practice, reinforcing his belief in adaptability, improvisation, and the racialized logic of environmental mastery. In 1889, Jenney made this point directly in an informal talk to the Chicago Sketch Club, a group of architectural draftsmen working in local offices, remarks later published in *The Inland Architect and News Record*.[29] Jenney begins by describing Darwin's theory of the survival of the fittest, and the need for the architect to adapt to the complex needs of the contemporary environment (by which he meant not only the physical landscape but also the business environment), and ends with an anecdote about his experience in the engineer corps of the Union army. Enlisting as a volunteer, Jenney had served on the staff of General Sherman as one of many engineer-soldiers quickly educated in the construction of field and permanent fortifications and the rapid construction of bridges and roads. Jenney was proud of this experience: On the title page of a book coauthored with Sanford Loring in 1869, he described himself as "Architect, Chicago. Graduate of the Ecole Centrale des Arts et Manufactures, Paris. Formerly Officer, Staffs of Generals Grant and

Sherman."[30] His wartime experience became part of his persona; as his employee Louis Sullivan noted, Jenney was known in the office as "the Major."[31]

In his talk to the Sketch Club, Jenney was explicit in describing his wartime experience as a part of his education, offering an anecdote about General Grant's Vicksburg, Mississippi, campaign of May 1863 (fig. 19.5). After retreating Confederate soldiers burned a railroad bridge crossing the nearby Big Black River, Jenney and his fellow engineers built new crossings, improvising from materials to hand, and soon "one entire division of Grant's Army had crossed it in safety with its artillery and baggage wagons."[32] Jenney notes that they used the timber frame of a cotton gin, the chimneys from nearby houses, and boards from a "negro hut." This story is confirmed by secondary literature: Union military engineers built three crossings across the Big Black River: a pontoon and two timber bridges. For the first bridge, at Coaker's Ferry, "boxworks of timbers from a dismantled cotton warehouse were constructed in three sections." The second, to the south, was "a 200-foot-long floating raft bridge made with materials provided by nearby cotton warehouses."[33] In this way, the industrial ingenuity of the Union army literally deconstructed and reconfigured Southern vernacular architecture for the purpose of conquest. This experience, Jenney claimed, "was an excellent school to learn expedients."[34] As a military engineer, he gained mastery over the defeated army by adapting established techniques to new situations, materials, and topographies.

The formative experience of warfare in developing organizational skills was a theme commonly repeated in biographies of "leading" American men published

FIGURE 19.5. *Big Black River Station, Mississippi, February 1864. The Battle of Big Black River Bridge took place nearby on May 17, 1863. Photo by William R. Pyewell. Prints and Photographs Division, Library of Congress.*

in the postbellum period. The profession of civil engineering, in particular, has deep roots in military construction. While Jenney was not yet prominent enough to be profiled in *Biographical Sketches of the Leading Men of Chicago* (1868), the positive influence of military experience is noted in several entries. For example, Arthur Charles Ducat, an Irish-born insurance underwriter, had served as an engineer under the Union General George H. Thomas. Invalided out of the army, Ducat was later "appointed by the Home Insurance Company of New York, to supervise the business of the company in the States of Ohio and Indiana, and afterwards as their agent in Chicago. . . . In these responsible duties, Colonel Ducat is daily illustrating the fact that service in the army, instead of demoralizing, has added to his executive ability and usefulness."[35] In his role as an executive of the Home Insurance Company and an authority on fire prevention, Ducat may well have encountered Jenney. Ducat's is just one of many entries citing the superior analytical abilities of Chicago's leading men. In these biographical sketches, the technological problems encountered during warfare were a prompt for higher industrial organization. Led by figures such as Ducat, the economic center of the nation would be reoriented away from the slave-owning South toward the industrial North. Gradually, industrial labor would take over from manual labor as the engine of national progress.

Jenney's experience in Sherman's army did not just supplement his French education; it expanded his understanding of architectural theory through practical experience. Architectural history has recorded the knowledge and experience that émigré architects brought to Chicago from Germany and elsewhere, and what American-born architects learned in France, but it has left relatively unexamined the expertise gained in the Civil War.[36] As Charles L. Davis II has noted, "An outward focus on European trends unduly masks some of the key domestic influences that determined the practical reality of architectural practices in the United States."[37] In the industrial and economic boom that followed the end of hostilities, building professionals greatly increased their knowledge of structural design, driven by the rapid expansion of railroad companies. Davis has discussed the Kansas City architect and critic Henry Van Brunt's experience as an architect for the railway, illustrating how the experiences of colonization and warfare provide the context of professionalization in architecture. Like Jenney, Van Brunt was an active writer, translating practical experience into an emerging theory of modern American architecture.

In this way, Jenney's wartime experience links the discourse of architectural evolution to broader narratives of national reconstruction and expansion, a theme echoed in the work of his contemporaries. In his 1889 essay "Architecture in the West," Van Brunt, like Jenney, claimed Viollet-le-Duc's theory of architectural evolution as the basis for a new architectural history that would best serve the American nation. Representing the country as an ever-westward-expanding frontier, Van Brunt wrote, "Civilization is advancing into the wilderness of the great west like a brimming and irresistible tide which knows no ebb. Its first waves of occupation bear upon their crests a human element of astonishing energy and force. It has planted cities and established civil order upon virgin soil in less than thirty days."[38] Just as Van Brunt's experience as an architect for the railways influenced his conception of American architectural progress, Jenney's remarks about the Vicksburg campaign must be seen in the context of the question of what the country wanted to be in the waning decades of the nineteenth century, a period of rapid national and global expansion. Projections of the future of the country relied on comparisons to an idealized, less constricted past—the concepts of freedom and democracy evident in the rhetoric of the early republic—and an aspirational, imperialist future, projected by a largely white, urban elite.

The gain of Vicksburg gave control of the Mississippi River to the Union army, which held it for the rest of the campaign. The blockade of the river empowered Chicago as a vital economic hub as the Northern entrepôt rushed to fill demand previously filled by the South.[39] After the war, the Illinois Central Railroad took advantage of this head start, expanding south along the Mississippi. In 1867, it extended into Iowa, and in the 1870s and 1880s, it reached as far as New Orleans and Louisville. In time, the Big Black River Bridge was replaced by the Illinois Central Gulf Railroad Bridge. The expansion of Chicago as a national and global industrial center in the second half of the nineteenth century helped realign the economy of the United States. As Diana Martinez has noted elsewhere in this volume, for abolitionists, slavery was a "relic of barbarism" that was "incongruous with the values of an advanced Anglo-Saxon civilization." Abolitionists and architects alike looked to an industrial future, one where machines could replace human labor.

Early skeleton-framed skyscrapers appeared in American cities about fifteen years after the Civil War. The massive growth in railroads and their associated technologies, especially iron and steel bridges, and the emergence of people with expertise in these technologies, such as engineers and ironworkers, inspired their application in other areas, including architectural design, when the economic demand for tall buildings appeared.[40] According to evolutionist narratives of architectural history, technologies that appeared first in railroad and bridge engineering, including steel production and steam power, modernized methods of construction, and in the process older craft traditions became obsolete. As historians have shown, however, the adaptation of technologies used on one kind of building to another was not necessarily linear and predetermined. Uptake of new building practices depended not only on professional knowledge and expertise but also on social and political constraints. In each city and region, architects, engineers, and builders dealt with not only local environmental conditions but also differing building regulations.

What is not in doubt, however, is the huge change in architecture and building culture that took place in the industrial cities of the Northeast and Midwest in the second half of the nineteenth century. There, a broad idea of professionalism developed, and the practice of building large structures no longer operated on a craft basis.[41] In the case of skyscraper construction, expertise was no longer vested in the traditional builder, who could take on almost any job, but in the "general contractor," who managed subcontractors and organized the flow of building materials to the site.[42] The use of iron and steel required different kinds of structural knowledge based on calculation tables rather than on-site experience, meaning architects could no longer work without guidance from civil engineers.[43] In turn, this change created markets for new building materials, such as iron, steel, terracotta tile, and plate glass. Traditional relationships between capital and labor were disrupted as new trades appeared to challenge older ones like bricklaying and carpentry.

Like many of his peers, Jenney understood these changes in evolutionary terms, based on his education in early nineteenth-century concepts of race and biology. In thinking of architecture as a series of discrete species of building types and styles built by distinct ethnographic peoples (influenced by Fergusson and Viollet-le-Duc), Jenney translated scientific processes lasting millennia into the short history of the United States in the postbellum period. This time frame, about a generation, is not even a blink of an eye on the timescale of biological evolution, yet the same principles were used to explain and rationalize recent changes in architectural form and practice: The "evolution" of larger, more lightweight buildings such as skeleton-framed skyscrapers was the product of a practical American race, one with the inherent capability to find sophisticated technological solutions to complex problems.

According to an ethnological schema of conjoined architectural and technological history, American architects, working closely with engineers and specialized building contractors, realized the innate abilities of the descendants of the hybrid Turanian-Celt-Aryan race, codified as "white," to adapt skillfully to a new environment and exploit its resources for their own advantage.[44] While canonical histories of American architecture emphasize assimilation, the "nation of immigrants" did not operate on a level playing field. In the process of creating a white professional class, craft builders—many European immigrants from ethnic backgrounds considered racially "other"—were rendered secondary agents in the Northern building industry. Although enslaved and free Black people had a major role in building in the South, in the North, barred from gaining expert qualifications, they were largely excluded from the process of skyscraper design.[45]

The explicit link between technological progress and racially defined capability found expression at the World's Columbian Exposition of 1893, whose elaborate fairgrounds were orchestrated by Daniel Burnham. Besides the well-known exhibits at the Court of Honor and the Midway Plaisance, the fair also included a series of full-scale ethnological exhibits, including representations of the past and current state of "American" architecture (fig. 19.6). These exhibits presented

FIGURE 19.6. *Penobscot Indian Camp, ethnographical exhibit at the World's Columbian Exposition, Chicago, 1891–1893. Photo by C. D. Arnold. Ryerson and Burnham Art and Architecture Archive, Art Institute of Chicago, 198902_140619-E20981.*

FIGURE 19.7. *Bird's-eye view of downtown Chicago, looking north from the Marquette Building, 1895. Photo by R. D. Cleveland. Chicago History Museum, ICHi-034608.*

the transfer of ideas of "American" identity from Indigenous Americans to settler colonialists. Held at the fair's Palace of Fine Arts in July 1893, the twenty-sixth annual American Institute of Architects convention featured papers by Van Brunt and the critic Barr Ferree, both of whom had built up a body of architectural writing based on the theory of environmental determinism and the evolutionary development of architectural form. Both argued that the true American architecture was the commercial building type found in the downtown Chicago Loop, describing it as the most advanced and natural response to the challenges of the modern urban environment (fig. 19.7).[46] In the translation of ideas from the "natural," geological and biological environment to the sociopolitical environment of capitalism, the skyscraper was naturalized as a superior method of construction based on local response to local conditions, and also a revolutionary improvement on traditional building practices. In the process, the skeleton frame could be seen as both a "vernacular" product of its environment and a "modern" technology, a radical break with the past.[47]

Skyscraper as Symbol: Ethnology, Nationalism, Modernity, and the Myth of the Chicago School

As ideas of racial hierarchy, technological progress, and national exceptionalism were translated into architectural discourse, the skyscraper emerged as both a symbol and an instrument of modernity, especially within the foundational texts that established the idea of the Chicago School. The identification of the first skyscraper is important in architectural historiography because it affirms the idea of radical rather than incremental change: This is the basis of modern architecture, the characteristic that separates it from the vernacular. Jenney's iconic building serves as a hinge point, a structure positioned as both vernacular, or "natural," and modern. At the turn of the twentieth century, historians of American architecture moved away from an evolutionary model based on assumptions of technological progress toward one that allowed for the role of individual authorship or genius. In the hands of art historians accustomed to thinking in terms of schools of aesthetic style, the concept of a cohesive Chicago School of architecture appeared, celebrated for its technological and aesthetic innovation and positioned as precursor to the modern or International Style.[48] In the 1920s, Henry-Russell Hitchcock constructed a familial lineage of American architecture from the simple forms of early nineteenth-century vernacular construction through to the protomodern experiments of H. H. Richardson, John W. Root, Louis H. Sullivan, and Frank Lloyd Wright.[49] William Le Baron Jenney holds a pivotal place in this historiographic transition, as the synthesizer of existing knowledge into a new structural system, one that other architects, notably his former employee Sullivan, raised to new heights of aesthetic expression.

Although the claim that the Home Insurance Building is the first skeleton-framed skyscraper was seldom made during Jenney's lifetime, it had begun to gain traction by the time of his death in 1907. It may be found in a biographical publication on the "leading living men in Chicago," published in 1905, and is repeated in an obituary of Jenney published in *The Inland Architect and News Record.*[50] Even there, the author of the obituary noted that the claim about the Home Insurance Building's structural primacy had been challenged by the Chicago architect Irving Pond, among others. But doubts expressed by those with firsthand knowledge, such as Pond, and evidence of experiments by others, including the Minnesota architect LeRoy S. Buffington (who patented a system of iron building construction in 1888), did little to stop the process of mythmaking—one in which the story of Jenney's inventiveness was a convenient shorthand for a more complicated history.[51] By 1929, Hitchcock confidently claimed that the Home Insurance Building was "the first true skeleton construction in metal."[52] In 1937, the German critic Walter Curt Behrendt cited Jenney's building as a new type of construction, an iron framework.[53] The same idea was cemented in books written by Sigfried Giedion and Carl Condit, published in 1941 and 1952, respectively.[54]

By the early twentieth century, the racial basis of claims about the Home Insurance Building's originality had all but disappeared. While the idea of the tall office building type as the natural product of its environment, the product of builders characterized by their ingenious use of materials, was repeated, overt references to the "white" race were erased. Yet other aspects of nineteenth-century racial evolutionary theories of architectural development persist: in particular, the idea that the invention of the skyscraper was the biggest change in architecture since the invention of the Gothic cathedral, an epistemic change that represented a dramatic jump forward in the evolution of building technique. In 1964, Condit described the skeletal structure of modern skyscrapers as "the most radical transformation of the structural art since the development of the Gothic."[55] By the time of Jenney's death, the version of the Gothic favored was not the pastiche of William Boyington's University of Chicago but an abstract idea of the Gothic as a "constructive principle," adaptable to modern materials. While this belief may be traced to American interpreters of Viollet-le-Duc such as Jenney and Van Brunt, who argued for the essential malleability of the Gothic, the racial basis of Viollet-le-Duc's theory, and the connection they drew between the adaptability of the Gothic style and racial aptitude for technical ingenuity, had been elided. While not expressed overtly, it remained in the conceptual link connecting modern American architects with the ingenuity and patrimony of European medieval builders.

The idea of the Home Insurance Building as the first skyscraper was overturned in the 1980s, when scholars pointed out that its structural attributes were not unique but were shared by a number of other buildings constructed around the same time. As Gerald R. Larson and Roula Geraniotis noted in a 1987 essay, the Home Insurance Building was not considered especially notable at the time of its completion.[56] (As Robert Bruegmann discusses, many of the attributes of the "skyscraper" were found in Burnham & Root's Montauk Building of 1881, which was often described by Chicago architects as the "first" of its type.[57]) Yet even though Larson and Geraniotis comprehensively debunked much of the mythology that has built up around the Home Insurance Building, their paper is titled "Toward a Better Understanding of the Evolution of the Iron Skeleton Frame in Chicago." As this title attests, the belief that architecture advances through a process of evolution endures in contemporary scholarship.

Even though the chronological primacy of the Home Insurance Building has been rejected, the analogy of evolution in architecture remains unchallenged. But for those who care to look, the basis of claims that the Home Insurance Building was the first skyscraper lies in ethnological and evolutionary theories of conjoined racial and technological development that are hiding in plain sight. Rewriting the history of nineteenth-century American architecture means looking back at iconic buildings and reexamining claims made for them in canonical texts. By reading Jenney's own words, we can see that the identification of the first skyscraper as a uniquely modern form of American architecture depended on the belief in a hierarchy of technical aptitude and cultural inventiveness, a hierarchy in which white Americans were considered biologically and psychologically superior to other races, and the American nation was considered the most advanced in the world. Revisiting the myth of the Home Insurance Building reveals how deeply nineteenth-century ethnology, nationalism, and modernity are entangled in the historiography of American architecture. By interrogating the ideological foundations of this narrative—its erasures, its evolutionary metaphors, and its racialized assumptions—we open the possibility for a more critical and inclusive architectural history.

Notes

This chapter was prompted by a series of conversations with Carol Willis, Thomas Leslie, Donald Friedman, and Gregory Dreicer about the mythology of the Home Insurance Building as the first skyscraper. I am indebted to their deep knowledge of skyscrapers and construction history, but the opinions presented here are my own.

1. Thomas E. Tallmadge, "Was the Home Insurance Building in Chicago the First Skyscraper of Skeleton Construction?," *Architectural Record* 76, no. 2 (1934): 113–118.

2. Museum of Modern Art, *Early Modern Architecture in Chicago 1870–1910*, exh. cat., 2nd rev. ed. (Museum of Modern Art, 1940), 2. On the exhibition, held at MoMA from January 18 to February 23, 1933, see Joanna Merwood-Salisbury, "American Modern: The Chicago School and the International Style at the Museum of Modern Art," in *Chicagoisms: The City as Catalyst for Architectural Speculation*, ed. Alexander Eisenschmidt and Jonathan Mekinda (University of Chicago Press, 2014), 117–129.

3. Colin Rowe, "Chicago Frame," in *The Mathematics of the Ideal Villa and Other Essays* (MIT Press, 1976), 89–117; originally published in *Architectural Review* in 1956.

4. Gerald R. Larson and Roula Mouroudellis Geraniotis, "Toward a Better Understanding of the Evolution of the Iron Skeleton Frame in Chicago," *Journal of the Society of Architectural Historians* 46, no. 1 (1987): 39–48. As Winston Weisman, Rosemarie Haag Bletter, and Tom Leslie have noted, respectively,

the designation of first skyscraper is a matter of definition. Winston Weisman, "New York and the Problem of the First Skyscraper," *Journal of the Society of Architectural Historians* 12, no. 1 (1953): 13–21; Rosemarie Haag Bletter, "The Invention of the Skyscraper: Notes on Its Diverse Histories," *Assemblage*, no. 2 (1987): 110–117; Thomas Leslie, "'Buildings Without Walls': A Tectonic Case for Two 'First' Skyscrapers," *International Journal of High-Rise Buildings* 9, no. 1 (2020): 53–60.

5. Dell Upton, "An American Architecture?," in *A Companion to American Art*, ed. John Davis, Jennifer A. Greenhill, and Jason D. LaFountain (Wiley Blackwell, 2015), 213.

6. Philip Steadman, *The Evolution of Designs: Biological Analogy in Architecture and the Applied Arts* (1979; Taylor & Francis, 2008).

7. Gregory K. Dreicer, "Building Myths: The 'Evolution' from Wood to Iron in the Construction of Bridges and Nations," *Perspecta* 31 (2000): 130–140; Irene Cheng, "Structural Racialism in Modern Architectural Theory," in *Race and Modern Architecture: A Critical History from the Enlightenment to the Present*, ed. Irene Cheng, Charles L. Davis II, and Mabel O. Wilson (University of Pittsburgh Press, 2020), 134–152.

8. This idea was promoted in Sigfried Giedion, *Space, Time and Architecture: The Growth of a New Tradition* (Harvard University Press, 1941); and in Carl Condit, *The Chicago School of Architecture: A History of Commercial and Public Buildings in the Chicago Area, 1875–1925* (University of Chicago Press, 1964).

9. Like the belief in the Home Insurance Building as the first skyscraper, the idea of a singular Chicago School of architecture has been subject to revision. See Robert Bruegmann, "The Myth of the Chicago School," in *Chicago Architecture: Histories, Revisions, Alternatives*, ed. Charles Waldheim and Katerina Rüedi Ray (University of Chicago Press, 2005), 15–29.

10. "Architectural and Building Notes," *Inland Architect and Builder* 3, no. 2 (1884): 23; "Synopsis of Building News," *Inland Architect and Builder* 3, no. 3 (1884): 42. See also Miles L. Berger, *They Built Chicago: Entrepreneurs Who Shaped a Great City's Architecture* (Bonus Books, 1992), 59–62.

11. Jenney is listed as a lecturer on architecture in the faculty of the Department of Liberal Arts. *Twenty-Fifth Annual Catalogue of the University of Chicago* (Chicago: R. R. Donnelley and Sons, 1884), 7. Jenney's lectures on architecture were reprinted in *The Inland Architect and Builder* from April 1883 to April 1884. On Jenney as a teacher and writer, see Theodore Turak, "The École Centrale and Modern Architecture: The Education of William Le Baron Jenney," *Journal of the Society of Architectural Historians* 29, no. 1 (1970): 40–47; Paul Kruty, "William Le Baron Jenney, Teacher," *Threshold: Journal of the University of Illinois at Chicago School of Architecture*, Fall 1991, 61–82.

12. James Fergusson, *History of Architecture in All Countries, from the Earliest Times to the Present Day*, 4 vols. (London: John Murray, 1862–1867); Eugène Emmanuelle Viollet-le-Duc, *Histoire de l'habitation humaine* (Paris: Typographie Lahure, 1875). On the influence of Fergusson and Viollet-le-Duc in the United States, see Robert R. Winter, "Fergusson and Garbett in American Architectural Theory," *Journal of the Society of Architectural Historians* 17, no. 4 (1958): 25–31; Daniel D. Reiff, "Viollet-le-Duc and American 19th Century Architecture," *Journal of Architectural Education* 42, no. 1 (1988): 32–47. On the biological analogy in the writings of Fergusson, Viollet-le-Duc, and other nineteenth-century architects, see Steadman, *Evolution of Designs*.

13. William Le Baron Jenney, "Architecture," *Inland Architect and Builder* 6 (January 1884): 158.

14. William Le Baron Jenney, "Architecture," *Inland Architect and Builder* 3 (April 1883): 33.

15. Jenney, "Architecture" (April 1883): 33.

16. Nathaniel S. Shaler, "The Law of Fashion," *Atlantic Monthly* 61 (1888): 397.

17. Nathaniel S. Shaler, *Nature and Man in America* (London: Smith Elder, 1891).

18. William Le Baron Jenney, "The Construction of a Heavy, Fireproof Building on Compressible Soil," in *Proceedings of the Nineteenth Annual Convention of the American Institute of Architects* (New York: American Institute of Architects, 1885), 96–102; William Le Baron Jenney, "The Construction of a Heavy, Fireproof Building on Compressible Soil," *Inland Architect and Builder* 6, no. 6 (1885): 100.

19. C. Jackson Martin, *History of the Home Insurance Company* (New York: Home Insurance Company, 1883), 30.

20. The Chicago architect and expert in fireproofing Peter B. Wight argued this point in a paper read at the 1893 American Institute of Architects convention. P. B. Wight, "Fireproof Construction and the Practice of American Architects," in *Proceedings of the Twenty-Seventh Annual Convention of the American Institute of Architects* (New York: American Institute of Architects, 1893), 302–312. On the role of fireproofing in driving innovation in tall-building construction, see Sara E. Wermeil, *The Fireproof Building: Technology and Public Safety in the Nineteenth-Century American City* (Johns Hopkins University Press, 2000).

21. William Le Baron Jenney, "The Chicago Construction, or Tall Buildings on a Compressible Soil,"

in *Proceedings of the Twenty-Fifth Annual Convention of the American Institute of Architects* (New York: American Institute of Architects, 1891), 30–37; William Le Baron Jenney, "The Chicago Construction, or Tall Buildings on a Compressible Soil," *Inland Architect and News Record* 18 (November 1891): 41. Subsequent notes cite the *Inland Architect* version.

22. Jenney, "Chicago Construction," 41. On the technology transfer from railway engineering to architecture, see Thomas Leslie, "Built Like Bridges: Iron, Steel, and Rivets in the Nineteenth-Century Skyscraper," *Journal of the Society of Architectural Historians* 69, no. 2 (2010): 234–261.

23. Frederick Baumann, *The Art of Preparing Foundations for All Kinds of Buildings, with Particular Illustrations of the "Method of Isolated Piers," as Followed in Chicago* (Chicago: J. M. Wing, 1873).

24. In 1893, the Chicago architect Peter B. Wight credited Burnham & Root with popularizing this type of construction in the buildings they erected for the Brooks Brothers Company, under the direction of their agent Owen F. Aldis. He did not mention Jenney. Wight, "Fireproof Construction," 307.

25. See, for example, "To What Extent Is It Necessary in Design to Emphasize the Essentially Structural Elements of a Building?," *Inland Architect and News Record*, no. 6 (May 1887): 59–62. This is a record of a debate held among Chicago architects.

26. *Industrial Chicago: The Building Interests* (Chicago: Goodspeed, 1896), 171.

27. Jenney, "Chicago Construction," 41.

28. Robert Mark and David P. Billington, "Structural Imperative and the Origin of New Form," *Technology and Culture* 30, no. 2 (1989): 300–329; Robert Mark, "Architecture and Evolution," *American Scientist* 84, no. 4 (1996): 383–389.

29. William Le Baron Jenney, "A Few Practical Hints," *Inland Architect and News Record* 13, no. 1 (1889): 7.

30. Sanford E. Loring and William Le Baron Jenney, *Principles and Practice of Architecture* (Chicago: Cobb, Pritchard, 1869).

31. Louis Sullivan, *The Autobiography of an Idea* (1924; Dover, 1956), 203–205.

32. Jenney, "A Few Practical Hints," 9.

33. Terry Winschel, "The Engineers at Vicksburg Part 18: Bridging the Big Black River," US Army Corps of Engineers, March 9, 2017, www.erdc.usace.army.mil/Media/News-stories. See also "The Battle of Big Black River Bridge," *Harper's Weekly*, June 20, 1863, 396; Michael Ballard, *Vicksburg: The Campaign That Opened the Mississippi* (University of North Carolina Press, 2004).

34. Jenney, "A Few Practical Hints," 9.

35. "Arthur Charles Ducat," in *Biographical Sketches of the Leading Men of Chicago* (Chicago: Wilson & St. Clair, 1868), 351. On Ducat, see *Portraits and Biographies of the Fire Underwriters of the City of Chicago* (Chicago: Chas. T. Rothermel, 1895), 258.

36. Roula Mouroudellis Geraniotis, "German Architectural Theory and Practice in Chicago, 1850–1900," *Winterthur Portfolio* 21, no. 4 (1986): 293–306; Turak, "École Centrale and Modern Architecture"; Robert Twombly, *Louis Sullivan: His Life and Work* (Viking, 1986), 56–76.

37. Charles L. Davis II, "Henry Van Brunt and White Settler Colonialism in the Midwest," in Cheng, Davis, and Wilson, *Race and Modern Architecture*, 99.

38. Henry Van Brunt, "Architecture in the West," *Inland Architect and News Record* 14, no. 7 (1889): 78.

39. Dominic A. Pacyga, *Chicago: A Biography* (University of Chicago Press, 2009), 50–65.

40. Thomas J. Misa, "The Structure of Cities, 1880–1900," in *A Nation of Steel: The Making of Modern America, 1865–1925* (Johns Hopkins University Press, 1995), 45–90; Carol Willis, *Form Follows Finance: Skyscrapers and Skylines in New York and Chicago* (Princeton Architectural Press, 1995); Thomas Leslie, *Chicago Skyscrapers, 1871–1934* (University of Illinois Press, 2013).

41. Mary N. Woods, *From Craft to Profession: The Practice of Architecture in Nineteenth-Century America* (University of California Press, 1999).

42. Jane Bonshek, "The Skyscraper: A Catalyst of Change in the Chicago Construction Industries, 1882–1892," *Construction History* 4 (1988): 53–74.

43. Joseph K. Freitag, *Architectural Engineering, with Special Reference to High Building Construction* (New York: John Wiley and Sons, 1895); William Birkmire, *Skeleton Construction in Buildings* (New York: John Wiley and Sons, 1893). For a contemporary view, see William Addis, *Structural and Civil Engineering Design* (Ashgate, 1999).

44. Alexander Saxton, *The Rise and Fall of the White Republic: Class Politics and Mass Culture in Nineteenth-Century America* (Verso, 1990); Theodore W. Allen, *The Invention of the White Race*, 2 vols. (Verso, 1994–1997).

45. Cedric de Leon, "Black from White: How the Rights of White and Black Workers Became 'Labor' and 'Civil' Rights After the U.S. Civil War," *Labor Studies Journal* 42, no. 1 (2016): 1–17.

46. Barr Ferree, "Economic Conditions of Architecture in America," and Henry Van Brunt, "The Growth of Characteristic Architectural Style in the United States," in *Proceedings of the Twenty-Seventh Annual Convention of the American Institute of Architects*, 230–253.

47. On the distinction between "vernacular" and "modern" architecture in anthropology, see Marcel Vellinga, "The End of the Vernacular: Anthropology and the Architecture of the Other," *Etnofoor* 23, no. 1 (2011): 171–192.

48. Robert Bruegmann, "Myth of the Chicago School," 15–29.

49. Henry-Russell Hitchcock, *Modern Architecture: Romanticism and Reintegration* (1929; Arno, 1972). See also James O'Gorman, *Three American Architects: Richardson, Sullivan, and Wright, 1865–1915* (University of Chicago Press, 1991).

50. John W. Leonard, *The Book of Chicagoans: A Biographical Dictionary of Leading Living Men of the City of Chicago* (A. N. Marquis, 1905), 313; "William Le Baron Jenney," *Inland Architect and News Record* 50, no. 1 (1907): 1, 8–9.

51. On Buffington's patent, see *Inland Architect and News Record* 11, no. 8 (1888): 89.

52. Hitchcock, *Modern Architecture*, 108.

53. Walter C. Behrendt, *Modern Building: Its Nature, Problems and Forms* (Harcourt Brace, 1937), 112.

54. Giedion, *Space, Time and Architecture*, 294; Carl Condit, *The Rise of the Skyscraper* (University of Chicago Press, 1952), 16.

55. Condit, *Chicago School of Architecture*, 79.

56. Larson and Geraniotis, "Evolution of the Iron Skeleton Frame."

57. Robert Bruegmann, *The Architects and the City: Holabird & Roche of Chicago, 1880–1918* (University of Chicago Press, 1997), 66–68.

20 "AMERICANS" AND OTHERS

A PREHISTORY OF FRANK LLOYD WRIGHT'S USONIA

Joseph M. Watson

OVER SEVERAL EVENINGS IN MAY 1939, Frank Lloyd Wright delivered the Sir George Watson Lectures of the Sulgrave Manor Board, hosted by the Royal Institute of British Architects, to a large, lively crowd of mostly young English architects.[1] Midway through the third lecture, Wright interrupted himself to offer some clarification. He realized belatedly that as part of his wide-ranging effort to "consider the place Architecture must have in Society if Democracy is to be realized," he had been using a term to refer to the United States with which his London audience might not be familiar.[2] He explained,

> I do not know whether some of you here tonight for the first time are familiar with this word "Usonia" for our country. "United Statesers" doesn't sound well and we are not really entitled to call ourselves "Americans," because we have not a monopoly on that title. The South Ameri-

> cans, as I found when I was in Rio de Janeiro several years ago, resent our use of it; the Brazilians say that they are the Americans. We have therefore to settle a dispute to find a good name for ourselves. Your Samuel Butler called us "Usonians." I think Usonian an excellent name, having its roots in union, as we have our national life in it. So I use the term and hope to get the country used to it in good time.[3]

This was not the first appearance of the term "Usonia" in Wright's lectures or publications, but it did constitute his most thorough effort to explain its meaning. His first usage came in a 1925 article in the Dutch journal *Wendingen*. Between 1925 and the late 1930s, he began using it with greater frequency and endowing it with greater meaning.

The meaning Wright attributed to Usonia in London in 1939 seems straightforward. "Usonian," unlike "American," was a more precise and deferential way of referring to the United States, since other peoples across the Americas could just as legitimately lay claim to being American. Yet, in other contexts, Usonia was not always so clear-cut. To cite just one relevant example, in the January 1938 issue of *Architectural Forum*, which was devoted entirely to his recent work, Wright lamented that "a small house on the side street might have charm if it didn't ape the big house on the avenue, just as the Usonian village itself might have great charm if it didn't ape the big town."[4] Elsewhere in the issue, he characterized his renewed interest in affordable single-family homes as a "new venture into space-concepts erected in slight materials by new methods," or, simply, as "modern architecture, Usonian."[5] For Wright, Usonia was a description and an aspiration. It encompassed his critiques of US urban-industrial society, the qualities of his own architecture, and the vision of a more "democratic" society his architecture would help bring into being. It was the United States as it was, and the United States as he intended to remake it.

These late 1930s writings give some sense of the range of meanings Wright attached to Usonia. They also point to a confusion, unresolved within the extensive literature on Wright but clarified here, regarding the term's origins. Contrary to Wright's claims, the English novelist and critic Samuel Butler never used the term. Much later, in *A Testament* (1957), Wright asserted, more specifically and just as erroneously, that he had taken Usonia from Butler's 1872 utopian satire *Erewhon, or Over the Range*.[6] In a 1961 essay on Wright's Broadacre City, the architectural historian George R. Collins appears to have been the first to realize that the word "is not to be found in any of Butler's works," which suggested that "actually Wright must have invented the term himself."[7] Collins goes on to speculate, however, that Wright may have found inspiration on "his first European trip in 1910 at which time there was considerable talk about addressing the States as U-S-O-N-A in order to avoid confusion with the new Union of South Africa."[8] Surprisingly, given the detailed attention nearly every facet of Wright's work and thought has received, Collins's claims more or less constitute the extent of scholarly efforts to explain Usonia's origins.[9] His speculation hints at a prehistory of Usonia, but it is a longer, more complicated history than his remarks suggest.

In what follows, I explore that history and Wright's relationship to it. While the term is most commonly associated with the affordable Usonian houses Wright built from the mid-1930s through the 1950s, Usonia was originally a late nineteenth-century phenomenon—a short-lived, relatively disorganized effort to forge a sense of national belonging among Anglo-Americans around the turn of the twentieth century. In that way, Usonia can be seen as a late addition to similarly fleeting efforts throughout the long nineteenth century to identify the most fitting name for the young nation. As early as 1804, for instance, the geographer Jedidiah Morse thought the annexation of Louisiana to the United States made "a fit time to introduce . . . a specific name for our country." "America," while preferable, was impracticable, since "other Americans" outside the United States could likewise claim the title. "Columbia" "would be honorary to the memory of the discoverer of America," but Morse preferred "Fredonia" because it lent itself to "all the variations"—"Fredonia," "Fredonian," and so forth—with "convenience and utility."[10] Advocates of "Fredonia," "Usonia," and various other proposals saw them as more accurate and, usually, uplifting alternatives to "America."[11] Recounting the earlier and largely forgotten history of the term "Usonia" helps fill a gap in the otherwise robust literature on one of the most prominent US architects. It also demonstrates the need to continue refocusing the historiographic lens, from inquiries into how an idea like Usonia "flourished in the mind of the artistic genius who conceived it," as Collins approvingly put it, to considerations of the complex social conditions that gave rise to both the term "Usonia" and the "genius" that appropriated it.[12] To do so is to grapple with the simple fact that across the Americas, as the scholar José F. Buscaglia puts it, "race and nation are one and the same."[13] Intriguingly, Buscaglia uses "Usonian" throughout his 2003 study "to refer to the peoples, nationalist ideology and imperial traditions of the United States of America" and credits Wright as his source.[14] Which is to say, he recovers something of the term's original meaning, albeit critically, which suggests there is more at stake here than just a better understanding of Wright. This prehistory of Usonia helps clarify the broader image of "America" that Wright himself and subsequent historians have constructed around his work and thought.

Race, Nationalism, and the Origins of Usonia

Usonia emerged in the late nineteenth century as a nebulous, racialized concept several decades before it became associated almost exclusively with the "democratic" ideals underpinning Wright's architecture.[15] Of the few sources, popular or scholarly, that have attempted to locate the term's first usage, most find it in a 1903 poem by James D. Law, an obscure Scottish American poet.[16] Law's elegy "The Sack of Auchindore" narrates the fiery demise of a minor Scottish noble and concludes with a veiled reference to Theodore Roosevelt as a descendent of the deposed clan ruling "in Usonia's mighty Lan'."[17] By way of explaining this unfamiliar term, Law includes a lengthy footnote that almost verbatim prefigures Wright's language in London three and a half decades later: "We of the United States, in justice to Canadians and Mexicans, have no right to use the title 'Americans' when referring to matters pertaining exclusively to ourselves."[18] He points to an earlier, unnamed writer who "first suggested 'Usona,' which is formed from the initials of 'United States of North America.'"[19] For Law, "the assonance of 'Usonans'" was "distasteful," but "designat[ing] our land, our people and our nation . . . 'Usonia,' 'Usonian' and 'Usonians'" would be "much more euphonious" and "represents in a similar way the 'United States of Northern *Independent* America.'"[20] Law was likely referring to a July 2, 1899, *St. Louis Republic* article by Sylvester Waterhouse, a classics professor at Washington University in St. Louis, which advocated that the United States adopt the name "Usona" and that its citizens become known as "Usonians." Waterhouse's proposal received national coverage—and in the process, "Usonians" was sometimes rendered as "Usonans"—but it is unlikely he originated the term. In a July 20, 1918, letter to the editors of *The New York Times*, the mathematician Christine Ladd-Franklin claimed that the term "Usona" "was first proposed by a Canadian, James P. Murray of Toronto, in 1885." She seems to be referring, with some confusion, to one J. P. Murray of Toronto, who wrote a letter to the editors of the journal *Canada* in 1907 noting that circa "1885 a Western Canadian called attention to the name formed from the initial letters of the title United States of North America—Usona."[21]

Sporadic incarnations of "Usona"—and, less often, "Usonia"—can be found throughout the late nineteenth and early twentieth centuries. Among other instances, these include Usona mining, manufacturing, and construction companies scattered across the country, from Connecticut to Colorado; a Usona yacht in Massachusetts; a Usonia Book Company in Chicago; a Usona Society for women at Brigham Young University; a line of Usona pottery from California; and a Usonia brand of hosiery sold at department stores nationwide (fig. 20.1). In 1901, the song "Usona" was debuted at a festival in Bloomington, Illinois. Its lyrics celebrated "the earth as a garden in bloom" and, in language evocative of Wright's, promised to "good, honest people / No need of crowding, there's plenty of room."[22] This was not Usona's only musical incarnation.[23] Perhaps because of Waterhouse's influence, St. Louis became a hub of Usonan activity. By 1902, the city boasted a Usona Dramatic Club, Usona Indemnity Society, Usona Social Club, Usona Supply Company, Usona Wire Company, and the fashionable, seventy-five-room Usona Hotel (fig. 20.2).[24] Elsewhere, architecturally speaking, an existing hotel in Fulton, Kentucky, was renamed the Usona in 1904, and an apartment building in the Bronx was christened Usona several years later.[25] Wright was

FIGURE 20.1. *Advertisement for B. Ott & Sons Company's Usona Power Brick Machine, La Crosse, Wisconsin.* Concrete *8, no. 6 (1908): 63.*

FIGURE 20.2. *Advertisement for the Usona Hotel, St. Louis, Missouri.* Gould's Blue Book for the City of St. Louis *(Gould Directory Co., 1913), 637.*

not even the first architect to make use of the term. In a paper titled "American Methods of Erecting Buildings," delivered at a November 1905 Royal Institute of British Architects meeting, the London-based, Chicago-born architect Reuben A. Denell began by "presum[ing] that by 'American methods' is meant the methods of the United States, or . . . U.S.O.N.A.," but then he reverted to "American" for the rest of his talk.[26]

This turn-of-the-century interest in an alternative to "America" must be understood within its historical context. The 1890s were marked by an increasingly intense and often violent nativism, a reaction to, among other things, southern and eastern European immigrants beginning to outnumber more "familiar" (and assimilable) arrivals from northern and central Europe; a deep, prolonged mid-decade economic depression; and labor unrest, punctuated by deadly strikes in Homestead, Pennsylvania, in 1892, and Pullman, Illinois, in 1894.[27] By the end of the decade, even as the intensity of this nativism had begun to ebb, the Spanish-American War introduced a new dimension. The US victory in December 1898 brought Guam, the Philippines, and Puerto Rico under US control, which introduced, at least among a vocal minority, fears that these new overseas dependencies would "pollute" the nation's supposed racial homogeneity.[28]

Waterhouse's piece in the *St. Louis Reporter* appeared just six months after the end of the war, suggesting that despite the explicit references to Canada and Mexico, the term "Usona" was undergirded by an unarticulated desire to differentiate the (white) citizens of the United States from the diverse inhabitants of its nascent empire.[29] At least some observers of the Usona debate made this imperial subtext explicit. One former resident of St. Louis's Usona Hotel, writing in response to Murray's letter in the journal *Canada*, observed that the question of "Usona" versus "America" was "bound to bob up more and more as the continent of North America increases in importance, and particularly as the different races of mankind each get a footing in the different sub-divisions."[30] More critically, the July 29, 1899, issue of the *Iowa State Bystander*, an African American newspaper in Des Moines, pointed out a contradiction between the term's conciliatory aspirations and the nation's colonialist reputation, observing wryly, "'Usona' may have a charm, but imperialists generally should consider the particularly appropriate nature of 'Expansia.'" Some critics simply did not see the point in exploring alternatives to "America," or they feigned confusion about how to pronounce "Usona."[31] Others understood this debate to center on questions of ethnic nationalism. An unsigned diatribe in the July 15, 1899, edition of the Lincoln, Nebraska, *Courier* warned that "all there is in a name or language is its history." The term "America" "means the Revolution, the civil war, the name is in literature and history. It means the landing of the pilgrims, the Indian wars, the Puritan inheritance and traditions." To adopt "Usona" would be to abandon the white Protestant heritage associated with "America." "Usona" may have been "an ingenious anagram," the author conceded, but "America" had been "christened in blood."

A second wave of interest in the term "Usonia" (as it was now more commonly rendered) emerged amid debates about US involvement in World War I, another period of nativist fervor, marked in particular by anti-German hysteria and nationalist arguments against US involvement abroad. Among the latter were proponents of the constructed language Esperanto. Christine Ladd-Franklin, a leading Esperantist, wrote to *The Nation* pondering alternatives to the term "American." She rejected "United Statesian" and "North American" because the former was cumbersome while the latter "is very suggestive of wild Indians, and it does not in any case enable us to separate ourselves from our neighbors, the Canadians and the Mexicans, with whom, in this age of wars, we may at any time have to be fighting."[32] She proposed "Usonian" as a derivative of the Esperantist colloquialism "Usono," which would clearly distinguish the United States of (North) America from the neighboring Estados Unidos Mexicanos (another United States) and the newly formed Union of South Africa (another USA).[33] As with the turn-of-the-century debates concerning "American" versus "Usonan," critics of Ladd-Franklin's proposal for "Usonian" focused on the term's lack of historicity. One response to her piece by the antiquarian Albert Matthews—titled "'Americans' and Others" and also published in *The Nation*—defended the use of "American" as "sanctioned by the use of one or two centuries." The name "originally meant an Indian," before designating "an English colonist in North America," until being "practically restricted" to "citizens of the United States."[34] Though perhaps not Matthews's intended meaning, it is worth noting that African Americans had been "practically restricted" from full US citizenship prior to ratification of the Fourteenth Amendment in 1868, and by the 1890s (just prior to the first wave of Usonan fervor), they had seen most Reconstruction-era civil rights stripped away. All of which is to say that the primary concern of both proponents and critics of "Usonia" and its variations was what best signified the identity and ideals of white US citizens over and against those other "Americans" who did not fit that description. If the terms of these debates were more often nativist or xenophobic than explicitly racist, Wright's appropriation of Usonia added a decidedly more racialized tone.

The Racial Rhetoric of Wright's Usonia

Wright only ever cited Butler as his source for the term "Usonia," but his usage beginning in the mid-1920s maps neatly onto the discourse sketched above. As previously noted, he often promoted "Usonia" because it more clearly differentiated those inhabiting the United States from inhabitants of other parts of the Americas, which borrowed the rationale (and even the phrasing) that Waterhouse, Law, Ladd-Franklin, and others had used since at least 1899.[35] If this shows Wright to be attuned to the now decades-long debate concerning Usonia, his very first usage of the term made a more explicit appeal to racial difference than the more thinly veiled ethnic nationalism of existing Usonian discourse.

"Usonia" first appeared in Wright's writings in "In the Cause of Architecture: The Third Dimension," published in two parts in the November 1925 and January 1926 issues of the Dutch journal *Wendingen*.[36] The *Wendingen* article argued that if the social and aesthetic potential of the Machine (always, for Wright, with a capital *M*) could be properly managed by architects, it could become an ideal means of overcoming the dehumanizing tendencies of industrialism and the creative encumbrances of stylistic revivalism. Like much of Wright's writing of the 1920s, this largely repurposed arguments from well-known, early-career publications such as "The Art and Craft of the Machine" (1901), "In the Cause of Architecture" (1908) (fig. 20.3), and his introduction to *Ausgeführte Bauten und Entwürfe*

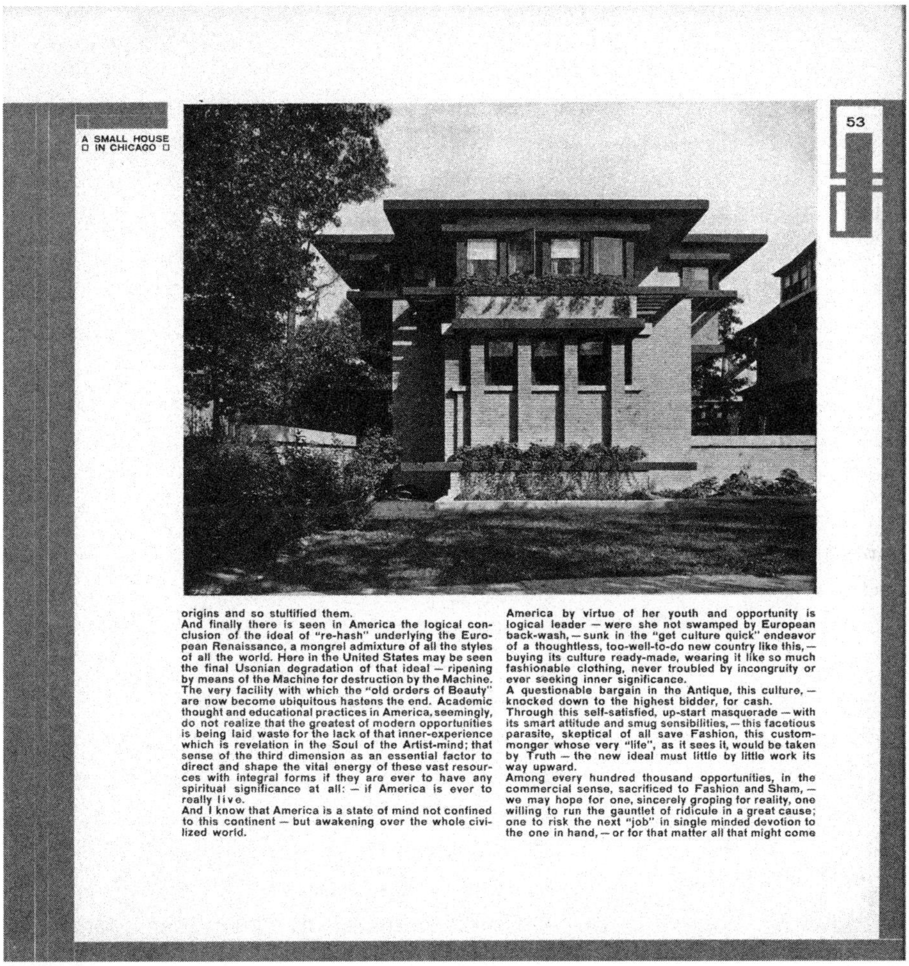

A SMALL HOUSE
IN CHICAGO

53

origins and so stultified them.
And finally there is seen in America the logical conclusion of the ideal of "re-hash" underlying the European Renaissance, a mongrel admixture of all the styles of all the world. Here in the United States may be seen the final Usonian degradation of that ideal — ripening by means of the Machine for destruction by the Machine.
The very facility with which the "old orders of Beauty" are now become ubiquitous hastens the end. Academic thought and educational practices in America, seemingly, do not realize that the greatest of modern opportunities is being laid waste for the lack of that inner-experience which is revelation in the Soul of the Artist-mind; that sense of the third dimension as an essential factor to direct and shape the vital energy of these vast resources with integral forms if they are ever to have any spiritual significance at all: — if America is ever to really live.
And I know that America is a state of mind not confined to this continent — but awakening over the whole civilized world.
America by virtue of her youth and opportunity is logical leader — were she not swamped by European back-wash, — sunk in the "get culture quick" endeavor of a thoughtless, too-well-to-do new country like this, — buying its culture ready-made, wearing it like so much fashionable clothing, never troubled by incongruity or ever seeking inner significance.
A questionable bargain in the Antique, this culture, — knocked down to the highest bidder, for cash.
Through this self-satisfied, up-start masquerade — with its smart attitude and smug sensibilities, — this facetious parasite, skeptical of all save Fashion, this custom-monger whose very "life", as it sees it, would be taken by Truth — the new ideal must little by little work its way upward.
Among every hundred thousand opportunities, in the commercial sense, sacrificed to Fashion and Sham, — we may hope for one, sincerely groping for reality, one willing to run the gauntlet of ridicule in a great cause; one to risk the next "job" in single minded devotion to the one in hand, — or for that matter all that might come

FIGURE 20.3. *A page from Frank Lloyd Wright's essay "In the Cause of Architecture: The Third Dimension," which includes his first use of the term "Usonia." The photograph is of the Emil Bach House (1915).* Wendingen *7, no. 5 (1926): 53.*

(1911). Midway through the essay, Wright zeroed in on what he saw as a destructive combination of unconstrained industrialization and Continental influences on US culture. He singled out the Renaissance in particular as an "admixture of ideals and races [that] necessarily confused origins and so stultified them."[37] He continued, warning somewhat repetitively that "there is seen in America the logical conclusion of the ideal of 're-hash' underlying the European Renaissance, a mongrel admixture of all the styles of all the world. Here in the United States may be seen the final Usonian degradation of that ideal—ripening by means of the Machine for destruction by the Machine."[38]

Wright did not clarify what exactly "Usonian" meant here, but it seems to have implied more than simply a desire to differentiate the United States from other American nations. Forgetting, it seems, that he had found early fame in Europe through publication of *Ausgeführte Bauten und Entwürfe* and that he was writing in a Dutch journal, Wright insisted that if architects in the United States could overcome their fascination with "European back-wash," they would become the natural leaders of a Machine Age revolution, because "America is a state of mind not confined to this continent—but awakening over the whole civilized world."[39] Whereas earlier generations of US architects argued for the superiority of their work because its neoclassical, Gothic, or Romanesque forms had evolved from (and superseded) old-world traditions, Wright offered his own architecture as a model of this transformative Usonian potential precisely because it was uncontaminated by such racially impure influences. He cited, among other examples, the Avery Coonley House (1907–1912), in Riverside, Illinois, because its horizontal forms, deep eaves, and free-flowing interiors seemed to "grow as part of its site," as a "natural" and "indigenous thing."[40] He also insisted that his Imperial Hotel (1913–1923) in Tokyo, which was built by Japanese labor to be enjoyed by Western diplomats, expatriates, and tourists, was "not a Japanese building—nor an American building in Tokio [*sic*]. It is simply a free interpretation of the oriental spirit."[41] In this first reference to Usonia, however fleeting and vague, Wright both made apparent its racial underpinnings, by differentiating it from "mongrelized" historical influences, and obscured them, by emphasizing, for example, the naturalness and indigeneity of an estate built for white industrialists on land cleared within living memory of its Native inhabitants.

In doing so, Wright also made clear his debt, conscious or not, to the existing contours of Usonian discourse. If his reference to Canadians and Brazilians also being American paraphrased earlier advocates of the terms "Usona" and "Usonia," the racialized rhetoric that accompanied Wright's introduction of "Usonia" into his lexicon—"mongrel admixture," "indigenous thing," "oriental spirit"—similarly cohered with those earlier advocates' (and their critics') ethnocentric anxieties. To be sure, the discourse on Usonia probably did not provide Wright's only source of inspiration here. His 1925 article appeared amid a particularly reactionary moment in US history, which took a variety of forms, from the nativism that thwarted plans for the League of Nations and inspired the discriminatory immigration quotas of the 1924 Johnson-Reed Act, to the white supremacy that fueled a revival of the Ku Klux Klan and popular interest in eugenics. Among the last, Lothrop Stoddard's *The Rising Tide of Color Against White World-Supremacy* (1920) proved especially popular. In it, Stoddard contended that "the cramped factory and the crowded city weeded out the big, blonde Nordic" and other "superior strains" in the United States, even as Latin America was overrun by the "mongrel—a walking chaos, so consumed by his jarring heredities that he is quite worthless."[42] In another sense, Wright's rhetoric resonated with that of his sometime employer and mentor Louis Sullivan. A well-known passage in Sullivan's *Kindergarten Chats* (1901) singled out H. H. Richardson's seven-story, red granite and sandstone–clad Marshall Field's Wholesale Store (1885–1887) in Chicago, which unlike the revivalist buildings surrounding it, was "a real man, a manly man; a virile force"; and an "oasis" "in a world of barren pettiness . . . for it sings the song of procreant power, as others have squealed of miscegenation" (that is, race mixing).[43] Sullivan was of course not alone in seeing the built environment through an inherently racial lens; he was one among several prominent late nineteenth-century architects who drew on the discourse of scientific racism to theorize what an "indigenous" architecture in the United States should look like.[44] Wright, for his part, offered a kind of synthesis of Stoddard and Sullivan. Aside from his concern about the "mongrel" architecture of the Renaissance in his 1925 *Wendingen* article, he lamented in *The Disappearing City* (1932) the "incongruities" and "abortions" resulting from "the advent of many nationalities" in the United States, which destroyed the potential that "had come to the new country with the decency of the early colonials," before promising that his "organic" vision would make manifest "a manly man, in Usonia, living in man-like freedom."[45] Usonia, in Wright's hands, was overdetermined by, among other things, the social environment in which he was writing, recurrent debates about the emergent US empire, cultural concerns he shared with other late nineteenth- and early twentieth-century architects, and racialized anxieties that permeated those social, political, and cultural contexts.

Conclusion

There are, as I see it, two primary conclusions to draw from this investigation into Usonia's origins. First are the insights it provides into Wright's work and thought. By working backward into the nineteenth century rather than forward from Wright's first usage of the term, and by shifting the focus from the "genius" and his ideas onto the overlapping contexts—social, cultural, political—within and against which those ideas were formed, it becomes clear that Usonia was not the singular invention of one man but a kind of late nineteenth-century assemblage of nationalist aspirations and racialized anxieties that Wright discovered and appropriated. Such an understanding of Usonia builds upon and extends recent work by a growing cohort of scholars, such as Charles L. Davis II, Dianne Harris, Elizabeth S. Hawley, and Mabel O. Wilson.[46] Their studies of Wright's Prairie style, Broadacre City, Nakoma Country Club, and Rosenwald School, respectively, have similarly reframed and recontextualized Wright's work, bringing previously unnoticed racial themes to the fore. Unlike these more project-specific studies, Usonia became the ethos of Wright's career after the 1920s. To see Usonia as a borrowed, racialized concept requires a rethinking, not just of individual projects but of the historical narratives that have been used to frame Wright's work broadly. This points toward a second, related conclusion—namely, what this reframing of Usonia can tell us about how "America" has been constructed through narratives that have had much to say about Wright's architecture but, until recently, very little about race. The desire to better circumscribe the United States, to more clearly differentiate its citizens from other "Americans," was rooted in the exclusionary logic of a racialized nationalism, whatever the conciliatory tone struck by Wright and other advocates of the term "Usonia." To better understand Wright's work and the "democratic" ideals it purports to uphold returns me to José F. Buscaglia's usage of "Usonia," rather than "America," to illustrate the racial nationalism and imperial machinations of the United States. There is a certain irony to this, since Buscaglia reclaims something of the term's original meaning but seems to do so unknowingly, since he cites Wright as his only source. Buscaglia uses "Usonia" to illustrate "the perils and the vices of nationalist thought."[47] If scholars, critics, and enthusiasts of Wright's work—as well as architectural historians interested in using Wright to rethink broader questions concerning "American" architecture—were to look beyond Wright himself, they would find that his Usonia, whatever its "democratic" aspirations, embodies similar perils and vices.

Notes

1. On the context of these lectures, see Andrew Saint, "Wright and Great Britain," in *Frank Lloyd Wright: Europe and Beyond*, ed. Anthony Alofsin (University of California Press, 1999), 129–136.

2. Frank Lloyd Wright, *An Organic Architecture: The Architecture of Democracy; The Sir George Watson Lectures of the Sulgrave Manor Board for 1939* (MIT Press, 1970), vii.

3. Wright, *Organic Architecture*, 27.

4. Frank Lloyd Wright, "Usonian House for Herbert Jacobs," *Architectural Forum* 88, no. 1 (1948): 78.

5. Frank Lloyd Wright, "'Honeycomb': Paul Hanna House," *Architectural Forum* 88, no. 1 (1948): 68.

6. Several sources, popular and scholarly, point to an essay titled "The Pictures We Make," written in 1927 but unpublished, as the first time Wright connected Usonia to Butler's *Erewhon*. It contains one fleeting reference to Usonia (compared with several to America and Americans) and no mention of Butler. See Frank Lloyd Wright, "The Pictures We Make," in *Frank Lloyd Wright: Collected Writings*, 5 vols., ed. Bruce Brooks Pfeiffer (Rizzoli, 1992–1995), 1:215–220. In 1941, Wright published a heavily revised version of "The Pictures We Make," which does include a reference to Butler but not to *Erewhon*. See Frederick Gutheim, ed., *Frank Lloyd Wright on Architecture: Selected Writings, 1894–1940* (Duell, Sloan and Pearce, 1941), 100. Wright's first documented reference to Butler was in *An Autobiography* (1932), reprinted in Pfeiffer, *Collected Writings*, 2:121. His first reference to *Erewhon* was in *A Testament* (1957), reprinted in Pfeiffer, *Collected Writings*, 5:199.

7. George R. Collins, "Broadacre City: Wright's Utopia Reconsidered," in *Four Great Makers of Modern Architecture: Gropius, Le Corbusier, Mies van der Rohe, Wright* [. . .] (Trustees of Columbia University, 1963), 70.

8. Collins, "Broadacre City," 71.

9. Most studies of Wright's work since the mid-1970s, if they attempt to clarify Usonia's meaning, have pointed not to Collins but to John Sergeant's paraphrase of Collins in his book on Wright's Usonian houses, but neither Sergeant nor subsequent scholars have added new insights. See John Sergeant, *Frank Lloyd Wright's Usonian Houses: Designs for Moderate Cost One-Family Homes* (Whitney Library of Design, 1976), 16.

10. Jedidiah Morse, *The American Gazetteer, Exhibiting a Full Account of the Civil Divisions, Rivers, Harbors, Indian Tribes, &c. of the American Continent* [. . .] (Boston: Thomas & Andrews, 1804), v, vi.

11. See H. L. Mencken, "Names for Americans," *American Speech* 22, no. 4 (1947): 241–256.

12. Collins, "Broadacre City," 74.

13. José F. Buscaglia-Salgado, *Undoing Empire: Race and Nation in the Mulatto Caribbean* (University of Minnesota Press, 2003), xxiv. My thanks to Charles Davis for bringing Buscaglia's work to my attention.

14. "José Buscaglia," College of Social Sciences and Humanities, Northeastern University, accessed February 10, 2022, https://cssh.northeastern.edu/faculty/jose-buscaglia/; cf. Buscaglia-Salgado, *Undoing Empire*, 266n34.

15. The following is an expanded, revised, and in several places corrected version of an account that appeared in Joseph M. Watson, "The Antinomies of Usonia: Neil Levine's *The Urbanism of Frank Lloyd Wright*," *Avery Review*, no. 25 (September 2017), https://www.averyreview.com/issues/25/the-antinomies-of-usonia.

16. See, for example, Wikipedia, "Usonia," accessed February 3, 2022, https://en.wikipedia.org/wiki/Usonia; Anthony Alofsin, *Wright and New York: The Making of America's Architect* (Yale University Press, 2019), 287n14; Catherine Maumi, *Usonia, ou, Le mythe de la ville-nature américaine* (Éditions de la Villette, 2008), 5.

17. James D. Law, "The Sack of Auchindore," in *Here and There in Two Hemispheres* (Home Publishing, 1903), 111.

18. Law, "Sack of Auchindore," 111.

19. Law, "Sack of Auchindore," 112.

20. Law, "Sack of Auchindore," 112.

21. J. P. Murray, "'Usona' v. 'America,'" *Canada: An Illustrated Weekly Journal* 4, no. 52 (1907): 526. The earliest extant use of the term "Usona" seems to be in a translation of a posthumously published travelogue by the Hungarian aristocrat Maurice Benyovszky. During a trek across the Pacific, Benyovszky describes landing on "the isle of *Usona*," which, based on other aspects of his account, seems to be the Japanese island Amami Ōshima. Pasfield Oliver, ed., *Travels of Mauritius Augustus Count de Benyowsky in Siberia, Kamchatka, Japan, the Liukiu Islands and Formosa* [. . .] (London: T. Fisher Unwin, 1893), 38; cf. L. L. K., "Mauritius Augustus Benyowszky," *Notes and Queries: A Medium of Communication for Literary Men, General Readers, Etc.*, no. 7 (May 25, 1895): 403. The earliest documented use of "Usona" to refer to the United States appears to be Waterhouse's.

22. See "Anniversary of Big Fire Is Marked by a Jubilee," *St. Louis Republic*, June 19, 1901, 2.

23. See the sarcastic retort to Ladd-Franklin's 1918 proposal in *The New York Times*, quoted in "A New Anthem," *Casper [WY] Daily Tribune*, July 19, 1918, 2; the entirely serious "Usona's Liberty Song," written and composed by Irene de S. Willis (Mission Music Publishing, 1918); and the secular cantata "Usona: A Paean of Freedom," music by Willard Patton, libretto by Sharlot Hall (Lloyd, 1919).

24. See "Usona Club Members Will Open Season of Amateur Theatrics," *St. Louis Republic*, September 25, 1902, 14; *The Insurance Year Book, 1910–1911* (Spectator, 1910), 497; "Social Clubs," *St. Louis Republic*, December 28, 1902; and the advertisement for Geo. B. Vashon & Co. in the *St. Louis Palladium*, August 18, 1906, 1. A Kansas City–based Usona Zinc Mining Company, founded in 1899, adopted its name at the suggestion of "a distinguished publicist of St. Louis." See *Age of Steel* 86, no. 17 (1899): 14.

25. For the Kentucky hotel, see the announcement in *Hotel Monthly* 12, no. 135 (1904): 39. For the Bronx apartments, see the Red Gum advertisement in *National Builder* 52, no. 8 (1911): 5.

26. R. A. Denell, "American Methods of Erecting Buildings: Read Before the Royal Institute of British Architects, Monday, 20th November 1905," *Journal of the Royal Institute of British Architects* 13, no. 2 (1905): 29.

27. See John Higham, *Strangers in the Land: Patterns of American Nativism, 1860–1925* (Rutgers University Press, 1955), chap. 4.

28. Higham, *Strangers in the Land*, 109.

29. It should be noted that Canadians were not exempt from certain strains of 1890s US nativism. A failed 1897 US immigration bill would have prohibited Canadians from crossing the border for work, part of an effort to defend the Anglo-Saxon race through restrictions placed on even Britain and its empire. See Higham, *Strangers in the Land*, 105, 96.

30. Jno. R. Kendrick, "'Usona' v. 'America,'" *Canada: An Illustrated Weekly Journal* 5, no. 60 (1907): 336.

31. These are scattered across numerous small papers in the months following publication of Waterhouse's proposal. A representative cross section, from enthusiastic to flustered to indifferent, can be found among the many responses to Murray's letter to the editors of *Canada*. See the letters in the January 12, 1907; January 19, January 26, February 2, February 9, February 23, March 2 and March 9, 1907, issues; and the editors' summary of the "controversy" in the March 16, 1907, issue.

32. Christine Ladd-Franklin, "The Usonians," *Nation* 102, no. 2638 (1916): 74; see also her earlier "Usonia Is Logical: A Suggestion That Esperanto Will Supply Our National Name," *New York Times*, June 12, 1915, 6.

33. Esperanto was invented by the Polish polymath L. L. Zamenhof around 1887. In 1905, the French Esperanto specialist Gaston Moch recommended "Usono" as the colloquial form of "Unuigitaj Ŝtatoj de Norda Ameriko," with "Usona" and "Usonano" as the adjective and pronoun forms. See Gaston Moch, *Historio resuma de l'arbitracio konstanta* (Instituto Internacia por la Paco, 1905), 48.

34. Albert Matthews, "'Americans' and Others," *Nation* 102, no. 2645 (1916): 282.

35. In addition to the lengthier explanation Wright offered in London in 1939, see, for example, the 1927 *Architectural Record* essay in which Wright warns, "America (or let us say Usonia—meaning the United States—because Canada and Brazil are America too)—Usonia is committed to the Machine and is Machine-made to a terrifying degree." Frank Lloyd Wright, "In the Cause of Architecture 1: The Architect and the Machine," in Pfeiffer, *Collected Writings*, 1:227.

36. Wright published an influential 1908 essay in *Architectural Record* titled "In the Cause of Architecture," followed by another, subtitled "Second Paper," in 1914. He would revisit many of the first article's themes in later writings, including the sixteen articles titled "In the Cause of Architecture" published during the 1920s—one each in *Wendingen* and *Western Architect*, plus fourteen in *Architectural Record*.

37. Frank Lloyd Wright, "In the Cause of Architecture: The Third Dimension" (1925/1926), in Pfeiffer, *Collected Writings*, 1:211.

38. Wright, "Third Dimension," 211.

39. Wright, "Third Dimension," 211.

40. Wright, "Third Dimension," 212. On Wright and the prairie, see Jennifer Gray, "Pattern Behind the Realism: The Jensen Graphic," in *Frank Lloyd Wright: Unpacking the Archive*, ed. Barry Bergdoll and Jennifer Gray (Museum of Modern Art, 2017), 24–32; Charles L. Davis II, *Building Character: The Racial Politics of Modern American Style* (University of Pittsburgh Press, 2019), 6–7.

41. Wright, "Third Dimension," 213. On the Imperial Hotel, see Ken Tadashi Oshima, "Reframing the Imperial Hotel: Between East and West," in Bergdoll and Gray, *Unpacking the Archive*, 60–68; Davis, *Building Character*, 214–226.

42. Lothrop Stoddard, *The Rising Tide of Color Against White World-Supremacy* (Charles Scribner's Sons, 1922), 164, 167, 166.

43. Louis H. Sullivan, *Kindergarten Chats and Other Writings* (Dover, 1979), 29, 30. The *Kindergarten Chats* originally appeared in serial form as a column in *Interstate Architect and Builder* from 1901 to 1902. They were subsequently edited and revised by Sullivan, but only published posthumously, in 1934, with further editing and an introduction by Claude Bragdon.

44. See Adrienne Brown, *The Black Skyscraper: Architecture and the Perception of Race* (Johns Hopkins University Press, 2017), chap. 3; Davis, *Building Character*, chap. 3; Joanna Merwood, "Western Architecture: Regionalism and Race in the *Inland Architect*," in *Chicago Architecture: Histories, Revisions, Alternatives*, ed. Charles Waldheim and Katerina Rüedi Ray (University of Chicago Press, 2005), 3–14.

45. Frank Lloyd Wright, *The Disappearing City* (William Farquhar Payson, 1932), 13, 12, 63.

46. In addition to works cited above, see Dianne Harris, "Where Was Jim Crow? Frank Lloyd Wright, Broadacre City, and the All-White American Suburb," in *Segregation and Resistance in the Landscapes of the Americas*, ed. Eric Avila and Thaisa Way (Dumbarton Oaks, 2023), 161–182; Elizabeth S. Hawley, "'Playing Indian' at the Nakoma Country Club," in Bergdoll and Gray, *Unpacking the Archive*, 78–85; Mabel O. Wilson, "Rosenwald School: Lessons in Progressive Education," in Bergdoll and Gray, *Unpacking the Archive*, 96–104.

47. Buscaglia-Salgado, *Undoing Empire*, xxiv.

ACKNOWLEDGMENTS

MANY HANDS GO INTO SUPPORTING a publication that has taken shape over years of symposia, panels, research seminars, and publication workshops.

The genesis of this project took place in the spring of 2019 with a one-day symposium titled "The Whiteness of Nineteenth-Century American Architecture." We would like to thank those who contributed funds and administrative support at the University at Buffalo School of Architecture and Planning, including Dean Robert Shibley, Hadas Steiner, and Jessie Fisher, and externally to Reinhold Martin, who provided support from the Temple Hoyne Buell Center for the Study of American Architecture at Columbia University. Mabel Wilson and Dianne Harris also gave keen and insightful keynotes to open and close this event.

This project would have been impossible without the convening of two complementary publication workshops. We would like to thank the Society of Architectural Historians (SAH) for accepting our proposal for an SAH Connects session titled "Race and the Historiography of American Architecture Publication Workshop." Special thanks go to Carla Yanni, Christopher Kirbabas, and Helena Dean for spearheading this effort. We are also grateful for the many comments that helped us refine the intellectual framing and scope of this project, as well as to the many junior scholars who expressed an interest in our work by responding to our call for papers. It is encouraging to see so many interested in reviving scholarly interest in nineteenth-century American architecture.

We would like to thank those who contributed funds and administrative support for the virtual publication workshop that took place at the University of Texas at Austin School of Architecture in the fall of 2022. Special recognition goes out to Dean Michelle Addington, Fernando Lara, and Sarah Lopez. Special thanks are due to the Office of the Vice President for Research, Scholarship, and Creative Endeavors at the University of Texas at Austin for a subvention grant to improve the quality of this book for publication. Thanks to Anjelyque Easley, doctoral candidate in architecture at the University of Illinois Urbana-Champaign, for editorial support.

We gratefully acknowledge the University of Illinois Urbana-Champaign and Victoria University of Wellington for their generous support for contributing authors, which helped make this collaborative publication possible.

INDEX

Note: *Italicized* page numbers indicate material in photographs or illustrations.

Abiff, Hiram, 104
abolition/abolitionism: and agricultural land grant colleges, 237, 250; and biblical Exodus analogies, 103; and Bulfinch's Massachusetts State House, 318; and crusade against one-room cabins, 149–150; and decorations of Library of Congress, 334, 338; Du Bois on, 1; and evolution of Mission and ranch styles, 303–305; and Indigenous anti-colonial opposition in Southern California, 290; and industrialization of American economy, 353; and influence of modernist historiography, 3; and Jefferson's influence on American architecture, 319, 323; and professionalization of American architecture, 26–27, 30, 32; and racial regimes and inversion, 100; and scope/structure of text, 11. *See also specific individuals*
Act for the Government and Protection of Indians, 294
Adam, Robert, 202
Adame, Modesto S., 179n57
Adams, Annmarie, 13
Adams, Carleton, 63, 73
Adams, M. B., 114
Adams, Robert, *203*
adobe structures, 71, *295*, 297–298
Adorno, Theodor, 319
Africa. *See specific countries*
Africa, decorations of Library of Congress, *337*, 338
African American Protestantism, 98–99
African-descended people, 67, 114–115, 165, 168, 174, 198, 206
African Methodist Episcopal (AME) Church, 11, 15, 127–143
Afro-Creole migrants, 177n34
Aggie Life, 254n69
agricultural colleges, 233–251, *235*, *237*, *244*, *246*, *249*, *250*, 251n2, 254n69, 284
Ahmed, Sara, 182
Aiken, South Carolina, 32
air circulation systems, 134, 140
Alabama, 152
Alabama A&M University, 138
Alabama College, 38
Alamo (merchant's house), 171
Alamo (mission), 73
Alaska Natives, 273
Alcalá de Bouis, Manuela, 171
Alderman, Derek, 114
Alexander, G. M., 133
Alexander, Zeynep Çelik, 327
Allcott, John, 42n25
Allen, Richard, 140
Allensworth, California, 115
Allen University, 130, *139*, 139–140
Allotment and Assimilation Era (1887–1934), 273
allotment of tribal land, 261–262, 264–265, 270, 289, 293, 301, 303–304. *See also* Dawes Act (General Allotment Act)
Alonzo, Armando C., 173, 179n64
AME Council of Bishops, 135
AME General Conference, *141*, 141–142
The American Architect and Building News, 35
"American" architectural style, 3, 4
American Architecture (Kimball), 2, 17
American Architecture Studies (Schuyler), 17
American Board of Commissioners for Foreign Missions (ABCFM), 215–216, *217*, 219
American Colonization Society, 105, 217
American Enlightenment, 312, 313
American exceptionalism, 17, 18, 344, 356
American Geographical Society, 219
American Indians, 273
American Institute/Institution of Architects (AIA), 13, 25, *28*, 29, 30–38, 42n22, 347, 356
"American Methods of Erecting Buildings" (Denell), 367
American modernism, 26
American Renaissance, 19

American Revolution, 99, 215
The American Spirit in Architecture (Hamlin), 2
Americas, decorations of Library of Congress, 337, 338
America's Architectural Roots (Upton), 5
"Americo-Roman" term, 31
Amherst, Massachusetts, 243–244
Amherst College, 243, 250
amusement parks, 185, *185*, 195n8
ancestral knowledge, 124
Ancient Monuments of the Mississippi Valley (Squier and Davis), 4
Anderson, Jennifer L., 200, 210
Andover Theological Seminary, 215
Andrew, John A., 236
Anglo-Americans, 4, 86, 226
Anglo-Saxons, 258–259, 334
annexation of Texas, 164
Anthony, Carl, 65, 313
Apache Indians, 277
An Appeal to the Colored Citizens of the World (Walker), 102
Arapaho Indians, 277
arbors, 123, 175n8
ArcGIS StoryMaps, 115
Architectural Forum, 363
Architectural Record, 374n35
The Architectural Record, 223
architectural symbolism, 99
Architecture and Utopia (Tafuri), 319–320, 324
"Architecture in the West" (Van Brunt), 352
The Architecture of H. H. Richardson and His Times (Hitchcock), 2
Argüelles de la Garza, Pedro, 177n35
Arizona, 275, *276*, *277*
Army of the Potomac, 242
Arnett Hall (Wilberforce University), 130, *138*, 138–139
Arnold, Edwin, 193
Arreola, Daniel, 164
"The Art and Craft of the Machine" (Wright), 369
Arts and Crafts style, 7, 196n23, 291
Asian influences and motifs, 181–182, 184–185, 187–191, 192–195, 337–338, *339*
aspens, 280
assimilation: and agricultural land grant colleges, 238–239, 245, 247; and architecture of South Texas border cities, 170–171, 174; and decorations of Library of Congress, 335; and ethnological schema of American architecture, 354; and evolution of Mission and ranch styles, 293–303; and goals of Reconstruction, 236; and Indian boarding schools, 273–274, 275, 277, 285–286; and mercantile colonialism in Texas border region, 168; and *negros* of Texas border region, 165; and the ranch house in Southern California, 289; and scope/structure of text, 10, 17–18; and white settlement of Indigenous lands, 257, 259, 261–262, 265; and Wright's "Usonia" term, 367
Athens, 74
The Atlantic Monthly, 129
Ausgeführte Bauten und Entwürfe, 369–370
Austin, Texas, 81, 82–84, 86–88, 89–92
authoritarianism, 317
Avery Coonley House, 370
Aztec motifs, 73

Babcock, Charles, 30
Bailey, Julius H., 131
Bailey, Liberty Hyde, 51
Baker, Jean, 40n5
Ballou's Pictorial Drawing-Room Companion, 205
Baltimore, Maryland, 34
Banham, Reyner, 2
Banivanua-Mar, Tracey, 257
barbed-wire fencing, 173
Barber, John Warner, *244*
Barnd, Natchee Blu, 258
Barra de Santiago, 164
Barrera y Garza, Tomás Sánchez de la, 177n35
Barrows, David P., 298, 300, 301
Barry, David F., 267
Battle of Bull Run, 241
Battle of Greasy Grass (Little Bighorn), 255, 267
Battle of Little Bighorn, 255, 267
Battle of the Big Black River, 351
Baumann Frederick, 348
Beard, Charles, xi
Beard, Mary, xi
Bear Dance, 278
Beaux-Arts style, 113, 181, 189, 329, 330
Beebe Lake, *44*
Behrendt, Curt, 357
Beirut, 216, 217, *218*
Belize, 204, 207, 208
Beltramini, Guido, 315
Benavides, Manuela Farías, 177n35

Bending the Future (Page and Miller), 147
Benjamin, Asher, 36
Bentel, Paul, 154
Bentham, Jeremy, 202, 208
Bentham, Samuel, 208
Benton, Thomas Hart, 166–167
Benyovszky, Maurice, 373n21
Bering Strait, 16
Bernal, Martin, 106
Bethel AME Church, Detroit, 134–135
Bexar County, Texas, 62
Bible, 102, 103, 118
biblical orientalism, 218
Bibliothèque Sainte-Geneviève, 329
Biden, Joseph, 274
Big Bethel AME Church, 130, 142, *142*
Big Black River Bridge/Station, 351, *351*, 353
Big Head, 266
Biographical Sketches of the Leading Men of Chicago, *351*
biological analogy for design, 344. *See also* evolution of building styles
Bishir, Catherine, 85
Bishop, Henry, 186
Bishop Museum, Honolulu, *190*
Bishop Playhouse, 186
Bismarck, Dakota Territory, 258–261, *260*, 270
The Bismarck Tribune, 260
bison, 264
Black Athena (Bernal), 106
Blackhawk, Ned, 11, 17
Black Reconstruction in America (Du Bois), xi, 6, 38
Blacks and African Americans: and agricultural land grant colleges, 239, 245–246, 251, 254n69; and alternative forms of historiography, 81, 82; and AME church design, 127–143; and "American architecture" label, 4; and architecture of fugitive spaces, 96–97; Black abolitionists, 103; Black Africans, 322; Black Codes, 68, 254n69; Black community in Matamoros, 177n34; Black cowboys, 68; Black diaspora, 15, 97, 103–105, 119, 168; and Black formalism, 15, 128–130, 133, 135, 137–139, 141–143; Black Freemasons, 98, 100, 102; Black history movement, 151–153; Black internationalism, 106; Black Seminoles, 114; and cattle brand registrations, 62–63, 68–71; and citizenship laws in Texas, 68; and crusade against one-room cabins, 146–157, 157n4; extension agents, 46; farmers, 250; freedom towns, 12, 15, 114; and free labor after Civil War, 238; and mahogany lumber industry, 208; military service in Civil War, 236; and naming of free Black communities, 114–115, 117, 124; and professionalization of American architecture, 28; and racialized historical narratives, 98–100, 105; ranchers, 69; and rural home economics, 45; and scope/structure of text, 9, 11, 14–15; settlement history, 111–115; and stonemasons of Texas, 89–91, *90*; and Wright's "Usonia" term, 367–368. *See also specific individuals*
Blau, Judith, 45
Bliss, Daniel, 217
board-and-batten architecture, *33*
boardinghouses, 249
boarding schools, 265, 273–277, *276*, 281–287, 289
Board of Agriculture, 234
Bogart, Michele, 340n11
Bohemian Club, 191
Boley, Oklahoma, 179n69
Bolland, O. Nigel, 200
Bond, Richard, 36
Bond, Scott, 153
border-brick style, 169–172, 174, 177n36, 179n56
border crossings, 16, 175
Born in Blackness (French), 106
Boston, Massachusetts, 34
Boston African Lodge No. 459, 99
B. Ott & Sons Company, 366
Bowie, Henry Pike, 191
Box, Russell, Sr., 284
Boyd, William, 332
Boyington, William, 357
Bradley, Rizvana, 11
branding, 176n16
Brandon, John, 82, 86
Brazil, 363, 370
Brewster, Earnol, 122
brickwork and brick masons: and architecture of South Texas border cities, 169, 171–172, 177n35; and stonemasons of Texas, 83, *83*, 86–87, 88–89, 91. *See also* masons and masonry construction
bridges, 350–351, 353
Bridgeton, New Jersey, 137
Brinton, Daniel, 333
British Crown Estate, 211
British Honduras, 204
British Museum Library, 328

Broadacre City, 363, 372
Brookings Institution's Meriam Report, 293
Brooklyn Bridge, 2
Brooks, Samuel W., 170
Brooks, S. W., 171
The Brown Decades (Mumford), 2, 210
Brownsville, Texas, 66, 163–175, 177n37
The Brownsville Herald, 172
Brownsville Town Company, 178n41
Brown v. Board of Education, 254n69
Bruner, Peter, 153
brush arbors, 123, 175n8
Buffington, LeRoy S., 357
building and loan associations, 152
building regulations, 353
Buildings and Landscapes, 5
Bulfinch, Charles, 26, 318
Bunch, Lonnie G., III, 156
Bureau of Home Economics, 13, 47, *50*, 51
Bureau of Indian Affairs, 17, 276, 290, 293, 302–303
Burnham, Daniel, 313, 354
Burnham & Root, 358
Burns, Howard, 315
Burns, Sara, 245
Burton, Thomas William, 153, *155*
Buscaglia, José F., 364, 372
Butler, Howard Crosby, 219, 222, 225, 372n6
Butler, Samuel, 363, 368
Byzantine style, 223, 225

cabinet maker, 200
Caddo Indians, 277
Cahaba, Alabama, 32, *33*
Cahuilla people, 300–301
Caldwell, Maria Louisa "Lou" Jones, 84
California, 192–193
California Gold Rush, 176n26, 193
California Mission–style, 173
California statehood, 294
Californios, 292, 297
Calvino, Italo, 126n16
Camargo, Tamaulipas, 166, 172, 178n37
camouflage, 280–281
Campbell, Emilia, 171
Canada, 365, 367–368, 370, 374n29
Canada (journal), 365, 367
Cantú, Eduardo Alarcón, 171
capitalism, 70, 172–173, 201–202, 206, 238, 319
Capitol Building Commission, 90
Capricci, 319–320
Carbajal, José María de Jesús, 178n37
Caribbean Basin, 200, 207, 210
Carlisle Indian Industrial School, 277, *278*
Carnegie, Andrew, 220
Carrasco, Jesús Franco, 165, 175n8
Carrió, Manuel Shvartzberg, 18
Casa Cross, 171
Casa Lojero, 167
Casey, Edward Pearce, 329–330, 336
Casey, Thomas Lincoln, Sr., 328
Catholic Church, 131, 239, 262, 290
cattle brands, 14, 61–71, *62*, 73, 75–76, 176n16
Cedar Hill, 155
Central America, 202
Central Deposit Vault Company, 345
Central Gulf Railroad Bridge, 353
Central Park, 234, 240, 241
Central Texas, 83
chapels, 118, 223
Chappelle Administration Building (Allen University), 130, 139, *139*
Charger, Chief, 264
Charles, Stillman, 169
Charles II, King of England, 205
Charles Keeler House, 188, 189
Charleston, South Carolina, 137
Charleston County, South Carolina, *156*
chattel slavery, 313, 334
Chattopadhyay, Swati, 11
Cheng, Irene, 200, 313, 344
Cheyenne River Agency, 264
Cheyennes, 277
Chicago, Illinois: Chicago Public Library, 328; Great Chicago Fire of 1871, 347, *347*
"The Chicago Construction, or Tall Buildings on a Compressible Soil" (Jenney), 348, *349*
"Chicago School" of architecture, 19, 342–343, 345, 356–358
Chicago Sketch Club, 350–351
Children's Aid Society of New York, 239
China, 338
Chinatown (San Francisco), 185, *186*
Chinese immigrants, 9, 182, 184, 187, 191
Chouin, Gérard, 120
Christianity, 15, 32, 217. *See also* African Methodist Episcopal (AME) Church; Catholic Church
The Christian Recorder, 15, 127, 129–132, 133–137, *135*, 140, 143, 144n9
"Church Antiquities," 131
churches, 32, *33*, 117. *See also* African Methodist Episcopal (AME) Church
Cincinnati, Ohio, 34
City Market House (Brownsville), 169, 170

City Park Square, 259
civil rights, 368
civil society, 322
Civil War: and agricultural land grant colleges, 236, 240, 245; and AME church design, 131, 136; and crusade against one-room cabins, 150; and Du Bois's critique of Reconstruction, 6; and evolution of skeleton-framed buildings, 345; and influence of modernist historiography, 3; Jenney's military service, 350–353; and occupation of Matamoros, 178n46; and postwar land-grant colleges, 233; and professionalization of American architecture, 30, 32, 34–35, 39; and racialized historical narratives, 103; and scope/structure of text, 9; Twain on causes of, 341n17. *See also* Reconstruction
Clarendon Bridge, 37
class hierarchies, 27, 55–56, 200
classicism, 314–316
Cleary, Richard, 170
Cleaveland, H. W., 30
Clemons, John, 123
Clemons, Patsy Ann, 123
Coahuila y Tejas, 68
Coahuiltecan peoples, 66
Cobb, Jasmine Nichole, 129
Cobb, John, 202
Cody, Jeffrey, 220
Coffey, Mary K., 75
Collier, John, 290, 293, 302, 304–305
Collins, George R., 363–364
colonialism, 64, 304, 341n19
colonial settlements, 193
colonial Spain, 72
colonization, 202
Colorado, 176n26, 275, *276*, *277*, 281
Colorado Desert, 298
Colorado Wickiup Project, 274
Columbia University, 217, 223, *224*, *225*, 226
Colunga, José, 179n57
Comanches, 66, 247, 277
Common Places (Upton and Vlach), 5
Comstock Lode, 176n26
Concord, Massachusetts, 244, *244*
Concord people, 193, 195, 196n29
Condit, Carl, 357
The Condition, Elevation, Emigration, and Destiny of the Colored People of the United States (Delany), 102, 105
Confederacy, 63. *See also* Civil War
Congregación del Refugio, 166. *See also* Matamoros, Tamaulipas
Congress Avenue (Austin, Texas), *87*
Congressional Record, 262
Constitution of the Republic of Texas, 68, 73
construction industry, 44
"The Construction of a Heavy, Fireproof Building on Compressible Soil" (Jenney), 347
contrabands, 245
Convent of the Incarnate Word and Blessed Sacrament, 171
convict leasing, *151*
Cook, Abner H., 82, 86
Cook, Lisa D., 116
"coolies," 193, 196n29
Cooper, Anna Julia, 152
Cooper Institute, 30
copyright law, 327
Corinthian columns, 337
Cornell University, 13, 43, *44*, 46–48, 51, 57
Cortina, Juan Nepomuceno, 168
cottages, 239
cotton, 167, 170–172, 240, 247
council circles, 265, *266*, *268*, 269
counterhistories, 105–107
Courier, 367
Coventry, George William, Earl of, 202, *203*
cowboys, 68, 298
The Craftsman, 291
craftsmen and artisans, 13, 199–200, 208
Crania Aegyptiaca (Morton), 102
Creoles, 168, 171, 174, 177n34
Crogman, William Henry, 148, 159n36
Croome Court, 202, *203*, 208, 210–211
Cross, John S., 171
Cross, Melitón H., 171, 174
cross-cultural themes, 184
Cruillas, Tamaulipas, Mexico, 69
Crusades, 71
Crystal Palace, 203–204, 208
cubism, 74
Culbertson, Margaret, 171
cultural diversity, 6–7
cultural dualism, 72
cultural eradication, 276
cultural style, 45
Curtis, Edward S., 301
Cushman, Ella, 49, 54–56

The Daily Picayune (New Orleans), 168, 177n35

Daily Ranchero (Brownsville), 168
Daily Time Record, *50*
Dairymen's League, 54
Dakȟóta people, 255, 257, 259, 264, 266, 270
Dakin, James H., 36–38
Dakota Access Pipeline, 270
Dakota Territory, 17
Dalton, Thomas, 100
Dante, 334
Dark Space (film), 96
Darwin, Charles, 350
Davis, Alexander Jackson, 35–37, 42n25, 340n11
Davis, Charles L., II, 16, 352, 372
Davis, Edwin H., 4
Davis, John, 218–219
Dawes, Henry L., 261–264
Dawes Act (General Allotment Act), 18, 264–266, 269–270, 289
Day, Thomas, 209
Decatur Street (New Orleans), 178n40
Decolonial Ecology (Ferdinand), 197
deforestation, 222. *See also* mahogany
Delany, Martin, 15, 97–107
Dell, Daisy, 185
Deloria, Ella Cara, 270
democracy, 19, 251n1, 317, 322, 344, 362–363, 364, 372
Democratic Party, 238
demolishing historic architecture, 146–157
Demosthenes, 334
Denell, Reuben A., 367
Department of Home Economics, 43
DeWitt, Lloyd, 315
Dialectic of Enlightenment (Adorno), 319
dialectics of liberty, 316–319
Dialektik der Aufklärung, 320
Dimerian Triad, 65, *65*, 67, 75–76
Dimery, Allen (Obidah), 62, 68
Dimery, Manuel, 68
Dimery, Margaret Smith, 14, 61–65, *62*, 66, 68–69, *70–71*, 75–76
The Disappearing City (Wright), 371
Division of Rare and Manuscript Collections, 51
Dodge, David Stuart, 217–221, 223
Dodge, Grace Hoadley, 217
Dodge, William, 216, 217
Dolores (*hacianda*), 176n17
Donaldson, Robert, 42n25
dormitories, 242, 249, 282
Douglass, Frederick, 32, 102, 155–156, 210
Downing, Andrew Jackson, 253n42, 340n11
Dred Scott decision, 32
Dreicer, Gregory, 344
Du Bois, W. E. B., xi, 6, 38, 97, 106, 148, 150–151, 158n23, 159nn35–36, 250
Ducat, Arthur Charles, 352
Dudley, Henry, 30
Dudley, Tara A., 14–15
Dunbar-Ortiz, Roxanne, 17
DuVal, Kathleen, 17

Eagle Pass, Texas, 172
Early Modern Architecture: Chicago, 1870–1910 (Museum of Modern Art), *343*
Eastern European settlers, 31
Eastern Seaboard, 27, 34
Eastville, Virginia, 137
École Centrale des Arts et Manufactures, 345
École des Beaux-Arts, 113, 329
Edinburgh, Texas, 177n37
Edmonds, Penelope, 257
Egypt, ancient, 103, 104–105
Eidlitz, Leopold, 30, 31
el-Bashe, Mahomet, 333
El Carmen, Texas, 177n36
El Chami, Yasmina, 17
Elements of Criticism (Kames), 321
elevators, 349
Elizabeth Street (Brownsville), 169
Ellicott, Henry J., 332
El Paso, Texas, 172
El Seno Mexicano / Nuevo Santander, 164
Elson, Isabel, 126n16
emancipation, 82, 88, 207, 236, 246
Emancipation Proclamation, 103, 122
Emanuel AME Church, 137
Emerson, Ralph Waldo, 334
Encumbrance (Rowland), 211
England, 210, 328
English landscape design, 253n42
English Navy, 205
English settlers, 17, 31. *See also* Anglo-Americans
Enlightenment, 20n15, 97, 313, 319, 321, 323, 327
Episcopal Reports, 135
Erewhon, or Over the Range (Butler), 363, 372n6
Ernest, John, 97
Escandón y Helguera, José de, 165
eschatology, 215
Escobar, Severiano, 179n57
Esperanto, 368, 374n33
Estados Unidos Mexicanos, 164, 368

Estes, Nick, 257, 270
Ethiopians, 103–104
ethnicity: and agricultural land grant colleges, 240; and "American architecture" label, 4; and architecture of South Texas border cities, 163; and border consciousness, 179n72; and Curse of Ham narrative, *101*; ethnic nationalism, 367; and ethnological schema of American architecture, 354; and evolution of Mission and ranch styles, 297, 300; and influence of modernist historiography, 3; and Maybeck's architectural regionalism, 188, 191, 195; melting-pot metaphor, 57; and racial hierarchy of South Texas border cities, 174; and racialized historical narratives, 103–104; and racial regimes and inversion, 100–102; and rural home economics, 57; and scope/structure of text, 16; and Wright's "Usonia" term, 369. *See also* ethnography/ethnology; race and racial identity
ethnography/ethnology: and "American architecture" label, 4; and American overseas missionary movement, 218, 220, 223; and decorations of Library of Congress, 326–340, *331*, *334*, *336*, 338, 340n11; ethnological exhibits, 354–356, *355*; ethnological exhibits at World's Columbian Exposition, 354–356, *355*; and ethnological schema of American architecture, 354; and evolutionary narrative in architecture, 345–350; and evolution of Mission and ranch styles, 294, *300*, 300–302, 305; and evolution of skeleton-framed buildings, 358; and Maybeck's architectural regionalism, 188; and naming of free Black communities, 115, 119, 125; and Wright's "Usonia" term, 370
Ethnography of the Cahuilla Indians (Kroeber), *300*
Eurocentrism and European influences: and "American architecture" label, 4; and decorations of Library of Congress, 337–338, *339*; and ethnological schema of American architecture, 354; European classicism, 316; European colonialism, 64; European immigrants, 16, 239, 354, 367; European Renaissance, 370; and evolutionary narrative in architecture, 345–346; and evolution of skeleton-framed buildings, 344, 357; Latrobe on, 40n2; and professionalization of American architecture, 26; and racialized historical narratives, 106; and scope/structure of text, 10, 13; telegraph line to America, *31*; vs. Civil War-era influences, 352
evangelicals, 104, 215–219, 221, 226, 268
Evans, Robin, 203
evolutionary theory, 357, 358
evolution of building styles, *343*, 344–350, 352–355, 357–358
Evolution of Farmers' Homes, *153*
Exodus analogy, 103
extension agents, 46

factionalism, 265–266
The Family Magazine, 205–206
Farías, Alfredo M. Passement, 177n35
Farías, Domingo V., 179n57
Farías, Irene Passement, 177n35
Farías, María Trinidad, 177n35
Farías-Sánchez, María Trinidad Sixtas, 177n35
farmhouses, 46–53, *49*, *52*, 56, 239
farming and agriculture, 244, 245, 264, 294, 322
Faust, Drew Gilpin, 34
Federal Hall National Memorial, 36
Federal Indian Boarding School System, 274–277
Federal Writers' Project, 123
"Felling Mahogany, Honduras" (McGahey), *207*
feminists/feminism, 56, 65
fencing, 67, 173, 176n16, 179n64
Ferdinand, Malcolm, 197, 206, 210
Fergusson, James, 2, 345
Ferree, Barr, 356
A Few Things to Be Thought of Before Proceeding to Plan Buildings for the National Agricultural Colleges (Olmsted), 237
A Field Guide to American Houses (McAlester), 4
Fifty-Fourth Regiment, 236
Finamore, Daniel, 200–201
fireproofing, 348, 349, 352
Fish, Cheryl J., 116
Fitch, James Marston, 39
Florida mahogany, 210
Floridian Black, 114
Floyd, George, 91
folk studies and architecture, 4, 11–12, 112, 293. *See also* vernacular architecture
forced labor, 204–208. *See also* slavery and enslaved persons
forestry, 199. *See also* mahogany
formal beauty, 321

Fort Brown, 169, 171
Fort Laramie Treaty, 264
Fort Lewis Indian Boarding School, 18, 274, 281–286, *283*, *284*
Fort Marion, 277, *278*
Fort Yates, 259, 262, *263*
Foster, Lafayette S., 245
fountains, 330
Four Corners region, 275–276, *276*, *277*, 281–282
Fourmile Branch, Tennessee, 32
Fourteenth Amendment, 368
Fox, Stephen, 16
France: and decorations of Library of Congress, 328; French Beaux-Arts movement, 113; French Enlightenment, 316; French law, 6; French settlers, 17, 31; and professionalization of American architecture, 28
Frankfort, Kentucky, 45
Franklin, Benjamin, 334, 335, *335*
Frederick Law Olmsted, a Critic of the Old South (Mitchell), 240
Frederick Law Olmsted: Landscape Architect, 1822–1903 (1922) (Olmsted and Hubbard), 240
Free, Gregory, 177n36
free Blacks: and agricultural land grant colleges, 254n69; and ethnological schema of American architecture, 354; freedmen's communities, 17, 93n2, 112, 114, 245–247; free labor, 236, 238, 247, 252n13; and Jefferson racial ideology, 322; and scope/structure of text, 14. *See also specific individuals*
"Freedman's Village Seen from the Road" (Waud), *246*
Freedmen's Bureau, *151*
Freedmen's Savings Bank, 210
Freedom Colonies, 115
Freemasonry, 15, 98–100, 102, 103–104
Free Soil Party, 236
French, Henry Flagg, 236, 246
French, Howard W., 106, 201
Frigga Fylgae society, 43, *44*
frontier architects, 2
Front Levee Street (Brownsville), 169
Fugitive Slave Act, 236, 341n18
Fuller, Buckminster, 313
functional beauty, 321
Furness, Frank, 6
furniture, 201–204

Gall, 266
Gallaud, Euphrosine, 177n35
Gallegos, Anjelica S., 18
Galveston, Texas, 66
Gardiner, Edward, 30
Gardner, Eric, 130
Garrison, William Lloyd, 241
gas lighting, 329
Gebhard, David, 291
gender divisions, 206
genealogical research, 14, 84, 102
General Allotment Act (Dawes Act), 18, 264–266, 269, 270, 289
general contractors, 354
General Land Office, 296
genocide, 28, 256, 262, 289
Geolas, Athanasiou, 13–14
George H. Boke House, 189
Georgia, 85
Geraniotis, Roula, 358
German immigrants and settlers, 17, 31, 239, 251, 252n13
Giedion, Sigfried, 2, 357
Gilbreth, Lillian, 54
Gilded Age, 216, 226
Giza funerary complex, 132
Glaevecke de Browne, María Josefina, 171
Goddess of Liberty statue, *90*
Goethe, Johann Wolfgang von, 334
gold, 176n26, 193
Golden Gate International Exposition, 185
Gonzalez, Aston, 129
Gooden, Mario, 96
Gordon, Lewis R., 11
Goseascochea de Cortinas, Estefana, 177n36
Gothic style, 132, 170, 188, 340n11, 357, 370
grange movement, 249
Grant, Ulysses S., 260–261, 351
Grass, John, 262–264, 266
Greasy Grass (Little Bighorn), 255, 267
Great Barrington, Massachusetts, 250
Great Exhibition of the Works of Industry of All Nations in London, 204
Great Sioux Reservation, 255, 257, 261, *263*, 264–265
Greco-Roman culture, 223
Greek Revival style, 36, 82
Green, Bernard, 328–329, 332, 336
Greene & Greene, 200
Greensward Plan (Central Park), 234
Gregorytown, Texas, 89
grounded normativity, 279
groves, 120
Guam, 367
Guangdong, China, 185, *185*

Guanzhou, China, 195n3
Guerrero Viejo, Tamaulipas, 166
Gullah language, 114
Gutman, Marta, 64

haciendas, 66, 69, 71, 73, 176n17, 292
Hafertepe, Kenneth, 319–321, 323–324
Halifax County, North Carolina, 85
Hall, Prince, 99
Hall, Stephen, 96
Hallet, Stephen, 26
Hamlin, Talbot, 2–3, 26, 39, 200
Handbook of Texas, 121
Handbook of Texas Online, 82
Handbook of the New Library of Congress, 332–333, 337–338, 340n11
Hanson, Martin, 170–172
Hanson, Martin, Jr., 172
Harper, Frances Ellen, 150
Harper, William, 248
Harper's Weekly, *260*, 260–261
Harris, Carmen V., 46
Harris, Dianne, 372
Harrison, Peter, 26
Harrison, William Henry, 150
Harrison County, Texas, *118*, 121–124, *122*, *123*
Hartman, Saidiya, 11, 64, 74
Harvard University, 107, 217, 248
Harvey-Fryar, Melanee C., 15
Haviland, John, 35
Hawaii, 187–191, *190*, 194
Hawley, Elizabeth S., 372
Hawthorne, Nathaniel, 244, 334
Hayden, Dolores, 13, 56
heating systems, 134, 140
Henderson, James M., 134
Hendrickson, John, 82
Henricks, Abram, 87
Hidalgo, Texas, 172, 177n37
Hidatsa people, 258
Higginbotham, Evelyn Brooks, 129
Hill, Jobie, 155
Hillside Club, 16, 191, 196n23
historically Black educational institutions, 138
historic preservation, 14, 146–147, 150–157
history-based theory, 74
History of the Negro Race in America (Williams), 105
Hitchcock, Henry-Russell, 2, 26, 343, 356
Hobart, Lewis, 181
Holliday, Kathryn E., 13
Holly, Michael Ann, 75
Holmes, Elijah H., 91
Holy Land, 215, 225
home economics, 13, 43–57, *49*, 60n44
Home Insurance Building, 19, 342, *343*, 344–345, 347, *348*, *349*, 352, 357–358
The Homemaker and her Job (Gilbreth), 54
Homestead, Pennsylvania, 367
Homestead Act of 1862, 289
Honduran mahogany, 202, 203–204
Honduras Almanack, 204–205, 207
hooks, bell, 126n16
Horkheimer, Max, 319
Houses and House-Life of the American Aborigines (Morgan), 4
Houston and Texas Central Railway, 88
Howells, John Mead, 217
Howells & Stokes, 218, 220, *221*, 223–224, *224*
Hubbard, Theodora Kimball, 240, 247, 253n29
Hugo, Victor, 329
Hunt, Richard Morris, 30, 31, 35
Huŋkpapȟa Lakȟóta people, 255, 258
hush arbors, 123
hybrid space and architecture, 73, 169–170, 174–175

Illinois Central Railroad, 179n69, 353
Immaculate Conception Church, 169–170
Imperial Hotel, 370
imperialism: and American overseas missionary movement, 219, 226; American soft imperialism, 214; and cultural influence of border areas, 64; and decorations of Library of Congress, 327, 340; and influence of modernist historiography, 3; and mahogany lumber industry, 200, 202–203; and Maybeck's architectural regionalism, 181, 189–191, 194; and mercantile colonialism in Texas border region, 167; and racial dynamics of architectural style, 71, 73; and racialized historical narratives, 104; and rural home economics, 45; and scope/structure of text, 18–19; and white settlement of Indigenous lands, 256, 260; and Wright's "Usonia" term, 364, 367, 370, 372. *See also* colonial settlements; settler colonialism
Indian New Deal, 293–294, *295*, 302, 304
Indian removal, 17, 276
Indian schools, 9, 273–277, 281–287
Indians of the Rio Grande Delta (Salinas), 165, 175n8
Indian territorial dispossession, 286
Indigenous peoples and lands: and crusade against one-room cabins, 147; and eth-

nological exhibits at World's Columbian Exposition, 354–356, *355*; and evolutionary narrative in architecture, 346–347; influence on architectural design, 19–20; and mahogany lumber industry, 198, 205; and Maybeck's architectural regionalism, 189; and mercantile colonialism in Texas border region, 165; and Mexican culture, 73; and professionalization of American architecture, 28; and racial dynamics of architectural style, 69; and scope/structure of text, 9, 17–18; and shortcomings of "American architecture" label, 6. *See also* Indian reservations; *specific Indian tribes*
Industrial Chicago, 349
Industrial Home School (Washington, DC), 252n24
informational learning, 278
The Inland Architect and Builder, 35, 346–347
The Inland Architect and News Record, 350, 357
Institute of Fine Arts, New York University, 35
intergenerational knowledge, 286
intergenerational wealth, 68
International Style, 4, 342–343, 356
"In the Cause of Architecture: The Third Dimension" (Wright), 369, *369*
intrinsic beauty, 321
"Inventory of Working Equipment," 48
Iowa State Bystander, 367
I quattro libri (Palladio), 315
Irish immigrants, 239, 251, 252n13, 252n23
Irish Military Lodge, 99
ironwork, 220, 329, 353
Irving, Washington, 334, 341n17
Islamic architecture, 72
isolated-pier foundations, 348
Israelites, 103–104
Italianate style, 340n11
Italian Renaissance style, 330, 340n8
Ivanhoe (Scott), 341n17
ivikani. *See* wickiups

jacals, 71
Jackson, J. B., 290
Jacksonian America, 26
Jamaica, 202, 204, 207–208, 210
James, George Wharton, 291
Japan, 338
Jarzombek, Mark, 5
jazz music, 184
Jefferson, Thomas: and agricultural land grant colleges, 242; and architectural influence of New Orleans, 179n69; and assimilation of Indigenous peoples, 275, 289; Enlightenment concepts in architecture of, 311–314; Hafertepe on Jeffersonian aesthetics, 321–323; and liberty/authority contradiction, 316–319; and professionalization of American architecture, 38–39; Rockfish Gap Report, 252n15; scholarly attention to architecture of, 314–316, 323–324; and scope/structure of text, 7, 18; and the University of Virginia, 238, 311, *312*, 314, 318–319
Jenney, William Le Baron, 19, 342, 344–350
Jennings, Jan, 51–53
Jerusalem, 216
Jim Crow segregation, 15, 93n2, 147–148, 150, 152, 154, 157, 157n4, 250
Jimmerson, G. D., 137
Johnson, Philip, 343, *343*
Johnson-Reed Act, 371
Johnston, George Barnett, 45
Jones, Edmund, 85
Jones, Isaac, 89
Jones, Maria Louisa, 86
Jones, Olivia "Lilly," 84, 89
Jones, Thomas H., 82–87, *87*, 89
Jordy, William H., 39
Joseph of the Nez Perce, 337
Journal of the Society of Architectural Historians, 5
A Journey in the Backcountry (Olmsted), 239
Journeys and Explorations in the Cotton Kingdom (Olmsted), 234
Joyner, Brian D., 114
junipers, 278, 280

Kames, Henry Home, Lord, 321–323
Kaplan, Amy, 194
Keeler, Charles, 188–189
Kenedy, John G., 173
Kenedy, Mifflin, 69–70, 173
Kenedy Ranch, 69–70
Kéralum, Pierre-Yves, 170
Kheel Center for Labor-Management Documentation and Archives, 51
Kilde, Jeanne H., 132
Kimball, Fiske, 2–3, 17, 19, 35, 159n35, 240, 253n29, 315
Kindergarten Chats (Sullivan), 371
Kineños, 69
King, Henrietta Chamberlain, 14, 63, 69–71, 73, 173
King, Richard, 63, 69–71, 73, 173
King Ranch, 14, 61–63, 65, 69–72, *71*, *72*, *74*, 75–76

Kiowas, 66, 277
"Kitchen Plan," 55, 56
Kleberg, Richard, 63, 73
Kleberg, Robert J., 173
Koeper, Frederick, 39
Korff Brothers, *31*
Kowalski, Louis, 171
Kramp, William C., 36
Kroeber, Alfred L., *300*, 300–301
Krotona Institute, 185
Ku Klux Klan, 371

labor unions, 3, 26, 32
Labrouste, Henri, 329
Ladd-Franklin, Christine, 365, 368
Lafever, Minard, 36
Lafon, Ramón, 166
Lake Placid, New York, 45
Lakȟóta people, 255, 257–258, 262, 265–267, 270
Lamarque, Marie Eduwiges, 171
Lambert, Crumell, 131–132
Lambeth, William, 314–315, 323
land-based sovereignty, 294
Land-Grant Agricultural and Mechanical College Act (Morrill Act), 46, 233–234, 238, 242–243, 248–249
land grant schools, 236, 238, 242, 244–245, 247, 249, 251, 251nn1–2
Land Ordinance, 312–313
landscape architecture, 253n29
Langston City, Oklahoma, 115
Lankford, John A., 15, 129–130, 137–143, 145n48
Lankford's Artistic Churches and Other Designs (Lankford), 130, 139–143, *142*, 145n48
Laredo, Texas, 66, 172
Larson, Gerald R., 344, 358
Larson, Magali Sarfatti, 45
Latin American architecture, 64
Latrobe, Benjamin Henry, 26, 40n2
Latta, Morgan London, 153
lattice truss, 36–37
Law, James D., 365
Lawrence, Abbott, 248
Lawrence, Ellis Fuller, 183, 192
Lawrence Scientific School (Harvard), 248
League of Nations, 371
Le Corbusier (Charles-Édouard Jeanneret), 74
Leffland, Jules, 71
Leggs, Brent, 147
Levee Street (New Orleans), 178n40
Lewis, Robert Benjamin, 15, 97–98, 100, 102–107
Lewis County, New York, 54
Lewis Mountain, 312
liberalism, 4, 10–11, 76, 216, 217, 226, 238–239, 290
liberation, 117
Liberia, 105, 225
Library of Congress, 19, 326–340, *329*, *331*, *334*, *335*, *336*, *339*
The Life, Travels and Opinions of Benjamin Lundy, Including His Journeys to Texas and Mexico (Lundy), 177n34
Life on the Mississippi (Twain), 341n17
Light and Truth (Lewis), 100–102, 105
The Light of Asia (play), 185, 193
Liliuokalani, Queen of Hawaii, 181, 187, 194
limestone, 83
Lincoln, Abraham, 103, 150, 245, 334
Lipan Apaches, 66
Litchfield, Connecticut, 244
literacy, 100, 117, 128
llanos mesteños, 172–173
Lockhart, Texas, 84
Logan, Trevon, 116
log cabins, 148–150, *154*
London Institute of Contemporary Arts, 211
Long, Robert C., Jr., 36, 37
Lopez-Whiteskunk, Regina, 280
Loring, Sanford, 350
Lost Cause, 6, 241
Louisiana Purchase, 169
Louis XVI, 315
Lowell, Massachusetts, 248
Lower Rio Grande, 165–166, 172
Lucas, George, 137
Lucking, Maura, 17
Luiseño people, 297–298, 305
lumber industry, 198–200, 204–207, 210
Lundy, Benjamin, 177n34
The Lutheran and Missionary, 131

Macaulay, Thomas Babington, 334
Machine Age, 370
MacMonnies, Frederick William, 336
Mad Bear, 266
Madero, Francisco I., 177n35
Madison County, Tennessee, 85
Maffly-Kipp, Laurie, 99
mahogany, 12, 16, 197–211
Mahogany Antique and Modern (Rogers), 197
"The Mahogany Tree" (Thackeray), 204
Main, F. P., 137
Maine, 242, 243

Maison Carrée, 315, 319, 321
Mandan, Dakota Territory/North Dakota, 255, *256*, *257*, 258–259
Manhattan, 208
manifest destiny, 2, 18, 193, 318
Manning, Warren, *235*, 314, 323
manumission, 11. *See also* abolition/abolitionism; emancipation
Maori, 188, 189
Mariano (Ute Chief), 285
Mark, Robert, 350
Marrant, John, 15, 97–100, 102–107
marronage, 11, 97, 106
Marshall Field's Wholesale Store, 371
Martin, Reinhold, 38, 320
Martinez, Diana, 19, 353
Martinko, Whitney, 146–147
Martin's Station, *33*
Martiny, Philip, 337–338
Marxist-feminism, 65
Mason, Charles, 88
Mason, Dicy, 81, 85, 88, 94n12, 95n44
Mason, George, 82, 85, 87–89, *88*, 91
Mason, Harriet, 88
Mason, Henry, 82, 85, 87, *88*
Mason, Laura, 88
Mason, Louisa, 88
Mason, Otis Tufton, 332
Mason, Raiford, 82, 85, 87–89, *88*, 91, *92*
Mason, Sam Jr., 82, 84–85, 87–88, *88*, 89–91, *92*
Mason, Sam Sr., 81, 84, *87*, 88–90, 93
Mason, Viny, 88
Mason family, 14, 81–93
masons and masonry construction, 83, *83*, 85, 87–91, 284, 348. *See also* brickwork and brick masons
Masontown, Texas, 82, 84, *88*, 88–89, 91, 95n49
masquerade balls, 183–184, 192
Massachusetts, 242, 249, 254n69
Massachusetts Agricultural College, 233–236, *235*, *237*, 239, 247–248, *249*, 250, *250*, 251n2, 254n69
Massachusetts Board of Agriculture, 246
Massachusetts Institute of Technology, 26, 183, 251n2
Massachusetts State House, 318
Matamoros, Mariano, 166, 170–172
Matamoros, Tamaulipas, 163–175, 177n34, 177n36, 178n40, 178n46, 179n56
Matthews, Albert, 368
Maximilian of Austria, Archduke, 178n46
Maybeck, Bernard, 16, 180–195, *185*, 195n3, 196n18
Mbembe, Achille, 98
McAlester, Virginia Savage, 4
McDonough, John P., 169
McGahey, J., *207*
McGehee, Charles L., 82, 86
McGill, Joseph, 155
McInnis, Maurie, 313–314
McKim, Mead & White, 173, 256, *257*, 258
McLaughlin, James, 255, 259, 261, 262
mechanization of agriculture, 245
melting-pot metaphor, 57
mercantile colonialism, 166–170
Merchants Exchange Building (New York City), 173
Merwood-Salisbury, Joanna, 19
Mescalero Apaches, 66, 281
metates, 279–280
Methodism, 136
Mexican American laborers, 70
Mexico: and evolution of Mission and ranch styles, 294; Mexican landholders, 70; Mexican law, 6; Mexican Revolution, 72; racial inequality in, 69; US-Mexico border, 61, 63–64, 66, 73; US-Mexico War of 1846-1848, 16, 164, 168–169, 176n26, 294; and Wright's "Usonia" term, 368
Michelle M. Mears, 82
The Mikado (Gilbert and Sullivan), 186–187
Miller, Marla, 147
Mills, Charles W., 45, 46, 48
Minosh, Peter, 19
missionary campus architecture, 12, 17. *See also* Syrian Protestant College
Mission Espada, 73
Mission Indian Agency, 294, *295*, *296*, 302
Mission Indian Federation, 303–305
Mission style, 18, 72, 291, 293–303
Mississippi River, 353
Missouri Compromise, *29*
Missouri River, 259, 270
Mitchell, Broadus, 240–241, 247
Mitchelville, South Carolina, 246
Mníšoše (Missouri River), 259
modernity and modernism: and Maybeck's architectural regionalism, 194; "modern" architecture, 4; modernist architectural style, 9; modernist historiography, 3; modernist mythologies, 9; modernist skyscrapers, 17; modern mythologies, 18–20; "modern vernaculars," 44
monoculture, 284
monopoly thesis, 45
Monroe Doctrine, 9, 64, 340
Montauk Building, 358

Montejano, David, 168
Montes, Tomás, 179n57
Monticello, 18, 312–314, 316–319, 321, 323–324
Moore, A. W., 82, 86
Moorish motifs, 215
More, George, 170
Morgan, Lewis Henry, 4, 261
Morrill, Justin, 234
Morrill Land Grant Act, 46, 233–234, 238, 242–243, 248–249
Morris Brown College, 137–138
Morrison, Toni, 97
Morse, Jedidiah, 364
Morton, Samuel, 102
Moses (biblical), 103
Mother Earth, 278
Mould, Jacob Wrey, 30
Mound Bayou, Mississippi, 115
Mountain, May Lee, 281–282
Mountjoy Prison, 239
Mount Vernon, 313
Mulroy, Kevin, 114
Mumford, Lewis, 2, 3, 38–39, 210
Murphy, Claudia Quigley, 60n44
Murray, James P., 365, 367
Museum of Modern Art (New York), 342, *343*
Museum of Natural History (New York), 219–220
My Bondage and My Freedom (Douglass), 32
The Mystery, 103

Nakoma Country Club, 372
Nashville, Tennessee, *84*
The Nation, 237, 368
National Association of Colored Women, 151–152
National City Bank, 173
nationalism, 9, 19, 356–358, 364–368
National Museum, 331–332
National Museum of African American History and Culture, 156, *156*
National Park Service, 154, 157n6
Native Americans, 3, 318, 322, 337. *See also* Indigenous peoples and lands; *specific Indian tribes*
Native Hawaiians, 273, 275
nativism, 367, 374n29
Navajo Indians, 73, 281
Near East, 215, 216
Needham, Paul, 196n23
The Negro in Our History (Woodson), 105–106
Negro Young People's Education Congress, 152
Nelson, Louis P., 65, 314, 316
neoclassical architecture, 113, 202, 208, 223, 315, 319–321, 370
neoteric societies, 114
Neu Braunfels, Texas, 247
Neutra, Richard, 291
Nevada, 176n26
Newcomb, Rexford, 291–293, 297, 302, 305
New Deal, 6, 18
New England, 243
New England-based regionalism, 39
The New England Farmer, 234
New Harmony, Indiana, 252n25
New Mexico, 275, *276*, *277*
New Negro movement, 141, 143
New Orleans, Louisiana, *28*, 28–29, 66, 166–172, 174, 177n35, 178n40, 179n69, 248
New South Wales, 239
New Testament, 118
Newton County, Texas, 119–120, *121*
New York City, 2, 17, 25–26, 28, 31, 34
New York City Hall, 31
New York Public Library, 311
New York State College of Home Economics Records, *49*
New York State College of Human Ecology, *55*
New York Times, 223, 365
New York University, 35
New Zealand, 188
Nicodemus, Kansas, 114–115
Nimrod, 100
Nochlin, Linda, 222–223
Nordhoff, Charles, 296–300, 302
Norfolk Island penal colony, 239, 252n23
Norsemen, 337
North America, 208
The North American Indian (Curtis), 301
North American Railway, 244–245
North Berkeley, California, 191, 196n23
North Carolina, 42n25, 85
North Carolina State Capitol, 36, 37
Northern California, 194
Northern Mexico, 71
Northern Pacific Railroad, 255–256, *257*, 260–261
Northern Ute Indians, 274, 282
Norway, 189
Norwood, Bryan E., 15
novohispano (colonial Spanish) practices, 174
Nueces River, 66

Nueces Strip, 69
Nuestra Señora del Refugio, 167, 168
Nuevo Laredo, Tamaulipas, 172, 178n37
Nuevo Santander, 164, 165–166
Nutting, Newton W., 328

Oahu, 187
Oakwood Cemetery, 91
Oblate Community House, 170
Očéti Ŝakówiŋ, 17, 257–262, 265–270
oculus (Library of Congress Building), 333–334
Odom, Elzie, 119–120
Odom, Harold, 120, *121*
O'Gorman, James, 3
Old Louisiana State Capitol, 38
The Old Mission Churches and Historic Houses of California (Newcomb), 291
Olmsted, Frederick Law, 6, 17, 233–251, *235*, *239*
Olmsted, Frederick Law, Jr., 240, 247, 253n29
one-room cabins, 147–157, 157n4
oral histories, 112
organicism, 74–75
orientalism, 192, 218
"The Origin and Objects of Ancient Freemasonry" (Delany), 99
"Origin of Negro Slavery," 200
Orono, Maine, 242
O'Rourke, Kathryn E., 14
Ottoman Empire, 216
Owen, Robert, 252n25

Pacific Theater of Operations, 194
Pae, Hyŏng-min, 125n3
Page, Max, 147
Pai, Hyungmin, 125n3
Painter, Nell Irvin, 334
Palace of Fine Arts (San Francisco), 180–181, 184–185, 189, 356
Palacio, José San Román, 169
Pala Indian Reservation, *295*
Palais Garnier, 341n20
Palatingiva (Pechanga), 298, *299*, 305
palazzos, 330
Palestine, 216, 219
Palladio, Andrea, 315
Palmito Ranch, 178n46
Pan-Africanism, 98, 104–105
Panama-Pacific International Exposition, 180–181, 195n3
Panic of 1893, 173
The Panopticon, 208
parade grounds, 242
Paredes, Américo, 70
Parman, John, 116
Parris, Alexander, 36
parti (*parti pris*), 15, 112–113, 115–117, 120, 124–125
Passement, Bartolo, 168, 174, 177nn35–36
Passement, Mateo, 167
Pateman, Carole, 45
paternalism, 208
patrón-péon system, 69
Payno, Manuel, 166, 167
Pechanga, 298, *299*, 305
Peeler, Henry A., 170
Pennsylvania Academy of Fine Arts, 35, 144n9
The Penny Magazine, 208
Penobscot Indian Camp, *355*
Perrault, Claude, 321
Perrilliat House, 167
Perry, Imani, 128–129
Persia, 222
Petersen, Frederick A., 30
Petrie, William Matthew Flinders, 132
Pexa, Christopher, 259
Phelps, Dodge & Company, 216
Phelps, Henry T., 173
Phelps-Stokes Fund, 225
"The Phenomenology of Whiteness" (Ahmed), 182
Philadelphia, Pennsylvania, 26, 34
Philadelphia Museum of Art, 35
Philippines, 341n19, 367
Philopappos Monument, 74
photography, 143, 150, 153–154, 158n23, 159n36, 291, 294, 298–302
Phyfe, Duncan, 208–209, *209*
"The Pictures We Make" (Wright), 372n6
Pierce, Charles C., 298, *299*, *301*
Pierson, William H., Jr., 39
Pike's Peak Gold Rush, 176n26
The Pilgrimage Play, 185
piñon pine, 278
Piper, Corey, 315
Piranesi, Giovanni Battista, 319–320
placemaking process, 122–125
place-naming, 12, 112–114, 117–118, 122–125
Plains Indian Sign Language, 258
plantations and plantation houses: and agricultural land grant colleges, 236–240, 243, 245–246, 248; and architecture of fugitive spaces, 96; and Black counternarratives in architectural history, 105; and crusade

against one-room cabins, *156*; and freedom colonies of Black Texans, 112; and Jefferson's influence on American architecture, 313, 316, 318–319, 323–324; and King Ranch main house, 73; and mahogany industry, 197, 209; and Maybeck's architectural regionalism, 191, 193; and naming of free Black communities, 119; and professionalization of American architecture, 37
Pleasant Hill, Texas, 121–124, *122*, *123*
Pleasant Hill Cemetery, *118*
Plymouth Rock, 259
Point of Pines Plantation, *156*
Polk, Willis, 187
Pond, Irving, 357
Poole, William F., 328
porciones, 165, 176n16
Porter Hall, 148
Port Royal, 245
Portscheller, Enrique, 179n56
Post, George E., 218–219
Post Hospital (Fort Brown), 171
postwar construction, 34
Potrero del Espíritu Santo grant, 178n41
poverty, 240–241, 247, 264, 297
Prairie-style architectures, 7, 372
Prairie View State Normal and Industrial College, 91
Pratt, Richard Henry, 265, 267, 269, 277
premodern architecture, 3–4
The Presbyterian Banner, 129
The Presbyterian Quarterly Review, 132
Priest, Josiah, 30, 100, *101*
primitive architecture, 17, 291. *See also* vernacular architecture
Princeton University, 217
Principia College, 189, *190*
printing press, 329
Pritchett, George, 122, 123
Pritchett, Neal, 123
private property, 289
professionalization of architecture, 9, 13, 30–38, 43–57. *See also* American Institute/Institution of Architects (AIA)
Progressivism, 2, 43, 46–47, 57, 182, 195, 216–217, 226, 250, 293, 303
Progress of a Race (Crogman), 159n36
Promised Land, 117, 215
property rights and ownership, 67, 304, 305
Protestantism, 103, 131–132, 215, 237
protomodern architecture, 4, 6
Psalms, 105
public health, 141
Public Land Survey System, 275
Pueblo architecture, 291
Puerto Rico, 210, 367
Pugin, Augustus, 32
Pullman, Illinois, 252n25, 367
Puritan colonies, 215
putti, 337–338, *339*

Queen Anne-style, 154

Rabassa v. Passement, 177n35
Race and Modern Architecture (Cheng, Davis and Wilson, eds.), 7
race and racial identity: aesthetic of whiteness, 214; and agricultural land grant colleges, 236–241, 245–251; and AME church design, 127–143; and American overseas missionary movement, 214–227; and architecture of South Texas border cities, 163, 166, 167–168, 171, 174; and crusade against one-room cabins, 146–148, 151–157; and decorations of Library of Congress, 327, 330–335, *331*, *334*, *335*, 335–338, *336*, 338–340; and evolution of Mission and ranch styles, 293–305; and evolution of the skyscraper, 356–358; and Jefferson's architecture, 313–314, 317, 320–324; and Jenney's architecture, 345–347, 354; and mahogany lumber industry, 200–201, 205–206; and Maybeck's architectural regionalism, 181–183, 187, 191, 194–195; and professionalization of American architecture, 27; racial advancement, 187; and racial assimilation of Native Americans, 290–293; and racial dynamics of architectural style, 67–70; racial epistemologies, 20n15; racialized power, 67; and racial regimes and inversion, 98–102; and the ranch house in Southern California, 289–305; and rural home economics, 45, 49–50, 56, 57; and scope/structure of text, 9, 15, 19; and white settlement of Indigenous lands, 256, 258–259, 261–264; and Wright's Usonia, 364–371. *See also* Blacks and African Americans; white supremacy
"Race and the Historiography of American Architecture" (workshop), 8
Races and Peoples (Brinton), 333
railroads, 37, 63, 173–174, 179n69, 244–245, 256, *256*, 259, 270, 353
Raleigh, Walter, 36, 200

ramada, 175n8, 298
Ramey, Elizabeth A., 47
rancherías (campsites), 166
ranch houses, 289–305
ranching, 172–173
ranchitos, 70
Rancho La Parra, 173
Rangers of the King Ranch, 70
Rebori, Andrew Nicholas, *343*
reciprocity, 280, 285, 305
Reconstruction: and agricultural land grant colleges, 236, 238, 248, 250; and AME church design, 128, 131, 139; and decoration of Library of Congress, 327; Du Bois on, xi, 1–2; and influence of modernist historiography, 3; and origins of freedmen's communities, 93n2, 114; and professionalization of American architecture, 38; and racial dynamics of architectural style, 68; and scope/structure of text, 9, 14, 19; and shortcomings of "American architecture" label, 6; and Wright's "Usonia" term, 368
reformatories, 239
refugee camps, 245–246
regionalism, 4, 39
Reichard, Charles F., 36
religio-racial identity, 143n3
Renaissance, 57, 89, 330, 336, 370–371
Rendón, Atilano, 179n57
Rennie, John, 198, *199*
Report on the Demoralization of the Volunteers, 241
Republican Party, 237–238, 246
Republic of Texas, 67–68, 86
Revett, Nicholas, 74
revivalist architecture, 6
Reynolds's Political Map of the United States, *29*
Reynosa, Tamaulipas, 166, 177n37
Richards, Joseph R., 236
Richardson, Heather Cox, 238
Richardson, H. H., 2, 6, 39, 179n69, 356
ring shouts, 123
Rio Grande, 66, 164, 169, 171, 176n12
Rio Grande City, Texas, 172, 177n37
Rise of American Civilization (Beard and Beard), xi, 1
The Rise of Masontown (Runcie), 91, 92
The Rising Tide of Color Against White World-Supremacy (Stoddard), 371
Roberts, Andrea, 15
Robinson, Cedric, 97, 106–107
Robinson, H. H., 187
Robinson, Willard B., 171
Rockefeller, James Stillman, 173
Rockfish Gap Report (Jefferson), 252n15
Roediger, David R., 56
Rogers, Isiah, 36
Rogers, Meyric R., 197
Roiphe, Rebecca, 41n12
Roma, Texas, 66, 172, 177n37
Romanesque style, 135, 138, 370
Romantic movement, 244, 329
Roosevelt, Theodore, 365
Root, John Wellborn, 2, 356
Rosenwald School, 372
Rowe, Colin, 343
Rowen, Jonah, 16
Rowland, Cameron, 211
Royal Institute of British Architects, 362, 367
Royal Oak, 205
Roycroft colony, 7
Runcie, Ryan, 91, 92
Running Antelope, 267
rural areas and communities: and agricultural land grant colleges, 234, 238–239, 243–245, 249; and architecture of the King Ranch, 63, 65, 69; and crusade against one-room cabins, 148, 152–154, *153*; and freedom colonies of Black Texans, 112, 124; and home economics training, 43–46, 47–49, *49*, 51, 53–54, 56–57; and industrial workers' towns, 252n25; and mahogany lumber industry, 201, 205; and mercantile colonialism in Texas border region, 172; and professionalization of American architecture, 27, 32; and ranch house of Southern California, 290, 297–298, 305; rural agricultural model, 244; rural farmhouses, 46–53, *49*, *52*, 56; and scope/structure of text, 5, 9
Rusert, Britt, 97
Russian Empire, 275

sabicu, 203–204
Sachse, Edward, 311
"The Sack of Auchindore" (Law), 365
Sadd, Joseph, 149, 150
Saint, Andrew, 26
Saint-Gaudens, Augustus, 336
Saldívar, José David, 175
Salem, Oregon, 137
Salinas, Martín, 165, 175n8
"salvage ethnography," 300

Samlesbury Hall, Lancashire, 196n18
Sampson, George W., 86–87
Sampson-Henricks Building, 83, *83*, 87, *87*, 91
San Antonio, Texas, 66, 73
Sancho, Ignatius, 323
San Domingo, 210
San Francisco Chronicle, 188
San Francisco Players Guild, 187
Sanitary Commission, 240, 241
sanitary engineer, 13
San Juan de los Esteros Hermosos, 166
San Marcos, Texas, 84
Santa Gertrudis House (King Ranch), *72*, 72–74, *74*, 173
Saving Slave Houses project, 156
Schindler, Rudolph, 291
Schmidt, F., 36
Schuyler, Montgomery, 2–3, 6, 17
Science Hall (Syrian Protestant College), 219–223, *221*, *222*, 226
Scientific American, 200
scientific knowledge, 216
scientific racism, 215
Scott, James, 100
Scott, Walter, 334
Scottish stoneworkers, 90
Scully, Vincent, 3, 19, 316–319, 323–324
Scurlock, Addison, 141
sectionalism, 11, 27, 237
sedition, 304
segregation, 10, 68, 148, 171, 174, 182, 195
Sergeant, John, 373n9
settler colonialism: and American overseas missionary movement, 214–216; ethnological exhibits at World's Columbian Exposition, 356; and evolutionary narrative in architecture, 350; and evolution of Mission and ranch styles, 302; and influence of modernist historiography, 3; and Jefferson's influence on American architecture, 318; and mercantile colonialism in Texas border region, 165–166, 168, 174; and racial dynamics of architectural style, 67, 73; and the ranch house in Southern California, 289–290; and scope/structure of text, 7–12, 17–18; and white settlement of Indigenous lands, 256–258, 270
Seuzeneau, Adolphe, 169
Seven Council Fires, 257
Shaler, Nathaniel S., 346–347
Shankle, Jim, 119
Shankle, Winnie, 119
Shankleville, Texas, 119–120, *121*
Shaw University, 137
S. H. Erlanger House, 196n18
Sherman, William Tecumseh, 350, 352
Sierra Leone, 209
silver, 167, 176n26
The Simple Home (Keeler), 188
Sims, Robert, 137
Singh, Nikhil Phal, 238
single-family home, 57
Sinophilia, 193–194
Sir George Watson Lectures, 362
Sitting Bull, 255, 259, 261–262, *263*, 266–267
Six Square, 95n49
skeleton-framed structures, 342–344, 347–348, 353–358
sketches, 113
skyscrapers, 2, 19, 342, *343*, 344, 353–358
Slave Dwelling Project, 155
Slavery, As It Relates to the Negro, or African Race (Priest), *101*
slavery and enslaved persons: and agricultural land grant colleges, 239; and American overseas missionary movement, 215; and Constitution of the Republic of Texas, 68; and "coolie" term, 196n29; and crusade against one-room cabins, 147–152; and decorations of Library of Congress, 334, 338; *Dred Scott* decision, 32; and ethnological schema of American architecture, 354; and evolutionary narrative in architecture, 347; and industrialization of American economy, 353; and Jefferson's influence on American architecture, 313, 314–324; and mahogany lumber industry, 198–199, 201–202, 204–208, 209–210; and Missouri Compromise, *29*; and naming of free Black communities, 114, 119; and professionalization of American architecture, 26–28, 30, 32, 37–38; and racial dynamics of architectural style, 67–69, 73; and scope/structure of text, 12, 14, 16, 18–19; and shortcomings of "American architecture" label, 6; slave cabins, 148, *151*, *153*, *154*, *156*, 158n13; slave narratives, 123; slavery in US in 1837, *28*; and stonemasons of Texas, 82–89. *See also* specific individuals
Smith, Ruby Green, 57
Smith, Shawn Michelle, 158n23
Smithmeyer & Pelz, 328–330, *329*, 340n8
social contract, 45
social mobility, 128
social-scientific surveys, 302, *303*, 304
Society of Architectural Historians, 8

sociology of professions, 45
soft imperialism, 214
Solomonson, Katherine, 17
Sorber, Nathan, 251n1
South Carolina, 156
South College, 248, *249*
Southern, Eileen, 158n13
Southern California ranch houses, 18, 289–305
Southern Ute Indians, 274, *276*, 278–282, *279*, 284–286
Southern Utes, 285
The Southern Workman (Du Bois), 150, 152
South Texas, 71
The Southwestern American, 86
Southwest US, 14
sovereignty issues, 304
Space, Time and Architecture (Giedion), 2
Spain: and professionalization of American architecture, 28; Spanish American architecture, 71; Spanish-American War, 340, 367; Spanish California, 292, 297; Spanish Colonial architecture, 290–293; Spanish colonialism, 73; Spanish law, 6; and US-Mexico border, 66
Spanish Town, Jamaica, 207
Sparrell, William, 36
spatial heterogeneity, 170
The Sphere and the Labyrinth (Tafuri), 320
Spofford, Ainsworth Rand, 327–328, 334–335, *335*, 338, 341n18
Spofford, Florence P., 35
Springfield Architectural Iron Works, 172
Squier, Ephraim G., 4
standard of living, 47
Standing Bear, Luther, 265, 269
Standing Rock Agency, 255, 257–259, 261–264, *263*, 264–270, *266*, *267*, *268*
Stanley, Louise, 47–48
steel construction, 220, 348–349, 353–354
Stevenson, Christine Wetherill, 185, 191
Stewart, Whitney Nell, 15
Stickley, Gustav, 291
stick lodges. *See* wickiups
Stillman, Charles, 173
Stillman, James, 173
St. John's church, 207
St. Joseph College, 171
St. Lawrence Riverway, 244–245
St. Louis, Missouri, 34, 365
St. Louis Reporter, 367
St. Louis Republic, 365
St. Luke's Episcopal Church, 33
Stoddard, Lothrop, 371
Stokes, Caroline Phelps, 218
Stokes, Isaac Newton Phelps, 217–220, 223–226
Stokes, Olivia, 218
Stowe, Harriet Beecher, 53
St. Paul's Chapel, 133, 218, 223–224, *224*, *225*, 225–226
street names, 169
Strickland, William, 36
Stuart, James, 74
Sturgis, Russell, 223, 225
submarine telegraph cables, *31*
suburban houses, 344
Sullivan, Louis H., 2, 179n69, 351, 356, 371
Sweet Auburn neighborhood, 142
Syria, 216
Syrian Protestant College, 216–223, *218*, *221*, 226–227

Tafuri, Manfredo, 19, 319–320, 324
Táíwò, Olúfẹ́mi O., 98
Tallmadge, Thomas, 342
Tamaulipas, Mexico, 68, 164, 168
Tampico, Tamaulipas, 168
Tanner, Benjamin Tucker, 144n9
Tanner, Henry Ossawa, 144n9
Taylor, Robert R., 138
Teachers Colleges, 217–218, 220
teak, 200
Teatro de la Reforma, 170
technological advancement, 342, 356–358
telegraph, *31*
Tennessee, 85, 250
Terrell, Mary Church, 150
A Testament (Wright), 363
Texas: Declaration of Independence, 67; Governor's Mansion, 82; King Ranch, 14, 61–76; and scope/structure of text, 14; State Capitol, 82, 87, *87*, 89–93, *90*; State Historical Association, 112, 121; State Library and Archives, 89; Texas flag, 73; Texas Freedom Colonies Project Atlas, 112, 115–117, 124; Texas Hill Country, 247; Texas-Mexico border, 9, 28; Texas Rangers, 70
Thackeray, William Makepeace, 204
theater culture, 192–193
Theatre Arts Alliance, 185
theatrical design, 181, 184, 195
Theory and Design in the First Machine Age (Banham), 2–3
Thomas, George H., 352
Thomas, Thomas, 36

Thomas, Thomas, Jr., 36
Thomas Burton House, *155*
Thomas H. Jones House, *83*
Thomas Jefferson, Architect (DeWitt and Piper, eds.), 315
Thomas Jefferson, Architect (Kimball), 315
Thomas Jefferson Building, *331*, *334*
Three American Architects (O'Gorman), 3
Tiffany, C. C., 132
Tiffany & Company, 72
"Time Study of New York Homemakers," 48, *50*, 50–51
Tlingit Indigenous people, 189
Tocqueville, Alexis de, 243
Torres, Baltasar, 172
Tosomock, 236
"Toward a Better Understanding of the Evolution of the Iron Skeleton Frame in Chicago" (Larson and Geraniotis), 358
Tower of Babel story, 100, *101*
Town, Ithiel, 36–37, *37*
Town & Davis, 36–37
town-planning, 112
Townsend, George Alfred, 330–332
trachoma, 285
traditional architectural history, 14
traditional knowledge, 285
transcontinental Pacific Railway Act, 289
transnational American culture, 9, 16–17
Trautwine, John, 36
Travis County Courthouse, 83, 86
treaties: Fort Laramie Treaty, 264; with Native Americans, 17, 264, 269, 273, 289, 294–295, 303–304; Treaty of Guadalupe Hidalgo, 164
Trinidadian mahogany, 204
Trinity Building, 25
tuberculosis, 285
Tubman, Harriet, 103
Tudor Gothic, 221
Tufton Farm, 313
Turcotte, Marie Stella, 173
Turner, Frederick Jackson, 16
Turner, Henry McNeal, 136, 138, 145n37
Tuskegee Institute (Tuskegee University), 107, 138–139, 148, *153*, 154
Tuskegee Negro Conference, 148, 151
Tuthill, Louisa, 26
Twain, Mark, 341n17

Uncle Tom's Cabin (Stowe), 53, 60n44, 149, *149*
Underground Railroad, 100
Union of South Africa, 368
United States Army, 70
United States Indian Industrial School, 265–270, *266*, *267*
University at Buffalo, 7
University of California, Berkeley, 16, 183, 188
University of Chicago, 345, 346
University of Illinois, 291
University of Illinois Urbana-Champaign, 35
University of Massachusetts, 233, 234
University of Oregon, 183
University of South Carolina, 248
University of Texas at Austin, 90
University of Virginia, 238, 311–314, *312*, 314, 318–319
Upjohn, Richard, 25, 30–32, *33*
Upjohn's Rural Architecture (Upjohn), 32
Upshaw, Charlotte Josephine, 138
Upton, Dell, 5, 45, 65, 313, 344
urbanism/urbanization: and architecture of South Texas border cities, 170; and evolution of Mission and ranch styles, 298, 300–302, 304–305; and evolution of skeleton-framed buildings, 356; and influence of modernist historiography, 3; and the King Ranch, 63; and professionalization of American architecture, 27; and the Progressive Era, 46, *46*; and racial dynamics of architectural style, 71; and scope/structure of text, 7, 13; urban commercial districts, 2
US Army, 164, 169, 274, 277, 281
US Army Corps of Engineers, 328
US Capitol dome, 37
US Census, 62
US Civil War, 32, 34, 170–172, 217
US Congress, 67, 327, 328, 338, 340n11
US Custom House, 36
USDA, 54
US Department of Agriculture (USDA), 47
US House of Representatives, 217
US-Mexico border, 61, 63–64, 66, 73
US-Mexico War of 1846–1848, 164, 168–169, 176n26
US Navy, 170, 178n46
Usona/Usonia, 19, 362–372
US Sanitary Commission, 234
US sectionalism, 13, 17, 26, 38
US Senate, 261
US Seventh Cavalry, 255
US Supreme Court, 32
Utah, 275, *276*, *277*, 281
Ute Mountain Ute Tribe, 274, 280

Van Brunt, Henry, 221, 352–353, 356–357
Vandervort, Helen, 54, 56
Van Rensselaer, Mariana Griswold, 2–3, 6
Van Rensselaer, Martha, 60n44
Van Zandt, Maria Louisa, 85, 89
Vaux, Calvert, 236
Vela, Petra, 173
Venetian Renaissance, 336
Venezuelan Commission, 340
Vermont, 29, 37
vernacular architecture, 4–12, 17, 44, 56, 63, 169, 291, 317
Vesey, Denmark, 137
Vesey, Robert, 137
Vicksburg campaign, 351, 353
View of the University of Virginia, Charlottesville, and Monticello Taken from Lewis Mountain, 311
Vile, William, 202
Villard, Henry, 256, 260–261
Villarreal, Roberto M., 69–70
villas del norte, 165–166, 168, 176n17
Viollet-le-Duc, Eugène Emmanuel, 2, 345, 352, 354
Virginia State Capitol, 7, 313, 315, 319
Vitruvian Triad, 65, *65*, 67, 75–76
Vitruvius, 76
Vlach, John Michael, 5
vocational education, 284

Walker, David, 102–104
walnut, 210
Walter, Thomas Ustick, 29–31, 35, 37, 41n11, 100, 102, 326
Walton, George L., 86
Walton, W. M., 86
wampum, 337–338
Ward, John Quincy Adams, 336
War Department, 276
Ward W. Willits House, 316–317
War Memorial Natatorium (Waikiki), 181, 187–188
Warner, Olin Levi, 336–337
Washington, Booker T., 152–154, 156, 158n23
Washington, DC, 37
Washington, George, 313
Washington Monument, 328
Waterhouse, Sylvester, 365
Waterloo, 82. *See also* Austin, Texas
Watson, Joseph M., 19
Waud, Alfred R., *246*
Waugh, Frank, 235
Webb, Walter Prescott, 70
Weisenfeld, Judith, 143n3
Welch, John, 30
Wells, Joseph C., 30
Wendingen, 363, 369, 371
West African burial practices, 120
West Coast modernism, 7, 16
Western Association of Architects, 34, 35, 346
Western United States, 68
West India Docks Mahogany Shed, 198, *199*, 201, 203, 208, 211
West Point, Mississippi, 137
westward expansion, 9, 318, 352–353
What Experience Has Taught Me (Burton), *154*
Whiffen, Marcus, 39
Whigs, 316
White, Stanford, 125n3
Whitefield, George, 98
"The Whiteness of American Architecture" (symposium), 7, 20n16
white preservationists, 15
White River Utes, 281
white supremacy: and Black counternarratives in architectural history, 97–98; and crusade against one-room cabins, 146, 157; and decorations of Library of Congress, 326, 332–335; and Indigenous anti-colonial opposition in Southern California, 290; and Jefferson's influence on American architecture, 314; and Lost Cause ideology, 241; and Maybeck's architectural regionalism, 182–183; and white settlement of Indigenous lands, 261–262; and Wright's "Usonia" term, 371
wickiups, 278–280, *279*, 283, 285
Wilberforce University, 130, 137–139, *138*, 142
Wilder, Craig Stevens, 251n1
SS *Wilhelmina*, 181–184, *182*, 192, 195
Willcox, Walter Ross Baumes, 183–184, 192
Willcox & Sayward, 183
Williams, George Washington, 105
Williams, Paul Kelsey, 145n37
Williston Davis House, 189
Wilson, Mabel O., 313, 315–316, 372
Wilson, Richard Guy, 315
Wilson, William M., 86
women's pageants, *44*
women's rights movement, 13
wood-based American housing, 16
Woods, Mary, 13, 26, 31
Woodson, Carter G., 105–106, 151
Works Progress Administration (WPA), 158n13
The World and Africa (Du Bois), 106

World's Columbian Exposition, 220, 333, 336, 345, 354–356, *355*
World War I, 47, 191, 280–281, 368
World War II, 194
Wright, Frank Lloyd: and evolution of skeleton-framed buildings, 356; and influence of modernist historiography, 3; and Jefferson's influence on American architecture, 313, 316–318; and scope/structure of text, 7, 19; and "Usonia" term, 362–372; and vernacular and "primitive" architectures, 291
Wright, Gwendolyn, 44
Wright, Josephine, 158n13
Yale University, 217, 318
Yellowstone National Park, 255–256
yeoman farmers, 239, 243, 289, 312–313
Yoo-Ka-Lucke, 333
Young, Ammi B., 36, 37
Young, Helen Binkerd, 51–53, *52*, *157*
Yturria, Francisco, 169, 170

Zamenhof, L. L., 374n33
Zapata, Texas, 177n37